# CONSTRUCTION PROJECT ADMINISTRATION

*Fifth Edition*

*EDWARD R. FISK, PE*

**Prentice Hall**
*Upper Saddle River, New Jersey        Columbus, Ohio*

**Library of Congress Cataloging-in-Publication Data**
Fisk, Edward R.,
      Construction project administration / Edward R. Fisk.—5th ed.
          p.        cm.
      Includes bibliographic references (p. 560) and index.
      ISBN 0-13-502279-7
      1. Construction industry—Management.   I. Title.
TH438.F57     1997                        95-49912
624′.068—dc20                             CIP

Editor: Ed Francis
Production Editor: Stephen C. Robb
Design Coordinator: Jill E. Bonar
Text Designer: Rebecca Bobb
Cover Designer: Julia Zonneveld Van Hook
Production Manager: Patricia A. Tonneman
Marketing Manager: Danny Hoyt

This book was set in Times Roman and Gill Sans Bold Italic by Carlisle Communications, Ltd. and was printed and bound by Quebecor Printing/Book Press. The cover was printed by Phoenix Color Corp.

 © 1997, 1992, 1988, 1982, 1978 by Prentice-Hall, Inc.
Simon & Schuster/A Viacom Company
Upper Saddle River, New Jersey 07458

Printed in the United States of America

10 9 8 7 6 5 4 3 2 1

ISBN: 0-13-502279-7

Prentice-Hall International (UK) Limited, *London*
Prentice-Hall of Australia Pty. Limited, *Sydney*
Prentice-Hall Canada, Inc., *Toronto*
Prentice-Hall Hispanoamericana, S. A., *Mexico*
Prentice-Hall of India Private Limited, *New Delhi*
Prentice-Hall of Japan, Inc., *Tokyo*
Simon & Schuster Asia Pte. Ltd., *Singapore*
Editora Prentice-Hall do Brasil, Ltda., *Rio de Janeiro*

# *Preface*

*T*he principal objective of this book is to provide those of us who are active in the construction industry with a single source of information that will help address the responsibilities and risks that we are likely to encounter. The book not only introduces students, design professionals, project managers, and owners to the special problems of construction, but also serves as a ready reference to experienced contract administrators and construction engineers as well.

The first edition was addressed to students of construction management, on-site representatives, engineers, and inspectors to provide them with a ready source of information in preparing for the responsibilities they could expect to confront on every modern construction project.

However, during the many seminars held by the author throughout the United States, Guam, Canada, and Mexico, and in the courses he teaches for the University of California, Berkeley, ITS Extension, University of Washington, Seattle, Engineering Professional Programs, and the American Society of Civil Engineers, it became evident that the project managers, contract administrators, and other management personnel who worked with or exercised control over the on-site project representatives had special problems which also needed to be addressed if the project team concept was to be realized. Thus, the concept for the second edition was born: to bring together the office and field personnel and present them with a workable system for operating as an effective construction team.

The third edition continued the concept of developing the project team approach, with the added consideration of claims avoidance methods to reduce claims losses. Each member of the project team needed to become intimately familiar with the principles of construction project administration. It was toward this end that the author strove to meet the particular needs of the project team in today's changing construction environment. A considerable amount of new material was added, and some of the chapters were reorganized for a more logical flow of information.

The fourth edition provided the updating necessary to remain current with state-of-the-art techniques in construction, and to add new material, including references to AIA, EJCDC, and FIDIC documents so that the book can literally become a single source for most construction-phase activities.

As a part of the continuing effort to stay abreast of the state of the art of the construction industry, and in recognition of the federal declaration to make the metric system (SI) the basic system of measurement in the United States and that federal agencies be required to use it exclusively, the fifth edition has been updated to emphasize its use and includes supplementary information to assist civil and construction engineers in utilizing metric (SI) civil engineering units in construction. In addition, all of the original material has been reviewed and updated, the subject of Partnering is addressed, and the index has been made more user friendly.

The author is grateful to the many contributions made through the years since this book was first published. Contributors to previous editions included Julius (Jim) Calhoun, Esq., Asst. General Counsel for Montgomery-Watson in Pasadena, CA; Gary L. McFarland, PE, and Charles H. Lawrance, PE, President and Vice-President, respectively, of Lawrance, Fisk, & McFarland, Inc., of Santa Barbara, CA; Wendell Rigby, PE, former Senior Civil Engineer of the City of Thousand Oaks, CA; Harold Good, CPPO, Procurement Manager of the City of Palm Springs, CA; Albert Rodriguez, CPCU, ARM, President, Rodriguez Consulting Group, Inc., Jacksonville, FL; Robert Rubin, Esq., PE, of Postner & Rubin, Attorneys at Law, New York, NY; Joseph Litvin, Esq., PE, Attorney at Law, Dayton, OH; Arthur Schwartz, Esq., General Counsel for the National Society of Professional Engineers, Alexandria, VA; Robert Smith, Esq., PE, of Wickwire Gavin, PC of Madison, WI, General Counsel for the Engineers Joint Contract Documents Committee (EJCDC); and the members of the EJCDC whose contributions to the tools of the contract administrator are without equal.

The author extends his particular thanks and appreciation to Prof. Wayne Reynolds of Eastern Kentucky University, Richmond, KY, for his careful, thorough review, corrections, and suggestions for this fifth edition; Donald Scarborough, President of Forward Associates, Ltd, of Novato, CA, for his valuable contributions to the updated chapters on CPM scheduling; William W. Gurry, President of Wm. Gurry & Associates, Atlanta, GA, for his contributions on design–build contracts; and the Associated General Contractors of America for their input on the concept of partnering.

Orange, CA                                                                    Edward R. Fisk, PE

# Contents

## 4   DOCUMENTATION: RECORDS AND REPORTS   67

## 5   SPECIFICATIONS AND DRAWINGS   109

**6**   **USING THE SPECIFICATIONS IN CONTRACT ADMINISTRATION    134**

**7**   **CONSTRUCTION LAWS AND LABOR RELATIONS    167**

**8**   **CONSTRUCTION SAFETY    185**

# 12 PLANNING FOR CONSTRUCTION    288

# 13 FUNDAMENTALS OF CPM CONSTRUCTION SCHEDULING    315

# 14 CONSTRUCTION OPERATIONS    352

# 18  CHANGES AND EXTRA WORK    452

# 19  CLAIMS AND DISPUTES    473

# 20  PROJECT CLOSEOUT    527

# *I*

## *Design/Construction Process*

*T*hroughout the ages, human beings have been building to meet the needs of their habitation on this earth. Then, just as now, the planning and building of each such project involved the collective efforts of many workers, all with different skills and types of specialized knowledge. At first the methods were primitive but effective. As the products of modern technology replaced the older, outdated tools of these early builders, the methods of construction and the types of skills and specialized knowledge required to complete a construction project had to change to keep pace.

## PROJECT PARTICIPANTS

Whether the project is a building, bridge, dam, pipeline, sewage treatment plant, water supply system, or any one of numerous other types of projects, it requires the skills and services of a project team comprised of three principal participants:

The owner
The designer
The builder

Each of these will normally involve other participants as a part of the team effort, as either a consultant, a quality control and assurance representative, a subcontractor, or a supplier of materials and equipment.

In practice, the owner usually enters into a contract with an architect/engineer to plan and design a project to satisfy the owner's particular needs. The owner participates during the design period to set criteria for design, cost, and time limits for completion and to provide decision-making inputs to the architect/engineer. Upon completion of the planning and design process, the project is ready for construction, and the advertising or selection process to obtain one or more qualified construction contractors begins.

After selection of one or more qualified construction contractors, or, as in the case of public works projects, selection of the lowest bidders, the owner enters into a contract directly with each prime contractor, who will then be fully responsible directly to the owner or the owner's designated representative for building the project in accordance with the plans, specifications, and local laws. The contractor has the further responsibility for the integrity of the new structure that has been built—in effect, the contractor must guarantee the work. Although the architect/engineer may be obligated to make field visitations to the construction site during the progress of the work, such periodic visits are for the purpose of observing materials and completed work to evaluate their *general* compliance with plans, specifications, and design and planning concepts only. Such basic services should not be interpreted as including full time inspection for quality control and assurance.

Thus, on the typical project, there are usually only two prime contracts with the owner: one with the architect/engineer for the design and planning of the project; the other with a single construction contractor or occasionally several prime construction contractors to build the project.

As is frequently the case on a modern complex project, numerous special types of construction are involved, and the contractor who entered into an agreement with the owner to build a project finds that the work can better be accomplished by subcontracting with a specialty contractor to do this portion of the work. Such subcontracts are agreements between the prime or "general" contractor and the subcontractor only, and involve no contractual relationship between any subcontractor and the owner. Under the owner's contract

**FIGURE 1.1**   Traditional construction contract relationships.

for construction, the general contractor is fully responsible for the entire work, whether or not subcontractors have been utilized to accomplish any portion of it. The traditional contractual arrangement is illustrated in Figure 1.1.

Figure 1.1 does not take into account the relationship between an owner with its own in-house engineering staff (such as many public agencies) and the construction contractor. However, by combining the functions of *owner* and *architect/engineer,* as in the diagram, the relationships would be similar.

## CONSTRUCTION ADMINISTRATION

Construction administration and contract administration are terms easily confused. As used in this book, the term *contract administration* means the management or handling of the business relations between the parties to a contract, which is popularly thought of as being limited to the administrative paperwork. In this book the term *construction administration* is used to refer to the much broader responsibility of relating to all project-related functions between the parties to a contract—not only the traditional contract administration duties, but the conduct of the parties, relations with the contractor, communications, business systems, procedures, responsibility, authority, and duties of all of the parties, documentation requirements, construction operations, planning and scheduling, coordination, materials control, payment administration, change orders and extra work, dispute and claim handling, negotiations, and all project closeout functions, including punch list inspections, final cleanup, and administrative closeout. Thus, as used in this book, contract administration is just a part of construction project administration.

It is not uncommon for the architect/engineer's or owner's Project Manager to function as the contract administrator, working out of the home office, who jealously guards the control of the job by reserving all meaningful project administration duties to him- or herself, while the authority of the Resident Project Representative at the project site is often limited to inspection and routine clerical duties. However, it is organizational hierarchies such as that which are the root cause of numerous construction claims losses to the owner or architect/engineer.

The mark of a good manager is the ability to select and hire qualified people and then to be willing to delegate as much authority as possible to such people. As long as a manager refuses to delegate and reserves all or most of the contract administration tasks to him- or herself, the capabilities of that manager will be severely inhibited, and furthermore, the Project Manager will be incurring considerable risk of loss to the parent organization through potential delay claim losses. A manager's authority is in no way diminished through delegation, but rather is strengthened.

As a means of implementing such a sound relationship between a Project Manager and a Resident Project Representative, the organizational chart shown in Figure 1.2 suggests a division of responsibility between field and office management personnel. A Project Manager can efficiently handle several projects without needlessly delaying any one of them by delegating the authority to make decisions on matters that should be decided at the Resident Project Representative's level. This contributes to the smooth and efficient operation of the construction activities and lessens the risk of contractor delay claims that would

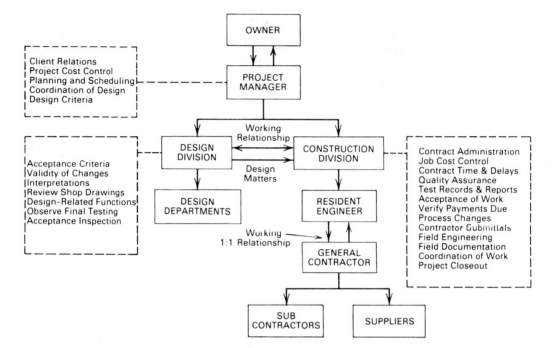

**Client Relations**
**Project Cost Control**
**Planning and Scheduling**
**Coordination of Design**
**Design Criteria**

**Acceptance Criteria**
**Validity of Changes**
**Interpretations**
**Review Shop Drawings**
**Design-Related Functions**
**Observe Final Testing**
**Acceptance Inspection**

**Contract Administration**
**Job Cost Control**
**Contract Time & Delays**
**Quality Assurance**
**Test Records & Reports**
**Acceptance of Work**
**Verify Payments Due**
**Process Changes**
**Contractor Submittals**
**Field Engineering**
**Field Documentation**
**Coordination of Work**
**Project Closeout**

**FIGURE 1.2**   Delegation of authority by the Project Manager during construction phase of a project.

normally follow the delays caused by routing routine matters through the home office as a prerequisite to obtaining permission to act.

The Resident Project Representative is under obligation to keep the Project Manager informed every step of the way. Where the Project Manager's decision is required, the Resident Project Representative should obtain a decision by telephone or FAX prior to issuing a consent order to a contractor to proceed with some particular work or corrective action. Then, of course, proper administrative paperwork must be completed to confirm the actions taken. Failure to expedite decisions often results in otherwise preventable claims which have a way of escalating into major claims the longer they take to be resolved.

The most effective Project Manager, or Contracting Officer on U.S. federal projects, is the person who is willing to delegate as many contract administration functions as possible to the Resident Project Representative in the on-site field office (the one-to-one concept). If unwilling to delegate, the Project Manager's only alternative to save the job is to relocate the Project Manager's office to the job site and run the project from there.

### The One-to-One Concept

One of the single most important philosophies in construction project administration, the *one-to-one concept,* is a vital administrative procedure that can eliminate much conflict, reduce exposure to claims-producing problems, and result in greater efficiency for all parties to the contract.

Under this concept, the owner or architect/engineer designates a single individual, preferably located at the project site, to be the sole spokesperson representing the owner's interests. This person should be the Resident Project Representative. Under this arrangement, *all* orders issued to the contractor must be issued through the Resident Project Representative, and no one in either the owner's or the architect/engineer's or construction manager's office should be permitted to make any commitments to or issue orders or instructions directly to the contractor or any of its subcontractors, except by communicating such orders to the Resident Project Representative for issuing to the contractor. Failure to follow this procedure may place the owner and the contractor in a difficult contractual position. Under the contract law principle of implied authority, it is generally held that the contractor may receive orders from any individual whom it has reason to believe has the authority to issue such orders on behalf of the owner (see "Apparent Authority" in Chapter 2). Thus, the project manager, department heads, vice presidents, city or county engineers, or other persons of authority might otherwise visit the site and make statements that result in the creation of constructive changes (see Chapter 18) and not only bind the owner, but lay the foundation for a contractor claim.

One situation where the author visited a construction site with a principal of an engineering firm was a classic example of what *not* to do. Upon arrival at the site, the principal went to the field office to confer with the Resident Project Representative. Then, accompanied by the Resident Project Representative, the principal toured the project site (one of his monthly site visits) with the Resident Project Representative and the contractor's representative. Up to this point, everything was done "by the book." However, from this point on, the principal's actions became a classic example of what not to do.

The principal listened to the contractor's side of the difficulties experienced during the previous month, including failure to achieve certain high standards of quality and workmanship in certain areas. The principal listened, then unbelievably made commitments to the contractor by accepting such nonconforming work without ever talking it over with the Resident Project Representative. In short, he gave away the store!

To complicate matters further, the principal's actions totally stripped the Resident Project Representative of his authority and ability to deal effectively with the contractor, as after that the contractor realized that all that would be necessary to avoid unpopular decisions made in the field would be to do an end-run around the Resident Project Representative and go directly to the principal to obtain concessions. Thus the principal's work load is increased, the effectiveness of the on-site inspection forces is diminished, and the risk of claims is greatly increased.

What should have been done would be for the principal to listen to the contractor's comments about the project without offering comment at that time, then go back to the field office with the Resident Project Representative and, behind closed doors, discuss the events and issue orders to the Resident Project Representative as to the acceptability or nonacceptability of the contractor's work. This would have placed the Resident Project Representative in a position of receiving backing from the home office, and the contractor would have realized that in the end, all orders will be received only from the Resident Project Representative.

The principal is still the only person with the authority to make the final determination, but is advised to issue those orders only through the Resident Project Representative to preserve the one-to-one relationship. One of the greatest difficulties, where a project is being administered by an architect or engineer on behalf of an owner, is to keep the owner from violating this vital management concept.

As a part of the one-to-one concept, the contractor, too, must organize so that a single management person located at the project site is designated as the contractor's sole agent. This is best set up as a provision of the specifications. Then, it should be arranged during the preconstruction conference that the contractor's agent should be designated in writing, and that no substitutions are permitted under the contract without the written authority of the corporate office. The designated person should be capable of speaking officially for the contractor, although it is certainly acceptable to use an on-site superintendent or project manager as the agent of the contractor, just as the engineer or architect uses his or her Resident Project Representative.

## The 5-Step Process of Initiating a Project

An important part of organizing a project so as to avoid later difficulties, which could include award disputes, charges of preference, loss of money due to bidder default, and later disputes over lost time and delays in the work, is the initiation of the project according to an orderly administrative procedure. This process is what the author calls the "5-step project initiation process" (Figure 1.3). It holds that there are five vital steps that must be followed when initiating a project, especially in public works projects:

1. Advertise or invite bids.
2. Open bids.
3. Award contract.
4. Sign agreement or "contract."
5. Issue Notice to Proceed.

While it is common for many owners and architects or engineers to follow most of these steps, items 4 and 5 are, unfortunately, often combined, sometimes even with the uninformed blessing of the owner's attorney, as well.

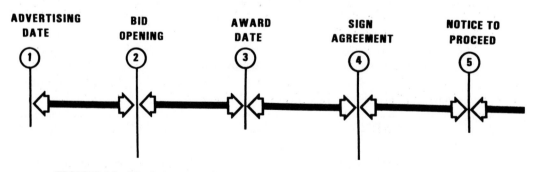

**FIGURE 1.3**   The 5-step process.

An important point should be noted here. The procedures for the signing of the agreement often take time. If a cautious contractor chooses to wait until it actually "sees" the agreement with the owner's signature, and if the project time is stated in the agreement as beginning as of the date of signing the agreement, there is the possibility of a valid delay claim against the owner even before the project begins. The contractor can rightfully claim that (1) it could not start until a signed contract was received, (2) the time lost in receiving the signed document was part of its construction time, and (3) it should be compensated with an extension of project time to cover the days lost while waiting for a signed agreement.

Throughout the book references will be made to the 5-step process and partial diagrams will retain the identification numbers in the foregoing list to identify any of the five tasks listed.

## CONTROL OF QUALITY IN CONSTRUCTION

Without definition, the term *quality control* in construction can have several meanings. To be sure, the actual quality of construction depends largely upon the control of the construction itself, thus involving the contractor to a great extent. What constitutes quality control and quality assurance appears to be the subject of dispute by some. For example, checking the placement of reinforcing steel in concrete formwork may be considered as quality control if the contractor does it, and as quality assurance if the owner observes or verifies that it has been done; yet the physical act of checking this work is exactly the same in either case.

Whether the subject is called quality control or quality assurance, the function performed is essentially that which has been recognized over the years as being construction inspection and testing of materials and workmanship to see that the work meets the requirements of the drawings and specifications. Inspection takes many forms, and its responsibilities vary somewhat depending upon the intended inspection objective. As an example, an inspector in the employ of the local building official is principally concerned with the safety and integrity of the structure being built, and whether it meets the local building code requirements. Quality of workmanship or aesthetics is largely beyond the inspector's responsibility and, because his or her salary is paid by the public, quality of workmanship is, to a great extent, left to the owner to control, using the owner's, contractor's , or designer's personnel. However, inspection by the owner's representative is intended to include concern not only for the structural integrity and safety of the structure, but also for the quality of workmanship, selection of materials being used, aesthetic values, and similar matters involving compliance with the provisions of the contract plans and specifications.

## ORGANIZATIONAL STRUCTURE OF A CONSTRUCTION PROJECT

There is no single organization chart that will remotely approximate the organizational structure of the field forces of the owner, the design organization, or the contractor on all projects. Before the internal structure of any of the principals to a construction contract can be examined, some understanding of the several basic types of contractual relationships must be gained. Of the several types of contractual relationships frequently encountered in construction, four of the principal types are:

1. Traditional architect/engineer (A/E) contract
2. Design/construction manager (D/CM) contract
3. Professional construction manager (PCM) contract
4. Design–build contract (similar to turnkey construction)

Under the provisions of the *traditional architect/engineer* contract illustrated in Figure 1.1, the owner usually engages the services of an architect/engineer to perform planning and design services, including preparation of plans, specifications, and estimates. Professional services of the architect/engineer during the construction are generally limited to performance of intermittent field visitations and certain contract administration functions such as review of the contractor's payment requests, review of shop drawings, evaluation of contractor claims, interpretation of plans and specifications during construction, change order requests, and final inspection.

A *design/construction manager* contract, illustrated in Figure 1.4, is quite similar to the traditional A/E contract with the exception that the architect/engineer's project manager is fully responsible to the owner during both the design and planning phases as well as the entire construction phase to provide for all project needs. This includes all scheduling, cost control, quality control, long-lead purchasing, letting of single or multiple contracts, and

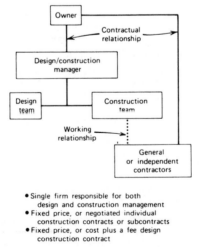

DESIGN/CONSTRUCTION MANAGER

- Single firm responsible for both design and construction management
- Fixed price, or negotiated individual construction contracts or subcontracts
- Fixed price, or cost plus a fee design construction contract

**FIGURE 1.4**   Contractual relationships under a design/construction manager-type contract.

coordination of the work. The design/CM responsibilities do not terminate until final acceptance of the completed project by the owner.

These responsibilities include the examination of cost-saving alternatives during both the design and construction phases of the project, and the authority to require the design or construction changes necessary to accomplish the owner's objectives.

A *professional construction management (PCM)* contract is based upon a concept pioneered several years ago by the General Services Administration of the federal government, and for a time was used extensively by that agency for the construction of public buildings. Although the functions performed by the professional construction manager may be no different than those of a design firm doing construction management, the responsibilities and contractual status are significantly different. Under the professional construction manager (PCM) concept, illustrated in Figure 1.5, the owner engages a construction management firm under a separate contract in addition to a conventional architect/engineer and construction contractor contract. Thus, instead of only two contracts for a project, the owner has actually executed three. In keeping with the principles of this concept, the professional construction management firm performs no design or construction with its own forces, but acts solely in the capacity of an owner's representative during the life of the project. In many cases, the PCM is responsible for reviewing the architect/engineer's payment requests in addition to those of the contractor. In any case, the PCM is responsible for total project time and cost control and coordination as well as quality control and, as such,

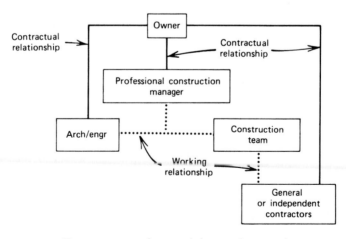

PROFESSIONAL CONSTRUCTION MANAGER

- Three party team of owner, designer, and construction manager
- Fixed price or negotiated individual construction contracts directly with owner
- Construction manager may act as owner's agent to extent delegated
- Negotiated professional fee for construction management services
- Negotiated professional fee for design services

**FIGURE 1.5**   Contractual relationships under a professional construction manager contract.

provides supervision and control over those functions of the architect/engineer and the contractor that relate to these important subject areas.

One important distinction is that a "construction manager" under this concept is an organization, not a single individual. Thus the construction management firm may provide a staff of both field and office personnel, including a project manager, estimators, schedulers, accountants, construction coordinators, field engineers, quality control personnel, and others.

A *design–build* contract, illustrated in Figure 1.6, popularly called *turnkey construction,* is based upon the owner entering into an agreement with a single firm to produce all planning, design, and construction with its own in-house capabilities. Some organizations recognize a further distinction between design–build and turnkey construction in that both provide both design and construction by a single organization, or joint venture, but the turnkey contractor also assembles the financing package. Such design–build firms are generally licensed as both architect/engineers and as general construction contractors in those states that require it, and offer a complete package deal to the owner. Its principal advantages, where its use is permitted, are the elimination of contractor claims against the owner resulting from errors in the plans or specifications and the ability to begin construction on each separate phase of a project as it is completed, without waiting for overall project design completion—the "fast-track" concept. It is in the design–build industry that fast-track construction was born.

There is one disadvantage in the system when public funds are involved in construction. Under most laws, a construction contractor must be obtained through a competitive bidding process, and the lowest bidder gets the job. Usually, design firms and construction management organizations are selected on the basis of their individual expertise and previous experience in the type of work to be designed. Under this concept it is felt that the greatest savings and cost benefits to the owner will be obtained by careful planning during the design stage, and that the occasional cost savings that might result from competitively bidding the design responsibilities would be more than lost in the resultant higher construction

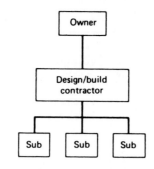

- Combined designer and construction contractor
- Numerous subcontractors
- Fixed price, guaranteed maximum or cost
  plus fixed fee designed/build contract
- No separate fee for design services

**FIGURE 1.6**   Design–build contract relationships (similar to turnkey construction).

cost that all too often follows a set of plans and specifications that had to be prepared in a hurry without checking.

### Staff Assignments for Construction Quality Assurance/Control

The staff requirements for the construction management and quality assurance/control activities of a construction project vary from job to job and from one employer to another. Although there seems to be a lack of uniformity in the structuring of many owners' or architect/engineers' field forces during construction, the average contractor organization seems to be extremely well organized in this area. This is probably to be expected, as the contractor organization is performing its primary function at the site, whereas the owner or architect/engineer is often on less familiar ground during the construction phase, even though the contract may call for the architect/engineer performance of some construction management functions.

In an attempt to compare job assignments and titles of positions of comparable authority from one organization to the next, the numerous titles of the same job emphasize the difficulty of determining position by title alone. Figure 1.7 is a chart of the normal functional relationships under a design/construction management contract, which will be used to illustrate the problem.

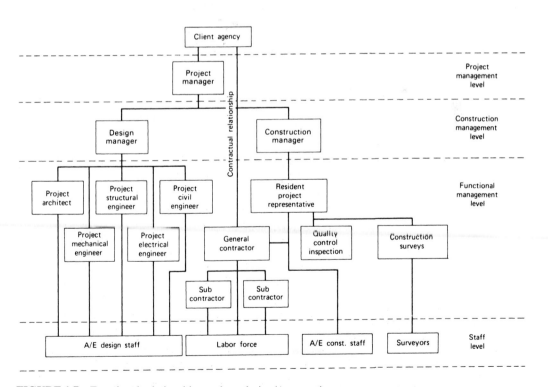

**FIGURE 1.7** Functional relationships under a design/construction manager contract.

An example of supervisory job titles of comparable authority is shown in the following table, which is based upon actual job titles used by some contractor and architect/engineer offices to designate the various levels of supervisory and management personnel utilized during the construction phase of a project. The levels indicated are those used in Figure 1.7.

| Level | Owner or Architect/Engineer | Contractor |
|---|---|---|
| Project Management level | Project Manager | Project Manager |
| | Project Engineer | |
| | Project Architect | General Superintendent |
| | Project Director | Construction Manager |
| Construction Management level | Construction Manager | Construction Manager |
| | Resident Engineer | Project Engineer |
| | Resident Architect | Superintendent |
| | Construction Coordinator | |
| | Resident Manager | |
| Functional Management level | Resident Project Representative | Project Engineer |
| | Project Representative | Superintendent |
| | Resident Engineer | CQC Representative |
| | Resident Inspector | |
| | Inspector | |
| | Quality Control Supervisor | |

All of these levels share in the responsibility of administering various provisions of the construction contract for their respective employers. In addition to the foregoing list of full-time personnel on the project site, numerous tasks remain to be performed by specialty inspectors and representatives of the various local government agencies having jurisdiction over the project. These include the following public and private specialty and code enforcement inspectors:

1. Local building department (code enforcement)
2. Soils inspectors
3. Inspectors of other agencies whose facilities are involved
4. Utility company inspectors
5. Specialty inspectors (concrete, masonry, welding, etc.)
6. Manufacturers' representatives (special equipment or materials)
7. OSHA safety inspectors

Each of the specialty and code enforcement inspectors is responsible only for its particular specialty task; thus, the overall responsibility for project administration and quality control falls on the shoulders of the Resident Project Representative of the owner or design firm or the contractor's quality control (CQC) representative.

### Full-Time versus Part-Time Project Representative

Not all construction projects subject to inspection by the owner or the design firm will require a full-time inspector. It is not infrequent for a single construction inspector to be assigned the responsibility of the Resident Project Representative for several projects at the same time. Usually, this is a method used to provide quality assurance inspections on smaller projects whose budgets or complexity of construction do not justify the financial burden of a full-time Resident Project Representative. The difference in responsibility is slight, as the administrative responsibilities are identical to those of the full-time Resident Project Representative on a single large project. As for the inspections performed, the inspector merely schedules field visits so as to be at each of the projects at key times during construction. Generally, an inspector should be on call and be able to respond to a specific field problem on short notice. Thus, in this book, the responsibilities and duties of the full-time Resident Project Representative should be understood to apply equally to a part-time project representative working directly out of the home office.

## PROFESSIONAL CONSTRUCTION MANAGEMENT

### The CM Controversy

CM by now has become a byword in the construction industry. But do most people actually know what it means? Even some industry giants seem to be confused.

The term *construction manager* is one of the most misunderstood titles of modern day construction and defies an accurate definition that is acceptable to everyone. Definitions have ranged from applying the term to the Resident Project Representative, to the other extreme of being a third prime contract with the owner (the other two prime contracts being those of the architect/engineer and the general construction contractor). In the latter case, the construction manager is the owner's agent and the duties of the position require supervision over some of the functions of both the design firm and the contractor. The American Society of Civil Engineers refers to this function as *professional construction management* to distinguish it from the type of construction management practiced by the design/construction management firms; others call it *third-party CM* or a *CM agency contract.* Both the American Institute of Architects (AIA) and the Associated General Contractors of America (AGC) simply refer to this type of contract as *construction management.*

Each of the major professional and technical organizations seems to agree in principle on the concept that the construction manager should be a firm that has no direct connection with either the architect/engineer firm that designs the project or the general contracting firm that constructs it. Even when a general contractor acts as construction manager, the AGC recommends that they enter into contract under a professional services agreement, and that the firm does not use any of its own construction forces to build the project. The principal difference between the professional services agreement proposed by the AGC and, for example, that of the AIA is that the AGC contract provides for quoting a guaranteed maximum project cost after the construction management team has developed the drawings and specifications to a point where the scope of the project is clearly defined. Under the AIA contract form, no price guarantees are made.

Yet, where many organizations seem to miss the point is that CM involves participation by the Construction Manager from the very conception of the project, through the investigation and design process, selection of feasible separate bid packages, value engineering, constructability analysis, bidability analysis, preparation of input into the specifications and other front-end documents, assistance in examining bids and awarding the contract, and finally, participation in the construction phase in the form of scheduling, cost control, coordination, contract administration, and final closeout of a project. Yet many in the construction industry are still confused by the rather ill-chosen name *Construction Management* and still only recognize the construction-phase tasks as being construction management. This is easily understandable, as the term in itself does suggest that its duties should occur during the construction phase only. This is precisely why, a number of years ago, the American Consulting Engineers Council (ACEC) began to refer to third-party CM as the *ACEC Project Management System.* Strictly speaking, it is just that—a project management system. However, the term *CM* sticks to this day, so the industry needs to understand it better.

Unfortunately, the problem is further complicated by the fact that even in the prestigious *Engineering News-Record (ENR),* in their annual list of top-rated CM firms, some of them are known by the author to never have done a single project that met the definition of third-party CM. The services they actually performed were better described as "services during construction." The firms in question simply performed contract administration and inspection and believed it to be CM. Other firms in the list performed the full range of services, beginning with the conceptual phase and continuing through the design phase before finally entering the construction phase. *ENR* has no way of determining the difference in interpretation by the various companies, as their reporting is based upon reported CM revenues claimed by the listed companies.

### Engineering Definition of Professional Construction Management

The Construction Management Committee of the American Society of Civil Engineers originally defined a professional *construction manager* as a firm or organization specializing in the practice of construction management or practicing it on a particular project as a part of a project management team consisting of the owner, a design organization, and the construction manager (usually referred to as CM). As the construction professional on the project management team, the CM provides the following services or portions of such services, as appropriate:

1. Works with the owner and design organization from the beginning of design through completion of construction; provides leadership to construction team on all matters that relate to construction; makes recommendations on construction technology, schedules, and construction economies.

2. Proposes construction alternatives to be studied by the project management team during the planning phase, and predicts the effect of these alternatives on the pro-

ject cost and schedule; once the project budget, schedule, and quality requirements have been established, the CM monitors subsequent development of the project to see that those targets are not exceeded without the knowledge of the owner.

**3.** Advises on and coordinates procurement of material and equipment and the work of all the construction contractors; monitors and inspects for conformity to design requirements; provides current cost and progress information as the work proceeds; and performs other construction-related services as required by the owner.

**4.** In keeping with the nonadversary relationship of the team members, the CM does not normally perform significant design or construction work with its own forces. (In a more recent action, the ASCE Committee on Construction Management also accepts the concept of CM being performed by the firm responsible for design.)

The typical functional relationships associated with a professional construction management contract are best shown in Figure 1.8, which was prepared by the General Services Administration, Public Buildings Service of the federal government.

### Fast-Track Construction

Frequently, a construction management contract is encountered that requires the letting and administering of multiple construction contracts for the same project, with each let at different times during the life of the project. Such staggered letting of construction contracts on the same project is referred to as *fast-track* contracting, and its principal objective is to shorten construction time for the overall project by starting some portions of the work as soon as it has been designed (Chapter 12), even though other portions of the project have not yet been designed. It is a risky process, depending heavily upon the careful selection of the various separate bid packages and the ability to schedule and control the design effort. Without this, fast-track can become the most costly method ever designed for completing a project late. Many times, such contracts also require purchase of special equipment or materials long before a contract has been let to install them. This is referred to as *long-lead procurement,* and such early purchases, along with the accompanying expediting and scheduling, is one of the functions required to be performed by the CM team. The Resident Project Representative is a vital link in the successful operation of a construction management contract and will be called upon to assist in many of the tasks described. When utilizing the fast-track process, the services of a construction management firm is essential, as the skills and experience required to complete a fast-track project successfully are seldom possessed by the design firm. On the other hand, if a single prime (general) contractor is used to build a project, the use of a construction management firm may actually be redundant, as many of the tasks that the CM is being paid for will ordinarily be done by the general contractor.

## DESIGN–BUILD CONTRACTS

The design–build concept, as originally conceived, was based on the concept that a single firm had the in-house staff and expertise to perform all planning, design, and construction tasks. Later, increased interest in the concept had engineers, architects, and conventional

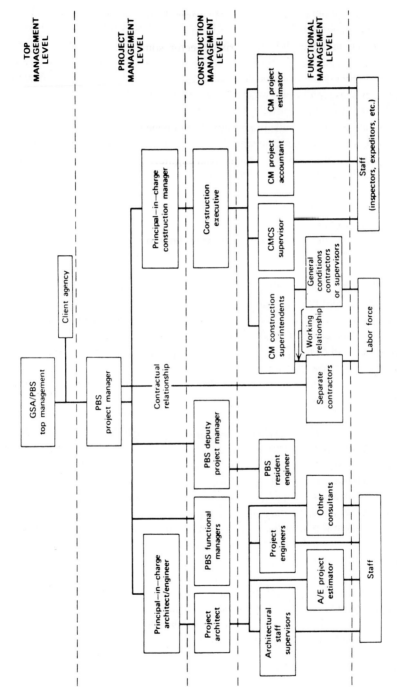

**FIGURE 1.8** Functional relationships under a General Services Administration professional construction management contract.

contractors seeking to compete with the original design–build firms to meet the growing interest by owners in the project delivery process.

While quite popular in the private sector, some public agencies find that the process still presents legal hurdles resulting from alleged conflicts between the design professional selection process under the Brooks Law and similar local regulations and the competitive bidding process traditionally used for contractor award.

Under the new approach, instead of limiting design–build to firms with in-house capability in both areas, the field has now been opened up to permit contracts with engineers who subcontract the construction portion to a contracting firm, with construction contractors that subcontract design services to an engineer or architect, and with engineers and architects in joint venture with contractor firms.

In recognition of the new relationships, a new group of standard contract documents for design–build projects was recently completed by the Engineers Joint Contract Documents Committee (EJCDC).[1] They are available from ASCE, NSPE, or ACEC. The documents, and an accompanying guide on how to use them, are probably the most comprehensive set of standard documents now available to those who work with design–build projects.

The new documents cover a variety of situations—for example, the relationship between owner and design–builder, which includes both general conditions and two agreements (one for a stipulated sum contract, another for a cost-plus contract that has a provision for guaranteed maximum price). For design–builders without a professional in-house staff to perform design services, EJCDC has prepared a subagreement to be used by both design–builder and engineer. To cover the relationship between design–builders and construction subcontractors, another document covers general conditions and two subagreements (one for stipulated price, the other for cost-plus).

Among the highlights of the new documents are descriptions of the selection process; scope definition; differentiation of design and construction work in several areas (such as providing for a general warranty and guarantee for construction work as well as a standard of care for design work); a dispute resolution process; responsibilities for subsurface conditions; remedies in the event an engineer is asked by design–builders to compromise an engineer's legal and professional responsibilities; and communications among engineer, design–builder, and owner.

An integral part of the new group of documents is a separate guide describing their use. The guide includes a commentary, a guide for preparing requests for proposals, a suggested proposal form, and a "how-to" guide on the preparation of supplementary conditions.

Because many owners don't have the in-house expertise to prepare proposal documents (or review design–builders' design submittals, observe the quality of construction, and so forth), EJCDC is now preparing another document for use by the owner (and an owner's consultant) to cover such services.

---

[1]EJCDC is a multidisciplinary group made up of American Society of Civil Engineers (ASCE), the National Society of Professional Engineers (NSPE), and the American Consulting Engineers Council (ACEC).

## DEFINITIONS OF INDIVIDUAL CONSTRUCTION RESPONSIBILITIES

Local building codes often require intermittent and sometimes "continuous" inspection on certain critical types of construction, such as structural concrete, structural masonry, pre-stressed concrete, structural welding, high-strength bolting, and similar work to be performed by special inspectors. The word *continuous* in this context is sometimes confusing because there are cases in which "continuous" is not synonymous with "constant" without a reasonable interpretation. Work on structural masonry or concrete work that can be inspected only as it is being placed requires the *constant* presence of the inspector. Placement of forms for concrete or reinforcing for concrete can fairly be interpreted as requiring continuous monitoring of the work so as to miss nothing, yet would hardly be interpreted as requiring the inspector's presence during the entire time that the steel is being placed. Generally, any special inspector coming onto the job will be under the authority of the Resident Project Representative and should be advised to follow his or her instructions.

### Project Manager

Every participating organization on a project has its *project manager.* Although the person is sometimes known by different names, the duties remain the same. Whether in the direct employ of the owner, the design firm, or the contractor, the project manager (PM) is usually the person responsible for the management of all phases of the project for his or her organization. For a design firm, the project manager controls the scheduling, budgeting, cost control coordination of design and construction, letting of contracts for the owner, and is normally the sole contact with the client as a representative of the design firm.

For the owner, a project manager is similarly responsible for all phases of a project, but may participate in architect/engineer selection and is the representative of the owner in connection with any business concerning the project. Where an architect/engineer firm has been engaged for design services only, the owner's project manager will provide construction contract administration and may employ a Resident Project Representative or other on-site quality control personnel to work under his or her supervision. Wherever this is the case, the architect/engineer may still be called upon to review shop drawings for the owner, and wherever a proposed design change is contemplated, the architect/engineer of record should always be consulted.

In a contractor's organization, "project manager" is also a frequently used title, although many very large firms still use the title "superintendent" for this function. As the title implies, the contractor's project manager is in complete charge of his or her project for the general contractor. This particular project manager or superintendent's responsibilities include coordination of subcontractors, scheduling, cost control, labor relations, billing, purchasing, expediting, and numerous other functions related to the project. To the owner, the PM or superintendent is the general contractor. Whether referred to as project manager or as superintendent, his or her duties are the same in many contractor organizations.

## Professional Construction Manager

The services performed by the professional construction manager cover a broad range of activities and, to some extent, overlap those traditionally performed by both the architect/engineer and the construction contractor, involving both the design and construction phases of a project. A comprehensive construction management contract may easily cover any if not all of the tasks included within the following six categories:

1. Participation in determining the bidding strategy involved in a fast-track, multiple-prime-contract project so as to avoid conflicts during the letting of the separate contracts.
2. Design phase review, including review of formal design submittals, review of contract documents, and overall constructability analysis.
3. Cost management, including estimates of construction cost and development of the project budget.
4. Scheduling for all phases of a project, generally incorporating critical path techniques.
5. Bid opening and evaluation, and assistance in contractor selection.
6. On-site, construction-phase management to provide contract administration, inspection, coordination, and field management.

On-site, construction-phase management may include coordination of separate contracts, phased construction (fast-track) contracts, monitoring of individual phases of the work, adjustment of the work to accommodate changed conditions or unanticipated interferences, determination of whether materials and workmanship are in conformance with the approved contract drawings and specifications, arrangements for the performance of necessary field and laboratory tests where required, preparation of change orders and change proposals, and review of progress payments and recommendations to the owner for payments to the contractors.

The construction manager (CM) may also, in some contracts, provide certain services that would normally have been provided by a general contractor, had there been one. These might well include establishment, maintenance, and operation of temporary field construction facilities, provisions for site security, cleanup, temporary utilities, and similar General Conditions items of work. Such items of work are generally paid for under this type of contract on a reimbursable basis and are not a part of the construction manager's professional fee for services. In certain respects, the professional construction manager's responsibilities may overlap or even preempt those of the contractor and the architect/engineer under some contracts.

## Quality Control Representative

Under the provisions of the construction contracts of numerous federal agencies, in particular the Corps of Engineers, Naval Facilities Engineering Command, National Aeronautics and Space Administration, and others, an inspection concept known as *contractor quality control* (CQC) is often implemented. While not favored by much of the construction industry, under this system the contractor must organize and maintain an inspection system within the organization to assure that the work performed by the contractor and subcontractor forces conforms to contract requirements, and to make available to the government adequate records of such inspections. Under the majority of such plans, as implemented by their respective agencies, a government representative is stationed on-site to provide quality assurance inspections. In some cases, the design firm may be engaged to provide quality assurance inspection in addition to contractor quality control. In such cases, the design firm may have a full-time Resident Project Representative and supporting staff on-site to perform this function.

## Resident Project Representative; Resident Engineer; Resident Inspector; Resident Manager

These titles usually refer to an on-site full-time project representative to whom has been delegated the authority and responsibility of administering the field operations of a construction project as the representative of the owner or the design firm. On some occasions, the inspection needs of a particular project may require that the Resident Project Representative be a qualified, registered professional engineer; in other cases, a highly qualified nonregistered engineer may be desired. Wherever a nonregistered engineer is permissible, it is often equally acceptable to use an experienced construction inspector for this purpose. The American Institute of Architects, in their documents, describe this individual as the "full-time project representative," whereas the Engineers Joint Contract Documents Committee[2] uses the term "Resident Project Representative." In this book the term *Resident Project Representative* is used to stand collectively for resident engineer, resident inspector, full-time project representative, resident manager, and project representative.

## Inspector; Field Engineer; Quality Assurance Supervisor

These titles usually refer to a staff-level, on-site representative of the owner, design firm, or contractor who has the responsibility of observing the work being performed and of reporting any variations from the plans and specifications or other contract documents. In addition, the inspector should call to the attention of the quality control supervisor or Resident Project Representative any unforeseen field conditions in time for remedial measures to be taken without creating delays in the work or changes in existing work to correct a problem. The inspector is the on-site eyes and ears of his or her employer, and although not empowered to make field changes that depart from the plans and specifications, the inspector should be capable of evaluating field problems and submitting competent recommendations to his or her supervisor. On projects using a Resident Project Representative, the inspector will normally work under that person's direct supervision.

---

[2]Comprised of American Consulting Engineers Council, American Society of Civil Engineers, National Society of Professional Engineers, and Construction Specifications Institute. Endorsed by Associated General Contractors of America.

Except for the responsibility for construction field administration, which is one of the principal functions of the Resident Project Representative, the inspector's job is identical in all respects to that of the Resident Project Representative. Inspection of construction is an occupation that requires a highly qualified person with a good working knowledge of construction practices, construction materials, specifications, and construction contract provisions. It is not in itself a job title, as the inspector may be a registered professional engineer or architect, a field engineer, a quality control specialist, or any of a host of other classifications. In this book the term *inspector* will be used to stand collectively for field engineer, inspector, quality control supervisor, or in some cases, the Resident Project Representative where the duties referred to apply to all field representatives on site, whether full- or part-time.

## DEFINING SCOPE OF WORK IN A CM CONTRACT

It is important, because of the differences in definition of the term *CM,* to clearly define the scope of the services to be performed in the CM contract with the owner. Without such definition, there are often claims and disputes between the architect/engineer as CM and the owner, due to a failure of the parties to achieve a meeting of the minds, as one party assumes that the term includes services that the other party never planned to provide for the basic fee agreed upon.

### Construction Administration Task List

It is recommended that all anticipated tasks be listed and included in any CM contract executed with the owner. A checklist of some of the tasks that may be involved follows:

**Conceptual Phase**
Develop conceptual estimates
Develop conceptual schedules
Provide input to program risk analysis

**Program Planning Phase**
Provide constructability analysis
Identify potential major construction problems
Develop project resource requirements
Inventory available area resources
Assist in development of capital budgets
Assist in development of cash flow projections
Develop parametric estimates and cost budgets
Update preliminary schedule
Develop preliminary project control system
Develop preliminary project management information system

Develop project safety program

Develop project labor relations program

Assist in development of insurance program

Administer electronic data processing (EDP) services

**Design Phase**

Oversee overall project planning

Assist in development of project life-cycle costs

Evaluate cost trade-offs

Provide value engineering function

Qualify potential bidders

Procure long-lead-time items

Finalize bid work packages

Finalize prequalified contractor lists

Finalize project schedules

Finalize physical layout of construction areas

Finalize project control systems and management information systems

Assist in obtaining required permits and licenses

Provide input and review of contract documents

**Construction Phase**

Develop and administer area transportation system

Administer project EEO program

Enforce project safety program

Coordinate labor relations

Receive and evaluate bids and award prime contracts

Manage and perform general conditions tasks

Implement time- and cost-control systems

Manage daily construction activities of the owner or architect/engineer

Administer prime contracts

Receive, review, and approve contractor's requests for progress payments

Administer contract changes and claims

Quality assurance and inspection

Interpret contract documents

**Closeout and Startup Phase**

Oversee project closeout

Oversee systems validation, testing, and startup

## RESPONSIBILITY FOR COORDINATION OF THE TRADES

Construction projects of any size usually require the efforts of several specialty contractors. Usually, of course, such work is performed under subcontract with a general contractor who is responsible for the coordination of all of the subcontractors.

A large number of claims involving changes, delays, and even site conditions result from coordination problems. As a result, the courts have been asked to determine who is responsible, as well as the scope of that responsibility. Changes in the methods of construction contracting, such as design–build and multiple prime contracts, have made the problem worse and increased the volume of litigation.

### Owner's Responsibility

Traditionally, the owner has had no responsibility for coordination of subcontractors. Scheduling and coordination of the trades has traditionally been the exclusive responsibility of the general contractor, and most standard construction contracts are clear on this issue. The owner's obligation is simply to avoid any active interference with the work of the various contractors.

As long as a single general contractor is used to construct a project, this will still hold true. However, if the owner awards more than one prime contract or elects to perform some of the work with its own forces, the owner inherits coordination responsibilities.

On a multiple-prime project, the owner is responsible for coordinating the various trade contractors with whom it has contracted in much the same way as a general contractor must coordinate its subcontractors. Few owners are equipped to do this, which has created the need for the professional construction manager.

Less apparent to owners is the fact that if they perform even a small portion of the work themselves, they have an implied obligation to coordinate the work in order to avoid economic harm to the prime contractors. Failure to meet this obligation can be expensive for the owners, as payment of delay damages will quickly offset the savings realized from performing the work with one's own forces.

On traditional projects, the project architect/engineer is not responsible for coordinating the various trades. The architect/engineer may be called upon to interpret the requirements of the contract documents to resolve scope-of-work problems, but will not become involved in the actual scheduling or coordinating of the work itself.

On a multiple-prime project, however, the owner's representative (usually called the construction manager) plays a very different role. In the absence of a general contractor, the owner must rely on the construction manager to provide overall scheduling and coordination of the trade contractors. In such a case, if improper coordination delays harm one of the contractors, the construction manager may be held liable.

The construction manager may be held directly liable to the contractor on a theory of negligence. More commonly, the contractor will sue the owner with whom it has contracted. The owner may then seek indemnification from the construction manager, arguing that any liability to the contractor is the result of the construction manager's failure to perform its duties properly, as established in the owner-construction manager agreement. This is part of what the owner pays for in awarding a lump sum contract to a single general contractor.

## THE PARTNERING CONCEPT[3]

The Partnering concept is not a new way of doing business; some have always conducted themselves in this manner. It is going back to the way people used to do business when their word was their bond and people accepted responsibility. Partnering is not a contract, but a recognition that every contract includes an implied covenant of good faith.

While the contract establishes the legal relationships, the Partnering process is designed to establish working relationships among the parties through a mutually-developed, formal strategy of commitment and communication. It attempts to create an environment where trust and teamwork prevent disputes, foster a cooperative bond to everyone's benefit, and facilitate the completion of a successful project.

For the most effective results, parties involved in the contract should conduct a Partnering workshop, ideally at the early stages of the contract. The sole agenda of the workshop is to establish and begin implementing the partnering process. This forum produces the opportunity to initiate the key elements of Partnering.

The key elements of Partnering include the following:

*Commitment.* Commitment to Partnering must come from top management. The jointly developed Partnering charter is not a contract, but a symbol of commitment.

*Equity.* All of the parties' interests need to be considered in creating mutual goals, and there must be a commitment to satisfying each of the parties' requirements for a successful project by utilizing win/win thinking.

*Trust.* Teamwork is not possible where there is cynicism about others' motives. Through the development of personal relationships and communication about each of the parties' risks and goals, there will be better understanding. Along with understanding comes trust, and with trust comes the possibility for a cooperative relationship.

*Development of Mutual Goals/Objectives.* At a Partnering workshop the parties should identify all respective goals for the project in which their interests overlap. These jointly-developed and mutually agreed upon goals may include achieving value engineering savings, meeting the financial goals of each party, limiting cost growth, limiting review periods for contract submittals, early completion, no lost time because of injuries, minimizing paperwork generated for the purpose of case building or posturing, no litigation, or other goals specific to the nature of the project.

*Implementation.* The parties jointly should develop strategies for implementing their mutual goals and the mechanisms for solving problems.

---

[3]*Partnering, a Concept for Success,* © copyright AGC of America, 1991, The Associated General Contractors of America, 1957 E. Street NW, Washington, DC 20006.

*Continuous Evaluation.* In order to assure effective implementation, the parties need to agree to a plan for periodic joint evaluation based on the mutually agreed upon goals to assure that the plan is proceeding as intended and that all of the parties are carrying their share of the load.

*Timely Responsiveness.* Timely communication and decision making not only save money, but also can keep a problem from growing into a dispute. In the Partnering workshop the parties must develop mechanisms for encouraging rapid issue resolution, including the escalation of unresolved issues to the next level of management.

## Partnering Benefits

For all of the parties involved in a project, Partnering is a high-leveraged effort. It may require increased staff and management time up front, but the benefits accrue in a more harmonious, less confrontational process, and at completion a successful project without litigation and claims. The Partnering process empowers the project personnel of each of the parties with the freedom and authority to accept responsibility; to do their jobs by encouraging decision making and problem solving at the lowest possible level of authority. It encourages everyone to take pride in their efforts and tells them it's OK to get along with each other.

Partnering is also an opportunity for public sector contracting, where the open competitive-bid process ordinarily keeps the parties at arm's length prior to award, to achieve some of the benefits of closer personal contact which are possible in negotiated or design–build contracts.

## Potential Problems

Partnering requires that all parties to a contract commit themselves to the concept. The Partnering concept is endangered if there is not true commitment.

Those people who have been conditioned in an adversarial environment may be uncomfortable with the perceived risk in trusting. Some may even find it impossible to adapt their thinking to a relationship based on trust. Giving only lip-service to the term or treating the concept as a fad is not true commitment.

For some, changing the myopic thinking that leads to thinking that it is necessary to win every battle, every day, at the other parties' expense will be very difficult. Win/win thinking is an essential element for success in this process. It must be remembered that the win/win concept, after all, is based upon the acceptance of the concept of compromise between the parties.

## The Partnering Process

The Partnering process emphasizes the need to educate your organization to the facts about the concept. It is important to make Partnering intentions clear from the beginning, and obtain a commitment from top management from the start.

The Partnering workshop must involve the following:

1. Creation of a Partnering charter
2. Development of an issue-resolution process
3. Development of a joint evaluation process
4. Discussion of individual roles and concerns
5. Presentation of a facilitated workshop

For success of the Partnering concept, it is necessary to provide for periodic evaluation. Occasional escalation of an issue may surface, of course, but the process is structured to accommodate such problems. In the end, final evaluations must be made, and refinements may be considered to improve future Partnering contracts.

## Closing

Many of us have witnessed the construction industry evolve into an adversarial, confrontational business where the parties' energies are misdirected away from the ultimate goal of constructing a quality product, on time, and within budget. Partnering changes mindsets. It helps everyone in the construction process to redirect his or her energies and to focus on the real issues associated with achieving our ultimate objective.

## Specifying Partnering

In the specifications, the owner needs to state its intention to encourage the formation of a cohesive Partnering relationship with the contractor and its subcontractors. This Partnering relationship must be structured to draw on the strengths of each organization to identify and achieve reciprocal goals. The objectives are effective and efficient contract performance, intended to achieve completion within budget, on schedule, and in accordance with plans and specifications.

The Partnering relationship must be bilateral in makeup, and participation must be totally voluntary. Any cost associated with effecting this partnership should be agreed to by both parties and should be shared equally with no change in contract price. To implement this Partnering initiative, it is anticipated that within 60 days of the Notice to Proceed, the contractor's on-site project manager and the owner's on-site representative should attend a Partnering development seminar followed by a team-building workshop to be attended both by the contractor's key on-site staff and the owner's personnel. Follow-up workshops should be held periodically throughout the duration of the contract as agreed to by the contractor and owner.

An integral aspect of Partnering is the resolution of disputes in a timely, professional, and nonadversarial manner. Alternative dispute resolution (ADR) methodologies need to be encouraged in place of the more formal dispute resolution procedures. ADR will assist in promoting and maintaining an amicable working relationship to preserve the partnership. ADR in this context is intended to be a voluntary, nonbinding procedure available for use by the parties to this contract to resolve any dispute that may arise during performance.

## PROBLEMS

1. What are the three principal concerns of a Resident Project Representative or inspector with respect to his or her project during the construction phase?

2. Ideally, a Resident Project Representative or inspector should be under the direct management control of whom? (Indicate job title.)

3. Who should have the authority to make design changes in the field during construction: the resident engineer, the owner's representative, the design engineer, or the inspector?

4. What type of organizational structure is best suited to fast-track construction?

5. True or false? If an inspector discovers that the work of a subcontractor is deficient, he or she should direct the subcontractor to make the necessary corrections, then tell the general contractor what was done.

6. Under a construction management (CM) contract, should the CM firm's responsibilities normally begin at the construction phase, the design phase, the planning phase, or the conceptual phase?

7. A design–build firm may be (check all that apply): (a) a single firm with both design and construction capability; (b) a joint venture contract between a contractor and a design firm; (c) a design firm that subcontracts the construction portion to a construction contractor; or (d) a construction contracting firm that subcontracts the design work to an architect or engineer firm.

8. True or false? Under the Partnering concept, all differences are intended to be resolved at the lowest management level—preferably in the field.

9. What type of relationships are intended to be established under a Partnering agreement?

10. What are the five steps necessary to set up a Partnering workshop?

11. Is Partnering a totally informal process, or should it be addressed in the specifications?

12. True or false? Under the CQC process, inspection is provided by the contractor.

13. What is the 5-step process of initiating a project? Name each of the steps in proper order.

14. Explain the one-to-one concept.

# 2

## Responsibility and Authority

### THE RESIDENT PROJECT REPRESENTATIVE AND INSPECTORS AS MEMBERS OF THE CONSTRUCTION TEAM

The effective management of a construction operation can only be achieved through a well-coordinated team effort. The Resident Project Representative and the inspectors are vital members of that team, for without them there would normally be no direct involvement in the construction of the project by the architect/engineer or the owner. The Resident Project Representative and the inspectors are the eyes and the ears of the architect or engineer and the owner. Their authority and responsibility on the project is largely based upon that concept. To be sure, one architect or engineer may delegate more or less authority to the Resident Project Representative or inspector than another architect or engineer; however, that is a matter of employer–employee relations between the Resident Project Representative or inspector and his or her employer. In addition, many federal construction contracts require a resident inspector in the employ of the contractor under the principle of *contractor quality control* (CQC). Generally, in the absence of specific instructions to the contrary, the guidelines in this chapter are considered by many members of the construction industry to be the normal standards.

### LINES OF AUTHORITY ON CONSTRUCTION PROJECTS

Almost all construction projects involve organizations. The participants—owner, contractor, subcontractors, and suppliers—are not individuals. They are corporations, partnerships, or other forms of business associations.

Organizational decision making can be ponderous. Yet decisions and approvals are required on a daily basis during the performance of a construction contract. It is obvious that each organization must establish lines of authority by designating the individuals who are authorized to make necessary decisions (see "The One-to-One Concept" in Chapter 1). If this is done in a careful, thoughtful manner, the project will benefit. If it is done in a haphazard manner, the likelihood of misunderstandings and disputes will increase.

## Agency Relationship

An agency relationship is established when one party, such as the owner or architect/engineer, designates another party, such as a Resident Project Representative or inspector (the agent), to act on its behalf. Once the agency relationship is established, the owner or architect/engineer is bound by the acts and omissions of its Resident Project Representative or inspector, as its agent. If on-site representatives are not designated and given the authority that they need, communication will break down and confusion will result. There will also be some unanticipated legal ramifications.

## Actual Authority

The most common way for an agency relationship to be established is by an express grant of actual authority. The contract documents simply state that a particular individual shall have the authority to make certain decisions. On public construction projects, the existence of actual authority is important because statutes protect public agencies against acts or decisions of unauthorized individuals.

## Apparent Authority

An agency relationship can also be created when the owner or architect/engineer allows another party to operate with the *appearance* of authority to act on behalf of the owner or architect/engineer. The contractors who reasonably believe that they are dealing with a duly authorized agent will be able to hold the owner or architect/engineer accountable for the acts or knowledge of that *apparent* "agent."

The doctrine of apparent authority does not apply to public agency owners, as statutes shield them from liability for the acts of anyone other than the actual designated agent. Private organizations can protect themselves by contractually designating an individual with authority to act for them and disclaiming responsibility for the acts of anyone else.

This is not totally foolproof, however, as the contractual disclaimer can be constructively waived by a persistent pattern of conduct that is inconsistent with the terms of the contract. A similar result may occur through *ratification.* An owner or contractor may, by its conduct, ratify the unauthorized actions of a person at the job site. The most common form of ratification is silence or acquiescence. In other words, if an owner or contractor sits silently by while one of its people takes charge at the job site, it will be difficult later to argue that the individual lacked authority to make a particular decision or issue a particular directive.

### Delegation of Authority

Once actual authority has been conferred on an agent, such as a Resident Project Representative, it is possible to allow that agent to delegate his or her authority, say, to one of the inspectors. It is sometimes common to grant certain authority to a specific individual "or his or her designated representative."

The phrase "or designated representative" may create problems, however. Other companies may not be able to determine whether there has been an effective delegation of authority. The option of delegating authority also increases the likelihood of creating the appearance of authority. It is then inconsistent with any disclaimer of "apparent authority."

Actual authority may be delegated even by a public agency. As an example, an excavation contractor was obligated to follow the directives of a resident inspector because the government contracting officer had delegated on-site responsibilities to the inspector [*Appeal of Stannard Construction Co,, Inc., ENG BCA No. 4767 (May 17, 1984)*][1]

### Limited Authority

It is also possible to grant limited authority to an agent. This can be done in order to give the Resident Project Representative certain responsibilities and authority without allowing that representative to make fundamental contract changes, changes in time or cost, or to waive legal rights. This arrangement is preferable to naming an authorized individual in the home office "or his or her designated representative."

To be effective, a grant of limited authority must include clear, objective contractual limitations on the scope of the agent's authority. For instance, a Resident Project Representative might be given the authority to approve changed or extra workup to a stated dollar amount.

### Summary

The foregoing provisions can best be summarized in the following four guidelines:

1. Establish actual authority in the contract with a specific individual. Do not designate a position, job title, or group of individuals.
2. Disclaim any apparent authority and establish administrative procedures consistent with the disclaimer language.
3. Do not give designated representatives the right to further delegate their authority.
4. When granting limited authority, state objective guidelines to delineate the scope of that authority.

---

[1]See *Construction Claims Monthly,* September 1984, p. 5, Business Publishers Inc., 951 Pershing Dr., Silver Spring, MD 20910-4464.

## WHY HAVE AN INSPECTOR?

It is not enough to leave the assurance of quality workmanship and materials entirely in the hands of the contractor. The architect/engineer or other design firm that was responsible for the determination of site conditions and for the preparation of the plans and specifications should be retained during the construction phase to provide field administration and quality assurance for the owner, the safety of the public, and the professional reputation of both the design firm and the contractor. Many architects and engineers seem to believe that if their design is adequate and the plans and specifications are carefully prepared, the field construction will take care of itself. Experience has proven this to be far from true.

Although a design firm acting as the agent of the owner during the construction phase of a project does not guarantee the work of the contractor, nor does such agent in any way relieve the contractor of any responsibilities under the terms of the construction contract, the design firm, through its field inspection forces, must endeavor to guard the owner against defects and deficiencies in the work. When, in the judgment of the designer, the plans and specifications are not being followed properly, and the design firm has been unable to obtain compliance by the contractor, the owner should be notified so that appropriate measures can be taken. Inspection should be performed during the progress of the work; inspection after completion defeats the purpose of providing quality control and assurance on the job, as many potential difficulties must be detected during construction; otherwise, they may be permanently covered. The result would be a latent defect that may not be discovered for years; then, when it is discovered, it may be too late, as it may have been instrumental in contributing to a structural failure or other disaster.

Often, the word *supervision* has been used in the past in connection with field inspection. It is a legally risky term, and as such, its use has long been discouraged by all technical and professional societies of the construction industry. In the case of *U.S. Home Corp. v. George W. Kennedy Construction Co.* [610 F. Supp. 759 (D.C.III.) 1985] a federal court ruled that if a project owner agrees to "oversee" or "supervise" a contractor's performance of the Work, the owner may share responsibility for defective work performed by the contractor. The bottom line is this: If the owner simply "inspects" the Work for compliance with the plans and specifications, the owner does not assume responsibility for the sufficiency of the contractor's work. If, on the other hand, the owner agrees to "supervise" the contractor's means and methods of performance, it gives rise to the issue presented in the *U.S. Home Corp. v. George W. Kennedy Construction Co.* case.

In the 1996 Edition of the Standard General Conditions of the Construction Contract of the Engineer's Joint Contract Documents Committee (EJCDC), published jointly by the American Consulting Engineers Council, the American Society of Civil Engineers, the Construction Specifications Institute, and the National Society of Professional Engineers, as approved and endorsed by the Associated General Contractors of America, the general contractor is allowed greater management control, whereas the engineer's involvement during the construction phase is lessened. The 1996 Edition of the EJCDC General Conditions (Article 9.10.B) states that the engineer "will not supervise, direct, control, or have authority over or be responsible for Contractor's means, methods, techniques, sequences, or procedures of construction, or the safety precautions and programs incidental thereto." The

AIA General Conditions makes similar reservations. Therefore, the Resident Project Representative for the design firm and the owner should not direct, supervise, or assume control over the means, methods, techniques, sequences, or procedures of construction except as specifically called for in the project specifications. Instead, the Resident Project Representative should exercise authority on behalf of the owner so that such activities will result in a project substantially in accordance with the requirements of the contract documents. The FIDIC documents are silent on this issue, stating only that "the Engineer shall have no authority to relieve the Contractor of any of his obligations under the Contract."

Construction administration and construction quality control by the contractor or quality assurance by the design firm or owner should include continuous on-site inspection during all structural construction of a building by one or more competent, technically qualified, and experienced inspectors. If employed directly by the owner or by the design firm, all such inspectors should be under the architect/engineer's supervision and direction and should report any discrepancies directly to the architect/engineer. If there is a staff of several inspectors on a project, all other inspectors should be under the direct supervision of the Resident Project Representative, and all communications between them and the owner or design firm should be through the Resident Project Representative. It is the responsibility of these other inspectors to see that all details of the engineer's or architect's design drawings, shop drawings, bar-placing drawings, and similar documents that have been approved by the engineer or architect are constructed in strict accordance with their respective requirements. In addition, each inspector must see that all the requirements of the specifications have been met and that all workmanship and construction practices are equal to or in excess of the standards called for in the construction contract documents. The inspector should also make certain, as the job progresses, that the mechanical and electrical installations are constructed in accordance with the approved drawings, and that nonstructural items do not adversely interfere with structural elements.

Supervision by the architect or engineer of record and by the Resident Project Representative or inspector are really quite different, particularly in one very important respect. Neither the Resident Project Representative nor the inspector should have the authority to change plans or specifications, or to make his or her own interpretations, even though he or she may be a qualified engineer with both design and construction experience. If any question of interpretation arises, or if there is a disagreement on a technical matter between the inspector and the contractor, or if there appears to be any possibility of error or deviation from good construction practice that is noticed by the inspector, it should immediately be brought to the attention of the architect/engineer's project manager for decision. Inspection by the contractor under a CQC contract should follow similar procedures. However, supervision by the architect/engineer or its designated project manager, as distinct from that of the Resident Project Representative (or resident inspector), may include the authority to modify the plans and specifications consistent with the contract provisions between the owner and the design firm and between the owner and the contractor, if job conditions indicate that a change would be in the interest of improvement of the structure or if such a change were otherwise justified and consistent with sound design principles followed in the original design. Any such change should be supported by a formal Change Order, however.

## *AUTHORITY AND RESPONSIBILITY OF THE RESIDENT PROJECT REPRESENTATIVE*

The Resident Project Representative can function effectively only when given certain specific authority. In addition, the contractor should be made fully aware of the authority of the Resident Project Representative. Although a number of documents have been published that set forth a recommended scope of an inspector's authority and responsibility, the following is recommended because it represents a set of standards that have been established as the result of evaluating the answers to numerous pertinent questions contained in questionnaires that have been circulated by the Task Committee on Inspection of the Construction Division of the American Society of Civil Engineers to a nationwide cross section of contractors; owners and owner representatives; engineers; federal, state, and local governmental agencies; independent inspection agencies; and others.

### *Responsibility[2]*

As the Resident Project Representative for a design firm or the owner, the resident engineer or inspector is responsible for seeing that the work being inspected is constructed in accordance with the requirements of the plans and specifications. This, however, does not confer the right to unnecessarily or willfully disrupt the operations of the contractor. In the performance of assigned duties, the resident project representative, who is referred to in the following guidelines simply as the "inspector," would normally assume the following responsibilities:

1. The inspector must become thoroughly familiar with the plans and specifications as they apply to the work to be inspected and should review them frequently. The inspector must be capable of immediately recognizing if the work being inspected conforms to the contract requirements.

2. If any material or portion of the work does not conform to the requirements, the inspector should so notify the contractor, explain why it does not conform, and record it in the daily diary. Should the contractor ignore the notice and continue the operation, the inspector should promptly advise the architect/engineer or the owner.

3. As a member of the construction team, the inspector must perform all duties in a manner that will promote the progress of the work. The inspector should be familiar with the construction schedule and should know how the work that is being inspected fits into the overall schedule. Completion of the work within the contract time is also of importance to the owner.

---

[2]Committee on Inspection of the Construction Division, "Recommended Standards for the Responsibility, Authority and Behavior of the Inspector," *Journal of the Construction Division,* Vol. 101, No. C02, June 1975. Proceedings of the American Society of Civil Engineers, pp. 360–363, inclusive. Reproduced by permission.

READ THE CONTRACT...

SOMEBODY PREPARED IT FOR A REASON,
AND IT WAS PROBABLY NOT TO HELP YOU

4. The inspector must studiously avoid any inspection, testing, or other activity that could be construed as a responsibility of the contractor; otherwise, the owner's position may be prejudiced in the event of a dispute or claim. This applies particularly to the contractor's quality control program for testing and inspecting the contractor's materials and workmanship, as a part of his or her contractual responsibility.

5. When the inspector is assigned to any operation, it should be covered as long as the work is proceeding or see to it that another inspector takes over should the original inspector have to leave. This applies particularly to work that will not be viewed again, such as driving piles, laying pipe in a trench, and placing concrete.

6. The inspector's daily report and diary should include a recording of the day's happenings, the contractor's activity on the work being inspected, instructions given the contractor, and any agreements made. The inspector must remember that in the event of contract disputes, the daily reports and diary may assume legal importance.

7. In the matter of on-site testing, tests should be performed expeditiously and carefully, test samples must be carefully handled and protected, and test failures must

be reported to the contractor without delay. It is a needless waste of time and money when a contractor is informed of an unsatisfactory result of a test that was performed two or three days previously.

8. Inspections and tests should be made promptly and timely:
   (a) Materials should be checked as soon after they are delivered as possible. An inspector who rejects material after they have been placed in their permanent position is not working in the best interest of the owner.
   (b) Preparatory work such as cleanup inside the forms, fine grading of footing areas, winter protection for concrete, and so on, should be checked promptly to minimize delay to subsequent operations.
   (c) Work should be inspected as it progresses. For example, postponing the inspection of the placing of reinforcing steel and other embedded items until they are 100 percent complete does nothing but delay progress.
   (d) An inspector has the responsibility to be available at all times to provide prompt inspection and a decision on acceptance when required. A contractor should not be required to delay his or her work while the inspector is locating the architect/engineer's or owner's project manager to make a decision. Of course, by the same token, the contractor is expected to give adequate notice to the inspector when the Work will be ready for inspection on an operation.

9. If any specific tolerance governing the contractor's work is found to be unrealistic, it is the responsibility of the inspector to so report it to the architect/engineer or owner.

10. Too literal an interpretation of the specifications can cause problems if it is not applicable to the particular situation. In such an instance, the inspector must review the conditions and seek guidance from the project manager, if necessary.

11. Whenever possible, problems should be anticipated in advance of their occurrence. The contractor's superintendent or foreman may seem to be unaware of a sleeve or other embedded item that must be set in the forms. It is incumbent upon the inspector to point this out to the superintendent or foreman. By this advance notice, the inspector contributes to maintaining the progress of the work.

12. Unacceptable work should be recognized in its early stages and reported to the contractor before it develops into an expensive and time-consuming operation. The notification should be confirmed in writing where necessary. For example, if the contractor is using the wrong form lining, stockpiling unacceptable backfill material, or placing undersized riprap material, the contractor should be informed of this at the first opportunity. An inspector who is thoroughly familiar with the contract requirements can recognize these situations almost immediately.

13. Occasionally, a problem may arise that the inspector is unable to handle alone. This should be reported to the architect/engineer or owner for prompt action. Unresolved problems can sometimes develop into critical situations and claims.

14. Rather than make a hasty decision, the inspector should thoroughly investigate the situation and its possible consequences. Many embarrassing situations

develop from decisions made prematurely. For example, a request by the contractor to be permitted to begin placing concrete at one end of a long footing while the crew is completing the reinforcing at the far end should be given consideration and not be automatically denied. If necessary, the inspector should seek advice from the architect/engineer or owner's engineering staff.

15. When work is to be corrected by the contractor, the inspector should follow it up daily. Otherwise, corrections may be forgotten or the work soon covered over.

16. The inspector should stand behind any decisions made on issues concerning the contractor's work. An untrue denial by the inspector can cause immeasurable damage to the relations between the contractor and inspection personnel.

17. In the course of his or her work, the inspector must be capable of differentiating between those items that are essential and those that are not, as defined by the architect/engineer or owner's engineering staff.

18. The inspector should be safety minded. If a dangerous condition is observed on the job, there is a responsibility to call it to the attention of the contractor and then note it in his or her daily diary. The mere physical presence of the owner's representative on the site creates a responsibility to report a recognizably unsafe condition.

19. The inspector has a responsibility to be alert and observant. Any situation that threatens to cause a delay in the completion of the project should be reported to the architect/engineer or owner.

## Authority[3]

The Resident Project Representative, referred to herein as the inspector, must be delegated certain authority to perform the required duties properly. The close working relations with the contractor demand it. The inspector should use the given authority when the situation demands it and should not abuse it. In addition, the contractor is entitled to know what the specific authority of the inspector is, and when the work is not proceeding in an acceptable manner.

1. The inspector should have the authority to approve materials and workmanship that meet the contract requirements and should give approvals promptly, where necessary.

2. The inspector should *not* be given the authority to order the contractor to stop operations. When a contractor is ordered to halt an active operation immediately, it becomes a costly item, particularly if expensive equipment and material such as concrete are involved. If the stop order is not justifiable by the terms of the contract, the contractor has just cause to demand reimbursement for the damage that has been suffered. Because of the nature of the inspector's duties, the inspector

[3]Committee on Inspection of the Construction Division, "Recommended Standards for the Responsibility, Authority, and Behavior of the Inspector," *Journal of the Construction Division,* Vol. 101, No. C02, June 1975. Proceedings of the American Society of Civil Engineers, pp. 360–363, inclusive. Reproduced by permission.

cannot be familiar with all the details of the contract nor with all the other contractual relationships. Authority for the issuance of a stop order should be left to the judgment of the architect/engineer's or owner's project manager (see Chapter 6 for possible exceptions to the rule). Furthermore, the power to "stop the work" is often interpreted by the courts as *control of the work*. This may expose the architect or engineer to tort liability for any accidents or injuries on the job.

3. The inspector should not have the authority to approve deviations from the contract requirements. This can be accomplished properly only with a Change Order.

4. The inspector should not require the contractor to furnish more than that required by the plans and specifications.

5. Under no circumstances should the inspector attempt to direct the contractor's work; otherwise, the contracting firm may be relieved of its responsibility under the contract.

6. Instructions should be given to the contractor's superintendent or foreman, not to workers or to subcontractors.

Although most documents that define the inspector's responsibility and authority are the result of studies and recommendations by professional societies such as the American Consulting Engineers Council (ACEC), American Society of Civil Engineers (ASCE), The Construction Specifications Institute, Inc. (CSI), the National Society of Professional Engineers (NSPE), and the American Institute of Architects (AIA), in at least one state such requirements have been incorporated into law for certain types of work.

When the Resident Project Representative is a licensed engineer and may properly be termed a *Resident Engineer,* it may be desirable to delegate greater authority and discretion to that position. The document illustrated in Figure 2.1 presumes that the Resident Project Representative is not a licensed engineer, and if more authority is to be delegated, some changes must be made in these documents. This document has important legal consequences, and consultation with an attorney is encouraged if questions arise.

## PROBLEMS

1. What is apparent authority?
2. Give an example of delegated authority.
3. What are the dangers of allowing the inspector to supervise the work?
4. When should materials be checked by the inspector?
5. True or false? It is better to specify absolute dimensions than to indicate allowable tolerances in construction.
6. How much authority should be allowed the Resident Project Representative or inspector—should he or she be permitted to approve Change Orders affecting time or cost?
7. Is it permissible for the owner's representative to issue instructions or orders to a subcontractor as long as they are directed to a management representative of that subcontractor?

# SUGGESTED LISTING OF DUTIES, RESPONSIBILITIES AND LIMITATIONS OF AUTHORITY OF RESIDENT PROJECT REPRESENTATIVE

*Prepared by*

ENGINEERS JOINT CONTRACT DOCUMENTS COMMITTEE

*and*

*Issued and Published Jointly by*

PROFESSIONAL ENGINEERS IN PRIVATE PRACTICE
*a practice division of the*
NATIONAL SOCIETY OF PROFESSIONAL ENGINEERS

*and by*

AMERICAN CONSULTING ENGINEERS COUNCIL

*and by*

AMERICAN SOCIETY OF CIVIL ENGINEERS

EJCDC No. 1910-1-A (1984 Edition)
© 1984 National Society of Professional Engineers

**FIGURE 2.1** Engineer's Joint Contract Documents Committee version of Duties, Responsibilities, and Limitations of Authority of Resident Project Representative. (Copyright © 1983 by National Society of Professional Engineers.)

EXHIBIT B TO AGREEMENT BETWEEN OWNER AND
ENGINEER FOR PROFESSIONAL SERVICES, dated
_____ ,19__ (for use with No. 1910-1, 1984 Edition).

### A LISTING OF THE DUTIES, RESPONSIBILITIES AND
### LIMITATIONS OF AUTHORITY OF THE RESIDENT PROJECT REPRESENTATIVE.

This is an Exhibit attached to, made a part of and incorporated by reference with the Agreement made on _____ ,
19_____ , between _____ (OWNER) and (ENGINEER)
providing for professional engineering services.

ENGINEER shall furnish a Resident Project Representative (RPR), assistants and other field staff to assist
ENGINEER in observing performance of the work of Contractor.

Through more extensive on-site observations of the work in progress and field checks of materials and equipment
by the RPR and assistants, ENGINEER shall endeavor to provide further protection for OWNER against defects
and deficiencies in the work of CONTRACTOR; but, the furnishing of such services will not make ENGINEER
responsible for or give ENGINEER control over construction means, methods, techniques, sequences or procedures
or for safety precautions or programs, or responsibility for CONTRACTOR's failure to perform the Work in
accordance with the Contract Documents and in particular the specific limitations set forth in paragraph 1.6 of the
Agreement are applicable.

The duties and responsibilities of the RPR are limited to those of ENGINEER in ENGINEER's agreement with
the OWNER and in the construction Contract Documents, and are further limited and described as follows:

## A. General

RPR is ENGINEER's agent at the site, will act as directed by and under the supervision of ENGINEER, and
will confer with ENGINEER regarding RPR's actions. RPR's dealings in matters pertaining to the on-site work
shall in general be with ENGINEER and CONTRACTOR keeping OWNER advised as necessary. RPR's dealings
with subcontractors shall only be through or with the full knowledge and approval of CONTRACTOR. RPR shall
generally communicate with OWNER with the knowledge of and under the direction of ENGINEER.

## B. Duties and Responsibilities of RPR

1. *Schedules:* Review the progress schedule, schedule of Shop Drawing submittals and schedule of values
   prepared by CONTRACTOR and consult with ENGINEER concerning acceptability.

2. *Conferences and Meetings:* Attend meetings with CONTRACTOR, such as preconstruction conferences,
   progress meetings, job conferences and other project-related meetings, and prepare and circulate copies
   of minutes thereof.

3. *Liaison:*
   a. Serve as ENGINEER's liaison with CONTRACTOR, working principally through CONTRACTOR's
      superintendent and assist in understanding the intent of the Contract Documents; and assist ENGINEER
      in serving as OWNER's liaison with CONTRACTOR when CONTRACTOR's operations affect OWN-
      ER's on-site operations.
   b. Assist in obtaining from OWNER additional details or information, when required for proper execution
      of the Work.

4. *Shop Drawings and Samples:*
   a. Record date of receipt of Shop Drawings and samples.
   b. Receive samples which are furnished at the site by CONTRACTOR, and notify ENGINEER of avail-
      ability of samples for examination.
   c. Advise ENGINEER and CONTRACTOR of the commencement of any Work requiring a Shop Drawing
      or sample if the submittal has not been approved by ENGINEER.

5. *Review of Work, Rejection of Defective Work, Inspections and Tests:*
   a. Conduct on-site observations of the Work in progress to assist ENGINEER in determining if the Work
      is in general proceeding in accordance with the Contract Documents.
   b. Report to ENGINEER whenever RPR believes that any Work is unsatisfactory, faulty or defective or
      does not conform to the Contract Documents, or has been damaged, or does not meet the requirements

**FIGURE 2.1** *continued*

of any inspection, test or approval required to be made; and advise ENGINEER of Work that RPR believes should be corrected or rejected or should be uncovered for observation, or requires special testing, inspection or approval.

    c. Verify that tests, equipment and systems startups and operating and maintenance training are conducted in the presence of appropriate personnel, and that CONTRACTOR maintains adequate records thereof; and observe, record and report to ENGINEER appropriate details relative to the test procedures and startups.

    d. Accompany visiting inspectors representing public or other agencies having jurisdiction over the Project, record the results of these inspections and report to ENGINEER.

6. *Interpretation of Contract Documents:* Report to ENGINEER when clarifications and interpretations of the Contract Documents are needed and transmit to CONTRACTOR clarifications and interpretations as issued by ENGINEER.

7. *Modifications:* Consider and evaluate CONTRACTOR's suggestions for modifications in Drawings or Specifications and report with RPR's recommendations to ENGINEER. Transmit to CONTRACTOR decisions as issued by ENGINEER.

8. *Records:*

    a. Maintain at the job site orderly files for correspondence, reports of job conferences, Shop Drawings and samples, reproductions of original Contract Documents including all Work Directive Changes, Addenda, Change Orders, Field Orders, additional Drawings issued subsequent to the execution of the Contract, ENGINEER's clarifications and interpretations of the Contract Documents, progress reports, and other Project related documents.

    b. Keep a diary or log book, recording CONTRACTOR hours on the job site, weather conditions, data relative to questions of Work Directive Changes, Change Orders or changed conditions, list of job site visitors, daily activities, decisions, observations in general, and specific observations in more detail as in the case of observing test procedures; and send copies to ENGINEER.

    c. Record names, addresses and telephone numbers of all CONTRACTORS, subcontractors and major suppliers of materials and equipment.

9. *Reports:*

    a. Furnish ENGINEER periodic reports as required of progress of the Work and of CONTRACTOR's compliance with the progress schedule and schedule of Shop Drawing and sample submittals.

    b. Consult with ENGINEER in advance of scheduled major tests, inspections or start of important phases of the Work.

    c. Draft proposed Change Orders and Work Directive Changes, obtaining backup material from CONTRACTOR and recommend to ENGINEER Change Orders, Work Directive Changes, and Field Orders.

    d. Report immediately to ENGINEER and OWNER upon the occurrence of any accident.

10. *Payment Requests:* Review applications for payment with CONTRACTOR for compliance with the established procedure for their submission and forward with recommendations to ENGINEER, noting particularly the relationship of the payment requested to the schedule of values, Work completed and materials and equipment delivered at the site but not incorporated in the Work.

11. *Certificates, Maintenance and Operation Manuals:* During the course of the Work, verify that certificates, maintenance and operation manuals and other data required to be assembled and furnished by CONTRACTOR are applicable to the items actually installed and in accordance with the Contract Documents, and have this material delivered to ENGINEER for review and forwarding to OWNER prior to final payment for the Work.

12. *Completion:*

    a. Before ENGINEER issues a Certificate of Substantial Completion, submit to CONTRACTOR a list of observed items requiring completion or correction.

    b. Conduct final inspection in the company of ENGINEER, OWNER, and CONTRACTOR and prepare a final list of items to be completed or corrected.

    c. Observe that all items on final list have been completed or corrected and make recommendations to ENGINEER concerning acceptance.

**FIGURE 2.1** *continued*

C. **Limitations of Authority**

Resident Project Representative:

1. Shall not authorize any deviation from the Contract Documents or substitution of materials or equipment, unless authorized by ENGINEER.

2. Shall not exceed limitations of ENGINEER's authority as set forth in the Agreement or the Contract Documents.

3. Shall not undertake any of the responsibilities of CONTRACTOR, subcontractors or CONTRACTOR's superintendent.

4. Shall not advise on, issue directions relative to or assume control over any aspect of the means, methods, techniques, sequences or procedures of construction unless such advice or directions are specifically required by the Contract Documents.

5. Shall not advise on, issue directions regarding or assume control over safety precautions and programs in connection with the Work.

6. Shall not accept Shop Drawing or sample submittals from anyone other than CONTRACTOR.

7. Shall not authorize OWNER to occupy the Project in whole or in part.

8. Shall not participate in specialized field or laboratory tests or inspections conducted by others except as specifically authorized by ENGINEER.

**FIGURE 2.1** *continued*

8. Who should have the sole authority to stop the work?

9. Which of the following is an acceptable practice by the engineer, the Resident Project Representative, or the inspector?
   (a) To control the work
   (b) To supervise the work
   (c) To have the right to stop the work

10. True or false? If requested by the contractor, the Resident Project Representative or inspector may offer suggestions as to how to do the work.

# 3

## Resident Inspection Office Responsibilities

### SETTING UP A FIELD OFFICE

The basic requirements concerning the setting up of a field office for the Resident Project Representative (resident engineer or inspector) will have been established in the contract documents long before either of them reports to the project site. It is normally the project specifications that call for a field office for the Resident Project Representative, and these same provisions often include requirements for field office furnishings, utilities, janitorial services, sanitary facilities, and telephone. However, if the specifier fails to call for field office facilities in the specifications for a project that requires the services of a full-time Resident Project Representative, the contractor that provided such extras at no extra cost would soon be out of business; after all, if the contractor was aware of the requirement for such facilities at the time the job was bid, money would have been allowed in the bid for this purpose—if not, it would be unfair to expect it.

Many agencies that are involved in frequent construction contracts already own their own trailer-type offices (Figure 3.1) and will normally have one moved to the construction site at the beginning of the work. Thus, the contractor has no reason even to suspect that the omission of field office facilities from the specifications was an oversight.

What is to be done if a field office is needed but was not specified? Perhaps the Resident Project Representative can prevail on the contractor to provide a prefabricated structure for the inspector's use, but the inspector and employer should be aware that this often takes the form of a tool shed structure that uses flap covers over side openings instead of windows. Under the circumstances, the field office probably would not be provided with power or lights either, so if it rains the resident engineer or inspector might be faced with three choices: leave the flaps open and get the plans wet; close the flaps and sit in the dark waiting for the rain to stop; or close the shed and stay outside in the rain. Thus, if the resident engineer or inspector has been hired prior to advertising the job for bids, it might be

**43**

**FIGURE 3.1**    Part of a large agency-owned construction field office complex (Aguamilpa Hydroelectric Project, Mexico).

wise to ask the design firm or the owner to assure that the proper facilities will be provided for the inspector in the specifications. It is not too late even if the job is already out for bids, for as long as the bids have not been opened, an addendum to the specifications may still be issued that can provide for these facilities. One other alternative presents itself. Generally, a contractor will provide a field office trailer for his or her own use (Figure 3.2). It is usually not too difficult to obtain permission to set up a corner for the Resident Project Representative's own trailer—it sure beats sitting in the rain.

Almost all construction contractors today are using the trailer-type offices that are either available for purchase or can be rented on a month-to-month basis. Most of the larger trailers have inside toilets, are air conditioned and heated, and are fairly easy to keep clean; some are even carpeted.

Where the specifications do call for a Resident Project Representative's field office, it is not uncommon for a contractor to offer to "share" the field office with the Resident Project Representative by partitioning it across the middle, setting aside one end for the contractor and the other end for the architect/engineer. If the specifications will support the Resident Project Representative in a request for a separate trailer for an office, there should be no compromise or settlement for a shared unit, as it is not a preferable arrangement. There can be numerous reasons in support of the need for a separate trailer and some of them are mentioned later in the book. One of the principal reasons is security for both architect/engineer or owner and the contractor and the respective records and property of each and the ability to hold confidential meetings in a separate unit. In a joint-use trailer office, there are no secrets—when someone wants a private conversation, whether it be the contractor or the architect/engineer, you will notice a desire to go for a walk around the site.

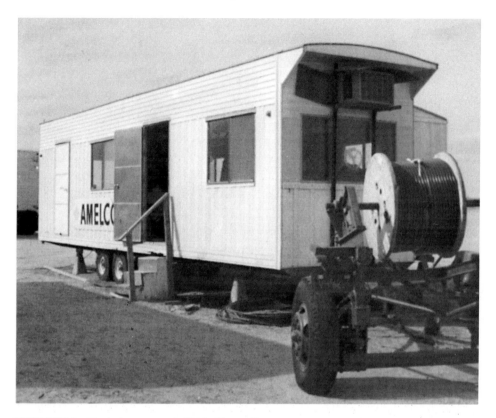

**FIGURE 3.2**   Typical contractor's field office trailer.

## *FAMILIARIZATION WITH CONSTRUCTION DOCUMENTS*

Upon being engaged to provide resident inspection on a project, the Resident Project Representative or inspector should obtain a complete set of all contract documents, including all contract drawings, standard drawings, specifications and specification addenda, and copies of all reference specifications, standards, or test requirements cited. Sufficient time should be spent carefully studying all of these documents, until the inspector is thoroughly familiar with all phases and details of the project as shown on the plans and specifications. This type of review should ideally take place in the office of the design organization so that the inspector can obtain firsthand responses to questions from the design staff. This enables a better understanding of the project by the inspector, and as a result, a more smoothly run project. The inspector should mark all areas containing key provisions and each area where special care must be taken. Cross-references should be carefully noted so that the affected sections in the specifications can be flagged to indicate locations where the different trades must interface or the work of different contractors must be coordinated. It is also wise to mark those areas where special tests or inspections are specified and where samples are required.

PROJECT No. 1553-04
SPECIFIED SUBMITTALS & EVENTS: CHRONOLOGICAL

| Submittal or Event Item | By | Reference |
|---|---|---|
| **PRE BID** | | |
| 1. Bidders Qualifications | NASA | IB |
| 2. Pre Work Conference | NASA | SP |
| **BID OPENING + 10 DAYS** | | |
| 1. Pre Award Survey | NASA | IB |
| **WITHIN 5 DAYS AFTER NOTICE TO PROCEED** | | |
| 1. Commence Work (Also Resident Engr on site) | Contr/A&E | IB 22 |
| **WITHIN 14 DAYS AFTER NOTICE TO PROCEED** | | |
| 1. Working Schedule | Contr | IB 29; SP 5.1 |
| **WITHIN 15 DAYS AFTER NOTICE TO PROCEED** | | |
| 1. CPM Job Schedule | Contr | IB 26 |
| 2. Shop Drawing & Equipment List Schedule | Contr | IB 23 |
| 3. Shop Drawing & Equipment List—1st Submittal | Contr | IB 33 |
| 4. Quality Control Program—1st Submittal | Contr | IB 70 |
| 5. Notify Contr Officer of Struct Steel Deliv Locn | Contr | SP 13.1 |
| 6. AC Water Pipe Materials List | Contr | TS 579 |
| **WITHIN 30 DAYS AFTER NOTICE TO PROCEED** | | |
| 1. Receive & Review Schedule of Submittals | NASA/A&E | IB 23 |
| 2. Report Status of Subcontr & Purchase Orders | Contr | IB 56 |
| 3. Schedule of Submittals (Final) | Contr | SP 9.2 |
| 4. Electrical Shop Dwgs & Lists | Contr | TS 587 |
| **WITHIN 45 DAYS AFTER NOTICE TO PROCEED** | | |
| 1. Quality Control Program Submittal (Final) | Contr/A&E | SP 4.5 |
| **WITHIN 60 DAYS AFTER NOTICE TO PROCEED** | | |
| 1. Plumbing: Proposed Matls List | Contr | TS 407 |
| 2. Electrical: Proposed Matls List | Contr | TS 470 |
| 3. Low Press Comp Air: Proposed Matls List | Contr | TS 480 |
| 4. Fire Protec Equipt: Prop. Matls List & Shop Dwgs | Contr | TS 507 |
| 5. Ventil. System: Proposed Matls List | Contr | TS 554 |
| **30 DAYS BEFORE COMPLETION** | | |
| 1. Equipment Manuals | Contr | IB 24; SP 9.5 |
| **BEFORE COMPLETION (NO SPECIFIED TIMETABLE)** | | |
| 1. Dwg. Change Incorporation (As-Built Dwgs) | Contr | IB 33; SP 1.5 |
| **NO SPECIFIED TIME FROM NOTICE OR AWARD** | | |
| 1. Report of Subcontractors over $10,000 Update annually | Contr | IB 54 |
| 2. 5 Days after award of subcontract: Statement to NASA of Subcontr and data | Contr | IB 53 |
| 3. 30 Days before starting specific phase of work: Detailed quality control plan | Contr | IB 71 |
| 4. Prior to fabrication (General items): Shop Dwg Approvals | Contr | SP 1.1 |
| 5. Return of Contr Submittals (Appr/Not Appr) | A&E | SP 1.6 |
| 6. Plan for tracking & processing contr Submittals | A&E | A&E Contract |
| 7. Concrete affidavits from Weighmaster Before Concrete Placement | Contr | TS 176; 102 |
| 8. Conc Matls Test Reports: As Work Progresses | Contr | TS 182; 185 |
| 9. Design Mix for Concrete: 15 Days before Start of Specified Work | Contr | TS 183 |
| 10. Hardware Samples | Contr | TS 344 |
| Contract Cost Breakdown & Payroll Reports | | IB 78 |
| **PERIODIC** | | |
| 1. Monthly: Reports on Tests and Inspections | Contr | SP 4.7 |
| 2. Monthly: Progress Payment Certification | A&E | A&E Contract |
| 3. Monthly: Quality Control Meetings | Contr/A&E | A&E Contract |
| 4. Twice Monthly: Const Schedule & Progress Mtg | Contr/A&E | A&E Contract |
| 5. Weekly: Construction Status Reports | A&E | A&E Contract |

**FIGURE 3.3**  List of project milestones.

At the same time, the Resident Project Representative must study the contract General Conditions ("boilerplate") of the specifications, as these provisions set the stage for almost all of the construction administration functions that will need to be performed. It is an especially good idea to set up a chart showing all the tests required, each type of test, the reference standard, the frequency of testing, and the specification section reference where these are called for (look ahead to Figure 11.8). This should be done prior to starting the work at the site.

Early in the project, a complete list should be compiled in chronological order that shows the date that every milestone event on the project is to take place (Figure 3.3). This should include meetings, submittals, tests, delivery dates for equipment, contractor partial payment requests, scheduling of surveys, final date for submittal of "or equal" items, and all other "milestone" events.

## EQUIPPING THE FIELD OFFICE

Field office equipment and supply requirements will vary from one job to the next, but on many public agency projects or larger private ventures such as high-rise buildings, hospitals, schools, and similar projects where the field management of the construction is more organized and formal, the Resident Project Representative's field office facilities may include any or all of the following:

1. Several desks and chairs
2. One or more plan tables and drafting stools
3. A plan rack or "stick file"
4. A four-or five-drawer filing cabinet
5. Telephone service (not coin-operated)
6. Bookcase
7. Inside toilet and lavatory (or adjacent portable unit)
8. Water, power, and lights
9. Heating and cooling facilities, as required
10. Janitorial services to clean the facility

In addition to furnishings, as listed above, it is not uncommon to require the following equipment for the owner's or architect/engineer's use during the life of the project:

1. Electrostatic copy machine
2. FAX machine with dedicated telephone line
3. Radio pagers
4. PC computer and printer (larger projects)

On larger projects, owners and architect/engineers often require the contractor to furnish a PC computer and printer along with a copy of their CPM scheduling program.

Most of the above might normally be specified to be furnished by the contractor and thus would be included in his or her bid price. In addition to the items provided by the contractor, the Resident Project Representative or inspector's employer would be expected to provide such additional items as a typewriter, adding machine (tape type), a small calculating machine, a postal scale, reproduction equipment, and all expendable office supplies.

On smaller projects, the facilities provided would be scaled down accordingly. The items just listed might reasonably be expected to be provided on a project involving a construction cost of somewhere over $1 million and involving over a full year of construction time.

### Ordering Supplies and Equipment

It is generally too late if the Resident Project Representative reports to the field office empty handed, only to find that the wheels of the construction process are already in motion. Before leaving the home office to take up residence in the new field office, the Resident Project Representative would draw as many office supplies and equipment as one might expect to need. The full list might conceivably include many, if not all, of the following items:

1. Report forms
2. Field books or "record books" for diaries
3. Stationery
4. Transmittal forms
5. Envelopes (all sizes)
6. Blank bond typing paper
7. Columnar pads (for estimating)
8. Loose-leaf notebooks (8½ × 11 three-ring type)
9. Pens, pencils, felt-tip pens, highlighter pens
10. Rejection or nonconforming tags
11. Minimum of two weeks' supply of film for all cameras.

In addition to the other supplies and equipment previously listed, the resident engineer or inspector should acquire all of the normal personal protective equipment required under OSHA for the types of work and environmental field conditions that are likely to be encountered.

## ESTABLISHMENT OF COMMUNICATIONS

Although this is one area in which the contractor almost always excels with regard to maintaining contact with members of its own field staff, some design firms and owners are beginning to realize the value to them, in both time and money, in investing in some means of direct communication with the Resident Project Representative at all times. The types of personal communications devices that offer the most value to the architect/engineer, owner, or contractor for maintaining contact with the field office include the following:

1. Field office telephones (not coin-operated)
2. "Beepers" or personal tone-signal radio paging devices
3. Cellular radio-telephones
4. Walkie-talkie radios
5. Voice or display pagers
6. Cordless telephones

Each of these pieces of communications equipment has its own particular best application and limitation, and it is seldom that all of them will be used on a single project.

### Field Office Telephone

The field office telephone is by far the most common device, and regardless of whether or not any other communications devices are provided, every field office should be provided with a telephone (not a pay phone) for voice communications. In addition, a second telephone line should be provided for a FAX machine. The design firm or owner should be careful in specifying its telephone needs, as it could find itself in the rather unique position of being furnished with a telephone that only connects to a private phone system. It may be necessary in some cases to specify that the contractor's field office must have a telephone and the Resident Project Representative's field office must also be provided with a telephone on a separate line connected to an established telephone exchange. If the contractor is connected to a private phone system, the Resident Project Representative's telephone should also be capable of being connected to the contractor's private phone system in addition to the established telephone system. The contractor should allow the design firm, the owner, or their authorized representatives or employees free and unlimited use of the field office telephone for all calls that do not involve published toll charges. Any toll charges received should be billed to the owner by the contractor at the rates actually charged the contractor by the telephone company.

### Tone-Signal Radio Pager

The use of a beeper (Figure 3.4) can be invaluable in maintaining one-to-one contact with an inspector who is frequently at some remote location at the construction site where the field office phone cannot be heard. In areas where such service is available, every inspector should have one. There are several services available in most urban areas, and some companies actually provide a service that covers several counties. With tone-signal pagers, or beepers as they are usually called, the party wishing to contact the inspector simply telephones the employer's office or other predetermined message center. The message center in turn telephones the paging service and says "please page 2543" or whatever the paging unit number happens to be. Some areas are on computerized systems in which the pager number is keyed directly from a pushbutton telephone. Upon hearing a beeping sound from the pager, the inspector simply turns off the signal and heads for the nearest telephone to call the message center. With a beeper, there is no way of communicating a message or determining the source of the call; thus, all calls must be returned to a central message center

**FIGURE 3.4**    Tone-signal pager ("beeper"). (Photo supplied by Motorola Communications and Electronics, Inc.)

to find out who called and what the message was, a distinct advantage to the project manager for one-to-one project control.

### Cellular Radio-Telephone

The value of a cellular radio-telephone is often somewhat overrated as far as a resident engineer or inspector is concerned unless they are provided with a portable unit. After all, an inspector who is at the site will seldom be in the vehicle and thus will not be able to receive a call directly on an automobile cellular telephone. Connecting the cellular radio-telephone to the auto horn is an alternative sometimes employed; however, this necessitates leaving the radio on standby at all times, even when the car is unattended. This can be a drain on the battery, although with modern solid-state equipment it is not as bad as it used to be. Even then, an inspector cannot know that a message was received without returning to the vehicle—which may be too late in case of an urgent message. Contrast this with the use of a beeper, which can let the inspector know immediately to call the office, regardless of where the inspector may be at the time. There are other situations, however, where a cellular radio-telephone can be of great service in construction. For a roving engineer or inspector who must serve the needs of numerous project sites, and spends a great deal of time on the road within range of a cellular receiving station, or for the inspector of a project such as a long pipeline, highway, or canal, a cellular radio-telephone used in a cellular service area can be an extremely useful tool, provided that uninterrupted service is available in the construction area.

There is a significant distinction between a *cellular radio-telephone* and a *two-way radio*. Both are in effect two-way radios; however, the terminology *radio-telephone* is reserved for those types of two-way radios that operate on assigned radio-telephone frequencies and have special equipment to make them compatible with standard land telephone equipment. The Resident Project Representative should forget CB radio for this purpose, as it is not sufficiently reliable unless served by repeater stations at strategic locations—and that *really* gets costly.

## Walkie-Talkie Radios

A walkie-talkie radio is a device best suited to on-site communications. Projects that involve a crew of several persons at remote locations within a large construction site, and operations that involve the issuance of instructions over relatively short distances, will find that walkie-talkie radios are great timesavers. They can eliminate the sometimes misunderstood hand signals, and a clear line of sight need not be maintained to communicate within reasonable distances.

## Voice Pagers

Voice pagers are quite useful in some situations; however, their limitations should be evaluated before considering replacing all beepers with voice pagers or display pagers. To be sure, a central message center is not needed, and a short voice message such as a telephone number can be transmitted directly. However, with voice pagers if the construction area is noisy, the message cannot be clearly heard, and without the convenience of a central message center the call could be lost—or at least difficult to confirm. Also, there is no privacy, and all messages received can be heard by anyone standing close to the receiver. If turned low, the inspector may not hear the message. Of course, most voice pagers can be switched over to a tone signal if message security is wanted at a special time. Yet unless the caller and the receiver knew that the audio was going to be turned off at any given time, how would either party know enough to call a central message center? In any case, to prevent misuse and abuse it would be in the best interests of the inspector and the employer to have all messages sent through a message center via a tone pager to preserve the one-to-one relationship so vital to effective job management.

## Cordless Telephone

For the small construction site, the cordless telephone appears to be the one of the best things invented for the one-person field office. Many different cordless telephones are on today's market, and no specific recommendations are offered, but with a reliable instrument, it can be the answer to the age-old problem of being able to reach the Resident Project Representative when away from the field office, but still on the site. A cordless telephone is *not* a substitute for a regular telephone in the field office, however, as the field office telephone is necessary to make the system work.

There are some limitations of use, however, that should be considered before investing in the system. Basically, it must be understood that all cordless telephones are in reality small hand-held radio transmitter-receivers with very short transmission ranges. The system is only suited to small jobs where the user is never very far from the location of the field office where the base radio set is installed. Thus, for a pipeline or highway job, it appears to be quite unsuitable. One must also understand its physical limitations. For example, there are sometimes radio-shielded areas on a construction site where transmission and reception is limited. This condition is remedied merely by moving the position of the cordless unit. However, if a call were to have been received while the instrument was in a shielded area, the user would have no knowledge of it. If the caller to the site is aware that a cordless telephone is being used, the appropriate thing is simply to redial the call a few minutes later when it can be presumed that the Resident Project Representative or inspector is out of the shielded area.

A cordless telephone set consists of two units. One is a small battery-powered hand unit that can be carried on the user's belt to anywhere on the site. The second is a larger 110-volt AC-powered base unit that can be plugged into the standard telephone outlet wherever the field office telephone has been installed. The incoming calls are first picked up by the base unit and relayed by radio to the hand-held unit being carried by the Resident Project Representative or inspector. For outgoing calls, you simply reverse the procedure.

Many people who have tried cordless telephones on construction projects have learned their limitations. However, the most common difficulty of reduced range from the advertised 200 to 250 m (700 to 800 ft) specified for most such telephones can usually be improved quite simply.

Cordless telephones require an antenna to operate within the specified range. This is normally built-in to the system by means of utilizing the third wire in the three-conductor power cord furnished with the unit. Thus, you cannot utilize a two-conductor extension cord for these units without seriously diminishing the effective range. Also, the majority of field offices are of the trailer office type. All such trailers, to meet local building code requirements, have their electrical wiring installed in EMT (electrical metallic tubing). This effectively functions as a radio shielding over the power cord that the unit requires as an antenna wire. Thus, again, the range is diminished. At local radio supply houses throughout the United States, there are prepackaged antenna sets designed for cordless telephones which, if installed outside the trailer unit, will allow maximum effective range of the cordless telephone unit at the project site. The cost should not be more than about $50 or $60 for the antenna itself, and when mounted at the top of a (20-ft) length of pipe attached to an outside corner of the field office trailer, the antenna will extend the phone range significantly.

## HANDLING JOB-RELATED INFORMATION

The establishment of communications on a project does not stop with the procurement of communications hardware. *Field communications* is a term that must also be applied to the procedures for handling and transmitting job-related information from one party to the other, the determination of who is authorized to receive and give project information, and the routing instructions for the transmittal of all communications, records, and submittals. At the beginning of a job, one of the first and most important things to be determined is the establishment of the authorized line of communications and authority, and the method of handling such information (Figure 3.5).

**FIGURE 3.5**   Lines of communication in construction.

Generally, it has been found preferable to establish the Resident Project Representative as the *only direct link* between the contractor and the design organization even though the matters being communicated may be intended for the project manager of either the owner or a separate firm. In this way, all transmittals will be received first by the Resident Project Representative, who will log them into the field office record book, and only then transmit them to the project manager. In the office of the design organization, a similar procedure is followed. All transmittals at that end should be received only by the project manager; if they are intended for other members of the design staff, they should be distributed through the project manager. In this way, there is always a single point of communication at each end: the Resident Project Representative in the field and the project manager at the design office.

Similarly, for the contractor, it is desirable to submit all data through the field office. No submittals should be permitted directly to the architect/engineer by any subcontractor or supplier at any time (see "Contractor Submittals" in Chapter 4).

All requests for deviations, Change Order claims, shop drawing submittals, and similar transmittals should be refused by the project manager if they are not transmitted to him or her through the Resident Project Representative. Otherwise, the records would be incomplete and, often, coordination is lacking because the information may have bypassed the project manager or Resident Project Representative, resulting in conflict or confusion in the field administration of the work. Similarly, submittals from subcontractors or materials suppliers should never be received by the Resident Project Representative directly, except through the hands of the general contractor. After all, it is the contractor's obligation to receive *and approve* all such transmittals before being considered for acceptance by the design firm. Officially, the subcontractor does not even exist, as far as the owner is concerned, because the owner entered into a contract with the general contractor only, and thus no contractual relationship exists between the owner and any subcontractors or material suppliers.

## STAFFING RESPONSIBILITIES

Staffing a field inspection office is usually not the responsibility of the Resident Project Representative, but is normally done by the design firm, the owner, or in the case of a CQC contract, the contractor. However, the Resident Project Representative should understand the types of persons required on some representative types of projects, because the Resident Project Representative will usually have the responsibility of supervising their activities.

Generally, on a project large enough to support a full time Resident Project Representative, the personnel needs of the project may vary from a single field representative of the owner or design firm under the responsible charge of a professional engineer or architect and backed up by occasional temporary special inspectors to ensure building code compliance, to a moderate-sized staff of three to five persons on a slightly larger project. Included as a part of this larger staff would be the Resident Project Representative, a full-time field inspector, possibly a field office assistant with estimating background, and a clerk-typist.

### Staffing Level of Field Office

On an exceptionally large number of projects where there were major claims, it was found that there was a failure by the architect or engineer and the owner to provide an adequate field force at the site during construction. It seems to be a popular myth that a Resident Project Representative is all that is necessary and that assigning more persons to the site is merely gilding the lily. Nothing could be further from the facts.

Generally, on small projects of $1 million or less a single on-site representative may be all that is necessary. On certain types of larger projects, however, consideration must be given to employing two, three, or more persons at the site, full-time. Although there is no known study of all types of projects, some investigation was made on the construction of treatment plant construction, and some guidelines were formulated by the State of California Division of Water Quality as administrators for the EPA (Environmental Protection Agency) Clean Water Grant Program in that state. Under their approach, only the *number* of on-site employees was addressed. In their analysis no distinction was made as to the types of persons at the site, or whether clerical help was necessary. The California DWQ DWO guidelines are summarized in the following table.

| Project Size | Inspection Person-Years/Year |
|---|---|
| Less than $1 million per year | 1.0 |
| $1 to $5 million per year | 2.5 |
| Over $5 million per year | 2.5 plus 2.0 for each add'l $5 million |

Subsequent to the development of these data, the author has done further study and determined qualitative guidelines as well. In the typical failure cases investigated, on-site representation was by a single but highly qualified registered professional engineer with significant field experience. The breakdown was traced to the demands upon the Resident Project Representative's time by both the administrative requirements and the on-site technical inspection requirements.

If you assume a situation involving one Resident Project Representative on a $6 million EPA Clean Water Grant Project, it is safe to say that over 80 to 95 percent of this person's time must be spent on administrative matters that preclude being in the field during many periods of critical need. Thus, serious problems can occur on site without the Resident Project Representative's timely knowledge. Unfortunately, the largest portion of these administrative matters involve tasks that do not require any knowledge or skill above the level of an ordinary clerk.

## Types of Personnel Assigned to Field Office

The usual method of solving the understaffing problem in the field is to assign another person to the site to help. But in a classic case of misguided good intentions, the second person is usually an inspector, because in the architect/engineer's or owner's mind, that is where the help is needed. This person also has a heavy load of paperwork to do in support of his or her own activities on site. As if to complicate the problem further, the Resident Project Representative now must add the burden of supervision and personnel administration to the already heavy administrative load. Thus, the Resident Project Representative, the highest-paid on-site person, is 95 percent occupied with administrative tasks, of which probably 70 percent could be performed more economically by a clerk. Meanwhile, an inspector is on the site who can devote perhaps no more than 75 percent of chargeable time to on-site inspection.

The answer by now should be obvious. In assignment of personnel to a job that justifies more than one person, based upon the foregoing table and the chart in Figure 3.6, the

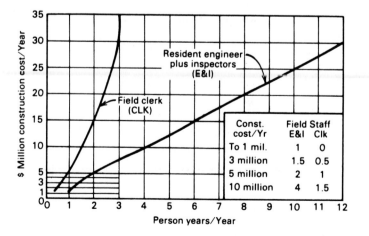

**FIGURE 3.6** Field office staffing guidelines.

first assignment is the Resident Project Representative. The second assignment should be a field clerk, not an inspector. The field clerk will relieve the Resident Project Representative of up to 70 percent of the routine paperwork burden, leaving the most qualified and highest-paid on-site person available to perform on-site inspections and troubleshoot to prevent field problems. This will leave the project with more time chargeable to inspection than the previous example utilizing an inspector as the second person, and at the same time it will substantially cut salary costs. As the work increases in complexity, inspectors can then be added as needed.

### Percent of Time Expended by Each Classification Toward Various Tasks

The following table illustrates the cost benefits of utilizing a clerk in the field.

| Case Type | Classification | Administrative Management/ | Clerical | Inspection | Field Cost Index* |
|-----------|----------------|------|----------|------------|-------------------|
| 1 | Res. Engr. | 25% | 55% | 20% | 0.20 |
| 2 | Res. Engr. | 30% | 65% | 5% | |
|   | Inspector | 5% | 20% | 75% | 0.28 |
| 3 | Res. Engr. | 30% | None | 70% | |
|   | Field clerk | None | 100% | None | 0.53 |
| 4 | Res. Engr. | 35% | None | 65% | |
|   | Field clerk | None | 100% | None | 0.59 |
|   | Inspector | 5% | None | 955 | |

*The field cost index (FCI) represents the value of inspection generated by each dollar spent on field staffing costs.

## DERIVATION OF THE FIELD COST INDEXES

The value of the FCI is based upon a benefit-to-cost relationship, wherein

$$FCI = \frac{benefits}{costs}$$

$$FCI = \frac{percent\ time\ spent\ in\ inspection \times respective\ pay\ rates}{all\ field\ pay\ rates}$$

where

$I$ = inspection time in percent of each individual's total daily time on the job

$I_e$ and $I_i$ = inspection time by the Resident Engineer and inspector, respectively

and

$R$ = pay rate for each respective field classification

$R_e$, $R_c$ and $R_i$ = pay rates for the Resident Engineer, clerk, and inspector, respectively

The FCIs in the following examples were based upon the assumption of the billing rates listed below for the Resident Engineer, clerk, and inspector. The index may vary slightly depending upon the relative costs in other firms. The higher the FCI value, the greater the savings.

To apply this principle to a numerical example, assume the following field billing rates for the Resident Engineer, inspector, and clerk, respectively:

$$R_e = \$58.00 \text{ per hour}$$

$$R_i = \$29.00 \text{ per hour}$$

$$R_c = \$18.00 \text{ per hour}$$

Then, based upon the work distribution percentages indicated in the table, we can calculate the following cases.

**Case 1: One Resident Engineer on site only**

$$FCI = \frac{I_e R_e}{R_e} = \frac{0.20 \times 58.0}{58.00} = 0.20$$

**Case 2: One Resident Engineer plus one inspector at the site**

$$FCI = \frac{I_e R_e + I_i R_i}{R_e + R_i} = \frac{(0.05 \times 0.58) \times (0.75 \times 29.00)}{58.00 + 29.00} = 0.28$$

**Case 3: One Resident Engineer plus one clerk at site**

$$FCI = \frac{I_e R_e}{R_e + R_c} = \frac{0.70 \times 58.00}{58.00 + 18.00} = 0.53$$

**Case 4: One Resident Engineer, clerk, and inspector at site**

$$FCI = \frac{I_e R_e + I_i R_i}{R_e + R_i + R_c} = \frac{(0.65 \times 0.58) + (0.95 \times 29.00)}{58.00 + 29.00 + 18.00} = 0.59$$

Then, by comparing the FCI values, it can be seen that if two persons were assigned to a field office, there would be an approximate 30 percent cost savings by utilizing a clerk as the second member of the field staff instead of an inspector, while providing approximately 88 percent of the total inspection hours that would have been available with an inspector.

As evidenced by the increase in the FCI through the use of a clerk at the project site, a significant cost savings can be achieved, while at the same time more technical expertise in construction is made available on site without added cost. A valuable benefit is the fact that not only is field morale increased, but project documentation is usually better and more consistent. Thus, in case of claims, the owner and architect/engineer are better protected.

The chart in Figure 3.6 provides a general guideline for the assignment of field personnel to a project similar in complexity to a wastewater treatment plant or plant addition. It must be emphasized, however, that project cost alone is not an indication of the level of field staffing required, and that each case must be examined upon its merits. Staffing

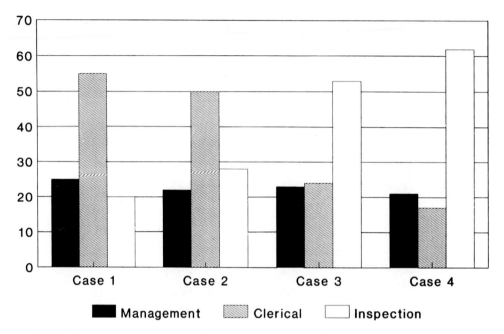

## AVERAGE DISTRIBUTION OF FIELD COSTS IN DOLLARS/100 DOLLARS BY ACTIVITY

**FIGURE 3.7**     Average distribution of field costs in dollars per 100 dollars by activity.

requirements for construction field offices will vary significantly depending upon the type of project, the number of areas in which the contractor will be working, the number of separate activities being concurrently pursued by the contractor, the type of construction contract (multiple prime, fast-track, etc.), and the complexity of the project. The average distribution of field costs under different staffing arrangements can be compared graphically in the chart in Figure 3.7.

The Resident Project Representative is the highest-paid member of the field team of the owner or architect/engineer, and thus it is incumbent upon the project manager to provide for the most effective utilization of his or her services. In Figure 3.8 two of the cases from Figure 3.7 are portrayed again graphically. It can be seen that the utilization of a field clerk in lieu of an inspector as the second assignment to a project (Case 3 in preference to Case 2) can improve project cost efficiency considerably.

## SELECTION OF TRAILER-TYPE FIELD OFFICES

When specifying the field office requirements in the project specifications, consideration must be given at that time as to the staffing requirements of the project to assure adequate

# RESIDENT ENGINEER UTILIZATION
## Allotment of Resident Engineer's Time

Case 2 - RE + Inspector

Clerical 50.0%
Management 22.0%
Inspection 28.0%

Case 3 - RE + Clerk

Clerical 24.0%
Managemen 23.0%
Inspection 53.0%

**FIGURE 3.8**  Allotment of resident engineer's time.

working space for all persons assigned to the project. Selection of office trailer size should be based upon the maximum ultimate occupancy load. The following guideline is suggested as a minimum based upon the use of trailer-type field offices:

**Field Office (Or Primary Field Office, If More Than One)**

| | |
|---|---|
| Resident Engineer only | 16 m² (2.4 m by 6.4 m body) 168 ft² (8 by 21 ft) |
| Resident Engineer and a clerk | 19.3 m² (2.4 m by 7.9 m body) 208 ft² (8 by 26 ft) |
| Resident Engineer, one inspector, and a clerk | 24 M² (2.4 m by 9.7 m body) 256 ft² (8 by 32 ft) |
| Resident Engineer plus two inspectors and a clerk | 39 m² (3.0 m by 12.8 m body) 420 ft² (10 by 42 ft) |

**Secondary Field Office**

| | |
|---|---|
| One inspector or field engineer | 12 m² (2.4 m by 4.9 m body) 128 ft² (8 by 16 ft) |

Figure 3.9 illustrates the typical floor plans and layout of field office trailers available from one major national organization dealing in sales, lease-purchase, and rentals of such equipment.

---

## *CONSTRUCTION SAFETY*

Although it is clearly understood that the Resident Project Representative's involvement in construction safety is limited (see Chapter 8), and that the general contractor has the

**FIGURE 3.9**   Typical floor layout of available construction field office trailers.

principal responsibility for all construction safety compliance, there are certain considerations that should be kept in mind by each inspector on the site. The degree of the Resident Project Representative or inspector's involvement may vary somewhat, depending upon the terms of the specific contract provisions and the actual circumstances surrounding each case of a potential hazard.

Occasionally, a contract for inspection may require the inspector to monitor the contractor's safety program to assure that an effective safety program is being provided (not uncommon in federal contracts). The inspector may be required to be involved in meetings with the contractor to discuss safety measures, and where project safety has been made one of the inspector's duties to observe, personal assurance should be obtained that safe practices are being followed. Some of the matters of concern in this type of responsibility are:

1. Review of the contractor's accident prevention program that is required by the local OSHA compliance agency.
2. A code of safe practices developed by the contractor and checked by the inspector for each project.
3. Various permits that may be required prior to starting specific work items, such as excavation, trench shoring, falsework, scaffolding, crane certifications, and similar requirements to be verified before allowing the contractor to begin.
4. Other safety items that may be pertinent to the contract, such as blasting operations, personal protective gear required, backup alarms for equipment, rollover protection guards on equipment, traffic control, and similar protective requirements to be confirmed.
5. The reporting of fatal accidents or disabling accidents to the local safety compliance agency as required.

The inspector's responsibilities with relation to the handling of hazardous conditions and the effect of various construction contract provisions on the administration of safety requirements are explored in greater detail in Chapter 8.

## DEVELOPMENT OF AN INSPECTION PLAN

It is desirable for each inspector to take a systematic approach to the quality control or quality assurance functions that are required for the project. Even if no formal plan is required to be submitted to the owner as a part of the quality control provisions of the contract, such as in a federal CQC (Contractor Quality Control) operation, such a plan is an excellent inspection tool, and the Resident Project Representative is urged to plan ahead by developing an outline of all the inspections that must be made, a checklist of points to look for, and a list of the types and frequencies of all tests that are required (see Chapter 11).

An inspection plan for submittal to the owner agency might reasonably be expected to cover all or some of the following items:

1. Establishment of detailed inspection procedures.
2. Outline of acceptance/rejection procedures.

3. Preparation of a chart showing all tests required, when they are needed, the frequency of sampling and testing, the material being tested, and who is obligated to perform the tests (Figure 3.10).

4. Establishment of who will be responsible for calling the laboratory for pickup of samples for testing, who will call for special inspectors when needed, and to whom such outside people will be directly responsible on the project.

5. Identification of who must physically prepare samples for testing, the contractor or the inspector; determination of whether the contractor will provide a laborer to assist the inspector in obtaining samples and transporting samples for testing.

6. Establishment of ground rules for acceptable timing of work operations after sampling and testing; mandatory scheduling must be provided to assure not only time to make samples and tests, but time to make corrections needed before work may be allowed to continue.

Often, on a federal project involving a CQC operation, if an architect/engineer firm is selected to provide quality assurance, it is required to submit a formal *construction sur-*

**TESTING PLAN**    S = Sampled    SHEET NO.    T = Tested

| SPEC SECTION & PARAGRAPH | ITEM OF WORK | TESTS REQUIRED (ASTM, ACI, COMM'L STDS, ETC) | SAMPLED BY | TESTED BY | ON SITE | OFF SITE | FREQUENCY OF TESTING |
|---|---|---|---|---|---|---|---|
| 02200 | EARTHWORK | | | | | | |
| 2.04B | Sieve Analysis | ASTM C-36 | ABC Lab | ABC Lab | | S/T | One passing test per Source |
| 2.0 | Standard Moisture Density | ASTM D-1557 (Mod.) | ABC Lab | ABC Lab | S | S/T | One - each source |
| 2.06E | In-place Density | ASTM D-1556 | ABC Lab | ABC Lab | S/T | | Min. 20 - (Random) |
| 03300 | CONCRETE | | | | | | |
| 1.04 | Mix Design | ASTM C-192; C-39 | ABC Lab | ABC Lab | | S/T | One per each req'd Strength - Aggregate Size |
| 1.05 | Test cylinders | ASTM C-31 | Inspector | ABC Lab | S | T | See Note #1 |
| 2.03 | Slump | ASTM C-143 | Inspector | Inspector | S/T | | One per batch |
| 2.01 | Air | ASTM C-231 | ABC Lab | ABC Lab | S/T | | One set of Cylinders |
| 04200 | MASONRY | | | | | | |
| 2.03 | Efflorescence | See Spec. Par. 2.03A | ABC Lab | ABC Lab | | S/T | One passing test |
| 2.05 | Mortar and Grout | See Spec. Par. 2.05 | Inspector | ABC Lab | S | T | See Note #2 |
| 2.07 | Drying Shrinkage | ASTM C-426 (See Spec.) | ABC Lab | ABC Lab | | S/T | One passing |
| 2.08 | Air dry Condition | ASTM C-427 | ABC Lab | ABC Lab | S/T | | One test per delivery |

Data used are fictitious for illustration only

EXPLANATORY NOTES

Note (1) 6 cyl per day per 40 m³   Test 3 AT 7 days; 3 AT 28 days

Note (2) One each design mix   Min. 3 ea day   Test one at 7 days; 2 ea at 28 days

FISK FORM 8-3

**FIGURE 3.10**   Example of a testing plan.

*veillance and inspection plan* prior to beginning the work. Under such a program, the architect/engineer must provide a Resident Project Representative and an appropriate field staff at the construction site, plus home office support as required. Implementation of such a program requires the architect/engineer, the construction manager, and the Resident Project Representative to meet the contractor prior to beginning each phase of the work and to define the responsibilities of each party under the contract. At that time, the contractor should be asked to submit and explain his or her established systems for quality control and his or her accident prevention program. These programs should then be reviewed by the architect/engineer or owner and the Resident Project Representative, and the programs compared with the specific requirements of the contract. Suggestions, if warranted, should be made by the Resident Project Representative at that time.

## OTHER JOB RESPONSIBILITIES

In addition to the items covered previously, there are numerous other field responsibilities that the Resident Project Representative must expect to cope with. These responsibilities in connection with the tasks described are only highlighted in this chapter, as the technical details of administering each of the listed subjects is covered more thoroughly in the chapters that follow. Naturally, much of the Resident Project Representative's work will have to be done in the field office. Unfortunately, in today's complex society, the resultant paperwork required means that a good portion of the Resident Project Representative's time must be spent writing and recording data. Administration of a construction project is no longer as simple as it was in days past, when all that was needed was a thorough knowledge of construction—today, the paperwork is just as vital as the inspections themselves.

### Construction Planning and Scheduling

A Resident Project Representative on a sizable project will most certainly become involved in construction scheduling, or at least in an evaluation of the construction schedules prepared by the contractor. An inspector who does not have a basic understanding of the principles involved will be hard-pressed to fulfill all administrative responsibilities. The two principal types of schedules that the inspector will be most likely to encounter are bar charts and network diagrams.

In a network diagram, the Resident Project Representative should be capable of recognizing logical and illogical construction of a schedule. In addition, realistic scheduling times, compatible delivery dates for equipment and materials, critical path operations, float (slack) times, and other related items of a network schedule must be checked. Also, frequent comparisons to see if the actual construction events are following the network diagram must be made, and the inspector should check to see that updated network data are provided as required.

### Contractor's Plant and Equipment

Although it is rare that the resident engineer or inspector will be required to check the contractor's equipment, it is an occasional requirement under the provisions of some public agency contracts. If equipment inspection is required, all that is normally expected of the inspector is a check of each piece of major equipment and a determination of whether it has the necessary safety devices and that such devices are all in good working order. This includes devices such as safety cages, backup bells, guards over moving parts, and similar items. In addition, the equipment check should include an evaluation of whether the exhaust emissions are excessive, and that there are no cracked windshields or bad tires on automotive or other heavy motorized equipment.

## Measurements for Progress Payments

One of the traditional responsibilities of the Resident Project Representative is the review of the contractor's monthly partial payment request to see that the quantities of materials and equipment delivered to the site or used in the work agree with the quantities for which the contractor has requested payment. It should be kept in mind that on a lump-sum project, the Resident Project Representative must still make monthly pay estimates of the contractor's work. However, the accuracy of the measurements are not as critical as they would be on a unit-price contract, because such differences will be made up in the end. This is not meant to suggest that the inspector can afford to be careless about quantities on a lump-sum job, as it is highly undesirable to allow the owner to pay for more work than has actually been accomplished as of the date of the payment request. Such overruns would completely defeat the purpose of the normal 5 to 10 percent retention that is usually held by the owner until the end of the project. If no retention money is held, even on lump-sum projects, the cumulative monthly progress payments must be carefully controlled to avoid overpayment.

On a unit-price contract, a precise measurement must be made of all construction quantities, and generally a system of measurement is spelled out in the specifications under the heading "Measurement and Payment," so that there can be no argument as to where, how, and when the measurements for pay purposes must be made. Errors in measurement or overlooked items under a unit-price contract can cost the owner an immense sum of money. Because of this fact, many measurements for such contracts are performed by the design firm utilizing the services of a survey crew to determine pay quantities of pipe; to cross-section a borrow area to determine the exact quantities of earth excavated; and to make similar measurements.

The subject of measurement and payment during construction is covered in detail in Chapter 16, where numerous methods are described and some of the typical pitfalls are discussed

## Filing of Notices and Certificates

Although the filing of legal notices is primarily the responsibility of the owner, that job may be delegated to the Resident Project Representative or project manager as an owner's representative. The notices and certificates themselves will normally have been prepared when the Resident Project Representative receives them; however, some knowledge of the process involved should be understood.

Such notices include the filing of the Notice to Proceed as well as the Certificate of Completion or Certificate of Substantial Completion at the close of construction. In addition, the inspector may be involved with the serving or filing of other forms of construction documents such as the Field Order and Deficiency Notice as well as special notices calling attention to imminent safety hazards that require immediate correction to remove a hazard to life or health.

## Evaluation of Construction Materials and Methods

The Resident Project Representative is frequently called upon to evaluate construction materials and methods. The responsibilities should be clear, however, and although the expertise of the Resident Project Representative is necessary for the good of the project, any such recommendations should be made *only* to the responsible architect or engineer, in writing, who will be the final authority as to what action to take. It is to be hoped that the architect or engineer will also recognize the value of following a formal transmittal procedure and, after reaching a decision, will submit all instruction or responses directly through the Resident Project Representative instead of mailing or delivering them directly to the contractor.

The work on a project may also involve the preparation of work statements, estimates, and data to contractor requested changes. The procedures are similar to those specified for evaluations of materials and methods. A fuller discussion of the handling of contractor submittals is covered under "Contractor Submittals" in Chapter 4.

## Record Drawings

A large portion of the work on many projects includes the posting of "as-built" information on a set of prints at the construction site. This is sometimes followed by a requirement that all such records of changes be drafted onto a set of reproducibles of the contract drawings. This is intended to provide the owner with a permanent record of each feature of a project as it was actually constructed. The normal construction contract usually calls for the *contractor* to make a set of *record drawings* by marking a set of prints with all changes from the original drawings as bid, including all Change Orders, alignment changes, depth changes of underground pipes and utilities, and all other items that are not the same as they were originally drawn.

The term *as-built drawings* should be discouraged because of the legal implications involved when the architect or engineer signs a certificate that says that everything shown on the drawings is exactly as constructed—this act could haunt the architect or engineer for years. The drafting of such data onto a set of transparencies is often required, but the resident engineer or inspector should be particularly careful when making commitments that the condition of the contract that requires the preparation of record drawings does not of itself mean that they will be drafted on reproducibles. It merely means that all changes will be marked (usually with colored pencil) on a set of record prints at the site. If work on the transparencies is required, it will be performed as a separate contract item by copying from the record drawings.

Many field people have been very lax in assuring that all record drawings are kept up to date, and unfortunately, the oversight may not be discovered for several years if no further work is constructed in the same area. It is a vital concern and should not be overlooked.

The most common procedure is for the contractor to prepare the record drawings as the project progresses, by clearly and legibly marking a set of prints that at the end of the project are turned over to the architect/engineer or to the owner's engineers for checking. After approval by the architect/engineer or owner, these record data are normally turned over to the owner, or if the contract calls for it, drafted on a set of tracings and then turned over to the owner.

## PROBLEMS

1. Evaluation of the contractor's schedule submittal should be limited to what three principal concerns?
2. What risk is the owner or the engineer exposed to if he or she tells the contractor how to construct the Work?
3. Why is it desirable to prepare an inspection plan prior to construction?
4. True or false? An inspector's construction diary may be in loose leaf form as long as the pages are numbered.
5. What are the three types of authority exercised by the Resident Project Representative?
6. What basic equipment (not furnishings) should be required in a construction field office?
7. A project has field trailers for the Resident Project Representative at the construction site and an off-site home office for the project manager. It is a traditional contract with an outside engineer/architect and a general contractor with three subcontractors constructing the work. From the following list specify, in numerical order, the routing of submittals from a subcontractor to the engineer/architect.
   A. _____ A/E project manager
   B. _____ Design reviewers
   C. _____ General contractor
   D. _____ Resident Project Representative
   E. _____ Subcontractors
8. You have been asked to plan the staffing of the Resident Project Representative's field office for a wastewater treatment plant that is going to be constructed. The estimated construction cost is $36 000 000.00 dollars for the project to be constructed over a two-year period. What is the probable total number of field personnel recommended? Based upon the chart in Figure 3.6, list their classifications and the number of personnel in each field classification recommended for the project.
9. For a project that will be staffed by a Resident Project Representative, two inspectors, and a field clerk, what is the minimum size recommended for the field office trailer?
10. What is the correct terminology for the final set of project drawings that have had all of the latest changes and field conditions marked on the drawing set?

# 4

## Documentation: Records and Reports

*I*n the earlier years of construction, all that seemed to be needed to assure quality construction was the assignment of a full-time Resident Project Representative who possessed many years of experience and a track record of successful projects. The philosophy was based upon the premise that the Resident Project Representative would ensure that the owner received his or her money's worth by applying the knowledge learned through the years of construction experience. No detailed records were kept; in fact, many decisions were made in the field that should have been made by the architect or engineer, and many "deals" were made involving construction trade-offs, without any documentation.

Unfortunately, too many of the old-time inspectors are still operating in this manner. In a recent case involving the installation of an underground pipeline with a special joint detail that was causing some trouble, an inspector "solved" the field problems (or thought he did) and, upon completing the project, proudly moved on to another project where the virtues of his technique of handling the previous job were extolled. Shortly after completion, unknown to the inspector, most of the joints were found to leak. Unfortunately, no daily reports were filed nor did the inspector maintain a daily diary. A couple of years later a lawsuit followed in which the contractor wanted to recover the additional costs, claiming that the engineer's design was wrong, that the manufacturer's product was deficient, and that changes had been made at the direction of the inspector that cost the contractor additional money without solving the problem. The engineer, without the benefit of any documentation to support a counter position, was forced to settle at a considerable disadvantage.

The engineer of record was placed in a very vulnerable position as a direct result of the failure of the inspector to maintain adequate records. If daily reports had been made out and submitted to the engineer regularly, it is quite probable that the engineer may have had the opportunity to review the problem and to take corrective action at an early date, possibly preventing the occurrence of the problem.

It was vital to the engineer's and owner's defense that they be capable of documenting the day-by-day events that led up to the problem, as well as the substance of conversations that took place between the inspector and the contractor, and what commitments, if any, were made by either party. Of prime importance was the issue of whether the inspector had actually warned the contractor of the possibility of leakage in the joint. This inspector had previous experience in the installation of the same kind of pipe and pipe joints on a previous job, and had noted its tendency to leak if installed in a certain manner.

The inspector was located and interviewed by the author for the engineers who had originally designed the job more than two years before. Upon careful questioning, the inspector admitted that he had recorded nothing, but claimed he could remember each incident fairly well. Subsequent questioning disproved this, and the engineer's office was left with little defense except the memory of a witness who could easily be discredited.

An interesting fact should be recognized by all inspectors. Any project could become involved in litigation, and it could be several years after the incident before testimony of the inspector as a witness is requested. Any record that the inspector makes in writing, which is recorded in a form that will retain its credibility, may be referred to by the inspector while on the witness stand. This is an allowable method of refreshing a witness's memory. There are some limitations, however, and one of them is that the notes recorded by the inspector must be made on the same day that the incident or conversation took place. It is *not* acceptable to write notes on scratch paper, then at a later date transcribe them into the inspector's diary or log book. Such personal records of the inspector, because they are not a part of the agency's regular business record-keeping system, may not be considered as evidence in themselves, except for records made by certain types of public officials in the course of their official duties, and, possibly, except for records that are ruled admissible under the principle of "normal records kept in the regular course of business." Thus, these notes may not be entered as evidence, but can only be referred to in court by the party who wrote them—and then only as a memory-refreshing device.

It cannot be emphasized too strongly that the modern construction job is beset with numerous potential disputes or legal problems. *Any inspector who fails to keep adequate records is not performing a competent job and should be replaced.* Instead of providing the services to the owner that the latter is paying for, such an inspector is simply adding to the overhead cost of the project, or worse, because the owner is lulled into the feeling that with an inspector on the job, its interests are going to be adequately protected. Had the owner known in time, corrective action could have been taken.

### Project Documentation as Evidence in Claims

Evidence of a written document made as a record of an act, condition, or event is normally admissible when offered to prove the act, condition, or event if:

1. The written document was made in the regular course of business (this may be applied to field diaries only if the owner or architect/engineer normally required that daily diaries be kept on all projects as a normal business record).
2. The document was written at or near the time of the act, condition, or event.

3. The possessor of the record or other qualified witness testifies to its identity and the mode of its preparation.
4. The sources of information and the method and time of preparation were sufficient to indicate its trustworthiness.

## FILES AND RECORDS

It is preferable to establish a filing system for an entire company or agency rather than to depend upon record-keeping systems designed for each individual project. Unfortunately, many organizations never have established a filing system broad enough to include the special problems of the construction phase of a project. Any effort to utilize a design-oriented filing system for construction is doomed from the start.

Elsewhere in this chapter, emphasis is placed upon the Resident Project Representative as the developer of a competent construction field office record-keeping system, because in the absence of an established company system of records filing, the Resident Project Representative may be the only person to whom we can turn to develop and maintain competent project records.

### Construction Filing System of a Major Engineering Firm

An example of the last six categories of the filing system of a major engineering firm in the United States is shown in the following example. Each of these categories relates exclusively to construction phase activities.

| | |
|---|---|
| 8.0 | BID PHASE ACTIVITIES |
| 8.1 | Advertisement for Bids |
| 8.2 | Bidder List (Documents Issued) |
| 8.3 | Bid Opening Reports |
| 8.4 | Summary and Evaluation of Bids |
| 8.5 | Preaward Submittals |
| 9.0 | PRECONSTRUCTION PHASE |
| 9.1 | Inspection and Testing Manual |
| 9.2 | R/W, Easement, and Permit Documents |
| 9.3 | Preconstruction Conference |
| 9.4 | Contractor Submittals |
| | 9.4.1 Bonds and Insurance |
| | 9.4.2 Bid Breakdown (Schedule of Values) |
| | 9.4.3 Preliminary Schedule (CPM, etc.) |
| 9.5 | Notices to Contractor |
| | 9.5.1 Award |
| | 9.5.2 Proceed |
| 10.0 | CONSTRUCTION PHASE |
| 10.1 | Inspection Records and Reports |
| | 10.1.1 Daily Construction Reports |

### Individual Project Records

It is often the Resident Project Representative's responsibility to determine what the specific needs of the employer are with regard to the types of construction records that must be established and maintained for a specific project. One principal exception is the conduct and administration of federal agency projects in which the government agency often provides a very specific list of all types of records, reports, and other documentation that is required, plus some specific requirements concerning the form in which such records must be maintained. Often the printed forms themselves are provided.

Many local public agencies, as well as some of the larger private architect/engineer firms, have preprinted forms to assist the inspector in the recording of pertinent job information, and many have procedures established for the handling, distribution, and storage of job records as well.

Without regard for whether an architect/engineer, public agency, owner, or other interested party has established such record keeping as a policy matter, *each* inspector, not just the resident engineer or inspector, should *always* maintain a daily diary in which notes and records of daily activities and conversations are kept. Such a diary should contain abstracts of all oral commitments made to or by the contractor, field problems encountered during construction, how such problems were resolved, notices issued to the contractor, and similar information. It should be remembered, however, that the daily construction diary is *not* a substitute for the Daily Construction Report, which describes the construction progress and normally receives wider distribution. The information recorded in the inspector's diary is generally of a private nature and is intended for the use of the inspector and his or her employer only.

### Construction Records

The following is a list of the principal types of construction records that the Resident Project Representative should maintain on every project:

1. *Progress of the work.* Maintain a Daily Construction Report (Figure 4.1) containing a description of the work commenced, new work started, status of work in progress, labor and equipment at the site, weather, and visitors to the site. If no work was performed at all, a daily report should still be filed, stating "no work." On projects where several inspectors are involved, this report is compiled from each inspector's Daily Record of Work Progress (Figure 4.2).

2. *Telephone calls.* All telephone calls made or received should be logged and a note made indicating the identities of the parties as well as a brief phrase indicating the nature or purpose of the call.

3. *Tests of materials.* A record should be kept of all material samples sent out to the laboratory for testing (Figure 4.3) as well as those tests performed at the site. The report should include space for later inclusion of the test results, as well as the location in the structure where the particular material was to be installed.

4. *Diary.* A daily diary should be maintained by each member of the field staff. This book may end up in court, so it should be neatly and accurately recorded. An entry

# DAILY CONSTRUCTION REPORT

DATE 31 JAN 1995

DAY: S M T(X) W TH F S

PROJECT RESERVOIR 1-D AND PUMP STATION
JOB NO. 95-90-00
CLIENT City of Fullerton, California
CONTRACTOR ABC Constructors, Inc.
PROJECT MANAGER E. R. Fisk, Project Manager

WEATHER: Brite Sun | Clear | Overcast (X) | Rain | Snow
TEMP.: To 0 | 0-10 | 10-21 (X) | 21-29 | 29 up
WIND: Still (X) | Moder | High
HUMIDITY: Dry (X) | Moder | Humid

Report No 219

### AVERAGE FIELD FORCE

| Name of Contractor | Non-manual | Manual | Remarks |
|---|---|---|---|
| ABC CONSTRUCTORS, INC. | 1 | 11 | PRIME |
| S&M CONSTRUCTION CO. | 1 | 2 | EARTHWORK SUB. |
| GLADMORE ENGRG | 0 | 2 | TEST LAB. |

### VISITORS

| Time | Representing | Representing | Remarks |
|---|---|---|---|
| 10:00 | RICHARD CARSON | ARMCO | |

Data used are fictitious for illustration only

### EQUIPMENT AT THE SITE

AC T-200 SCRAPER; (2) AC HD-16 DOZERS; CAT D-8 (IDLE/UNER REPAIR)

### CONSTRUCTION ACTIVITIES

EXCAVATION: SECOND STAGE EXCAVATION OF ACCESS RAMP WAS CONT'D WITH THE HD 16 DOZER. EXCESS MATL IS BEING PICKED UP WITH THE T200 SCRAPER AND DISTRIBUTED ON SITE TO BRING TO FIN. GRADE; ROUGH SLOPE TRIMMING IS CONTINUING WITH THE DOZER.

PIPE LAYING: LAYING OF 400mm RCCP FOR THE BY-PASS LINE HAS PROGRESSED TO NW COR. OF SITE. AS OF 08:30 HRS CORNER BENDS WERE BEING LAID. SAND BACKFILL IS BEING PLACED ON TOP OF PIPE ZONE AND CONSOLIDATED BY FLOODING.

BASIN AREA: SLOPES ARE BEING HAND TRIMMED TO FIN. GRADES AND THICKENED EDGE SECTIONS ARE BEING CUT TO TEMPLATE. BOTTOM OF BASIN IS BEING TRIMMED TO GRADE WITH A SKIP-LOADER.

TRENCH BACKFILL: MUD THAT WAS BEING WASHED INTO THE 1D-2 PRESSURE LINE TRENCH DURING PREV. RAIN IS BEING REMOVED AND REPLACED W/SAND.

THRUST BLOCKS: THRUST BLOCK CONCRETE WAS PLACED IN THE TWO 45-DEG. BENDS IN THE 400mm BY-PASS LINE, AND CONC. ENCASEMENT OF THE CROSSOVER RISER WAS CAST USING CLASS "C" CONC. PER SPEC.

DISTRIBUTION: 1. Proj. Mgr.
2. Field Office
3. File
4. Client

PAGE 1 OF 1 PAGES

BY R. E. Barnes
TITLE Res. Engr.

Fisk Form 8-1

**FIGURE 4.1** Daily Construction Report. (From *Construction Engineer's Complete Handbook of Forms* by Edward Fisk. Copyright © 1992 by Prentice Hall. Reprinted by permission of Prentice Hall.)

# INSPECTOR'S DAILY RECORD OF WORK PROGRESS

For submittal to Resident Project Rep. to compile Daily Construction Report

Project Title _AMHERST RESERVOIR_ Project No. _95-174_

Feature _EMBANKMENT CONST._ Date _7-24-95_

Contractor _S&M CONST. (SUB.)_ Type of Work _EARTHWORK_

**DAY:** S [M X] T W TH F S

**WEATHER:** Brite Sun | Clear [✓] | Overcast | Rain - | Snow
**TEMP.:** To 0 | 0-10 | 10-20 [X] | 21-29 | 29 up
**WIND:** Still [✓] | Moder | High | Report No
**HUMIDITY:** Dry [✓] | Moder [✓] | Humid | **417**

**CONTRACTOR'S WORK FORCE** (Indicate classifications, including Subcontractor personnel)

ONE FOREMAN
TWO EQUIPT. OPERATORS

**EQUIPMENT IN USE OR IDLED** (Identify which)
MS 120-B BACKHOE IN USE; NO EQUIPT. DOWN
ONE CAT D-9 AND ONE CAT D-6 IN ACTIVE USE

**MATERIALS OR EQUIPMENT DELIVERED** _VCP PIPE DELIVERED TO SITE_

**NON-CONFORMING MATERIALS OR WORK** (Describe reason for non-conformance)
VCP DELIV. TODAY INCL 14 LENGTHS W/REJECTABLE DEFECTS
(CRACKS IN BELLS; OUT-OF-ROUND; BLISTERS)

**FIELD PROBLEMS** (which could result in delay or claim) _DISCOVERY OF EXPANSIVE CLAYS IN EAST_
EMBANKMENT AREA NOT PREVIOUSLY NOTICED BY SOILS ENGRS. REPORT
TO ENGR FOR FURTHER INSTRUCTIONS.

**QUANTITIES OF PAY ITEMS PLACED** _96m PIPE TRENCH EXCAVATED; 45m PIPE BEDDED,_
LAID, & JOINTED; 27m OF PIPE FULLY BACKFILLED & COMPACTED; 12m PIPE
ZONE B.F. PLACED (SAND). NO PAVING OVER ANY TRENCHES YET.

**SUMMARY OF CONSTRUCTION ACTIVITIES** _EXCAVATION OF BASIN AREA CONTINUING._
TRENCH EXCAV. & B.F. FOR INLET/OUTLET PIPE; DELIVERY OF PIPE MATLS
TO THE SITE; CONST. FENCING CONTINUING.

Data used are fictitious
for illustration only

**FOLLOWUP INSPECTIONS OF PREVIOUSLY REPORTED DEFICIENCIES**
RECHECKED EXCAV. & RECOMPACTION OF TRENCH B.F. OVER 600mm RCCP
INLET/OUTLET LINE TO ASSURE 90% PER SPEC. IT IS NOW OK.
CHECKS OUT AT 92% AND 93% AT ALL LEVELS

**DISTRIBUTION**
1. Field Office
2. Inspector

Inspector _R. E. Barner_

Fisk Form 8-5

**FIGURE 4.2** Inspector's Daily Record of Work Progress. (From *Construction Engineer's Complete Handbook of Forms* by Edward Fisk. Copyright © 1992 by Prentice Hall. Reprinted by permission of Prentice Hall.)

# Twining Laboratories of Southern California, Inc.

3310 Airport Way / Mailing Address P.O. Box 47 / Long Beach, CA 90801 / (213) 426-3355 / (213) 636-2386 / (714) 828-6432
BRANCH OFFICE: 1514-D North Susan Street / Santa Ana, CA 92703 / (714) 554-2645

EXAMINATION NO. 87-19685

## COMPRESSION TESTS ON CONCRETE CYLINDERS

E.R. Fisk & Associates
1224 East Katella
Suite 105
Orange, CA 92667

| | | | |
|---|---|---|---|
| PROJECT ADDRESS | Galaxy Office Tower 12891 Galaxy Way, El Segundo, CA | | |
| ARCHITECT | J.K. Jones Association | CONTRACTOR | Smith Construction |
| ENGINEER | Martin & Brayton | SUBCONTRACTOR | Blayman Concrete |
| SAMPLE FROM | Second floor slab, A–C to 7–9 | | |
| MIX | LB 87-1061 | SPECIFIED STRENGTH | 4000 @ 28 days |
| DATE CAST | 1-28-87 | SLUMP 4½" | SPECIMEN SIZE 6" x 12" |

| | | | |
|---|---|---|---|
| DATE TESTED | 2-4-87 | 2-25-87 | 2-25-87 |
| SPECIMEN NO. | 2A | 2B | 2C |
| COMPRESSION | 7 days | 28 days | 28 days |
| TOTAL LOAD LBS. | 86,000 | 122,500 | 125,000 |
| POUNDS PER SQ. IN. | 3,040 | 4,330 | 4,420 |
| AREA. SQ. IN. | 28.27 | | |

28 day average = 4,375

COMPLIANCE    28 day test complies with specified strength

| | MADE BY: | DELIVERED BY: | RECEIVED ON: |
|---|---|---|---|
| SPECIMENS | Harold Johnson | TLSC | 1-29-87 |

DISTRIBUTION
  E.R. Fisk & Assoc. - 2
  Smith Construction -1
  Blayman Concrete - 1
  El Segundo Building Dept. - 1
  C & C Ready Mix - 1

**FIGURE 4.3**  Laboratory test report.

should be made every day, whether or not work was performed. The detailed contents and form of the diary will be described later in this chapter (see Figure 4.7).

5. *Log of submittals.* All material being transmitted to the architect/engineer through the Resident Project Representative should be logged in and out on a submittal log such as illustrated in Figure 4.4.

## Construction Field Office Files

All field office files should be kept up to date and should be maintained for ready reference at the job site during the entire construction phase of the project. Upon completion of the work, the files should be turned over to the architect/engineer, who will retain some and forward others to the owner for retention. The field office files should include the following categories:

**CONTRACTOR SUBMITTAL LOG**

Project: 5 MGD TREATMENT PLANT ADD'N   Project Mgr. R. E. BARNES
Job No. 95-87-075   Contractor ABC CONSTRUCTORS, INC.

| Date Rec'd. | Trans-mittal No. | Description | Subcontractor / Ref. Spec. Section | Con-tractor Trans. No. | No. Copies Rec'd | No Exceptions Taken | Make Corrections Noted | Revise & Resubmit | Rejected | Date Ret'd. | No. Copies Ret'd. | Remarks |
|---|---|---|---|---|---|---|---|---|---|---|---|---|
| 6-12-95 | 78 | Plan View - Aeration Basin / Secondary Sed. Tanks / Dissolved Air Flot. Thickener | 11200 | | 6 | | X | | | 6-21-95 | 5 | |
| 6-13-95 | 79 | Electrical Materials List | A. J. Peterson / 16050 | | 6 | X | | | | 7-17-95 | 5 | |
| 6-13-95 | 80 | Warranty Covering Acme Kitchen Unit | 11400 | | 6 | | | | X | 6-15-95 | 5 | |
| 6-13-95 | 81 | Metal Compartment Dwgs. Color Card | 10600 | | 6 | | | | | 7-19-95 | 5 | |
| 6-13-95 | 82 | Cellite Resin System | 03300 | | 6 | | X | | | 6-19-95 | 5 | |
| 6-13-95 | 83 | Pumps, Flow Detector, Motors, Frequency Drive | Harris & Foote / 11200 | | 6 | | | | | 7-19-95 | 5 | See Change Order C.O. 003 |
| 6-13-95 | 84 | Chlorination Equipment | Wallace & Tiernan / 11200 | | 6 | | | X | | 6-16-95 | 5 | |
| 6-13-95 | 85 | Curing Compound | 03370 | | 6 | X | | | | 6-19-95 | 5 | Approved "Or Equal" item |
| 6-19-95 | 86 | Wall Spool Blower Solids Bldg. | 11200 | | 6 | X | | | | 6-21-95 | 5 | |
| 6-21-95 | 87 | S. Primary Sludge Digester Slab | 11200 | | 6 | X | | | | 6-22-95 | 5 | |

Contractor Submittal Log provides a permanent record of all submittals by the contractor of shop drawings, samples, and other requested data received during construction.
Fisk Form 7-2

**FIGURE 4.4** Contractor submittal log. (From *Construction Engineer's Complete Handbook of Forms* by Edward Fisk. Copyright © 1992 by Prentice Hall. Reprinted by permission of Prentice Hall.)

1. *Correspondence.* Copies of all correspondence concerning the project that have been sent to the Resident Project Representative should be maintained and filed by date.

2. *Job drawings.* Drawings of clarification or change, or drawings that contain supplemental information should be filed at the field office, in addition to a complete set of all contract drawings as bid.

3. *Shop drawing submittals.* The Resident Project Representative should maintain a drawing log and should maintain a shop-drawing file of submittals that have received final review and approval (Figure 4.4).

4. *Requisitions.* Copies of all approved requisitions for payment should be kept at the site for field reference and as a guide for initial review of the next month's partial pay requisition from the contractor.

5. *Reports.* Copies of all reports of all types should be filed by date.

6. *Samples.* All approved samples showing material and/or workmanship should be kept at the job site as a basis of comparison, and should be appropriately tagged and logged.

7. *Operating tests.* The Resident Project Representative is responsible for seeing that all required tests are performed at the proper time. The files should include the results of all such testing.

8. *Deviation requests.* Whenever a request for deviation is received, a copy should be maintained with the disposition of the request.

## CONSTRUCTION PROGRESS RECORD

The most commonly accepted form of construction progress record is in the form of a Daily Construction Report, which is filled in by the Resident Project Representative or, if applicable, by the contractor's CQC representative on a daily basis even if no work was performed at the site that day. Usually, such reports are executed in carbon copies or by the use of forms printed on NCR paper that will provide the necessary number of copies.

The daily report is highly necessary as a progress record, and the use of this report in combination with an inspector's daily diary allows two types of information to be recorded in separate documents. In this manner, the more privileged type of information can be restricted to recording in the diary, and the true work progress can be recorded on the Daily Construction Report, where it will receive wider distribution.

## CONSTRUCTION REPORTS

### Daily Construction Reports

The content of a Daily Construction Report should include the following information (however, it should be remembered that as long as a separate daily diary is being kept, the Daily Construction Report should contain items relating to work progress, not to conversations or to other transactions):

1. Project name and job number.
2. Client's name (name of project owner).
3. Contractor's name (general contractor only).
4. Name of the project manager for the design organization.
5. Report number and date of report (use consecutive numbering).
6. Day of the week.
7. Weather conditions (wind, humidity, temperature, sun, clouds, etc.).
8. Average field force, both supervisory and nonsupervisory.
    - (a) Name of each contractor or subcontractor on the job that day.
    - (b) Number of manual workers (journeymen and apprentices) at the site.
    - (c) Number of nonmanual workers (superintendents and foremen) at the site.
9. Visitors at the site; include names, employers, and time in and out.
10. List identity, size, and type of all major pieces of construction equipment at the site each day. Indicate if idle, and reason, if applicable.
11. Log all work commenced; status of all work in progress; and all new work started. Identify location of the work as well as its description, and which contractor or subcontractor is performing it.
12. Sign the daily report with your full name, title, and date.

On large projects, items 1 through 4 are often preprinted on the Daily Construction Report form to avoid needless duplication of effort by field personnel.

## Monthly Reports

In addition to Daily Construction Reports, it is not uncommon to require monthly reports as well. Generally, such reports are grouped in two categories: Monthly Report of Contract Performance, as in Figure 4.5; and a General Project Status Report, as illustrated in Figure 4.6.

The *Monthly Report of Contract Performance* is intended to supplement the Daily Construction Reports, and as such summarizes the work progress for the immediately preceding month both graphically (S-Curve diagram), and verbally, through a summary of contract time and change orders, and in a brief narrative report summarizing the work progress during the past month.

The *General Project Status Report* is a monthly statement of time and cost and should be of special interest to the project manager. The document not only places all time and cost figures in one handy document, but documents all changes that accrued since the beginning of the project. This is a strongly recommended document for whomever is responsible for management of the contract on behalf of the owner or architect/engineer.

**MONTHLY REPORT OF CONTRACT PERFORMANCE**

City of Thousand Oaks

| | | | DATE 7-31-89 |
|---|---|---|---|

| PROJECT | Amherst Reservoir & Pumping Plant | WORK ORDER NO. | CONTRACT NO. 89/90-00 |
|---|---|---|---|
| OWNER | City of Thousand Oaks | CONTRACTOR | XYZ Constructors, Inc. |
| LOCATION | Old Conejo Road | PROJECT A & E | LFM, Inc. | NO. WKG. DAYS 220 |

PERCENT OF WORK COMPLETED

100 90 80 70 60 50 40 30 20 10 0

1 2 3 4 5 6 7 8 9 10 11 12 13 14 15 16 17 18 19 20 21 22 23 24

ELAPSED CONTRACT TIME IN MONTHS

| STARTING DATE: | OFFICIAL 3-28-89 | ACTUAL 4-03-89 | COMPLETION DATE: | OFFICIAL 1-31-90 | ACTUAL |
|---|---|---|---|---|---|
| TIME EXTENSIONS RECOMMENDED THIS MONTH: | | none | REASON | | |
| TOTAL EXTENSIONS ACCUMULATED: | | 12 days | NUMBER OF CHANGE ORDERS: | APPROVED 3 | PENDING 1 |
| PERCENT OF WORK COMPLETED: | | 42.0 | PERCENT OF TIME ELAPSED: | | 40.00 |

CONTROLLING OPERATIONS AND OTHER REMARKS

Deliveries of prestress concrete cylinder pipe has fallen behind schedule.

Trenching contractor will shut down operations until deliveries catch up.

Release on retention funds authorized under escrow agreement No. 89/90-00 dated 31 Aug 1989.

| DISTRIBUTION: | 1. Project Manager 2. Project Accounting 3. Resident Project Representative | SIGNATURE | R. E. Barnes |
|---|---|---|---|
| | | TITLE | Resident Project Representative |

Wiley-Fisk Form 8-8

**FIGURE 4.5**  Monthly Report of Contract Performance.

**GENERAL PROJECT STATUS REPORT**

PROJECT  Hydroelectric Project
OWNER  City of Thousand Oaks, CA                    PROJECT NO.  89/90-00
CONTRACTOR  XYZ Constructors, Inc.                  CONTRACT NO.  22 Dec 1988
PROJECT MANAGER  R. E. Barnes                       DATE  1 Mar 1990

| | |
|---|---:|
| Amount of Original Contract. . . . . . . . . . . . . . . . . . . . . . . . . . . . . . . . . . . . . . . $ | 65,123,405.00 |
| Approved Change Orders to Date . . . . . . . . . . . . . . . . . . . . . . . . . . . . . . . . . | 62,037.00 |
| Anticipated Over-run or (Under-run) in Uncompleted Work. . . . . . . . . . . . . . . . . . | 25,622.00 |
| Actual Over-run or (Under-run) in Completed Work. . . . . . . . . . . . . . . . . . . . . . . | ---- |
| Rental Revenue from Contract Owner not included above . . . . . . . . . | |
| Estimated Total Amount of Principal Contract . . . . . . . . . . . . . . . . . . . . . . . $ | 65,211,164.00 |
| Other Contract Work not Included in Principal Contract. . . . . . . . . . . . . . . . . . . . | ---- |
| Total Estimated Contract Volume . . . . . . . . . . . . . . . . . . . . . . . . . . . . . . . . $ | 65,211,164.00 |

| | | |
|---|---:|---:|
| Contract Revenue to Date. . . . . . . . . . . . . . . . . . . . . . . . . . . $ | 27,176,039.00 | |
| Less: Contract Advances for Materials on Hand. . . . . . . . . . . . | (-2,657,123.00) | |
| Contract Advances for Plant and Move-in. . . . . . . . . . . . | (-1,058,416.00) | |
| Revenue Reduction for Uncompleted Work . . . . . . . . . . | (-806,014.00) | |
| Other . . . . . . . . . . . . . . . . . . . . . . . . . . . . . . . . . . . . | ---- | |
| Total Amount of Work Completed to Date. . . . . . . . | 22,584,486.00 $ | 22,584,486.00 |
| Uncompleted Contract Volume . . . . . . . . . . . . . . . . . . . . . . . . . . . . . . . . . . . . . $ | | 42,646,678.00 |

| | |
|---|---:|
| Percent Complete Based on Original Contract. . . . . . . . . . . . . . . . . . . . . . . . . | 34.66 % |
| Percent Complete Based on Total Estimated Contract . . . . . . . . . . . . . . . . . . | 34.03 % |
| Time Allotted by Original Contract. . . . . . . . . . . . . . . . . . . . . . . . . . . . . . . . | 1,400 Days |
| Extension of Contract Time . . . . . . . . . . . . . . . . . . . . . . . . . . . . . . . . . . . . | 10 Days |
| Total Contract Time . . . . . . . . . . . . . . . . . . . . . . . . . . . . . . . . . . . . . . . . . | 1410 Days |
| Contract Time Elapsed. . . . . . . . . . . . . . . . . . . . . . . . . . . . . . . . . . . . . . . . | 434 Days |
| Percent of Original Contract Time Elapsed. . . . . . . . . . . . . . . . . . . . . . . . . . | 31.00 % |
| Percent of Total Time, Including Extensions, Elapsed. . . . . . . . . . . . . . . . . . | 30.78 % |
| Date Contract was Physically Completed—If Completed . . . . . . . . . . . . . . . . | ---- |
| Expected Date of Physical Completion—If Not Complete . . . . . . . . . . . . . . . . | 2 Nov 1992 |

Wiley-Fisk Form 8-7

**FIGURE 4.6**  General Project Status Report.

## CONSTRUCTION DIARY

Often called by different names, the construction diary (Figure 4.7) is an important document. The requirements for maintaining an unimpeachable legal record in the form of a daily diary are indicated in the list that follows shortly. Although variations may occur without destroying the credibility of the document, the recommendations provided here should assure the greatest degree of reliability.

It should be remembered that it is frequently necessary to consult a field diary to give testimony during a court trial. In some cases, the book itself may not be generally admissible as evidence but could be used as a memory refresher by the person who made the original entries while giving testimony on the witness stand. It is because of this provision that certain basic record-keeping rules are considered mandatory to preserve the integrity of the record.

Mention is sometimes made of the "privileged" nature of some of the contents of the construction diary. This is *not* meant to imply that it is a private document to be seen and possessed by the inspector alone. On the contrary, the record normally belongs to the design firm or owner, and although it is wise for the inspector to retain a copy of its contents, the diary must normally be turned in with the job records when it is full or at the end of the construction project. During the progress of the work, it may be advisable to submit the daily diary at regular intervals to the project manager of the design organization or owner to allow inspection of its contents. In this manner the project manager can be advised of all the transactions that have been taking place in the field. Normally, the project manager may want to make copies of its pages at that time; however, that does not preclude the requirement that the filled books be turned in to the project manager at the end of the job, at which time they are often stored in the vault with other permanent job records.

The diary requirements can be grouped into two significant categories: *format* and *content.* Each is equally important in its own way.

### Format of the Construction Diary

1. Use only a hard-cover, stitched-binding field book such as used by surveyors for their note keeping, or a "record book" obtainable at stationers.
2. Pages should be consecutively numbered in ink, and *no* numbers should be skipped.
3. No erasures should be made. In case of error, simply cross out the incorrect information and enter the correct data next to it.
4. No pages should be torn out of the book at any time. If a page is to be voided, place a large "X" through the page and mark "void."
5. Every day should be reported, and every calendar date should be accounted for. If there is no work performed on a given date, the date should be entered on the page followed by the words "no work" or similar wording. It is still desirable to record the weather on "no work" days, as it may have later bearing on *why* no work was performed in a case involving a claim for liquidated damages.

FIGURE 4.7 Sample diary page.

**6.** All entries *must be made on the same date that they occur.* If notes are kept on separate scratch paper and later transcribed into the diary, and this fact is disclosed during a trial, the credibility of the entire diary comes into question.

### Content of the Diary

**1.** Record telephone calls made or received, and a substantial outline of the nature of such calls, including any statements or commitments made during the call. Identify the parties calling.

**2.** Record any work or material in place that does not correspond with the drawings or specifications, as well as the action taken. List any other problems or abnormal occurrences that arose during each day, including notations of any particular lack of activity on the part of the contractor. Note corrective actions taken.

**3.** Record time and the name of the contractor's representative to whom field orders are delivered, and the nature of the contents of the field order.

**4.** Note unforeseen conditions observed by the inspector that may cause a slowdown by the contractor.

**5.** Where a contractor is performing extra work because of an unforeseen underground obstruction, make a careful field count of all personnel and equipment at the site and how they are occupied. Log the number and craft of each person idled by such work, as well as any idle equipment *that would otherwise be capable of working.*

**6.** Record the content of all substantive conversations held with the contractor at the site, as well as any trade-offs, deals, or commitments made by either party.

**7.** Record all field errors made by *any* party at the site. Identify in detail and indicate probable effect.

**8.** Show name of the job at the head of every page.

**9.** Sign every diary entry and indicate your job title immediately under the last line of entry on each day's report. This will preclude claims that additional wording was added later.

## WHO SHOULD MAINTAIN DIARIES AND DAILY REPORTS

A construction diary should be kept by every individual involved in the project. The Daily Construction Report, by comparison, is prepared and submitted only by the Resident Project Representative, utilizing the Inspector's Daily Record of Work Progress reports submitted by each of the inspectors as an information source. These interim inspectors' reports serve also as a check of contractor work progress when it becomes necessary to review the contractor's partial pay request.

## DOCUMENTATION OF INTERMITTENT INSPECTION

Sometimes a project representative is responsible for monitoring the construction of several smaller projects instead of serving as a Resident Project Representative on a single, large project. In such cases, the project representative usually makes intermittent field visits to each project site, as needed, to meet the individual project requirements.

The documentation requirements for construction progress reporting of multiple projects by the same project representative calls for an approach different from the traditional daily report. A more practical approach under the circumstances is to prepare a weekly project report for each project for which the project representative is responsible (Figure 4.8). In this manner, the activities of the entire week of each project can be summarized in a single project report for each project being monitored.

## SPECIAL FEEDBACK REPORTS

Although not generally a contract requirement or even a common practice among most architect/engineer offices, a highly desirable practice would be the establishment of communications feedback systems between the various field forces and between the field and office. Such communications can minimize the number of repeated errors or field problems that often occur as a result of the traditional failure of communication between the construction forces and the designers of a project.

### Report of Field Correction

Whenever the need for any corrective change is recognized in the field that would require a departure from the plans and specifications as originally issued, a complete detailed report should be prepared by the Resident Project Representative and submitted to the project manager for evaluation by the design and specifications departments to see if the problem can be prevented in the future by design or specifications changes.

A convenient document for this purpose is illustrated in Figure 4.9. It provides for the necessary information needed by the office forces in their evaluations and possible corrections, if merited. The report should be in sufficient detail to allow the engineer or architect to understand the problem, make a determination, and issue instructions to the field personnel. This document is intended as a source of information only, and must not be used as an authorization to perform work nor as a change order. Wherever changes are required, the normal procedures for accomplishing such changes within the terms of the contract must be observed. The document should do the following:

1. Identify the problem. Indicate why originally specified construction is not recommended.
2. Offer a solution. Describe in detail the recommended change or changes that are suggested.

# INSPECTOR'S WEEKLY PROGRESS REPORT

Feature Inspected ___CONCRETE RESERVOIR LINING & SITEWORK___

Item No. ___

Project ___CARTER RESERVOIR___                                    Date ___10-13-94___

Project No. ___94-27___                          Contract No. ___94-27___

Work Order No. ___                               Purchase Order No. ___

Contractor ___L&M CONSTRUCTION CO., INC.___      Location ___IRVINE, CA___

Subcontractor ___WARNER CONCRETE CO.___          Location ___ORANGE, CA___

---

CONTRACT REQ'D DELIVERY DATE ___2-20-95___       ESTIMATED DELIVERY DATE ___2-20-95___

(EXPLAIN DIFFERENCE) ___AUTH. C.O. 003 AND 007 EXTENDED COMPLETION DATE BY___
___15 WORKING DAYS. ALSO 3 DA. EXCUSABLE WEATHER (22 CAL. DAYS)___

ENGINEERING STATUS:

DESIGN COMPLETE % _____                    CONTRACTOR COMPL. % _____

INCOMPLETE _____        ~~Data used are fictitious~~PLETE _____
                             ~~for illustration only~~

PRODUCTION STATUS:

CONTRACT NOT YET SCHEDULED _____  WILL BE SCHEDULED _____  SCHEDULED _____

CONTRACT IN PRODUCTION _____

CONTRACT PROGRESSING TO PRESENT SCHEDULE _____ INSPECTOR'S ESTIMATE OF % COMPL. ___24%___

SHIPPING INFORMATION:

TOTAL SHIPPED THIS WEEK ___NONE___

TOTAL PREVIOUSLY SHIPPED ___5.43T REBAR; 457M WATERSTOP___

TOTAL SHIPPED TO DATE ___8.46T REBAR; 610M PVC WATERSTOP___

---

REMARKS

BACKFILLING CONTINUED TO 400MM RCCP DOWNHILL LINE. GUNITE REPAIR
TO EAST HALF OF RES. ROOF BEGUN ON MONDAY 10/10/94. SLOPE PANELS
WERE PREPARED FOR CONC. PLACING. 3 PANELS COMPL. ON TUE 10/11/94 AND
ANOTHER 2 ON FRI 10/14/94. THIS COMPLETES ALL SLOPE PAVING. POWER CO.
SET 4 POLES TO SERVE THE SITE, BUT TRANSF. & RACKS HAVE NOT BEEN
ERECTED. ELEC. PAD WAS CAST ON MON. 10-3-94 USING MIX # CRP-1020 AT
75MM SLUMP.
WATERSTOP JOINTS IN 2ND STAGE PANELS WERE BONDED WED 10/12/94.
JT FILLER MATL BEING REMOVED FROM FINISHED PANELS AND GROOVE IS
BEING PREPARED FOR POLYURETHANE SEALANT.
IN VALVE PIT, ALTITUDE VALVES WERE PLACED AND DRAWN INTO FINAL POSITION
USING CAST-IN-PLACE PULLING EYES, DRESSER COUPLINGS SET JUST OUTSIDE
VALVE VAULT.
SITE GRADING BEGUN THUR 10/13/94 USING MOTOR GRADER AND A CAT AT
CURB & GUTTER AREAS.
FRI 10/14/94 THE FLANGE WAS ATTACHED TO THE COPPER SENSING LINE
TO THE ALTITUDE VALVE.

By ___R. E. Beemer___                    Title ___INSPECTOR___

Inspection Agency ___LFM, INC.___

Fisk Form 8-6

---

**FIGURE 4.8**  Inspector's Weekly Progress Report. (From *Construction Engineer's Complete Handbook of Forms* by Edward Fisk. Copyright © 1992 by Prentice Hall. Reprinted by permission of Prentice Hall.)

# REPORT OF FIELD CORRECTION

PROJECT _CHAMPLAIN RESERVOIR No. 3_

LOCATION _THOUSAND OAKS, CA._  PROJECT NO. _94-13_

CONTRACTOR _ABC CONSTRUCTION, INC._

SPECIAL REPORT NO. _2_

PAGE _1_ OF _1_ PAGES

DATE _4-25-94_

CROSS REFERENCE TO
DAILY REPORT NO. _153_

### INSTRUCTIONS

Whenever any corrective change is made in field construction which is at variance with the specifications and drawings as originally issued, a complete detailed report shall be filed, listing the following items, so that specifications or drawings storage data can be corrected.

1. Identify the problem: Indicate why originally specified construction was not used.
2. The Solution: Describe, in detail, the recommended change or changes that were made, as applicable.
3. Indicate whether this is an isolated case or a general condition which could be improved by changing future specifications or drawings.
4. Submit sketches as necessary.

### REFERENCE DATA

SPECIFICATION SECTION No. _03300_ PAGE No. _____ PARAGRAPH No. _3.4.5A_

DRAWING No. _S-401_ ENTITLED _RESERVOIR BASIN STRUCTURE_

SKETCH No. _____ DATED _____ ENTITLED _____

### DESCRIPTION

1. DETAILED IDENTIFICATION OF THE PROBLEM _BLEEDING ALONG ALL VERTICAL JTS OF STEEL PANEL WALL FORMS. ALL VERTICAL JOINTS IN STEEL WALL SURFACES SHOW EXTENSIVE EVIDENCE OF EXPOSED AGGREGATE AT ALL VERTICAL WALL JOINTS. EXAMINATION OF STEEL PANEL FORMS SHOWS TYP 1mm GAPS AT ALL VERTICAL JOINTS, BUT TIGHT JOINTS AT ALL HORIZONTAL JOINT LINES. FASTENING DOGS SEEM UNABLE TO DRAW FORM JOINTS TIGHTLY TOGETHER TO ELIMINATE LOSS OF CEMENT PASTE AT VERTICAL JOINTS._

2. DETAILED SOLUTION PROPOSED OR ACCOMPLISHED _PRE-ASSEMBLE ALL PANEL UNITS WHILE CLEAN. REPLACE FASTENING DOGS WITH BOLTED JOINTS AND DRAW TIGHT BEFORE INITIAL FORM USE. CALK ALL DEFECTS IN PANEL JOINTS AND TAPE ALL JOINTS. NO JOINTS SHOULD BE TIGHTENED WITHOUT DISASSEMBLY AND CLEANING OF FORM PANEL EDGES. REJECT PANELS WITH WARPED OR DAMAGED EDGES._

_ALTERNATIVE: USE NEW PLYWOOD FORM MATERIAL INSTEAD OF METAL PANS, OR USE FULL-FACE METAL FORMS_

Data used are fictitious for illustration only

3. IS THE PROBLEM AN ISOLATED CASE OR GENERAL? _GENERAL- PROBLEM HAS BEEN ENCOUNTERED ON 3 RESERVOIRS. REVISE SPEC TO ALLOW CONTROL OVER FORM DESIGN._

4. SUBMIT SKETCHES AS NECESSARY _PHOTOS ATTACHED_

DISTRIBUTION
1. Design/Spec Depts.
2. Proj Mgr.
3. Field Office
4. File

(Attach extra sheets as necessary)

BY _R. E. Barnes_  TITLE _RES. ENGR._

Fisk Form 8-4

**FIGURE 4.9**  Example showing proper use of the Report of Field Correction form.

3. Indicate whether the case appears to be an isolated one or whether it appears to be a general condition that could be improved by changing specifications or drawings.

Whether it will facilitate an understanding of the problem or its solution, the Resident Project Representative is encouraged to submit sketches along with the Report of Field Correction.

At this point, the Resident Project Representative should be cautioned.*The foregoing instructions are not meant to imply that the inspector is to take any corrective action that will result in a variation from the plans and specifications without the approval of the architect or engineer of record.* By definition the architect or engineer of record is that individual whose signature appears on the plans as evidence that he or she, either personally or as a representative of a design firm, public agency, or owner, bears legal responsibility for such plans. The authority of anyone to take field action without consulting the architect or engineer of record is limited to cases when such action would *not* result in a variance from the approved plans and specifications. Otherwise, all such actions must be preapproved by the architect or engineer of record. A possible exception might be during emergency conditions, wherein a field decision must be made immediately. Even then, it is wise to telephone ahead to describe the condition and the solution recommended, followed by a written FAX report to the architect/engineer and execution of a formal Change Order. In any case, if forced into a decision-making role, the inspector should inform the contractor that an inspector is not authorized to make such a determination, but that the inspector will not prevent the contractor from taking unilateral emergency action based upon the contractor's own judgment, provided that the contractor fully understands that such actions are subject to confirmation and approval by the architect/engineer; and furthermore, that in case of disapproval, the contractor may be required to take corrective action to remove portions of the work affected by the emergency at the contractor's own expense.

## Concrete Batch Plant Daily Reports

Whenever critical concrete batching control is necessary, such as is often required for the construction of hydraulic structures, a separate inspector may be assigned to the concrete batch plant during all concreting operations. The data recorded by the batch plant inspector are forwarded to the Resident Project Representative and the project manager daily, and should be compared at the job site with the corresponding delivery ticket data. All such information may be conveniently recorded on a prepared form such as illustrated in Figure 4.10. This information should be carefully recorded and stored with the other permanent project records, as it may be utilized later to determine probable causes of field problems with concrete.

## Plant Inspector's Report to Field Inspector

The plant inspector should maintain regular communication with the on-site inspector, who should be informed of any special circumstances or messages in connection with the current placing operations. Ideally, this should be in a report format (Figure 4.11) and is an

**LAWRANCE, FISK & McFARLAND, INC.**
CONSULTING CIVIL & ENVIRONMENTAL ENGINEERS
Santa Barbara, California

**CONCRETE BATCHING PLANT
DAILY REPORT**

PROJECT _BEAR CANYON HE_ FEATURE _FISH BARRIER DAM_ SHIFT _DAY_ DATE _4·24·95_
CONTRACTOR _ABC CONSTRUCTORS INC._ PROJ. NO. _62-02_ INSPECTOR _PRS_
AGGREGATE SOURCE: COARSE _SAN GABRIEL RIVER_ FINE _SAN GABRIEL RIVER_
CEMENT BRAND _RIVERSIDE_ TYPE _II_ LOT NO. _BIN-7_ FALSE SET _NO_
NAME OF: AEA _PROTEX_ WRA _KRL-40_ CACL$_2$ _—_ POZZOLAN _AIROX_
TEMP: AIR _24°-39°_ WATER _(ICE)_ CEMENT _49°_ SAND _28°_ GRAVEL _29°_ CONCRETE _14°_

**MOISTURE ADJUSTMENTS FOR CORRECT BATCH WEIGHTS**

| | MIX NO. _1020_ | | | | MIX NO. | | | | MIX NO. | | | |
|---|---|---|---|---|---|---|---|---|---|---|---|---|
| | Basic Batch M. S.S.D. kg | Probable Free Water % | Free Water kg | Actual Batch M. kg | Basic Batch M. S.S.D. kg | Probable Free Water % | Free Water kg | Actual Batch M. kg | Basic Batch M. S.S.D. kg | Probable Free Water % | Free Water kg | Actual Batch M. kg |
| AEA | 0.06 | — | — | 0.06 | | | | | | | | |
| WRA | 1.5 | — | — | 1.5 | | | | | | | | |
| POZZOLAN | 64 | — | — | 64 | | | | | | | | |
| CEMENT | 213 | — | — | 213 | | | | | | | | |
| SAND | 825 | +4.0 | +33 | 858 | | | | | | | | |
| COARSE AGG 4.75 mm | 690 | +0.5 | +3.6 | 694 | | | | | | | | |
| 38.1~19.0 mm | 769 | 0 | 0 | 747 | | | | | | | | |
| 4.75-38.1 mm | 1193 | -0.1 | -1.4 | 1192 | | | | | | | | |
| | | | | | | | | | | | | |
| WATER ICE | 172 | — | 35 | 137 | | | | | | | | |
| WATER (LITERS) | | | | | | | | | | | | |

*Data used are fictitious for illustration only*

**TEST BATCH DATA**

| Mix No. | Time | Test Cyl Nos. | Slump mm | Conc. Temp °C | Unit M. kg/m³ | % Air (Meter) | Actual Mass SSD, kg | | | | | Total Water kg | Net W / C+P (by Wt) | Yield m³/ Batch | Cement/ m³ kg |
|---|---|---|---|---|---|---|---|---|---|---|---|---|---|---|---|
| | | | | | | | Sand | 19.0 | 38.1 | 100 | | | | | |
| 1020 | 9:20 | FX-5 | 38 | 14 | 2629 | 2.4 | 416 | 346 | 388 | 600 | | 86 | 0.28 | 1.52 | 2.0 |
| | | | | | | | | | | | | | | | |
| | | | | | | | | | | | | | | | |

**CONCRETE PRODUCTION DATA**

| Spec. Item No. | Mix No. | Total No. Batches | Per Batch | | | Batched | | | Waste | | | Used | | |
|---|---|---|---|---|---|---|---|---|---|---|---|---|---|---|
| | | | Cement kg | Pozz. kg | Vol. Batch m³ | Total m³ Conc. | Cement kg | Pozz. t | Conc. m³ | Cement kg | Pozz. t | Conc. m³ | Cement kg | Pozz. t |
| 9 | 1020 | 64 | 213 | 64 | 1.5 | | | | 1.5 | | | | | |
| | | | | | | | | | | | | | | |
| | | | | | | | | | | | | | | |
| | | | | | | | | | | | | | | |
| Total | | | | | | | | | | | | | | |

WATER BATCHER CHECKED_____
AEA DISPENSER CHECKED___ 07:45 HRS; 10:35 HRS 13:00 HRS
WRA DISPENSER CHECKED___ 07:45 HRS

Over for Screen Analyses and General Remarks

**FIGURE 4.10** Example of a daily report from the concrete batch plant inspector. (From *Construction Engineer's Complete Handbook of Forms* by Edward Fisk. Copyright © 1992 by Prentice Hall. Reprinted by permission of Prentice Hall.)

| SCREEN ANALYSIS OF AGGREGATES - PERCENT RETAINED EACH SIZE | | | | | | | | | | | | |
|---|---|---|---|---|---|---|---|---|---|---|---|---|
| SCREEN SIZE | 150 mm -75 mm | | | 75 mm - 38.1 mm | | | 38.1 mm - 19.0 mm | | | 19.0 mm - 4.75 mm | | |
| | M + Tare | Mass | % Each | Wt + Tare | Mass | % Each | M + Tare | Mass | % Each | M + Tare | Mass | % Each |
| 177 mm | | | | | | | | | | | | |
| 152 mm | | | | | | | | | | | | |
| 125 mm | | | | | | | | | | | | |
| 90 mm | | | | 0 | 0 | 0 | | | | | | |
| 75 mm | | | | 9.3 | 6.3 | 4 | | | | | | |
| 63 mm | | | | 66.3 | 63.3 | 41 | | | | | | |
| 45 mm | | | | 57.0 | 54.0 | 35 | 3.4 | 0.4 | 1 | | | |
| 38.1 mm | | | | 32.3 | 29.3 | 19 | 6.1 | 3.1 | 6 | | | |
| 31.5 mm | | | | 4.5 | 1.5 | 1 | 21.1 | 18.1 | 35 | | | |
| 22.4 mm | | | | | | | 23.7 | 20.7 | 40 | 0 | 0 | 0 |
| 19.0 mm | | | | | | | 11.3 | 8.3 | 16 | 5.2 | 2.2 | 9 |
| 16.0 mm | | | | | | | 4.0 | 1.0 | 2 | 11.7 | 8.7 | 36 |
| 9.5 mm | | | | | | | | | | 11.5 | 8.5 | 35 |
| 4.25 mm | | | | | | | | | | 7.8 | 4.8 | 20 |
| 4.00 mm | | | | | | | | | | 3.1 | 0.1 | 0 |
| pan | | | | 0 | 0 | 0 | 3.2 | 0.2 | 0 | 0 | 0 | 0 |
| TOTAL | | | 100 | — | 154.4 | 100 | — | 51.8 | 100 | — | 24.3 | 100 |

| SCREEN SIZE | SAND | | | | | | | | | | | |
|---|---|---|---|---|---|---|---|---|---|---|---|---|
| | M + Tare | Mass | % Each | Cum. % Ret. | M + Tare | Mass | % Each | Cum. % Ret. | M + Tare | Mass | % Each | Cum. % Ret. |
| 4.75 mm | 191 | 6 | 3 | 3 | | | | | | | | |
| 2.36 mm | 215 | 24 | 11 | 14 | | | | | | | | |
| 1.18 mm | 241 | 26 | 12 | 26 | | | | | | | | |
| 600 μm | 287 | 46 | 21 | 47 | | | | | | | | |
| 300 μm | 356 | 69 | 32 | 79 | | | | | | | | |
| 150 μm | 395 | 39 | 18 | 97 | | | | | | | | |
| 75 μm | 400 | 5 | 2 | | | | | | | | | |
| pan | 402 | 2 | 1 | | | | | | | | | |
| TOTAL | 215 | 217 | 100 | | | | 100 | | | | 100 | |
| F.M. | | | | | | | | | | | | |

Data used are fictitious for illustration only

Items needing attention _____

Items of special interest _____

General Comment _____

Inspector _____

Fisk Form 16-1

**FIGURE 4.10**   *continued*

## PLANT INSPECTOR'S REPORT
## TO FIELD INSPECTOR

PLANT NAME
UNITED ROCK & SAND

INSTRUCTIONS TO PLANT INSPECTOR:
Fill out the upper half of this form, attach to load ticket, and send to Field Inspector with first load.

PLANT LOCATION
ORANGE, CA

FOR CONCRETE MIXTURES:

| CLASS OF CONCRETE A-3500 | SOURCE OF COARSE AGGREGATE SAN GABRIEL |

| BRAND OF CEMENT RIVERSIDE | TYPE I/II | SOURCE OF FINE AGGREGATE SAN GABRIEL |

BRAND OF ADMIXTURE
NONE

FOR BITUMINOUS MIXTURES

*Data used are fictitious for illustration only*

| TYPE OF MIX | GRADING |

| AR GRADE OF ASPHALT | SOURCE OF BITUMEN |

| PLANT INSPECTOR M. COLLINS | DATE 6-07-94 |

REMARKS: HELD 60 L WATER FROM EA. 5m³ BATCH
— WILL YOU BE RUNNING TOMORROW ?

PROJECT TITLE
RESERVOIR 1-D

INSTRUCTIONS TO FIELD INSPECTOR:
Fill out this lower portion and return to the plant inspector immediately.

LOCATION
FULLERTON, CA

| PROJECT NO. 95-90-00 | SPECIFICATIONS OR CONTRACT NO. F 3057-556 |

(CONCRETE)(ASPHALT) USED FOR
VALVE VAULT STRUCTURE

GALLONS OF WATER ADDED ON THE JOB
45 L/5m³ LOAD

| FIELD INSPECTOR R.E. BARNES | DATE 6-07-94 |

NOTES: HAD ALL DRIVERS RUN AT MIXING SPEED FOR 3 MIN. AFTER ARRIVAL AT SITE TO ASSURE FULL MIXING TIME AFTER RECEIVING TIP FROM ONE OF THE DRIVERS THAT MOST LOADS ARE FORCED TO LEAVE PLANT WITH INADEQUATE MIXING TIME.

BE SURE TO CHECK DRUMS BEFORE BATCHING TO BE SURE THAT ALL WASHDOWN WATER HAS BEEN REMOVED.

WE EXPECT TO PLACE 150 m³ TOMORROW

Fisk Form 16-2

**FIGURE 4.11** Plant Inspector's Report to Field Inspector. (From *Construction Engineer's Complete Handbook of Forms* by Edward Fisk. Copyright © 1992 by Prentice Hall. Reprinted by permission of Prentice Hall.)

intermittently prepared memorandum designed for easy exchange of information between the plant inspector and the field inspector or Resident Project Representative. If a form similar to the one illustrated is used, an easy means of recording two-way communications is provided. The information should also be retained in the permanent project files.

Delivery of the memorandum is normally accomplished by sending it to the project site with one of the drivers leaving the batching plant. In this way it is even possible to send commentary that concerns the concrete load that the message was actually delivered with so that no time is lost in communications.

### Field Investigation Report

On numerous occasions in construction, situations arise that cannot be resolved until more facts are known. Under such conditions, an investigation should be made by the project manager or Resident Project Representative, and the findings recorded. This information is then available for use in efforts to determine future courses of action where they are justified.

## DOCUMENTATION OF DANGEROUS SAFETY HAZARD WARNINGS

In Chapter 8, the procedure for the handling of serious contractor safety violations is described. In addition to the action described there, certain additional precautions should be taken to document the action taken by the owner's field personnel and the contractor. This is vitally important for the Resident Project Representative because failure to do so could result in serious charges being unfairly lodged against the design organization or owner for failure to take affirmative action in case of a death or serious injury resulting from the hazard.

It is recommended that in each case involving an "imminent hazard," the resident inspector take the following steps *after seeing that persons in the immediate area of the hazard are removed from danger:*

1. Notify the contractor's superintendent or foreman.
2. Issue written notice to the contractor to take immediate action to correct the hazard, and record this action in the inspector's diary, including the exact time of day that the notice was given. Also, inform the contractor that unless immediate action is taken to correct or remove the hazard, the matter will be immediately referred to the OSHA compliance officer serving that area.
3. Upon failure or refusal of the contractor to take immediate steps to correct or remove an "imminent hazard," note the exact time of day, and telephone the OSHA compliance officer and make a full oral report. After completing the call, enter into the diary or log that the contractor either failed or refused to effect immediate correction of the hazard; describe all steps taken to alleviate the hazard, including orders given to remove personnel from the danger area; record all field orders (written and oral) given to the contractor; record the exact time of the day that

      (1) persons were ordered out of the danger area, (2) a correction order was issued to the contractor, and (3) the OSHA compliance officer was notified.

4. Upon completion of the foregoing, write a full report to the design firm or owner, including a summary of all pertinent data recorded in the construction diary.

5. Upon mailing the field report to the design firm or owner, telephone the firm or owner to advise of the forthcoming report, describe the incident briefly, indicate the action taken, and record the call in the construction diary.

## MISCELLANEOUS RECORDS

There are numerous types of individual records that are important to log and retain for future reference. Many of the records that must be maintained are primarily of a technical, not an administrative nature. Thus, no detailed coverage will be attempted here. However, as a reminder, the following will serve as a partial list of some of the many technical records that must be maintained on a job, as applicable (once compiled, the handling of these records becomes an administrative matter):

1. Manufacturers' certificates for products
2. Laboratory test certificates (Figure 4.3)
3. Concrete transit-mix delivery tickets (Figure 4.12)
4. Records of pile driving (Figure 4.13)
5. Record of inspection of structural welding (Figure 4.14)
6. Sewer infiltration test reports
7. Fabricating plant inspection reports
8. Special inspector reports
9. Weld radiographs
10. Acceptance certificates by public agency inspectors
11. Discrepancy reports
12. Deviation requests and action taken
13. Concrete mix designs

## LABOR STANDARDS REVIEW RECORDS

On contracts where any federal funds are to be used, the Davis-Bacon Act applies. There are two types of situations where this will occur: contracts with local cities, counties, or special districts where the projects are being constructed with federal grant money, such as the EPA Clean Water Grant Program, EDA, HUD, or on contracts directly with a federal agency, such as military construction, the Postal Service, or GSA projects.

      The project administrator has additional responsibilities on all such work, and checks with the contractor must be made for the following items:

**FIGURE 4.12**   Transit-mixed concrete delivery ticket.

1. On military projects, employee interviews must be conducted to determine classifications and rates of pay, including fringe benefits. All such data must be recorded on "Labor Standards Interview," Form No. DD-1567.

2. On federal grant programs, certified payrolls must be obtained from the contractor on Labor Department Form WH-347 (or similar forms), and the Resident Project Representative must check them for compliance with wage rates in the specifications and report any errors to the contractor.

3. On-site checks must be made of the type and classification of all work performed at the site and the number of workers in each category. Payroll reviews of prime and subcontractors' payroll submittals should be made.

4. On military construction, the previously described information with all available data should be recorded on the daily Report to Inspector and the CQC report to assure consistency.

5. On grant-funded projects, the agency administering the grant program will make periodic inspections to check for compliance with labor laws. This inspection includes checking payrolls and interviewing employees to ascertain working hours and actual payment received.

6. Checks must be made that all equal employment opportunity laws are being followed.

**City of Thousand Oaks**

**PILE DRIVING RECORD**

| 1 Project Title  CHLORINATION FACILITY | 2 Structure  ADMIN BLDG/LABS | Date 4-17-90 |

| 3. Pile Material and Type  STEEL "H" | 6. (Hammer (Make and Size)  McKIERNAN-TERRY DIESEL DE-20 | 7 Contract No  89/90-00 | Inspector Signature  O.R.Bailey |
| 4. Minimum Penetration  50 FT | 6a. Blows per minute  48-52 | 6b. Stroke  6-FT | 8. Reference Dwg  C-314 122 | Shift  DAY |
| 5. Resistance Required  40 BLOWS/FT THRU LAST 4 FT | 6c. Weight of ram  2,000 # | 6d. Rated Striking Energy  16,000 FT-LB | 9. Datum Elevation  +10' ABOVE MLW | SHEET NO.  1  OF  3 |

| PILE DATA | | | | ELEVATIONS | | | PENETRATION (BLOWS/FT) Last 4 Feet | | | | DATE DRIVEN | REMARKS |
|---|---|---|---|---|---|---|---|---|---|---|---|---|
| COL. OR BENT LINE | ROW | SIZE (BUTT TO TIP) | ORIGINAL LENGTH | GROUND | TIP | CUT-OFF | 2" to 3" | 3" to 4" | 4" to 1' | 1' to Tip | | |
| A | B | C | D | E | F | G | H | I | J | K | L | M |
| C3 | 3 | 14×14 | 40' | 283 | 248 | 4' | | | | | 4-17-90 | |
| C4 | 4 | 14×14 | 40' | 283 | 247 | 3' | | | | | 4-17-90 | |
| C5 | 5 | 14×14 | 40' | 283 | 253 | 9' | | | | | 4-17-90 | TO REFUSAL |
| | | | | | | | | | | | | |
| | | | | | | | | | | | | |
| | | | | | | | | | | | | |
| | | | | | | | | | | | | |
| | | | | | | | | | | | | |
| | | | | | | | | | | | | |
| | | | | | | | | | | | | |
| | | | | | | | | | | | | |
| | | | | | | | | | | | | |
| | | | | | | | | | | | | |
| | | | | | | | | | | | | |
| | | | | | | | | | | | | |
| | | | | | | | | | | | | |
| | | | | | | | | | | | | |
| | | | | | | | | | | | | |

Wiley Fisk Form 12-4

**FIGURE 4.13**  Pile Driving Record.

---

6-29-76

BANK BLDG
6420 WILSHIRE-LA

INSPECTED FULL PEN WELDING
OF COLUMN SPLICES-14TH FLR

| COL G-5 | PREHEAT | OK |
| | N. FLG | OK |
| | S. FLG | OK |
| | WEB | INC. |

| COL H-5 | PREHEAT | OK |
| | N. FLG | OK |

INSPECTED REPAIR OF N. FLG
WELD COL. F-4            OK

---

7-22-76

SO CAL RAPID TRANSIT
AT DELTA STEEL-SANTA FE SPRINGS

U/T FULL PEN SPLICES IN
TAPERED GIRDERS

| T.G #3 | WEB SPLICE | - 3 OK |
| | FLG SPLICE | - 4 OK |
| #6 | WEB " | - 3 OK |
| | FLG " | - 3 OK |
| (MIDDLE BOT FLG) LE | - 1 REJ |
| #2 | WEB SPLICE | - 3 OK |
| | FLG " | - 2 OK |
| (TOP) FIGS L.F. | - 2 REJ |
| #4 | WEB SPLICE | - 3 OK |
| | FLG " | - 4 OK |

**FIGURE 4.14**  Inspector's records of welded joints. (Courtesy of Smith-Emery Company, Los Angeles.)

Normally, tasks 1, 2, and 3 are the responsibility of the on-site project representative (CQC representative or Resident Project Representative), whereas tasks 4, 5, and 6 are normally performed by the agency administering the grant program, or in the case of direct federal contracts, by the federal agency construction office staff.

## JOB CONFERENCES

Often overlooked, but no less important, is the task of recording the proceedings of job conferences. This includes management meetings, safety meetings, coordination and scheduling meetings, and similar functions. The Resident Project Representative should attend all such functions, fully prepared to document for personal information the business transacted at each such meeting. The notes should include the time, date, and location of the meeting, the name and employer of each person in attendance, and the time the meeting ended. During the meeting, careful notes should be taken to have a complete record of the substance of all important statements made at the meeting. Where statements are made by more than one person, the identities of all speakers should be listed.

## CONTRACTOR SUBMITTALS

The normal recommended procedure for the handling of submittals from the contractor is to require that *all* such submittals (e.g., shop drawings, samples, certificates, or other similar items) be submitted directly to the Resident Project Representative by the general contractor (see Figure 3.5). Thus, if a submittal is mailed directly to the design firm or owner, it should be returned unopened, with the request that it be transmitted through the Resident Project Representative's field office. Similarly, if a submittal is made to the Resident Project Representative directly from a subcontractor, it should be returned to the subcontractor unopened, with the request that it be transmitted through the general contractor. Such practices are not created out of a love of red tape but rather, to make use of a proven system that can prevent disputes or even field errors resulting from lack of communication between the parties to the contract (see "Handling of Job-Related Information" in Chapter 3).

Each such submittal, upon receipt by the Resident Project Representative, should be logged in before forwarding to the office of the design firm or owner. All such material should be forwarded to the design firm or owner without action by the Resident Project Representative, unless specifically directed to do so in any particular case. As far as contractor submittals are concerned, the Resident Project Representative simply serves as a central receiving point and recorder for such information. As long as all submittals follow this orderly procedure, there should be no excuse for loss or delay in a transmittal. If all such material is properly logged in and out, claims by the contractor of excessive holding time by the design firm or owner, or claims of submittals that were in fact never made, can be quickly and effectively confirmed at the site.

There is often some confusion during the setting up of a contractor submittal log sheet to decide whether to assign transmittal numbers on the basis of the order *received* or on the order *returned* to the contractor. Most offices seem to find that less confusion results from assigning a transmittal number immediately upon *receipt* of a submittal. In the illustrated submittal log (Figure 4.4), spaces are provided for indicating the action taken on each submittal as well. Although this may seem to be an unnecessary bit of added work, as such information can also be found by searching for a copy of the transmittal itself, the time saved from making searches of the files and wading through the many drawing sheets that may form a part of each such transmittal may soon make it all seem worthwhile. In the submittal log, it is important that the "action taken" wording conform *exactly* to the term used on the submittal being returned to the contractor.

It is generally undesirable to attempt to utilize the contractor's submittal numbers as a "convenience"; often the contractor may submit several dissimilar items all grouped under a single transmittal, with a single reference number. For efficient processing by the engineer/architect, it is desirable to separate each such submittal item and assign each item a separate incoming transmittal number. In this manner, if only a portion of the contractor's submittal is subject to delay, it will not negatively affect the other items that were grouped into the single transmittal. This will avoid the confusion that might result if an attempt was made to describe the various actions taken by the engineer/architect relative to each item submitted when some of the items are ready to return and others must be held for further evaluation.

## CONSTRUCTION PHOTOGRAPHS

More and more reliance is being placed upon the use of photography to document construction progress, damage, technical detail, types of materials, methods of installation, evidence of site conditions before starting work, and similar tasks. Basically, it is the Resident Project Representative who will probably be called upon to do the photography. Thus, an understanding of the types of photographs normally used in construction as well as the purpose of each is beneficial.

1. *Public relations photography.* Subject matter as well as the composition of the picture and the lighting are selected on the basis of artistic composition. The photograph is intended to appeal to the layperson and show what an impressive structure is being built. An example is a view inside a reservoir under construction: The photographer will use an extra-wide-angle lens, accent the perspective, and may even use filters and special lighting to create striking lighting effects. No technical details can normally be noted, but it does produce a beautiful photograph (Figure 4.15). In Figure 4.16, the positioning of the aircraft in front of the hangar was for visual effect. The actual project for which the author was the Construction Manager appears partially behind the aircraft. The total project consisted of the hangar and repair shops, tow-way, fire pump station, underground piping, the mating device, fuel and oxidizer facilities, and an office building. However, this approach is typical of public relations photographs, as all that is necessary is to suggest the project concept, not necessarily to show all of its components or details.

**FIGURE 4.15**   Typical public relations photograph of construction. Greystone Reservoir, City of Beverly Hills, California. Engineers: Montgomery-Watson Consulting Engineers, Pasadena, California. (Photo by J. Allen Hawkins, Pasadena, California.)

2. *Progress photography.* Selection of the subject matter is based upon the need to show as much detail of the construction as possible. Photo composition is secondary, as the primary intent is to disclose the quantity and kind of work that was completed since the last progress photographs were taken. In addition, some photos are intended simply to document kinds of materials used and the method of installation. Thus, the photographer may sacrifice beauty and composition in the photograph to assure legibility of a material label or identifying mark in a finished photograph. It is considered undesirable to strive for striking lighting effects in progress photographs as they all too often obscure details in shadow areas of the picture (Figures 4.17 and 4.18).

3. *Time-lapse photography.* The subject of job progress photography would not be complete without some mention of "time-lapse" or interval photography. Simply stated, it is just a means of using automatic equipment to take photographs at regular intervals from the same point each time. This is normally accomplished with professional equipment, using an electric motor-driven camera connected to an electric interval timer or "intervalometer." Such equipment can be used with either still cameras or movie cameras, and by setting the delay interval between subsequent pictures to anywhere from seconds to days, a unique sequence of

**FIGURE 4.16**   Public relations photograph of the NASA ALT Facilities at the Hugh L. Dryden Flight Research Center, Edwards AFB, California. (Photo courtesy of NASA.)

construction events can be recorded to show the exact nature and amount of construction work completed as of any given day or other interval. When adapted to a movie camera, this technique can also be used to simulate a speeded-up construction operation. Time-lapse photography can also be accomplished manually, using inexpensive equipment, provided that a camera can be fixed on a tripod and allowed to remain in this position during the entire sequence time. The camera can be operated manually, but must be operated faithfully on a predetermined schedule each day (Figure 4.19).

## Identification of Photographs

Although the data required for a public relations photograph may be minimal, the progress photograph must be considered as a reference source or even as potential evidence in case of later claims or disputes. To be of greatest value, certain information should be recorded on the back of each progress photograph taken:

### Identification of Photographic Prints
1. Date photo was taken
2. Identity of the subject
3. Photo or negative number (for reorder)

**FIGURE 4.17**   Typical construction progress photograph.

If it is known that the specific photographs being taken are going to be used in evidence as claims-defense photographs, the list should be continued to indicate the following additional data that should be recorded on each print:

**Claims-Defense Photographs: Additional Data**
4. Time of day, name of photographer
5. Direction in which camera was pointed
6. Where photographer was standing

### Photographs as a Defense against Claims

A camera is an important and often vital tool of all field personnel, whether in the employ of the design firm, the owner, or the contractor. It is often the only means of establishing a condition of fact at any given occasion prior to its being permanently covered. The camera could well be the tool that might save the Resident Project Representative, the design firm,

**FIGURE 4.18**    Aguamilpa Hydroelectric Project, Mexico.

**FIGURE 4.19**    Long-interval-time-lapse progress photograph of the Harry Cochrane Hydroelectric Project for the Montana Power Company.

the owner, or the contractor from charges that might be based upon one person's word against another had it not been for a photographic record.

Some pipeline contractors who regularly construct large underground pipelines beneath city streets in residential and business areas send a photographic crew to the site before the start of any work to photograph all of the curbs, sidewalks, and frontage of every residence and business place along the pipeline route. Every foot of frontage is photographed as a permanent record of the condition that existed prior to the beginning of construction as evidence against frivolous damage claims filed after work is completed. It is remarkable that so many honest people can have cracks in their sidewalks or curbs and never notice them until a contractor starts tearing up the street in front of the house. For some reason, the homeowner is invariably convinced that all such cracks or other damage were caused by the new construction. The Resident Project Representative or the CQC representative of the contractor should be able to find a lesson in this example that will indicate a means of protection for the design firm, the owner, or the contractor from the hazards of frivolous claims.

## PHOTOGRAPHIC EQUIPMENT AND MATERIALS

### Types of Equipment Used

Where field personnel are expected to take the progress photographs, they are generally asked to use a 35mm camera and possibly, a Polaroid camera. Usually, use of a Polaroid camera is limited to photographing field problem areas so that they may immediately be available to discuss with the architect/engineer. Some firms will allow the use of a Polaroid camera for progress photography, but its disadvantages outweigh its advantages. There is no negative possible with color-pack Polaroid. Although Polaroid offers a P/N (positive/negative) film for some models, it is not commonly available for most popular Polaroid cameras; thus, copying of an original photograph must be done by rephotographing the print itself—seldom an ideal process. Also, if the architect/engineer wishes to retain copies of the prints and forward other print copies to the owner, both the versatility of a negative film plus the higher quality of the photographs taken with the 35mm camera will pay off.

### Camera Handling

Although the subject of photographic technique is somewhat beyond the scope of this book, some helpful hints are offered that may assist the construction inspector in resolving some of the problems of recording his or her project progress on film.

Exposure times are important, as an error in estimating the light conditions can lead to the loss of a picture, and in construction you will seldom get a second chance to repeat the scene. Because of this, it is recommended that field personnel either have an automatic exposure camera or at least one with a built-in light meter to assure proper shutter speed and lens aperture. This is especially important in the case of color films, as an error of as little as one shutter speed or one f-stop can sometimes result in an unsuccessful photograph.

## Selection of Still Camera Equipment

The most commonly used cameras for construction are still cameras. Video cameras, while quite useful in construction, are not that widely used, nor are they a valid substitute for the permanent record provided by still-camera photographic prints.

In the choice of still (nonvideo) cameras, do not be misled by cameras with extremely "fast" lenses, because the measure of the quality of a camera, or of a lens for that matter, is not in the speed of the lens but in its quality. Although the added lens speed may allow the taking of pictures under extremely low light conditions, it is not worthwhile if the results are not sharp and clear, or if the sharpness falls off at the edges.

A camera with an f3.5 lens is quite adequate for most field uses and can generally be obtained at a reasonable cost. Also, as the ability of the average person to estimate distances accurately is somewhat less than that person is usually willing to admit, it is essential that the camera selected be either an auto-focus camera or have a range finder that allows the Resident Project Representative or inspector to focus the camera accurately.

If the Resident Project Representative or inspector plans to select a 35mm camera for work progress photography, it may be desirable to obtain one that allows the use of inter-changeable lenses, if the somewhat added cost of this feature is not objectionable. Many of the subjects that an inspector must photograph will involve the inclusion of wide viewing areas, which if a normal 50mm lens is used (standard on 35mm cameras) would require backing up too far, or there may be insufficient space to back up any further. A wide-angle lens of 28mm or 35mm is better for such conditions, as it will allow the inspector to cover adequately the entire project area when necessary.

Occasionally, a close-up detail may be needed of a portion of the work that is inaccessible to the photographer without turning into a human fly and walking up the side of a tall building. A long-focal-length (telephoto) lens can allow the same effect as actually being up close. A 135mm lens is an ideal telephoto for this purpose. If the Resident Project Representative or inspector plans to have only one lens, however, a 35mm focal length lens is ideal. If two lenses are to be used, both the 50mm and the 35mm lens are a good combination, although a 28mm would be a good substitute for the 35mm. An example of the same subject as photographed from the same location, but using three different focal-length lenses, is illustrated in the three photographs of the NASA mating device structure at the Hugh M. Dryden Flight Research Center in California. In this example, the structure was photographed first with a 35mm wide-angle lens, then with a 50mm normal lens, and finally with a 135mm telephoto lens (Figure 4.20).

When selecting a camera for use in construction, do not underestimate the capability of the inexpensive 35mm autoexposure, autofocus cameras currently on the market. Many such cameras have been used to produce excellent progress photos. For a few dollars more, you can get a fully automatic camera with a lens that adjusts to two preselected focal lengths. The usual combination is 35mm to 70mm. One manufacturer, however, offers a 28mm to 48mm lens instead. You will find that a wide-angle lens offers more opportunities for good photographs than a telephoto lens, so the 28mm to 48mm might be a good buy. The 48mm covers the angle of view that reasonably approximates that of the human eye.

A helpful hint: when you are working with any automatic camera, remember that they are battery powered. Therefore, when the batteries lose their power, the photography ses-

**With 35mm lens**

**FIGURE 4.20**    Same subject photographed with three different lenses.

sion is over. Find out what size and type of batteries are needed for your camera and keep several spares in the field office, as they may not be readily available everywhere.

If you are a camera buff and choose to bring your own high-priced, 35mm reflex camera into the field, it is suggested that you budget from $300 to $400 for cleaning by a authorized professional camera repair shop after the project is over. Such cameras are sensitive to dust and moisture and will probably have to be completely disassembled, cleaned, readjusted, and reassembled in order to operate properly in the future.

### Transporting Films through Airport Security

Often, construction people are required to travel by air and frequently bring their cameras and film with them. Thus, they will experience firsthand the intricacies of protecting their unexposed film during a security check of their carry-on baggage. There appears to be a considerable amount of misinformation about the effect of airport x-ray equipment on photographic films. They may tell you that the amount is so slight that it will have no effect on the film. This is patently false. The person who tells you this is usually the security person at the screening location, who is merely repeating what he or she has been told by their superiors. They are not scientists or photographic engineers, and are generally unqualified to make such statements.

**With 50mm lens**

*(c)*

**With 135mm lens**

**FIGURE 4.20** *continued*

Guidelines released by Eastman Kodak Company some years ago state that a cumulative x-ray exposure not exceeding 5 milliroentgens will not affect most films provided that the exposure is made in increments not exceeding 1 milliroentgen, and that the orientation of the film or luggage in which the film is placed is changed between exposures. However, the effect of small amounts of radiation will be greatly influenced by the film speed as well. High-speed films such as any film with a speed of ISO(ASA)400/ISO°(din)27° or especially, ISO(ASA)1000/ISO°(din)31° should always be hand checked and never allowed to pass through x-ray at any radiation level.

Some airport x-ray machines only expose film to a dosage of approximately 0.05 milliroentgen for each inspection. The maximum possible dosage that might occur for each inspection of carry-on baggage with such equipment could possibly be as low as 0.01 milliroentgen. However, do not be misled into thinking that you can protect your film by storing it in the checked baggage. On many flights, all checked baggage is x-rayed routinely, and the dosage used for checked baggage is frequently far higher than that of inspection stations at the airport gates.

An important fact to remember, however, is that the effect of x-ray exposure on film is cumulative, so that the total number of x-rays received by the film during each inspection is added to the x-ray count received by the same film on other inspections. Keep in mind that some x-ray equipment exposes the film to a much larger dosage at each inspection. This is particularly true of international inspection points. Even atmospheric radiation has a cumulative x-ray effect on film, though it is minimal. Of special concern to the discriminating photographer is the fact that while some exposure to x-rays may not cause a visible blemish on the film, it definitely can affect the color balance and thus the final effect on the prints or slides. Only undeveloped film, exposed or not, can be affected by x-ray radiation.

Another recommended precaution is that if you go on more than 10 flights with the same roll of film, you should ask the baggage inspector to hand-inspect your camera case and film. In the United States, on all flights regulated by the FAA, you have a legal right to demand that your cameras and film be hand-checked. Storage of film in lead containers has not produced consistently satisfactory results, so reliance on such precautions should be seriously reconsidered.

### Video Cameras in Construction

A video camera can be an extremely useful tool in construction management. Used properly, it can be used to document field problem areas for showing and discussion at regular job management meetings in the field, it can be used as a training tool for inspectors, it can be used as a marketing tool during proposal presentations, and it can serve to document work progress and delays in anticipation of possible future litigation. This is especially true in cases involving delay claims.

On the down side, however, a video camera is somewhat bulky to carry around, and it is also quite demanding on the available time of the Resident Project Representative, and thus there is often a tendency to pass by video opportunities that might otherwise be a valuable record.

Although the selection of video camera equipment is beyond the scope of this book, it should be kept in mind that most facilities for playback of videotapes are designed to play

VHS videocassettes. Smaller cameras are convenient, but smaller cassettes will require special adapters to play on VHS equipment.

Video cameras are generally capable of fully automatic operation, including exposure control and focusing, and most also have power-operated zoom lenses as standard equipment. Beyond the automatic features, modern video cameras seem to be capable of operations that are well beyond human comprehension except, perhaps, to a computer programmer.

## Selection of Film

The choice of color films is often based on the answer to the question, "Do you want slides or color prints?" Generally, slides cost less initially, because there are no prints to make—all that you get back is the original film that was in the camera. In case of color print film, however, you receive both a color negative (the film that was in the camera) and color prints that were made from those negatives—thus, the added cost. It is wise to choose color negative film over color positive (slide) film for a very practical reason. Exposure errors in color negative film can be corrected in the final prints; however, in the case of slide film, there is no chance for compensating for exposure errors. For construction, color prints are recommended. From the color negatives, slides can still be made if needed; color prints and enlargements can be made, and even black-and-white prints can be made if desired. Thus, it is a truly versatile film. However, if prints are wanted from a slide, the processor must first rephotograph the slide to make a negative, then make prints in the ordinary way. This is a considerably more costly process than if color print film had been used in the first place.

For general usage in construction, the following 35mm color films are recommended. The Ektar films are particularly recommended where sharpness of image is an issue:

| Color Slide Films | | | | | |
|---|---|---|---|---|---|
| Film | Code | ASA/Din | Sharpness | Resolving Power | Grain |
| Kodachrome | KR | 64/19° | Extremely high | high | Extremely fine |
| Kodachrome | KL | 200/25° | Very high | high | Fine |

| Color Print Films | | | | | |
|---|---|---|---|---|---|
| Film | Code | ASA/Din | Sharpness | Degree of Enlargement | Color Saturation |
| Kodak Ektar | CJ | 1000/31° | Medium | Moderately low | High |
| Kodak Ektar | CW | 125/22° | Extremely high | Very high | n.a. |
| Kodacolor Gold | CG | 400/27° | Medium | Moderate | High |
| Vericolor Prof. | VPH | 400/27° | n.a. | n.a. | Medium |
| Kodak Pro-400 | PPF | 400/27° | High | Moderate | High |

## Film and Camera Storage

Security is always a problem on a construction site and, in particular, items such as cameras, pocket calculators, and similar pocket-sized items of considerable value are always in jeopardy. Cameras should be locked up; however, this usually presents a problem. They are sensitive to temperature, particularly when they have film inside. Usually, the only available secure areas at a construction site are locked file cabinets in the field office (a rarity) or the locked trunk of the inspector's automobile. If the field office is cooled in the summer and heated in the winter, the file cabinet is best. The auto trunk is a high-risk area for film and cameras unless special precautions are taken to prevent damage from the high heat concentrations usually present there. One method of protecting the camera and film in an automobile trunk in hot weather is to keep the camera and film in one of the popular Styrofoam beverage containers designed to keep a six-pack cool on a picnic. If film or cameras are subject to such conditions for several hours, serious consideration should be given to the use of one of the popular Styrofoam containers that are provided with special freeze-pack covers. When stored in the refrigerator freezer overnight, these will maintain safe film and camera temperatures all day long, even under the most severe conditions.

In any case, neither film nor cameras should be left in the trunk without taking special precautions. In winter months, there is little substitute for a heated field office, as nothing you can do to your auto trunk is likely to keep the camera and film from freezing when the temperature drops to these ranges.

If a camera is taken out of a heated enclosure into a very cold atmosphere, be sure to let the camera adjust to the cold air for awhile before attempting to take pictures; otherwise, the condensation that may form will cause problems.

Color films require storage in cool, stable temperatures if the color balance is to be maintained. Try to keep them about 18° to 21° C (65° to 70° F) at all times, if possible. Polaroid film can be an even greater problem in the field. It has been the author's experience that Polaroid color film under hot weather conditions requires special care and handling during extremely hot weather and during extremely cold weather. As with hot temperature photography, the ideal arrangement is to keep the camera in a controlled temperature inside the Resident Project Representative's or inspector's automobile or field office until the actual time of exposure.

---

## PROBLEMS

1. True or false? An inspector's diary may be in loose leaf form as long as the pages are numbered.
2. List at least four types of information that should be documented in the Daily Construction Report.
3. Who should keep a construction diary?
4. What is the purpose of preparing a "feedback" report?
5. What types of transactions between the contractor and the owner or engineer/architect should be documented?
6. How long should project records be saved by the owner?

7. Name the four principal applications of photography to construction documentation.

8. What type of information is recommended to be documented in the Daily Construction Report and in the diary?

9. What are the six principal concerns in the format of a construction diary?

10. If the Daily Construction Report is electronically stored in a computer, what must be done to protect the integrity of the document?

# 5

## Specifications and Drawings

### WHAT IS A SPECIFICATION?

The specifications are the part of the contract documents that define the qualitative requirements of the project that is to be built. The dictionary defines *specification* as "a detailed description of requirements, dimensions, materials, etc., as of a proposed building, machine, bridge, etc.," and further as "the act of making specific."

The role of the drawings is to define the geometry of a project, including dimensions, form, and details. The specifications are intended to complement this by defining the nature of the materials that are to be used and the description of the workmanship and procedures to be followed in constructing the project.

All too often an inspector, just like many people in the building trades, expects the drawings to provide all the information required, incorrectly assuming that the specifications are needed by the lawyers only in case of dispute. To be sure, the specifications may be needed in cases of dispute, but if used properly and referred to throughout the construction work, they can also serve to minimize disputes. Even more important to the Resident Project Representative and the contractor is the fact that the specifications are the only documents that will spell out the obligations for administration of the project during its construction. By far the majority of the administrative tasks that the Resident Project Representative will be required to perform are covered by the specific terms of the *General Conditions* of the contract and by nothing else. Even years of past experience cannot serve as a substitute, as the rules of the game change from project to project. What may have been proper on a previous job may be wrong on the next, and only the specifications will tell it as it should be.

## CONFLICTS DUE TO DRAWINGS AND SPECIFICATIONS

It should be brought out here that neglecting the specifications can lead to serious problems. In case something is shown or noted one way on the drawings and described differently in the specifications, which will govern? The answer to that question is easy. The specifications will normally take precedence unless it says *in the specifications* that the plans will govern. Thus, it is still the specifications that set the controlling criteria. Normally, it is easy to determine the relative importance of one document over another, as most specifications specify the relative order of importance of the different parts of the contract documents in the General Conditions of the construction contract. However, it should be of interest that in the absence of such a specific provision, the courts have repeatedly held that the provisions of the specifications will take precedence over the drawings in case of a conflict between the two [*Appeal of Florida Builders, Inc.*, ASBCA No. 9013, 69–2 BCA 8014 (1969)].

Therefore, if the specifications are the most important single document, the inspector can hardly perform in a competent manner without being thoroughly familiar with both the specifications and the construction drawings.

### Conflicts between Drawings and Specifications

In some cases, the same data are covered in both the drawings and the specifications—not a great arrangement, but it happens often enough. The problem here is that frequently one document is changed during design and the other is overlooked. This generally creates the problem just referred to. The unfortunate situation is that usually where such a problem exists, it is the drawings that were updated to receive the latest changes or corrections, and the specifications may in fact be outdated and incorrect. The basic philosophy still controls, however, and the inspector has no authority to force the contractor to provide that which is shown on the drawings when the bid may have been based upon the article contained in the specifications. In case of any such conflict, the contractor is obligated to notify the owner's representative before continuing. However, it is well for the inspector to monitor carefully any such possibilities personally, as the contractor may honestly miss recognizing the presence of a conflict. It would also be possible for a dishonest contractor merely to *claim* to miss the conflict so as to furnish the cheaper of the two items, knowing full well that if the design firm wants it changed after the contractor has already built it in accordance with the specifications, in all likelihood, he or she will be able to claim successfully extra compensation for such additional work.

It should be remembered that some items will appear only in the specifications and not on the drawings; others will appear only on the drawings and not be mentioned in the specifications. This is not necessarily an oversight, nor is it to be considered as a flaw in the specifications or drawings. Many architectural and engineering firms as a matter of policy prefer not to repeat data on both documents. This is done intentionally as a means of preventing conflicts due to late changes that may be made to one document alone and not to the other. The Resident Project Representative should make certain that the trade supervisor doing the work uses the specifications also, as it will minimize construction problems and conflicts.

## Scope-of-Work Disputes

The contract documents for a typical construction project consist of the Agreement itself, the General Conditions, Technical Specifications, and numerous Drawings. Additionally, some provisions are covered by reference to another document. Unfortunately, contract documents often fail to adequately describe, define, or delineate the work to be performed. This generates some of the so-called "scope-of-work" disputes. Such disputes center on the nature and extent of the performance obligation.

The most frequent cause of such disputes is the lack of detail in drawings or lack of specifics in specifications. The problem with drawings is most common on small projects where design costs, and therefore the number of drawings, are held to a minimum. If the drawings lack sufficient detail, the contractor will have to rely on what it understands is expected. This may or may not coincide with the intentions or expectations of the owner or designer.

Specifications problems usually result from lack of attention during the specification process. The widespread use of "canned" or "off-the-shelf" specifications and manufacturer's specifications is another large contributor to the number of disputes occurring. Errors of omission or ambiguity are frequent, and unfortunately for the owner, are generally interpreted in favor of the contractor.

Problems also occur when specifiers resort to broad, subjective generalities (e.g., "in accordance with highest industry standards") rather than describing the work objectively and in detail.

## Avoiding Scope-of-Work Problems

The best but most difficult way to avoid scope-of-work problems is outlined in the following guidelines:

1. Provide adequate budget for drafting specifications.
2. Work with a set of carefully prepared, carefully coordinated front-end documents.
3. Place control of each set of project specifications in the hands of a single, qualified specifications engineer, or require that all specifications be subject to his or her review and editorial control.
4. Do *not* mark up previous job specifications to create another set of job specifications; always work from the same set of master specification documents for every job.
5. Update the master specification at least annually to keep current with industry standards, codes, and laws affecting construction.
6. Use the same set of front-end documents on all projects to minimize contract administration problems and to ensure that there has been no contractual variation in the owner's risk posture.
7. Front-end documents should not be edited by project engineers. All changes to front-end documents should be subject to review of both legal and construction management personnel with specific experience in construction contracts management.

While the foregoing will go a long way toward improving the specifications product, it is important that every office either establish a specifications department or at the very least designate a Specifications Engineer to control specification standards and policies.

### The Use of Generalities in Specifications

It is in the owner's best interests to keep designers from indulging in generalities in specifications. It may be tempting for designers to use vague, catch-all language or to graft general performance standards onto what are otherwise proprietary specifications.

It is equally important to avoid the use of vague and unenforceable subjective terms in specifications. When preparing specifications for some federal projects, the author was furnished with a list of phrases typically found in specifications, which we reproduce in the list in the next section. The agencies' instructions were that such terms would not be permitted on their specifications. Needless to say, there are more specifications that contain such phrases than there are examples that avoid them.

The specifications are one of the most important tools of the inspector or Resident Project Representative. Often, professional engineers have taken the position that the sole mission of their Resident Project Representative and inspectors is to provide a project constructed in strict accordance with the plans and specifications. Upon issuing this profound proclamation, they lean back and assume that all should go well if their inspector or Resident Project Representative simply follows the plans and specifications.

Perhaps in many cases, he or she can do just that. However, as is often the case, the problem began in the office. All too often, specifications are not properly prepared, nor are they often prepared by engineers or architects who specialize in such work so problems are just built-in from the outset.

## UNENFORCEABLE PHRASES

There are many pitfalls that can be encountered in the preparation of specifications, and the following represents a simple list of words and phrases often encountered which have no enforceable meaning and should not be allowed to be used in specifications. A few are actually unbiddable. There are two or three others that can be used in proper context but must be used only with great care. The list was originally compiled by a federal agency and may include some phrases only used by them. If a Resident Project Representative or inspector encounters this type of specification language, it is suggested that diplomacy and compromise are in order, as they are virtually impossible to administer in an objective, literal sense:

1. To the satisfaction of the engineer
2. As determined by the engineer
3. In accordance with the instructions of the engineer
4. As directed by the engineer
5. In the judgment of the engineer
6. In the opinion of the engineer

7. Unless otherwise directed by the engineer (unbiddable)
8. To be furnished if requested by the engineer (unbiddable)
9. In strict accordance with
10. In accordance with the best commercial practice
11. In accordance with the best modern standard practice
12. In accordance with the best engineering practice
13. Workmanship shall be of the highest quality
14. Workmanship shall be of the highest grade
15. Accurate workmanship
16. Securely mounted
17. Installed in a neat and workmanlike manner
18. Skillfully fitted
19. Properly connected
20. Properly assembled
21. Good working order
22. Good materials
23. In accordance with applicable published specifications
24. Products of a recognized reputable manufacturer
25. Test will be made unless waived (unbiddable)
26. Materials shall be of the highest grade, free from defects or imperfections, and shall be of grades approved by the engineer
27. Links and bends may be cause for rejection
28. Carefully performed
29. Neatly finished
30. Metal parts shall be cleaned before painting
31. Suitably housed
32. Smooth surfaces
33. Pleasing lines
34. Of an approved type
35. Of a standard type
36. When required by the engineer (unbiddable)
37. As the engineer may require (unbiddable)
38. In accordance with the standards of the industry

If phrases such as those in the foregoing list are encountered in a specification draft, a careful study should be made of methods of rewording the document to avoid the probability of disputes with the contractor over the interpretation of what the terms mean. Remember, too, that the basic rule of contracts is that in case of ambiguity, the intent of the contract will generally be interpreted in favor of the party who did not draft the contract— which, in short, means that the contractor's interpretation will carry greater weight than that of the owner or the architect/engineer. It is wise to avoid the habit of using such terms. Although some of the foregoing phrases can occasionally be justified, their use is usually a sign of a specifications engineer who either does not understand what he or she is calling for, is working under severe budget constraints, or is too lazy to research the issues properly and establish more specific, unambiguous requirements.

## CONTENT AND COMPONENT PARTS OF A SPECIFICATION

### Content of the Specifications

In addition to the well-known *technical* provisions contained in the specifications, it should be clear that the term *specifications* is not necessarily limited to the technical portions alone. In many organizations, everything that is bound into the specifications document is referred to as the "specifications." This may include the notice of invitation to bid on the project; the bidding documents and forms, including the bid bond where required; contract (agreement) forms, including performance and payment bonds where required and noncollusion affidavits where required; the conditions of the contract, often referred to simply as the "boilerplate" because it provides a protective shield around the contract by anticipating most of the areas of discussion or dispute that might arise and provides for an orderly way of resolving each such case; and finally, the technical provisions. If the term *contract documents* is used, it legitimately includes everything, including the drawings, and sometimes includes a book of "standard specifications" by reference, as well. Usually, some of the boilerplate documents will specify a list of all items that are to be officially classed as a part of the contract documents.

Another often misunderstood characteristic of a set of specifications is that the size of a specification is in no way related directly to either the size or cost of a project, but is actually more influenced by how many different trades or materials are involved in the work. Thus a public restroom building in a park with only one room and a single set of plumbing fixtures may require as thick a set of specifications as a two-story building. On the other hand, a highway construction job costing ten times the price of either of the two buildings described may involve a specification of only three or four sections and possibly as few as eight or ten pages of technical provisions.

Most contractors, inspectors, or other construction administrators have, at some time or another, questioned the wisdom of the specifications writer. If it will give the inspector any peace of mind, the author readily believes that all specifications writers are not necessarily knowledgeable in some of the subjects about which they write (sometimes an understatement). In a recent ASCE (American Society of Civil Engineers) questionnaire circulated on a national basis by its National Task Committee on Specifications to engineers, contractors, public agencies, owner-developers, suppliers, and attorneys, the general response from the contractors was that a specifications writer should have field construction experience before becoming a specifications writer. Every construction worker has undoubtedly run into specifications at some time where it seemed obvious that the specifications writer did not possess this background. Part of the problem lies in the procedures often used by architects and engineers in selecting personnel for, and budgeting time and costs for, the production of specifications. All the standardized specification formats in the world cannot cure the problem of a skimpy budget. If each of the items specified is properly covered, the Resident Project Representative or CQC representative will have the tools for and sufficient authority to assure the owner of quality in construction. The inspector is deprived of a primary tool if these important considerations are neglected.

## Component Parts of a Specification

Generally, most specifications can be divided into three main elements, or parts. Although these parts are not necessarily arranged on each job in the same order in which the resident engineer or inspector will encounter them, the various design firms or public agencies responsible will generally keep the content of the specifications within the classifications shown in Figure 5.1

In addition to the classifications indicated in Figure 5.1, all publicly funded projects require a listing of minimum wage rates. These are normally listed in the specifications.

If a public project has federal funding as well as being subject to state labor code requirements, then, in addition to the requirements for state wage rates, a complete copy of

```
PART I—BIDDING AND CONTRACTUAL DOCUMENTS

Notice Inviting Bids                                        (mostly public works)
Instruction to Bidders
Proposal (or Bid) Forms
    Proposal
    Bid Sheets
    Contractor Certificates                                (mostly public works)
    List of Subcontractors                                 (Calif. public works)
    Bid Bond Form                                          (mostly public works)
    Non-Collusion Affidavits                               (mostly public works)
Agreement and Bonds
    Agreement (contract)
    Performance Bond Form                                  (mostly public works)
    Payment Bond Form (labor & materials)                  (mostly public works)
PART II—CONDITIONS OF THE CONTRACT

        General Conditions (the "boilerplate")
        Supplementary General Conditions (special for the project)
        (In some specifications the supplementary general conditions are referred to as "Special
        Conditions")
PART III—DETAIL (TECHNICAL) SPECIFICATIONS

        (From this point on, the architect/engineer provides technical sections covering the various
        parts of the project.)
```

**FIGURE 5.1**   Three-part specifications format.

the applicable federal wage rates must also be bound into the specifications, and the contractor is obligated to pay the higher of the two rates if there is a difference. The federal wage rates are normally reproduced directly from the *Federal Register,* which lists wage rates all over the nation. Every Friday, new listings appear in the *Federal Register* of all wage rate schedules or changes. Any specifications containing federal wage rates should also have the sheets containing the current modifications to the general wage rate determination.

The Instructions to Bidders is usually a preprinted document and on public works projects is normally considered as one of the contract documents. Thus, the provisions of the Instructions to Bidders are as binding upon the bidder and the contractor as are the provisions of the technical specifications. Failure to comply with its terms can render a contractor's bid as "informal," or "nonresponsive," which may be used as justification for rejecting it. The general subject area usually covered by an Instructions to Bidders document includes the following.

Form of bid and signature

Interpretation of drawings and specifications

Preparation of the proposal

List of documents to be submitted with the bid

Bonding requirements

What is expected of the successful bidder

Insurance policies required

Basis for selection of the successful bidder

The General Conditions, or "boilerplate" as it is often called, is the most overlooked, yet one of the most important documents in the specifications to the resident inspector. It is this document that establishes the ground rules for administration of the construction phase of the project. The subject matter generally covered in General Conditions is fairly consistent from job to job wherever "standard" preprinted documents of a governmental agency or AIA, EJCDC, FIDIC, or similar organizations are used. Whenever an architect or engineer or a public agency elects to prepare its own General Conditions, the resulting document frequently lacks many of the essentials and, worse yet, has never been "proved" in court. The general subjects covered in most so-called "standard" General Conditions documents include:

Legal definitions of terms used in the contract

Correlation and intent of the documents

Time and order of the work

Assignment of contracts

Subcontracts

Where to serve legal notices

Authority of the architect/engineer

Change orders and extra work

Extensions of time for delays

Right of the owner to terminate the contract

Right of the contractor to terminate the contract

Right of the owner to take over work

Obligations of the contractor

Supervision by the contractor

Handling of claims and protests

Lines, grades, and surveys; who performs and who pays

Defective work or materials

Materials and workmanship

Provisions to allow access to all parts of the work

Inspection and tests; how administered and who pays

Coordination with other contractors at the site or nearby

Suspension of all or part of the work

Liquidated damages for delay

Stop notice procedures

Right of owner to withhold payment

Provisions for public safety

Changed conditions (sometimes called "unforeseen conditions")

Estimates and progress payments

Final payment and termination of liability

Protection and insurance

Disputes; settlement by arbitration

Part III of the specifications, as outlined in Figure 5.1, refers to that portion of the specifications that a layperson usually thinks of when one speaks of specifications. In this portion of the document are the detailed technical provisions that relate to the installation or construction of the various parts of the work and to the materials used in the work. There are several ways of logically dividing these sections into subject areas so as to lend some sort of order to the final document. Most of the systems, however, generally group specifications sections into trade-related functions as a means of easy grouping. This sometimes prompts the complaint from contractors that the sections do not accurately represent the responsibility areas of the various trades. Actually, there is usually no attempt made to conform exactly to trade jurisdictions, as they vary significantly from one part of the nation to the other; in fact, in some cases, jurisdictional differences may be evident from one adjacent country to the other within the same state.

It should be recognized that on any project there are usually a few technical requirements that would apply to *all* sections equally. In such cases, it has been found desirable to provide a section of the technical specifications, usually at the front of the technical portion, that may be entitled "General Requirements" and that spells out the various requirements of a *technical* nature that apply generally to the entire project. This section should not be confused with any of the text of Part II—Conditions of the Contract; there the General Conditions and Supplementary General Conditions are matters of a legal/contractual nature—*not technical provisions*. A common error made by general contractors in their dealings with subcontractors is to hand them a single technical specifications section relating to their trade, without copies of either the General Requirements or the General and Supplementary General Conditions of the Contract. This has often created serious problems in the conduct of the work, as all of the boilerplate sections apply to all of the work of each subcontractor as well.

## WHAT DO THE SPECIFICATIONS MEAN TO THE INSPECTOR?

The specifications, in short, are one of the inspector's vital tools. Without them, an inspector cannot possibly perform in a competent manner. To be able to use these tools effectively, however, the inspector should have an idea of the relative importance of each of the various component parts of the contract documents. The following is a condensed list of some of the contract document components and their relative importance. For a more complete list, refer to Chapter 17.

> Agreement governs over specifications.
> Specifications govern over drawings.
> Detail specifications govern over general specifications.

Each month, on larger projects, the contractor normally applies for and receives monthly partial payments (progress payments) for work completed thus far. The amount of each payment must be in direct proportion to the amount of work completed during the preceding month. It is the responsibility of the Resident Project Representative to check the quantities of such work completed, estimate its value, and review the monthly payment request of the contractor prior to submitting it to the design firm's project manager or sometimes the owner, along with a recommendation for payment, if justified. In the handling of such matters, the terms of the General Conditions must be strictly followed, as the procedures for handling such payment claims must follow an orderly, prearranged plan. There are no provisions for allowing terms or creating restrictions that were not written into the original contract.

In short, the entire policy for the administration and conduct of the work at the job site is established under the terms and conditions of the General and Supplementary General Conditions of the construction contract. The remaining portions of the specifications more properly relate to quality control or quality assurance functions, which are a subsidiary function of the Resident Project Representative.

## CSI SPECIFICATIONS FORMAT—ITS MEANING AND IMPORTANCE

Briefly mentioned in earlier paragraphs was the fact that the technical portions of the specifications were generally structured in whatever manner suited the architect or engineer who prepared them. In the past years, this problem was even worse, and a contractor would indeed have to be versatile to be required to work from one type of contract documents on one job and at the same time be constructing another similar project nearby, from another set of documents that bore no resemblance to the first.

In recent years, an organization called the Construction Specifications Institute (CSI) tackled the task of attempting to inject some degree of uniformity and standardization into the general arrangement and method of writing construction specifications. To this end they have been enormously successful, although it can be seen that the format or arrangement and classification system they have devised was created by architects and engineers whose experience was limited to the construction of *buildings,* and the resulting format shows very little influence of engineers engaged in heavy engineering and similar types of construction. The CSI Format was indeed intended for buildings, but once entrenched, no one seemed to be able to change or even alter the system when it became desirable to extend it to other types of engineered construction as well. Thus, when the system is used for certain types of heavy engineering projects, some serious formatting conflicts present themselves. In any case, the system *did* create order where none existed before by setting forth a list of 16 standardized "divisions," which were supposed to work for everything, and with a little imagination it could indeed be adapted to many, though not all, nonbuilding construction projects, even though it may be somewhat cumbersome and awkward in certain types of work.

## CSI 16-Division Format

The CSI 16-Division Format was adopted by the AGC (Associated General Contractors), the AIA (American Institute of Architects), the NSPE (National Society of Professional Engineers), and others in the United States and Canada in the form of a document entitled *Uniform System for Building Specifications.* Note that word *building* again—no mention of heavy engineering projects. Nevertheless, it is widely used both for building and some engineering work, and is popularly known as the CSI Format. This system has been officially adopted for *all* construction work by the U.S. Army, Corps of Engineers; the U.S. Navy (NAVFAC); National Aeronautics and Space Administration (NASA); the state of New York for public works projects; and by numerous other public and private agencies; however, it has not been adopted nor endorsed by the ASCE (American Society of Civil Engineers) for heavy construction projects. In fact, that organization considered working on an alternative format that will be better suited to heavy construction.

Eventually, all the manufacturers followed suit, and now most, if not all, building materials are identified with the CSI classification number for filing purposes, which corresponds to the CSI division number under which each such product is intended to be grouped. Thus, most of the time, if you pick up a specification it will be under CSI Format, and even without a table of contents, you should be able to find the section you are searching for. As an example, you should automatically turn to Division 3 if you are looking for concrete, or Division 16 if you are looking for electrical work (Figure 5.2). Note that under the CSI 16-Division Format, whenever a job does not use a certain division, it is simply skipped, but the numbers of the remaining divisions never change.

From a civil or mechanical engineer's standpoint, there are still some problems to be solved in devising a uniformly adaptable specification "division" list. Whenever this fact is

 1. General Requirements
 2. Site Work and Utilities (includes all civil work)
 3. Concrete
 4. Masonry
 5. Metals
 6. Wood and Plastics
 7. Thermal and Moisture Protection
 8. Doors and Windows
 9. Finishes
10. Specialities
11. Equipment
12. Furnishings
13. Special Construction
14. Conveying Systems
15. Mechanical
16. Electrical

> Note that whenever a job does not use a certain Division, it is simply skipped . . . but the numbers of the remaining Divisions still never change.

**FIGURE 5.2**    List of CSI 16 divisions.

recognized and the matter studied objectively from the standpoint of those professionals who construct buildings as well as heavy engineering works or systems, the industry may yet see an ideal system. Nevertheless, the CSI Format is here to stay, and all inspectors should learn to use it. Memorize all 16-Division titles, as they never change, even from one job to the next.

## CSI Division/Section Concept

Whenever the term *division/section concept* is heard with regard to the CSI Format, it is an expression of the relationship of the fixed-title divisions to the subclassifications under each division called "sections." Although division titles *never* change from job to job (although some divisions may be omitted from a project if they are not applicable) the titles of the sections that are grouped under them are adapted to the specific needs of each individual project. In Figure 5.3 all 16 fixed-division titles may be used under each appropriate division. In addition to the short list illustrated, the CSI also publishes a document that provides a ready index of section titles to fit the CSI 16-Division Format.

## CSI Three-Part Section Format

One of the most valuable contributions of the CSI to the work of the contractor and the inspector is the adoption of the three-part *section format* (Figure 5.4). It is a time-honored concept first observed by the author on the published specifications standards for a Federal Aid Road Act project dated in 1917. Under this arrangement each *section* is divided into three parts, each containing one type of information only. With this system, fewer items are

## BIDDING REQUIREMENTS, CONTRACT FORMS, AND CONDITIONS OF THE CONTRACT

| | |
|---|---|
| 00010 | PRE-BID INFORMATION |
| 00100 | INSTRUCTIONS TO BIDDERS |
| 00200 | INFORMATION AVAILABLE TO BIDDERS |
| 00300 | BID FORMS |
| 00400 | SUPPLEMENTS TO BID FORMS |
| 00500 | AGREEMENT FORMS |
| 00600 | BONDS AND CERTIFICATES |
| 00700 | GENERAL CONDITIONS |
| 00800 | SUPPLEMENTARY CONDITIONS |
| 00850 | DRAWINGS AND SCHEDULES |
| 00900 | ADDENDA AND MODIFICATIONS |

**Note:** Since the items listed above are not specification sections, they are referred to as "Documents" in lieu of "Sections" in the Master List of Section Titles, Numbers, and Broadscope Explanations.

## SPECIFICATIONS

### DIVISION 1—GENERAL REQUIREMENTS

| | |
|---|---|
| 01010 | SUMMARY OF WORK |
| 01020 | ALLOWANCES |
| 01025 | MEASUREMENT AND PAYMENT |
| 01030 | ALTERNATES/ALTERNATIVES |
| 01040 | COORDINATION |
| 01050 | FIELD ENGINEERING |
| 01060 | REGULATORY REQUIREMENTS |
| 01070 | ABBREVIATIONS AND SYMBOLS |
| 01080 | IDENTIFICATION SYSTEMS |
| 01090 | REFERENCE STANDARDS |
| 01100 | SPECIAL PROJECT PROCEDURES |
| 01200 | PROJECT MEETINGS |
| 01300 | SUBMITTALS |
| 01400 | QUALITY CONTROL |
| 01500 | CONSTRUCTION FACILITIES AND TEMPORARY CONTROLS |
| 01600 | MATERIAL AND EQUIPMENT |
| 01650 | STARTING OF SYSTEMS/COMMISSIONING |
| 01700 | CONTRACT CLOSEOUT |
| 01800 | MAINTENANCE |

### DIVISION 2—SITEWORK

| | |
|---|---|
| 02010 | SUBSURFACE INVESTIGATION |
| 02050 | DEMOLITION |
| 02100 | SITE PREPARATION |
| 02140 | DEWATERING |
| 02150 | SHORING AND UNDERPINNING |
| 02160 | EXCAVATION SUPPORT SYSTEMS |
| 02170 | COFFERDAMS |
| 02200 | EARTHWORK |
| 02300 | TUNNELING |
| 02350 | PILES AND CAISSONS |
| 02450 | RAILROAD WORK |
| 02480 | MARINE WORK |
| 02500 | PAVING AND SURFACING |
| 02600 | PIPED UTILITY MATERIALS |
| 02660 | WATER DISTRIBUTION |
| 02680 | FUEL DISTRIBUTION |
| 02700 | SEWERAGE AND DRAINAGE |
| 02760 | RESTORATION OF UNDERGROUND PIPELINES |
| 02770 | PONDS AND RESERVOIRS |
| 02780 | POWER AND COMMUNICATIONS |
| 02800 | SITE IMPROVEMENTS |
| 02900 | LANDSCAPING |

### DIVISION 3—CONCRETE

| | |
|---|---|
| 03100 | CONCRETE FORMWORK |
| 03200 | CONCRETE REINFORCEMENT |
| 03250 | CONCRETE ACCESSORIES |
| 03300 | CAST-IN-PLACE CONCRETE |
| 03370 | CONCRETE CURING |
| 03400 | PRECAST CONCRETE |
| 03500 | CEMENTITIOUS DECKS |
| 03600 | GROUT |
| 03700 | CONCRETE RESTORATION AND CLEANING |
| 03800 | MASS CONCRETE |

### DIVISION 4—MASONRY

| | |
|---|---|
| 04100 | MORTAR |
| 04150 | MASONRY ACCESSORIES |
| 04200 | UNIT MASONRY |
| 04400 | STONE |
| 04500 | MASONRY RESTORATION AND CLEANING |
| 04550 | REFRACTORIES |
| 04600 | CORROSION RESISTANT MASONRY |

### DIVISION 5—METALS

| | |
|---|---|
| 05010 | METAL MATERIALS |
| 05030 | METAL FINISHES |
| 05050 | METAL FASTENING |
| 05100 | STRUCTURAL METAL FRAMING |
| 05200 | METAL JOISTS |
| 05300 | METAL DECKING |
| 05400 | COLD-FORMED METAL FRAMING |
| 05500 | METAL FABRICATIONS |
| 05580 | SHEET METAL FABRICATIONS |
| 05700 | ORNAMENTAL METAL |
| 05800 | EXPANSION CONTROL |
| 05900 | HYDRAULIC STRUCTURES |

### DIVISION 6—WOOD AND PLASTICS

| | |
|---|---|
| 06050 | FASTENERS AND ADHESIVES |
| 06100 | ROUGH CARPENTRY |
| 06130 | HEAVY TIMBER CONSTRUCTION |
| 06150 | WOOD-METAL SYSTEMS |
| 06170 | PREFABRICATED STRUCTURAL WOOD |
| 06200 | FINISH CARPENTRY |
| 06300 | WOOD TREATMENT |
| 06400 | ARCHITECTURAL WOODWORK |
| 06500 | PREFABRICATED STRUCTURAL PLASTICS |
| 06600 | PLASTIC FABRICATIONS |

### DIVISION 7—THERMAL AND MOISTURE PROTECTION

| | |
|---|---|
| 07100 | WATERPROOFING |
| 07150 | DAMPPROOFING |
| 07190 | VAPOR AND AIR RETARDERS |
| 07200 | INSULATION |
| 07250 | FIREPROOFING |
| 07300 | SHINGLES AND ROOFING TILES |
| 07400 | PREFORMED ROOFING AND CLADDING/SIDING |
| 07500 | MEMBRANE ROOFING |
| 07570 | TRAFFIC TOPPING |
| 07600 | FLASHING AND SHEET METAL |
| 07700 | ROOF SPECIALTIES AND ACCESSORIES |
| 07800 | SKYLIGHTS |
| 07900 | JOINT SEALERS |

### DIVISION 8—DOORS AND WINDOWS

| | |
|---|---|
| 08100 | METAL DOORS AND FRAMES |
| 08200 | WOOD AND PLASTIC DOORS |
| 08250 | DOOR OPENING ASSEMBLIES |
| 08300 | SPECIAL DOORS |
| 08400 | ENTRANCES AND STOREFRONTS |
| 08500 | METAL WINDOWS |
| 08600 | WOOD AND PLASTIC WINDOWS |
| 08650 | SPECIAL WINDOWS |
| 08700 | HARDWARE |
| 08800 | GLAZING |
| 08900 | GLAZED CURTAIN WALLS |

### DIVISION 9—FINISHES

| | |
|---|---|
| 09100 | METAL SUPPORT SYSTEMS |
| 09200 | LATH AND PLASTER |
| 09230 | AGGREGATE COATINGS |
| 09250 | GYPSUM BOARD |
| 09300 | TILE |
| 09400 | TERRAZZO |
| 09500 | ACOUSTICAL TREATMENT |
| 09540 | SPECIAL SURFACES |
| 09550 | WOOD FLOORING |
| 09600 | STONE FLOORING |
| 09630 | UNIT MASONRY FLOORING |
| 09650 | RESILIENT FLOORING |
| 09680 | CARPET |
| 09700 | SPECIAL FLOORING |
| 09780 | FLOOR TREATMENT |
| 09800 | SPECIAL COATINGS |
| 09900 | PAINTING |
| 09950 | WALL COVERINGS |

**FIGURE 5.3**  CSI MASTERFORMAT master list of section titles and numbers. (Reproduced with the permission of the Construction Specifications Institute.)

## DIVISION 10—SPECIALTIES

| | |
|---|---|
| 10100 | CHALKBOARDS AND TACKBOARDS |
| 10150 | COMPARTMENTS AND CUBICLES |
| 10200 | LOUVERS AND VENTS |
| 10240 | GRILLES AND SCREENS |
| 10250 | SERVICE WALL SYSTEMS |
| 10260 | WALL AND CORNER GUARDS |
| 10270 | ACCESS FLOORING |
| 10280 | SPECIALTY MODULES |
| 10290 | PEST CONTROL |
| 10300 | FIREPLACES AND STOVES |
| 10340 | PREFABRICATED EXTERIOR SPECIALTIES |
| 10350 | FLAGPOLES |
| 10400 | IDENTIFYING DEVICES |
| 10450 | PEDESTRIAN CONTROL DEVICES |
| 10500 | LOCKERS |
| 10520 | FIRE PROTECTION SPECIALTIES |
| 10530 | PROTECTIVE COVERS |
| 10550 | POSTAL SPECIALTIES |
| 10600 | PARTITIONS |
| 10650 | OPERABLE PARTITIONS |
| 10670 | STORAGE SHELVING |
| 10700 | EXTERIOR SUN CONTROL DEVICES |
| 10750 | TELEPHONE SPECIALTIES |
| 10800 | TOILET AND BATH ACCESSORIES |
| 10880 | SCALES |
| 10900 | WARDROBE AND CLOSET SPECIALTIES |

## DIVISION 11—EQUIPMENT

| | |
|---|---|
| 11010 | MAINTENANCE EQUIPMENT |
| 11020 | SECURITY AND VAULT EQUIPMENT |
| 11030 | TELLER AND SERVICE EQUIPMENT |
| 11040 | ECCLESIASTICAL EQUIPMENT |
| 11050 | LIBRARY EQUIPMENT |
| 11060 | THEATER AND STAGE EQUIPMENT |
| 11070 | INSTRUMENTAL EQUIPMENT |
| 11080 | REGISTRATION EQUIPMENT |
| 11090 | CHECKROOM EQUIPMENT |
| 11100 | MERCANTILE EQUIPMENT |
| 11110 | COMMERCIAL LAUNDRY AND DRY CLEANING EQUIPMENT |
| 11120 | VENDING EQUIPMENT |
| 11130 | AUDIO-VISUAL EQUIPMENT |
| 11140 | SERVICE STATION EQUIPMENT |
| 11150 | PARKING CONTROL EQUIPMENT |
| 11160 | LOADING DOCK EQUIPMENT |
| 11170 | SOLID WASTE HANDLING EQUIPMENT |
| 11190 | DETENTION EQUIPMENT |
| 11200 | WATER SUPPLY AND TREATMENT EQUIPMENT |
| 11280 | HYDRAULIC GATES AND VALVES |
| 11300 | FLUID WASTE TREATMENT AND DISPOSAL EQUIPMENT |
| 11400 | FOOD SERVICE EQUIPMENT |
| 11450 | RESIDENTIAL EQUIPMENT |
| 11460 | UNIT KITCHENS |
| 11470 | DARKROOM EQUIPMENT |
| 11480 | ATHLETIC, RECREATIONAL AND THERAPEUTIC EQUIPMENT |
| 11500 | INDUSTRIAL AND PROCESS EQUIPMENT |
| 11600 | LABORATORY EQUIPMENT |
| 11650 | PLANETARIUM EQUIPMENT |
| 11660 | OBSERVATORY EQUIPMENT |
| 11700 | MEDICAL EQUIPMENT |
| 11780 | MORTUARY EQUIPMENT |
| 11850 | NAVIGATION EQUIPMENT |

## DIVISION 12—FURNISHINGS

| | |
|---|---|
| 12050 | FABRICS |
| 12100 | ARTWORK |
| 12300 | MANUFACTURED CASEWORK |
| 12500 | WINDOW TREATMENT |
| 12600 | FURNITURE AND ACCESSORIES |
| 12670 | RUGS AND MATS |
| 12700 | MULTIPLE SEATING |
| 12800 | INTERIOR PLANTS AND PLANTERS |

## DIVISION 13—SPECIAL CONSTRUCTION

| | |
|---|---|
| 13010 | AIR SUPPORTED STRUCTURES |
| 13020 | INTEGRATED ASSEMBLIES |
| 13030 | SPECIAL PURPOSE ROOMS |
| 13080 | SOUND, VIBRATION, AND SEISMIC CONTROL |
| 13090 | RADIATION PROTECTION |
| 13100 | NUCLEAR REACTORS |
| 13120 | PRE-ENGINEERED STRUCTURES |
| 13150 | POOLS |
| 13160 | ICE RINKS |
| 13170 | KENNELS AND ANIMAL SHELTERS |
| 13180 | SITE CONSTRUCTED INCINERATORS |
| 13200 | LIQUID AND GAS STORAGE TANKS |
| 13220 | FILTER UNDERDRAINS AND MEDIA |
| 13230 | DIGESTION TANK COVERS AND APPURTENANCES |
| 13240 | OXYGENATION SYSTEMS |
| 13260 | SLUDGE CONDITIONING SYSTEMS |
| 13300 | UTILITY CONTROL SYSTEMS |
| 13400 | INDUSTRIAL AND PROCESS CONTROL SYSTEMS |
| 13500 | RECORDING INSTRUMENTATION |
| 13550 | TRANSPORTATION CONTROL INSTRUMENTATION |
| 13600 | SOLAR ENERGY SYSTEMS |
| 13700 | WIND ENERGY SYSTEMS |
| 13800 | BUILDING AUTOMATION SYSTEMS |
| 13900 | FIRE SUPPRESSION AND SUPERVISORY SYSTEMS |

## DIVISION 14—CONVEYING SYSTEMS

| | |
|---|---|
| 14100 | DUMBWAITERS |
| 14200 | ELEVATORS |
| 14300 | MOVING STAIRS AND WALKS |
| 14400 | LIFTS |
| 14500 | MATERIAL HANDLING SYSTEMS |
| 14600 | HOISTS AND CRANES |
| 14700 | TURNTABLES |
| 14800 | SCAFFOLDING |
| 14900 | TRANSPORTATION SYSTEMS |

## DIVISION 15—MECHANICAL

| | |
|---|---|
| 15050 | BASIC MECHANICAL MATERIALS AND METHODS |
| 15250 | MECHANICAL INSULATION |
| 15300 | FIRE PROTECTION |
| 15400 | PLUMBING |
| 15500 | HEATING, VENTILATING, AND AIR CONDITIONING (HVAC) |
| 15550 | HEAT GENERATION |
| 15650 | REFRIGERATION |
| 15750 | HEAT TRANSFER |
| 15850 | AIR HANDLING |
| 15880 | AIR DISTRIBUTION |
| 15950 | CONTROLS |
| 15990 | TESTING, ADJUSTING, AND BALANCING |

## DIVISION 16—ELECTRICAL

| | |
|---|---|
| 16050 | BASIC ELECTRICAL MATERIALS AND METHODS |
| 16200 | POWER GENERATION |
| 16300 | HIGH VOLTAGE DISTRIBUTION (Above 600-Volt) |
| 16400 | SERVICE AND DISTRIBUTION (600-Volt and Below) |
| 16500 | LIGHTING |
| 16600 | SPECIAL SYSTEMS |
| 16700 | COMMUNICATIONS |
| 16850 | ELECTRIC RESISTANCE HEATING |
| 16900 | CONTROLS |
| 16950 | TESTING |

**FIGURE 5.3**  *continued*

PART I—GENERAL

Scope; Related Work; Submittals; Inspection
Requirements; Testing; Certificates; etc.
PART II—PRODUCTS

Technical specifications for all materials, equipment, fabricated items, etc.; In *no case* is it proper
to show any installation requirements in this part, or specify quality of workmanship in this part.
PART III—EXECUTION

Qualitative standards relating to workmanship, etc.; covers installation, erection, construction, etc.;
In *no case* is it proper to cover any product, materials, equipment, or fabricated item requirements
in this part.

**FIGURE 5.4**   Three-part section format.

overlooked simply because the specifications for a particular product were sandwiched between some unlikely paragraphs dealing with the installation of some totally unrelated item—which just happened to be located there because some architect or engineer happened to think of it while writing that portion of the section.

In the three-part section format, all technical sections of the specification are divided into three distinct parts, always in the same order: (1) general, (2) products, and (3) execution. If followed faithfully, as most users of the system will do, it makes the reading of the specifications a simple, orderly process and eliminates many an error due to oversight.

## ASCE CIVIL ENGINEERING SPECIFICATIONS FORMAT

In 1994 the American Society of Civil Engineers formed a new Committee on Civil Engineering Specifications Format Standards under its Special Standards Division. The new committee concluded at its first meeting that although the commercial sector is well served by the CSI and the highway/bridge sector is well served by state DOTs and the FHWA, civil engineering and heavy construction projects are not well served by existing formats. The objective of the new committee is to develop a new specifications division-level structure to replace the CSI Masterformat and DOT formats on civil engineering and heavy construction projects such as airports, treatment plants, landfills, waterways, tunnels, power plants, electrical T&D, industrial process plants, railroads, dams, and underground utilities.

## STATE HIGHWAY DEPARTMENT FORMATS

Long before the coming of the CSI Format, the various state highway departments established specification formats of their own in response to the needs of the type of construction in which they were engaged. Most states have settled on a uniform format based on the AASHTO (American Association of State Highway and Transportation Officials) model.

The basic similarity among all state highway specifications is the fact that they all use a published, bound book of "standard specifications." This book covers in detail all general contract conditions as well as the technical specifications for all types of construction that could reasonably be anticipated in any highway department project. The subject matter covered is not as narrow as one might at first expect, and to add complications to the specification, it frequently covers several alternative methods of completing the work.

To adapt these standard specifications to a specific project requires an additional document, for the standard specifications themselves cover far too broad a subject area. Furthermore, they do not indicate whether a specific method should be used on a particular project. This adaptation is accomplished by the preparation of a small supplementary specification called the *Special Provisions* or *Supplemental Specifications*. This document clearly defines the changes to the Standard Specifications or any additions to or deletions from the Standard Specifications that might be necessary to adapt it to the specific project being constructed. For the sake of uniformity, the Special Provisions follow a "standard" format adopted by each using agency, so that all users throughout that state will produce a document that is in the same format, and all contractors will have prior knowledge of the basic requirements and conditions for highway construction in their state.

In the previous cases referred to, when "specifications" were mentioned, the term was interpreted to include all documents, General Conditions, and technical provisions. On a state highway project, this definition must be revised. Here the "specifications" are the Standard Specifications, and the document issued for the specific project contains only supplementary material. The usual title for the book containing the documents plus the special technical conditions is "Special Provisions."

## AASHTO Standard Format for Highway Construction Specifications

The majority of the state highway departments of the United States closely follow the standards of the American Association of State Highway and Transportation Officials (AASHTO).

Rather than refer to the basic or "general" standards of the AASHTO, the example used here as an AASHTO-type specification will be the Road and Bridge Standards of the Virginia Department of Highways and Transportation. Just as used in all other states, the Virginia standard specifications cover all potential types of highway and bridge construction that may be encountered, along with all of the possible acceptable alternatives. These must be supplemented by a book of Special Provisions to adapt the Standard Specifications to a particular project. In addition, as a means of keeping the Standard Specifications up to date, the State of Virginia also issues Supplemental Specifications, which are modifications sheets needed to update the Standard Specifications. These are normally bound into the set of Standard Provisions.

As with other state highway specifications, the arrangement of the subject matter in the technical portions of the Special Provisions closely parallels that of the contents of the book of Standard Specifications, wherever possible. The Virginia Road and Bridge Specifications are initially divided into seven main divisions:

I    General Provisions (Sections 101 to 110; contractual relationships)
II   Materials (Sections 200 to 258; for the work of Divisions II through VII)
III  Roadway Construction (Sections 301 to 321; execution only)

IV    Bridges and Structures (Sections 401 to 426; execution only)
V     Incidental Construction (Sections 501 to 519; execution only)
VI    Roadside Development (Sections 601 to 610; execution only)
VII   Signing (Sections 702 and 703; execution only)

In similar fashion, the Florida Department of Transportation Standard Specifications for Road and Bridge Construction are divided into four main divisions:

I     General Requirements and Covenants (Sections 1 to 9; contractual relationships)
II    Construction Details (Sections 100 to 715; execution only)
III   Materials (Sections 901 to 995; for the work of Division III)
IV    Contract Forms (printed under separate cover)

As in both the California and the Virginia Standard Specifications, the Florida Standard Specifications divisions are further broken down into sections related to the majority of construction materials and methods expected to be encountered in normal road and bridge construction. Anything needed for a project that is not contained in the standard specifications is specified in the Special Provisions.

What most state highway specifications have in common with the CSI Format (long before the formation of the CSI) is the strict separation of materials and execution in their specifications. Thus, in all execution portions of a state highway specification, the materials are covered by reference to the detailed specifications in the division provided for that purpose.

Numbering of the special provisions technical sections in the Virginia highway specifications uses a fixed number system that retains the numbers used in the original book of Standard Specifications, unlike the California example described later, in which a fixed numbering system is used that is wholly independent from the numbering system used in its standard specifications.

## Other Department of Transportation Formats

The State of Washington Standard Specifications for Road, Bridge, and Municipal Construction is somewhat of a departure from the AASHTO standard, as they do not separate the technical sections into separate discrete sections or divisions. In some respects they follow the concept used by the CSI in that they utilize separate divisions to cover the various basic construction materials or types. They further depart from typical state highway department specifications by addressing municipal construction as well as state highway work.

The Washington Standard Specifications are separated into nine Divisions:

1. General Requirements
1. APWA Supplement
2. Earthwork
3. Production from Quarry and Pit Sites and Stockpiling

**4.** Bases

**5.** Surface Treatments and Pavements

**6.** Structures

**7.** Drainage Structures, Storm Sewers, Sanitary Sewers, Water Mains, and Conduits

**8.** Miscellaneous Construction

**9.** Materials

The principal difference is in the organization of the technical subject matter. Otherwise, as with all other State Highway specifications, they are formatted for the Special Provisions concept rather than Project Specifications.

The California Department of Transportation, or "Caltrans," standard specifications also are a departure from the AASHTO standard, having predated AASHTO. They were designed to meet the specific needs of the construction industry in California for street, highway, and bridge construction projects and, as such, were adopted by many cities and counties throughout that state that administer similar projects at local levels. As with the AASHTO standard specification format, they must be supplemented by a book of special Provisions. The format used in these Special Provisions has been standardized, and a uniform format with fixed-number sections and standard section titles has been adopted.

The arrangement of a typical California Department of Transportation "Special Provisions" document is shown in Figure 5.5. The list of subjects covered, as well as the standardized title of each section, remains unchanged from one project to the next.

There were rumors in the industry that the California Department of Transportation is considering a conversion of their specifications to the CSI Format. If this actually happens, it will be a somewhat revolutionary departure from the traditional approach used by all other state transportation agencies throughout the United States.

## NONSTANDARD CONSTRUCTION SPECIFICATIONS FORMATS IN USE

There are different approaches to the problem of separating a project specification into seemingly logical units of construction. The two most common concepts are:

**1.** Separation into trade-group and material classifications, as in the CSI Format

**2.** Separation by project features, wherein each significant feature of a project is described completely within a single section, including all the materials and methods involved to complete the specified structure or feature

Depending upon the nature of a specific project, each concept may have something good to be said of it, and each could serve to special advantage if used properly. If the two systems would ever be mixed in the same specification, however, the job of field administration could become chaotic! The problems resulting from such an unwise choice include the inability reasonably to control payments to the contractor for the various portions of the work, difficulty in defining interfaces in construction, and duplication of specification provisions in different parts of the work—often with varying and conflicting requirements. An

NOTICE INVITING BIDS

SPECIAL PROVISIONS

Section 1 Definitions and Terms
Section 2 Proposal Requirements and Conditions
Section 3 Award and Execution of Contract
Section 4 Beginning of Work: Time of Completion; and Liquidated Damages
Section 5 Control of Work
Section 6 Control of Materials
Section 7 Legal Relations and Responsibility
Section 8 Prosecution and Progress
Section 9 Measurement and Payment
Section 10 Construction Details (technical provisions that vary from the Standard Specifications)

PROPOSAL AND CONTRACT

Proposal and Bid Sheets
Bid Bond
List of Subcontractors
Non-Collusion Affidavit
Agreement
Performance Bond
Payment Bond
Worker's Compensation Certificate

**FIGURE 5.5** California Department of Transportation format for Special Provisions. (Other state DOT Special Provisions are similar.)

engineer or inspector who is assigned to a project like this should be prepared for a lion-sized job of maintaining cost control, especially if it turns out to be a unit-price job.

A graphic example of the complicated relationships involved can be determined from Figure 5.6, which takes the various project features of a recreational park project as an example and superimposes them in matrix form with the various trade-group and material classifications that apply to the same work.

It becomes obvious from the chart that any project that included all these various project features would be most benefitted by using the CSI Format, which is based upon the separation of the specification technical provisions into sections corresponding to the *vertical* columns in the chart in Figure 5.6. Thus, there would be only one concrete section, one metals section, one electrical section, and so forth, no matter how many separate structures or units of construction were included in the project.

However, if a project only involved street paving and parking lots, street lighting and signals, landscaping and irrigation, and a storm drain system, as many municipal improvement projects do, it might be perfectly practical to divide the specifications into sections describing project features corresponding to the *horizontal* lines on the chart in Figure 5.6. This is primarily because the materials of construction and the trades used in this case are peculiar to the unit being built, and the material specification for one of these units is not equally applicable to any of the other sections.

| Item | Project Features | CSI Division Categories | | | | | | | | | | | | | | |
|---|---|---|---|---|---|---|---|---|---|---|---|---|---|---|---|---|
| | | 2 | 3 | 4 | 5 | 6 | 7 | 8 | 9 | 10 | 11 | 12 | 13 | 14 | 15 | 16 |
| A | Site Grading | x | | | | | | | | | | | | | | |
| B | Site Utility Lines | x | x | | x | | | | | | | | | | x | |
| C | Storm Drain System | x | x | | x | | | | | | | | | | | |
| D | Valve Chamber | x | x | x | x | | x | | x | | x | | | | x | x |
| E | Streets & Parking | x | x | | x | | | | x | | | | | | x | x |
| F | Snack Bar Building | x | x | x | x | x | x | x | x | x | x | | | | x | x |
| G | Rest Room Building | x | x | x | x | x | x | x | x | x | x | | | | x | x |
| H | Administration Bldg. | x | x | x | x | x | x | x | x | x | x | | | | x | x |
| I | Landscaping & Irrig. | x | x | | | | | | | | | | | | x | |

**FIGURE 5.6**    Comparison of trade group versus project feature formatting.

## PROJECT SPECIFICATIONS (PROJECT MANUAL) VERSUS SPECIAL PROVISIONS CONCEPT

This subject was touched on slightly in earlier paragraphs, but it is of great importance for the resident engineer or inspector to know the relative importance of the documents that must be used in the field and to understand the very important difference between these two concepts.

### Project Specifications (CSI Project Manual)

The *project specifications* concept (or *Project Manual* in CSI terminology) is based upon the issuance of a single, all-inclusive project specifications book containing all of the contract provisions that apply to the job, although *references to* outside sources are permissible. The effect of such outside references in this type of specification, however, is to bind the contractor only to the extent of the specific reference specification named. Thus, if a project specification states that "portland cement shall be Type II cement as specified in Section 90 of the Standard Specifications," it limits control of the cited reference to the *portland cement specifications only* and does not bind the contractor to any other provisions of that same section, such as the grading of aggregates for concrete.

### Special Provisions or Supplemental Specifications

The *Special Provisions* or *Supplemental Specifications* concept is based upon the idea that a previously published book of Standard Specifications is the actual detailed specification for all applicable work on the project, and that the Special Provisions or Supplemental Specifications are merely a supplemental document to provide for those items on a particular project that the design engineer wanted changed from the provisions of the Standard Specifications, or where he or she made a specific selection of options provided in the Standard Specifications (Figure 5.7). Thus, for example, although it has already been established that the entire concrete section of the Standard Specifications will control the project (insofar as it is applicable, of course) the reference in the Special Provisions or Supplemental Specifications that "portland cement shall be Type II cement as specified in Section 90 of the Standard Specifications" merely controls the choice of option as to the *type of cement* required for the work. The total provisions of the rest of "Section 90" still apply to the concrete work. The exact specification phrase used in the *project specifications* can have a vastly different meaning when used in a *Special Provisions* or *Supplemental Specifications* document.

## INSPECTOR TRAINING AND KNOWLEDGE OF SPECIFICATIONS

Inability to interpret specifications was next to the top of the contractor's list of complaints about inspectors in an ASCE study. These were generally felt to be "go-by-the-book" type inspectors. The usual reason offered for the go-by-the-book philosophy is lack of sufficient field experience to risk the slightest departure from the exact wording of the specifications—right or wrong.

Anyone who has ever had to work both in specifications and in field construction will know that there is little possibility that the information generated in the "sterile" design office environment can be followed literally during the construction phase of a contract. Field conditions vary frequently from the assumed design conditions, and many adjustments must be made. To accomplish this requires not only an experienced, well-qualified inspector, but an enlightened project manager and specifications staff who can recognize the validity of these claims, respond to field suggestions to improve their own product, and work effectively with the inspectors as team members instead of as adversaries.

Of the contractors who claimed to have had to work with incompetent inspectors, some felt that their construction problems were the result of the inspectors' attempts to impose excessive requirements upon them as a form of "play-it-safe" engineering.

The two principal items that the contractors named as having been the cause of the greatest number of problems were (1) specifications interpretation and (2) lack of inspector experience and proper training.

The offshoot of the study was that inspection should be recognized as the principal problem and that poor inspection is prevalent. It was the recommendation of the contractors contacted that inspectors should improve themselves through education, training, certification, and frequent liaison with contractor organizations. It was also stated, in all fairness to inspectors, that the specifications were also in great need of improvement and that the engineers and architects should be held more accountable for their own professional errors. Finally, the study concluded, a means should be developed to provide for more effective coordination and communication between the inspectors and the contractors, and between the inspectors and the specifications engineers.

| PROJECT SPECIFICATIONS (CSI) | SPECIAL PROVISIONS (Federal/State DOT) |
|---|---|
| **PART I - PROPOSAL AND CONTRACT**<br><br>    Notice Inviting Bids<br>    Instructions to Bidders (Preprinted)<br>    Proposal (Bid) and related forms<br>    Agreement and related forms<br>    Contract Administration forms (optional) | **STANDARD SPECIFICATIONS**<br><br>    DOT Standard Specifications<br>    (Includes General Provisions and technical<br>    specifications for typical highway, bridge, or<br>    street improvement project). |
| **PART II - CONDITIONS OF THE CONTRACT**<br><br>    General Conditions (Preprinted)<br>    Supplementary General Conditions<br>    Federal Requirements (if applicable) | **PART I - PROPOSAL AND CONTRACT**<br><br>    Notice Inviting Bids<br>    Proposal (Bid) and related forms<br>    Agreement and related forms<br>    (No separate Instructions to Bidders). |
| **PART III - TECHNICAL SPECIFICATIONS**<br><br>    Division 1 - General Requirements<br>    Division 2 - Site Work and Utilities<br>    Division 3 - Concrete<br>    Division 4 - Masonry<br>    Division 5 - Metals<br>    Division 6 - Wood and Plastics<br>    Division 7 - Thermal and Moisture<br>                        Protection<br>    Division 8 - Doors and Windows<br>    Division 9 - Finishes<br>    Division 10 - Specialties<br>    Division 11 - Equipment<br>    Division 12 - Furnishings<br>    Division 13 - Special Construction<br>    Division 14 - Conveying Systems<br>    Division 15 - Mechanical<br>    Division 16 - Electrical<br><br>End of standard Division titles; the specifier<br>may add additional Divisions as necessary. | **PART II - SPECIAL PROVISIONS**<br><br>    1. Definitions and Terms<br>    2. Bidding Requirements and Conditions<br>    3. Award and Execution of Contract<br>    4. Scope of Work<br>    5. Control of Work<br>    6. Control of Material<br>    7. Legal Relations and Responsibility to Public<br>    8. Prosecution and Progress<br>    9. Measurement and Payment<br>    10. Construction Details (Technical)<br><br>Section 10 is intended to cover ONLY those<br>technical provisions that modify, delete, or add<br>to the provisions of the Standard Specifications.<br>Otherwise the Standard Specifications will<br>govern all work.<br><br>Sections 1 through 9 only require sufficient<br>editing to make them job-specific. |

COMMENTARY

1. Widely used nationally in public & private sectors for all types of construction; primarily for buildings.

2. Adopted by all federal agencies except Transportation

3. Not used by any state DOT agencies, nor by most local agencies on street & bridge work.

4. Uniform national standard format recognized by EJCDC, ACEC, ASCE, NSPE, AIA, AGC, ABC, USCE, USBR, NAVFAC, NASA, and many others.

5. Readily adaptable to published national front-end documents of AIA and EJCDC (NSPE)

1. Concept used by Federal Highway Administration and all state DOT's for roads & bridges.

2. Widely used by cities & counties for street improvements, utilities, and bridge construction.

3. Not suitable for building construction, water & wastewater treatment facilities, pump stations, power projects, etc.

4. Generally limits specifier to materials covered in Standard Specifications and contract admin. principles adapted to roads & bridges.

5. Format is a uniform national standard, but specific terms vary from state to state.

**FIGURE 5.7**  Comparison of documents of two commonly used formats: Project Specifications vs DOT Special Provisions.

### Specifications and the Inspector

One of the principal weaknesses of some inspectors is their general lack of a good working knowledge of specifications. It is only fair at this point to mention also that some of the principal weaknesses among the specifications engineers is their general lack of specific knowledge of construction methods.

As an arbitrator over a number of years, the author has often discovered situations where the case involved a contractor versus a subcontractor, or an owner versus a contractor on a case where the root cause was flaws in the specifications. In such cases, the fault lay not with the parties to the arbitration or litigation, but with the engineer or architect who was responsible for the preparation of the specifications.

For many years the remark has been heard from specifications writers that "if only those people in the field would follow the specifications, we wouldn't have gotten into this problem." At the same time, the field people were saying "someone ought to send those specifications writers into the field for a while where they can be introduced to the real world." Therein lies the essence of a serious problem involving a failure to communicate. Each side suspects the other and challenges their competence.

Actually, there is some justification for each of their viewpoints. Field situations involving design or specifications difficulties should be reported in writing to the specifications department and, wherever justified, changes should be made in the master specifications (guide specifications) to assure that the problem will not be continually repeated.

The fault does not lie wholly with either the inspectors or the specifications engineers. The point is that there must be an effective channel of communications between them. There must also be provisions for educating each group to the needs and problems of the other. In the author's own office, this was accomplished by occasionally transferring specifications writers into the field to work under proper supervision as an inspector. This was done during periods of slowdown in the specifications department, which usually occurs during periods of increased activity in the field.

The logic of this approach is based upon the fact that one of the major elements of each technical specification is that portion dealing with the "execution" of the work. It is in this area that many specifications writers are weakest, since the knowledge necessary to write an effective execution provision can only be obtained through actual field experience. Yet firms continue to have specifications written by people who have never worked in the field and who are simply copying material from old specifications which, to their eyes, appear to be from a "similar" project. Remember the old adage: "Methods used on other projects only work on other projects."

### Specification General Conditions, or Boilerplate

The education of the inspector must be expanded to include careful study and understanding of the General Conditions of the Contract. Unfortunately, many seem to believe that the General Conditions were created by the lawyers for other lawyers to read only if, and when, a dispute goes to court.

Actually, the entire administration of the contract is based upon the provisions contained in this document. While the technical portions of the specifications, or "project manual" as it is called by the Construction Specifications Institute, describe the qualitative requirements of the final product that is to be constructed, the General Conditions provide for an orderly means of handling situations or problems that arise in the contractual relationship with the contractor. In preparing the General Conditions, an attempt is made to anticipate the various types of contractual situations that might arise during the course of the project, and by signing the agreement the owner and the contractor have agreed that should any of the described problems arise, they will be handled as set forth in the general conditions. This provides for the orderly resolution of construction difficulties without the necessity of resorting to the filing of claims that must be resolved through arbitration, litigation, or other dispute resolution alternative.

There is a need in today's complex construction environment for continuing education programs designed to meet the needs of both inspectors and specifications writers. Inspection and specifications are inseparable. The specifications are not only one of the principal elements of the contract documents, but serve as one of the principal tools of the inspector as well.

## ALLOWANCES AND TOLERANCES IN SPECIFICATIONS

One of the factors that should be considered in the efforts to involve the specifications writer and the inspector in an effective working relationship is the inclusion in the specifications of tolerance limits, instead of the traditional methods of specifying absolutes. Some problems for which the inspectors have been blamed can actually be traced to the fact that the specifications either provided for no tolerance at all, or the tolerances provided were either unreasonable or unenforceable. An excellent example of properly specified tolerances can be seen in paragraph 3.3 "Suggested Tolerances" in the American Concrete Institute's Standard on "formwork" (ACI 347). Tolerances for Concrete Construction expressed in metric (SI) units can be found in the U.S. Bureau of Reclamation *Metric Manual,* published by the U.S. Government Printing Office, Denver, CO. Where tolerances are specified, the inspector can be more secure in taking a stand with a contractor on an issue. The specifying of tolerances further eliminates many disputes with contractors who otherwise felt that rejections for nonconformance based upon the inspector's interpretation of absolute values was too subjective. As an absolute value is impossible to obtain consistently, an even greater burden is placed upon the inspector who is obligated to administer such a contract, for the inspector is then always being placed in the position of deciding "how close is close enough?"

All too often, such absolute values are not even well justified by the design computations, but may have been specified solely because the specifier lacked sufficient knowledge of actual construction materials, methods, and practices. Place the specifier in the field for a while and his or her attitude will most certainly change.

Even in a machine shop, where most people will admit that the demand for precision far exceeds that of construction in the field, the dimensions for machined parts are shown on the drawings, with tolerances shown for each dimension. Thus, even in precise work, it is recognized that an absolute dimension without an indicated tolerance is not only impractical, it is virtually impossible. Let the construction industry take heed and reduce construction bid prices by applying reasonable tolerances, and at the same time minimize disputes with the contractor. Furthermore, by specifying tolerances during the design phase, the control is placed in the hands of the engineer or architect, where it rightfully belongs.

## PROBLEMS

1. What are the three principal "parts" of the contract specifications document (or CSI "Project Manual" or "Contract Book" as some public agencies call the document);

2. What are the three parts of a technical section under the CSI Format?

3. Prioritize the following documents in their traditional order of precedence:
   a. _____ Technical Specifications
   b. _____ Agreement
   c. _____ General Conditions of the Contract
   d. _____ Reference Documents
   e. _____ Contract Drawings
   f. _____ Supplementary General Conditions

4. May changes to the documents be done by Addenda after opening bids, but prior to Award?

5. Give three examples of unenforceable phrases if used in specifications.

6. If you were working with a set of project specifications prepared in CSI format, under what section numbers would you find the following subjects?

   _____ Plumbing                        _____ Roof flashing and sheet metal
   _____ Utility piping                  _____ Sheet metal fabrications
   _____ Project meetings                _____ Hardware
   _____ Contractor submittals           _____ Butler buildings
   _____ Restoration of underground      _____ Painting
            pipelines                      _____ Piling

7. Describe the function of the Special Provisions or Supplemental Specifications as used in a DOT project as opposed to the CSI Format.

8. Although CSI Format specifications are widely used, name one type of construction where they are seldom used.

9. Under CSI Format, explain the difference between the documents referred to as "General Conditions" and "General Requirements."

10. Under the CSI Format, the definition of *Contract Documents* does not include the Notice Inviting Bids, Instructions to Bidders, or the Bid itself. Name the principal exception to this rule, wherein the term *Contract Documents* may include the Notice Inviting Bids, Instructions to Bidders, and the Bid itself.

# 6

## Using the Specifications
## in Contract Administration

### GENERAL CONDITIONS OF THE CONSTRUCTION CONTRACT

The *General Conditions,* sometimes called the *General Provisions,* specify the manner and the procedures for implementing the provisions of the construction contract according to the accepted practices within the construction industry. These conditions are intended to govern and regulate the requirements of the formal contract or agreement. They do not serve as a waiver of any legal rights that either party to the contract may otherwise possess. The General Conditions of the Contract are intended to regulate the functions of either party only to the extent that his or her activities may affect the contractual rights of the other party or the proper execution of the work.

Although the General Conditions of most construction contracts vary somewhat from one set to another, depending upon the requirements of the agency that originated the document, most address similar issues, although not always in the same manner. The following examples will allow you to compare the content of three major national and international General Conditions documents. The following subjects addressed in the "Standard General Conditions of the Construction Contract" EJCDC[1] Document No. 1910-8 (1996 Edition) may well be considered as somewhat typical of many engineering documents:

1. Definitions (terms used in the contract documents)
2. Preliminary matters (starting the project; preconstruction matters)
3. Contract documents, intent, amending, and reuse
4. Availability of lands, physical conditions, reference points (differing site conditions; soils reports)

[1]Engineers Joint Contract Documents Committee, c/o National Society of Professional Engineers, 1420 King Street, Alexandria, VA 22314.

**5.** Bonds and insurance

**6.** Contractor's responsibilities

**7.** Other work (related work at site; coordination)

**8.** Owner's responsibilities

**9.** Engineer's status during construction

**10.** Changes in the work (procedures)

**11.** Change of contract price (pricing provisions)

**12.** Change of contract times

**13.** Warranty and guarantee; tests and inspections; correction, removal, or acceptance of defective work

**14.** Payments to contractor and completion

**15.** Suspension of the work and termination

**16.** Dispute resolution

**17.** Miscellaneous

The EJCDC General Conditions are used mostly on engineering projects and by many public agencies, such as city and county governments, with supplements to adapt it to local state laws governing the conduct of public contracts in that state. In many instances it is used as a base document upon which to develop a proprietary document for a particular agency. The EJCDC documents were jointly prepared and endorsed by the following organizations:

American Consulting Engineers Council

American Society of Civil Engineers

National Society of Professional Engineers

Construction Specifications Institute

Associated General Contractors of America

Other standard sets of General Conditions have been developed by various segments of the construction industry, notably those of the American Institute of Architects for building construction. Although most published documents bear a superficial similarity to one another, some of the various documents do have serious differences.

The following subjects are addressed in the "General Conditions of the Contract for Construction" AIA[2] Document A201, 1987 Edition, which is used almost universally on all architectural projects. If they are to be used on public building projects, however, they, too, would require a supplement to adapt it to local state laws governing the conduct of public contracts in that state:

**1.** General Provisions (definitions of terms)

**2.** Owner (rights and obligations)

---

[2]American Institute of Architects, 1735 New York Avenue, N.W., Washington, DC 20006.

**3.** Contractor (obligations)

**4.** Administration of the contract (by the architect)

**5.** Subcontractors (owner's and architect's rights to control selection)

**6.** Construction by owner or by separate contractors (mutual responsibility)

**7.** Changes in the work (change process)

**8.** Time (delays; extensions; progress and completion)

**9.** Payments and completion (payment administration)

**10.** Protection of persons and property (by contractor)

**11.** Insurance and bonds

**12.** Uncovering and correction of work

**13.** Miscellaneous provisions (laws; notice; tests)

**14.** Termination or suspension of the contract
(Approved and endorsed by the Associated General Contractors of America.)

## INTERNATIONAL CONSTRUCTION CONTRACTS

International projects have their own standards, usually FIDIC.[3] The documents of the "FIDIC Conditions of Contract for Works of Civil Engineering Construction, 4th Edition, 1987" are used almost universally on international engineering projects financed by the international banking industry, the United Nations, and others. The scope of coverage of the FIDIC General Conditions includes:

**1.** Definition and interpretation

**2.** Engineer and engineer's representative

**3.** Assignment and subcontracting

**4.** Contract documents

**5.** General obligations

**6.** Labor

**7.** Materials, plant, and workmanship

**8.** Suspension

---

[3]International Federation of Consulting Engineers (FIDIC), 9 Carel van Bylandtlaan, The Hague, Netherlands (available in the United States from American Consulting Engineers Council, 1015 Fifteenth St., N.W., Washington, DC 20005).

FIDIC represents the interests of independent consulting engineers worldwide. It serves as the liaison for its membership with international banks and agencies, such as the International Bank for Reconstruction and Development, the Inter-American Development Bank, the African Development Bank, the Asian Development Bank, the United Nations Development Programme, the Food and Agriculture Organization of the United Nations, the World Health Organization, the United Nations Office of Technical Cooperation, the European Development Fund, the Kuwait Fund for Arab Economic Development, the Arab Fund for Economic and Social Development, and others. FIDIC documents are available in the United States from American Consulting Engineers Council, Washington, DC 20005.

9. Commencement and delays
10. Defects liability
11. Alterations, additions, and omissions
12. Procedure for claims
13. Contractor's equipment, temporary works, and materials
14. Measurement
15. Provisional sums
16. Nominated subcontractors
17. Certificates and payment
18. Remedies
19. Special risks
20. Release from performance
21. Settlement of disputes
22. Notices
23. Default of employer
24. Changes in cost and legislation
25. Currency and rates of exchange

Just as there are numerous differences in nomenclature between owners, architect/engineers, and contractors in various types of organizations, there are numerous diffences between the terminology of international construction contracts in the United States and other countries.

For illustration, the following list compares terms of similar meaning from conventional American contracts and those from international contracts under FIDIC documents, widely used outside the United States.

| United States | International (FIDIC) |
|---|---|
| Addenda to Notice Inviting Bids | Appendix to Tender |
| Award of Contract | Letter of Acceptance |
| Beneficial Use | Taking-over |
| Bid | Tender |
| Bid Forms | Forms of Tender |
| Bid Schedule (unit price projects) | Bill of Quantities |
| Changes in the Work | Variations |
| Date of Notice to Proceed | Commencement Date |
| Differing Site Conditions | Adverse Physical Obstructions |
| Guarantee Period | Defects Liability Period |
| Owner | Employer |
| Partial Payment | Provisional Sum |
| Quantity changes in excess of 15% | Variations in excess of 15% |
| Schedule | Programme |
| Schedule of Values | Breakdown of lump-sum items |

| **United States** | **International (FIDIC)** |
|---|---|
| Supplementary General Conditions | Conditions of Particular |
| Time-and-Materials work | Daywork |
| (sometimes called "force account") | |

With the exception of those items that relate to matters of international currencies and assurances, it can be seen that all three documents—the EJCDC, the AIA, and the FIDIC—share many of the items of common concern to all people in the construction industry.

Standard forms of General Conditions have many advantages. Not only are they generally the result of collaboration with industry and government leaders, and thereby should represent a fair and equitable method of handling a construction contract, but they have normally had the advantage of being thoroughly critiqued by members of both the architect/engineering profession and the legal profession. Furthermore, many have been tested in court and can be relied upon to provide similar protection to all who use them. Another, and frequently overlooked advantage, is that such documents have evolved into a form that has withstood the test of time and experience and have become familiar to the contractors who use them. After repeated usage, a contractor will clearly understand all of its terms, meaning, and implications. This is often reflected in a stability of bid prices, as the full effect of the document's provisions on the contractor has already been established, as far as costs are concerned.

It must be remembered, however, that the mere fact that a document *is* so "general" in nature means that certain types of specific data cannot be included; otherwise, it would not be applicable to all of the projects on which it is used. For example, a provision in the General Conditions for "liquidated damages" or for "bonds" will normally only cover the limitations, procedures, or other unchanging elements—but *not* the actual monetary amount. The specific dollar amounts must be referred to in the Supplementary General Conditions, a document that will be discussed later.

Some of the well-known standardized General Conditions documents in current usage are those of the following organizations:

| | |
|---|---|
| AIA | American Institute of Architects |
| EDA | Economic Development Administration, Department of Commerce |
| EJCDC | Engineers' Joint Contract Documents Committee |
| EPA | Environmental Protection Agency |
| FHA | Farmers Home Administration, Department of Agriculture |
| FIDIC | Fédération Internationale des Ingénieurs-Conseils (International Federation of Consulting Engineers) |
| HUD | Housing and Urban Development |
| JPL | Jet Propulsion Laboratories |
| NASA | National Aeronautics and Space Administration |
| NAVFAC | Department of the Navy, Naval Facilities Engineering Command |
| SCS | Soil Conservation Service |
| USBR | U.S. Bureau of Reclamation |

| USCE | Corps of Engineers, U.S. Army |
|------|-------------------------------|
| (Joint) | EJCDC Standard General Conditions of the Construction Contract and Standard Form of Agreement. Funding agency edition endorsed by U.S. Department of Agriculture, Rural Development Administration, Farmers Home Administration, and Rural Utilities Service |

Obviously, there is no shortage of "standards" and the choice of which to use on any given project may be influenced by many things, including the specific owner requirements, source of construction funds, type of work to be constructed, whether the project is being built by a public or a private agency, and last but not least, whether a particular set of General Conditions contains provisions with which the owner and architect/engineer are willing to live.

From the multitude of standard General Conditions available, there would seem to be little valid reason to generate a new one, yet many architects and engineers and owners are doing just that when they type their own General Conditions to fit a particular job. Each time that a new set is written, there is always the danger that its provisions may contain subtle wording that may not afford the same contractual protection as that contained in the existing standard forms that have had their days in court—and survived.

### General Conditions Portions of Standard Specifications

On some projects where the basic contract is written around a set of Standard Specifications, such as those used by the state Departments of Transportation, the General Conditions of the contract are usually contained in the early chapters of the Standard Specifications book. For example, a project for construction of a bridge under the Virginia Road and Bridge Specifications has its General Conditions specified in Division I, General Provisions, which includes Sections 101 through 110 of that document.

Similarly, the American Public Works Association, in cooperation with the Associated General Contractors, published a book of Standard Specifications entitled *Standard Specifications for Public Works Construction,* usually simply referred to as the "Green Book." Here, as in the standard state highway specifications, the General Conditions are actually Part I, General Provisions, Sections 1 through 9 of the standard specifications book. The principal difference between the two books lies in two areas: (1) the Green Book contract provisions are designed to accommodate a broader type of construction, whereas the state highway and bridge specifications are designed primarily for highways, bridges, and drainage facilities; and (2) the state highway standard specifications are designed for use by the state alone and therefore contain all of the special legal requirements that must be a part of state agency contracts in that state, whereas the Green Book is written for use in Southern California, and attempts to include those legal requirements that apply to contracts by cities, counties, and other local agencies in California. Similar publications of APWA have been published in various regions of the United States.

## DIFFERING SITE CONDITIONS

### Unforeseen Underground Conditions

Several of the provisions of the General Conditions deserve special discussion because of their importance to the inspector and to the contractor as a result of the possible interpretations of their provisions. One of the most misunderstood of all contract provisions, and the one that is frequently the cause of large contractor claims for additional work and change orders, is the provision for *differing site conditions.*

Subsurface and latent physical conditions at the site present a special problem. If they differ significantly from what is printed in the contract documents, the contractor may well be entitled to additional payment for any increased work involved. When this happens, it usually comes as a great surprise to the owner. Architects or engineers should explain the possibility of such claims to the owner before the construction contract is signed. They should also be particularly careful that they give no assurance as to the accuracy of any subsurface exploration, even when a special soils consultant was employed. Failure to advise the contractor of any available data regarding subsurface conditions may not only entitle the contractor to additional payment, but may possibly be the cause of a significant delay in the project when underground conditions are discovered that are quite different from those shown on the plans.

One can no longer say that the responsibility for all such conditions and the delays that accompany them will always be that of the contractor. There are recent court decisions relieving the contractor from such responsibility even where the wording of the contract documents states that the contractor must be familiar with all conditions at the site that might affect the performance of the Work. In fairness to the contractor and to avoid risk of blame for causing delays on the job, the design firm or the owner should make available to the contractor all data used in design.

### Federal Guidelines

A contracts policy in the federal government as it relates to unforeseen underground conditions is becoming a widely accepted standard of the industry and is highly recommended for all construction contracts, both public and private, because it provides for a fair and equitable approach to an otherwise difficult problem.

The provisions of federal contract forms call for the making of adjustments in time and/or price where unknown subsurface or latent conditions at the site are encountered. The purpose is to have the government accept certain risks and thus reduce large contingency amounts in contractors' bids to cover such unknown conditions.

The federal government includes provisions in their construction contracts that will grant a price increase and/or time extension to a contractor who has encountered subsurface latent conditions.

The wording of the "Differing Site Conditions" clause in federal contracts reads as follows:

(a) The Contractor shall promptly, and before such conditions are disturbed, notify the Contracting Officer in writing of: (1) Subsurface or latent physical conditions at the site differing materially from those indicated in this Contract, or (2) Unknown physical conditions at the site, or of an unusual nature, differing materially from those ordinarily encountered and generally recognized as inherent in work of the character provided for in this Contract. The Contracting Officer shall promptly investigate the conditions, and if he or she finds that such conditions do materially so differ and cause an increase or decrease in the Contractor's cost of, or the time required for, performance of any part of the Work under this Contract, whether or not changed as a result of such conditions, an equitable adjustment shall be made and the Contract modified in writing accordingly.

(b) No claim of the Contractor under this clause shall be allowed unless the Contractor has given the notice required in (a), above; provided, however, the time prescribed therefore may be extended by the government.

(c) No claim by the Contractor for an equitable adjustment hereunder shall be allowed if asserted after final payment under this Contract.

## Types of Differing Site Conditions

It is common to refer to a differing site condition as being either a Type 1 or a Type 2 Differing Site Condition, based upon the definition given in the federal contract provisions and summarized here.

### Type 1-Differing Site Condition

Subsurface or latent physical conditions at the site which differ materially from that indicated in the contract documents

### Type 2-Differing Site Condition

Unknown unusual physical condition at the site which differs materially from conditions ordinarily encountered and recognized as inherent in this type of work

## Bidder's Obligations

The premises upon which a differing site conditions clause in federal grant-assisted construction contract rests are as outlined in the following paragraphs.

1. Each bidder is not expected to perform an independent subsurface site investigation prior to submittal of its bid. However, bidders are generally advised in the contract documents to make a site inspection of their own.

2. The contract bid price is proportional to the degree of risk that the construction contractor must provide for in its competitive bid.

3. The most cost-effective construction is obtained by accepting certain risks for latent or subsurface site conditions.

It should be noted, however, that other clauses of the contract documents may impact upon the resolution of a change order that was originally initiated under a differing site conditions clause, such as a requirement to make a site inspection before bidding.

### Sharing the Risk

One of the major risks on any construction project is the possibility that physical site conditions will differ from those expected by the parties to the contract. Regardless of whether the project involves new construction or modifications of an existing structure, it is impossible to predict accurately every physical condition that will be encountered in the field.

To a great extent, the level of detail and accuracy of the site information will depend upon the amount of time and money expended by the owner. On the other hand, the contractor has the opportunity, and usually the obligation, to inspect the site prior to bidding. Despite the good-faith efforts of both parties, it is almost certain that some unanticipated condition will be encountered that will affect the time or cost of construction, or both. This leads to the question of who should bear the risk of increased construction costs necessitated by site conditions that were not indicated in the contract documents.

While many owners were able to place the differing site conditions risk with the contractor, other owners began to question the wisdom of this approach. Careful contractors were forced to carry sizable contingencies in their bids as insurance against differing site conditions. This led some owners to the conclusion that the concept of contractual risk sharing would not only be more equitable, but more economical as well.

The pioneer in this risk-sharing concept has been the federal government. The "Differing Site Conditions" clause under the Federal Acquisition Regulations System (48 CFR 52.236-2) is the prototype for similar clauses in both the public and private sectors. In fact, the government's definition of a compensable differing site condition has become the standard throughout the construction industry.

### Traditional Rule of law

The traditional rule of law has been that the contractor has no implied contractual right to recover additional compensation for differing site conditions. The contractor's obligation is simply to complete the project, as designed, for the contract price. The rationale is that the contractor had the opportunity to inspect the site prior to submitting its bid. Therefore, the risk of differing site conditions is presumed to have been factored into the contractor's bid price.

The rather harsh effects of this doctrine gave rise to an exception created by the courts: To the extent that the owner includes specific site conditions in the contract documents, the owner is extending an implied warranty that the information is accurate.

If the contractor relies on the information in the contract documents during bid preparation, and that information proves to be inaccurate, the owner must bear the responsibility. The contractor is still obligated to complete the contract but may sue for the increased cost of performance on the theory of breach of contract.

### Use of Disclaimers of the Accuracy of Site Information

Owners often attempt to include express disclaimers in the contract documents to counter the doctrine of implied warranty, as shown in the following example:

> Information regarding subsurface conditions and quantities is solely for the use of the owner. It is provided to bidders not as a representation of fact, but for general guidance only. Actual subsurface conditions encountered shall be at the sole risk of the successful bidder. Each bidder is responsible for thoroughly investigating the site and satisfying itself of the accuracy of the estimated quantities in the Bid Schedule. After all bids have been submitted, the bidder shall not assert that there was a misunderstanding concerning quantities of Work or the nature of the Work to be performed.

Another example of such a disclaimer is that used by the federal government in fixed-price contracts where physical data such as test borings, hydrographic, or weather conditions data will be furnished or made available to the bidders (48 CFR 52.236-4):

> Data and information furnished or referred to below is for the contractor's information. The Government shall not be responsible for any interpretation or conclusions drawn from the data or information by the contractor.

Generally, such disclaimers are enforceable unless the owner intentionally or negligently misrepresents site conditions or withholds site information. It should be noted, however, that the use of such exculpatory clauses will be strictly construed by the courts against the owner. Some courts have refused to enforce site data disclaimers on the grounds that investigation by the contractor was physically impossible due to lack of time between bid solicitation and bid submittal. In general, however, such disclaimers are considered as enforceable, and a wary contractor should proceed on that assumption [*Jahncke Service, Inc. v. Department of Transportation,* 322 S.E.2d 505 (Ga. App. 1984)].

An example can be seen in that decision handed down by a Georgia court. It enforced a public owner's disclaimer of the adequacy of designated borrow pits and disclaimer of the accuracy of accompanying boring logs. Jahncke Service, Inc., had been awarded a unit-price contract by the Georgia Department of Transportation to construct 10.6 km (6.61 miles) of highway embankment. The contract documents designated several nearby borrow pits where the department had obtained the right to remove gravel and other fill. Soil boring reports for each pit were also available. The contract documents disclaimed the department's responsibility for borrow materials in the following terms:

> The Department, in making this borrow pit available to contractors, assumes no responsibility if the Contractor relies on this information. . . . The quantity of material shown on the plans as available in the borrow areas is not guaranteed. The obligation is upon the Contractor, before making its Bid or Proposal, to make its own investigation.

During construction, Jahncke discovered that the designated borrow pits did not provide the quantity or quality of materials that Jahncke anticipated from the boring reports. Forced to obtain materials from other sources, Jahncke submitted a claim for an increase in the unit price per cubic yard.

The department relied upon the contract disclaimers in denying the claim. The Court of Appeals of Georgia agreed that as a matter of law, the contract provisions precluded Jahncke from recovering additional compensation for insufficient material or inaccurate reports. The court stated: "It is undisputed that Jahncke was on notice as to the possibility of errors or discrepancies in the boring report and as to the necessity, before submitting a bid, of making an independent investigation rather than contenting themselves with relying on the boring report."

## MATERIALS AND EQUIPMENT

One of the most common occurrences during construction is the constant search by the contractor to obtain products that cost less than those actually specified, and offer them to the architect/engineer as substitutes (sometimes without offering a share of the savings to the owner). The ever-present desire to use cheaper materials that frequently have not had the test of time to show that they will perform as well as a specified product frequently leads to claims against the architect or engineer for negligence if it is determined later that the product did not perform as required. Great care must be used in the approval of new, substitute products as well as in the application of some established ones. The architect or engineer has the duty to see that the products furnished in compliance with his or her drawings and specifications are actually suitable for the particular uses intended. Reliance on producer's sales literature is hazardous at best. There are several court decisions in which the architect or engineer has been held liable for failure to have a new material tested, or an established item tested for a new application prior to approving it. Thus, it is easy to understand his or her occasional reluctance to try new products.

It may even be desirable to require that the manufacturer of such new products furnish guarantees that extend beyond the usual time. The refusal of a producer to provide such guarantees may be sufficient reason for rejecting the product. In any case, the authority for acceptance of a product offered as an "or equal" item is reserved to the architect or engineer of record—not to the Resident Project Representative or other inspector. Consideration of a product as an "equal" should be deferred until after execution of the contract, and *not considered during the bidding phase* of a project.

## THE CONTRACTOR AND SUBCONTRACTORS

Almost all of the construction contract General Conditions are based upon having the Resident Project Representative deal solely with the general contractor, not directly with the subcontractors, material suppliers, or fabricators. The General Conditions usually state that the general contractor is fully responsible for all the acts and omissions of the subcontractors, and nothing in the General Conditions is intended to create any contractual relationship between any subcontractor and the owner or design firm or any obligation to assure that the contractor has paid the subcontractors or material suppliers.

The fact that only the *general* contractor is recognized should end the frequent disputes of subcontractors that revolve around definitions of the scope of their portion of the work (usually, the result of the failure of the general contractor to provide its subcontractors with a complete set of specifications and drawings). The general contractor may complain that it is the design architect's or engineer's fault because they failed to include certain items in a specification section that would be performed by a specialty subcontractor, and thus the contractor believes that additional funds should be paid to cover the added charges to the general contractor by the specialty subcontractors. Obviously, the answer is simple from a contractual standpoint—only one contract was let; the total scope of the work was specified; and it is not the responsibility of the architect or engineer to determine how the successful bidder plans to subcontract the work. Furthermore, the scope of any one class of work can often vary significantly even from one county to the next, because of differences in trade union contracts and the resultant jurisdictional agreements. One contract means one job; it is the general contractor's responsibility to contract properly with his or her subcontractors to assure a clear understanding of the scope of each such subcontract.

## SHOP DRAWINGS AND SAMPLES

### The Function of Shop Drawings

The shop drawing is the connecting link between design and construction. Because of the increasing complexity of today's construction, shop drawings in recent years have become one of the largest sources of professional liability claims against the designer. Unreasonable delay in processing shop drawings and ambiguous wording in the shop drawing approval stamps are the principal source of trouble. Most specifications require that the contractor refrain from ordering material until the results of the review of the shop drawing submittal from the design organization have been received. Any delay in processing of shop drawings affects the contractor's scheduling and, in turn, may result in extra cost to the owner.

Normally, the contractor is obligated to submit a preliminary schedule of the submittals of shop drawings and other submittals required under the contract. This schedule should be reviewed by the design firm or the owner's engineering staff and finalized prior to construction. Shop drawing submittal procedures are one of the topics for discussion at the *preconstruction conference* described in Chapter 11. Careful attention to these preliminary matters can avoid misunderstandings at a later date, and an agreed-upon procedure should be set out on paper and copies circulated to all affected parties.

Shop drawings are drawings submitted to the owner's architect/engineer by a contractor or subcontractor. Shop drawings usually show in detail the proposed fabrication or assembly of project components. They are also used to indicate the installation, form, and fit of materials or equipment being incorporated into the project. Shop drawings are needed because it is impossible for the plans and specifications to spell out every detail of every aspect of the work. This is particularly true of large construction projects.

While the plans and specifications usually define the overall nature of the project, the means and methods of construction are expected to be determined by the contractor. Owners and their architect/engineers expect this expertise from the contractor. Shop drawings also provide a way for contractors to propose and architect/engineers to approve a particular method of accomplishing a special requirement.

### Approval of Shop Drawings

One of the most important and misunderstood facts about shop drawings is that a shop drawing approval does not normally authorize changes from the contract provisions

[*Appeal of Whitney Brothers Plumbing & Heating, Inc.,* ASBCA No. 16876, 72-1 BCA 9448 (1972)]; these must properly be accomplished by a *change order.*

The review and approval of shop drawings involves some considerable risk to architect/engineers and owners. In an effort to maintain flexibility in determining the acceptability of the work, as well as some leverage over the contractor, architect/engineers frequently use shop drawing approval language that is evasive or ambiguous at best.

This language, which is usually found on the shop drawing approval stamps applied to each drawing, contains typical "approval" language, such as:

> Review is only to check for compliance with the design concept of the project and general compliance with the contract documents. Approval does not indicate the waiver of any contract requirement. Changes in the work may be authorized only by separate written change order.

The Design Professionals Insurance Company of Monterey, California, one of the major underwriters of errors and omissions insurance for architect/engineers, in their book *The Contract Guide,* advocates:

> . . . the review and approval of contractor submittals, such as shop drawings, product data, samples, and other data, as required by the engineer or architect, but only for the limited purpose of checking for conformance with the design concept and the information expressed in the contract documents. The review should not include review of the accuracy or completeness of details, such as quantities, dimensions, weights or gages, fabrication processes, construction means or methods, coordination of the work with other trades or construction safety precautions, all of which are the sole responsibility of the contractor. The engineer's or architect's review should be conducted with reasonable promptness, while allowing sufficient time in their judgement to permit adequate review. Review of a specific item must not indicate that the engineer or architect has reviewed the entire assembly of which the item is a component. The engineer or architect should not be held responsible for any deviations from the contract documents not brought to their attention in writing by the contractor, nor should they be required to review partial submittals or those for which submittals of corrected items have not been received.

However, in a case heard by the General Services Administration Board of Contract Appeals in 1985, the board ruled that "when a contractor clearly calls out a deviation from the original specifications, the government will be bound by its shop drawing approval regardless of disclaimers in the stamped language" [*Appeal of Montgomery Ross Fisher and H. A. Lewis, a Joint Venture,* GSBCA No. 7318 (May 14, 1985)].

Both the AIA in Articles 3.12.8 and 4.27 of General Conditions Document A201 (1987 Edition) and the EJCDC in Article 6.26 of General Conditions Document 1910-8 (1996 Edition) refer to the obligation of the architect or engineer to review *and approve* shop drawings. FIDIC documents do not use the term "shop drawings," but refer to such documents under the category of "Permanent Works Designed by the Contractor"; there, in Sub-Clause 7.2 of the "Conditions of the Contract" (1987 Edition), they require such documents to be submitted to the engineer "for approval."

### Misuse of Shop Drawings

*A shop drawing must not be used as a change order,* and any variation from the design drawings and specifications must be the result of a formal change order. Otherwise, it is not authorized [*Appeal of Community Science Technology Corp., Inc.,* ASBCA No. 20244, 77-1 BCA 12,352 (1977)].

In a recent example, a reservoir was to have a precast, prestressed (pretensioned) concrete roof provided under a contract with a fabricator who specialized in furnishing such work as a complete package; that is, they provided the design (within the criteria set by the architect/engineer); the fabrication of all the prestressed, precast concrete structural members; and the erection at the site of all such members into a complete roof system. On shop drawings transmitted during the execution of this contract, a small but significant design detail was changed from that shown in the original design concept that was approved by the engineer and the local building and safety department. The contractor contended that approval of shop drawings with the design change on them meant that they should build according to the shop drawings instead of the contract drawings. However, the contract provided that any change from the contract drawings must be accompanied by an authorized change order, and therefore the contractor was required to conform to the original detail as shown on the contract drawings. Again, only a *change order* should be used to authorize a deviation from the contract provisions, and a change order must normally be signed by the owner, as it is the owner who is a party to the contract, not an outside design firm. It cannot be done legally simply by showing changes on a shop drawing unless the architect/engineer creates an informal change order out of the shop drawing by adding the proper authorization and signature of the owner to the drawing sheets. This, of course, would be somewhat irregular and certainly undesirable from the record-keeping viewpoint.

## DISAPPROVING OR STOPPING THE WORK

Some General Conditions allow the Resident Project Representative, as a representative of an outside design firm, the right to stop the work. This is a very sensitive area and can lead to serious legal consequences if it can be shown that the action was unjustified and subjected the contractor to added cost. However, upon receipt of information from the architect or engineer that the work is defective, the *owner* may order the contractor to stop the work on these grounds. In any case, the more risky right to stop the work should be left to the owner, as a party to the construction contract, not to an outside design firm or their Resident Project Representative.

In some cases where the owner is relatively "unsophisticated," as the term relates to construction, there is a tendency to allow an architect/engineer or its field representative to exercise greater control over the project. It should be kept in mind at all times, however, that certain additional risks accompany such added responsibility.

One prime exception to the foregoing "stop the work" discussion is the case where the work is being carried on in an unsafe manner. Under these conditions, moral standards or the law may impose a duty on both the Resident Project Representative and the contractor for the benefit of employees and third parties to stop such work as a means of lessening the risk of death or serious injury that could result if such conditions were allowed to continue (see the discussion of Imminent Hazards in Chapter 8).

Any disapproval or rejection of the work should be communicated to the contractor in writing, stating the reasons for the disapproval. This should be done as early as possible after rejecting the work. In addition, the Resident Project Representative normally has the power to require special testing or inspection of all work that has been covered up without his or her consent, including work that has been fabricated, installed, or completed. In its Standard General Conditions of the Construction Contract, EJCDC Document 1910-8 (1996 Edition) provides for the owner's right to stop the work in Article 13.10 as follows:

### Owner May Stop the Work

13.10. If the Work is *defective,* or CONTRACTOR fails to supply sufficient skilled workers or suitable materials or equipment, or fails to furnish or perform the Work in such a way that the completed Work will conform to the Contract Documents, OWNER may order CONTRAC-TOR to stop the Work, or any portion thereof, until the cause for such order has been eliminated: however, this right of OWNER to stop the Work shall not give rise to any duty on the part of OWNER to exercise this right for the benefit of CONTRACTOR or any surety or other party.

The unanticipated legal exposure resulting from giving the power to stop the work to the engineer resulted in a change to the National Society of Professional Engineers (NSPE) contract documents in 1967. Under Article 13.10 of the Standard General Conditions of the Construction Contract of the EJCDC,[4] only the owner has the right to stop the work, and then only if that work is defective. It was believed that the right to reject defective work was a sufficient weapon for the engineer, and the severe and more risky right to stop other work should be left to the owner. Where the owner does not have sufficient technical sophistication, great reliance is placed on the engineer or architect to "do it all," but in so doing, the engineer or architect should be aware of the additional legal exposure assumed.

Similarly, in the General Conditions of the Contract for Construction, AIA Document A201 (1987 Edition), Article 2.3.1., provides for the owner's right to stop the work. The principal difference between the EJCDC provisions and the AIA provisions for owner's right to stop the work appears to lie in the requirement in the AIA documents that a stop work order from the owner to the engineer must be delivered in writing and signed personally by either the owner or an authorized agent, who must also be designated in writing.

The FIDIC, in its Conditions of Contract for Works of Civil Engineering Construction (Fourth Edition 1987) places no such limitations on the authority of the engineer. It addresses the subject of work stoppage under the heading "Suspension of Work" in Article 40.1, where it states:

### Suspension of Work 40.1

The Contractor shall, on instructions of the Engineer, suspend the progress of the Works or any part thereof for such time and in such manner as the Engineer may consider necessary and shall, during such suspension, properly protect and secure the Works or such part thereof so far

---

[4]*EJCDC, Standard Forms of Agreement,* Publication 1910-8, 1985, the National Society of Professional Engineers, 2029 K Street, Washington, DC 20006.

as necessary in the opinion of the Engineer unless such suspension is (a) otherwise provided for in the Contract, or (b) necessary by reason of some default of or breach of contract by the Contractor for which he is responsible, or (c) necessary by reason of climatic conditions on the Site, or (d) necessary for the proper execution of the Works or for the safety of the Works, or any part thereof (save to the extent that such necessity arises from any act or default by the Engineer or the Employer or from any of the risks defined in Sub-Clause 20.4), Sub-Clause 40.2 shall apply.

It can be noted in the FIDIC handling of work suspension (stopping the work) that the engineer may be obligated to "protect and secure" the work during the period of such suspension or stoppage, an obligation not imposed under either EJCDC or AIA documents. It further permits the engineer to stop the work, which in the United States could expose the engineer to the risk of tort liability under the principle that a party who has the right to stop the work is in *de facto* control of the work; thus if someone were injured on the job site, argument could be made that the engineer was under an obligation to prevent the injury by stopping the work beforehand to correct whatever defect resulted in the injury.

For further discussion of suspension or termination of the work, see Chapter 14.

## SUPPLEMENTARY GENERAL CONDITIONS

As the name implies, the Supplementary General Conditions are simply an extension of the General Conditions. It is in this document that the special legal requirements of the contract are expanded to include provisions that apply solely to the project at hand. In some cases, the titles of articles within the Supplementary General Conditions will duplicate titles already mentioned in the General Conditions. This is neither repetitious nor necessarily a superseding provision. In most cases, both such paragraphs still apply. However, the provisions in the General Conditions may contain only procedural and responsibility clauses, whereas the same subject in the Supplementary General Conditions will add specific requirements that apply only to this job, such as amounts of liquidated damages or the amounts of bonds, or amounts of insurance required.

The Supplementary General Conditions portion of the contract documents may appear under several titles, without actually changing the nature of the document. Often, under older formats, this portion of the specifications was known as "Special Conditions" or on some of the newer formats, Supplementary General *Provisions* instead of *Conditions*.

In addition to items that are expansions of Articles already specified in the General Conditions, there are numerous other subjects that may, in all likelihood, be encountered in the Supplementary General Conditions. A sample of the contents of one such document follows:

1. Scope (of the entire project)
2. Supplementary Definitions (not covered in the General Conditions)
3. Legal Address of the Architect/Engineer and the Owner (needed for service of legal documents)
4. Amounts of Bonds (actual dollar or percentage values)
5. Amount of Liquidated Damages (actual dollar value)

6. Permits and Inspection Costs (who pays what)
7. Contract Drawings (complete list, by number and title, of all drawings that are made a part of the contract)
8. Applicable Laws and Regulations (specific requirements for this job)
9. Insurance (amount of coverage; additional insurance not specified in the General Conditions, and amount of its coverage)

## TECHNICAL PROVISIONS OF THE SPECIFICATIONS

It should be noted that two of the three parts into which the specifications document is usually divided have "general" clauses in them. They are Part II, Conditions of the Contract, and Part III, Technical Provisions. To avoid confusion, some distinction should be noted between these two portions of the specifications.

First, the "general" provisions of the *Conditions of the Contract* relate to the contractual relationships and legal obligations of the parties to the contract. However, the "general" provisions of the *technical* portion of the specifications should relate to those requirements of a technical nature that apply generally to the work of the entire project rather than to work of one trade, for example. Thus, the General Conditions of the Contract refer to legal and contractual relationships, whereas the General Requirements Section of Part III, Technical Provisions, relates to construction details, project features, procedural requirements for handling the work, and similar project-related functions.

Under the CSI Format, Division I of the 16-Division Format was reserved for this purpose, and the subjects generally included (if applicable to the project) would usually be either those shown in the following list, or similar subjects that the architect/engineer deems necessary to perform the work of the project properly (see also Figures 5.2 and 5.3):

### GENERAL REQUIREMENTS—DIVISION I

**01010. Summary of Work**
    Work by others
    Items provided by owner
    Work included in this contract
    Work to be performed later

**01025. Measurement and payment**

**01030. Alternatives**

**01200. Project meetings**
    Preconstruction conferences
    Progress meetings
    Job site administration

**01300. Submittals**
    Construction schedules
    Network analyses
    Progress reports

Survey data

Shop drawings, product data, and samples

Operation and maintenance data

Layout data

Schedule of values

Construction photographs

**01400. Quality Control**

Testing laboratory services

Inspection services

**01500. Temporary facilities and controls**

Temporary utilities (power, lighting, water, phones, sanitary)

Construction elevators and hoists

Guards and barricades

Shoring, falsework, bracing, scaffolding, and staging

Access roads

Control of dust, noise, water, vapors, pollutants

Traffic control; parking; storage of materials

Temporary field offices

**01600. Material and Equipment**

Quality transportation and handling

Storage and protection

**01700. Project closeout**

Cleaning up

Project record documents

Touch up and repair

Operational testing and validation

Maintenance and guarantee

Bonding requirements during guarantee period

These and similar provisions are generally representative of the types of subject matter that are expected to be contained in Division I of the Technical Provisions where the CSI Format is being used. A comparison of these subjects with the subject area covered under the General Conditions of the Contract, Part II of the specifications, should give some idea as to the accepted grouping of the various subject matters.

## Provisions for Temporary Facilities

During the preparation of the specifications, it is desirable to provide input data that are necessary for effective contract administration. These data should include provisions for certain temporary facilities and services so that they can be required of the contractor by a specific date.

It should be emphasized that it is the contractor's basic responsibility to provide all plant and equipment that is adequate for the performance of the work of the contract, within the time specified. All such plant and equipment must be kept in satisfactory operating condition and must be capable of performing the required work safely and efficiently. It is sometimes desirable to have all such items subject to the inspection and approval of the Resident Project Representative at any time during the duration of the contract.

A number of specific issues should be covered in the specifications to facilitate these requirements.[5] The following is a suggested list of items that may be appropriately covered where the item is applicable to the project being constructed:

- Temporary electrical services
  *(Include: construction lighting, wiring, and circuit separation)*
- Fire protection
  *(Include: connections to contractor's water supply system)*
- Temporary utility services
  *(Include: water supply development and connections; later removal of such connections; power supply and connections; free local telephone service for both the contractor's and the owner's or architect/engineer's field offices; type of telephone service required, and cost of toll calls; time of installation of such temporary facilities)*
- Sanitation
  *(Include: toilet facilities and disposal of waste materials)*
- Site access and storage provisions
  *(Include: highway limitations, marine transportation provisions including pier and landing facilities and small boat launching facilities, and contractor's work and storage area limitations)*
- Environmental controls
  *(Include: explosives and blasting, dust abatement, chemical use and disposal, and misplaced or discharged materials into waterways)*
- Cultural resources
  *(Include: historical, architectural, archeological, or other cultural resources endangered by the project; the owner's right to stop the work in case of a cultural resource "find")*
- Field office facilities
  *(Include: type of structure or facility; office equipment and furnishings to be provided; utility services to be provided; date of installation and completion of field office facility; and cleanup services required)*

---

[5]As a part of the specifications provisions for temporary facilities, the specifications should also provide for some of these items to be included under a separate line item in the bid sheet, or as a part of a "mobilization" line item. In this manner, failure to provide such facilities on a timely basis can be reflected in the contractor's entitlement to the first progress payment. (See Chapter 16, for further details regarding Payment for Mobilization Costs.)

## ADDENDA TO THE SPECIFICATIONS

*Addenda* to the specifications (or in singular form, an *addendum* to a particular set of specifications) are documents setting forth the changes, modifications, corrections, or additions to the contract documents that have been issued after the project has been advertised for bids, but *before* the time of opening bids—sufficiently in advance of the bid opening date, one hopes, to allow the bidder time to make the necessary changes in his or her bid.

The addenda may be specified as "Addendum to the Specifications" or as an "Addendum to the Notice Inviting Bids." Each has the same legal effect. Many public agencies prefer the latter (Figure 6.1). Normally, the addenda must be delivered to each party who has obtained a set of specifications in such manner as to provide the owner with written assurance of completed delivery before the opening of bids. This may be accomplished by sending a copy to each person who has obtained a set of plans and specifications, via certified mail with a return receipt requested. The return receipt is the confirmation of receipt by the bidder and it should be carefully filed. A further safeguard to assure that all parties who bid the job are using the same edition of the documents is to use one of the following methods of assurance:

1. Require that the bidder sign an acknowledgment for the receipt of each addendum issued. Then, at bid-opening time, all such acknowledgments are checked before considering the bid as admissible or responsive.

---

CITY OF PALM SPRINGS
ENGINEERING DIVISION

**ADDENDUM NO. 1**

To all prospective bidders under Specifications for Reroofing the Police Department Building, City Project No. 93-52, for which bids are to be received by the City of Palm Springs at the office of the Purchasing Manager at 3200 E. Tahquitz Canyon Way, Palm Springs, California 92262, until 4:00 p.m. on Tuesday, 21 March 1995.

I.  The existing three bid schedules in the Specifications and Drawings for this contract have been revised. Bid Schedules"A," "B," and "C" have been changed, and revised bid shedules have been included as a part of this Addendum No. 1. Said rovicod Bid Schedules "A,""B," and "C" shall be used in submitting bids.

II. The Specifications as originally issued shall be used in submitting bids, and an acknowledgement of receipt of this Addendum No. 1 shall be entered on Page 1 of the Bid. Failure to provide such acknowledgement shall render the bid as non-responsive and subject to rejection.

BY ORDER OF THE CITY OF PALM SPRINGS

13 March 1995                    By      Robert J. Rockett, PE
                                         City Engineer
                                         Civil Engineer C 28209

---

**FIGURE 6.1** Specifications addendum.

**2.** Require that the bidder simply submit copies of all addenda along with the bidding documents at the time of opening bids. This is a fairly common procedure by many public agencies, which frequently require that the bid forms not be removed from the specification document, and that the entire book be submitted intact with the bid.

One of the first things to be done upon receipt of addenda is to check the specifications and drawings carefully, and mark all corrections, changes, modifications, or additions to the original documents. The next step is to cross-check to see if any of the data that were changed involve interfacing with other sections of the specifications or any other drawings. In the issuance of addenda, the architect or engineer seldom if ever provides cross-references. The Resident Project Representative's copy must be checked for this and the set of contract documents should be marked to reflect all such changes by addenda.

It should be remembered that addenda can only be issued *during the bidding period;* any changes that are made after the opening of bids should be issued as change orders during the construction phase. Thus the Resident Project Representative will have access to all such changes by addenda long before reporting to the project site.

Of prime importance is the fact that an addendum to the specifications (or to the *Notice Inviting Bids,* as it is sometimes called) will always take precedence over any portion of the plans or specifications that is in conflict with it. The Resident Project Representative should always check all addenda before requiring compliance with provisions of the original specifications or drawings.

## STANDARD SPECIFICATIONS

By definition, a set of *Standard Specifications* is a preprinted set of specifications, usually comprising both a set of General Conditions and complete technical specifications for all types of construction and materials that the originating agency expects normally to cover in their kind of work. When adopted by a public agency or by a design firm working on a project for a public agency, the total content of the Standard Specifications becomes a part of the contract documents, subject only to changes set forth in a separate project-related document called the *Special Provisions* or *Supplemental Specifications,* which adapts the rather general treatment of the Standard Specifications to the specific needs of a particular project. In this manner, where alternatives are offered in the Standard Specifications, the Special Provisions or Supplemental Specifications serve to indicate which of the available choices apply to this specific project. Under this type of contract, contractually anything not modified by the terms of the Special Provisions or Supplemental Specifications is required to comply with all applicable provisions of the Standard Specifications.

In direct contrast, if a project does not cite the Standard Specifications as the principal contract document, but merely references certain sections from it, then nothing in the Standard Specifications will apply to that project except those items specifically referenced in the specifications. To assure proper application, the resident engineer or inspector must be very careful with regard to citations from Standard Specifications.

Particular attention should be paid to the exact numerical designation of a citation as well. For example, if a citation reads

per Section 223.02(d) of the Virginia Road and Bridge Specifications

such a specific reference would preclude the use of anything that is not in that particular subsection (d); in this case it would mean that concrete must be cured solely by the use of the "liquid membrane seal" method, which is specified in detail. However, if the citation reads

per Section 223 [or 223.02] of the Virginia Road and Bridge Specifications

the contractor would be free to select any of four specified acceptable methods of curing concrete; it would be the contractor's option.

Under California Department of Transportation Specifications, the coverage of each Section is broader; Section 90 of the document includes not only portland cement, but also aggregates, curing materials, admixtures, and similar items. The effect of making a reference as general as

per Section 90 of the Caltrans Standard Specifications

in a contract where the standard specifications was the principal document would be to require the contractor's compliance with all provisions of that section, including a choice of each alternative provided. If the engineer wanted to limit the use of curing methods, for example, the Special Provisions or Supplemental Specifications would have to include a qualifying statement to that effect.

The use of a set of Standard Specifications without an accompanying set of Special Provisions or Supplemental Specifications is like asking to read a copy of a book, and being handed a dictionary instead with the comment "all the words are here; just read the ones that apply."

## MASTER SPECIFICATIONS (GUIDE SPECIFICATIONS)

A *Master Specification* or *Guide Specification* is another matter entirely. It is equivalent to a Standard Specification only in that it is a preprinted set of specification provisions. It is never used on a job in the preprinted form, however. Each time it is to be used, the Master Specification must be physically modified to meet the specific job requirements. This precludes any need to issue a set of Special Provisions or to issue sections of specifications that do not apply to the project at hand. Masterspecs are in-house tools to enable the architect/engineer or other agency to produce more effectively project specifications that reflect a fixed corporate or agency policy, and that may readily be updated to reflect current changes in construction methods, materials, and laws.

The Masterspec concept is based upon the same principle as that used in the old Corps of Engineers' Guide Specifications. Each subject area is separated into separate sections and a specification is prepared leaving blank areas or a selection of choices to be made to adapt the section to any specific project. After marking the guide or Masterspec, it may be typed as a part of the project specification.

One of the principal advantages of this system is the fact that old job specifications are not used to prepare specifications for a new project. Instead, the Masterspec is utilized each time as the basic document from which to begin. In this manner, too, updated material changes, legal requirements, ASTM references, and similar items subject to constant change can readily be incorporated in the Masterspec as the changes are noted. Thus, all subsequent project specifications will be up to date, without the commonly observed outdated phrases, materials that are no longer available, and similar faults inherent in the system of utilizing a previous project specification as a base to write a new one.

## SPECIAL MATERIAL AND PRODUCT STANDARDS

If every time an item were specified for a project the specifications would have to contain all of the provisions that were necessary to assure that the product met all physical, chemical, geometrical, or performance standards required, every project specification would have to be from 10 to 100 times bulkier than it is now, and some would look like a set of encyclopedias. Worse yet, every architect/engineer without the benefit of coordination would have enough subtle differences in the description of a product as compared with another architect or engineer's description of the same product that the manufacturers would be solely in the business of manufacturing "custom" materials for every different project. Even if this could be accomplished, construction costs would skyrocket.

As a means of providing the uniformity necessary, various nonprofit associations as well as government agencies and manufacturers have established voluntary standards that are actually Standard Specifications for separate individual products. Thus, by referring to the published data for each of these products, an architect or engineer can design each project subject to the specified product limitations, with full assurance that such products are not only marketed, but carefully regulated by each manufacturer to assure compliance with the previously established standards.

The agencies that issue such standards are sometimes governmental, sometimes industry trade associations, and sometimes independent standards associations whose only function is the preparation of such industry standards with the voluntary cooperation of industry, of course. In each case, the standards have been established as a coordinated effort between the manufacturer, architect/engineer, academic community, and other influences, as applicable.

Such standards become a part of a construction contract only if specifically called out in the specifications or drawings—and then only to the degree referred to. If a specification calls for a particular product by its ASTM designation, but includes something that was not a part of that ASTM standard, the product must conform to the cited standard *subject to the modifying provision.* Thus, it would actually be a "special" product requiring the manufacturer to make a "custom" item with appropriate increase in cost and delay in delivery schedule.

Such standards may be loosely divided into two basic classifications: (1) government standards and (2) nongovernment standards. Of the first category, the following are most commonly used.

### Government Standards

***Federal specifications.*** Federal specifications describe essential and technical requirements for items, materials, or services that are normally bought by the federal government. They are also referred to extensively in specifications for nonfederal projects when commercial standards are not available for a particular item. They are generally characterized by the unique letter–number type of designations used, such as "SS-C-1960/3B" for portland cement concrete in Figure 6.2.

**178**     **NUMERIC LIST OF FEDERAL SPECIFICATIONS & COMMERCIAL ITEM DESCRIPTIONS**

| DOCUMENT NUMBER | QPL | TITLE | FSC | PREP | DATE | PRICE |
|---|---|---|---|---|---|---|
| RR-W-670D | | Wringer, Mop | 7920 | FSS | 17 Oct 72 | |
| RR-W-1101A | | Waste Receptacle, Swinging Doors | 7240 | FSS | 31 Oct 72 | |
| RR-W-001588 | | Waste Receptacle, Wall Or Post Mounted | 7240 | FSS | 20 Mar 70 | |
| RR-W-1817A | | Warning Device, Highway, Triangular, Reflective | 9905 | FSS | 30 Jul 75 | |
| SS-A-281B(1) | | Aggregate; (For) Portland-cement-concrete | 5610 | ME | 25 Jan 57 | |
| SS-A-666D | | Asphalt, Petroleum (Built-up Roofing, Waterproofing, And Dampproofing) | 5610 | FSS | 7 May 68 | |
| NOTICE 1 | | | | | 24 Jul 68 | |
| SS-A-671C | | Asphalt, Liquid; Slow-curing, Medium Curing, And Rapid Curing | 5610 | FSS | 8 Sep 66 | |
| SS-A-694D | | Asphalt Roof Coating (Brushing And Spraying Consistency) | 5610 | FSS | 9 Mar 73 | |
| SS-A-701B | | Asphalt, Petroleum (Primer, Roofing, And Weatherproofing) | 5610 | FSS | 15 Jul 74 | |
| SS-A-706D | | Asphalt, Petroleum' road And Pavement Construction (Asphalt Cement) | 5610 | YD | 25 Sep 78 | |
| SS-B-656B | | Brick, Building, Common (Clay Or Shale) | 5620 | ME | 18 Feb 66 | |
| SS-B-663B | | Brick, Building, Concrete | 5620 | FSS | 9 Jun 65 | |
| SS-B-668B | | Brick, Facing, Clay, Or Shale | 5620 | FSS | 20 May 74 | |
| SS-B-671C | | Brick, Paving | 5620 | FSS | 2 Jun 65 | |
| SS-B-681B | | Brick, Building, Sand-lime | 5620 | FSS | 22 Dec 65 | |
| SS-B-755A(1) | | Building Board, Asbestos Cement' flat And Corrugated | 5640 | FSS | 21 May 68 | |
| SS-C-153C | | Cement, Bituminous, Plastic | 5610 | FSS | 13 Dec 74 | |
| SS-C-160A(2) | | Cements, Insulation Thermal | 5640 | FSS | 11 Jan 79 | |
| SS-C-161A | | Cement' keene's | 5610 | FSS | 23 Jan 74 | |
| SS-C-255 | | Chalk, Carpenters' And Railroad | 7510 | FSS | 30 Aug 49 | |
| SS-C-00255A | | Chalk, Carpenters' And Railroad | 7510 | FSS | 10 Jan 69 | |
| SS-C-266F | | Chalk, Marking, White And Colored | 7510 | FSS | 20 Aug 73 | |
| SS-C-450A | | Cloth, Impregnated (Woven Cotton Cloth, Asphalt Impregnated; Coal Tar Impregnated) | 5650 | FSS | 10 Apr 67 | |
| SS-C-466E | | Cloth, Thread, And Tape; Asbestos | 5640 | SH | 2 Jul 64 | |
| INT AMD 2 | | | | | 22 Sep 76 | |
| SS-C-540B | | Coal Tar (Cutback) Roof Coating, Brushing Consistency | 5610 | FSS | 11 Jun 75 | |
| SS-C-621B | | Concrete Masonry Units, Hollow (And Solid, Prefaced And Unglazed) | 5620 | FSS | 19 Jan 68 | |
| INT AMD 2 | | | | | 18 Jun 70 | |
| SS-C-635B | | Crayon Assortment, Drawing, Colored | 7510 | FSS | 7 Dec 66 | |
| SS-C-646B(2) | | Crayon, Marking, Lumber | 7510 | FSS | 31 Oct 63 | |
| SS-C-661A | | Crayon, Marking | 7510 | FSS | 11 Jan 74 | |
| SS-C-1783 | | Cloth, Asbestos | 5640 | FSS | 29 Mar 73 | |
| SS-C-1960/GEN | | Cement And Pozzolan (General Requirements For) | 5610 | YD | 2 Dec 75 | |
| SS-C-1960/1A | | Cement, Masonry | 5610 | YD | 24 May 77 | |
| | | | 5610 | YD | 28 Aug 78 | |
| SS-C-1960/3B | | Cement, Portland | 5610 | YD | 28 Aug 78 | |
| | | | 5610 | YD | 24 May 77 | |
| SS-C-1960/5A | | Pozzolan, For Use In Portland Cement Concrete | 5610 | YD | 28 Aug 78 | |
| SS-F-001032 | | Floor Covering, Asphaltic Felt (Bituminous Type Surface) | 7220 | FSS | 19 Oct 66 | |
| SS-G-659A | | Graphite, Dry (Lubricating) | 9620 | FSS | 1 Mar 67 | |
| SS-J-570B | | Joint Compounds And Tape, Wallboard (For Gypsum Wallboard Construction) | 5640 | FSS | 9 Aug 77 | |
| SS-L-300 | | Lath, And Board Products, Gypsum | 5640 | FSS | 27 Feb 74 | |

**FIGURE 6.2**   Federal Specifications index.

***Military specifications (Department of Defense).***   Military specifications, or *Mil-Specs* as they are often called, specify products that are usually unique to the needs of the military; however, in some rare cases such as certain electrical devices, they may be the only source of an appropriate material specification. Their use is generally discouraged in civil projects because of the difficulty in obtaining copies of the standards as well as the restricted availability of manufacturers who produce to these standards. Mil-Specs are characterized by designations such as "MIL-R-0039016A" for an electrical relay (Figure 6.3).

## UBC Standards

Although technically not a governmental agency, the UBC Standards, wherever referred to, are actually backed up by local ordinances, thus carrying the force of law. All cities and counties that have adopted the Uniform Building Code include the UBC Standards as a part of their requirements by virtue of the fact that they are covered by reference in the Uniform Building Code. The majority of UBC Standards are, in fact, other commercial standards that have been adopted as UBC Standards and renumbered. The UBC designations are characterized by the following type designation: "UBC Standard 26-1-91" for Portland Cement and Blended Hydraulic Cements. This standard is based upon ASTM Designation C150-94 and C 595-81a.

**ALPHABETICAL LISTING**

| TITLE | | DOCUMENT NUMBER | FSC | PREP | DATE | | CUSTODIAN | |
|---|---|---|---|---|---|---|---|---|
| Valves, Aircraft Hydraulic Shuttle | Q | MIL-V-5530B (4) | *1650 | 71 | 24 Mar 70 | AV | AS | 71 |
| Valves, Aircraft Hydraulic Unloading | Q | MIL-V-5519C (1) | 1650 | 71 | 05 Aug 64 | | | 71 |
| Valves, Aircraft Power Brake | | MIL-V-5525C | 1630 | AS | 21 Oct 59 | AV | AS | 11 |
| Valves, Aircraft, Hydraulic Pressure Relief, Type II Systems (Asg) | Q | MIL-V-8813 | *1650 | AS | 20 Nov 57 | | AS | 71 |
| Valves, Aircraft, Hydraulic Thermal Expansion Relief (Supersedes AN-V-28) | Q | MIL-V-5527A | 1650 | AS | 14 May 51 | | AS | 71 |
| Valves, Angle, Shut-off, Packed, Receiver, REFRIGERANT-12 | | MIL-V-22854A (1) | 4130 | GL | 30 Sep 68 | GL | YD | 82 |
| Valves, Astern (For Shipboard Use) | L | MIL-V-22682A (2) | 4820 | SH | 15 Aug 63 | | SH | |
| Valves, Ball | L | MIL-V-23611 | 4820 | YD | 19 Mar 63 | | YD | |
| Valves, Ball. Naval Shipboard, For Air, Nitrogen, Helium Or Hydraulic Service (Sizes 2-1/2 Inches I.p.s And Below) | Q | MIL-V-22687B (1) | 4820 | SH | 16 May 66 | | SH | |
| Valves, Blocking | L | MIL-V-21517D (3) | 1440 | OS | 17 Oct 63 | | OS | |
| Valves, Blow Off, Boiler | L | MIL-V-18406A | 4820 | YD | 11 Jan 68 | | YD | |
| Valves, Boiler Blow. Shipboard Use | L | MIL-V-17737D | 4820 | SH | 01 Feb 71 | | SH | |
| Valves, Check | | MIL-V-18436C | 4820 | YD | 30 Apr 70 | ME | YD | 82 |
| Valves, Check Swing. Cast-iron And Steel | | MIL-V-10386B (3) | 4820 | ME | 17 Feb 67 | ME | YD | 82 |
| Valves, Check, Controllable. Hydraulic, Aircraft, Type II Systems (Asg) | Q | MIL-V-19067A | 1650 | AS | 30 Apr 57 | | AS | 71 |
| Valves, Check, Oxygen, High Pressure (Asg) | Q | MIL-V-5027D | 1660 | AS | 12 Mar 68 | AV | AS | 71 |
| Valves, Combined Vent check For Submarine Mbt Blow Lines | QL | MIL-V-23953A (2) | 4820 | SH | 12 Feb 70 | | SH | |
| Valves, Compressor Service. REFRIGERANT-12 | | MIL-V-22862B | 4130 | GL | 30 Jul 68 | GL | YD | 82 |
| Valves, Control. Air Diaphragm-operated | L | MIL-V-18030C (1) | 4820 | SH | 26 Jan 70 | | SH | |
| Valves, Cylinder. Gas. Carbon Dioxide Fire Extinguisher | | QPL-17360-13 | 4210 | SH | 20 Nov 68 | | | |
| Valves, Diaphragm. Stop | L | MIL-V-82026 | 4820 | YD | 13 Jul 64 | | YD | |
| Valves, Expansion. Thermostatic, REFRIGERANT-12 | | MIL-V-23450 | 4130 | GL | 10 Jun 71 | GL | YD | 82 |
| Valves, Fuel Selector | | MIL-V-5018A (2) | 4530 | AS | 31 Oct 63 | MO | AS | 84 |
| Valves, Fuel Shutoff Solenoid Operated, 28 Volt, D c (Asg) | | MIL-V-8610A (1) | 2990 | 82 | 05 Nov 71 | | AS | 82 |
| Valves, Fuel Shutoff, Electric Motor Operated | | MIL-V-8608A (2) | 2915 | 11 | 09 Nov 66 | AV | AS | 11 |
| Valves, Gate. Bronze, 300 Psi | L | MIL-V-18827A | 4820 | YD | 15 Dec 71 | | YD | |
| Valves, Gate. Cast Or Forged Steel And Alloy Steel. Outside Screw And Yoke (Basically Commercial Valves) | Q | MIL-V-1811GD | 4820 | SH | 24 Jul 61 | MO | SH | 82 |
| Valves, Gate. Globe And Angle. Steel | | MIL-V-18434B | 4820 | YD | 28 May 71 | | YD | |
| Valves, Gate, Rising Stem. Double Acting Aluminum | | MIL-V-58039B | 4820 | ME | 20 Jun 66 | GL | MC | |
| Valves, Globe. Angle And Y. Flanged Bonnet, Manually Operated (Sizes 1-1/2 Inches And Below) | | MIL-V-22094B (1) | 4820 | SH | 3 Oct 61 | MO | SH | 82 |
| Valves, Globe, Angle, And Y. Cast Or Forged, Steel, And Alloy Steel, Outside Screw And Yoke (Sizes 2-1/2 Inches And Above) (Basically Commercial Valves) | Q | MIL-V-22052C (3) | 4820 | SH | 24 Aug 64 | | SH | |
| Valves, Globe, Angle, Quick Change Cartridge Trim, High Pressure (H.p.) Hydraulic And Pneumatic (Sizes 1/8 - 1 1/4 Inches) | QL | MIL-V-24109A | 4820 | SH | 31 Aug 71 | | SH | |

**FIGURE 6.3**   Index of Mil-Spec standards.

## Nongovernmental Standards

**ASTM (American Society for Testing and Materials).** These are by far the most recognized of all American standards. They cover not only materials specifications, but contain testing requirements and, in rare cases, some performance standards as well. The listings are characterized by designations such as "ASTM Designation C150-94," where the "94" denotes the year of the particular edition or revision of that particular standard (Figure 6.4). All ASTM standards are divided systematically into groupings with separate letter prefixes that enable a user to identify the type of material referred to from the number designation alone. The following is a complete listing of all current letter prefixes and the material categories to which they refer:

| | |
|---|---|
| A | Ferrous metals |
| B | Nonferrous metals |
| C | Cementitious, ceramic, concrete, and masonry materials |
| D | Miscellaneous materials |
| E | Miscellaneous subjects |
| F | Materials for specific applications |
| G | Corrosion, deterioration, and degradation of materials |
| ES | Emergency standards |

**FIGURE 6.4** Typical page from ASTM Index of Standards.

***ANSI (American National Standards Institute).*** This is perhaps the second most commonly known commercial and industrial standards organization. It is often mistaken for a governmental entity because of its name; however, it is a voluntary, nonprofit organization without any governmental connections whatever.

ANSI is a coordinating organization for a federated national standards system. The ANSI federation consists of 900 companies, large and small, and some 200 trade, technical, professional, labor, and consumer organizations. In cooperation with its councils, boards, and committees, ANSI coordinates the efforts of many organizations in the United States that are developing standards.

ANSI does not develop any standards of its own, but does provide means for determining the need for them and ensures that organizations competent to fill these needs undertake the standards-development work. Most of the standards listed by ANSI are developed by trade, technical, professional, consumer, and labor organizations. Each of these standards is then submitted to ANSI for recognition as a national consensus standard.

The system of standards identification used by ANSI prior to 1979 is no longer in use, and currently all ANSI standards are identified by the sponsor's own numbering system, prefixed by "ANSI" and the letters identifying the sponsoring agency (Figure 6.5).

Coal
    preparation plants, ANSI/NFPA 120
    pulverizers, ANSI/ASME PTC4.2
Coated abrasives—*see* Abrasives
Coating and dipping, ANSI/NFPA 34
Coatings
    organic, ANSI/NFPA 35; ANSI/UL 1332
    steel water pipelines, ANSI/AWWA C203
    underbody, surface vehicles, ANSI/SAE
        J671
    viscosity, ANSI/ASTM D3236
COBOL (programming language), ANSI
    X3.23, X3.23a
Codes
    bar, print quality, ANSI X3.182
    carriage positioning characters, ANSI
        X3.78
    communities in U.S., ANSI X3.47
    counties in U.S., ANSI X3.31
    dates, ANSI X3.30
    geographic point locations, ANSI T1.205,
        X3.61
    hydrologic units, ANSI X3.145
    input/output to microprocessors, ANSI
        X3.95
    ISO registration, ANSI X3.83
    keyboard arrangements, ANSI X3.114
    states in U.S., ANSI X3.38
    time, ANSI X3.51
    time of day, ANSI X3.43
    videotex/teletext, ANSI X3.110
    weights and measures, ANSI X3.50
Codes, ASCII
    character sets, ANSI X3.4, X3.41
    controls, ANSI X3.64
    graphic representation, ANSI X3.32
Coding, color
    identification, ANSI/EIA 359-A, 359-A-1
    physical hazards marking, ANSI Z535.1
    semiconductor devices, ANSI/EIA 236

Communication systems
    electric power stations, ANSI/IEEE 487
    inductive coordination, ANSI/IEEE 776
    interconnection circuitry, ANSI/NEMA SB3
    optical fiber, ANSI Z136.2
    transmitters, ANSI/IEEE 377
Communications, fire services, ANSI/NFPA
    1221
Compactors, surface vehicles, ANSI/SAE
    J1017, J1472
Compactors, waste, ANSI Z245.2
Components, surface-mount, ANSI/EIA 481-1
    NECQ system, ANSI/EIA 601
Composites
    insulators, ANSI/IEEE 987
    slabs, ANSI/ASCE 3
    structures (aerospace), ANSI/SAE ARP
        1643A
    welding rods, ANSI/AWS A5.21
Compressors, ANSI/ARI 510
    air, motor-operated, ANSI/UL 1450
    air systems, ANSI/ASME B19.1
    centrifugal, ANSI/API 617
    displacement, ANSI/ASME PTC9
    performance test code, ANSI/ASME
        PTC10
    process industries, ANSI/ASME B19.3
    refrigerant, ANSI/ARI 520, 530; ANSI/UL
        984
    trucks and buses, ANSI/SAE J1340
Computer automated measurement and
    control—*see* CAMAC
Computer graphics
    glossary of terminology, ANSI/IEEE 610.6
    graphical kernel system, Ada binding,
        ANSI X3.124.3
    graphical kernel system, FORTRAN
        binding, ANSI X3.124.1
    graphical kernel system, functional
        description, ANSI X3.124

Computers (aerospace) ECS program, ANSI/
    SAE ARP 1623A
    flight management systems, ANSI/SAE
        ARP 1570
    performance, ANSI/SAE AS 8002
COMTRADE, ANSI/IEEE C37.111
Concrete
    canal linings, ANSI/ASAE S289.1
    curing, ANSI/ACI 308
    heavyweight, selecting proportions, ANSI/
        ACI 2 11.1
    lightweight, selecting proportions, ANSI/
        ACI 211.2
    no-slump, selecting proportions, ANSI/ACI
        211.3
    reinforced, ANSI/ACI 315, 318, 318M
    structural, ANSI/ACI 301, 318.1, 318.IM
Concrete construction
    columns, ANSI/CRSI A38.1
    forms for joints, ANSI/CRSI A48.1
    forms for joists, ANSI/CRSI A48.2
    masonry, ANSI/ACI 531
    nuclear, ANSI/ACI 349
    safety requirements, ANSI A10.9, A10.9a
    tolerances, ANSI/ACI 117
Concrete pipe—*see* Pipe, concrete
Condensate removal devices, ANSI/ASME
    PTC39.1
Condensers, refrigerant, ANSI/ARI 490;
    ANSI/ASHRAE 22, 64
Conductors
    aluminum, wire connectors, ANSI/UL
        486B
    copper, wire connectors and soldering
        lugs, ANSI/UL 486A
    overhead, ANSI/IEEE 738
    self-damping measurements, ANSI/IEEE
        563
    underground, ANSI/UL 486D
    wiring terminals, ANSI/UL 486E

**FIGURE 6.5**   ANSI Index of Standards.

***AWWA (American Water Works Association).***   This is not as well known as ASTM or ANSI, except in the public works sector, where it has been the standard of the water industry. Its standards are broad, and many specify a single fabricated item, or an entire project feature, such as the designation "AWWA D100" [full designation is ANSI/AWWA D100-79(AWS-D5.2-79)] for the construction of welded steel elevated water tanks, standpipes, and reservoirs. AWWA publishes their data in several forms, including reference books, handbooks, manuals, standards, and periodicals and pamphlets, and some of their standards have also been adopted by ANSI, as in the example cited previously. As with the other standards organizations, a system of letter prefixes has been established for the orderly grouping of subject matter for easier recovery of data:

| | |
|---|---|
| A | Source |
| B | Treatment |
| C | Distribution |
| D | Storage |
| E | Pumping |

***ACI (American Concrete Institute).***   This possibly represents the most respected of concrete standards in the United States. Most of the ACI provisions have been adopted into all other codes and regulations, with minor changes. ACI is a nonprofit technical society. It is not industry-supported [its nearest industry supported counterpart is the Portland Cement Association (PCA)]. ACI publications are produced by standing committees, each of which is identified by a committee number. All publications are identified by a numbering system in which the ACI committee number forms the publication number, followed by the revision date. Thus committee 318 is the code committee, and each new revision of the ACI Building Code carries the same number 318, followed by the latest revision date.

There are numerous other standards that have not been mentioned, but the methods of identifying their publications are similar to the organizations already mentioned. The following is a partial list of other organizations that publish standards:

| | |
|---|---|
| AASHTO | American Association of State Highway and Transportation Officials |
| AISC | American Institute of Steel Construction |
| AISI | American Iron and Steel Institute |
| AITC | American Institute of Timber Construction |
| APA | American Plywood Association |
| ASHRAE | American Society of Heating, Refrigerating, and Air Conditioning Engineers |
| ASME | American Society of Mechanical Engineers |
| AWPA | American Wood Preservers Association |
| AWPI | American Wood Preservers Institute |
| AWS | American Welding Society |
| CRSI | Concrete Reinforcing Steel Institute |
| IES | Illuminating Engineering Society |
| NEMA | National Electrical Manufacturers Association |
| NFPA | National Fire Protection Association |

SSPC        Steel Structures Painting Council
UL          Underwriters' Laboratories, Inc.
WIC         Woodwork Institute of California
WRI         Wire Reinforcement Institute, Inc.

### Access to Special Standards by Resident Project Representative and Contractor

All too often the specifier cites publications and standards that are not in the normal field library of the Resident Project Representative or the contractor. Although there are companies specializing in the sale of copies of such documents in many major cities that serve the needs of the contractor, often the Resident Project Representative of the architect/engineer or owner is the only party in the field who has no access to such information, and thus is placed at a considerable disadvantage in the field. It is important to remember that if it is important enough to specify that an item must conform to a certain set of standards, it should be important enough to see that the field office obtains a copy of this standard—otherwise, why even bother with inspection? There are certain popular standards that may be excluded from this, as they are so widely used and well understood that only a manufacturer's certificate of conformance with the cited standard should suffice.

Some firms solve the problem in an ideal fashion. A volume of photocopies of all the cited standards in a specific project is compiled and furnished to the Resident Project Representative at the beginning of the job. In this manner, the information is always accessible in the field when needed.

## BUILDING CODES, REGULATIONS, ORDINANCES, AND PERMITS

Building codes have been adopted by most cities, counties, and states. They are adopted by each governmental entity by ordinance or other means at their disposal to impart the force of law behind them. The codes carefully regulate design, materials, and methods of construction, and compliance with all applicable code provisions is mandatory. Most of these codes are based in whole or in part on the various national codes that are sponsored by different national groups. Changes, where made in the parent code, have generally been to accommodate local needs and conditions and to make portions of the code more stringent than may have been provided for in the code as it was originally written.

There are, of course, many codes that are not based upon such national codes, but have been specifically written for a particular locality. Many large cities do this.

Although the Uniform Building Code is the basis for the majority of codes in use in the western states, there are several prominent codes in use throughout the United States that are equally important in the areas that they serve. Some of the more prominent codes are listed below:

1. *National Building Code:* compiled by the American Insurance Association; adopted in various localities across the country.
2. *Uniform Building Code:* compiled by the International Conference of Building Officials (ICBO); widely used in the western states.

3. *Basic Building Code:* compiled by the Building Officials and Code Administrators International (BOCA); used mainly in the eastern and north central states.

4. *Southern Standard Building Code:* compiled by the Southern Building Code Congress (SBCC); used in most southern and southeastern states.

5. *National Electric Code:* compiled by the National Fire Protection Association (NFPA); widely adopted in all parts of the country.

6. *National Plumbing Code:* compiled by the American Public Health Association and the American Society of Mechanical Engineers; used widely in all parts of the country.

7. *Uniform Plumbing Code:* compiled by the International Association of Plumbing and Mechanical Officials (IAPMO); widely used in the west.

8. *ICBO Plumbing Code:* compiled by the International Conference of Building Officials (ICBO); used principally in the western states.

9. *ICBO Uniform Mechanical Code:* compiled by the International Conference of Building Officials (ICBO) (mostly HVAC and gas piping) used principally in the western states.

Of particular importance to the inspector as well as the contractor is the edition date on the code. Even though a new code edition has been published, there can be no assurance that a particular jurisdiction will adopt it at any certain time, if at all. A case in point is a city that for years used an old edition of the Uniform Building Code, which it kept updated by adopting a series of city ordinances annually to meet the requirements of the local building official. Thus, in fact, it was a special code, and only by carefully studying the basic old code edition plus all ordinances adopted afterward could an inspector be aware of the conditions that affected his or her project in that jurisdiction. That particular city has since adopted a newer version of the Uniform Building Code, and the cycle must begin all over again.

In addition to the provisions of any applicable codes, the contractor is obligated to conform to the provisions of all permits issued by public agencies having jurisdiction. Many of these permits are several pages long, and resemble a small specification.

## Projects Subject to Control by More Than One Agency

Often a project will involve property or facilities that are under the jurisdiction of another public agency. If a pipeline project, for example, crossed an interstate freeway route, a flood control right-of-way, or the pipeline of another public agency or utility, the contractor could well be facing the prospect of having not only the regularly assigned resident inspector on the job, but a battery of other inspectors who represent each of the other affected agency properties. In each such case, a permit may be required from each affected agency, and the contractor would be bound not only by the terms of the contract documents for the project, but by the terms of each such permit as long as the work was in an area within the jurisdiction of the issuing agency. Whenever the pipeline mentioned crosses any of these other improvements, the requirements of the agency owning such improvement will usually

govern over the terms of the project specifications, unless their requirements are less stringent than those of the project specifications, in which case the affected agency may agree
to the project specification requirements in lieu of their own.

The basic authority in such cases still lies with the Resident Project Representative.
Inspectors representing any affected jurisdictional agencies should exercise their proper authority by working through the Resident Project Representative, and should not be instructed to communicate their requirements directly to the contractor.

## TYPES OF DRAWINGS COMPRISING
## THE CONSTRUCTION CONTRACT

The drawings or plans that were prepared especially for the project, generally referred to as
the *contract drawings*, are for the express purpose of delineating the architect or engineer's
intentions concerning the project that they have conceived and designed. The drawings normally show the arrangement, dimensions, geometry, construction details, materials, and
other information necessary for estimating and building the project.

Occasionally, *standard drawings* of public agencies are defined as being a part of the
contract documents. These drawings usually portray the repetitive details of certain types
of construction that may be required by the local public agency for all similar work in their
jurisdiction. A typical example is the design of drop inlet structures and other drainage
structures that have been standardized in each community throughout the years. Instead of
redrawing the same details over and over, the architect or engineer simply refers to a certain standard drawing of the jurisdictional agency involved.

*Shop drawings* are those details and sketches prepared by the contractor or the material suppliers or fabricators that are necessary to assure the fabricator that the basic concept
is acceptable before beginning costly fabrication. Shop drawings frequently contain information that is not related to the design concept, or information that is relative only to the
fabrication process or construction techniques in the field, all of which are outside the scope
of the duties and responsibilities of the architect or engineer. In approving shop drawings,
the architect or engineer only indicates that the items conform to the design *concept* of the
project and compliance with the plans and specifications prepared (see "Shop Drawings
and Samples" in this chapter). The contractor remains wholly responsible for dimensions
to be confirmed in the field, for information that pertains solely to the fabrication process
or to techniques of construction, and for coordination of the work of all the trades.

Change orders are issued to accompany a written agreement to modify, add to, or otherwise alter the work from that originally set forth in the contract drawings at the time of
opening bids. A change order is normally the only legal means available to change the contract provisions after the award of the contract, and normally requires the signature of the
owner.

Some confusion seems to accompany the use of the terms *record drawings* and *as-
built drawings.* Generally speaking, *record drawings* are a marked set of prints prepared by
the contractor or the Resident Project Representative in the field. Record drawings are contract drawing prints upon which the contractor or inspector records all variations between
the work as it was reported by the contractor as having been actually constructed and the

work as it was shown in the original contract drawings as they existed at the time the contract was awarded. All change orders should be reflected in appropriate marks on the record drawings. The term *as-built drawings* is unpopular because of some of the legal difficulties that have resulted in attempting to have the architect or engineer certify that a set of drawings truly represented the project "as built." If, some years later, an underground pipeline is struck because it was not at the location or depth indicated in the certified as-built drawings, the architect, or engineer could be the defendant in a civil action pressed by the one-time client.

## ORDER OF PRECEDENCE OF THE CONTRACT DOCUMENTS

Where a discrepancy exists between the various parts of the contract documents, legal precedent has established some degree of order. However, many General Conditions cite the specific order anyway so that a dispute may be settled without the need for interpretation or arbitration.

Although, if specified in the contract documents, a listing of order will govern, the general policy follows, in order of decreasing authority:

1. Agreement
2. Specifications
3. Drawings

For further discussion of this subject, see "Order of Precedence of Contract Documents" in Chapter 19.

## PROBLEMS

1. On most public works projects, if products are referred to by brand name, what additional phrase is required?
2. Is it still possible, under contracts involving separate inspections by other agencies having jurisdiction, to maintain the one-to-one relationship with the contractor?
3. What types of bonds are required to be provided by a bidder/contractor on a public works contract?
4. What happens when the terms of the Supplementary General Conditions are in conflict with the General Conditions?
5. Can the Supplementary General Conditions be used to modify the Agreement form?
6. Which of the following listed documents is the preferred location for specifying the amount of liquidated damages? Which document normally is used to specify the terms and conditions of the liquidated damages?

   Notice Inviting Bids

   Instructions to Bidders

Bid or Proposal

Agreement

General Conditions of the Contract

Supplementary General Conditions

Division 1 General Requirements

7. True or false? Changes on shop drawings are meant to supersede the original contract drawings.

8. Should an existing soils report be included as part of the contract documents?

9. Name the international (FIDIC) equivalent to the following terms commonly used in U.S. construction contracts:

Differing site conditions

Bid or Proposal

Changes in the Work

Date of Notice to Proceed

Addenda

Guarantee Period

Bid Schedule (unit price projects)

Schedule

Supplementary General Conditions

# 7

## Construction Laws and Labor Relations

### COMPLIANCE WITH LAWS AND REGULATIONS

As with most endeavors, the performance of construction contracts is regulated by law. The difference between construction and other enterprises seems to lie in the fact that there are more jurisdictional agencies involved, and thus more laws to contend with.

Simply stated, it can be said in general that these laws fall into four major categories:

1. Contract law—those laws and regulations that affect the making of contracts, both public and private.
2. Laws governing the execution of the work being performed under the contract—including the issuance and conformance to the conditions of the various permits, regulation, ordinances, and other requirements of the many jurisdictional agencies that are frequently involved.
3. Laws that relate to the settling of differences and disputes that may develop out of the performance of the contract.
4. Licensing laws that govern not only the business practices but also the personal qualifications standards of the various people involved in the construction process.

The latter include the licensing of architects and professional engineers in every state in the United States, as well as the licensing of contractors in many states, the licensing of construction managers in a few states, and the licensing of inspectors in some states. In addition to these licenses, all of which require the demonstration of proficiency by some type of examination, there are the local business licenses, permits to do business in certain areas, and sales tax permits that authorize the collection of sales tax by businesses.

**167**

Of the more common laws that are encountered on most projects are the following:

Americans with Disabilities Act (ADA) of 1990

Davis-Bacon Act requirements (for federal or federally funded projects)

OSHA and state safety requirements for industrial applications

OSHA and state safety requirements for construction

State Labor Code requirements

U.S. Department of Labor requirements, as applicable

State housing laws

Local building codes and ordinances

Sales and use tax regulations

Air pollution control laws

Noise abatement ordinances

Business licenses to conduct business in *each* locality

Mechanic's lien laws of the state

Unemployment insurance code requirements

Worker's compensation laws

Corps of Engineers and Coast Guard regulations for work in navigable waterways

Subletting and subcontracting laws

Licensing laws for architects, engineers, surveyors, contractors, and inspectors

Permits by special local agencies for construction, including building permits, grading permits, encroachment permits, street work permits, police permits for interrupting traffic, excavation permits, Environmental Protection Agency permits, special hauling permits, Department of Agriculture permits, and many others

Civil Rights Act of 1964 (federally assisted programs)

Civil Rights Act of 1991

All local city and county codes and ordinances

There are, of course, many others; but this list serves as a means of calling attention to the fact that a project cannot be built without regard for the regulations of the many jurisdictional agencies affected by the work. These include federal, state, county, city, special districts, including the many federal and state bureaus that have a legal interest in the effects of the proposed work on the area they have a legislative mandate to control, and all others who have a legitimate interest in the work that affects facilities or improvements over which they have legal jurisdiction and responsibility.

## PUBLIC VERSUS PRIVATE CONTRACTS

As a means of protecting the public interest in projects involving the expenditure of public funds, or the public administration of projects built with private funds but intended for public use, the majority of all public contracts are required to conform to the general laws governing the execution of public contracts in that state.

Although every contractor has a legal obligation to observe the law in the conduct of business, many state and federal regulations are required to be spelled out in the project documents, even though the failure to repeat their terms and conditions would not relieve the contractor of the responsibility to conform to their requirements.

Some of the significant differences between the requirements for public contracts and private projects can be noted by observing the following restrictions that apply to public contracts in most jurisdictions:

1. The Project must be publicly advertised.
2. Bids must be accompanied by a bid bond, usually 5 or 10 percent.
3. The Notice Inviting Bids must normally contain a list of prevailing wage rates for all crafts to be used in the work. If federal funds are involved, an additional listing of the federal wage rates must be published.
4. Insurance policies and bonds covering public liability and property damage are required.
5. In some jurisdictions, a list of all subcontractors who will perform work on the project must be listed and filed with the general contractor's bid.
6. Wherever a brand name product is specified, the specifications must give the names of the brand name products, *plus* the words "or equal."
7. A performance bond and a payment bond (for labor and materials) must be provided in the amounts specified by law.

Some states can be classified as *code states* because they regulate virtually everything by specific code provisions. In principle, only Louisiana's legal system was not based upon English common law. However, some states that were supposedly under common law principles have evolved into code states. California is a notable example. As it applies to construction contracts, public works is most heavily regulated in that state. It is fruitless to list all of the applicable code requirements in a book such as this, for as the author learned in a law course many years ago: "Learn where to find the law; do not attempt to memorize it, for otherwise, with one sweeping move, the legislature could repeal your entire education." When asked to draft front-end documents for a set of construction specifications, it is wise to seek a review of the documents by competent legal counsel; however, be certain that the attorney is a specialist in contract law, especially as it applies to construction.

### Limitations of Authority of a Public Agency

While the contract entered into between the contractor and the public agency responsible for a given public works project will generally define the relationship between them, it is also important for the parties to be aware of the limitations of the public agency's authority to enter into contracts in order to perform certain acts. As stated previously, a governmental agency has no power to enter into an act that it is not properly authorized to perform. Under certain circumstances, that fact can have a major impact on a contractor.

A public agency has only the ability to do what it has been granted the authority to do. Whatever a public agency wishes to do by way of a public works construction contract, it must be authorized to do under the laws of that particular jurisdiction. A public entity cannot act in excess of its jurisdiction, and any action taken by a public agency without the legal power to do so is without legal force and effect. In other words, a public agency can do only what the law allows or prescribes. The contractor, by knowing the particular laws that apply when dealing with a public agency, can use that knowledge to its advantage in order to force the public agency to do what is required by law.

The way that a limitation of authority can ultimately affect a contract is shown in the case of *Zottman* v. *The City and County of San Francisco* [(20 Cal. 96 (1862)]. In that case, the city of San Francisco properly entered into a valid contract with a contractor to make improvements to a certain town square. After the contract was entered into, the scope of the contract was changed by the city, and the contractor was ordered to do certain additional work. The contractor was paid for the contract work, but the city refused to pay for the extra work. The contractor then brought legal action against the city for payment. The court denied payment because the contract for extra work was not let to the lowest bidder after proper notification as required by law. The court also said that the acts of the city officials in demanding that the work be done did not ratify the contract for the extra work, as the city had no authority to make such a contract in the first place. While the court acknowledged that denying payment to the contractor that performed the work might be a hardship, the court found that the contractor was aware of the law and would suffer only what should have been anticipated. The city was allowed to retain the work without paying for it. According to later decisions, had the contractor received any payments for any portion of the extra work, the city would have been entitled to demand that the contractor return such progress payments to the city. The risks that a contractor takes in working with a public agency outside the law or in violation of the law can easily be seen.

## TRAFFIC REQUIREMENTS DURING CONSTRUCTION

Often the work on a project involves a degree of restriction on the local traffic in the project area. The contractor is obligated to get a permit from the local agency empowered to enforce traffic regulations whenever it becomes necessary to close a street or intersection, or to restrict its traffic. The terms and conditions of this permit will become a part of the contract provisions, and must be enforced. The inspector should take careful note of the specific restrictions, which are sometimes spelled out in the project specifications as well. Frequently, as in cases involving streets that handle rush-hour traffic, the traffic requirements may vary depending upon the time of day. The inspector should watch in particular for requirements that a flagger be provided and used by the contractor to direct traffic through restricted traffic lanes, and to be certain that the conduct of the flagger is in full accordance with the traffic requirements of the jurisdiction having control. Whenever there is only one lane of traffic open on a street that must provide two-way travel, a flagger or a detour route will generally be required. In general, the minimum number of lanes allowed during construction affecting a city street is one 3-m (10-ft) traffic lane *in each direction*. The inspector should watch for requirements that excavations be continually fenced or covered, as might be the case in the vicinity of schools; or that not less than a specified length of pipe trench be allowed open at any one time ahead and behind a pipelaying operation; or that the contractor be required to provide temporary "bridges" over excavations that might otherwise prevent safe access to businesses and residences in the vicinity of the work.

## CODE ENFORCEMENT AGENCY REQUIREMENTS

Whenever privately owned buildings are to be constructed, and frequently in the case of most public buildings or public works projects, the building code enforcement agency will be involved. In some jurisdictions, a public project built by another agency within the same jurisdiction enjoys immunity from the regulations imposed by another agency of the same government. Thus, a project constructed by that agency might apply its own rules to govern design and construction. Generally, however, it will be found that even the structures of agencies not obligated to conform to a sister agency's requirements will design in accordance with its code requirements and, in some cases, will even submit to its inspection requirements. If a permit fee is levied, however, it would simply be a paper transaction between departments.

Wherever the code enforcement agency has jurisdiction over a project under the Uniform Building Code, the provisions of Section 305(a) specify the conditions under which a project must be under the continuous inspection of a "special inspector" approved by the building official. In some jurisdictions, such approval is granted only after passing a written examination administered by the local department of building and safety. Where such programs are provided, even an architect or registered engineer may not be allowed to perform the inspections unless the building department's examination has been passed. In other jurisdictions, no formal program exists, and the process of "approval" of the inspector by the building official is an informal one, usually simply upon recommendation of the architect or registered engineer of record on the project.

A complete listing of all specialty areas that require the employment of a special inspector is found in Section 305 of the Uniform Building Code, and found in some other codes as well.

## WORK WITHIN OR ADJACENT TO NAVIGABLE WATERWAYS

It may not be frequent that an inspector will encounter a project subject to these requirements, but every now and then the inspector may be called upon to provide inspection of offshore construction as illustrated in Figure 7.1 or a project at a waterfront, such as where barge-mounted pile drivers or similar equipment may be used. On such work, some items that might not otherwise be thought of can be encountered.

For one thing, the contract documents should provide that the contractor must furnish, at the request of the design firm, the owner, or any inspector assigned to the work, suitable transportation from all points on shore designated by the design firm or owner to and

**FIGURE 7.1**    Example of offshore construction subject to Corps of Engineers' jurisdiction.

from all offshore construction. If these provisions are not in the specifications, they should be arranged for with the contractor at the preconstruction meeting.

As for the transportation of the contractor's personnel and equipment to offshore sites, it is the contractor's own responsibility to obtain boat launching facilities, or to make arrangements with local water carriers. The contractor is similarly obligated to avoid the creation of navigation hazards or interference in any way with navigation routes except upon special permit from the agencies having jurisdiction.

If a contractor, during the course of the work, throws overboard, sinks, or misplaces anything overboard that could be interpreted as a hazard to navigation, the contractor must be required to recover such items as soon as possible. The contractor's first requirement after such an incident is to give immediate notice to the inspector, along with a description and location of such obstructions. If necessary, the contractor may also be required to place a buoy or other mark at the location until recovery. It is an item that must be conducted at the contractor's sole cost and expense unless specifically provided otherwise in the contract. Liability for the removal of a *vessel* wrecked or sunk without fault or negligence of the contractor is limited to that provided in Sections 15, 19, and 20 of the Rivers and Harbors Act of March 3, 1899, which is still very much alive and enforced.

All work being constructed in or involving the use of "navigable waterways" is subject to the orders and regulations of the Department of the Army, Corps of Engineers, and to the U.S. Coast Guard as they apply to the construction operations affecting property or improvements within the jurisdiction of these agencies. The principal jurisdiction on all construction matters lies with the Corps of Engineers, whereas the Coast Guard is concerned primarily with the movement of vessels. The term *navigable waters* is much broader now than in previous years, and is administratively defined in *Permits for Activities in Navigable Waters or Ocean Waters* on page 31324 of the *Federal Register* of 25 July 1975.

In addition, the Federal Water Pollution Control Act amendments of 1972 (Public Law 92-500) requires a Corps of Engineers permit, under Section 404 of the act, for the discharge of any more than one cubic yard of dredged or fill material into any navigable waters. A word of caution—the list of waterways defined as navigable under this act is different from those defined in the Rivers and Harbors Act of 1899. Stripped of its regulatory language, the *404 Permit* as it is commonly referred to in the industry, states that whenever a party deposits more than 1 cubic yard of anything in, on, or encroaching on any portion of the historic high water line of any "navigable waterway," a Corps of Engineers 404 Permit is required. This, as interpreted by the District Engineer of one of the major Corps of Engineers Districts, includes portions of dry land that carried flood flows and to previous streambeds even where, after a flood, a stream followed a new watercourse after the flood. Take into account, also, that the lead time in obtaining a 404 Permit is at the very least several months. Generally, it is preferable to plan construction operations to avoid such encroachment entirely.

An owner or architect/engineer should take into account the potential delays in the work that could result from expecting the contractor to obtain this permit.

## FAIR SUBCONTRACTING LAWS

For work on public projects in some areas of the United States, laws have been enacted to protect subcontractors and the public against the practice of *bid shopping* or *bid peddling* by general contractors. Such laws were prompted by the realization that projects that had been subject to bid shopping practices often resulted in poor-quality material and workmanship to the detriment of the public, and because it deprived the public of the full benefits of fair competition among prime contractors and subcontractors, and in addition it led to insolvencies, loss of wages to employees, and other evils.

Generally, such laws provide that any bidder on a public project must list all subcontractors that the bidder intends to use on the work, whose work, labor, or services exceed a specified percentage of the prime contractor's total bid.

Under the provisions of such *fair subcontracting* laws, if the general contractor fails to list a subcontractor for any portion of the work, the general contractor must perform all such work itself.

It is the Resident Project Representative's responsibility when construction begins to check carefully the identity of all subcontractors on projects subject to such laws to ensure that their provisions have not been violated. This may have to be monitored at intermittent intervals to assure compliance at all times.

## THE HAZARDOUS WASTE PROBLEM

Hazardous waste management practices are influenced and, in many cases, controlled by a number of environmental laws and regulations. As the direct result of damage to life and the environment through mismanagement of hazardous wastes, Congress, in 1976, enacted Subtitle C of the Resource Conservation and Recovery Act (RCRA), which imposed controls on the management of hazardous wastes.

Each state is encouraged to develop its own program, following the EPA's guidelines. The major provisions under RCRA for controlling hazardous waste are:

1. Definition of hazardous waste
2. A system to track hazardous waste from its generation to its point of final disposal
3. Standards for generators and transporters of hazardous waste
4. Permit requirements for facilities that treat, store, or dispose of hazardous waste
5. Requirements for state hazardous waste programs

The subject of hazardous wastes has become a sensitive construction issue, as owners are coming under fire to provide full disclosure of hazardous materials that a contractor may come into contact with in the course of construction of a project, and specify the means and methods for disposal of such wastes.

Contract wordings are varied, as it is a relatively new untested area of risk for a construction contractor and project owner. In California, one of the states that did develop its own program within the guidelines of the EPA, any public works project of a local public entity which involves digging trenches or other excavations that extend deeper than 4 ft below the surface *must* contain the following clause in the contract documents:

a. In any public works contract which involves digging of trenches or other excavations that extend deeper than four feet below the surface, the Contractor shall promptly, and before the following conditions are disturbed, notify the public entity, in writing, of any:

1. Material that the Contractor believes may be material that is hazardous waste, as defined in Section 25117 of the California Health and Safety Code, that is required to be removed to a Class I, Class II, or Class III disposal site in accordance with the provisions of existing law.

2. Subsurface or latent physical conditions at the site differing from those indicated.

3. Unknown physical conditions at the site of any unusual nature, different materially from those ordinarily encountered and generally recognized as inherent in work of the character provided for in the Contract.

b. The public entity shall promptly investigate the conditions, and if it finds that the conditions do materially so differ, or do involve hazardous waste, and cause a decrease or increase in the Contractor's cost of, or the time required for, performance of any part of the Work shall issue a Change Order under the procedures described in the Contract.

c. That, in the event that a dispute arises between the public entity and the Contractor whether the conditions materially differ, or involve hazardous waste, or cause a decrease or increase in the Contractor's cost of, or the time required for, performance of any part of the Work, the Contractor shall not be excused from any scheduled completion date provided for by the Contract, but shall proceed with all work to be performed under the Contract. The Contractor shall retain any and all rights provided either by Contract or by law which pertain to the resolution of disputes and protests between the contracting parties.

In addition, the California Department of Transportation (Caltrans) prescribes a construction hazardous waste contingency plan (Figure 7.2) for the orderly handling of unknown wastes discovered during construction. Although the foregoing applies only to California public works, similar requirements exist in other jurisdictions.

## FEDERAL LABOR LAWS

### Labor–Management Relations Laws

The history of federal labor laws goes back to 1890, when the Sherman Anti-Trust Act was enacted. This provided the statutory beginnings for labor management legal policy. Although it is debatable whether the act was ever intended to apply to labor unions, a Supreme Court decision in 1908 ruled that the labor unions were indeed covered by the act.

During the intervening years, Congress passed other labor-related laws that more clearly outline federal labor policy. Today's labor policy is the outcome of the combined provisions of the Norris-LaGuardia Act of 1932 (Anti-Injunction Act), the National Labor Relations Act of 1935 (Wagner Act), the Labor Management Relations Act of 1947 (Taft-Hartley Act), and the Labor Management Reporting and Disclosure Act of 1959 (Landrum-Griffin Act).

### Equal Employment Opportunity Laws

In recent years, many of the federal labor laws have been aimed at eliminating discrimination in employment for any cause, such as age, sex, race, religion, or nationality. The first of these was the *Civil Rights Act of 1964,* in which Congress confirmed and established certain basic individual rights with regard to voting; access to public accommodations, public facilities, and public education; participation in federally assisted programs; and opportunities for employment. Administration is handled through the Equal Employment Opportunity Commission (EEOC) that was created by the act. Under this act it is unlawful for any employer to refuse to hire or to discharge any individual or otherwise discriminate against him or her with regard to conditions of employment because of race, color, religion, sex, or national origin.

**FIGURE 7.2** Construction hazardous waste contingency plan

In 1965, the President issued *Executive Order 11246,* which applies to contracts and subcontracts exceeding $10,000 on federal and federally funded construction projects. Under this executive order, the contractors not only are prohibited from discrimination but also must take positive action to see that applicants are employed and that employees are treated during their employment without discrimination. Originally limited to discrimination based upon race, creed, color, or national origin, it was supplemented in 1968 by *Executive Order 11375,* which prohibits discrimination in employment based upon sex in all federal and federally funded contracts. Any contractor who fails to conform may be barred from future contracts involving federal funds, the present contract can be canceled or suspended, and the OFCC has the additional power to withhold progress payments from contractors who appear to be in violation.

In 1967, the *Age Discrimination in Employment Act* was passed. This act prohibits arbitrary age discrimination in employment. The act protects persons 40 to 65 years old from age discrimination by all employers of 25 or more persons in an industry affecting interstate commerce. Employment agencies and labor organizations are also covered. The prohibitions against age discrimination do not apply when age is a valid occupational qualification, when differentiation is based upon reasonable factors other than age, when differentiation is caused by the terms of a valid seniority system or employee benefit plan, or when the discharge or discipline of the individual is for good cause.

## Americans with Disabilities Act

The *Americans with Disabilities Act* (ADA) of 1990 is a federal ban on disability-based employment discrimination (both physical and mental disabilities) covering all but the smallest employers. Insofar as the Act applies to employers, it applies to all employers with 15 or more employees. It is enforced by the Equal Employment Opportunity Commission (EEOC). Enforcement is through use of the Civil Rights Act of 1964 powers, remedies, and enforcement procedures.

Basically, the ADA makes it unlawful to discriminate against a qualified individual with a disability. A "disability" is defined in the Act, along with exclusions.

Because of the publicity accorded the ADA, it is highly likely that its provisions will be vigorously enforced, along with a significant increase in litigation.

## Wage and Hour Laws

The *Davis-Bacon Act* of 1931, as subsequently amended, is a federal law that determines the minimum wage rates and fringe benefits that must be paid to all workers on all federal and federally assisted projects. The law applies to all projects over $2000, and it states that the wages of the workers must not be less than the wage rates specified in the schedule of prevailing rates of wages as determined by the Secretary of Labor for similar work on similar projects in the vicinity in which the work is to be performed. Under its terms, the contractor is required to pay once a week to all workers employed directly on the site of the work, at wages no lower than those prescribed. The federal minimum wage rates are currently published every Friday in the *Federal Register,* and all changes are reflected in the various trades and areas of the United States.

As passed in 1934, the *Copeland Act* (Anti-Kickback Law) forbids an employer to deprive any employee on a federal or federally assisted construction job of any portion of the compensation to which that employee is entitled under federal law. Other than deductions provided by law, the employer may not require kickbacks from its employees. Violation may be punished by fine, imprisonment, or both. The Copeland Act applies to all projects on which the Davis-Bacon prevailing wage law applies.

The Fair Labor Standards Act, usually known as the *Wage and Hour Law,* was enacted by Congress in 1938 and has since been amended several times. The act contains provisions governing minimum wage, maximum hours, overtime pay, equal pay, and child labor standards. An employer who violates the wage and hour requirements is liable to his employees for double the unpaid minimum wages or overtime compensation, plus associated court costs and attorneys' fees. Willful violation is a criminal act and may be prosecuted as such. Several classes of employees are exempted from coverage under the act, such as executive, administrative, and professional employees who meet certain tests established for exemption.

The Fair Labor Standards Act, as amended by the *Equal Pay Act of 1963,* provides that an employer may not discriminate on the basis of sex by paying employees of one sex at rates lower than he or she pays employees of the other sex for doing equal work on jobs requiring comparable skill, effort, and responsibility and performed under similar working conditions.

The basic minimum age for employment covered by the act is 16 years, except for occupations declared to be hazardous by the Secretary of Labor, to which an 18-year age minimum applies. Construction, as such, is not designated as hazardous, although some of its specific work assignments are designated as such by name.

The *Contract Work Hours and Safety Standards Act* passed by Congress in 1962 (Work Hours Act of 1962), which has since been amended, applies to federal construction projects and to federally assisted projects. It does not apply if the federal assistance involved is in the form of a loan guarantee or insurance. Its main requirement is that workers be paid not less than $1\frac{1}{2}$ times the basic rate for all hours worked in excess of 8 hours per day *or* 40 hours per week.

## The National Apprenticeship Act

In 1937, Congress passed the National Apprenticeship Act. One of its prime objectives was to promote cooperation between management and organized labor in the development of apprenticeship programs. Traditionally, apprenticeship programs have been a joint effort between union-shop contractors and the AFL-CIO building trades unions. However, in 1971, the Bureau of Apprenticeship and Training approved national apprenticeship standards for the employees of open-shop contractors. This was the first time a unilateral apprenticeship program was approved on a national basis and placed under the direct supervision of employers only.

### Ethnic Minorities and Women in Construction

Affirmative action to increase participation of women and ethnic minorities in the construction force came about with the Public Works Employment Act of 1977, which made available $4 billion of federal subsidies for construction projects through local governments, but required that at least 10 percent of the work be awarded to ethnic minority companies, subcontractors, subcraftsmen, or suppliers. When bidding on a project involving such funds, the contractor must be aware of what is required to comply with the Equal Employment Opportunity (EEO) and Minority Business Enterprise (MBE) provisions. In many circumstances, a woman-owner business qualifies as an MBE.

While a history and full explanation of the effect of affirmative action programs such as these on construction is beyond the scope of this book, it is sufficient to say that bidding on many projects depends upon complete compliance with all such requirements. Particular attention should be paid to the sources of funding being used on any project to ensure that the contractor is aware of any such program requirements. If they are applicable, a contractor must scrupulously comply with every requirement in order to prepare a responsive bid and to stand a chance of being awarded the contract. Remember the Golden Rule: "He who has the gold make the rules." Thus, the source of construction funds is an important issue to the bidder.

### Worker's Compensation and Employer Liability Insurance

The contractor's Comprehensive General Liability Insurance policy normally excludes coverage of any liability incurred under state Worker's Compensation laws. The laws of every state require employers to be responsible for the payment of compensation benefits to employees who sustain job-related illnesses or injuries. Contractors normally finance such payments through the purchase of Worker's Compensation Insurance. Under Worker Compensation schemes, the insurance carrier then pays benefits to an injured employee at rates set by state law.

Very often Worker's Compensation Insurance is the most expensive type of insurance that a contractor must secure. There are numerous reasons for the high cost: the hazardous nature of construction work in general and the many job-related accidents that occur, long duration of payments, the statewide nature of Worker's Compensation programs, the pro-claimants on the Worker's Compensation boards, and the ease and simplicity of filing a claim.

While some states require contractors to purchase Worker's Compensation Insurance from state-administered insurance trust funds, contractors in most other states are free to purchase such insurance from private insurance carriers. There are significant variations in the administration and levels of benefits paid out from state to state that can pose a problem for contractors doing business in more than one state. When a contractor *does* have operations in more than one state, private carriers often provide "all states" endorsement to cover the contractor for every state listed in the policy. To ensure continued Worker's Compensation Insurance coverage, the contractor must supply updated information to the carrier, as required.

The costs of premiums for Worker's Compensation Insurance vary greatly, as they are geared in part to the contractor's safety record. If a contractor has a good record of job site safety, it will pay very small premiums in comparison to those paid by a contractor with a consistent loss record. The opportunity for a safety-minded contractor with a good job site safety record to save money on reduced premiums is significant. When purchasing such insurance, a contractor should seek a policy from a carrier that will provide comprehensive loss prevention services as well as standard claim services.

## LABOR RELATIONS

The involvement of the Resident Project Representative in the labor relations for a project is seldom extensive. In most cases, the Resident Project Representative plays the part of an impartial observer, able to enjoy the advantage of being close to the work and feel the undercurrents operating there. Because of this closeness, the Resident Project Representative can be invaluable to the owner and the design firm as a barometer of on-site labor conditions. If employed on a construction management contract, this insight may be of even greater value, as the construction manager may be directly involved in the labor relations processes on the project.

One of the most important rules for the inspector to follow is to remain in an observer category only. No opinions should be expressed at the site with anyone except the project manager, and then only while in confidence. Neither should the Resident Project Representative or other inspector take sides on any labor issue, or even express any sympathy for either side of a potential controversy.

All direct relations of the resident inspector on the job are to be conducted through the foremen and superintendents only, with the one possible exception of the emergency handling of an "Imminent Hazard," defined in Chapter 8.

The resident inspector, although not expected to take part in labor negotiations, may be called upon to confirm that the contractors and their labor forces are in conformance with both the contract provisions and the labor laws of the state and federal governments.

### Construction Unions

The labor union movement is deeply involved in the construction industry. There is no denying that their contribution has been an important one. They have had a stabilizing influence on what is a potentially unstable industry, although this is viewed as having both its good and its bad points. The unions do provide direct access to a pool of skilled and experienced labor from which a contractor can draw, as his or her needs require, and through the medium of negotiated labor contracts, fixed wage levels have been established, thus serving the dual purpose of upholding the living standard for the labor force as well as providing added stability to the bids of the contractor by eliminating the labor rates as a competitive bid item. The unions also help by maintaining discipline among their membership as well as setting achievement standards for the different skill levels.

## Contractor–Employee Relationships

Since the advent of the large labor union in the construction industry, the old personal relationships that formerly existed between an employer and employees are all but gone. Loyalties of a building tradesman are now largely to the union, which handles all of the employee's business relationships on a scale well beyond the confines of a single employer's shop. Thus, the rates of pay, holidays, overtime, and other employment conditions are not negotiated with the employee himself or herself, but with the union business agents. Thus, each employee is bound by the terms of the resultant labor contract just as the contractor is.

As a result of such relationships, the employees are not generally "company minded," but feel that they owe their allegiance to their respective unions, instead. Even their social lives are intertwined with their unions. In a manner of speaking, it could be said that the tradesmen are employees of a single large employer—their union—who contracts with various contractors to provide their services. The paternalistic attitude of the unions to their members through the retirement benefits and similar allowances seems further to bear this out.

## Collective Bargaining in Labor Relations

Under the provisions of the National Labor Relations Act, both management and labor are required to bargain in good faith. This does not necessarily mean that concessions must be made or that the two sides even agree, for that matter—just that they bargain in good faith.

Lack of good faith on the part of a contractor could be interpreted from ignoring a bargaining request, failure to appoint a bargaining representative with power to reach an agreement, attempts to deal directly with employees during negotiations, refusal to consider proposals, failure to respond with counterproposals, antiunion activities, or refusal to sign an agreement.

Although some contractors bargain with unions independently by dealing directly with them, the most prevalent form of labor negotiations in the construction industry is for contractor associations to bargain with the unions for all of the members of the association. In this manner, the contractor has greater bargaining power than as an individual. Local associations of general contractors generally bargain with the locals of the basic trades: the carpenters, cement masons, laborers, operating engineers, and construction teamsters. In some areas, iron workers are also included. The basic trades may bargain either as individual locals or as a group of locals affiliated with the same international union, or even through groups of locals of different unions such as building trades councils. The resulting labor agreements are generally referred to as *Master Labor Agreements*. The resulting agreements apply only within the jurisdiction of the union locals involved, and then only to the extent of the particular trades involved.

## Administration of the Union Contract

The matter of union–contractor labor relations is not closed simply because a labor agreement has been reached, however. There is still the matter of administering the labor contract and assuring that all its provisions are being met. Any project is likely to have some disputes or disagreements between either the union and the contractor, or between two unions representing different crafts. The labor agreements typically contain procedures for the settlement of such disputes. When a dispute occurs that cannot be resolved by a conference of the steward, business agent, superintendent, and any other party directly involved, the grievance procedure set forth in the agreement is followed. This procedure generally forces the matter up to progressively higher echelons of the contractor and the union, during which time no work stoppage is supposed to occur. If the matter cannot be resolved, arbitration of the matter may or may not be provided for in the labor agreement. Generally, the unions have resisted the concept of binding arbitration; however, there is a greater tendency now to provide for arbitration as a means of resolving or settling contract disputes without resort to work stoppages.

## PREJOB LABOR AGREEMENTS

On some projects where special employment conditions exist, and where the project is large enough to justify the procedure, a prejob conference is held with the local labor officials to establish standard conditions for field operations for the life of a particular project. The intended purpose is to establish a meeting of minds between the contractor and the unions involved regarding job conditions of employment, work rules, or jurisdictional responsibilities. In a project located in a remote area, for example, the contractor is interested in running the job in as economical a manner as possible, whereas the unions want fair labor standards to be maintained. The locals having jurisdiction must be checked to see that they have enough people available to do the job. If not, arrangements must be made to bring workers in from the outside, either by the union local or by the contractor. Although some contractors are tempted to resist prejob labor conferences on the grounds that the unions will be tempted to make exorbitant demands, most available evidence seems to indicate that the unions are more reasonable at this stage because they do not feel that the contractor is trying to hide anything. On one project in which the author was involved, such cooperation with the local building trades council allowed an open-shop condition to exist at a federal project, involving both union subcontractors and nonunion subcontractors on the same project, thus preserving the jobs of the members of an otherwise economically depressed community. Through an agreement involving mutual understanding of the various problems involved, no union member of the community with the skills necessary for this particular project was deprived of a livelihood as a result of the agreement, and thus the purposes of the owner, the contractor, and the labor force were realized.

### Open-Shop Contracting

Open-shop contracting, so called because it is unhampered by union agreements or representation, has suffered more than its share of troubles in its lifetime. In recent years, however, it appears to have made rapid and possibly lasting strides to where it is now established as a fact of life in the labor market. There is a strong movement by many smaller contractors and subcontractors to embrace the open-shop concept, and it is estimated that close to 40 percent of the annual construction volume is now done by nonunion contractors. In recent years, even some of the larger contractors have gone nonunion.

Contrary to the first impression usually received, open-shop contractors are not necessarily anti-union. Although they do usually pay somewhat less than the union scale, the average nonunion worker is provided with full-time employment instead of working by the job. Thus, the income comes closer to being a guaranteed annual income, and as such often exceeds that of union counterparts. The fringe benefits of most of the companies are similar to those paid by union contractors. This does not mean that none of an open shop's employees are union members. Many such shops have a mixture of union and nonunion help. One of the basic rights an open-shop contractor stands for is the right of the contractor to decide on the size of his work crews and to what job a worker may be assigned. Similarly, they are free to use prefabricated materials and are not subject to jurisdictional disputes, featherbedding, forced overtime, and work slowdowns. Workers are paid according to their work and performance. If, however, an open-shop contractor bids a federal job subject to the Davis-Bacon Act, the employees must be paid the same minimum wage rates published in the Federal Wage Rate Determination, and the bids will have to be computed accordingly. Thus, competing in some markets for a project may be difficult. If a federal job is won, however, there is nothing in the federal law to prohibit an open-shop contractor from being awarded a contract.

## PROBLEMS

1. If a contractor entered in contract with a public agency to construct a pipeline from points A to B, then later decides to construct a pump station at one end of the pipeline, may this be done with a change order or must it be separately advertised for bid under separate contract?

2. If in the project in question 1 the public agency, instead of building the pump station, decides to reroute the pipeline, but still run it between points A and B, may this be done with a change order?

3. What is the purpose of a payment bond in a construction contract?

4. What is the purpose of requiring a bid bond on a public contract?

5. What is the usual criterion that governs selection of the successful bidder in a public works contract?

6. True or false? Within those jurisdictions where public contracts are subject to "Fair Subcontracting Laws" to prevent bid shopping, each bidder is required to list its subcontractors as a part of its bid.

7. On a public contract covered under state laws regulating the payment of prevailing wages to all workers, what will be the effect if federal grant funds are involved in the project?

8. Every state in the United States with the exception of Louisiana and every province in Canada with the exception of Quebec is based upon English Common Law. What is the basis of law for Louisiana and Quebec?

9. True or false? A public agency can do only that which the law allows or prescribes.

10. Executive Order 11375 prohibits discrimination in employment based upon sex on all federal and federally funded contracts. If a contractor fails to conform, what are the remedies open to the agency?

# 8

## Construction Safety

**A**s mentioned in Chapter 4, the contractors have the prime responsibility for construction safety; however, there are certain areas of concern for construction safety that the Resident Project Representative should not ignore. The degree of the inspector's involvement is, to some extent, influenced by the specific terms of the construction contract, but some recent court decisions point out the need for concern by the inspector on the job.

In the Illinois case of *Miller* v. *DeWitt* (37 Ill. 2d 273, 226 N.E. 2d 630), where a steel roof had to be shored up while construction took place beneath it, the roof fell and injured a worker. In this case, the court stated: "As a general rule it has been said that the general duty to 'supervise the work' merely creates a duty to see that the building when constructed meets the plans and specifications contracted for." Thus, the court said, under ordinary circumstances, the architect would not be regarded as a person in charge of the work. But in the *DeWitt* case, the courts added that despite the argument of the architects that the shoring was "a method or technique of construction over which they had no control, we believe that under the terms of the contracts the architects had the right to interfere and even stop the work if the contractor began to shore in an unsafe and hazardous manner."

In the New York State case of *Clinton* v. *Boehm* (124 N.Y.S. 789), it was ruled that the architect owed no duty to the workers to supervise the contractor's methods to assure the workers' safety, and in 1960 the rule was again upheld [*Olsen* v. *Chase Manhattan Bank,* 175 N.E.2d 350]; however, this rule was seriously challenged in Arkansas in 1960 when the court said that the "supervising" architect who saw that an excavation wall was badly shored had a duty to the workers to *stop the work* to make repairs and that failure to do so made the architect liable for the death of three workers in a cave-in [*Erhart* v. *Hummonds,* 334 S.W. 2d 869].

In southern California, an unsupported wall of a 4.26-m (4-ft) deep trench caved in, resulting in the death of a laborer who was in the trench at the time. The project was a large residential development involving separate construction contracts not only for the various types of structures being built, but also for underground pipelines for water and sewer. An inspector was assigned to the entire project to monitor the progress of several of the different contracts then under construction. One of these projects involved a large underground sewer main, and it was on this project that the disaster occurred. It was reported that the inspector had observed in unshored trench prior to the accident and knew that workers were in the unshored trench. The widow of the deceased worker filed suit, and in the resulting decision, the court held that the excavation contractor had contributed to the accident through negligence, but also held that the engineer's office must share the responsibility. In the view of the court, the engineer had an inspector on the job during construction and although the inspector saw the contractor's employee "descend into the trench, he voiced no objection" [*Widman v. Rossmoor Sanitation, Inc.*, 1965–70, 97 Cal. Rptr. 52].

Both the Arkansas and the California cases seem to support the proposition that an architect/engineer who has knowledge of a safety problem has a duty to the workers to prevent harm to them. Without the knowledge of a safety hazard, it appears that the architect/engineer has no such duty to them. Thus, if a design or construction management firm has a contract for construction management or continuous inspection, as might be the case where a Resident Project Representative is employed, there would seem to be no way of pretending no knowledge of such conditions.

Thus, judging by the preceding examples of the inspector's involvement simply due to his or her presence on the project, it can be seen that the inspector has an important involvement in construction safety hazards that pose a threat to life or health. It is of particular note that the case just mentioned involved an inspector who was providing only *part-time* inspection on that particular project. It is from cases such as the one just mentioned that policies have been adopted by many agencies, both public and private, that spell out the obligations of an inspector with regard to personal knowledge of safety hazards on the job.

## OSHA AND CONSTRUCTION SAFETY

In 1970 Congress found that personal injuries and illnesses arising out of work situations imposed a substantial burden upon, and were a hindrance to, interstate commerce in terms of lost production, wage loss, medical expenses, and disability compensation payments. Consequently Congress passed the Williams-Steiger Occupational Safety and Health Act of 1970 (OSHA) [Title 29 USC 451, et seq.]. With the passing of the Act, the federal government imposed nationwide safety standards on the construction industry. Under the Act, each of the states was allowed to pass its own version of OSHA, as long as the state's plan was at least as strict as the federal standards. OSHA imposes strict employee safety and health standards to protect covered employees and enforces the same provisions for inspections, investigations, record-keeping requirements, and enforcement procedures. Under OSHA, logs of accidents as well as supplementary information and inspection may be involved.

If a state exercises its right under the Act to enact a safety plan at least equivalent to the federal OSHA regulations, it retains the right to be the sole safety enforcement agency within that jurisdiction. If a state does not come up with such a plan, construction in that state will be subject to inspection by federal safety inspection agencies as well as state inspection agencies.

The Act established the Occupational Safety and Health Administration, U.S. Department of Labor, Washington, DC 20210. Regional offices are found in various cities throughout the country. OSHA is responsible for the establishment of safety and health standards and for the rules and regulations to implement them. Such rules and regulations are published in the *Federal Register* and can be obtained from local OSHA offices or federal bookstores. *OSHA Safety and Health Standards,* Code of Federal Regulations, Title 29, Part 1910, contains regulations relating to the safety features to be included by the agency or architect/engineer in the design of any project. *Construction Safety and Health Regulations,* Code of Federal Regulations, Part 1926, pertain specifically to construction work.

It was OSHA's intent in preparing Part 1926 to place in one volume all of the rules and regulations applicable specifically to construction work. It is suggested that each of the contractor's superintendents, foremen, or other supervisors have a copy for reference. To the extent that Part 1926 contains standards that are incorporated by reference, copies of applicable referenced material should be made available to the supervisors for reference as well.

In order to ensure compliance with applicable regulations, contractors should assemble copies of the pertinent regulations that are incorporated by reference, as they relate to those regulations that apply to the specific project under construction. OSHA documents can be inspected at OSHA in Washington or at any of their regional or field offices.

The Act deals with all working conditions and includes the following broad categories:

General Safety and Health Provisions
Occupational Health and Environmental Controls
Personal Protective and Life Saving Equipment
Fire Protection and Prevention
Signs, Signals, Barricades
Materials Handling, Storage, Use, and Disposal
Tools—Hand and Power
Welding and Cutting
Electrical
Ladders and Scaffolding
Floors and Wall Openings and Stairways
Cranes, Derricks, Hoists, Elevators, and Conveyors
Motor Vehicles, Mechanized Equipment, and Marine Operations Excavations, Trenching, and Shoring
Concrete, Concrete Forms, and Shoring
Steel Erection
Tunnels and Shafts, Caissons, Cofferdams, and Compressed Air

Demolition

Blasting and Use of Explosives

Power Transmission and Distribution

Rollover Protective Structures; Overhead Protection

Recording and Reporting Work Injury Frequency and Severity Data and Accident Cost

These categories are further divided into sections listing specific requirements, including the posting of certain notices that projects are covered by the law and submittal of certain data within the time limits on standardized forms.

## GENERAL RESPONSIBILITY FOR CONSTRUCTION SAFETY

Construction sites can be considered as being one of the most hazardous types of working environments in the nation. In order to assure an accident-free environment, an accident prevention program aggressively supported by the management of the responsible organizations is essential.

The foremost area of critical concern is the relationship among the general contractor and its subcontractors. Regardless of the legal responsibility of the general contracting firm or its counterpart for a project, each subcontractor also has the legal obligation to assure the health and safety of its own employees. Each subcontractor, as well as the general contractor, will be held liable by OSHA if they allow their employees to be exposed to hazards that could cause serious physical harm or death. Of course, there will be those subcontractors who (1) do not require their workers to follow safety and health regulations; (2) do not provide personal protective equipment; and (3) permit the use of unsafe equipment. In general, these individuals consciously choose to ignore recognized safety and health standards. Prime contractors and construction managers should be acutely aware of this problem and should include a safety and health requirement in their own contracts with subcontractors.

## SAFETY RESPONSIBILITY UNDER CONSTRUCTION MANAGEMENT AND TURNKEY CONTRACTS

Although the Resident Project Representative is often spared the more detailed responsibilities of the general contractor and subcontractors in assuring safe working conditions at a construction site, there are two types of contracts for construction in which the Resident Project Representative may well be as involved in matters involving on-site construction safety as a general contractor under a conventional contract:

1. Professional Construction Management (PCM) contracts, depending on the specific contract provisions and scope of responsibility at the site.
2. Design–build and turnkey construction contracts.

### Professional Construction Management Contracts

Under a Professional Construction Management (PCM) contract, the Resident Project Representative's responsibilities are extremely difficult to define, as they may vary widely from one firm to the next. There is no way of determining the exact limits of such responsibility under a PCM contract, as the specific scope and terms governing such arrangements vary significantly (see Chapter 1 for further details on PCM responsibilities). In many cases, however, the PCM firm can incur obligations and responsibilities that were previously reserved to the general contractor.

Where multiple prime contracts are being managed, as in fast-track construction, the PCM functions are very similar to those of a general contractor and the PCM might do well to include the following items in each of the various separate construction contracts:

1. All unsafe or unhealthy conditions observed should be reported to the Resident Project Representative so that immediate corrective action can be initiated.
2. Compliance with all applicable safety and health laws, codes, ordinances, and regulations should be made mandatory.
3. Recognized safety and health work practices should be made mandatory.
4. Safety equipment should be inspected regularly and should be properly maintained.
5. The PCM or design–build/turnkey contractor should reserve the right to approve all conditions and practices.
6. In his or her own best interests, the PCM or design–build/turnkey contractor should require that an ongoing accident prevention program be implemented at the work site by each contractor and subcontractor.
7. Each contractor and subcontractor should be required to properly maintain all necessary personal protective equipment.
8. There should be a continuing communication channel open between the PCM or design–build/turnkey contractor and each of their prime or subcontractors concerning safety and health matters.
9. Periodic on-site inspections, including follow-up procedures, should be conducted by the PCM or design–build/turnkey contractor to guarantee continuance of acceptable accident prevention procedures by each contractor and subcontractor.

To establish a meaningful and successful accident prevention program, it is necessary to accept the premise that the PCM or design–build/turnkey contractor management has the legal and moral responsibility to ensure a safe and healthful workplace. The top executive, whether the president, manager, or owner, must outline policies, stimulate thinking, and exhibit personal concern and interest in such a program before expecting others to follow and cooperate. This same top management should show this personal interest and give positive evidence of a sincere commitment by personally informing all employees that accident prevention is good business, and everyone is expected to be an active participant. In larger organizations, the administration of such a safety program is a full-time job, and is generally handled by a person designated as a Safety Engineer, Hazard Control Engineer, Safety and

Health Director, or a similar title. The duties of the safety professional should be administrative and advisory, and implementation should be through the regular line management staff.

The safety engineer should advise the operating management staff on safety and health matters of interest or importance to them. Although the safety engineer must have sufficient management backing to take action when the responsible operations management staff fails to respond, care must be exercised that this authority is not used to circumvent the authority of the other members of the management staff.

### Elements of a Safety and Health Program

There are several key considerations to be taken into account in the development and implementation of an effective safety program. A brief summary follows:

1. Commitment by top management to the development of a feasible program
2. Establishment of a safety and health policy by top management
3. Provision for a reasonably safe and healthful environment
4. Provision for competent supervision
5. Delegation of adequate authority
6. Provision for training and education
7. Conduction of accident prevention inspections
8. Investigation of accidents to determine cause (not blame)
9. Measurement of accident prevention performance
10. Maintenance of proper documentation and records of construction accidents (Figures 8.1 and 8.2)
11. Provision of continuing support

### Design–Build/Turnkey Contracts

Generally, a design–build/turnkey contractor's responsibilities for safety are inseparable from those of a general contractor. In some states, the risks have been found to be even higher. Under a principle of law referred to as *strict liability,* design–build and turnkey contractors have been held liable for injury and damages where the injured party need prove only that an injury or loss was sustained. Fortunately, this principle has not yet found wide acceptance across the country.

## EFFECT OF INCLUDING CONTRACTOR'S SAFETY OBLIGATIONS IN THE SPECIFICATIONS

The Resident Project Representative is the person who is most directly involved in the administration of contract provisions and should have the responsibility of assuring that the contractor is in full compliance with all aspects of the contract, including applicable major

## RESIDENT PROJECT REPRESENTATIVE'S
## REPORT OF CONTRACTOR'S ACCIDENT

Date **21 JUNE 1994**

DAY

| S | M | T | W | TH | F | S |
|---|---|---|---|---|---|---|
| | | X | | | | |

Project **5 MGD TREATMENT PLANT ADDITION**

Unit _____

Proj. No. **IRV-100**      Contract No. **K-0933-21**

WEATHER — Bright ✓ Clear / Overcast / Rain / Snow

TEMP — To 32 / 32-50 / 50-70 ✓ / 70-85 / 85 up

WIND — Still ✓ / Moderate / High      No. **1**

Contractor: **ABC CONSTRUCTORS, INC.**

Sub-Contractor: **N.A.**

Date of Accident: **6-21-94**      Time: **09:20 HRS.**      Location: _____

Description of Accident: **SITE CLEANUP WAS IN PROGRESS AFTER FORM REMOVAL. LABORER (VICTIM) WAS SWEEPING A LEDGE 9m ABOVE CONC. FLOOR. RECTANGULAR HOLE IN LEDGE, WHICH WAS PREVIOUSLY COVERED WITH PLYWOOD, WAS UNCOVERED TO SWEEP DIRT INTO. LABORER BACKED INTO HOLE & FELL**

Primary Cause: **BY SWEEPING BACKWARD WITH A PUSH-BROOM, LABORER WALKED BACKWARD AND FELL THRU HOLE TO HIS DEATH ON CONC. SLAB 9 METERS BELOW.**

### Contractor's Personnel or Equipment

Name of Injured Employee: **JAMES L. MARTIN**      Age: **29**

Occupation: **LABORER**      Sex: **M**

Nature of Injury: **SKULL FRACTURE**

Degree of Injury: _____ First Aid ☐      Doctor Visit ☐      Hospital ☐      Fatality ☒

Type of Equipment: _____

Extent of Damage: _____

### Other Persons or Property

Name of Injured Party: **NONE**      Age: ___

Address: _____      City: _____      State: _____

Nature of Injuries: _____

*Data used are fictitious for illustration only*

Name of Property Owner: _____      Address: _____

Nature and Extent of Damages: _____

Was Use or Lack of Safety Equipment a Factor in This Accident: **NO**

If so, Explain: _____

What Safety Regulations Were Violated: **NONE KNOWN. WALKWAY WAS PROPERLY PROTECTED WITH GUARD RAILS. FLOOR HOLE HAD BEEN PROPERLY COVERED.**

What Corrective Action Has Been Taken by the Contractor: **CAUTIONED OTHER EMPLOYEES ABOUT USING GREATER CARE. WATCH WHERE THEY WALK.**

DISTRIBUTION:
1. Project Manager
2. Legal Staff
3. Engineer/Architect
4. Project File

Report by: _(signature)_

Title: **CONSTRUCTION MANAGER**

Fisk Form 8-13

**FIGURE 8.1** Report by Resident Project Representative of contractor's accident. (From *Construction Engineer's Complete Handbook of Forms*, 2nd edition by Edward Fisk. Copyright © 1992 by Prentice Hall. Reprinted by permission of Prentice Hall.)

**FIGURE 8.2**    Example of a photograph documenting a fatal accident to accompany the report illustrated in Figure 8.1.

safety requirements. The degree of control that the inspector may have over the contractor in requiring compliance with the OSHA construction safety requirements depends at least partly on the following conditions:

1.  If no mention is made in the contract documents, whether on the drawings or in the specifications themselves, safety obligations of the contractor are primarily a legal obligation between himself/herself and the state or federal agency administering the provisions of OSHA. Although an inspector would seem to be obligated to call attention to observed deficiencies that constitute a serious hazard, and to notify the contractor that they should be remedied, the contractor's failure to respond can only be handled by the inspector through the service of a written notice to the contractor, with copies to the organization administering the construction contract and by filing an official notice to the local OSHA enforcement agency, which is administered at state level in many areas. Otherwise, the contractor's fail-

ure to comply is difficult to control, as the inspector normally possesses no special powers over the work.

2. If, however, the contractor's compliance with the safety requirements of OSHA is specified in the contract specifications, the inspector's subsequent demand that a contractor comply with certain OSHA provisions takes on a different light. In this case, the safety requirements, in addition to being the legal obligation of the contractor, have become a *contractual* one as well. Thus, the contractor's failure to comply can be interpreted as a breach of contract, and the design firm may recommend that the owner withhold payments for that portion of the work until the contractor complies. This does not take the place of the official notice mentioned in the preceding paragraph, but merely provides an additional recourse to the design firm and the owner beyond the steps already mentioned. Furthermore, under these conditions, assurance that the contractor is living up to safety obligations is now a part of the inspector's responsibility because it is written into the specifications and must therefore be considered as one of the inspector's field administrative responsibilities. This also functions as an allocation of a portion of the safety hazard risk to the inspector's employer.

Wherever the construction safety provisions are written as a part of the terms of the construction contract, the inspector in the administration of his or her part of the contract is required to see that the contractor properly provides for the safety of the workers. Under no circumstances should the contractor be instructed orally or in writing as to *how* to correct a deficiency. The unsafe condition should simply be *identified* and the specific regulation, if it is known, should be cited.

As mentioned previously, it is quite probable that the inclusion of safety requirements in the construction contract will incur additional responsibility on the part of the architect/engineer to assure that proper safety precautions have been taken. It must also be recognized that there may be some additional liability to the architect/engineer in case of a job-related injury involving the failure of a contractor to observe safety requirements. However, such a provision is the only means readily at the disposal of the architect/engineer to assure performance of the contractor's safety obligations, and the risk of loss to the architect/engineer could be even greater in the absence of such controls if a fatal or crippling accident did occur, as one may be certain that the architect/engineer, the owner, and the Resident Project Representative would all be named in any resulting litigation.

## APPLICABILITY OF STATE AND FEDERAL OSHA PROVISIONS TO A PROJECT

As a way of setting the groundwork, it should first be mentioned that the federal OSHA provisions are in two volumes. The first book, "*OSHA Safety and Health Standards,* Code of Federal Regulations Title 29, Part 1910," deals with safety features that are intended to be included in the design of the project. This is the responsibility of the designer to include on the plans as a part of the project design. The second book is the one that relates to the construction phase of the work and generally concerns the temporary hazards and conditions that exist as a direct result of the construction activities. This volume is entitled *"Construction Safety and Health Regulations,* Code of Federal Regulations Title 29, Part 1926." In addition, under the federal safety program, each state has the right to enact a safety code that is at least equivalent to the federal OSHA provisions and, by so doing, retains the right to be the sole safety enforcement agency within its jurisdictional borders. If a state does not choose to exercise this option, construction in that state will be subject to inspection by both federal and state safety inspection agencies. If a state elects to upgrade its safety code to meet the OSHA requirements, it has a 3-year period to accomplish this. Under these conditions, local safety enforcement will be by state agency only, both during and after enactment.

## SPECIAL APPLICATIONS

Although ordinarily it would be assumed that a state safety program would not have jurisdiction within the confines of a federal reservation, and that only the federal OSHA program would govern there, an interesting state government interpretation has been made on this subject, as described in the following paragraph.

A federal military reservation was the site of a construction project that was planning to base its safety requirements on federal OSHA requirements administered by federal safety inspectors. The state announced jurisdiction, based upon the fact that its safety provisions were a part of its labor code, which was enacted to protect workers in their various occupations. It was further stated that none of the construction workers on the military base were federal employees, and as such were all subject to the provisions of the State Labor Code. This appears valid, as all other provisions of the State Labor Code apply to the contractor's employees, and the fact that a particular construction project takes them into federal property does not strip them of the protection afforded by the labor code.

It appears, then, that a project on a federal reservation, if built by nonfederal employees from off the reservation, will be subject to local state safety regulations—possibly in addition to federal OSHA if the state involved has failed to meet, or has not participated in, the OSHA upgrading program.

## PROCEDURAL GUIDELINES

In carrying out the owner's and the design firm's responsibilities of assuring safety compliance as a contract requirement, the following guidelines are suggested where the owner feels that inspector monitoring of the contractor's safety program is desirable:

1. IMMINENT HAZARD (Figure 8.3): a condition that if not corrected would probably result in an accident causing severe or permanently disabling injury or death.

   PROCEDURE: When an imminent hazard condition is known to exist, or when a contractor either delays in correcting or permits repeated occurrences of a hazardous condition, the Resident Project Representative should immediately order the contractor to suspend the operations affected and not permit work to resume

**FIGURE 8.3**   Photographic documentation of an imminent hazard.

on these operations until the condition has been corrected. The hazard should be photographed, and the project manager of the design firm and the owner and the state or federal agency having jurisdiction over construction safety should be notified of the hazardous condition and of the action taken. In addition, a letter giving all the details should be prepared, covering all the events leading up to the suspension, and this letter should be submitted to the project manager.

2. DANGEROUS CONDITION (Figure 8.4): a condition that does not present an immediate danger to workers, but if not corrected could result in a disabling injury and possibly death, or could develop into an imminent hazard as just described.

PROCEDURE: When a dangerous condition is known to exist, the resident inspector should notify the contractor in writing of the conditions and allow a reasonable period of time for correcting the condition. If the resident inspector is not certain of the remedial measures proposed or taken by the contractor, the services of a construction safety engineer should be requested. If the contractor does not correct the dangerous condition, or if the condition is deteriorating into an imminent hazard, the design firm should consider recommending that the owner suspend the affected operations.

**FIGURE 8.4**    Photographic documentation of a dangerous condition.

**3.** MINOR OR NONSERIOUS CONDITION: Conditions that could result in minor
or less serious injuries, or that are small in nature, but that may still be classified
as a threat to health.

PROCEDURE: When a minor or nonserious condition is known to exist, the
Resident Project Representative should advise the contractor of the conditions and
of the necessity of eliminating them. If the contractor fails to correct the problem
or permits its repeated occurrence on subsequent operations, the design firm or
owner should be notified.

The construction safety activities of both the contractor and all project personnel
must be documented in the inspector's diary. It is important for inspectors to realize that
their duties only include responsibility for seeing that the contractor complies with the pro-

ject safety requirements through the use of normal administrative procedures. The legal enforcing agency is the federal or state OSHA officers. The inspector should keep the name and telephone number of the local safety compliance officer handy—it is often a most effective compliance tool.

It should be noted that the mention of suspension of portions of the work in the foregoing procedural guidelines *relate to the immediate area* of the hazardous condition only. Nothing described here is intended to suggest that the inspector, the design firm, or the owner would be justified in closing down an entire project or even a significant portion of a project for such local conditions.

References to the capability of payment retention by the owner upon the recommendation of the design firm on contracts where safety provisions have been made contractual requirements as well as legal obligations are presented solely as a matter of interest to the inspector. It must be kept in mind that only the project manager has the authority to approve or recommend that part or all of a contractor's monthly progress payment be withheld. However, recommendations of the Resident Project Representative may bear a heavy influence on the decision of the project manager in such cases.

## SHORING AND BRACING

The federal OSHA Part 1926 *Construction Safety and Health Regulations* requires that all trenches and earth embankments over 1.5 m (5 ft) deep be adequately protected against caving in by a system of sheeting, shoring, and bracing or by sloping the sides of the trench or other excavation to an acceptable angle.

Trench and excavation shoring is one of the critical safety hazards referred to in the OSHA Construction Safety and Health Regulations. Numerous fatalities have resulted from failure of the contractor to provide adequately for worker safety under these conditions. The inspector should take particular note of the fact that all trenches or other excavations on any project, public or private, require sheeting, shoring, or bracing if they are 1.5 m (5 ft) deep or deeper (1.2 m (4 ft) in some states). Details of safety codes vary somewhat from state to state, but there is a trend toward greater uniformity and the safety codes of each jurisdiction should be carefully checked prior to beginning work in another state to confirm the specific limitations and regulations that will control.

It is quite probable that all of the excavation cave-ins of record could have been prevented if there had been proper engineering design and inspection of the support system. The additional cost of engineering may well be compensated by lower construction costs when contingency and liability costs are minimized through reduced risk of construction hazards.

As a result of research conducted by the Associated General Contractors of America (AGC) and reported in the American Society of Civil Engineers *Journal of the Construction Division,* some revealing facts were discovered regarding excavation cave-ins:[1]

---

[1]L. J. Thompson and R. J. Tannenbaum, "Survey of Construction-Related Trench Cave-ins," *Journal of the Construction Division,* Vol. 103, September 1977, p. 511. Proceedings of the American Society of Civil Engineers. Reprinted with permission.

1. At least 100 fatalities occur each year from cave-ins. At least 11 times as many receive disabling injuries.
2. The majority of these cave-ins are in shallow excavations, primarily sewer trenches.
3. No part of the country is immune to cave-ins.
4. Every type of soil is susceptible to cave-ins.
5. Most cave-ins occur in unsupported excavations.
6. Major factors influencing trench failure are the presence of construction equipment near the edge of an excavation and adverse climatic conditions.
7. Usually, engineers do not specify shoring requirements prior to bidding.
8. Approximately 50 percent of the contractors surveyed would prefer that engineers specify the shoring requirements prior to bidding.
9. Virtually no one is designing support systems for shallow excavation based on soil properties and site conditions. "Traditional" or "standardized" methods are the present governing procedures.
10. Engineers are not investigating cave-ins to determine the causes by soils investigation and engineering analysis.
11. Any time an excavation fails, there should be an engineering investigation to determine the cause of the accident. This information should be published to aid other engineers in preventing future failures.

## SAFETY REQUIREMENTS IN CONSTRUCTION CONTRACTS

Many public agencies include safety standards as a part of the construction contract documents, which then become a contractual obligation as well as a legal one, as explained previously. Many state highway departments include a safety code in their construction contracts. Several federal agencies, including the U.S. Army Corps of Engineers, the Naval Facilities Engineering Command, and the U.S. Bureau of Reclamation include health and safety standards in their construction contracts. OSHA provides that such federal agencies may continue to provide their own safety inspection and enforcement; however, this does not preclude the state from requiring compliance through its own safety enforcement officer. Thus it can be seen that the inclusion of safety requirements as a part of the contractual obligations of the contractor is a growing practice. Upon beginning a project the inspector should make a careful study of the plans and specifications to determine whether or not such safety provisions are included as a contractual requirement, thus placing an additional burden of responsibility upon the inspector to assure compliance and to take appropriate administrative action in case of default by the contractor.

## PROBLEMS

1. What party to a construction contract normally has primary responsibility for construction safety unless otherwise covered under the contract, the owner, the engineer/architect, or the contractor?

2. What are the three hazard classifications discussed in the text?
3. The recommended procedure to deal with an unshored trench hazard is initially to:
   a. Stop the work
   b. Order the workers out of the trench
   c. Call OSHA
   d. Do nothing (it is the contractor's problem)
4. Does the Resident Project Representative have a duty to document accidents by the contractor or its personnel? If so, what kind of documentation should be used?
5. Many contracts require the engineer/architect to review the contractor's safety program and to monitor the contractor's safety performance. Discuss the merits or demerits of that approach.
6. Federal and state contracts generally require their agencies to take part in the project safety program and accept a portion of the responsibility for project safety. What are the risks, benefits, and obligations of the owner under this arrangement?
7. On a Professional Construction Management contract, can the Construction Manager be cited by OSHA for safety violations or is the contractor the only one that can be cited by OSHA?
8. Who sets minimum standards for occupational safety and health in construction?
9. If safety requirements are not specified in the contract, is the contractor relieved of its safety obligations on the contract?
10. If not contractually obligated to accept safety responsibility, can the Resident Project Representative or inspector still be at risk?

# 9

## *Meetings and Negotiations*

*T*he meeting is the communications center of every organization. It is a decision-making body where the best prepared member's ideas are accepted because such a member is more direct, thinks more quickly, and knows how to use effective communications methods. As in any other organized group, the meeting displays a blending of a number of individual talents. When the objectives of the meeting are to formulate in-house decisions relating to project design, construction, or administration, the concept of performing individual roles in the meeting format can lead to better decisions and prevent later problems. In negotiations, the meeting *team* concept is preferable, where all of the talents of each individual member of the negotiation team are put together to function as a formula for success.

Any dispute or conflict can be negotiated successfully if the parties are willing to engage in good-faith discussions on mutually defined issues in an attempt to reach an acceptable settlement. Each party must be willing to compromise and accept less than its total demands. Negotiation involves a series of compromises. A person must have a thorough understanding of the basic elements of the bargaining process to negotiate effectively. Likewise, a person must adequately prepare for and competently conduct negotiations to avoid poor performance, fragmentation, mistakes, and miscalculations. The outcome of a negotiation should be satisfactory to both parties and should promote good relationships. The key to a successful negotiation is to satisfy the needs of all parties: Everyone should gain something.

## TYPES OF MEETINGS IN CONSTRUCTION

Most construction projects involve numerous types of meetings. Some are in-house meetings of the owner, the architect/engineer, or the contractor; others are meetings between representatives of these organizations as they meet the challenges of the various problems that are thrust upon them regularly throughout the construction process. Generally, in-house meetings are organization, coordination, or decision-making meetings, whereas meetings between different organizations may also involve negotiations. Some of the many different purposes for holding meetings for construction are summarized in the lists that follow. Meetings of an in-house nature are generally attended only by members of the same firm, and their principal functions are fact finding, decision making, and coordination. Some examples are:

1. Project conceptual design meetings (in-house)
2. Project presentation meetings (to potential client)
3. Project "kickoff" meetings (in-house project team)
4. Project manager's organization or coordination meeting
5. Project budget meetings for production
6. Project design meetings (technical coordination)
7. Project constructability meetings (design/construction interface)
8. Planning and scheduling meetings for project work load
9. Value engineering meetings
10. Prenegotiation meetings (in-house preparation)

As a project enters into the construction phase, the owner or the owner's architect/engineer may also become involved in a series of meetings with the contractor. Such meetings may be for the purpose of communication, coordination, resolution of difficulties, or to negotiate prices or other terms. Such meetings may include:

1. Prebid conference (information—not recommended for public works projects because of risk exposure)
2. Preconstruction conference (communication and coordination)
3. Requests for substitutions of materials or products
4. Change Orders and Extra Work (negotiations)
5. Unforseen underground work (negotiations)
6. Corrective work required (negotiations)
7. Scheduling changes (coordination; negotiation)
8. Mediation of construction difficulties
9. Protests and disputes (negotiations)
10. Difficulties caused by conflicts in plans and specs
11. Contractor-sponsored Value Engineering Proposal costs
12. Punch list meetings
13. Project acceptance and transfer of responsibility

Although there may be numerous reasons for holding meetings, these lists represent some of the more frequent reasons. Some of the meetings listed are design phase meetings and are not considered to be within the intended scope of this book. Several of the others, however, will be discussed further.

Basically, it should always be remembered that depending on the purpose of the meetings and the types of people who will be in attendance, the philosophy of conduct at some meetings may be required to be quite different from what it is at others. Most in-house meetings are not negotiation sessions; therefore, each individual will probably be called on to contribute ideas. In that context, one should be prepared to offer ideas without regard for whether the viewpoint is in keeping with the consensus. In meetings held with a potential client, however, as in the making of a presentation, or meetings between the contractor and the owner or architect/engineer that have been arranged for the purpose of negotiating, it is important for each group to maintain an appearance of unity. This can be done effectively only after careful preparation, rehearsal, and previously established position policy.

### Who Should Attend

Often, the success or failure of a presentation or negotiation meeting is determined before the first word has been spoken. Careful selection of those who will be in attendance is of vital importance to the success of the meeting objective.

The types of persons and the specific parties represented at each type of meeting will vary somewhat depending upon the purpose of the meeting and the type of organization represented. However, it is vital that certain key persons be present and, for maximum effectiveness, the attendees should be limited to just those key persons.

In a few cases, notably where disputes or potential claims are involved, one of the parties may bring an attorney to the meeting. If this should happen, the meeting should be delayed long enough to enable the other party's attorney to be present also. Never conduct a meeting with anyone when his or her attorney is present without contacting your own attorney to receive instructions as to the course of action to take.

---

## HANDLING YOURSELF AT A MEETING

One of the first and most basic rules of conduct at a meeting is to become familiar with the meeting agenda. It is important to learn in advance as much as possible about the subject of the meeting if you expect to turn it to your advantage. Some guidelines follow:

1. Determine who called the meeting.
2. Find out the reason for the meeting.
3. Understand the background of the subject.
4. Establish your own position on the subject.
5. Determine your goals or objectives before the meeting.

The most important point brought out by these guidelines is that of establishing your own position on the subject. Then, at the meeting, direct all of your efforts toward reaching that objective during the meeting, while carefully observing the responses of the others in attendance.

If you receive mixed reactions to a proposal, a vote may be premature, so while confidently holding your position, you may suggest the need for a recess or deferred action on the issue until a consultant can be heard, or that more information is required and should be reviewed before a final decision is arrived at. Then, slowly, the subject may be eased out by withdrawing your push and pointing to the fact that the question may be easy to resolve at the next meeting or after a meeting recess.

After the recess is a good time to begin a little lobbying. Each apparent dissenter may then be approached individually to put the point across. There may be some compromises needed, but if they fit your objectives, they may be well worth a reasonable compromise. After mustering sufficient support, the issue is ready to be reintroduced to the floor for a general vote.

A delayed meeting has other advantages. It allows preparation time to strengthen your position after your opponent has tipped his or her hand. No amount of advance preparation can offer the advantages of being able to study the issues and plan your position after your opponent has made full disclosure of his or her position. If you succeed in obtaining the delay, it can place you on the offensive where you have a distinct tactical advantage.

## Importance of Your Image

Appearance is of considerable importance at meetings and negotiation sessions. The best general advice is to dress conservatively and maintain an appearance of authority. At the meeting, speak to others in a confident, objective way and never give the appearance of begging or patronizing your opponent.

## Seating Advantage

Seating position is seldom spoken of as having an influence on the outcome of a meeting. Yet its subtle psychological advantages are felt if not actually observed. Unless place markers are provided, it is to your considerable advantage to position yourself very carefully at the conference table.

Many people attempt to put themselves in as unobtrusive a position as possible. This approach can work to your disadvantage, as it will minimize your effectiveness at the meeting. If you have a point to get across, you will never make it that way. The position that you occupy at the meeting table can also have a significant psychological effect upon whether your ideas will get attention or whether you come out ahead on a negotiation session. A few brief suggestions are offered that might allow you some advantage at the conference table.

1. Sit at the opposite end of the meeting room table from, or on the side closest to the leader.
2. If, however, the leader is the type who frequently consults the person next to him or her, sit next to the meeting leader.

Some seating positions to avoid at a meeting include any seat where visual contact with the leader is obstructed. If you happen to be late in arriving, this may not be possible to avoid, but that is another reason for arriving on time. If the Resident Project

Representative attends a meeting accompanied by the project manager, where the meeting is presided over by higher management, it is advisable to seat yourselves in such a way that will not place either party between the leader and the other party. If you do, and the leader directs a question your way, one party can simply field the question and leave the other party invisible. It is advisable for the Resident Project Representative and the project manager to seat themselves at opposite sides of the table, facing each other. In this manner, either party could add to the other's statement and, while doing so, all those present would have their eyes upon both members of your team. High visibility is important. For with high visibility goes attention, and with attention goes authority.

### Determine the Opponent's Motivation

Part of your group's success at a meeting will be based upon your ability to correctly assess the opponent's motivation at the meeting. The opponent's drive toward their objective can offer clues as to their probable reaction to any point brought to a vote.

### Methods and Techniques

The first and basic rule to turn the meeting to your team's own advantage is to take a positive approach. Ideas should always be presented in a systematic and orderly fashion. It is not enough merely to present the facts; they must also follow a logical course toward the point that you are attempting to put across. Often, the problem in presentation meetings where the architect/engineer is attempting to present a proposal for a project to the owner is that each member will respond individually as the opportunity seems to arise. It is of vital importance in this type of meeting to prepare carefully ahead of time, coordinate the activities of each of the people who are involved, and rehearse the presentation just as though it were a theatrical production. Many a disaster has been precluded by this simple expedient.

## PRECONSTRUCTION CONFERENCE[1]

The optimum time for the *preconstruction conference,* also known as a *construction coordination conference,* is after all of the subcontracts have been awarded but prior to the beginning of actual construction. This will permit the subjects discussed at the conference to form a background of understanding of the intended operational plan for each of the members of the construction team.

It is essential that all key members of the construction team be represented at this meeting. The presence of the owner will enable him or her to better appreciate the potential operational problems encountered by the project team, and will aid the total construction team by providing greater insight on specific owner needs and will help the archi-

---

[1]Adapted from *Construction Coordination Conference,* Copyright 1974 by the American Subcontractors Association, the Associated General Contractors of America, and the Special Contractors, Inc. All rights reserved. Used with permission.

tect/engineer to secure and translate team cooperation into a good quality job that is consistent with the scheduled time and costs.

The preconstruction conference is a logical method by which the problems of economic waste and disruptive construction problems can be discussed and possibly prevented. It is designed to benefit all concerned by recognizing the responsibilities for the various tasks *before* the project is begun. The benefits include the following:

1. Recognition and elimination of delays and disagreements.
2. Establishment of agreements that curb increases in construction costs.
3. Predisposition of gray-area responsibilities that, if left unassigned, can cause later disputes.
4. Unification of management requirements and the establishment of clear understanding of these requirements.

## Definitions

The *preconstruction conference,* or *construction coordination conference,* is a meeting of the principal parties involved with the planning and execution of the construction project, and should include:

- The owner or authorized representative
- The architect/engineer and Resident Project Representative
- The general and all prime contractors and their superintendents
- The subcontractors and their superintendents
- Key suppliers
- Public agency representatives, as necessary

Full attendance and participation by all key team members can be assured by including a requirement in the conditions of the contract that all contractors and subcontractors attend this meeting.

## Purpose

The primary purpose of the conference is to establish acceptable ground rules for all parties concerned, and to assure that each contractor understands the complete job requirements and coordinates the work to produce a completed job in a minimum amount of time, with maximum economic gain, and in harmony with the owner, architect/engineer, prime contractors, and all subcontractors.

## Time for the Conference

The Preconstruction Conference should be scheduled to permit sufficient time to cover the total agenda. This could involve from one to several days. In any case, whatever time is spent should be considered as *preventive* rather than corrective.

## Topics for Discussion

The topics of the discussion will depend on the nature, size, and complexity of the project. It is necessary, however, to assign priorities to the tasks. Although each job is different, there are certain factors that are common to all types of construction. As an aid to the development of an agenda, or as a handy means of listing all of the subjects discussed and determinations reached, it may be helpful to utilize a preprinted form for this purpose, such as that illustrated in Figure 9.1 or in Figure 11.2.

## Agenda for a Typical Preconstruction Conference

1. *Progress payments.* When, how, and to whom are payments to be made? State in exact terms so that no questions remain about requirements and responsibilities. The subject of retention and final payment should also be discussed at this time.

2. *Form of payment requests.* Identify the form that is required to apply for progress payments. Also, are suppliers and subcontractors lien waivers required? Can supplier and subcontractor waivers be one payment behind? (See also Chapter 16 regarding partial payments to the contractor.)

3. *Payroll reports.* Specify the requirements, if any, for payroll reports, as required on projects subject to Davis-Bacon Act provisions.

4. *Shop drawing and sample submittal requirements.* These include the form and procedure for the submittal of shop drawings and samples, identity of parties authorized to receive submittals, where submittals are to be delivered, number of copies required of each submittal, turnaround time required to return submittals by the architect/engineer, precedence of contract drawings over shop drawings, type of action indicated by the architect/engineer, and the limits of responsibility for review of submittals.

5. *Requirements for interference and/or composite drawings.* Who initiates them, and what will be the order of progression of these drawings? What is the impact on construction time if composite drawings are required?

6. *Insurance requirements; permits required.* Identify the time for providing insurance; who obtains and pays for permits?

7. *Job progress scheduling.* A preconstruction conference affords an opportunity for the essential involvement of subcontractors in the development and correlation of the individual schedules that make up the construction schedule for the project. Many large projects are conducted on an overall, or "master" schedule, using CPM or the PERT systems. Such scheduling is useless unless it is understood and followed by all of the parties in the construction team.

8. *Temporary facilities and controls.* These are the utility services that are essential to the construction process but do not form a part of the finished project. (See also Chapter 14 regarding temporary facilities provided by the contractor.) Under the CSI Format, these requirements are spelled out in Division 1, General Requirements. Under other specifications formats this may not be as well defined. This is often a gray area, requiring clear definitions of responsibility at the

```
┌─────────────────────────────────────────────────────────────────────┐
│                    PRECONSTRUCTION CONFERENCE                         │
│              Checklist of Subjects to be Considered for Agenda        │
│                                                                       │
│  Construction Coordination (Preconstruction) Conference               │
│   •   Participants                                                    │
│   •   Time required for conference                                    │
│   •   Use of an agenda—topics for discussion                          │
│   •   Minutes of the meeting                                          │
│   •   Acknowledgement or correction of minutes                        │
│                                                                       │
│  Identification of Key Personnel of All Parties                       │
│   •   Names and 24-hour telephone numbers of contractor, engineer,    │
│       and owner                                                       │
│   •   Define authority and responsibility of key personnel            │
│   •   Designate sole-contact for administration of contract           │
│                                                                       │
│  Authority and Responsibilities                                       │
│   •   Methods of construction (methods may be challenged)             │
│   •   Rejection of work by inspector                                  │
│   •   Work performed in absence of inspector (unacceptable)           │
│   •   Work performed in absence of contractor's superintendent        │
│       (unacceptable)                                                  │
│   •   Stopping the work (right reserved to owner alone)               │
│   •   Safety at the site                                              │
│   •   Issuance of field orders from engineer/owner                    │
│   •   Authority of the inspector                                      │
│                                                                       │
│  Conformance with Plans and Specifications                            │
│   •   Call attention to areas of special concern                      │
│   •   Answer contractor inquiries                                     │
│   •   Clarification of specification provisions                       │
│                                                                       │
│  Contract Administration                                              │
│   •   Notice to Proceed                                               │
│   •   Time of the contract                                            │
│   •   Liquidated damages                                              │
│   •   Insurance requirements and bonds                                │
│   •   Record drawings (procedure, responsibility for)                 │
│   •   Mobilization (identify scope)                                   │
│   •   Contractor submittal procedure (through resident engineer)      │
│   •   Surveys and staking                                             │
│   •   Bid allocation of lump sum bids (not valid as cost-basis on     │
│       extra work)                                                     │
│   •   Environmental requirements (cleanup; sanitary; dust; blasting;  │
│       chemicals)                                                      │
│   •   Change Orders and extra work procedures                         │
│   •   Unforeseen underground conditions procedures (public agency     │
│       responsibility)                                                 │
│   •   Coordination with utilities                                     │
│   •   Closeout procedures                                             │
│   •   Progress payments and retainage procedures                      │
│                                                                       │
│  Materials and Equipment                                              │
│   •   Substitutions of "or equal" items                               │
│   •   Long lead (prepurchase) items                                   │
│   •   Assignments of procurement contracts to contractor              │
│   •   Owner-furnished materials or equipment                          │
│   •   Storage and protection                                          │
│   •   Concealed shipping damages                                      │
│   •   Payment for materials not yet used in the work                  │
└─────────────────────────────────────────────────────────────────────┘
```

**FIGURE 9.1**   Checklist of subjects to be considered for preconstruction conference agenda.

Contractor's Schedule
- Owner/engineer rights to approve
- Submittal requirements
- Owner/engineer can set milestone date

Change Orders and Extra Work
- Who has authority to issue
- Effect on time and cost
- Field order vs change order
- Cumulative change order

Subcontractors and Suppliers
- Contractual relationship
- Submittal requirements
- Owner/engineer: No direct contact alone
- Fair subcontracting act requirements

Coordination with Other Agencies and Contractors
- Interface requirements
- Testing and validation of systems
- Highway departments and railroads
- Code enforcement agencies
- Other regulatory agencies of government

Handling of Disputes, Protests, and Claims
- Must exhaust all contractual means
- Resolution by the engineer

Labor Requirements
- Davis-Bacon Act
- Documentation and audit requirements
- Federal, state, and local requirements

Rights-of-Way and Easements
- Permanent easements for project
- Temporary easements for construction
- Dumping sites and storage areas
- Access to the site by heavy equipment

Owner protection
- Warranties and guarantees
- Bond protection during guarantee
- Security
- Extended maintenance of landscaping

Punch list procedures
- Contractor certification of completion
- Punch list inspections
- Final acceptance inspection (run-up; testing; final walk-through)
- Withheld funds for remaining punch list items

**FIGURE 9.1** *continued*

time of the conference. Some of the questions that must be answered on this subject are:

(a) Who provides the services?

(b) Who maintains them?

(c) Who pays for these services?

(d) If shared cost, in what proportion?

(e) What are the *contractual* responsibilities, if any, under OSHA?

9. *Storage facilities and staging area.*

10. *Job site security during nonworking hours.* Losses from vandalism and theft at unguarded construction sites are rapidly mounting sources of expense to the entire construction industry. An agreement sharing the costs of better security measures might be worthy of discussion.

11. *Cleanup and trash removal.* Consider containers, scraps, sanitary wastes, and so on.

12. *Available hoisting facilities.* Who supplies hoisting facilities? If the general contractor supplies them, what will be the arrangement to make the hoist available to individual subcontractors?

13. *Change Orders.* Because Change Orders are the subject of more disputes than any other single aspect of construction, they should be discussed in complete detail (see Chapter 18). Typical items for discussion relating to Change Orders are:

(a) Percentages for overhead and profit to be applied to Change Orders. What costs will or will not be included in the Change Order price?

(b) Length of time that a Change Order proposal price is to be considered firm.

(c) Identify individuals who are authorized to approve Change Orders.

(d) Procedures to be followed when submitting initiator Change Orders or Change Order proposals.

(e) Change Order forms that must be used.

(f) Time extension requests made by subcontractors due to changes in drawings or specifications.

(g) Amount of detail required of subcontractors when submitting Change Order proposals or initiator Change Orders. Will a complete breakdown of all costs be required? Brief description. Descriptive drawings.

(h) Overtime resulting from Change Orders; consideration of decreased productivity.

(i) *When* materials or equipment are to be removed because of a change, which party owns the removed material or equipment, and who removes it from the site of the job.

(j) Responsibility for preparation of Record Drawings brought about by Change Orders.

14. *Warranty requirements.*

15. *Employment practices.*

16. *Listing and identification of all tiers of subcontractors.*

17. *Punch lists.* Establish timely punch list items and avoid an excessive number of punch lists.

**18.** *Record drawings* and final document submittals.

**19.** *Final payment* and retainage.

The establishment of meaningful communications between the parties involved on a construction project is essential for its successful development. Only with such a basis of understanding can the necessary planning and work proceed without conflict or costly disputes. The preconstruction conference, or construction coordination conference, as some call it, is a logical means toward this end.

A suggested checklist of subjects to be considered for inclusion in a preconstruction conference agenda is shown in Figure 9.1. Obviously, no agenda will contain all of the listed items, but with the list as a reference while compiling the actual agenda, there is less chance that an item will be omitted.

## IN-HOUSE DECISION-MAKING MEETINGS[2]

Meetings are the means of group decision making, a popular but not always effective means of responding to the issues confronting an organization. Group decision making often comes up with a less than ideal answer because group psychological pressures tend to cloud basic issues. To improve the process, it is necessary to understand how groups think, and why. Although each of us may have often regretted the decisions of some groups, committees, or task forces in which we have participated or have been associated, we continue to spend long hours in group decision making that might better have been handled on an individual basis.

One reason for continuing the practice of decision making in groups is that a group may be less likely than individuals to make bad decisions. This appears to be particularly important when the cost of a wrong decision may be especially high. Although more labor-hours may be employed to reach a group decision, the resulting decision seems more likely to be the correct one—which may be one of the reasons why many high-level decisions made in business and government are made in groups.

A decision is seldom successful unless it is accepted by those who must act upon it. In fact, the advocates of group decision making cite increased commitment to group-inspired decisions as one of the advantages of that concept. People are more likely to accept and use decisions that they or their representatives have helped to develop.

### Other Group Benefits

Group inputs are sought because the quality of the contributions may be more in keeping with accepted values of credibility and candor than if they came from an individual. This is particularly true for organizational development activities directed toward improvements in communication and resolution of conflicts.

---

[2]Adapted from C. W. Von Bergen and R. J. Kirk, "Groupthink: When Too Many Heads Spoil the Decision," *Management Review,* March 1978, pp. 44–49 (New York, AMACOM, A Division of the American Management Associations).

Another reason for favoring group decision making has to do with responsibility. Spreading of responsibility may appear very attractive when a good decision calls for actions that are unpopular, unpleasant, or risky. An individual may be reluctant to pursue a course of action if he or she alone will be held accountable for any negative consequences, whereas a group may decide to go along with an unpleasant or risky action because the responsibility is shared among its members. The group takes on an identity of its own, as if it were an individual third party. In this way members can achieve some degree of anonymity.

Group meetings also affords a relatively captive audience for those who like to hear themselves, a friendly "club" for those who want social contacts, satisfaction for those who are eager to deflate rivals, and a base for those who want power and status. For some individuals, satisfying those personal needs in a group is more important than the actual goals of the group.

Finally, group decision making may be preferred because of the belief that "two [or more] heads are better than one." Although this concept may not be entirely true, this belief holds that the group's multiple viewpoints, talents, and areas of expertise brought together to solve problems, set goals, establish policies, and carry out projects or activities will result in a better product.

### The Collective Thinking Problem

Unfortunately, many groups do not function properly, and sometimes their conclusions may be poorer than those an individual might have reached. The major barriers to effective group problem solving are those conditions that prevent the free expression of ideas in a group. Restraints can decrease the likelihood that the correct solution or elements of such a solution will be made available to the group. Both obvious and subtle factors can work against the group's use of its own resources.

Obvious factors, such as embarrassment and fear of reprisal, tend to restrict free expression of ideas in groups. However, there are other more subtle constraints, such as high regard for the psychological need for obtaining a unanimous decision on all issues sought by the members of groups. Most groups tend to produce unanimous decisions, and their discussions tend to increase the uniformity of their members' individual judgments.

Social-psychological studies have suggested that the better the group members get along with one another, the less its members will deliberately hold back what they think out of fear of being punished socially for arousing the resentment of the leader or a fellow group member. The closer a group feels socially, however, the more its members will unwittingly hold back what they think because of their newly acquired motivation to preserve the unity of the group and to adhere to its standards. Thus, although the members of a closely bonded group feel much freer to deviate from the majority, they also desire genuine concurrence on all important issues. A desire to match their opinions and conduct themselves in accordance with each other's wishes often results in their reluctance to use this freedom to express a negative viewpoint.

The danger is not that each will fail to reveal his or her strong objections to a proposal, but that each will think the proposal is a good one without even attempting to carry out a careful evaluation that could reveal grounds for strong objections. The insecurity generated by possible rejection provides a strong incentive to agree with the other members.

The more *esprit de corps* exhibited by a group of policy-makers, the more likely it is that independent thinking will be replaced by *collective thinking*.

As a group becomes excessively close-knit, collective thinking develops. The process is characterized by a marked decrease in the exchange of potentially conflicting data and by an unwillingness to examine carefully such data when they surface.

This type of group process emphasizes team play at all costs and often increases the probability that the collective attendees will tend to seek unanimity, become overoptimistic, and exhibit a lack of vigilance. This often results in a strategy that is ineffective and not in keeping with existing realities.

### Symptoms of Collective Thinking

Collective thinking may be characterized as involving a number of symptoms, and one could argue that collective thinking exists only in a group to the degree that these eight symptoms are present:

1. The illusion of togetherness regarding the viewpoint held by the majority in the group and an emphasis on team play.
2. A view of the "opposition" as generally inept, incompetent, and incapable of countering effectively any action taken by the group, no matter how risky the decision or how high the odds are against the plan of action succeeding.
3. Self-censorship of group members in which open disagreements are avoided, facts that might reduce support for the emerging majority view are suppressed, faulty assumptions that are not questioned, and personal doubts that are suppressed in the form of group harmony.
4. Collective rationalization to comfort one another to discount warnings that the agreed-upon plan is either unworkable or highly unlikely to succeed.
5. Self-induced constraints within the group that tend to prevent anyone from undermining its apparent unanimity and to protect its members from unwelcome ideas and negative information that may threaten a unanimous agreement.
6. Reinforcement of consensus and direct pressure on any dissenting group member who expresses strong reservations or challenges, or argues against the apparent unanimous thinking of the group.
7. An expression of self-righteousness that leads members to believe that their actions are moral and ethical, thus inclining them to disregard any ethical or moral objections to their beliefs.
8. A shared feeling of invulnerability, along with a high degree of *esprit de corps,* characterized by total faith in the wisdom of the group and by an unsupported optimism that tends to allow members of the group to take excessive risks.

### Preventing Collective Thinking

Whereas most project managers have probably experienced collective thinking at one time or another, it is not inherent in all group decision-making activities, and it can be avoided.

The following guidelines, although not all inclusive, may be useful in preventing the appearance of collective thinking in *decision-making* meetings:

1. *Leader encouragement.* In most organizations, group members need encouragement to feel free to disagree with the boss or a group leader. The subordinates in the group must feel free to disagree if they are to contribute the best of their thinking. The leader should encourage free expression of minority viewpoints. Although group members holding minority views are more likely to be on the defensive and more hesitant in voicing their opinions, to introduce balance into the situation, the group leader must do all that he or she can to protect individuals who are attacked and to create opportunities for them to clarify their views.

2. *Diversity of viewpoints.* Attempt to structure the group so that there are different viewpoints. Diverse input will tend to point out nonobvious risks, drawbacks, and advantages that might not have been considered in a more homogeneous group.

3. *Legitimized disagreement and skepticism.* Silence is usually interpreted as consent in a meeting. It should be explained that questions, reservations, and objections should be brought before the group and that feelings of loyalty to the group should not be allowed to obstruct expression of doubts. Genuine, personal loyalty to the group that leads one to go along with a bad policy should be discouraged. Voicing of objections and doubts should not be held back for fears about "rocking the boat" or reluctance to "blow the whistle." Each member of the meeting group should take on the additional role of a critical evaluator and should be encouraged by the group leader and other members to air all reservations.

4. *Idea generation versus idea evaluation.* A major barrier to effective decision making is the tendency to evaluate suggested solutions as soon as they appear instead of waiting until all suggestions are in. Early evaluation may inhibit the expression of opinions, and it tends to restrict freedom of thinking and prevents others from profiting from different ideas. Early evaluation can be particularly destructive to ideas that are different, new, or lacking in support. The group leader should encourage initial emphasis on problem solving at the expense of early concentration on solutions.

5. *Advantages and disadvantages of each solution.* The group should try to explore the merits and demerits of each alternative. The process of listing the sides of a question forces discussion to move from one side of the issue to the other. As a result, the positive and negative aspects of each strategy are brought out into the open and may become the foundation for a new idea with all its merits and few of its weaknesses.

6. *New approaches and new people.* In many cases, thinking about the problem by oneself or discussing it with another person can result in refreshing new perspectives. Any belief that one should be able to generate correct answers to complex problems and issues the first time that they are dealt with should be done away with. In fact, the norm, during the design phase at least, should be to "think about it again" and "think about it in a new way." This implies remembering the answer derived by one approach, putting it aside for a while, then coming back to the problem afresh. Also, it may be helpful if, in the intervening time, each of the

group participants consults a trusted colleague, who is not a member of the group, to bounce it off him or her for a reaction. Ideally, these colleagues should be someone different in expertise and background from the rest of the group members, so that they can offer critical, independent, and perhaps fresh ideas that can be reported back to the group. These recommendations, although desirable in decision-making meetings, such as design phase meetings in an engineering organization, are quite unsuited to the method of handling the implementation meetings involving the decision-making process during construction when time is of the essence and a quick response is necessary.

## PRINCIPLES OF NEGOTIATION

Generally, negotiation may be considered as the art of arriving at a common understanding through bargaining on the essentials of the contract, such as specifications, prices, time of performance, and terms. A negotiator, when fully aware of his or her bargaining strength, can know where to be firm and where to make concessions on prices or terms. The negotiation occurs when both parties with differing viewpoints and objectives attempt to reach a mutually satisfying agreement. The negotiation process involves:

1. Presentation of each party's position
2. Analysis and evaluation of the other party's position
3. Adjustment of one's own position to as many of the other party's views as are reasonable

If one party, after thoroughly analyzing the position of the other party, acknowledges the fairness of the other party's position and that it is in the best interest of both parties, this concurrence represents an equitable agreement.

It should be understood from the beginning, however, that both sides have not only the right but the obligation to obtain the best deal that they can for their own firm. Generally, the best negotiation strategy is based upon being reasonable within the rules of the game. This involves objectivity in negotiations and an awareness that the negotiator's prime purpose is to obtain the best possible deal for the employer. We talk of knowing the rules of the game, yet it must be appreciated that complete disclosure is not necessarily desirable nor practical (nor are you likely to encounter much of it). In short, each party is there to *win*. Nevertheless, a reputation for honesty is certainly useful, as it improves the image of the negotiator and therefore the chance for winning. Remember, negotiation is an adversary action, and complete disclosure of one's position may be counterproductive.

The person chosen to negotiate on behalf of the owner, architect/engineer, or contractor organization must be a strong individual who is capable of controlling the members of the negotiating team. The chief negotiator must also be acquainted with the broad details of the issue, the work to be done, and the method by which the cost information was developed. The negotiator must have freedom of action so that the various factors involved in any negotiation may be considered. It is equally important for the negotiator to be capable of organizing the team into a harmonious group, planning the objective, and explaining the objective to the negotiating team members so that they will be able to coordinate their efforts effectively.

### Contractor's Position on Change Orders and Extra Work

If the contractor is in a sole source position, knows it, and is sure to be assigned the work eventually, an attempt to hold the line at the negotiation table may be delayed. However, if in an unsound or weak position, the contractor may assign the most alert and aggressive people as representatives in negotiations to take advantage of any opportunities that might arise during the course of the negotiations. Some organizations attempt to obtain a psychological advantage by a show of force, such as having several members of their top management or their attorneys represent them at the negotiations. Sometimes this can be to an organization's disadvantage as well, for it emphasizes the importance of the issue to it, and thus places the other party at a tactical advantage.

### The Philosophy of Team Playing

Both sides in the negotiations will generally select participants in the negotiation process on the basis of special positions or skills that they possess. In many cases, these specialists may have authority and positions within their organization that are superior to those of the person selected as the principal negotiator. Although the project manager, and sometimes the Resident Project Representative, may be a part of the negotiation team, it is important to understand that the authority of the principal negotiator must take precedence during negotiations, and that negotiation is not intended to be a discussion among individual specialists.

At the beginning, an in-house meeting of the negotiation team should be held, at which time the subject of team conduct and communication at the bargaining table should be discussed. Each member of the negotiation team must know what he or she can and cannot do during negotiations. The negotiator must not assume that all members of the team will know how to act, but must instruct them beforehand. Project managers and other team members who are accustomed to leadership roles in their own organizational environment often find it quite difficult to play secondary or supporting roles during negotiations. It is essential that each team member be constantly reminded that the principal negotiator is the team leader and spokesman, and that this negotiator is the only one who actually negotiates with the other party.

Sometimes a team member will forget this and become overeager, resulting in an active discussion with the other party. The principal negotiator should not hesitate to call for a recess if it is felt that there is a developing loss of control over the team members. Even if another team member feels that the principal negotiator failed to take advantage of an opportunity that the other party inadvertently provided, that team member should remain silent during the session. A few missed opportunities are preferable to an undisciplined team.

The principal negotiator should be careful about asking for a recess, however, as it can also become a disadvantage. It can serve as a red flag to the other party; they will sense your position on the issue at hand. One strategy is to delay calling for a recess until another subject is brought up, or as some prefer, call for an occasional recess at random times, just as a break, so as not to give any indication to the other party that any specific issue is involved.

## Basic Negotiation Policy

There are two basic methods of approaching a negotiation. First, you may consider the package as a whole, an overall method; second, you may elect to resolve each of the elements of the package separately, in sequence, as the negotiations progress.

Inherent difficulties of the sequential method of negotiation are the facts that it is necessary to reach separate agreements on each of the items before progressing to the next item, and to agree upon the order in which each item will be considered. Another problem is that there is no later opportunity for making trade-offs of one item for another.

The basic principles of negotiation do not require that an agreement be reached on individual items, but that compromises may be made by each party to reach an overall determination. Sometimes a contractor's main interest may fall into an area that the architect/engineer is willing to concede. Therefore, negotiations should not be conducted on the basis of reaching a firm agreement on each issue but, rather, on the basis of discussing each issue in sequence and arriving at a general meeting of the minds. The final solution then will represent, not an agreement on individual items, but a resolution of all of the points of disagreement within the total contract.

One advantage of the overall method of negotiating is that it does not require a specific agreement on an issue before moving on to the next subject. Instead, a general meeting of the minds or an implied acceptance of the issue is understood and each party may then move on to the next item of the negotiation. Under this principle, it is understood that the implied agreement is binding only in the context of the entire negotiation.

Occasionally a contractor, for example, may attempt to bypass the negotiator and negotiate directly with the management of the architect/engineer or the owner. This is a practice that must be discouraged, as a precedent will have been set that will have the effect of undermining the negotiator's effectiveness. If successful in this ploy, the contractor may subsequently insist upon conducting all future negotiations that way. The solution is for the management to reiterate the position taken by the negotiator. Another method, which was used by a contractor on one of the author's projects, was to drive toward the home office of the architect/engineer after failure to win a point in the field, with the intent of negotiating with the principal. After telephoning the engineer's office to announce the contractor's visit so that the principal could be properly prepared with the position taken in the field, it just so happened that on the contractor's arrival, the principal of the firm was always tied up in conference. After several hours of waiting in the outer office, the contractor would give up and leave. After about three or four incidents of this type, the contractor was resigned to the fact that the matters would have to be negotiated with the Resident Project Manager, as originally provided for in the contract.

### Negotiation Guidelines

As a means of obtaining a tactical advantage over the opponent in any negotiation, the following principles are suggested:

1. Keep the objective in mind.
2. Adjust your end to suit your means.
3. Exploit the line of least resistance.
4. Take an approach that offers alternative objectives.
5. Keep your plan adaptable to changing circumstances.
6. Do not put your weight behind an approach while your opponent is on guard.
7. Do not renew an attack along the same lines or in the same form after it has failed once.

In the early stages of a negotiation, an architect/engineer, owner, or contractor will find it to their advantage to plan their overall strategy as an offensive one. There is a choice, however, of various tactics to use. The strategist may elect not to reveal its position and maneuver the other party from one position to the other until its objective has been reached; or, more often, after an initial fact-finding session, the strategist may reveal its minimum position as a counter proposal. In this case, the counter proposal must be a realistic one. Another tactic is to reveal the minimum figure, then immediately offer the objective. This provides the user of this method with very little bargaining room, however, and may be considered as a sign of weakness by the other party.

## TECHNIQUES OF NEGOTIATION[3]

Numerous times during the conduct of a construction project, the project manager and the Resident Project Representative will be called on to become involved in some form of implementation meetings and negotiations with the contractor. At any meeting where a decision must be made that will influence the financial position of either the contractor or the owner, it is quite likely that the meeting will involve some form of negotiation, even if the symptoms were not recognized.

Negotiation is an art. Let no one tell you otherwise. However, some of the basic rules and guidelines of the art can be acquired by observing and learning from the experts.

It is said that in the marketplaces of the Middle East, there often comes a point in the haggling when the buyer starts walking away to signal that there is to be no deal. This action in itself does not impress the seller, but tradition holds that when the customer has walked 30 paces, he or she will not return. So if the merchant is willing to offer a better

---

[3]Adapted from G. W. Harrison and B. H. Satter, "Negotiating at 30 Paces," *Management Review,* April 1980, pp. 51–54 (New York, AMACOM, a Division of American Management Associations).

price, he or she waits until the customer has gone 28 paces or so and then runs after him. An amusing game to an observer, perhaps, but similar games are played for much higher stakes around the construction conference table. Price is usually the key issue for both the contractor and the owner.

Without going into the psychological analysis of the art of negotiating, we should take a practical look at some of the ploys that surface on both sides. The *30 paces* ploy is a last-ditch maneuver that should never be used on minor obstacles to reaching an agreement. It is equivalent to saying "do it my way or else," and it is dangerous if cooperation is needed at a later stage in the negotiations.

Another approach is the *commissar's technique,* which is said to be somewhat typical of the iron curtain countries. Under this ploy, a team of people of impressive credentials and corporate titles negotiates a deal. But if on reflection, the team is not fully satisfied, more negotiators will come in the next day, saying that they are superiors to the first group and that the first group did not have the authority to make a final commitment (sounds like some car salesmen I have heard). Then the process may be repeated. Obviously, it is not likely to work a third time, as the credibility of the offending negotiating team probably has been stretched as thin as it can get.

What is the point? It is that you should know the exact authority of the negotiator at the table, even if it is the chairman of the board, for even that person may have to obtain approval of the Board of Directors before he or she can make a binding commitment. It is also wise to make sure that the issues to be discussed have already passed through the appropriate management committees, lawyers, auditors, or any others whose judgments or approvals are necessary before final consideration.

Who, and how many, will attend the negotiating session is also important. Too many people present on either side makes it difficult to get a consensus. Although the collective thinking phenomenon is unlikely to be present at the average negotiation session, as all of the position policies of each side should have been well established in prenegotiation meetings, the adversary relationship that may be present between the two groups may complicate efforts to reach a consensus. In addition, always remember that a "handshake" deal may be a stronger weapon for one side than for the other. Think out in advance how an agreement should be arrived at and make sure that you are in control on all of the issues that are important to you.

### Bargaining Strategy

The substance of good strategy is something that must be tailored to the specific circumstances and facts. However, there are certain basic practices which can lead to the formulation of strategies. The most important step is to determine your objective by discussing it with your negotiating team, and compare that with what you perceive is the objective of the other party. Seek out common ground that can be settled without disagreement, and isolate key issues. The negotiator must recognize the weaknesses of his or her own arguments as well as emphasize their strong points.

### Negotiating Tips

The following is a list of negotiating tips from *Presenting the Claim to the Contracting Officer and Appeals Board,* Government Contracts Claims Course Manual (Federal Publications, Inc.):

1. Strive to determine the real objectives of the other party.
2. Do not let personality differences frustrate the progress of the negotiations.
3. Avoid being too dogmatic or inflexible.
4. List and discuss your side's objectives with all members of your team.
5. Be prepared when you begin negotiation.
6. Recognize the consequences to your side if negotiations should fail.
7. Many successful negotiations are easier in a better environment.
8. Maintain a written record of the negotiations on a daily basis.
9. Continually verify the information being presented and received during the course of the negotiations.
10. Never walk out on a negotiation unless you are prepared to terminate it.
11. Patience is a virtue, but progress is a necessity.
12. Be prepared to make reasonable concessions.
13. Be prepared to turn a disadvantage into an advantage.
14. Quit when you are ahead. You don't always have to knock something off an offer. If the offer is good, take it.

Once a settlement has been reached, the owner or architect/engineer should prepare a written memorandum of agreement which clearly spells out the terms of the settlement. This should be done as soon as a basic agreement is reached; send a copy to the other party requesting that they sign it, indicating confirmation of the agreement. Details may be worked out in subsequent meetings and need not be included in the basic agreement letter.

Negotiations that have broken down should also be detailed in writing, since statements of fact constituting an admission can be used in court. Also, interim agreements reached during negotiations can serve as a basis for final award in court.

### Psychology of Negotiation

The story is told of a shrewd country lawyer in the South who always asked the big-city lawyers who came down South to negotiate, "When are you taking the plane back to New York?" If the answer was "this afternoon," he knew they were eager for an agreement. But if they were booked into the motel for a week, he knew that he was in for a siege. Finding out the other party's timetable for making a deal is always one of the objectives of a good negotiator, as it can have a decided effect on the outcome. Never rush anyone who is not ready to make a quick decision.

A knowledge of *real values* of the work to be accomplished is essential to negotiate intelligently, although the owner and the contractor may choose not to use the same basis of comparison. The determination of the real value of work does not always dictate the price, but it does keep both sides in the same ballpark. Getting someone to come down in the asking price is a big accomplishment only if the final price is not $50,000 or $100,000 more than the work was worth.

A tale has been told about the boy who told his father that he had decided to sell his dog for $1 million. The amused father gave his permission, and a few days later his son told him that he actually had sold his dog for $1 million. The surprised father asked the boy if he had been paid in cash. "No," the son said, "I traded him for two $500,000 cats."

Some negotiators, unfortunately, fail to compute the cash equivalent of what is being offered in payment for the work in question. Anything other than cash must be carefully analyzed to determine its real worth. This includes bonds, stocks, and other instruments.

## Strategic Ploys

Throwing up obstructions or creating distractions with minor issues is sometimes a deliberate strategy in negotiations, but can be a dangerous one. Negotiations should be directed at the settling of major issues, without getting bogged down in technicalities that the lawyers and the accountants can deal with after a broad agreement has been reached. As much as possible, both the contractor and the owner should concentrate on the prospects of making a deal, not breaking one. A good negotiator always labels a participant as a "deal maker" or "deal breaker," depending on how the outcome would affect the negotiator's own position.

It was a wise person who advised never to bargain for the last possible penny but always "leave a little something on the table." The other side must have the opportunity to save face, both at the negotiating session and back at the home office. It is not a good idea to alienate everyone through overzealous haggling, especially if those present at the session must also stay on to run the operation. Develop a sense of how far the other party can go, and when to back off a little.

## Setting the Pace

Contractors and owners, or their architect/engineer representatives, frequently engage in gamesmanship of who will make the first move in the negotiations, neither wanting to be typecast as the anxious one. Normally, such maneuvering produces no real advantages, and there are really no rules of protocol about such matters. From a practical standpoint, the initiator of a particular deal or step in the negotiation process is out to take the lead in supplying information, suggesting a price, and so on.

Whether a party to the negotiations establishes itself as a professional or a newcomer at the negotiation table strongly influences how the session is conducted. Here are some guidelines:

1. Make sure that you know the scope of the meeting, the issues to be discussed, and the amount of time available to discuss them.

2. Start off with some smaller issues to get the "feel" of the personalities involved.

3. Do not get into the position of waiting for the other shoe to drop. Know all of the issues before reaching a compromise.

4. Decide in advance whether it is to your advantage to reach a rough or a precise agreement, and if publicizing the conditions before a commitment would work for or against you.

5. Make sure that you are bargaining with someone who has the authority to sign for his or her organization.

6. Have a walk-away price in mind that is consistent with the realities of the circumstances.

7. Bear in mind that there is no one "best" negotiating strategy other than good common sense.

8. If the other side brings legal counsel, contact your side to see whether or not your attorney wishes to be present. In some cases, unexpected arrival of the other party's lawyer at a meeting was cause for delay of the meeting until the owner could be afforded similar representation.

### Who Won?

It is often impossible to know who wins in a negotiation. The mere fact that a contractor came down in price, or an owner or architect/engineer increased the offer, proves nothing without knowing what they were really willing to settle for. Although one lawyer is reported to have said that if both sides say they are unhappy, it was probably a fair deal, the fact is that in any transaction based upon sound analysis and realistic negotiation, both sides should be satisfied. Often, in winning the point, a good negotiator will leave something "on the table" for the other party. A face-saving gesture, perhaps, but a valuable concept for maintaining a continued amicable relationship with the other party. Thus, each will come away from the bargaining table with a little something and may well be prompted to say, after conclusion of the negotiations, "I like doing business with you."

## PROBLEMS

1. List at least five important types of in-house meetings occurring prior to the construction phase.

2. List at least five important types of meetings held during the construction phase of a project.

3. Should any of the parties bring an attorney to a construction meeting? If one does, what should the other party do?

4. What are the five types of information that you should determine prior to attending a meeting?

5. Is there any advantage to be obtained by choosing a seating position at a meeting, if the opportunity presents itself?

6. Name two recommendations for selection of good position at a conference room table.
7. Name the benefits of holding a preconstruction conference.
8. Name the principal parties that should be asked to attend the preconstruction conference.
9. What is collective thinking?
10. Name three important principles of negotiation, with reference to your own preparation.
11. Name at least five principles that should guide you in obtaining and maintaining a tactical advantage over the opponent.

# 10

## Risk Allocation and Liability Sharing

*I*n recent years, a great deal of lip service has been paid to the concept of risk allocation and liability sharing. It seems to be the inevitable result of the many losses suffered by owners and engineers alike in connection with the projects they build, due to a new emphasis on the resolution of construction disputes through litigation and arbitration. Many of the risks were there all the time, but in earlier years, the contractors were always expected to bear the responsibility for as many construction risks as the owners could pass off on them through indiscriminate use of exculpatory clauses for everything from risks of unforseen underground conditions to substandard designs and specifications.

Far from trying to operate in a risk-free environment, a contractor understands that risk is part of the business. All that is wanted is a fair reimbursement for taking such risks. However, the modern contractor is no longer content to sit idly by and take all of the risks while being locked into a guaranteed maximum price but now stands ready to fight back. Contractors have come to realize that they have the means and often the right to recover the losses that are the result of the imposition of unfair contract conditions or administration.

Whereas part of the job of the Resident Project Representative is to minimize exposure of the owner and the architect/engineer to risk of claims losses, there are other risks that are rightfully within the responsibility area of the project manager to control. Some of the risks may be transferred to others by contract. However, it should be recognized that all risks are rightfully the owner's unless transferred or assumed by another party for fair compensation. The principal guideline in determining whether a risk should be transferred to another is whether the party assuming the risk has both the competence to assess the risk and the expertise necessary to control or minimize it. The choice must be made before the allocation of risk takes place. One such approach to the decision-making process is outlined in the flowchart in Figure 10.1.

LOGIC FLOW CHART FOR RISK DECISIONS

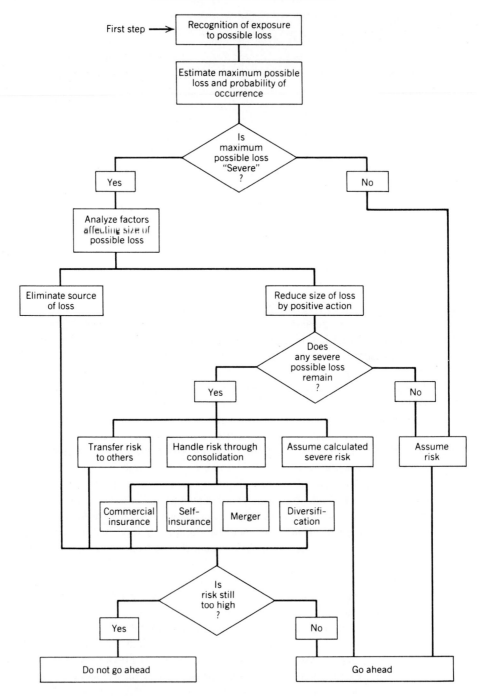

**FIGURE 10.1**   Logic flowchart for risk decisions.

## RISK MANAGEMENT

The first thing that must be recognized is that risks, especially in construction, do exist but are not necessarily fairly distributed. Some kinds of risks must be recognized as being inevitable in engineering and construction and therefore must be accepted philosophically and realistically as a part of the situations to be dealt with. Managing risks means minimizing, covering, and sharing of risks—not merely passing them off onto another party.

Although some risks can be avoided, risk management deals primarily with the following concepts:

1. Minimizing risks—regardless of whose risk it is
2. Equitable sharing of risks among the various project participants

The parties must be able to sit down together, prior to the start of the work, to come to a better understanding of the realities of the risk responsibility, assumption, and allocation. The parties must be prepared to discuss and to decide on the following issues:

1. What levels of risk are realistic to assume?
2. Who can best assume each risk?
3. What levels and kinds of risks are properly and most economically passed on to insurance carriers?

Risk exists wherever the future is unknown. Because the adverse effects of risk have plagued humankind since the beginning of time, individuals, groups, and societies have developed various ways for managing risk. Because no one knows the future exactly, everyone is a risk manager, not by choice but by sheer necessity.

### Definition of Risk

Risk has been defined in various ways. There is no single "correct" definition. In order to emphasize the major objective of risk management, we will choose to define *risk* as the *variation in the possible outcomes that exist in nature in a given situation.* Another way to clarify this definition of risk is to distinguish between risk and probability. Risk is a property of an entire probability distribution, whereas there is a separate probability for each outcome.

Both risk and probability have their objective and subjective interpretations. The true state of things is different from the way it appears. Because a person acts on the basis of what is believed to be correct, it is important to recognize this distinction. To the extent that a person's estimates are incorrect, that person's decisions are based on false premises. Consequently, risk managers must constantly strive to improve their estimates. Even with perfect estimates, decision making about risk is a difficult task. Uncertainty is the doubt that a person has concerning his or her ability to predict which of the many possible outcomes will actually occur. In other words, it is a person's conscious awareness of the risk in a given situation.

### Scope and Applicability to Construction

Risk, as such, is present in all situations and businesses. As applied to construction, we will use the categories detailed by the American Society of Civil Engineers at the Specialty Conference on Construction Risks and Liability Sharing in Scottsdale, Arizona, in January 1979, where the principal categories listed included:

1. Construction-related risks
2. Physical risks (subsurface conditions)
3. Contractual and legal risks
4. Performance risks
5. Economic risks
6. Political and public risks

As it may well be imagined, not all of these items are considered in the same order of priority by owners, architect/engineers, and contractors, and there are also considerable differences of viewpoint as to the percentage of each item that should be shared by the various parties.

As a means of defining the range or spectrum of risk and liability sharing in construction, consider that at one end of the spectrum, the contractor is assigned the entire risk or liability with no risk to the owner. This usually results in high cost; in effect, the contractor is acting as the insurer of the owner.

At the other end of the spectrum, the contractor is released from all risks or liability, and the burden is assumed by the owner. This usually results in a lower cost; in effect, the owner assumes a self-insured role.

Either end of the spectrum has both advantages and disadvantages. Owners must thoroughly assess their own situations to determine what allocation or distribution of risks would serve them best. For instance, the viewpoint of a large city, with an excellent engineering force of its own, might be that it is to its advantage to minimize contractor risk and assume more of the risk itself. An owner with a large amount of engineering resources and a thorough and expert design staff could afford to assume a larger portion of the risk to obtain the overall benefit of lower costs. Other factors that should influence the owner's assessment are the type of construction (does it include high-risk construction such as underground work?), the degree of detail; accuracy and/or completeness of the plans and specifications, in some cases the urgency of the project, and similar considerations.

## IDENTIFICATION AND NATURE OF CONSTRUCTION RISKS

Although construction risks can be categorized in many ways, only four groupings are presented here: physical, capability, economic, and political and societal. In the process of identifying risks, only those that are created by the parties themselves in their attempts to transfer risks are included.

## CONTRACTUAL ALLOCATION OF RISK

In the absence of contractual provisions to the contrary, our legal system already allocates most construction risks between the designer, owner, and contractor. Therefore, when we speak of risk allocation, we really mean risk reallocation, risk spreading, or reaffirmation of the existing allocation of risk so that the risk stays where it otherwise would be.

There are two basic precepts or guidelines that should be recognized as criteria for the sharing of risks inherent in a construction project.

1. All risks are rightfully those of the owner unless and until contractually transferred to or assumed by the contractor or insurance underwriter for a fair compensation.
2. The principal guideline in determining whether a risk should be so transferred is whether the receiving party has both the competence to assess the risk fairly and the expertise necessary to control or minimize it. An additional guideline is the determination of whether the shift of the risk from the owner to another party will result in a savings to the owner and the public.

The principal means available for contractual allocation or reallocation of risk are the construction specifications for the construction contract and the owner/architect/engineer agreement for the design of the project. Under the format endorsed by the Engineers Joint Contract Documents Committee,[1] which has been approved and endorsed by the Associated General Contractors of America, such provisions would logically be spelled out in the General Conditions or the Supplementary General Conditions. In the case of a public works contract, the contractor does not have the opportunity to participate in the wording of the agreement between the parties. However, in private contracts risk allocation could become a valid bargaining consideration. The wording should in any case be prepared by competent legal counsel—avoiding the attitude adopted by some attorneys that their client is best served by exculpatory clauses that would seem to relieve their client of any responsibility for anything, including the negligence of their own personnel. The weakness of this attitude may become more evident during the settlement of some of the large claims that frequently follow such issues.

### Exculpatory Clauses

An exculpatory clause is one that attempts, by specific language, to shift a risk or burden of risk from one party to another. As the impacts of such clauses can be very great, a contractor must be very careful to review the contract for such exculpatory clauses to determine what risks are being shifted to it and how the bid should be adjusted to reflect that risk.

---

[1]Standard Forms of Agreement, Engineer, Owner, and Construction Related Documents prepared by Engineer's Joint Contract Documents Committee (American Consulting Engineers Council, American Society of Civil Engineers, Construction Specifications Institute, and National Society of Professional Engineers.

A contract, for example, may contain an exculpatory clause that is intended to shift the responsibility for the engineer's errors and omissions to the contractor, such as the clause illustrated in the following example:

> If the Contractor, in the course of the work, becomes aware of any claimed errors or omissions in the Contract Documents, it shall immediately inform the Engineer. The Engineer will then promptly review the matter and if an error or omission is found, the Engineer will advise the Contractor accordingly. After discovery of an error or omission by the Contractor, any related work performed by the Contractor shall be done at its own risk unless otherwise authorized in writing by the Engineer.

Under such a provision, the owner may claim that work done by the contractor in accordance with incorrect plans or specifications will not be paid for. While it is the intent of the clause to prevent the contractor from knowingly exploiting any errors or omissions the contractor may have become aware of to the detriment of the owner, one can see how such a clause could also be easily used against the unwary contractor.

In the following example of an exculpatory clause, a similar situation is created:

> The Contractor shall give all notices required by law and shall comply with all laws, ordinances, rules, and regulations pertaining to the conduct of the work. The Contractor shall be liable for all violations of the law in connection with work provided by the Contractor.

Under the terms of the foregoing provision, the contractor can be held liable for violations of the law, *even though those violations were the result of building the project in accordance with the plans and specifications that violated the law.* It is clearly the responsibility of the design professional to prepare plans and specifications that comply with all applicable laws; this clause unfairly shifts the responsibility for such compliance over to the contractor.

Although most exculpatory clauses are viewed by both state and federal courts on the basis of what is equitable to the parties as well as the specific language of the clause, some courts on occasion disregard the equitable considerations and apply only the harsh terms of the clause. In a recent New York court decision, Kalisch-Jarcho, Inc. was a successful bidder on an $8 million heating and air-conditioning contract for the construction of a new police headquarters in New York City. The contract included a provision in which Kalisch agreed to make no claim for damages for delay in the performance of the contract occasioned by an act or omission of the City, and any such claim would be compensated by an extension of time. Kalisch sued the city for breach of contract, claiming damages for 28 months of delay. The trial court awarded Kalisch approximately $1 million, but the decision was reversed upon appeal. The court found that the exculpatory clause protected the city from a claim of damage as there was no evidence that the delay had been intentional [*Kalisch-Jarcho, Inc.* v. *City of New York,* Ct. App. N.Y. (March 29, 1983)].

## WHO SHOULD ACCEPT WHAT RISKS?

There is no fixed rule to help answer this question, but Figure 10.2 suggests a starting position for determining who should bear what risks. It should be recognized, however, that

| Type of Risk | Contractor | Owner | Engineer | Comments |
|---|:---:|:---:|:---:|:---:|
| Site Access | | • | | |
| Subsurface Conditions | | • | | a |
| Quantity Variations | • | • | | b |
| Weather | • | | | c |
| Acts of God | | • | | |
| Financial Failure | • | • | • | |
| Subcontractor Failure | • | | | |
| Accidents at Site | • | | | |
| Defective Work | • | | | |
| Management Incompetence | • | • | • | |
| Inflation | • | • | | d |
| Economic Disasters | | • | | |
| Funding | | • | | |
| Materials and Equipment | • | | | |
| Labor Problems | • | | | |
| Owner-Furnished Equipment | | • | | |
| Delays in the Work | • | • | • | e |
| Environmental Controls | | • | | |
| Codes and Regulations | | • | | |
| Safety at Site | • | | | |
| Public Disorder | | • | | |
| Union Strife | • | | | |
| Errors and Omissions | | | • | |
| Conflicts in Documents | | | • | |
| Defective Design | | | • | |
| Shop Drawings | | | • | |

a—Can be transferred to the contractor; however, owner has obligation to undertake precontract exploration measures, and the designer has the responsibility to design for the conditions expected

b—Contractor can be expected to assume risk up to 15 to 25 percent. Where quantities are dependent upon unforseen subsurface conditions, owner must assume the risk.

c—Normal weather for the time and location only. Unusual inclement weather which delays the work is the owner's responsibility.

d—Sharing of escalation risk should be limited to 12 to 18 month span.

e—Usually the contractor's risk; however, owner could incur some liability.

**FIGURE 10.2**　Construction risk allocation to participants.

in some cases more than one party to the contract may share a common risk. In such cases, though, the risk may be shared in name only, as the specific risk carried by each party may differ materially in terms of the specific details of the risk they carry.

## TYPES OF RISKS AND ALLOCATION OF THOSE RISKS[2]

*Site access* is obviously an early risk and one that the owner should retain. The contractor lacks the capacity to influence those in control of the site to render it available. However, permit requirements that relate to a contractor's capacity or safety control program can be rightfully assumed by the contractor.

*Subsurface conditions* of soils, geology, or groundwater can be transferred to the contractor, who is in a better position to assess the impact of these conditions on the project cost and time. However, as an essential party of the transfer process, the owner has the responsibility to undertake precontract exploration measures and the designer has the responsibility to design for the conditions expected. The extent that this is not feasible should determine the degree to which the owner retains a portion of the risk under an "unforeseen conditions" clause.

*Weather,* except for extremely abnormal conditions, is a risk for the contractor to assume, as its impact on construction methods can be better assessed by the contractor.

*Acts of God,* such as flood or earthquake, are exposures that have no purpose in being transferred beyond the owner, except that the architect/engineer can assume the responsibility for designing to minimize their impact. However, to the extent that it can be occasioned by the contractor's operations, fire may be one shared with the owner.

*Quantity variations* are another form of risk frequently encountered. Within reasonable tolerances, quantities of work can be reasonably estimated and any variances assumed by the contractor for all quantities in excess of, for example, 15 to 25 percent. Where quantities are dependent upon subsurface or other lesser known conditions, significant variations should be shared only to the extent that exploratory information is available. Quantity changes triggered by late changes in the owner's requirements, however, should be at the owner's risk. Some types of variation, such as tunneling overbreak, are contractor controlled and should be borne by the contractor.

*Capability-related* risks are the result of the different capacity and expertise that each of the parties brings to the construction project. The consequences of failure of any party to measure up to these standards should be borne by the failing party. Unfortunately, this is not always the case. Too often the contractor who has the practical task of building the project carries the burden of the owner's or architect/engineer's failure. This, in turn, renders the contractor's performance task either unfeasible or feasible only at considerable extra cost.

*Defective design* is a risk usually associated with the architect or engineer. The tremendous expansion of construction has placed great burdens upon the design profes-

---

[2]This section follows J. Joseph Casey (President, Gordon H. Ball, Inc., Danville, CA), *Identification and Nature of Risks in Construction Projects: A Contractor's Perspective,* presented at the ASCE Specialty Conference on "Construction Risks and Liability Sharing," Scottsdale, AZ, January 24-26, 1979.

sions. Maintaining performance standards in the face of this is quite difficult, and occasionally, design or specification defects occur that create construction problems. Unfortunately, it is usually the owner and the contractor who suffer the consequences of such failures instead of the architect/engineer who created the problem in the first place. Design failures or constructability errors are becoming more and more apparent, and the architect/engineer should bear the true cost of such failures. Often, ill-advised use of performance specifications are provided as an escape from the responsibilities of design.

*Subcontractor failure* is a risk that is properly assumed by the contractor except where it arises from one of the other listed risks attributable to the owner or architect/engineer. The prime or general contractors are in the best position to assess the capacity of their subcontractors, and therefore it is they who should bear the risk of not assessing the risk properly.

*Defective work of construction,* to the extent that the problem is not caused by a design defect, should be the contractor's risk.

*Accident* exposures are inherent to the nature of the work and are best assessed by the contractors and their insurance and safety advisors. Furthermore, the contractors have the most control over site conditions that can increase or decrease accident exposure.

In the viewpoint of some, the recent trend toward "wrap-up" insurance coverage is a mistake. The safety record on a construction project is so heavily affected by the contractor's methods, site conditions, worker attitudes, and supervisor awareness that the owner will quite possibly obtain the opposite of what is sought for. Ultimately, the cost of insurance is the cost of the losses plus the cost of administering the compensation for these losses.

*Managerial competence* is a risk that must be shared by each party, as they each have their own set of managers. It is an ongoing challenge for each organization to assign personnel according to their respective competence levels.

*Financial failure* is a risk not frequently mentioned and can happen to any of the parties to a contract. Although infrequent, the order of magnitude of such failure should be considered. It is a shared risk, as the parties need to look at the financial resources of themselves, their partners in joint undertakings, and the other parties to the contract.

*Inflation* is one of the world's realities. Every owner is conscious of its impact on the viability of any project. It is important that the owner retain the true cost of a project. Government experts in finance have so far been unable to predict where the country will be a few years from now, so it is unfair to expect the contractor to do better than so-called government experts. The contractor's apprehensions will result in higher cost to the owner, or unwarranted optimism will result in the contractor's own financial harm. A default resulting from such a failure will result in even greater costs to the owner. The sharing of the escalation risk should therefore be limited to a short span of time, approximately 12 to 18 months, when union agreements usually expire and beyond which is pure speculation.

*Economic disasters,* as referred to herein, are periodic economic disasters of such magnitude that a contractor could not properly assess either their probability or their cost impact. An example might be OPEC decisions, nationwide strikes, devaluation, tax rate changes, and similar large-scale incidents. The owner should retain the risk of such disasters.

*Funding* is obviously a risk beyond the capacity of the contractor to control. Improper sources of these funds may occasion delays or create interest costs that are not anticipated and financing problems that to many contractors are unbearable. There is no moral justification for a competent contractor being driven out of business by delayed compensation for services rendered. This is especially true in the protracted negotiation of changes. All too often the owner plays the cash-flow game to lever dispute negotiations to the owner's advantage. Some large contractors with financial capability may be able to fund these delays, with great outlay of interest, but all too often, the smaller contractor cannot even survive.

*Labor, materials, and equipment* involve considerable risks. The availability and productivity of the resources necessary to construct the project are risks that it is proper for the contractor to assume. The expertise of the contractor should follow the assessment of cost and time required to obtain and apply these resources. This is the basic service that the owner is paying for.

*Acceleration or suspension of the work* is a risk properly retained by the owner, but is all too often pushed onto the contractor in the form of "constructive acceleration" or "constructive suspension." An objective appraisal of the facts underlying the situation and acceptance of responsibility where it belongs is necessary. It is important to realize that this applies to legitimate acceleration, however, and not to false claims of acceleration as described in Chapter 13 under the heading "Who Owns Float?"

*Political and societal* is an area of growing importance to any effort at risk allocation. It is an area in which political and social pressures from parties having little interest in a project but having a great impact on such a project greatly influences its outcome. This is an unclear area and deserves much careful thought as to how the risk should be allocated—in some cases it is clear, in others it is vague.

*Environmental* risks rightfully belong to the owner alone and should be retained by the owner except to the extent that they are influenced by construction methods determined by the contractor, or created by suppliers controlled by the contractor.

*Regulations* by government in the social area, such as safety and economic opportunity, are the rules under which the contractor rightfully must operate. Although there is additional risk in this less known and interpretive area, it is similar to the work rules established by union contract or agreements.

*Public disorder and war* are political catastrophes of such impact that their risk is best retained by the owner, lest it becomes necessary to pay an unusually high price for transferring the risk to another party.

*Union strife* and all that it entails are risks that are properly taken by the contractor. Unjustified work rules and similar problems are all risks that the contractor must assess and provide for.

## Risk Distribution

To many contractors, risk management is the nature of their business. That is what they are paid to do. Management of risk first involves a "go/no-go" decision on risk assumption. To the extent that this process is complicated by unwarranted "risk dumping," the costs in time and money eventually find their way to the owner in the form of higher prices.

There have been some construction contracts where total physical risk was assigned to the contractor, including the risk of unforeseen (changed) conditions and of variations of quantities required to complete the work. Even under such extreme allocation of risk, the owner still retains a very substantial risk that the contractor may not comply with the terms of the contract and properly complete the work within the allotted time. Even if a claim is made under a performance bond, substantial damage may certainly have already occurred. Under the best of circumstances, from the owner's viewpoint, the owner will retain material risk. It is therefore important that the owner recognize the existence of this risk and not be lulled into the false sense of security that it has somehow been passed on to the contractor or the contractor's surety. Unreasonably burdening the contractor does not necessarily rid the owner of the risk. Default on the part of the contractor in whole or in part is also a very real risk that the owner can be left with.

Inclusion in a contract of the frequently used (or "misused") disclaimer provision relating to geological information furnished the bidders for underground construction may not be as effective in passing risk to the contractor as some might think, because such clauses are of questionable enforceability. Despite this, such exculpatory clauses continue to be used, and such use actually places the risk upon all of the parties to the contract, without at the same time providing any relief to anyone. Under such circumstances, a dispute will frequently arise if the geological formation does not coincide with what is found in the field. Such a dispute may not be resolved until many years have passed, and then only at great expense to all of the parties to the contract, with the resulting effect of creating a substantial increase in the cost of the project. The final result is that the owner may have to bear certain risks anyway, despite any contract clauses to the contrary. In view of this, it may be wiser for the owner to recognize these facts at the beginning and provide contractually for the owner's assumption of such risks.

The fact that the contractor carries a substantial burden of risk is beyond dispute. Unfortunately, it seems that the viewpoint of many who design and administer construction contracts is that the contractor should carry virtually all of the risk, whether provided in the contract or not, and it is precisely this attitude that has contributed to the inevitable litigation that will follow.

## The Contractor's Viewpoint[3]

It is not sufficient to establish policy on how risk is to be allocated among the parties. Follow-up is required to insure that these policies are actually being implemented. The owner may determine that it is in its own interest to undertake extensive geological investigation for an underground project. However, this effort may be wasted if the frequently used disclaimer provision regarding geological information furnished to the bidders is included in the contract documents.

---

[3]Adapted from Norman A. Nadel (President, MacLean Grove & Company, Inc., New York, NY), *Allocation of Risk—A Contractor's View,* presented at the ASCE Specialty Conference on "Construction Risks and Liability Sharing," Scottsdale, AZ, January 24-26, 1979.

In the specifications for a recent subway construction contract that involved underground rock tunneling, there was a "changed condition" clause included. The borings generally indicated reasonably sound rock with ample cover over the roof of the tunnel. Despite this, the specifications writer saw fit to include the following paragraph:

> The contractor's procedures for tunnel excavation shall provide for such construction techniques, including but not limited to, reduced heading advance, multiple narrow drift excavation, forepoling, pumping of cement or grout to reduce water inflow, and any other techniques applicable to rock tunneling, that may be required due to the nature of the rock encountered.

Here, any benefit thought to be obtained from the use of the changed conditions clause by the owner was clearly lost when that paragraph was added.

Contractors sometimes find themselves at the mercy of contract administrators who lack the courage to implement the contract in accordance with its terms. For example, a contractor was engaged in the construction of a rock tunnel for a subway in which the borings indicated sound rock with substantial cover over the tunnel roof. In actuality, the rock cover disappeared and approximately 30 meters (100 ft) of the tunnel had to be excavated utilizing soft-ground techniques. Before encountering the area of reduced cover, the rate of progress was such that the excavation for the stretch of tunnel in question would have taken approximately 8 days. Actually, more than 6 months were required to redesign the support system, to secure the necessary materials, and to excavate the tunnel utilizing a much slower and costlier procedure. Despite these facts, the contract administrator refused to find that a changed condition existed. Instead, it was determined that "extra work" was being performed for which, under the terms of the contract, the contractor could be paid only for certain direct costs.

The contractor had been denied payment for the very great costs that resulted from the delay of the work. Under the provisions of the changed conditions clause of the contract, the contractor was very clearly entitled to payment for the costs of the delay. The contractor was left with no alternative but to seek relief in court, a process that is going to be very expensive and time consuming to both the contractor and the engineering firm and owner.

As an intelligent application of the risk allocation procedures, it would seem that the application of the following guidelines could be helpful to produce construction at the lowest possible cost:

1. If a risk is imposed upon a party, an opportunity for reward to that party should exist for properly dealing with the risk.
2. Allocation of the risk to the party who is in the best position to control it.
3. Allocation of the risk to a party in whose hands the efficiency of the system is best promoted.
4. Allocation of the risk to the party who is best able to undertake it financially.
5. Steps should be taken to assure that risks are actually allocated as intended.

Occasionally, it may not be apparent how a given risk should be allocated. In such a case, careful consideration of what may be the motivation of the parties involved may be productive.

## How Are Risks Allocated?[4]

How are risks allocated, and how should they be allocated? The allocation is initially made by the owner's legal department or its specifications department, which prepares the contract forms that are offered to the bidders on a take-it-or-leave-it basis. To the extent that such persons or departments are sensitive to practical construction and contract administration problems, possibly some contractor organizations or engineers may be capable of exerting some influence upon them in the preparation of these documents and the resultant reallocation of risks. More coercive and effective (and more expensive) allocations are the kinds made through the courts.

In the traditional construction contracting practice, the owner would allocate almost all of the risks to the contractor, saying in effect: "You deal with all of the construction problems and all the third parties, and don't bother me." In this same tradition, the architect/engineer would design a structure in its finished condition, and if any thought was given to the construction problems that might be involved in building it, considerable care was taken not to express any opinions on these matters in the contract documents.

This one-sided attitude fostered two results:

1. Contractors added high contingencies to their bids to cover the costs of the risks
2. Litigation of construction contract claims followed.

Broadly speaking, the owners lost; the courts reallocated many risks that the owners thought they had laid on the contractor and, as a result, the owners paid for their risks *twice*—once in bidding contingencies and a second time in court. Meanwhile, the contractors were not profiting either. They were losing money on delays and disputes, and often just breaking even (if they were lucky) in court. Construction law, as a result, is rapidly becoming a very profitable field—for lawyers.

## Risks Reserved to the Contractor

In addition to the types of risks referred to under "Types of Risks and Allocation of Those Risks," the following are typical of the risks reserved to the contractor:

1. The contractor should bear all risks over which the contractor can exercise reasonable control. These include all matters relating to selection of construction methods, equipment, and prosecution of the work except as this control is affected by the action of third parties.
2. In the area of third-party effects, risks should be allocated to those best able to deal with the third party. This principle would assign to the owner the risks related to government agency regulations and to agreements with adjacent property owners.

---

[4]Following Thomas R. Kuesel (Senior Vice President, Parsons, Brinckerhoff, Quade, & Douglas, Inc., New York, NY), *Allocation of Risks,* presented at the ASCE Specialty Conference on "Construction Risks and Liability Sharing," Scottsdale, AZ, January 24-26, 1979.

    Risks associated with labor and subcontractor agreements and disputes should be assigned to the contractor.

**3.** Construction safety should be the responsibility of the contractor, although financial risk with regard to third parties is properly allocated to insurers (either the contractor's or the owner's).

Construction is a highly complex business. Guidelines, recommendations, regulations, contracts, and even legal rulings can only provide direction for judging a particular situation. Among the most difficult and important to define factors in evaluating and allocating risk are the reputations of the parties to the contract. Some owners and some architect/engineers have earned reputations such that reputable contractors will not bid on their projects. Others have reputations that even attract bidders who would pass up similar work in other jurisdictions. Conversely, some contractors have earned reputations that invite contract administration "by the book," whereas others enjoy the ability to secure many contract modifications by negotiation. The risk of an unfavorable reputation (or the benefit of a favorable one) is earned by all parties over a long period. It is not allocable, and it is not rapidly changed.

## MINIMIZING RISKS AND MITIGATING LOSSES[5]

The provisions and methods used in allocating risks should be clear and straightforward enough so that all of the parties know in advance what risks they have assumed, how they will be compensated, and that they can monitor the process. Otherwise, the owner may lose the benefit of the allocation and may even end up paying for the risk twice.

    In the allocation of risks, it is important not to discourage designer innovation or production of ultraconservative, defensive designs. Designers cannot innovate if placed in a position where the amount of their fee does not cover their risks, unless the owner will protect them as a means of encouraging new concepts.

    The concept of minimizing risks and mitigating losses can be implemented initially by the adoption of a set of management policy positions that are vital to the success of the program. Whereas any one policy item may in itself appear to be somewhat insignificant, collectively they can save a company a considerable amount of trouble.

    The following principles are essential to an effective risk management program:

**1.** Thorough engineering, with competent advance planning to minimize the delays

**2.** Adequate subsurface exploration and interpretation of the data as it affects both design and construction

**3.** Full disclosure of all information available to the owner and the designer to the contractor

---

[5]Adapted from Henry J. Jacoby (Chairman, Grow Tunneling Corporation, New York, NY), *Summary Session,* and David G. Hammond, *Minimizing Risks and Mitigating Losses,* presented at the ASCE Specialty Conference on "Construction Risks and Liability Sharing," Scottsdale, AZ, January 24-26, 1979.

4. Permits and rights-of-way obtained in advance by the owner
5. Strong, competent management by all parties
6. On-site decision-making ability to minimize delays
7. Adequate procedures for handling disputes promptly, as the work progresses
8. Adequate financial security of all parties
9. Contractor participation during design phase, or for public agency contracts, contractor value-engineering clauses in the contract with shared savings provision
10. Good labor contracts and conditions to improve productivity

No attempt was made in the foregoing list to assess the effect of regulatory agencies and the interagency disputes that delay and increase the cost of projects. These are recognized as major risks and are considered beyond the ability of the owner, architect/engineer, or contractor to control or minimize except through the legislative or political process.

## Contractor Participation in Value Engineering

Value engineering by the contractor is a subject that is viewed as controversial by some, but the concept has potential benefits as a means of minimizing risks and cost overruns. Value engineering by the contractor (see Chapter 15) involves contractor proposals for changing construction methods or designs as a means of reducing project construction costs. Generally, such concepts involve a cost-sharing provision on any savings realized. Many designers resist such potential intrusions of the contractor into their hallowed ground. They often feel that their design approach was the proper one in the first place, and it is a reflection upon their design ability if the contractor dares to question it. Nevertheless, it should be recognized that for most projects, the identity of the contractor will not be known at the time of design. Obviously, what an architect/engineer might call for or permit to be done by a contractor whose qualifications were known and trusted might be quite different from that which could be allowed for a contractor who is known to the designer only as the "low bidder" with bonding capability, but otherwise unknown virtues.

## Management Structures

Of major importance in the minimizing of risks and mitigating of losses is the management structure used for prosecution of the project. This includes all management, supervisory, and working levels of the owner, architect/engineer, construction manager, and the contractor.

## Long-Lead Procurement

Before making a final decision about prepurchase of materials or equipment by the owner, the impact should be considered of the added risks that are thus assumed by the owner, such as latent defects, damage in transit, storage costs, compatibility problems, maintenance, and others. There can be several valid reasons for owner prepurchase, but saving money on the purchase price is not generally one of them. The contractor must still add a percentage for handling and installation and, after the project is ready for testing and operation, if the pre-purchased equipment does not work properly and substitutions or replacements must be ordered, the owner will become liable for the added cost of project slowdown and delays. Thus, instead of liability reduction, liability has only increased.

There are certain cases, of course, where it may be necessary to prepurchase equipment, such as in the case of long-lead factory-fabricated items. Here again, the owner must consider the risks and costs and the ability to furnish the equipment to the contractor when it is needed; what handling and erection costs will be, and whether there is warehousing and maintenance capability available. As an alternative, on long-lead purchases, the owner may include an assignment of contract provision in the construction contract. In this manner, the cost of the prepurchase can be included in the project cost as an allowance, and the successful contractor contractually agrees to accept assignment of the prepurchase contract as soon as the construction contract has been executed. In this manner, the contractor makes payment directly to the manufacturer or fabricator of the item at the prescribed time, expedites delivery, and arranges for delivery, unloading, storage, maintenance, and installation just as would have been done had the contractor personally initiated the order in the first place. This reduces the owner's risk and places it in the hands of the contractor who generally has more experience and ability in the handling of such transactions. The cost will be reflected in the contractor's bid just as if the purchase had been a sole source procurement in the construction contract.

## Permits and Rights-of-Way

Another way to minimize losses is for the owner to obtain permits and rights-of-way in advance of construction. Some permits can often be better obtained by the owner than by the contractor. In addition, there will be some savings to the owner by not having the contractor's markup added to the task of obtaining them and paying the fees. Some permits can be better handled by the contractor, and some judgment must be exercised in the allocation of these responsibilities. Permits for things such as haul routes, disposal sites, and similar items are better handled by the contractor, who has a better understanding of the plan of work.

It is generally agreed by all that whenever possible, it is better to have the owner obtain rights-of-way in advance of construction and make them available to the contractor upon notice to proceed. Although this is the ideal arrangement, often the complete rights-of-way are not available at the time that the construction should start. Here the owner must weigh the somewhat known risk of delaying the contractor while the contract is in force until the rights-of-way become available for the contractor to start, knowing full well that there may be some negative effect on the contractor's efficiency of operation and therefore on the project cost to both the owner and the contractor.

## Disputes

Even in the area of disputes there is still some leeway for cost-saving measures. After a difference of opinion has been expressed, adequate machinery must be put into action for the resolution of such problems. The *second worst* way to handle claims is to ignore them; the *worst* way is to allow them to go to litigation. If handled promptly and vigorously, most disputes can be resolved without their being permitted to degenerate into large problems affecting not only the cost to the project, but the progress of the work. It is important to both the efficient progress of the work and the lowest cost to both the owner and the contractor in the performance of "changed conditions" work that such changes be negotiated and settled as soon as possible.

## Disclosure of Information

It has been common until recently for owners to keep design or site information in their possession to themselves, providing the contractor only with so-called "factual information." Only recently has this been recognized as not in the best interest of the owner or the architect/engineer. On the Baltimore Subway Project, for example, complete disclosure was made to the contractor in the bidding documents not only of factual data, such as boring logs and cores, but of the designer's interpretation of how the ground or rock was expected to act during construction. A complete geotechnical report including both factual data and design analysis was made available to the bidders in the form of a geotechnical report. It is considered probable that the furnishing of such complete information enabled and forced the owner and engineer to do a more complete subsurface exploration and thus avoided some surprises. The evidence to date appears to support the premise that lower bids may be anticipated from bidders when this approach is taken. Low bids on this project averaged 10 percent below the engineer's estimate.

In contrast, on the Chicago TARP Project, where the initial philosophy was that all risks were to be assumed by the contractor, the contract did not provide any provisions such as those for changed conditions and the geotechnical information provided to the contractor was factual only, for which the owner further disclaimed any responsibility. Initial bids taken on early contracts resulted in few bids being submitted, and those that were submitted were in amounts more than double the engineer's estimates. Subsequent modifications in the philosophy in the contract documents resulted in an improvement in that situation.

## PROBLEMS

1. True or false? All risk belongs to the owner unless transferred by contract.
2. Describe the two primary concepts involved in risk management.
3. What are principal issues that should be considered in the allocation and assumption of risk responsibility?
4. Name the six categories of risk.
5. In a construction contract, which is the best party to bear the various risks?
6. What are the four guidelines for allocation of risk in construction contracts?
7. Name one alternative to long-lead purchase and issuance to the contractor of products as "owner-furnished equipment".
8. Name four types of construction risks that are properly allocated solely to the contractor.
9. Name four types of risks that are properly retained solely by the owner.
10. Name four types of risks that are properly allocated solely to the engineer or architect.

# 11

## *Preconstruction Operations*

### DESCRIPTION OF APPROACH

On a project involving a field staff of two or more persons, the organizational structure of the Resident Project Representative's field office is often determined by a design or construction management firm as the representative of the owner of the project. It should be clearly understood before work on the project begins that all assignments and limits of authority and responsibility are as delegated to the Resident Project Representative by his or her employer. On larger projects, it might be desirable to draft an organizational diagram or chart that clearly defines all levels of responsibility and authority on the proposed project. Such a chart can be of immeasurable help in expediting the work when new tasks must be done and the normal procedures are not applicable.

Preconstruction operations can generally be grouped into five phases.

1. Advertise and award phase
2. Development of quality control program or construction surveillance and inspection plan on CQC projects
3. Field office organization phase (planning)
4. Preconstruction conference
5. Establishment of a field office at the construction site for the administration and quality assurance of the work for the owner

Frequently, the Resident Project Representative is not involved in the project during the advertise and award phase at all; however, this phase of the work will be covered in this chapter for the benefit of those whose obligations do include this phase of the work. In cases where that obligation is not included, the Resident Project Representative's tasks may be limited to the performance of items 3, 4, and 5 only of the foregoing list.

**240**

## CONSTRUCTABILITY ANALYSIS

Often overlooked, except by some large engineering organizations such as the Corps of Engineers, a constructability analysis is an essential element in the plan to provide competent plans and specifications and avoid or, at the very least, minimize the owner's exposure to preventable claims.

Although the value of a constructability analysis was discovered by the rest of the construction industry rather belatedly, constructability is evolving as one of the most significant enhancement opportunities in the construction industry. Although practiced for many years by a few organizations, only recently has it come to focus as offering major benefits in construction cost and schedule. The Business Roundtable's Construction Industry Cost Effectiveness (CICE) Project identified constructability as an area with a major potential for improved cost-effectiveness.

There is no single method to achieve the desired results. The type of contract in which to implement constructability is on turnkey (design–build) projects; it is much more difficult to do on projects where design and construction are accomplished by distinct and separate contracts. Each discipline seems to resent the intrusion of the other into what it considers as its "turf."

If constructability is to work, there must be a bridge between the traditional separation of design and construction. This is sometimes accomplished through the involvement of Professional Construction Management firms, which often possess these areas of expertise, and when acting as direct representatives of the owner have the clout to carry it through with the design organizations.

As proposed by the Business Roundtable, systems were examined that have proven to be the best for implementing constructability. Company or project size is no barrier to constructability, as it is equally valuable to both large and small organizations. However, some smaller companies have elected to combine some constructability functions.

One of the most effective means of achieving involvement of constructability specialists into the planning and design process is to bring in the construction discipline as a component of the project team, starting the first day. In order to be effective, the construction discipline must be accorded full participation in the planning design sessions.

One of the biggest obstacles to good constructability is the *review syndrome*. This occurs when construction personnel are excluded from the planning process and are invited only to "review" completed or partially completed work received from the designers. This prevents construction knowledge and expertise input in the early planning, when cost sensitivity is at a maximum and construction should be making its most important contributions.

When constructability is approached solely on a review basis, it inevitably becomes inefficient and ineffective. The designer becomes defensive because he or she has already committed publicly on the drawings and specifications being reviewed, and the reviewer is reluctant to comment lest he or she be perceived as being overly critical.

The most effective approach is to place the entire constructability team into active roles in an integrated planning and design development process. In that environment, the whole array of alternatives is discussed up front and jointly evaluated. One excellent technique is to hold a series of project constructability brainstorming sessions as the first project activity. Analyses and trade-offs can be made before the project design is finalized.

## ADVERTISE AND AWARD PHASE

During the advertising phase, the Resident Project Representative should review the contract documents carefully to make certain that all important field considerations have been provided for in the specifications. If, during the award phase, omissions are noted in the plans or specifications or if conditions are specified that may create conflicts in the field, there is still time to provide written notice to the design firm of any such omissions or conflicts so that it can issue an addendum to the specifications prior to bid opening time. Thus the problem can be corrected in time to eliminate the need of a change order during construction.

An example of such omission might be the failure of the design firm to specify that the contractor shall furnish a field office for the Resident Project Representative's use throughout the life of the project, unless the design firm or owner intends to provide such facilities. The omission of a requirement for a field office in the specifications was once the cause of the author spending a long uncomfortable year at a project site in a prefabricated tool shed that the contractor was talked into providing as a field office at no additional cost. Anyone who has ever had this experience will realize its shortcomings. In rainy weather the choice was to close the window flaps and keep dry—in the dark, or to leave the flaps open and get plenty of light—and get wet. It was hot in the summer and freezing in the winter, and the dirt was often so thick that the floor was obscured.

Another thing to look for in the specifications is a requirement for a field telephone. If a free telephone is not specified, the contractor will either provide none in the inspector's field office, or if a telephone is provided, he or she will invariably provide a pay phone—after all, if a telephone was not in the specifications, there is no valid reason for the contractor to have included the cost of a free one for the resident project representative in the bid. If a pay phone is installed, the Resident Project Representative will have to keep a pocket full of change at all times to be capable of communicating with the home office. The ideal approach is to require that the contractor provide, maintain, and pay for, for the full term of the project, a field telephone in the Resident Project Representative's field office as well as in the contractor's field office. This is fair to the contractor as well as to the owner, for it allows a fixed telephone cost to be bid as part of the proposal. This telephone should also be specified to be connected to an established exchange for toll service and with all other phones that may be used by the contractor. This may sound like an unnecessary precaution, but consider the fix the author found himself in some time ago when the telephone in the field office was part of a private telephone system of the contractor and *could not be connected* to a regular public telephone service for local or toll calls! It is equally important to see that the telephones provided in the contractor's field office and in the Resident Project Representative's field office be on separate trunklines. A party-line or extension telephone, including key phones that allow selection of both the contractor's and the inspector's trunkline, is undesirable, as it allows no security of communications for either party.

Naturally, the mention of toll service may scare the contractor unless some pre-arranged agreement has been reached concerning the use of the telephone for long-distance calls. It is recommended that the contractor permit the Resident Project Representative, the design firm, the owner, or any of their authorized representatives to use the telephone without cost for all calls that do not involve published toll charges. Calls that do involve toll charges should then be billed to the owner by the contractor *at the actual rate charged* by the telephone company.

There are many other points to watch for in the specifications; many of them involve technical matters. In all cases, if a description of the problem can be submitted to the design firm in time, and if they agree with the inspector's recommendations, this item can become a part of the contract requirements before bid-opening time.

Prior to bid-opening time, the Resident Project Representative should meet with the project manager to develop an agenda and a list of key subjects to be discussed at the pre-construction conference. In addition, the project manager should contact the owner to see if assistance will be wanted during the preparations for and during the bid opening.

During the bid-holding period following the opening of all bids, but prior to determination of the award of the construction contract, the Resident Project Representative should be available, if requested by the design firm or the owner to assist in the evaluation of bid data, costs, and other contractually significant items. In this manner, the architect's or engineer's job of making recommendations to the owner for award of the contract can be made much simpler and easier.

## ISSUANCE OF BIDDING DOCUMENTS

At first, the subject of issuing bidding documents (plans and specifications and related materials) seems like a minor one. Yet if not properly handled, particularly on public works projects, serious claims or project delays can result. The following summarizes just a few of the more important details that must be handled during the bidding phase of a project:

1. After advertising for bids, keep an accurate log of all sets of contract documents issued, the firm name and legal address of each bidder, the name and position of the party picking up the documents for the firm, the date picked up, the amount of fee or deposit received and whether it was in the form of cash or check, the number of sets picked up by each bidder, and if the sets are numbered, the serial numbers of the sets delivered to each bidder. This log, in the form of a preprinted form, can be kept by a receptionist and construction documents can be issued at the front desk. One recommended format is shown in Figure 11.1.

2. Whenever there are changes in the drawings that are issued as an addenda to the bidding documents, a copy of the addenda should be mailed to each holder of a set of contract documents. Where a single bidder has obtained more than one set of documents, a copy of the addenda should be sent for each set obtained. All such addenda should be sent to each bidder by certified mail, with a "return receipt requested," and should be addressed to each bidder's legal address (preferably *not* a post office box). Meanwhile, all as-yet-undistributed sets of documents should

# RECORD OF BID DOCUMENTS

Project Name: Parker WWTP Expansion
Project No.: 3-704
Project Manager: G. F. Albrecht
Phone ext. 544

Am't req'd per set $ 50.00   fee [X]   deposit [ ]
Must sets be returned? No

| DATE ISSUED | FIRM NAME & ADDRESS OF RECIPIENT (Legal Address of Firm - Street Address) | NAME OF INDIVIDUAL RECIPIENT TELEPHONE NO. OF FIRM (Include Area Codes) | FEE OR DEPOSIT AMOUNT | Cash | Check | DATE REC'D | DATE RET'D | DOCUMENTS NO. SETS | SET NUMBERS | ADDENDA ISSUED 1/6 | 2/7 | 3/8 | 4/9 | 5/10 |
|---|---|---|---|---|---|---|---|---|---|---|---|---|---|---|
| 3/3/80 | LMN Contractors 1000 Argus St. Centerville, MO 63100 | G. F. Edwards (314) 000-0000 | 50 |- | | x | 3/3 | | 1 | 001 | ✓ | ✓ | | | |
| 3/3/80 | ABC Construction, Inc. 1000 N. Tustin Orange, CA 92600 | L. M. Ciabottoni (714) 000-0000 | 150 |- | | x | 3/3 | | 3 | 002 003 004 | ✓ | ✓ | | | |
| 3/3/80 | T & G Paving 2765 Columbine Ave. Suburbia, MO 63100 | H. F. Jorgensen (816) 000-0000 | 50 |- | x | | 3/2 | | 1 | 005 | ✓ | ✓ | | | |
| 3/4/80 | Concrete Specialties, Inc. 50 Samsone St. Centerville, MO 63100 | H. Bedrosian (314) 000-0000 | 50 |- | x | | 3/3 | | 1 | 006 | ✓ | ✓ | | | |
| 3/5/80 | Emerson & Farnsworth 1000 Any Street Dallas, TX | Geo. F. Carson (214) 000-0000 | 100 |- | | | 3/2 | | 2 | 007 008 | ✓ | ✓ | | | |

CM 101

**FIGURE 11.1**  Example of a Record of Bid Documents.

be brought up to date simply by including a copy of the addenda with each set so that all bidders picking up sets of documents after issuance of an addenda will receive theirs along with the initial issue.

3. At the time that a project is advertised for bidding and the estimated number of document sets have been reproduced, all project drawings should be sent out to have reproducible copies made so that there will be a permanent record of the set as originally issued, and in case of a sellout on all preprinted sets of documents, additional identical sets can still be reproduced, even though later changes may already have been posted on the original transparencies. In this manner, if later changes are made to the drawings and you run out of bid document sets, another set of drawings *in their original form* can still be printed.

It is of vital importance that all bidders receive *identical* sets of bidding documents. It is not proper to issue later drawings where changes covered in a previous addenda have already been posted, as charges of bidding irregularity may well be made and sustained. If this were to happen, the first group of bidders would have received the old drawings with a copy of an addenda that instructs the bidders as to what changes are to be made—and the bidders would have to post them on their own drawings. This means that the addenda was subject to the bidder's interpretation. However, if a bidder picked up an updated set of drawings later, the later bidder would have received a set of documents upon which the architect/engineer had posted the corrections, and thus the addenda would have been subject to the architect/engineer's interpretation—an obvious irregularity. Not only that, but problems in drafting errors can cause difficulty, and often do. When the architect/engineer posts all corrections, as on the later sets of drawings referred to, a drafting error could easily be the cause of the later set of drawings being not even technically the same as the earlier set plus its addenda.

Such irregularities can be sufficient cause to have all bids set aside and the entire project forced to be rebid. This can not only lead to costly delays in getting a project started, but might also influence the amounts of each bid after each bidder has had the opportunity for full disclosure of the amount of each of the other bids. Frequently, this is not to the financial advantage of the owner.

## PREQUALIFCATION OF BIDDERS

Some states provide for prequalification of bidder on public contracts. In fact, in Massachusetts a court held that "bidder prequalification is not mere formality; it is a cornerstone of the competitive bidding statute," and ruled that the statute must be construed strictly [*Modern Continental Construction Co.* v. *City of Lowell,* 465 N.E.2d 1173 (Mass. 1984)].

Several states employ prequalification requirements for public works bidding. These include California [Govt Code §14310 et seq (1980)]; Colorado, [Colo. Rev. Stat. § 24-92-107 (1982)]; Delaware, [Del. Code Ann. tit. 29, §6905 (1983)]; Hawaii, [Hawaii Rev. Stat. § 103-25 (1976)]; Indiana, [Ind. Code § 5-16-1-2 (1974)]; Maine, [Me. Rev. Stat. Ann. tit. 5, §1747 (1979)]; Massachusetts, [23 B.C.L.Rev. 1357 (Mass. 1982)]; Michigan, [Mich.

Comp. Laws Ann. §123.501 (1967)]; Nebraska, [Neb. Rev. Stat. §73-102 (1981)]; Pennsylvania, [Pa. Stat. Ann. tit. 71, §642 (1962)]; Virginia, [Code of Va. §11-46 (1984 Supp.)]; and Wisconsin, [Wis. Stat. Ann. §66.29 (1965)].

## BONDS

### Bid Bonds

When an owner decides that some security is needed to protect it against the financial disadvantages that may occur because a bidder later refused or was unable to sign an agreement to construct the work after submitting a bid, there are a couple of alternatives open. In any case, the bid security should amount to at least 5 percent and is often 10 percent of the contractor's bid price. Bid bonds, certified checks, cashier's checks, and sometimes negotiable securities may be accepted as bid security. The security assures the owner that if the contract is awarded to the successful bidder, that bidder will enter into contract with the owner. After the bids are opened and an award made, bid securities are returned to all bidders. If, however, the selected bidder cannot or will not enter into contract, the bid security is forfeited and award is made to the next bidder in line on the same basis.

The bid bond is far preferable to other securities, as it is less of a burden upon the contractor. Bid bonds should preferably be in an amount of 10 percent of the bid price for the project.

A surety company makes only a nominal charge to a contractor for a bid bond, and although writing one does not commit the surety to write a performance and payment bond later, it is a good indication that they are willing to do so. Bid bonds should be of the "forfeiture" type that gives the owner a direct right of action under the bond.

Although optional on private contracts, all public works contracts require the contractor to post a bid bond as security with the bid. Under the terms of a bid bond, the surety company agrees to pay a stipulated sum of money to the owner, as a forfeit, if the bidder is awarded the contract and fails to enter into an agreement with the owner to construct the work.

### Performance and Payment Bonds

After award of the contract, the contractor is required to provide performance and payment (labor and materials) bonds on all public works contracts. Although this is not common in private works, and is actually actively opposed by some groups, there is a current move toward the utilization of bonds on private works as a hedge against potential lien claims and failure to complete the work.

Under a performance bond, the surety has an obligation to the owner for any additional costs to complete the contract due to the contractor's failure to comply with its contract requirements. The most common reason for a contractor not completing a contract is insolvency. Therefore, sureties are interested in the contractor's financial condition as well as other qualifications before writing a performance bond. Generally, a contractor's ability to take a large contract is a function of bonding capacity, as the bonding company will only risk a slight increase over previous bond amounts. In this manner, the road from being a small contractor to becoming a large contractor doing $20 million projects is a long, slow, step-by-step process with the bonding company.

Under a payment bond, the surety guarantees the payment of all legitimate labor and materials bills that result from the performance of the contract. The surety has an obligation to the owner for the additional costs that are the result of failure of a contractor to pay the labor and materials bills due to the performance of work on the contract.

Combination payment and performance bonds, which include in one instrument the obligation for both the performance of the contract and the payment of laborers and material suppliers, have resulted in difficulties and delays in the handling of claims. It is recommended that where bonds are to be provided, they should be separate bonds issued by the surety as a "package," for which no additional charge is made. Under the two-bond system, the surety is enabled to make payment without awaiting a determination as to owner's priority. The customary amount of public works bonds the author has seen are in an amount of 100 percent on performance bonds and 50 percent on payment bonds. However, the Construction Industry Affairs Committee of Chicago, with membership spanning both the design profession and the contractor associations, recommends that both the payment and performance bonds be written in the amount of 100 percent of the contract price.

When prime contractors require a surety bond from their subcontractors, the prime contractor's position is similar to that of an owner. Prime contractors should be careful to obtain bonds from their subcontractors that are of the same form and not less than the guarantee that the prime is giving the owner under the owner's own bond.

Where awards can be made to prequalified contractors, such as on private work, surety bonds might be eliminated if the financial stability and record of performance of the contractor are known to be satisfactory. Performance bonds and payment bonds are not guarantees of trouble-free jobs but do protect the owner from additional costs due to the contractor's failure to complete a contract or to pay bills.

## Time of Submittal of Bonds

Under the 5-step project initiation process described in Chapter 1, a bid bond must be submitted at the time of submitting bids (item 2 in Figure 11.2). Upon being awarded the contract, the successful bidder is obligated to enter into contract with the owner for construction of the work. If the awardee fails to enter into contract with the owner, the bid bond is forfeited and the owner will then award to the next-lowest bidder.

On public works projects, after award of the contract, a bidder who enters into a contract with the owner must submit a performance bond and a payment bond to the owner. This should be submitted to the owner at the time of submitting the signed agreement form to the owner for its signature (item 4 in Figure 11.2). Upon receipt of the signed agreement from the successful bidder, the owner releases all remaining bidders' bonds and affixes its own signature to the agreement. Then, subsequent to execution of the agreement by both parties, a Notice to Proceed may be issued (item 5 in Figure 11.2).

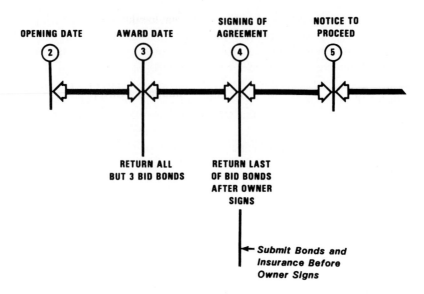

**FIGURE 11.2**   Flow diagram for bond submittal.

## LIABILITY FORMS OF INSURANCE

### Comprehensive General (Public) Liability Insurance

This type of insurance protects against legal liability to the public. There are many forms of liability insurance, but the one usually recommended for construction is the Broad Form Comprehensive Liability Policy (Automobile included). Under this type, all forms of liability insurance are combined in one contract. Physical damage may also be included on all owned automobiles.

The following forms of liability insurance may or may not be included in the comprehensive form. If not, separate policies may be arranged.

**Premises—operations.**   This coverage protects against the legal liability for bodily injury to persons other than employees, and damage to the property of others that is not in the contractor's care, custody, or control.

Exclusions should be checked carefully. For example, explosion, collapse, and underground damage are normally excluded from coverage under the basic policy for most types of work. These are usually designated exclusions "x," "c," and "u," respectively. Although in some cases these exclusions cannot be removed, each project should be carefully examined for exposure to these hazards, and coverage secured where possible and necessary.

*Personal injury.* This protects against legal liability for claims arising from false arrest, libel, wrongful entry or eviction, and related wrongs against a person. A check of the policy will reveal exclusions.

*Independent contractors—protective liability.* Coverage provides for the insured's legal liability that may arise from acts or operations of a subcontractor or its employees and damage to property of others if that property is not in the care, custody, or control of the contractor. Certificates of insurance should be secured from all subcontractors and the scope of their insurance coverage verified.

*Completed operations—product liability.* This is an optional coverage which, subject to exclusions, protects against liability to persons or property of others that may arise after a project is completed: for example, from an accident due to faulty workmanship or materials. Actual replacement of faulty work cannot be covered.

*Contractual or assumed liability.* Many construction contracts include a clause in which the contractor assumes the liability of someone else toward third parties. Such clauses can usually be recognized by the words "hold harmless" or "indemnify." It is recommended that insurance policies of contractors and subcontractors provide blanket contractual liability in such cases. Assumed liabilities can then be covered automatically.

*Umbrella excess liability.* This insurance provides catastrophe coverage for claims in excess of the limits of liability afforded by other policies, and also for some hazards normally excluded in underlying liability policies. It may be subject to a large deductible feature, $10,000 to $25,000, and is a reasonably inexpensive way to protect a business from claims that could arise from a disastrous occurrence.

*Automobile.* All liability from existence or operation of any owned, hired, or nonowned vehicle may be included in this provision. This insurance should be on an automatic basis to provide coverage of newly added equipment. A special endorsement may be needed if employees or their families use company cars. A "use of other car" endorsement, naming each person so protected, would provide coverage for individuals using cars not owned by them or their employer.

*Automobile medical payments.* This may be added to a policy. In some states it is required.

*Automobile physical damage.* This covers damage to property of others and may also be endorsed to include comprehensive and collision coverage on owned vehicles. A high deductible of $250 to $500 or more can result in a considerable savings in premiums.

## PROPERTY FORMS OF INSURANCE

### Standard Builder's Risk Insurance

This type of coverage protects against physical damage to the insured property during the construction period, resulting from any of the perils named in the policy. This coverage provides reimbursement based upon actual loss or damage rather than any legal liability that may be incurred. There are three principal methods used to establish amounts of coverage and to determine the premium.

1. *Completed Value.* This method is based upon the assumption that the value of a project increases at a constant rate during the course of construction. While the policy is written for the value of the completed project, the premium is based upon a reduced or average value. The dollar coverage provided is the actual value of completed work and stored materials at any given time. This form of builder's risk must be taken out at the start of construction. It is recommended that this method be used for the typical building project.

   During construction the contractor must notify the insurance carrier periodically of the increase in value of a project. Coverage and premiums are based upon the reported value. This method is advantageous where completed value is low during most of the construction period but increases very rapidly toward the end. However, failure to report an increase in value may result in lack of proper coverage.

2. *Automatic Builder's Risk.* This policy form gives a contractor temporary protection automatically, pending the issuance of a specific policy for each project.

3. *Ordinary Builder's Risk.* This seldom-used type of policy form is written for a fixed value. Coverage may be increased by endorsement at the request of the insured.

Within the framework of the preceding methods of writing a builder's policy, the following perils may be covered:

1. Fire and lightning.
2. Extended coverage—covers windstorm, hail, riot, civil commotion, nonowned aircraft, smoke, and explosion (other than that from boilers, machinery, or piping).
3. Vandalism and malicious mischief—excludes pilferage, burglary, larceny, theft, and damage to glass (other than glass block).
4. Additional perils—The standard builder's risk policy may be endorsed to provide for specific additional perils. These may include collapse (not caused by design error, faulty materials, or workmanship), landslide, groundwater, surface water (other than flood), sprinkler leakage, explosion or rupture of boilers, machinery or piping, breakage of glass, pilferage, and theft.

It may be possible to obtain endorsements or separate policies to cover perils of flood and earthquake; however, such coverage can be difficult to obtain. For these perils it is recommended that the contractor request the project owner to secure this coverage in conjunction with its permanent insurance for the completed structure.

Some of these additional perils can be covered by adding an "all-risk" type of endorsement, or a multiple-peril builder's risk policy (as described in the next section) may be preferred. These additional coverages generally require a deductible clause.

### Multiple-Peril (All-Risk) Builder's Risk Insurance

This is a nonstandard type of policy, which provides similar but broader coverage than the standard builder's risk policy. Although the name "all risk" is widely used, all perils are *not* covered—it is a relative term denoting the broader-than-usual coverage. Generally, each insurance carrier writes its own form of multiple peril.

Rather than naming the perils insured, this type of policy insures against all risks of direct physical loss or damage to property from any external cause *except* those specifically excluded in the policy. Thus, coverage is determined by what is excluded, not included, and the policy must be checked closely to determine the coverage provided. Some forms will require a deductible clause for some of the perils covered.

This type of policy (written on a completed-value basis) is recommended over a standard builder's risk policy *if* sufficient care is taken at the outset to make sure that all desirable coverage is included. Protection can be tailored to an individual contractor's needs.

### Submittal of Evidence of Insurance

The contract documents should require that evidence of specified insurance be submitted at the time of submitting the performance and payment bonds (item 4 in Figure 11.2). This should be in the form that will disclose the total policy coverage (Figure 11.3), not merely a statement certifying that coverage was obtained by the contractor. During the submittal phase, the project manager should maintain a Bond and Insurance Record such as that illustrated in Figure 11.4.

## OPENING, ACCEPTANCE, AND DOCUMENTATION OF BIDS

In the administration of private contracts, where informality may be the preferred or at least accepted choice of the architect/engineer, no rigid procedures are necessary, nor, for that matter, is the issue of bid irregularity or responsiveness a subject of critical concern unless desired by the owner or architect/engineer.

The administration of a contract for a public agency, however, whether it be by the public agency itself or a private architect/engineering firm under contract to the agency, does invite a number of somewhat inflexible rules for the opening, acceptance, and documentation of all bids received.

**MINIMUM INSURANCE REQUIREMENTS**

<u>TYPE OF COVERAGE</u>                                           <u>LIMITS OF LIABILITY</u>

<u>Comprehensive General Liability</u>

                               Bodily Injury                                $300,000
                                                                                Each Occurrence

|  | Each Occurrence | Aggregate |
|---|---|---|
| Property Damage | $100,000 | $100,000 |

Including:

Coverage for damage caused by blasting, collapse,
underground damage or explosion:

Independent Contractors:

Products, completed operations:

Contractual Public Liability and Property Damage
covering liability assumed in the contract between
the Insured and the owners/agents designated in the contract.

<u>Comprehensive Automobile Liability</u>

| | Each Person | Each Occurrence |
|---|---|---|
| Bodily Injury | $100,000 | $300,000 |
| Property Damage | | $50,000 Each Occurrence |

Including:
Coverage for all owned, hired or non-owned licensed
automotive equipment. Coverage to comply with Motor
Carrier Act of 1980.

<u>Excess Liability</u>

                                                         $1,000,000
                                                       Combined Single Limit

Including Employer's Liability

<u>Workers' Compensation</u>                                     Statutory
                  and
<u>Employer's Liability</u>                                       $100,000

See Certificate On Reverse Side

REVISED 1-2-84

**FIGURE 11.3a**   Examples of a Certificate of Insurance showing policy coverage.

**252**

# Certificate of Insurance

FORM NO 4500-0008

THIS CERTIFICATE IS ISSUED TO THE OWNERS/AGENTS LISTED BELOW DESIGNATED IN THE CONTRACT WITH THE INSURED

**Texas Utilities Company**
**Its Subsidiaries:**
    **Texas Utilities Services Inc.**
    **Texas Utilities Mining Co.**
    **Texas Utilities Fuel Co.**
    **Basic Resources Inc.**

**Texas Utilities Electric Company**
**Its Divisions:**
    **Dallas Power & Light Co.**
    **Texas Electric Service Co.**
    **Texas Power & Light Co.**
    **Texas Utilities Generating Co.**

NAME AND ADDRESS OF INSURED

**INSURANCE COMPANIES AFFORDING COVERAGE**

COMPANY **A**
**B**
**C**
**D**

TYPE OF WORK PERFORMED & LOCATION

| COMPANY LETTER | TYPE OF INSURANCE | POLICY NO | POLICY EXP DATE | Limits of Liability In Thousands (000) | | |
|---|---|---|---|---|---|---|
| | | | | | EACH OCCURRENCE | AGGREGATE |
| | **COMPREHENSIVE GENERAL LIABILITY** Including: ☐ EXPLOSION AND COLLAPSE ☐ UNDERGROUND DAMAGE ☐ PRODUCTS/COMPLETED OPERATIONS ☐ CONTRACTUAL INSURANCE ☐ BROAD FORM PROPERTY DAMAGE ☐ INDEPENDENT CONTRACTORS ☐ PERSONAL INJURY | | | BODILY INJURY $ PROPERTY DAMAGE $ or BODILY INJURY AND PROPERTY DAMAGE COMBINED $ PERSONAL INJURY $ | $ $ $ | |
| | **COMPREHENSIVE AUTOMOBILE LIABILITY** Including: ☐ OWNED ☐ HIRED ☐ NON-OWNED ☐ MOTOR CARRIER ACT | | | BODILY INJURY EACH PERSON $ EACH ACCIDENT $ PROPERTY DAMAGE $ or BODILY INJURY AND PROPERTY DAMAGE COMBINED $ | | |
| | **EXCESS LIABILITY** Including: ☐ EMPLOYER'S LIABILITY | | | BODILY INJURY AND PROPERTY DAMAGE COMBINED $ | | |
| | **WORKERS' COMPENSATION** and **EMPLOYER'S LIABILITY** Including: ☐ LONG SHOREMEN'S AND HARBOR WORKERS | | | STATUTORY E L $ | | (EACH ACCIDENT) |
| | **OTHER** | | | | | |

The undersigned certifies that he is the representative of the above listed insurance companies, that he has authority to execute and issue this certificate to Certificate Holder, and, accordingly, does hereby certify on behalf of said insurance companies that policies of insurance listed above have been issued to the insured named above and are in force at this time. Notwithstanding any requirement, term or condition of any contract or other document with respect to which this certificate may be issued or may pertain, the insurance afforded by the policies described herein is subject to all the terms, exclusions and conditions of such policies. Copies of the policies shown will be furnished to the certificate holder upon request.

This Certificate does not amend, extend or alter the coverage afforded by the policies listed.

**Cancellation:** Should any of the above described policies be cancelled before the expiration date thereof, the issuing company will mail 30 days written notice to the below named certificate holder.

NAME & ADDRESS OF CERTIFICATE HOLDER

DATE ISSUED _____

BY _____
AUTHORIZED REPRESENTATIVE OF INSURANCE COMPANIES AFFORDING COVERAGE

ADDRESS _____

REVISED 1-2-84

**FIGURE 11.3b**   Reverse side of Certificate of Insurance.

**BOND AND INSURANCE SUBMITTAL**

City of Palm Springs

| | | | |
|---|---|---|---|
| PROJECT NO. | C4308.002 | CONTRACT NO. | NSY15309 |
| PROJECT | 15 MGD Water Treatment Plant | | |
| OWNER | City of Palm Springs | | |
| ENGINEER | C. H. Lawrance, P.E. | | |
| CONTRACTOR | ABC Constructors, Inc., Oakland, CA | | |

| INSTRUMENT | COMPANY | AMOUNT | EXP. DATE |
|---|---|---|---|
| PERFORMANCE BOND | Colonial Indemnity Co. | 100% | 10-1-90 |
| LABOR AND MATERIAL BOND | Colonial Indemnity Co. | 50% | 10-1-90 |
| MAINTENANCE AND GUARANTEE BOND | Colonial Indemnity Co. | 10% | 10-1-90 |
| PL AND PD INSURANCE | Aetna Casualty & Surety | Per Section 8.02 | 10-1-90 |
| WORKERS' COMPENSATION INS. | Aetna Casualty & Surety | Per Section 6.05(3) | 10-1-90 |
| BUILDER'S RISK INSURANCE | not required | | |
| WRAP-UP INSURANCE | | | |
| | | | |
| | | | |

DISTRIBUTION: 1. Owner
2. Project Engineer
3. Resident Project Representative
4. Project Files

CM-107

**FIGURE 11.4**  Example of a Bond and Insurance Submittal record.

Several primary matters of concern during this phase include:

1. Receipt of sealed bids at the designated time and place
2. Confirmation that all bids are responsive
3. Acceptance and logging of each bidder's name and the bid amount for all responsive bids
4. Summary of all line-item prices for all unit-price bids of responsive bidders

## Bid Shopping or Bid Peddling

It is sometimes the custom in the construction industry where there are no protective laws to shield a subcontractor from the unfair practice of bid shopping, for the prime contractor, after being notified of selection, to shop around to other potential subcontractors and offer to substitute them in the general contractor's bid if they will underbid the subcontractors originally used in determining the bid price. Where local laws prohibit this bid shopping, or "bid peddling" as it is sometimes called, the custom is varied so that the prime contractor may withhold submittal of its bid until the very last moment allowable before the closing of the bid acceptance period. The contractor, having previously been provided with a copy of the bid with penciled-in prices, will often spend the last few moments of time before bid opening in an attempt to negotiate last-minute price concessions from the subcontractors and suppliers, or even solicit new subcontractors or suppliers to replace those who originally quoted the job. Then, just before closing of the bid acceptance period, the contractor will ink-in the final prices, insert the bid in its envelope, seal it, and submit it. All details of the contractor's original bid will have been carefully prepared in the office before arriving at the bid opening, and only a minor amount of work is involved in any last-minute changes. All that needs to be done is to replace the originally penciled-in figures with the latest figures—in ink—and compute the new bottom-line price before submitting the bid.

## Bids Must Be Responsive

A responsive bid is one that meets all of the requirements specified in the Notice Inviting Bids and the Instructions to Bidders. To be responsive, a bid must be submitted on time, including all required documents; all forms must be completely and properly filled out, signed by a responsible party, and dated; any required bid bond must be executed on the prescribed form and attached to the bid; on unit-price bids, all line items must be filled out; no changes or alterations of any of the documents is permitted; no changes or conditions may be attached to the bid; and all addenda must be properly acknowledged.

In addition, where required by the terms of the bid solicitation, the documents may be required to be filled out and left bound in the bound volume of specifications for submittal to merit consideration. Also, in some cases, instead of a simple written acknowledgment that all addenda have been received, a bidder may be asked to submit the actual copies of all addenda received. One reason for requiring that bids be executed in the bound set of specifications and the original addenda returned with the contractor's bid is that many public agency owners prefer to assemble a legal record bid set by drilling a hole through the corner of all bid documents and inserting a wire with a lead seal. Often, where this procedure is used, the owner will also require that one of the original agreements be executed on the documents bound in the same specifications copy. Normally, when this system is used, additional loose sets of bidding documents and agreement forms are provided for additional originals.

### Acceptance and Recording of Bids

Prior to opening the bids, the architect/engineer or owner should prepare a checklist of all items that must be confirmed before a bid can be considered as responsive. The terms *responsive* and *responsible* should not be confused, however. A bidder may be determined to be *nonresponsible* (sometimes referred to as "informal") after having been ruled as properly *responsive*.

The bid opening can be conducted most efficiently using two persons, each with a specific task to perform during the bid opening. One person should be responsible for opening and extracting all of the bids from their packages and recording the name of each bidder on a log sheet such as the bid-opening report illustrated in Figure 11.5.

Each bid should then be carefully checked for being responsive. This is accomplished by taking each bid, in turn, and having one person read from the check list while the second person checks the bid for conformance. After completing each review, an appropriate entry is made after the name of any bidder on the log whose bid has been found to be nonresponsive or informal.

Next, one of the two persons, usually the project manager, will read each bidder's name and total bid price aloud to the assembled bidders. The second person should then enter all bid totals opposite the names of the responsive bidders previously recorded in the Bid-Opening Report.

Finally, after all of the bids have been opened, the nonresponsive or informal bids rejected, and all responsive bids received, the project manager may, by inspection, determine the identity of the *apparent* low bidder, subject to later confirmation after a careful bid review and evaluation. It is important that any mention made at the time of the bid opening be referred to as only the *apparent* low bidder. A better system would be to provide copies of all tabulated bids, as received, and let the other bidders draw their own conclusions, just in case the bid evaluation process turns up an error that could change the identity of the low bidder.

The issue of whether or not a bid is responsive can be potentially far more serious than it might seem to be at first. The author was involved in one case, involving a city water department, where failure of the apparent low bidder to sign one of the minor documents prior to submittal of the bid was challenged by the second-lowest bidder as being a nonresponsive bid and should thus be disqualified. Each threatened to sue the city if the contract was awarded to the other party and, in the end, the city attorney ruled that all bids would be rejected and the project readvertised, even though this would create a delay in beginning the project, and even though it was understood that there was a strong possibility of receiving higher bids on the project the second time around. Under the circumstances, the city would most certainly have been involved in litigation if an award had been made to either one of the original two lowest bidders.

**Purpose:** Documentation of all bids received, including the name of each contractor and the amount of each bid.

**Prepared by:** Administrator at the bid opening.

**Directed to:** Project Manager; owner.

**Copies to:** Project Manager for engineering review; official files.

**Comments:** Bids must be carefully examined at the time of opening to determine if they are responsive prior to recording. Nonresponsive bids must be rejected without being entered into the record.

**FIGURE 11.5**   Bid-Opening Report for recording bids.

## Summary of Bids for Evaluation

Following the close of the bid-opening session, the individual bids must be tabulated and evaluated, and each bidder must be checked for financial responsibility, licensing (where required), and integrity. Where unit prices form the basis of the bid, every individual line item must be tabulated for each bidder in preparation for a detailed, item-by-item evaluation, analysis, and comparison of bids. This information is normally entered onto a specially prepared form (spreadsheet) such as that illustrated in Figure 11.6, and all line-item amounts are entered opposite the corresponding engineer's estimate for that item. Additional information on the subject of bid evaluation is presented in Chapter 14.

## Cost Breakdown of Lump-Sum Bids (Schedule of Values)

Traditionally, contractors are understandably reluctant to provide unit price breakdowns of their lump-sum bids. However, the problem of determining the value of work performed

**FIGURE 11.6**   Summary sheet for recording the engineer's estimate and all bids received.

each month for the purpose of making fair progress payments is quite difficult without some reasonable basis for allocating portions of the total contract price to the various individual tasks represented.

The contractor may not want to make a commitment on unit-price amounts for various reasons. One reason, of course, is the fear that in case of later negotiations for possible extra work, the contractor would be at a disadvantage at a bargaining session if unit-price estimates were offered on a project in which the contractor is entitled to a fixed price for doing the work, regardless of cost distribution.

It is generally necessary to specify that such a price allocation be made representing the major task items if it is to be obtained at all. Even then, it must be fully understood that its only purpose is to allow monthly evaluations of work performed for the determination of progress payment amounts, and must *not* be considered as a commitment to prices in case of later negotiations. To accomplish this through specifications provisions, the contract documents should include copies of price allocation forms (schedule of values) similar to the one illustrated in Figure 11.7, with the line items already determined by the architect/engineer. Thus the contractor need only fill in a price representative of an allocation of portions of the lump-sum contract price to the specific tasks listed.

## DEVELOPMENT OF A QUALITY CONTROL OR ASSURANCE PROGRAM

On many federal projects, one of the construction phase requirements is that the architect/engineer or its field representative develop a *construction surveillance and inspection plan* for submittal to the contracting officer (Figure 11.8). A prerequisite to the development of a surveillance and inspection plan is the development of a *quality requirements control system*. The purpose of this system is to develop a method of control for all specification requirements that are required to be done in writing, plus some other items that the architect/engineer may add. The *quality requirements control system* should contain a record of all quality control requirements in tabular form or other equivalent method.

In addition, such federal contracts often include the requirement that the architect/engineer's Resident Project Representative review the *construction contractor quality control (CQC) plan*. This involves a review of the contractor's CQC plan for clarity and completeness and a recommendation to the owner's contracting officer for acceptance, rejection, or revision.

Initially, to develop a successful quality control program, a complete definition of each and every task must be determined. This is done in coordination with the drawings and specifications and other controlling documents. Following completion of the quality control program, personnel assignments must be made, along with a definition of the duties and responsibilities of each person on the quality control team.

Prior to the time when the need actually arises, arrangements should be made for the selection of the testing laboratory that will provide testing services under contract and, if required, supplementary inspection personnel for specialized tasks of short-term duration.

| | | |
|---|---|---|
| **E.R.FISK CONSTRUCTION**<br>GENERAL ENGINEERING CONTRACTOR<br>Anaheim, California | | **ALLOCATION OF TOTAL CONTRACT PRICE**<br>(Lump Sum Bid Breakdown) |

| PROJECT TITLE | PROJECT NO. | SPEC. OR CONTRACT NO. | SHEET | OF |
|---|---|---|---|---|
| Reservoir 1-D and Pump Stations 1d-2 and 1D-3 | 95/91 | --- | 1 | 6 |

| NAME OF CONTRACTOR | CONTRACT TYPE | CONTRACT DATE |
|---|---|---|
| ABC Constructors, Inc. | Lump Sum | 14 March 1995 |

| SCHEDULE & ITEM | DESCRIPTION OF COMPONENT PARTS | | ALLOCATION* | | TOTALS |
|---|---|---|---|---|---|
| | | | MATERIAL | LABOR | |
| 1 | Temporary Fence | 1 460 M | | | |
| 2 | Earthwork (a) Excavation 1st stage (common) | 14 000 M3 | | | |
| | (b) Excavation 2nd stage (common) | 1 660 M3 | | | |
| | (c) Excavation (structure) | 525 M3 | | | |
| | (d) Embankment | 11 300 M3 | | | |
| | (e) Backfill (trench) | 1 574 M3 | | | |
| | (f) Backfill (structure) | 180 M3 | | | |
| | (g) Disposal of excess material | LS | | | |
| | (h) Excavation (trench) | 1 965 M3 | | | |
| 3 | Concrete (a) Reservoir peripheral walls | 155 M3 | | | |
| | (b) Footings and foundations | 50 M3 | | | |
| | (c) Miscellaneous structures | 155 M3 | | | |
| | (d) Reservoir paving | 770 M3 | | | |
| | (e) Prestressed precast conc. roof | LS | | | |
| | (f) Grout and drypack | 1 M3 | | | |
| | (g) Concrete drain and curbs | 70 M3 | | | |
| 4 | Waterstops (a) PVC bulb type (Durajoint #5) | 2 960 M | | | |
| | (b) PVC flat type (Duraseal #11) | 1 950 M | | | |
| | (c) Expansion joint filler (12 mm x 178 mm) | 4 760 M | | Data used are fictitious for illustration only | |
| | (d) Elastomeric joint sealer (Thiokol) | 3 175 M | | | |
| | TOTALS | | | | ** |

\* Allocation shall be in percents of total contract price of the items allocated or in dollars and cents.
\*\* This total shall be equal to the total contract price of all items allocated

FISK FORM 6-5

**Purpose:** Use to determine value of work performed each month on lump-sum contracts.

**Prepared by**: Contractor.

**Directed to**: Resident Project Representative; Project Manager.

**Copies to**: Project Manager; Resident Project Representative; contractor.

**Comments**: On lump-sum contracts it is difficult to determine value of work performed without a bid breakdown prepared by the contractor. These cannot be considered as firm prices, however, and cannot be used as a basis of determining the value of extra work.

**FIGURE 11.7** Contractor's allocation (schedule of values) of lump-sum bid price to specified construction tasks for computing partial payments.

## INSPECTION AND TESTING MANUAL

Although not universally done on private or local public agency projects, a requirement of many federal agency construction services contracts calls for the preparation of a *quality control plan,* as mentioned earlier. Actually, this is a good idea to use on any job, and it not only eases the work burden during the job but also provides for a more orderly administration of the entire construction phase of the job. It does call for a great deal of effort at the

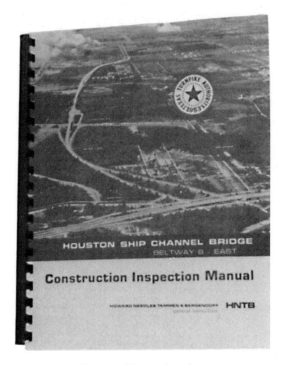

**FIGURE 11.8** Construction surveillance and inspection plan.

beginning of a project, however, as it not only requires that all the policy matters that apply to the quality control functions be set out in writing, but it also requires the preparation of technical checklists for all work on the project as a means for reminding the inspector of each item that must be checked, as well as setting forth the standards for each such inspection. Normally, a quality control plan also sets out, in tabular form, a complete listing of all testing that is required on all materials and equipment for which tests are specified, and it further specifies the frequency of such tests (see again Figure 3.3). It can be said that a quality control plan is actually a separate "specification" for the testing and inspection phase of an entire project, and such a document can easily run to over a hundred pages of typewritten text.

Work flow diagrams should be developed before the work on the project has begun. In this manner, preliminary planning efforts will not interfere with the orderly flow of the inspector's work after the contractor has mobilized at the site. The inspector's work flow diagrams are intended solely for the use of the field office staff and should include reminders to the Resident Project Representative as to when certain important events are to happen, as well as the assignment and responsibility for them. Generally, all these things can be shown in a simple chart form with a few explanatory sentences.

A significant part of the input data needed to prepare the work flow diagrams can be obtained from the contractor's CPM or bar charts. These charts are the keys to each significant construction event, as no other document can provide so much data in such a usable form. To be sure, adjustments will be required throughout the life of the job, but in general, the CPM or bar chart will set the stage for all construction events to follow.

## *Preparation of an Inspection and Testing Manual*

The engineer or architect should take a systematic approach to the quality control and assurance functions that are required for the project. The actual task of developing such a document may rightly fall upon the shoulders of the Resident Project Representative, whose firsthand knowledge of construction can be of immeasurable value in the preparation of a workable inspection plan.

The Resident Project Representative should plan ahead by developing an outline of all the inspections that must be made, a checklist of points to look for, and a list of the types and frequencies of all tests that are required. An inspection plan might reasonably be expected to cover all or some of the following items:

1. Establishment of detailed inspection procedures
2. Outline of acceptance/rejection procedures
3. Preparation of a chart showing all tests required, when they are needed, the frequency of sampling and testing, the material being tested, and who is obligated to perform the tests
4. Establishment of who will be responsible for calling the laboratory for pickup of samples for testing, who will call for special inspectors when needed, and to whom will such outside people be directly responsible on the project
5. Identification of who must physically prepare samples for testing—the contractor or the inspector; determination of whether the contractor will provide a laborer to assist the inspector in obtaining samples and transporting samples for testing
6. Establishment of ground rules for acceptable timing of work operations after sampling and testing; mandatory scheduling to assure not only time to make samples and tests, but also to make corrections needed before work may be allowed to continue.

A prerequisite to the development of a surveillance and inspection plan is the development of a quality requirements control system. The quality requirements should be shown in tabular form or other equivalent method. Typical examples of the data that must be presented in the form of tables or lists as a checking method throughout the job are:

1. Proofs of compliance (from the various specification sections)
2. Qualifications for soil-testing service
3. Tests for proposed soil materials
4. Reports required
5. Excavation methods (approval of)
6. Concrete testing and inspection service (approval of)

Prior to the time when the need actually arises, arrangements should be made for the selection of the testing laboratory that will provide testing services under contract and, if required, supplementary inspection personnel for specialized tasks of short-term duration.

A Testing Plan (Figure 11.8) should be developed to provide for the orderly administration of the construction phase of the work and as a means for reminding the inspector of each item that must be checked, as well as setting forth the standards for each such inspection. Normally, a quality control plan also sets out, in tabular form, a complete listing of all testing that is required on all materials and equipment for which tests are specified, and it further specifies the frequency of such tests. As a part of an inspection plan, it is desirable to include a flow diagram (Figure 11.9) for guidance of the Resident Project Representative, inspector, and contractor in administering the inspection of nonconforming work or test results.

# FIELD OFFICE ORGANIZATION OF THE OWNER OR THE FIELD REPRESENTATIVE

## Mission of the Field Engineer or Inspector

The mission of the Resident Project Representative or inspector as the design firm's or the owner's resident project representative is to assure compliance with the plans and specifications and to cause the end product to meet the needs of the ultimate user. In certain cases, where public agencies are involved, the resident project representative is further charged with the responsibility of checking on the compliance by the contractor with certain legislation, such as that pertaining to labor and the use of domestic materials.

## The Planning Stage

In the early stages of design or, in some cases, prior to that time, the owner must decide who is going to operate its field office to monitor construction. There are many current practices, some of which are described in the following paragraphs.

As practiced in many cases, the owner may engage its own Resident Project Representative to monitor the construction phase of the project (under the responsible charge of an architect or professional engineer), or the owner may hire an architect/engineer or construction management firm to perform this function. Another approach is to engage the services of an independent agency such as a testing laboratory or, on public projects, one governmental agency may solicit the help of another government agency for furnishing construction services. An example of this was the employment of the U.S. Corps of Engineers in the early postwar hospital construction program of the Veterans Administration, and later for Post Office construction.

Another practice is for the owner to enter into a professional construction management (PCM) contract wherein the construction manager oversees both design and construction and may actually contract with the construction contractor. Or, the owner may hire a single contractor to perform design, construction, and supervision of construction on either a lump-sum or a cost-plus-fixed-fee (CPFF) basis. The latter is a combined engineer-

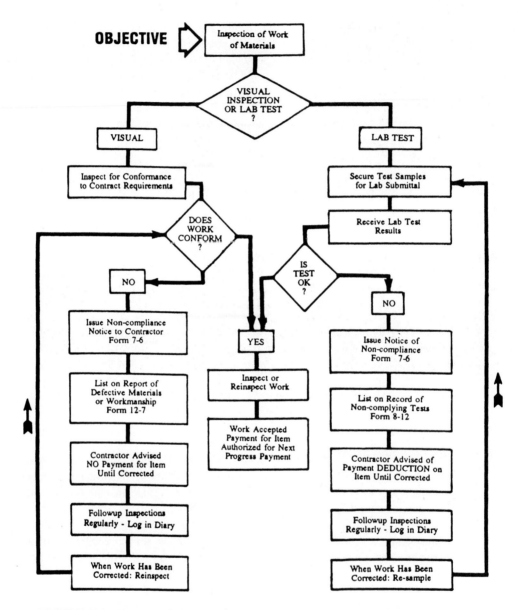

**FIGURE 11.9**  Flowchart for handling nonconforming work or test results.

ing and construction contract often called a design–build or turnkey job. For special inspection, the services of a testing laboratory may be hired for testing soils, aggregates, lum-
ber, masonry units, steel, and concrete. Similarly, there are expert freelance technicians who
inspect steel framework to assure soundness of connections (riveted, bolted, or welded) as
well as the leveling and plumbing of beams and columns.

Having decided who is to perform the inspection, the extent and scope of the inspection services must be determined. Sometimes contracts provide that the builder will arrange

**FIGURE 11.10**    Large fixed-type field office. (Aguamilpa Hydroelectric Project, Mexico)

for inspection by a testing laboratory and furnish test results to the owner or its architect/engineer. The degree of inspection required often depends upon the importance of the work or the function of the item in question. For instance, it is hardly worthwhile to take test cylinders on 2000-psi concrete used for sidewalks around a single-story residence, but it is absolutely essential that it be done on a prestressed concrete bridge girder. The inspector should be cautioned at this point, however, as the determination of the frequency and level of tests required is a decision that must be made by the engineering staff of the design firm or owner, not by field personnel unless specifically authorized to do so by the project manager of the owner or design firm, as applicable. The extent of the inspection is a major factor in the cost of operating the owner's field office. Another item to be considered by the owner in the construction planning stage is the provision of adequate funds to cover the field office costs of whatever agency is chosen to inspect the project.

### Establishment of the Field Office

Arrangements will have to be made to set up the field office for the Resident Project Representative and field staff prior to the beginning of the work on the project (Figure 11.10). If it is the contractor's responsibility to do this under the project specifications, the inspector should monitor this provision closely, as there are often last-minute field problems that tend to delay implementation; also, the contractor may make last-minute attempts to offer facilities that do not meet the provisions of the specifications, such as setting up one-half of the contractor's field office trailer for the use of the inspector—even though the specifications may call for a separate structure.

The Resident Project Representative should make certain that the field office telephone has been ordered in time if it is the contractor's responsibility to provide such utilities to the inspector's field office. Without it, the Resident Project Representative will be out of communication with the design firm's or the owner's office during the early portion of the job. In addition, if the contractor is obligated under the provisions of the specifications to provide an electronic pager (radio "beeper") or other communications equipment, be sure that such equipment is provided in time to cover the critical early part of the job.

Finally, a requisition should be made and sent to the office of the design firm or the owner by the Resident Project Representative in sufficient time to enable them to make up a supply order on a routine basis, and to be able to obtain the office equipment that may be needed in the field office.

## Field Office Responsibilities

In the establishment of a field office, the owner, or its design or construction management firm, is guided by many of the criteria that are considered by the contractor for setting up its own field office: the delegation of authority, the functions to be performed, the remoteness of the work site, and the extent and complexity of the job.

The delegation of authority from the design firm or the owner to the Resident Project Representative or from the contractor to its CQC representative can vary within wide limits. In some cases, it is merely to inspect the work; in others, the greater task of construction project administration is assigned. Costs of field office operation will vary widely with the extent of the work delegated. Usually personalities, experience, remoteness of the job site, and functions performed are serious considerations governing the delegation of authority. With respect to the Resident Project Representative's or CQC representative's *delegated* functions, the following factors must be considered:

1. What specific functions of the Resident Project Representative or CQC representative are specified in the contract?

2. How much testing will be performed by the Resident Project Representative or CQC representative and his or her staff, and how much will be contracted out to commercial testing laboratories?

3. How much of the materials specified will require preinspection at the factory before being shipped to the job site?

4. How much use will be made of special inspectors, such as for concrete, masonry, or structural steel and welding inspections?

5. Is the contract lump-sum, unit-price, or cost-plus-fixed-fee?

6. What is the authority of the architect/engineer to initiate, estimate, negotiate, and execute contract modifications?

7. What authority will be granted to the design or construction management firm by the owner to approve partial and final pay estimates?

8. How much of a check on the contractor's costs must be maintained by the Resident Project Representative, particularly on unit-price and cost-plus-fixed-fee contracts?

9. What responsibilities will the Resident Project Representative have, in the case of public agency contracts, for enforcement of such labor laws as the Davis-Bacon Act, the 8-hour law, and the Copeland Act or similar laws?

Other questions more specifically related to the *direct* responsibilities of the Resident Project Representative or CQC representative include the following:

1. To what degree must testing be conducted? In cases such as cement or steel, will mill certificates be accepted or will specific tests be required?

2. How much surveying must be supplied by the design firm or owner's field office?

3. Will record drawings be required to be prepared by the contractor or by the Resident Project Representative of the owner or design firm?

4. What reporting and other documentation requirements will be imposed on the Resident Project Representative or CQC representative and their field office staff?

5. What will be the responsibility of the Resident Project Representative or CQC representative with regard to intermediate and final acceptance of test results?

6. Will the Resident Project Representative or CQC representative be asked to participate in any portion of the review phase of shop drawings? If so, to what degree?

7. What, if any, safety responsibilities will be expected of the Resident Project Representative or CQC representative?

In the establishment of the Resident Project Representative's field office, the matter of staffing should be considered together with the assignment of individual responsibilities (Figure 11.11). The number of personnel needed to perform the administrative and quality control functions normally associated with the Resident Project Representative's field office may vary from one part-time construction administrator/inspector to a staff of 10 to 40 key people on an exceptionally large project. Most commonly, the small projects involve the use of one part-time construction coordinator who provides construction administration and general technical inspection, supplemented by special inspectors where necessary. On slightly larger projects, a full-time Resident Project Representative may be justified. Although the Resident Project Representative may be the only full-time member of the field office staff, special inspectors may be utilized where necessary. Beyond this level, the full-time Resident Project Representative is usually provided with a full-time clerk-typist to assist in the numerous routine office tasks involved. In addition, one or more full-time field inspectors may also be assigned to the project, supplemented by part-time special inspectors as necessary.

Projects of a size and complexity that require a larger or more specialized staff are generally under the direction of a resident engineer who is a registered professional engineer or architect as the Resident Project Representative (Figure 11.11).

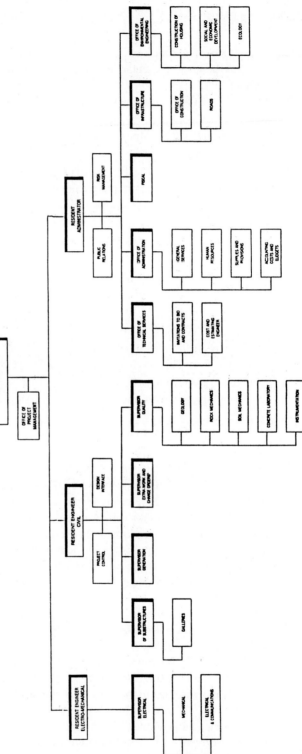

**FIGURE 11.11** Representative operational diagram for a large project.

## Outline of Field Office Cost Items

Among the items contributing significantly to the cost of establishing and operating a construction field office for the owners or design firm are the following:

1. *Supervision.* Usually, on the larger projects, a full-time Resident Project Representative is assigned to each job site. The Resident Project Representative may work under the direct supervision of a project manager in an architect/engineer's office who often is in charge of several projects and many different contracts. The project manager *is* the architect/engineer as far as the project is concerned. A Resident Project Representative may be assigned to supervise the inspection of more than one project on an intermittent basis—usually for the same project manager. In addition to supervising the inspection forces, the Resident Project Representative maintains liaison with the contractor's project superintendent and sometimes with a representative of the owner, and is often asked to conduct on-the-job conferences.

2. *Operations.* This generally comprises the inspection (quality) group. It may be subdivided into functional areas such as the dam, the spillway, or the powerhouse; or on a contract basis such as the paving contract, the drainage facilities contract, the pump station contract, or similar tasks. Also to be considered are the various special inspectors such as the mechanical, electrical, control systems, welding and structural steel, masonry, concrete, soils, and paving inspectors. Laboratory operations may also be assigned to test soils, aggregates, concrete masonry units, sealants, asphalt, and other construction materials.

   Keeping a daily diary is the duty of each inspector (Chapter 4), and all activities must be documented thoroughly. The Resident Project Representative is also responsible for checking the contractor to assure that all insurance, bonding, and permits are in order. The operations tasks also include review of payment requests, measurements of work completed as a means of verifying payment requests (Chapter 16), the evaluation of requests by the contractor for change orders (Chapter 18), and the submittal of recommendations to the design firm or the owner regarding the recommendations of the Resident Project Representative for action to be taken on such requests. The Resident Project Representative, although not performing any construction surveys personally, should be involved to the extent of coordinating the survey tasks required for the project.

   The field office operations include estimating of costs of construction for partial and final payments, change order requests, and value engineering proposals. All transmittals of samples, shop drawings, and other material intended for the design firm or the owner should be routed through the Resident Project Representative, who should log all such submittals prior to forwarding to the design firm or the owner for action. The responsibility of the Resident Project Representative does *not* include approval of shop drawings, samples, approval of substitutions of materials, *nor* the interpretation of the intent of the plans and specifications—these should be reserved for the architect or engineer's project manager. On a very large project, a professional engineering staff may be assigned the job of field administration of the project, in which case, exceptions to the afore-mentioned responsibilities may be established by the design firm.

3. *Administration.* In addition to the administrative tasks included in the foregoing paragraph, the Resident Project Representative and the field office staff must per-form general clerical services, communications services, limited personnel func-tions, mailing and shipping, ordering and maintaining of supplies and equipment, administration of transportation and travel of personnel, expense account submittals, minor purchasing, maintenance of company owned vehicles, and sim-ilar functions. In addition, on some governmental projects, particularly federal work, the Resident Project Representative field office may be required to check the contractor's payrolls for compliance with labor legislation, and assist in nego-tiations with craft unions and labor relations. Wherever owner-furnished equip-ment is to be installed by the contractor, the Resident Project Representative also may be called upon to expedite delivery and control, and provide for the storage and issuance to the contractor of such owner-furnished equipment.

## THE PRECONSTRUCTION CONFERENCE

In communicating with the contractor and the contractor's personnel, it is important that the design firm or the owner and their Resident Project Representative make their positions very clear right from the start of the job. It is far better to get started on a basis of administering the contract firmly in accordance with the plans and specifications than it is to correct a dif-ficult situation later in the job that is the result of a lax relationship with the contractor.

As a means of establishing the "ground rules" and calling the contractor's attention to the critical areas of construction, the preconstruction conference is an invaluable tool. Initially, it allows the key personnel of both sides to be introduced, and the responsibilities and authorities of each can be defined at that time. It also allows the parties to get a clear understanding of the procedures involved in contractor submittals, sampling and testing, construction surveys, inspections by outside agencies, payment requests, procedures for claims and disputes, unforeseen job conditions, change order requests, and similar items. The contractor can take this opportunity to raise questions about any of these items and clear up any misunderstandings.

During the course of the preconstruction meeting, mention can be made of the con-tractor's responsibility to provide insurance documents as specified and all required bonds as well as to obtain (and usually pay for) all permits from building departments, street de-partments, police departments (for traffic control), flood control districts, environmental protection agencies, or other agencies having jurisdiction. The contractor should be re-minded at the preconstruction meeting that all such documentation is required to be sub-mitted before work can begin, and that the contract has a specified length of time after the signing of the contract or the issuance of a Notice to Proceed within which time the con-tractor is to begin the work.

Another item that should be brought up at the preconstruction conference is the schedule of job site and management meetings, the location and frequency of such meet-ings, and who should be in attendance.

Before closing the conference, the subject of the construction schedule should be raised. It may be necessary to remind the contractor that the initial project schedule submitted at the beginning of the project will require periodic adjustment, and that all such adjustments must meet with the approval of the design firm and the owner. It should also be emphasized that the design firm or the owner, through the Resident Project Representative, has the right to require the contractor to revise the work schedule, increase the work hours or personnel, or to make other adjustments that will assure completion of the project within the agreed-upon time schedule. Before making any such demands upon the contractor, however, be certain that the provisions of the contract will allow the architect or engineer to exercise such authority. Also, check both the time allowed to complete the job and whether the exact wording of the contract makes specific reference to "time" as "the essence of the contract." Failure to specify time as the essence of the contract may place the owner in a weak position for requiring the contractor to accelerate the work to complete the work "on time" [cf. *Kingery Construction Co.* v. *Scherbarth Welding, Inc.,* 185 N.W.2d 857 (1971)].

## PRECONSTRUCTION CONFERENCE AGENDA

### Checklist of Subjects to Be Considered for Agenda

#### Construction coordination (preconstruction) conference
- Participants
- Time required for conference
- Use of an agenda—topics for discussion
- Minutes of the meeting
- Acknowledgment or correction of minutes

#### Identification of key personnel of all parties
- Names and 24-hour telephone numbers of contractor, engineer, and owner
- Define authority and responsibility of key personnel
- Designate sole contact for administration of contract

#### Authority and responsibilities
- Methods of construction (methods may be challenged)
- Rejection of work by inspector
- Work performed in absence of inspector (unacceptable)
- Work performed in absence of contractor's superintendent (unacceptable)
- Stopping the work (right reserved to owner alone)
- Safety at the site
- Issuance of field orders from engineer/owner
- Authority of the inspector

### Conformance with plans and specifications
- Call attention to areas of special concern
- Answer contractor inquiries
- Clarification of specification provisions

### Contract administration
- Notice to proceed
- Time of the contract
- Liquidated damages
- Insurance requirements and bonds
- Record drawings (procedure, responsibility for)
- Mobilization (identify scope)
- Contractor submittal procedure (through resident engineer)
- Surveys and staking
- Bid allocation of lump-sum bids (not valid as cost basis on extra work)
- Environmental requirements (cleanup; sanitary; dust; blasting; chemicals)
- Change orders and extra work procedures
- Unforeseen underground conditions procedures (public agency responsibility)
- Coordination with utilities
- Closeout procedures
- Progress payments and retainage procedures

### Materials and equipment
- Substitutions of "or equal" items
- Long-lead (prepurchase) items
- Assignments of procurement contracts to contractor
- Owner-furnished materials or equipment
- Storage and protection
- Concealed shipping damages
- Payment for materials not yet used in the work

### Contractor's schedule
- Owner/engineer rights to approve
- Submittal requirements
- Owner/engineer can set milestone date

### Change orders and extra work
- Who has authority to issue
- Effect on time and cost
- Field order versus change order
- Cumulative change order

## Subcontractors and suppliers

- Contractual relationship
- Submittal requirements
- Owner/engineer: no direct contact alone
- Fair subcontracting act requirements

## Coordination with other agencies and contractors

- Interface requirements
- Testing and validation of systems
- Highway departments and railroads
- Code enforcement agencies
- Other regulatory agencies of government

## Handling of disputes, protests, and claims

- Must exhaust all contractual means
- Resolution by the engineer

## Labor requirements

- Davis-Bacon Act
- Documentation and audit requirements
- Federal, state, and local requirements

## Rights-of-way and easements

- Permanent easements for project
- Temporary easements for construction
- Dumping sites and storage areas
- Access to the site by heavy equipment

## Owner protection

- Warranties and guarantees
- Bond protection during guarantee
- Security
- Extended maintenance of landscaping

## Punch list procedures

- Contractor certification of completion
- Punch list inspections
- Final acceptance inspection (run-up; testing; final walk-through)
- Withheld funds for remaining punch list items

A careful record should be kept of all matters discussed at the preconstruction conference, and a copy of the record should be provided to all who attended the conference (Figure 11.12).

## RECORD OF PRECONSTRUCTION CONFERENCE

**City of Thousand Oaks**

DATE 6 APRIL 1990

Page 1 of 4

| NAME OF OWNER | ADDRESS (Including Zip Code and Telephone) |
|---|---|
| City of Thousand Oaks<br>Utilities Department | 2150 West Hillcrest Drive; Thousand Oaks<br>(805) 497-8611 |
| NAME OF ENGINEER | ADDRESS (Including Zip Code and Telephone) |
| Lawrance, Fisk & McFarland, Inc.<br>Consulting Engineers | 328 Garden Street, Santa Barbara<br>(805) 564-2441 |
| NAME OF CONTRACTOR (FIRM) | ADDRESS (Including Zip Code and Telephone) |
| XYZ Constructors, Inc. | 100 Conejo Drive - Thousand Oaks<br>(805) 000-0000 |

| PROJECT TITLE | JOB NUMBER |
|---|---|
| Beatty Canyon Water Treatment Plant | 89/90-00 |

### SUBJECTS TO BE DISCUSSED

1. Identification of Official Representatives of Owner, Engineer, Contractor and Other Interested Agency:

OWNER: H. F. PAULSEN, GEN. MGR.    ENGINEER: C. H. LAWRANCE, VICE PRES.

ADDRESS: 18100 SIERRA MADRE, AZUZA, CA    ADDRESS: 328 GARDEN ST., SUITE 1 SANTA BARBARA, CA

CONTRACTOR: G. ALBRECHT, VICE PRES.    OTHER AGENCY:

ADDRESS:    ADDRESS:

2. Responsibilities of the Engineer: (Engineer does not "Supervise" the Contractor's employees, equipment, or operations)

PER GEN. COND. ARTICLES 1.02, 1.03, AND 3.01. ALL COMMUNICATIONS TO CONTRACTOR WILL BE SUBMITTED AT CONST. SITE THRU RES. ENGR. ALL ORDERS IN WRITING. ONLY RES. ENGR. HAS AUTHORITY TO ISSUE ORDERS.

3. Responsibilities of Owner's Governing Body (Actual Contracting Organization.)

OWNER WILL WORK THRU ENGINEER ON ALL PROJECT MATTERS. OWNER'S APPROVAL REQUIRED ON ALL CHANGE ORDERS INVOLVING A CHANGE OF PROJECT TIME OR COST.

4. Responsibilities of the Contractor: (Review contract terms for specifics)

PER GEN. COND. ARTICLES 1.04, 1.05, AND 3.05 PRINCIPALLY. CONTR. MUST KEEP AUTH. SUPT. ON JOB AT ALL TIMES. MUST DO NOT LESS THAN 20% WITH OWN CREW

5. Responsibilities of Materials Testing Organization:

UNDER DIRECT CONTRACT W/ OWNER, BUT ASSIGNED TO WORK WITH RES. ENGR. REQUIRES MIN. 24-HR NOTICE OF NEED

6. General Discussion of Contract:

A. Contractor Submittals: (Shop Drawings; Samples; Record Drawings; Schedules; Insurance & Bonds; etc.)

ALL SUBMITTALS PER SECTION 130 OF SPEC. ALL SUBMITTALS MUST BE MADE DIRECTLY TO RES. ENGR. AT SITE, WHO WILL FORWARD TO ENGR.

B. Notice to Proceed; Mobilization:

NOTICE OF AWARD DOES NOT AUTHORIZE SITE ACCESS. WORK TO START WITHIN 10 DA OF NOTICE TO PROCEED. MOBILIZATION PER SEC. 110; NO PRORATION.

**FIGURE 11.12** Sample record of a preconstruction conference.

274

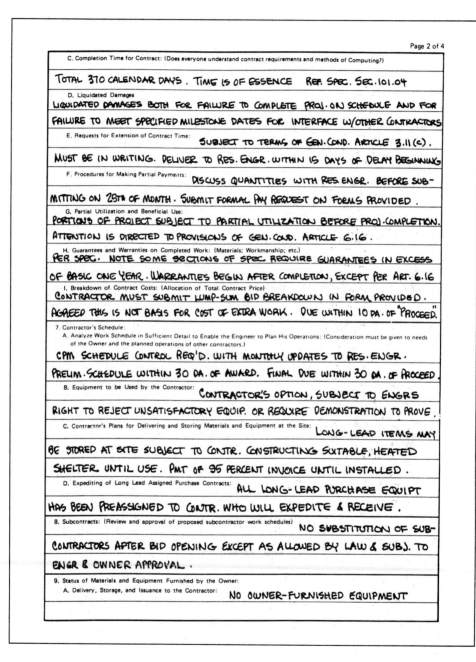

**C. Completion Time for Contract:** (Does everyone understand contract requirements and methods of Computing?)

TOTAL 370 CALENDAR DAYS. TIME IS OF ESSENCE  REF. SPEC. SEC. 101.04

**D. Liquidated Damages**

LIQUIDATED DAMAGES BOTH FOR FAILURE TO COMPLETE PROJ. ON SCHEDULE AND FOR FAILURE TO MEET SPECIFIED MILESTONE DATES FOR INTERFACE W/OTHER CONTRACTORS

**E. Requests for Extension of Contract Time:**  SUBJECT TO TERMS OF GEN. COND. ARTICLE 3.11(c).

MUST BE IN WRITING. DELIVER TO RES. ENGR. WITHIN 15 DAYS OF DELAY BEGINNING

**F. Procedures for Making Partial Payments:**  DISCUSS QUANTITIES WITH RES. ENGR. BEFORE SUB-

MITTING ON 25TH OF MONTH. SUBMIT FORMAL PAY REQUEST ON FORMS PROVIDED.

**G. Partial Utilization and Beneficial Use:**

PORTIONS OF PROJECT SUBJECT TO PARTIAL UTILIZATION BEFORE PROJ. COMPLETION. ATTENTION IS DIRECTED TO PROVISIONS OF GEN. COND. ARTICLE 6.16.

**H. Guarantees and Warranties on Completed Work:** (Materials; Workmanship; etc.)

PER SPEC. NOTE SOME SECTIONS OF SPEC REQUIRE GUARANTEES IN EXCESS OF BASIC ONE YEAR. WARRANTIES BEGIN AFTER COMPLETION, EXCEPT PER ART. 6.16

**I. Breakdown of Contract Costs:** (Allocation of Total Contract Price)

CONTRACTOR MUST SUBMIT LUMP-SUM BID BREAKDOWN IN FORM PROVIDED. AGREED THIS IS NOT BASIS FOR COST OF EXTRA WORK. DUE WITHIN 10 DA. OF "PROCEED."

**7. Contractor's Schedule:**
   **A.** Analyze Work Schedule in Sufficient Detail to Enable the Engineer to Plan His Operations: (Consideration must be given to needs of the Owner and the planned operations of other contractors.)

CPM SCHEDULE CONTROL REQ'D. WITH MONTHLY UPDATES TO RES. ENGR.

PRELIM. SCHEDULE WITHIN 30 DA. OF AWARD. FINAL DUE WITHIN 30 DA. OF PROCEED.

**B. Equipment to be Used by the Contractor:**  CONTRACTOR'S OPTION, SUBJECT TO ENGRS

RIGHT TO REJECT UNSATISFACTORY EQUIP. OR REQUIRE DEMONSTRATION TO PROVE.

**C. Contractor's Plans for Delivering and Storing Materials and Equipment at the Site:**  LONG-LEAD ITEMS MAY

BE STORED AT SITE SUBJECT TO CONTR. CONSTRUCTING SUITABLE, HEATED SHELTER UNTIL USE. PMT OF 95 PERCENT INVOICE UNTIL INSTALLED.

**D. Expediting of Long Lead Assigned Purchase Contracts:**  ALL LONG-LEAD PURCHASE EQUIPT

HAS BEEN PREASSIGNED TO CONTR. WHO WILL EXPEDITE & RECEIVE.

**8. Subcontracts:** (Review and approval of proposed subcontractor work schedules)  NO SUBSTITUTION OF SUB-

CONTRACTORS AFTER BID OPENING EXCEPT AS ALLOWED BY LAW & SUBJ. TO ENGR & OWNER APPROVAL.

**9. Status of Materials and Equipment Furnished by the Owner:**
   **A.** Delivery, Storage, and Issuance to the Contractor:  NO OWNER-FURNISHED EQUIPMENT

**FIGURE 11.12**  *continued*

B. Transportation and Shipping to Project Site:

NO HIGHWAY OR BRIDGE RESTRICTIONS

10. Change Orders and Extra Work: (Outline procedures to be followed and who has authority to issue)

NO CHANGES FROM PLANS & SPECS EXCEPT ON WRITTEN AUTHORITY OF RES. ENG. ALL SUCH CHANGES MUST ULTIMATELY BE SUPPORTED BY FORMAL CHANGE ORDER. EMERGENCY FIELD ORDERS OK, BUT MUST BE CONFIRMED.

11. Staking of Work: (Clearly define responsibilities of Engineer and Contractor. Line and Grade must be furnished by Engineer.)

ENGR. WILL PROVIDE LINE & GRADE ONLY (2 POINTS & ONE ELEVATION)

12. Project Inspection:
A. Functions of the Engineer, including Records and Reports: RES. ENGR. IS DESIGNATED AS SOLE ON-SITE REP. OF ENGR. & OWNER. AUTH. PER NSPE FORM 1910-1-A.

B. Responsibilities of Owner:
EXERCISE PROJECT CONTROL THRU ENGR.

C. Safety and Health Obligations of the Contractor: (Cite Engineer's procedures in handling an imminent hazard)
CONTR. HAS TOTAL RESPONSIBILITY. ENGR RESERVES RIGHT TO ORDER IMMEDIATE CORRECTION OF OBSERVED MAJOR HAZARDS, HOWEVER.

13. Final Acceptance of the Work: (Include requirements for tests and validation of systems and project cleanup)
CONTR. TO PROVIDE LIEN RELEASES & AFFIDAVIT OF PAYMENT. OWNER WILL HOLD RETAINAGE PLUS TWICE VALUE OF OUTSTANDING PUNCH LIST ITEMS.

14. Labor Requirements:
A. Equal Employment Opportunity Requirements:

PER SPEC REQUIREMENTS — SUPPL. GEN. CONDITIONS

B. Davis-Bacon Act: PROJECT SUBJECT TO FEDERAL WAGE REQUIREMENTS.
IF STATE MINIMUMS ARE DIFFERENT, CONTR MUST PAY HIGHER RATES.

C. Other Federal Requirements:

CORPS OF ENGINEERS 404 PERMIT FOR DUMPING OR STOCKPILING

D. State and Local Requirements: STATE HIGHWAY ENCROACHMENT PERMIT REQ'D.
STREET DEPT EXCAVATION PERMIT; TRAFFIC CONTROL; BLDG PERMIT

E. Permit Responsibilities: AS LISTED THEREIN. ALL REQUIRE CLEANUP,
NIGHT COVERING OF OPEN TRENCHES & TRAFFIC PER ANSI D6.1-1968

F. Union Agreements:

NO SPECIAL AGREEMENTS

15. Insurance Requirements: PER. GEN. COND. ARTICLES 6.05 AND 6.06, ALSO SUPPL. GEN. COND. ARTICLE 8.02. MUST SUBMIT TO OWNER AT TIME OF AGREEMENT SIGNING

**FIGURE 11.12** *continued*

16. Rights-of-Way and Easements:

A. Explain any Portion of Project Site Not Available to Contractor: CONTR. NOT PERMITTED TO MOVE ONTO PRIVATE PROPERTY UNTIL COPIES OF EASEMENTS ARE OBTAINED

B. Contractors Responsibilities During Work Covered by Contract: NO TEMP. CONST. EASEMENTS HAVE BEEN OBTAINED. IT IS CONTR. RESPONSIBILITY TO ARRANGE THESE & PAY.

17. Coordination with Utilities, Highway Departments, and Railroads CONTR. MUST NOTIFY AFFECTED UTILITIES WHEN WORKING NEAR THEIR FACILITIES. FOLLOW UTIL. INSTRUCTIONS

18. Placement of Project Signs and Posters: PER SPECIFICATION & EPA STANDARD. SIGN MUST BE ERECTED WITHIN 30 DA AFTER NOTICE TO PROCEED

19. Handling of Disputes, Protests, and Claims: FIRST STEP: RES. ENGR; SECOND STEP: PROJECT ENGINEER. REF. GEN. COND. ARTICLES 3.06 AND 3.07.

NOTED AND CONCURRED WITH, But understood not to be a modification of any existing contracts or agreements:

_____
(Contractor Representative)

_____
(Contractor Representative)

_____
(Engineer Representative)

_____
(Engineer Representative)

_____
(Owner Representative)

_____
(Owner Representative)

OTHERS IN ATTENDANCE at Preconstruction Conference

ORGANIZATION Represented

_____

ABC CONSTRUCTORS, INC.

_____

PARKSIDE ENGRG CORP

_____

LAWRANCE, FISK & McFARLAND, INC.

DISTRIBUTION: 1. Contractor
2. Project Engineer
3. Resident Project Representative
4. Owner
5. Project File

**FIGURE 11.12** *continued*

## STUDY PLANS AND SPECIFICATIONS

Prior to the beginning of any actual work on the project, and preferably prior to mobilization by the contractor, the Resident Project Representative or CQC representative *and all other inspectors* assigned to the project should obtain a complete set of project plans and specifications, *plus all addenda* and all key reference books or standards that are cited in the specifications. The plans, specifications, addenda, and references should be carefully studied and the inspector's copy of the plans and specifications should be marked with a highlighter pen or other marker to identify all key inspection provisions. The placing of index tabs at the beginning of each section of the specifications is also a good idea, as it will facilitate rapid reference to each section when needed. If the construction documents review can be conducted in the office of the architect/engineer, it is even better, as the inspector will be in a better position to get factual answers to specific questions from the project manager and the design engineers and architects themselves. In addition, this one-to-one level of communication allows the supervisor of each design discipline to meet the project field representative and to develop a working relationship. At the same time, contacts can be made with the mechanical and electrical department heads to determine their schedules for requesting special inspections of those portions of the work for which they are personally responsible.

## KEY DATES

The Resident Project Representative or CQC representative should note on the field calendar every date that has special significance on the project, whether it be for tests, special inspections, payment request due dates, delivery dates, or other important milestones. All such data should be obtained from either the specifications (if listed there) or from the contractor's CPM or bar chart schedule.

## LISTING OF EMERGENCY INFORMATION

It is quite important to maintain an up-to-date list of all key personnel of the owner, the engineer, and the contractor to be contacted in case of a project emergency (Figure 11.13). Each person listed should provide telephone numbers where he or she may be contacted at any time, day or night, as well as on weekends and holidays.

Review the list from time to time to confirm and update names and telephone numbers. In addition, the Resident Project Representative should keep a list of emergency and utility services and the corresponding telephone numbers.

Distribution of the key personnel list should be restricted to those key personnel on the list and management personnel of their respective organizations. No general posting of the list should be made.

**City of Thousand Oaks**

# UTILITIES AND SERVICES INFORMATION

PROJECT ___La Crescenta Reservoir and Pumping Plant___  PROJECT NO. ___89/90-00___

OWNER ___City of Thousand Oaks___

CONTRACTOR ___XYZ Constructors, Inc., Thousand Oaks___

ENGINEER ___Lawrance, Fisk & McFarland, Inc. 928 Garden St., Suite 1, Santa Barbara CA___

## KEY PERSONNEL

| | Business | Residence |
|---|---|---|
| **OWNER REPRESENTATIVE** | | |
| C. P. Owens, Project Manager | (805) 000-6391 | (805) 000-3110 |
| **CONTRACTOR'S SUPT/PROJECT MANAGER** | | |
| Everet K. Jefferson | (805) 000-2632 | (805) 000-9431 |
| **PROJECT MANAGER/ENGINEER** | | |
| Charles M. Parker | (805) 000-9141 | (805) 000-6152 |
| **RESIDENT PROJECT REPRESENTATIVE** | | |
| R. E. Barnes | (805) 000-4426 | (805) 000-3716 |

## PROJECT UTILITIES AND SERVICES

| | | |
|---|---|---|
| **OSHA REPRESENTATIVE** | Cal-OSHA Consultation Service | (213) 786-3870 |
| | Cal-OSHA (Enforcement) | (213) 736-3071 |
| **GAS** | Southern California Gas Co. | |
| | Excavation Pipeline Locations | 1-800-422-4133 |
| **POWER** | Southern California Edison Co. | |
| | Santa Barbara | (805) 000-0000 |
| **TELEPHONE** | Pacific Telephone & Telegraph Co. | |
| | Underground Service Alert | 1-800-422-4133 |
| **WATER** | | |
| **SANITATION** | | |
| **STREETS & HIGHWAYS** | City of Thousand Oaks | |
| | Department of Public Works | (805) 000-0000 |
| **FIRE PROTECTION** | Thousand Oaks Fire Department | |
| | Thousand Oaks | 9-1-1 |
| **POLICE PROTECTION** | Thousand Oaks Police Department | |
| | Thousand Oaks | 9-1-1 |

All key personnel should have a copy of this information, and a copy should be posted in each field office in a prominent location.

**FIGURE 11.13**  Example of a project emergency services information sheet.

## AGENCY PERMITS

At the beginning of the job, the Resident Project Representative should see that all required permits have been obtained and should prevent any construction work from proceeding whenever a required permit controlling such work has not been obtained. It should be noted that sometimes the terms of a permit may be quite lengthy and the permit conditions may read like a specification in itself. Such terms and conditions of a permit must be considered as binding upon the contractor and will normally take precedence over the terms of the project specification in case of conflict.

## STARTING A PROJECT

The beginning of a construction project normally starts with the award of the construction contract. This may be accomplished in the minutes of a city council or county board of supervisors action, by letter, or by issuance of a preprinted *Notice of Award* form (Figures 11.14 and 11.15). The giving of a Notice of Award is similar in its legal effect to the issuance of a letter of intent, as it obligates the owner to sign the construction contract if the contractor does what is required of it within the time specified. The Notice of Award *does not authorize the start of construction,* because no work is supposed to start until after the owner/contractor agreement has been signed by both parties. Under the terms of the EJCDC General Conditions, the contract time will begin running on the thirtieth day after the owner has signed and delivered a fully executed agreement, but it may start sooner if a formal Notice to Proceed is issued. Under the AIA General Conditions, if no Notice to Proceed is issued, the contract time will begin as of the date of signing of the agreement. Under FIDIC Conditions of Contract, the Work must begin "as soon as is reasonably possible after receipt of a notice" (to proceed).

The issuance of a *Notice to Proceed* (Figures 11.16 and 11.17) formalizes the date that the project is to begin and sets the stage for computation of the total project construction time. This will greatly facilitate the establishment of an accurate count of construction time for the computation of liquidated damages. It is considerably more reliable than relying solely upon the Notice of Award, as can be seen by the variation in terms within the contract provisions of the two major societies who offer standardized General Conditions to be used in the project specifications. Many public agencies allow a 10-day period after the issuance of a formal Notice to Proceed for the contractor to begin work at the site.

A construction contract can but should not designate a specific commencement date because of the uncertainty of when the work can begin. Before the contractor can begin it must be given access to the site. This can require that easements be obtained, public approvals be given, and funds be obtained.

As a result, the commitment to begin work is usually expressed in terms of a number of days after access to the site. The owner also uses this approach to avoid responsibility for delay in its ability to grant access to the site.

Some owners attempt to establish a date to proceed by basing the starting date upon the date of execution of the agreement. This can be unfair to the contractor, who may not

**NOTICE OF AWARD**

**City of Palm Springs**

Dated ___MARCH 22___ 19_91_

To: ___Walsh Construction of Illinois dba Walsh Pacific Construction___
(Bidder)

Address: ___791 Foam Street, Suite 200___

___Monterey, CA 93940___

Project:     1991 EXPANSION OF PALM SPRINGS CONVENTION CENTER

City's Project No.     90-38

Contract for ___1991 Palm Springs Convention Center Expansion___

You are hereby notified that your Bid dated ___MARCH 19___ 19_91_ for the above Contract has been considered. You are the apparent successful bidder and have been awarded a contract for the above-named project.

The Bid Price of your contract is $___Five million, Six hundred, seventy-eight thousand dollars___

___($5,678,000.00)___ Dollars

Three copies of each of the proposed Contract Documents (except drawings) accompany this Notice of Award. Three sets of the Drawings will be delivered separately or otherwise made available to you immediately.

You must comply with the following conditions precedent within 10 days of the date of this Notice of Award; that is, by:

___APRIL 2,___ 19_91_ .

1.   You must deliver to the City ~~three~~ four fully executed counterparts of the Agreement, including all the Contract Documents. This includes the ~~triplicate~~ duplicate sets of Drawings. Each of the Contract Documents must bear your signature on the cover page.

2.   You must deliver with the executed Agreement, the Payment and Performance Bonds and the Insurance Certificate as specified in the Instructions to Bidders, the General Conditions (Article 5), and the Supplementary General Conditions.

Failure to comply with these conditions within the time specified will entitle the City to consider your Bid abandoned, to annul this Notice of Award, and to declare your Bid Security forfeited.

Within 10 days after you comply with the foregoing conditions, the City will return to you one fully signed counterpart of the Agreement with the Contract Documents attached.

CITY OF PALM SPRINGS

By ___Harold E. Hood, CPPO___

Title ___Purchasing Manager___

Copy to Architect by Certified Mail

_____Return receipt Requested

*Data used are fictitious for illustration only*

Palm Springs Project 90-38
Convention Center Expansion
A00670-022391
© 1990 by E. R. Fisk

NOTICE OF AWARD
CONTRACT ADMINISTRATION
FORMS - PAGE 1

**FIGURE 11.14**   Example of a Notice of Award (From *Construction Engineer's Complete Handbook of Forms* by Edward Fisk. Copyright © 1992 by Prentice Hall. Reproduced with permission of Prentice Hall.)

# NOTICE OF AWARD

Dated _____, 19_____

TO: _____
                    (BIDDER)

ADDRESS: _____

_____

_____

PROJECT _____

OWNER's CONTRACT NO. _____

CONTRACT FOR _____

_____
        (Insert name of Contract as it appears in the Bidding Documents)

You are notified that your Bid dated _____, 19_____ for the above Contract has been considered. You are the apparent Successful Bidder and have been awarded a contract for_____

_____

_____
        (Indicate total Work, alternates or sections or Work awarded)

The Contract Price of your contract is_____

_____Dollars ($        ).

[Insert appropriate data in re Unit Prices. Change language for Cost-Plus contracts.]

_____ copies of each of the proposed Contract Documents (except Drawings) accompany this Notice of Award. _____ sets of the Drawings will be delivered separately or otherwise made available to you immediately.

You must comply with the following conditions precedent within fifteen days of the date of this Notice of Award, that is by

_____, 199_____.

1. You must deliver to the OWNER _____ fully executed counterparts of the Agreement including all the Contract Documents. This includes the triplicate sets of Drawings. Each of the Contract Documents must bear your signature on (the cover) (every) page (pages _____).

2. You must deliver with the executed Agreement the Contract Security (Bonds) as specified in the Instructions to Bidders (paragraph 18), General Conditions (paragraph 5.1) and Supplementary Conditions (paragraph SC-5.1).

EJCDC No. 1910–22 (1990 Edition)
Prepared by the Engineers Joint Contract Documents Committee and endorsed by The Associated General Contractors of America.

**FIGURE 11.15a** Example of a Notice of Award keyed to the documents of the Engineer's Joint Contract Documents Committee (ACEC, ASCE, CSI, NSPE). (Copyright © 1990 by National Society of Professional Engineers.)

3. (List other conditions precedents).

_____

_____

_____

_____

_____

_____

_____

_____

_____

_____

_____

_____

Failure to comply with these conditions within the time specified will entitle OWNER to consider your bid in default, to annul this Notice of Award and to declare your Bid Security forfeited.

Within ten days after you comply with the above conditions, OWNER will return to you one fully signed counterpart of the Agreement with the Contract Documents attached.

_____
(OWNER)

By: _____
(AUTHORIZED SIGNATURE)

_____
(TITLE)

## ACCEPTANCE OF AWARD

_____
(CONTRACTOR)

By: _____
(AUTHORIZED SIGNATURE)

_____
(TITLE)

_____
(DATE)

COPY to ENGINEER
(Use Certified Mail,
Return Receipt Requested)

**FIGURE 11.15b** Reverse side of EJCDC Notice of Award.

**E. R. FISK & ASSOCIATES**
P.O. Box 6448 • Orange, CA 92613-6448

# NOTICE TO PROCEED

To

XYZ CONTRACTORS, INC.
5892 First Street, Suite 104
Santa Barbara, 93000

Project __Caldwell Reservoir__ No. __1134-57__

Construction Contract No. __CN07-8976-4366__

Type of Contract __Unit Price__

Amount of Contract __$423,975.00__

You are hereby notified to commence work on the referenced contract on or before __23 April__ 19__90__, and shall fully

complete all of the work of said contract within __365__ consecutive calendar days thereafter. Your completion date

is therefore __23 April__ 19__91__ .

The contract provides for an assessment of the sum of $ __500.00__ as liquidated damages for each consecutive calendar
day after the above established contract completion date that the work remains incomplete.

Dated this __9th__ day of __April__ 19__90__ .

*Data used are fictitious
for illustration only*

By __W. Ke_____

Title __Project Manager__

### ACCEPTANCE OF NOTICE

Receipt of the foregoing Notice to Proceed is hereby acknowledged

By __XYZ Contractors, Inc.__

this __11th__ day of __April__ 19__1990__ .

By __J. P. Campbell_____

Title __President,__
__XYZ Contractors, Inc.__

Wiley-Fisk Fo. 6-1

**FIGURE 11.16** Example of a Notice of Proceed (From *Construction Engineer's Complete Handbook of Forms* by Edward Fisk. Copyright © 1992 by Prentice Hall. Reproduced with permission of Prentice Hall.)

## NOTICE TO PROCEED

Dated _____ , 19 _____

TO: _____
(CONTRACTOR)

ADDRESS: _____

_____

PROJECT _____

OWNER's CONTRACT NO. _____

CONTRACT FOR _____

_____
(Insert name of Contract as it appears in the Bidding Documents)

You are notified that the Contract Times under the above contract will commence to run on _____ , 19 _____ . By that date, you are to start performing your obligations under the Contract Documents. In accordance with Article 3 of the Agreement the dates of Substantial Completion and completion and readiness for final payment are _____ , 19 _____ and _____ , 19 _____ .

Before you may start any Work at the site, paragraph 2.7 of the General Conditions provides that you and Owner must each deliver to the other (with copies to ENGINEER and other identified additional insureds) certificates of insurance which each is required to purchase and maintain in accordance with the Contract Documents.

Also before you may start any Work at the site, you must
(add other requirements)

_____

_____

_____

_____
(OWNER)

By: _____
(AUTHORIZED SIGNATURE)

_____
(TITLE)

ACCEPTANCE OF AWARD

By: _____
(CONTRACTOR)

_____
(AUTHORIZED SIGNATURE)

_____
(TITLE)

_____
(DATE)

Copy to ENGINEER
(Use Certified Mail,
Return Receipt Requested)

EJCDC No. 1910-23 (1990 Edition)
Prepared by the Engineers Joint Contract Documents Committee and endorsed by The Associated General Contractors of America.

**FIGURE 11.17** Example of a Notice to Proceed keyed to the documents of the Engineer's Joint Contract Documents Committee (ACEC, ASCE, CSI, NSPE). (Copyright © 1990 by National Society of Professional Engineers.)

be given access to the site until long after the date on the agreement. Often, the contractor will not receive a signed copy of the Agreement until one or more weeks after execution by the owner, thus using construction time that should have been available for the contractor. If the contractor runs into a period of liquidated damages, it will more assuredly file a claim to recover the time lost by failure to receive confirmation of the execution of the agreement. EJCDC documents provide that the contract time will begin to run on the 30th day after the effective date of the Agreement, or if a Notice to Proceed is given, on the day indicated in the Notice to Proceed. There are many complications possible; however, all of the risks could be avoided if the owner fixed a starting date in the Notice to Proceed or upon receipt of the Notice to Proceed.

## PROBLEMS

In each of the following three questions, insert the letter from the following list of multiple-choice answers that represents the proper time to accomplish the indicated task.

    **A.** during the bid phase
    **B.** after Agreement, but before the Notice to Proceed
    **C.** prior to advertising for bids
    **D.** after bid opening, but before Award of Contract
    **E.** after Notice to Proceed
    **F.** after award, but before owner signs the Agreement

1. A prebid conference should be held when? _____
2. A preconstruction conference should be held when? _____
3. When should the bidder submit the payment bond, the performance bond, and the certificate of insurance? _____
4. What is the proper method of responding to bidder inquiries during the bid phase of a project?
5. True or false? A builder's risk "all-risk" policy of construction insurance covers all perils without additional endorsement.
6. What is a nonresponsive bid?
7. Explain the nature and purpose of a price allocation form, or schedule of values.
8. Is it the responsibility of the Resident Project Representative to review shop drawings, evaluate sample submittals, approve substitute materials, or interpret the intent of the contract plans and specifications?
9. What is the significance of a Notice of Award? What does it do? Is access to the site authorized thereby?
10. Is it an acceptable contract administration procedure to permit access to the site or issue a Notice to Proceed after Award but prior to execution of the formal Agreement?

11. On a project which supports a full-time Resident Project Representative at the site, with the project manager located in the home office, to whom should all contractor submittals be submitted first?

12. Should an inspector always try to get the contractor to give the owner the highest quality materials and workmanship, regardless of the quality level called for in the specifications?

13. Who should be the only party with the authority to "stop the work"?

14. If the specifications are silent on the subject, but a contractor asks you, as the Resident Project Representative or inspector, how to perform the work, which of the following is the recommended procedure?

    a. Be ready to help by telling the contractor your opinions, because as a member of the construction team, it is your responsibility.

    b. Politely decline because construction means and methods are the sole prerogative of the contractor.

    c. Direct the contractor how to perform the work because you know that if he asked you, it meant that he did not know how, and the project may otherwise suffer delays or failures.

15. True or false? "Front loading" of a bid is always an illegal or unethical form of unbalancing a bid.

# 12

## Planning for Construction

### PLANNING FOR CONSTRUCTION

Construction planning and scheduling should not be considered as one of the deep mysteries of life, but rather as an application of common sense, a logical analysis of a construction project together with all of its parts, and a thorough knowledge of construction methods, materials, and practices.

The process of planning is simply an application of the thought process that must be entered into before the actual scheduling can begin. The planning process should include answers to the following *preliminary* questions:

1. *Long-lead purchases.* Are there any items that will require purchase orders to be placed long in advance of the time that the item is needed on the job because of material shortages, fabrication time, or similar delay factors?

2. *Utility interruptions.* Is there any part of the project that will involve an outage of utility services such as water, power, gas, or other essential services? If so, has the utility owner been contacted to determine the maximum length of the outage, the time of day that outages will be permitted, the calendar dates during which outages will be permitted, or similar restrictive controls?

3. *Temporary utilities.* Will temporary utility lines be required to be built to bypass the construction area, and will temporary roads be required to provide detour routes for street traffic?

4. *Temporary construction utility service.* Who provides temporary construction utility service, and from where must it be obtained?

5. *Labor.* Have representatives of labor been contacted in the area of construction to establish the jurisdictional responsibilities of the various trades to be used in the work, as well as to determine the union work rules in the affected area?

6. *Work and storage areas.* Have provisions been made for contractor's work and storage areas?

7. *Traffic requirements.* Have local traffic control regulations been investigated? Will construction equipment be allowed to operate on public streets, will street closures in the construction area be permitted, and will special traffic control and flaggers be required to direct traffic around construction?

8. *Temporary access.* Will temporary access, including temporary bridges, be required to provide continued access to residences and places of business during the construction period?

9. *Other contractors.* Will other contractors be working in the same area, thus requiring schedule coordination with them to complete the work of this contract?

10. *Interdependency of tasks.* Are some of the tasks in this project dependent upon the completion schedule of another contractor or utility owner before they can be started?

11. *Environmental controls.* Will special environmental controls be required; if so, which ones?

12. *Special regulations.* Are there special regulations, such as FAA requirements for work at airports, that may affect the construction scheduling or construction time?

13. *Special construction equipment.* Will special equipment be required for construction? If so, is it off-road equipment that will require special haul routes? What are the load limits and bridge clearances for roads in the area?

14. *Time for construction.* Is the time allowed to complete the project adequate for the location and the seasons, or will it require increased crew sizes or premium time?

Each of these items is an important consideration in the planning stage of a project. After determination of the various limitations and constraints on the conduct of the work, the task of planning the actual construction effort can begin. Many large contracts can be divided into separate stages of construction. In some cases there may be a single general contractor responsible for the construction of all the stages, which may simply have been planned to accommodate a fixed order or sequence of construction. In other cases, it may be possible that portions of a construction project may begin even before the entire work of design has been completed. This is generally accomplished by the owner entering into phased construction contracts ("fast-track"), in which each stage of the work is let for construction as soon as the design effort on that particular phase of the work has been completed (Figure 12.1).

As mentioned previously, this approach has the added advantage that it can result in completion of a project at an earlier date than would be possible if it were necessary to wait until all design work had been completed. It may also offer a distinct financial advantage to the owner in many cases by allowing the early bidding of completed portions of the work to avoid the added costs that could result from the cost inflation spiral if the work were to be delayed. The fast-track method of construction is often a money saver for the owner despite added field administration costs, as the earlier construction completion date is often money in the owner's pocket.

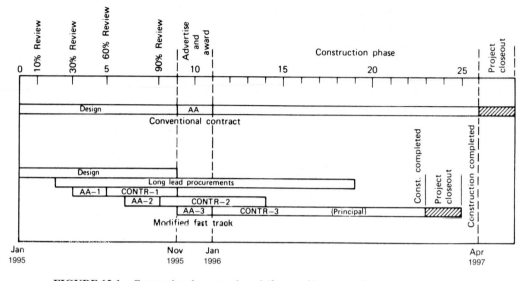

**FIGURE 12.1**   Conventional versus phased (fast-track) construction.

Phased construction (fast-track) has its disadvantages, too, as it creates considerably more work for the project manager and the Resident Project Representative, and may require a larger field staff to administer. One of the difficulties that may have to be overcome is created by the fact that under a fast-track system of construction, numerous other prime contractors are on the job. Because of this, the added responsibility for coordination of each of these various *prime* contractors falls upon the shoulders of the contract administrator and the Resident Project Representative as there would be no general contractor with this responsibility. Similarly, interfaces between the various scopes of the work of each of the separate prime contracts have been very carefully worked out in the contract documents. Furthermore, if the project in which these various separate contractors are involved concerns separate elements that must ultimately become a part of a single operational system, the question of responsibility for the proper functioning of the overall system may pose a serious problem for the owner.

Generally, under a system of fast-track contracts, it is most desirable to operate under a design–build/turnkey or a construction management contract, wherein such responsibilities can be handled by the construction manager and his or her project team. In such cases, the task of administration of the construction will be carried by an on-site project manager, and the resident inspector will normally be performing the functions of a quality control supervisor.

Another approach to the problem of responsibility over fast-track contract operations that has not yet come into common use is one in which all but one of the prime contracts awarded contains an assignment clause that allows one of the other prime contractors to function as a lead contractor. In this capacity, the lead contractor will have responsibility

Separate fast—track prime contractor agreements include an assignment clause to allow principal (coordinating) contractor, when he is brought onto the project, to have authority for coordination and interface responsibility. This is NOT AN ASSIGNMENT OF CONTRACT.

Principal (coordinating) contractor's agreement will contain a clause requiring him to provide overall coordination between his own forces and those of all fast—track prime contractors as well as maintain interface control between the work of all tasks.

**FIGURE 12.2**   Phased (fast-track) construction with assigned coordination.

for coordinating the work of all the contractors on the project and assuring that all work will interface properly without gaps or overlaps of responsibility (Figure 12.2).

The planning problem is further complicated by the fact that consideration must be given to the work of each of the trades to assure that there will be no interference by others whose work takes them into the same construction area; nor will the work of one trade be held up because of the failure of another to complete its work. Costs of mobilization must also be considered, as it would certainly be both uneconomical and time consuming to move heavy earthmoving equipment to a site for construction of the work of one phase and move off the site, only to be moved back again to execute the earthwork requirements of another phase of the work if all of the earthwork could have been completed at the same time.

Obviously, to get a clear picture of all the interrelated problems at a construction site, some kind of a graphic picture must be drawn to enable the contractor and the Resident Project Representative to get a clear understanding not only of the sequence of events, but also of their times of beginning and anticipated completion.

## CONSTRUCTION SCHEDULES AS RELATED TO BUILDING COSTS

Unrealistic completion dates, coupled with exorbitant liquidated damages charges against the contractor for failure to meet such requirements, impose severe financial burdens and undeterminable risks on the contractor. Furthermore, the owner, as a direct result, pays more than the building is worth, with no guarantee that the job will be completed by the stipulated deadline.

Some of the reasons are stated here. To cope with an unrealistic completion schedule, a contractor must do everything possible to attract adequate labor from a current short supply of workers, and must add to the bid sufficient money to cover the daily costs of liquidated damages for the days that are expected to run over the completion date. In addition, the contractor must figure in the premium costs of overtime work rates, which run from one and one-half to two times the normal rate.

Another result will be evident in the disparity of bids received, as no two bidders are likely to evaluate the unknown and uncontrollable factors in the same manner. The essence of proper bidding is an accurate estimate of determinable costs within the power and judgment of the bidder. Unrealistic completion schedules and liquidated damages charges also force the bidder to guess as to the availability of materials and equipment, over which the contractor has no control. Thus, another added cost must be considered.

In addition, disputes and seemingly endless paper work seem to result from the inevitable claims for extensions of time due to causes outside the scope of the contract.

## SCHEDULING METHODS

There are relatively few basic scheduling systems in use today, although numerous variants of each are in use. Generally, scheduling methods can be classed in four major categories:

1. Bar charts
2. Velocity charts (S-curves)
3. Line-of-balance charts
4. Network diagrams

Bar charts seem to have been with us since the beginning of time, and they are still in extensive use today. They are still an extremely useful tool and may often be seen accompanying a network diagram. The bar chart as it is used today is somewhat similar to the charts discussed by one writer in the nineteenth century involving a work versus time graphical representation. It was Henry L. Gantt and Frederick W. Taylor, however, who popularized its use early in the twentieth century. Their Gantt charts are the basis of today's bar graphs or bar charts. Although their work was originally aimed at production scheduling, it was readily accepted for planning construction and recording its progress. One of its principal advantages is that it is readily understood by all levels of management, supervision, and laypersons.

The velocity diagram used as a management tool predated network techniques; however, the method is not too well known in the United States. The velocity diagram is similar in many respects to the well-known S-curve, which is customarily used in the United States for project cost control and progress reporting (Figure 12.3). The velocity diagram as a scheduling tool shows the relationship between time and output of a construction project in a straightforward and simple way. It represents the determined route of a construction process, or the construction volume on one axis and time on the other. The construction advance rate or *production velocity* is indicated by the slope of the production line. As with the traditional S-curve, the user can determine at a glance whether a project is proceeding on schedule or whether it is behind but catching up or falling further behind.

For that reason, the velocity diagram lends itself efficiently to projects that are linear in nature. On a project such as a pumping station or water treatment plant, there are no rational means of gaging work progress except as a function of cost. However, in a linear project, progress can be related to units of length. Examples of projects ideally suited to velocity diagram scheduling control are linear construction sites such as pipelines, canals, and highways. Although adaptable as a time/progress *reporting* tool for projects involving vertical linearity, it is not as well suited to the *control* of a vertical project such as a high-rise building because of the complex dependencies.

Line of balance is a specialized technique for repetitive work. It was derived from the manufacturing industry and has been found to be effective in planning construction work that is truly repetitive. Examples of successful applications include planning and construction of identical floors in high-rise construction and large housing developments.

Line of balance has been found to be difficult to use on projects that require a large number of trades or operations to construct each identical unit. The problems result not from the technique itself but from the difficulty of showing all of the information on one chart, especially when using the technique to monitor progress. When used to plan, it can be an effective means of relating resources, activity durations, and the general pace of work on the site.

The technique is not widely used in the United States, however, and most contractors in this country either utilize bar (Gantt) charts or network scheduling techniques. Network diagrams represent the development of systems that not only record the graphical work-versus-time relationships of each phase of the work, but also enable the user to see the interrelation and dependencies that control the project. Network planning did not come into being until the middle of the 1950s, when the U.S. Navy Special Projects Office set out with their consultants to devise a new method of planning for special weapons systems. The result was called the *Program Evaluation Review Technique,* now universally called PERT. It was an *event-oriented* system and was designed primarily as a project monitoring system. The attempt to apply PERT to the construction industry was not too successful, primarily because of event orientation, the use of three time estimates instead of one, and the technique of starting at the end and working toward the beginning. Consequently, further research was done by others in the construction field, and the result was the *Critical Path Method,* known as CPM. This method was *activity oriented,* used single time estimates, and usually started at the beginning and worked to the end of the project.

In actual practice, the CPM and PERT techniques are very similar in principle, except for the emphasis on probability in PERT. Network planning is the basis for both sys-

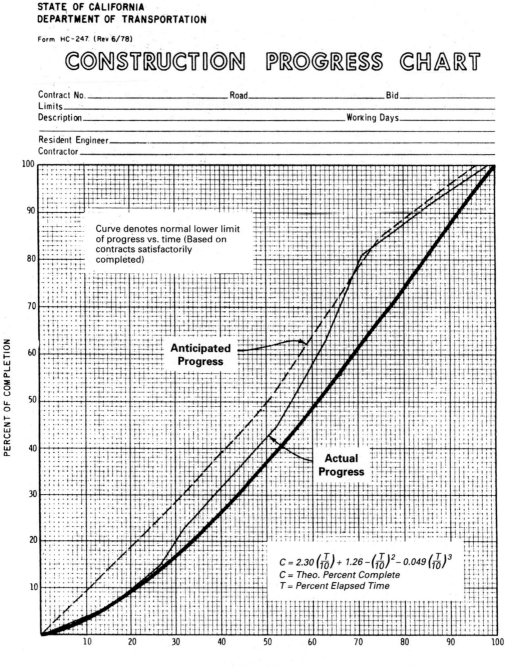

FIGURE 12.3   Construction progress S-curve.

**294**

tems, and although in contemporary usage a computer is generally used, they can be done by manual methods as well.

By comparing the bar chart methods with network diagramming methods, the user can see the advantages of one system over the other. With a network diagram, it can be shown to be obvious that work item E could not proceed until work item D had been completed, whereas a bar chart could only indicate the scheduled date that task E was to be performed, and if task D was late there was no way of determining from the bar chart that task E would be delayed also because of the interrelationship between the two tasks. In the preparation of a bar chart, the scheduler is almost necessarily influenced by the desired completion dates, often working backward from the completion dates. The resultant mixture of planning and scheduling is often no better than wishful thinking.

By comparison with the bar chart and network diagram systems, the velocity chart appears to share few of the advantages of either system, yet, in turn, offers some distinctive advantages of its own. Whereas both the bar chart and the network diagrams identify specific project tasks or activities and provide the user with progress information relative to the individual activities, and whereas the network systems go even further by providing additional control by means of established activity dependencies, the velocity chart is only capable of tracking the project as a whole. What it *can* offer that neither of the other systems can, however, is the ability to display the *rate* of completion and a graphic indication of whether an off-schedule project is catching up, falling behind, or accelerating its scheduled completion date. Some engineers and contractors find it an extremely useful tool for smaller projects and seem to prefer it to either bar chart scheduling or network scheduling.

## BAR CHARTS

If a bar graph is carefully prepared, the scheduler goes through the same preliminary thinking process that the network planner does. However, a bar graph does not show or record the interrelations or dependencies that control the progress of the project, and thus cannot be used alone in scheduling a project. At a later date, even the originator of a bar graph may find it difficult to explain the plan using the bar graph. In the example in Figure 12.4, a simplified bar chart shows the stages of construction of a small one-story office building. Suppose that after this 10-month schedule has been prepared, the owner asks for a 6-month schedule instead. By using the same time for each activity, the bar chart can be changed as shown in Figure 12.5. Although this may look correct at first, it is not based upon logical planning; it is merely the juggling of the original bar graph. In the case of *Mega Construction Co., Inc.* v. *United States* 29 Fed.Cl. 396 (1993), involving the construction of a post office building in Canoga Park, California, the Court of Federal Claims denied a claim because the contractor's bar charts failed to establish the interrelationship between disrupted tasks and other activities on the schedules's critical path. In the words of the court, the "Plaintiff's bar chart depicted its version of the numerous work items. However, it failed to prove that the claimed delays occurred along the critical path, because it does not indicate the interdependence of any one or more of the work items that were on the critical path while the project was ongoing, but offered no credible evidence of the interdependence of the project's activities."

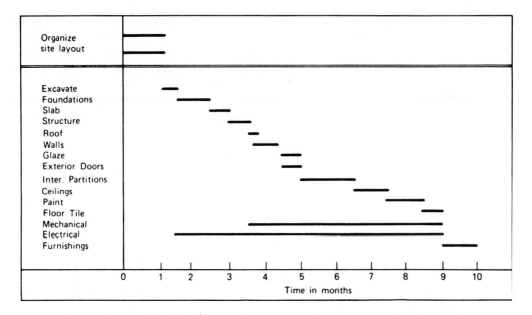

**FIGURE 12.4**   Bar chart of small one-story office building.

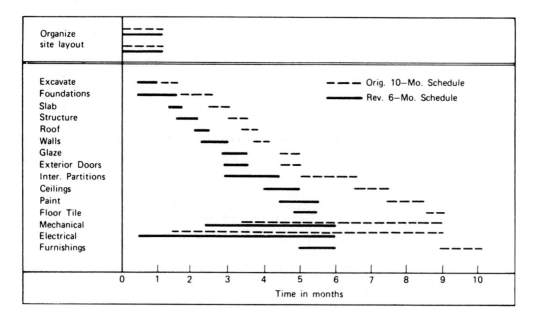

**FIGURE 12.5**   Revised bar chart of a small one-story office building.

In Figures 12.4 and 12.5, note that the general contractor's work is broken down in some detail, while the mechanical and electrical work are each shown as a continuous line, starting early and ending late. In conformance with the bar chart, the general contractor often pushes the subcontractor to staff the project as early as possible with as many mechanics as possible, although the subcontractors would like to come on the project as late as possible with as few mechanics as possible. The general contractor often complains that the subcontractor is delaying the job through lack of interest in the progress of the work. At the same time, the subcontractor is complaining that the general contractor is not turning over work areas and that the subcontractor will have to go into a crash effort to save the schedule. As in most matters, the truth is probably somewhere between both extremes. Network diagrams offer the means to resolve many of these differences with specific information rather than with generalities.

The bar chart is often actively used early in the project, but seems to be nowhere to be found later in the project. One can assume that the reasons for this may be that somewhere before the construction phase the design firm and owner are all trying to visualize the project schedule to set realistic completion dates and, once this is accomplished, lose interest in the specifics of the schedule. Most specifications require the submittal of a schedule in bar graph form by the contractor soon after the award of the contract. When the project begins to take shape in the field, the early bar charts become as useful as last year's calendar, because the bar graph does not lend itself to planning revisions.

In one form, the bar chart persists, and rightfully so. As a means of communicating job progress information to nontechnically trained people, or even to construction experts whose need to know is limited to progress data only, the bar chart excels as a means of showing such data in a clear and concise manner. Such charts record the progress in each of the major elements of construction as a solid bar along a corresponding time scale, and are generally updated monthly (Figure 12.6).

## S-CURVE SCHEDULING OR VELOCITY DIAGRAMS[1]

Although it was stated earlier in the chapter that a velocity diagram (Figure 12.7) is essentially a form of the popular S-curve, it is how the diagram is used as a scheduling tool that makes it unique, and thus deserving of its own identity. As with the S-curve, the construction advance rate is indicated by the slope of the line. During the actual construction process, the Resident Project Representative or project manager must compare the scheduled construction velocity with that of the actual construction velocity (rate of progress). From the updated velocity diagram, surplus or deficit can be recognized easily. Therefore, decisions such as starting construction at a second place on the project can be made, in case the actual velocity is lower than the scheduled velocity, and compliance with the time deadline has first priority.

A simplified illustration of a velocity diagram applied to a pipeline project is illustrated in Figure 12.7. Here, if a pipeline must be built from station A to station B, a distance

[1]J. Dressier, "Construction Management in West Germany," *Journal of the Construction Division, ASCE,* Vol. 106, No. C04, Proceedings Paper 15878, December 1980, pp. 477–481.

FIGURE 12.6  Bar chart progress schedule for unit price project.

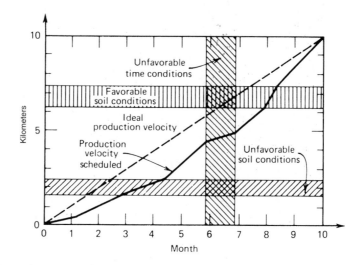

**FIGURE 12.7**    Velocity diagram as time scheduling tool.

of 10 kilometers (6.2 miles) in 10 months (100 percent), the ideal production velocity would be 1 kilometer per month (dashed line in Figure 12.7). However, as there will be changing soil or other environmental conditions, and one will also encounter changing weather conditions, the most probable schedule must be developed according to the solid line.

Figure 12.7, of course, represents a greatly oversimplified example. However, the velocity diagram has proved its efficiency for complicated operations as well, in particular when schedules depend on minimum time lags between parallel operations, or minimum distances relating to space, and so forth. In that context, the velocity diagram was used as a management tool for the first time during the planning and construction of the St. Gotthard Tunnel in Switzerland about 100 years ago.

As a reporting device, instead of a tool for *control,* the popular S-curve is frequently used as a management reporting tool to show comparisons of anticipated progress with actual progress, even where bar charts or network diagrams are being used to schedule the work in the field. An example was shown in Figure 12.3, where an S-curve was used by the California Department of Transportation as a monthly progress reporting device. Another variation of the S-curve is based upon cost instead of time and is used as a cost control tool (see Figure 14.1).

## LINE-OF-BALANCE CHARTS

Line-of-balance charts (Figure 12.8) are used to plan the construction of a number of similar items. The technique is used to analyze the application of labor and plant resources to assure that each resource can progress from one item to the next in an orderly way, completing its own work on all the items without being delayed in waiting for the preceding work to be completed. Thus, the technique is based upon the concept of keeping all of the resources in balance, each following the other productively.

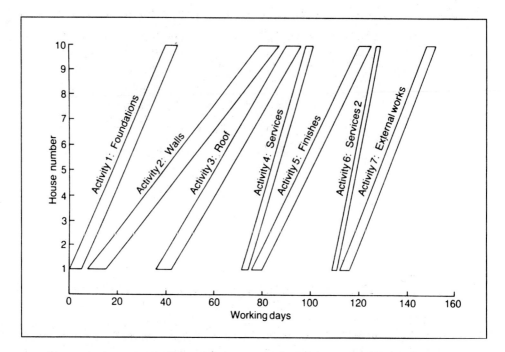

**FIGURE 12.8**    Example of a line-of-balance schedule diagram for a 10-house project.

The main objective of using line-of-balance is to make optimum use of all resources. To accomplish this, it is important that the activities and resources are related closely (i.e., the job is planned on a trade basis).

The purpose of a line-of-balance analysis is to balance the rate of progress of the activities, and to schedule the activities to eliminate interference. This is done by:

1. Adjusting the rate of production for each activity so that this approximates to a common rate of production for all activities
2. Delaying the start of those activities that (even after adjustment) proceed faster than the activity immediately preceding it, to maintain at least the minimum buffer specified at all times

In the classical, factory-based line-of-balance analysis, it is assumed that individual resources make equal contributions to progress, regardless of the number of resources used. For example, if a task takes 10 person-hours, one person would complete the task in 10 hours, whereas 10 people would complete the task in 1 hour. Thus, the rate of progress of each activity may be adjusted quite finely; consequently, the activities may be made to work at almost the same rate of progress.

In construction, such an approach is unrealistic. Tradesmen rarely work as individuals or in large groups. Years of experience and practice have established the most effective size for a group.

In construction, estimates of activity duration are only approximate. In repetitive construction where the activities and trades follow in succession, any delay in the planned completion of an activity will result in the following trades having to wait unproductively for its completion. Therefore, it is considered as wise to plan a short delay or buffer between each activity. The estimate of buffer times is related to the project manager's assessment of the reliability of the estimate of activity durations. Where the reliability is poor, large buffers must be used.

## NETWORK DIAGRAMS

### General Summary of Systems in Use

Network diagrams, so called because of the net effect of the interconnecting lines used to indicate dependencies and interrelationships, can be divided into two basic categories.

1. *CPM* or *Critical Path Method,* which was originally developed specifically for the planning of construction from PPS (Project Planning and Scheduling), which was originated by du Pont.
2. *PERT* or *Program Evaluation Review Technique,* which was originated by the Special Projects Office of the Navy Bureau of Ordinance, and with few exceptions is used almost exclusively in military, aerospace, and project management work. Adaptations of the basic technique have been developed for use in construction.

Occasionally, modifications are used that utilize some of the separate features of the previously mentioned systems. Contractors for construction of ground support and launching facilities for missiles in space may encounter PERT in construction; otherwise, it appears that little will be seen of it in construction in an unmodified form.

### Critical Path Method

The workhorse of network scheduling methods used in construction is the popular critical path method (CPM), which is used almost universally wherever network scheduling methods are called for. The CPM system shows the order and interdependence of activities and the sequence in which the work is to be accomplished. The basic concept of the network analysis diagram is to show the start of each given activity and its dependence upon the completion of preceding activities, and how its completion also restricts other activities to follow. The CPM network provides for the construction phase only, using either manual or automated methods, involving the following activities:

1. Long-lead purchases and deliveries of critical materials
2. Fabrication, installation, and testing of critical equipment
3. Submittal and approval of material samples and shop drawings
4. All activities that affect progress on the job
5. Required dates of completion for all activities

If a project is of such size that a single network cannot be easily shown on a single sheet, a summary network diagram will probably be provided. The summary sheet is usually a network of from 50 to 150 activities and is based upon the detailed diagrams of all the remaining tasks. The mathematical analysis of the CPM network diagram includes the following information for each activity:

1. Preceding and following event numbers
2. Activity description
3. Estimated duration of activities
4. Earliest start dates (calendar dates)
5. Earliest finish dates (calendar dates)
6. Scheduled or actual start date
7. Scheduled or actual finish date
8. Latest start date (calendar date)
9. Latest finish date (calendar date)
10. Monetary value of activity
11. Responsibility for activity (prime; subs; suppliers; etc.)
12. Labor required
13. Percentage of activity completed as of each report
14. Contractor's earnings based upon portion of work completed
15. Bid item of which the activity is a part

In addition to the tabulation of activities, the CPM computer printout should also include an identification of activities that are planned for expediting by the use of overtime or double shifts to be worked, including possible Saturday, Sunday, or holiday work. It should also provide an on-site manpower loading schedule and a description of the major items of construction equipment planned for operations on the project. Where portions of the work are to be paid for under unit costs, the estimated number of units in an activity that was used in developing the total activity cost should be shown.

The computer printout generally sorts certain classes of frequently used data into groups or "sorts." Generally, the data on a CPM will be grouped into the following sorts:

1. By the preceding event number from the lowest to the highest, and then in order of the following event number.
2. By the amount of slack, then in the order of earliest allowable start dates.
3. In order of the latest allowable start dates, then in order of preceding event numbers, then in order of succeeding event numbers.

The data provided must be timely, must be responsive to the needs of management at all levels, and must be fully capable of providing a sound basis for management decisions. The computer printouts, in which automated methods are used, will include the following:

1. Sorts by early and late start, criticality, responsibility, and building area.
2. Allocation of material and labor costs to each work item.
3. Generation of cash-flow projections and contractor payment request verifications.
4. Master schedule; design schedule; preconstruction schedule; and occupancy schedule.
5. Separate reports, including summary and bar charts, contractor payments, purchase orders, shop drawings, and samples.

## PERT Management Control Systems

PERT as a Management Control System is a network system for management control developed by the Special Projects Office of the Navy Bureau of Ordnance. The system can be used by private architect/engineers in the project management of numerous projects. PERT provides for the design phase of a project using both manual and automated procedures as a support for the following functions:

1. Planning
2. Organizing
3. Scheduling
4. Budgeting
5. Reporting of design and construction progress
6. Reporting of design and construction expenditures
7. Accounting
8. Documentation
9. Identification of variances and problems
10. Decision making
11. Decision implementation

## Learning to Use a Network Diagram

Network diagrams may seem unduly complicated to read at first, and if you happened to be called upon to try to develop one, they would indeed *be* complicated. Fortunately, the Resident Project Representative's responsibility in network diagramming is limited to reading, understanding, and using the diagrams to good advantage on the project. The skill of learning to read and understand them is not that complicated and can be acquired by anyone willing to learn a few of its basic principles. These are explained in more depth in Chapter 13.

It is essential that the Resident Project Representative should become reasonably familiar with the principles of network diagramming so as to perform effectively the associated duties and responsibilities involved with those projects that use them. The inspector must not only understand the network diagrams themselves, but should be capable of reading and interpreting the computer printouts of all CPM data received by the field office.

Admittedly, the system may only be encountered on larger projects, but a basic knowledge of the general principles of network diagramming should be a part of every Resident Project Representative's education.

## SPECIFYING CPM FOR A PROJECT

There are a number of sources for guide specifications for preparing a meaningful CPM specification, but the one favored by the author is a slightly modified version of the guide specification published by the Associated General Contractors of America in their book *Using CPM in Construction*. The principal modifications made by the author were to require time-scaled network diagrams; provide columns of both free float and total float on the report form, and specify frequency of printouts not exceeding 4 weeks apart. In addition, the author ties in the submittal of the schedule to the owner or engineer with the contractor's initial mobilization payment to assure that the contractor will abide by the requirements to submit the proposed schedule in time. A sample specification meeting these requirements can be seen in Figure 12.9.

## PERSONAL COMPUTERS FOR CPM NETWORK SCHEDULING

The age of the manually prepared CPM schedule is fast disappearing from the construction scene. Computerized project scheduling on personal computers using critical path techniques is simpler, cheaper, and yields such a large array of reporting and tracking documentation that the successful project manager will ultimately find it indispensable. As recently as 1981, CPM required a cool hand, a quick eye, and plenty of patience to get even a rudimentary critical path out of some mainframe computer systems, and the personal computer (PC) market had not yet awakened. To be sure, there were exceptions. However, until the advent of the IBM/PC and other compatible PCs using a PC/DOS or MS/DOS operating system, the demand for personal-computer-based CPM had not yet arrived.

Now the situation has changed. There are many good project scheduling programs designed for the IBM/PC-compatible computers, some of them excellent. Most such software can be customized to some degree, and at least those reviewed by the author give identical critical paths for the same input data. The basic requirement for CPM logic is the ability of replicability of programs. Unless they are capable of producing identical output, they are useless. Worse yet, failure of a program to be able to provide this can lead to construction claims and operating losses in real dollars.

### Computer Hardware

Ideally, for maximum versatility and potential compatibility with data generated on another computer outside your own office, it is desirable to provide hardware that is compatible with the industry standard microcomputer.

**1.01 General**

A. The project management scheduling tool "Critical Path Method," a network scheduling system commonly called CPM, shall be employed by the Contractor for planning and scheduling of all work required under the Contract Documents. All schedule reports shall be in the form of computer printouts. The Contractor may elect to use bar charts (Gantt Charts) as an onsite scheduling tool; provided, that all such bar charts shall be generated from the approved CPM network.

B. Summary of types and schedule submittals required:

   1. Preliminary Construction Schedule: Submit within 7 days after date of commencement specified in the Notice to Proceed (See Section 01500 Mobilization, Item 9); must be a detailed schedule conforming to Paragraph 1.05, herein.

   2. Initial Construction Schedule: This is the revised and approved version of the Preliminary Schedule. Submit within 30 days of date of Notice to Proceed. (See Section 01500 Mobilization, Item 10). This is the working schedule for the project until a revised schedule is required to be submitted.

   3. Revised Construction Schedules and Additional Network Diagrams: Updated revisions of the Initial Construction Schedules and network diagrams as required by the Engineer.

**1.02 Qualifications**

A. A statement of computerized CPM capability shall be submitted in writing prior to the award of the Contract and shall verify that either the Contractor's organization has in-house capability qualified to prepare and use the CPM scheduling technique, or that the Contractor employs a CPM consultant who is so qualified.

**1.03 Submittal Procedures**

A. Time of submittals: Within 7 days after the date of commencement as stated in the Notice to Proceed, the Contractor shall submit for acceptance by the Engineer the Preliminary Construction Schedule, a detailed schedule which shall consist of a network diagram describing the work activities and procurement to be accomplished in the project and their dependency relationships as well schedule reports (as defined following). The schedule produced and submitted shall indicate a project completion date on or before the contract completion date. The Engineer, within 7 days after receipt of the network diagram, shall meet with a representative of the Contractor to review the proposed plan and schedule.

B. Within 7 days after the conclusion of the Engineer's review of the Preliminary Construction Schedule, the Contractor shall revise the network diagram as required and re-submit the network diagram and the schedule reports produced therefrom. The revised network diagram and schedule reports shall be revised and approved or rejected by the Engineer within 7 days after receipt. The network diagram and schedule reports when accepted by the Engineer shall constitute the Initial Construction Schedule until a Revised Construction Schedule is required to be submitted.

C. Acceptance: When the Initial Construction Schedule network diagram and schedule reports have been accepted by the Engineer, the Contractor shall submit to the Engineer 4 copies of the time-scaled network diagram, 4 copies of a computerized schedule report in which the activities and procurement have been sorted by activity number, 4 copies of a computerized schedule in which the activities have been sorted by Early Start Date, 4 copies of a computerized schedule report in which

**FIGURE 12.9**   Sample guide specification for CPM scheduling based upon AGC recommendations.

activities have been sorted by Total Float, and one copy of the <u>Initial Schedule Report</u> on computer disks.

D. <u>Additional Network Diagrams:</u> The Contractor, if requested by the Engineer, shall provide revised network diagrams if, at any time, the Engineer considers the completion date to be in jeopardy because of "activities behind schedule." The <u>Additional Network Diagrams</u> shall include a new arrow or precedence diagram and schedule reports conforming to the requirements of Paragraph entitled "CPM Standards," herein, designed to show how the Contractor intends to accomplish the Work to meet the completion date. The form and method employed by the Contractor shall be the same as that required for the original <u>Initial Construction Schedule.</u>

E. <u>Schedule Revisions:</u> The Contractor shall modify any portions of the construction schedule that become infeasible because of "activities or procurement behind schedule" or for any other valid reason. An activity that cannot be completed by its original latest completion date shall be deemed to be behind schedule.

**1.04 Change Orders**

A. Upon issuance of a Change Order or Work Change Directive, the approved change shall be reflected in the next submittal of the <u>Revised Construction Schedule</u> by the Contractor.

**1.05 CPM Standards**

A. <u>Definition:</u> CPM scheduling, as required by this Section, shall be interpreted to be generally as outlined in the Associated General Contractors publication, "The Use of CPM in Construction," except that either arrow diagramming or activity-on-node precedence diagramming format is acceptable.

B. <u>Construction Schedules:</u> Construction schedules shall include a computer-generated graphic network and computerized, construction schedule reports, as described below.

C. <u>Networks:</u> The CPM scheduling network shall be in the form of a time-scaled arrow or precedence diagram, shall be of the customary activity-on-arrow or activity-on-node type, and may be divided into a number of separate pages with suitable notation relating the interface points among the pages. Individual pages shall not exceed 1000mm × 1414mm (39-inch by 56-inch). Notation on each activity arrow shall include a brief work description and a duration estimate (see below).

D. All construction activities and procurement shall be indicated in a time-scaled format and a calendar scale shall be shown on all sheets along the entire sheet length. Each activity arrow or node shall be plotted so that the beginning and completion dates and free float time of said activity can be determined graphically by comparison with the calendar scale. All activities shall be shown using the symbols that clearly distinguish between critical path activities, non-critical activities, and free float for each non-critical activity. All non critical path activities, shall show estimated performances time and free float time in scaled form.

E. <u>Duration Estimates:</u> The duration estimate indicated for each activity shall be computed in working days, converted to calendar days, and shown on the construction schedule in calendar days, and shall represent the single best estimate considering the scope of the Work and resources planned for the activity. Except for certain non-labor activities, such as curing concrete, paint drying, procurement, or delivering of materials, activity durations shall not exceed 10 working days (14 calendar days) nor be shown as less than one working day unless otherwise accepted by the Engineer.

**FIGURE 12.9** *continued*

F. The requirement for activity durations not in excess of 10 working days (14 calendar days) shall apply to all schedule submittals excepting the Proposed Construction Schedule required to be submitted prior to the Notice to Proceed.

G. Schedule Reports: Schedule Reports shall be prepared from the Initial Construction Schedule and from all subsequent Revised Construction Schedules, and shall include the following minimum data for each activity:

1. Activity Numbers or i-j Numbers.

2. Estimated Activity Duration.

3. Activity Description (including procurement items).

4. Early Start Date (Calendar Dated).

5. Early Finish Date (Calendar Dated).

6. Late Start Date (Calendar Dated).

7. Late Finish Date (Calendar Dated).

8. Status (Whether Critical).

9. Total Float for Each Activity.

10. Free Float for Each Activity.

H. Project Information: Each Schedule Report shall be prefaced with the following summary data:

1. Project Name.

2. Contractor Name.

3. Type of Tabulation (Initial or Revised; if revised, show revision number or date).

4. Project Duration.

5. Project Scheduled Completion Date.

6. The date of commencement of the Work as stated in the Notice to Proceed.

7. If an updated (revised) schedule, cite the new project completion date and current project status.

**1.06 Construction Schedule Monitoring**

A. At not less than monthly intervals, and when specifically requested by the Engineer, the Contractor shall submit to the Engineer a computer printout of a Revised Schedule Report for those activities that remain to be completed.

B. Each Revised Construction Schedule, including an updated network diagram, if required, shall be submitted in the form, sequence, and in the number of copies requested for the Initial Construction Schedule.

**FIGURE 12.9** *continued*

The microcomputer should meet the following requirements as a minimum.

**1.** Minimum of 8 megabytes of RAM.

**2.** One 1.44-megabyte $3\frac{1}{2}$-inch disk drive.

**3.** One 200-megabyte hard disk drive as a minimum.

**4.** Capable of running software written for DOS or Windows operating systems.

**5.** MS/DOS Version 5.0 or later or Windows 95 operating system.

**6.** Operate on 110/220 volts AC, 50/60 Hz.

**7.** One printer port.

**8.** Hayes-compatible, 2400-baud or greater internal or external modem with communications software. If an external modem is used, the computer will also need one serial communications port.

The printer should be a 356 mm (14-inch) carriage, 24-pin, dot-matrix, tractor-feed printer running off the parallel port, with the capability of printing a 132-column width, or a laser printer that can use both letter size and legal size paper.

## Scheduling Software

Today even some of the most sophisticated CPM software has been made available for the PC user, particularly IBM compatibles. Construction management professionals can now enter daily production figures on a portable PC, compute the updated CPM schedule in the field, and communicate reports generated by the software directly to a home office located almost anywhere in the world, almost instantaneously.

## Selected Features

The most attractive feature of project scheduling software to the new user is the hard-copy reports that can be used in communicating changes in the project and its completion schedule. For obvious reasons, the nature of computer-generated reports suggest a note of credibility to most people. Although this may be somewhat unfounded, the effect is the same. The reports can be logically presented, and support documentation is becoming rapidly available at the push of a button. In a competitive marketplace of shrinking profit margins and escalating costs, the successful PC advocates have already established firm controls, including sophisticated project scheduling.

A second feature is the ease with which the PC can make many changes in the same project while saving the original project file and produce a series of scheduling alternatives for the user to evaluate. This is commonly referred to as playing "what if?" games. Depending upon the type of network schedule format used, whether activity-on-arrow or precedence diagramming, this can be an extremely valuable tool on large, complex projects. Other features that are valuable but not always available are graphic plotting, cost accounting, custom report generation, and file transfer capability.

Graphic plotting is almost universal, probably because of its visibility. Depending on what you are illustrating, some software may be considerably better than others. Without graphics capability, the software can be hampered in its ability to communicate to the casual user.

Cost accounting may be the single area that separates the excellent from the good systems. It is in this area alone that the profitability of any project can be tracked. Conversely, it is the most hazardous playground for "what if?" games. A project with little potential for profit can be miraculously saved by playing "what if?" games with the accounting module: all on paper and before the facts. Of course, on judgment day when all the bills are paid, the true accountability will be made.

Custom reports have some very pleasant benefits. Typically, the manager gets to see just what is wanted and nothing more. This is good for presentations. Extraneous information that seems only to clutter up other standard reports can be judiciously expunged from the documentation. This can effectively speed up an otherwise tight meeting agenda.

One last feature, almost insignificant but valuable in the extreme when needed, is file transferring capability. Different systems may operate the same critical path project schedule, but they do it in different ways. Usually, this results from programming requirements and the type of screen entry system for data input. In the end, what you may have to do is either reenter data for use on a different system or acquire and educate yourself on the original system. Some software comes with file translation programs that cause a common filing language, such as ASCII, to facilitate the transfer of input data. This is definitely not an arena for the casual user but is the province of the in-house programmer.

Computerized project scheduling using a PC is here to stay. The available software is quite good, and prices range from several hundred dollars to several thousand dollars for PC versions, and from several thousand to hundreds of thousands for mainframe licenses. Most software in the good-to-excellent range can be had for PC computers.

### Problems with Some PC Software for CPM Scheduling

Unfortunately, most of the software on the marketplace today that is intended for the PC market has one serious flaw. This includes some of the more popular programs, such as Primavera P3. Earlier versions of P3 were written to print only one column of float (e.g., total float only). To be sure, the program is capable of printing free float if you do a little reprogramming, but unfortunately you cannot program it to produce the free float in the form of a parallel column next to the total float column. If you did succeed in getting a free float printout on the report format, it was reproduced as a separate line instead of a column. This is a very inconvenient way of showing free float and denies the user the visual advantage of comparing the total and free float value for each activity side by side. Later versions (4.0) of P3 and P4 are designed to accommodate the user who wishes both free and total float to be printed in parallel columns. The inexpensive SureTrak program also published by Primavera has always been capable of printing float in two parallel columns.

Why is free float so important anyway? First, it is invaluable in evaluating contractor change orders to determine whether or not to allow additional time on the contract for each change order. Second, it is invaluable at the end of the job to assist in evaluating impacts on the contractor's schedule. Neither of these can be accomplished with total float alone.

---

## COMPUTERIZED PROGRESS PAYMENTS

Progress payments are a logical extension of the project scheduling environment. If the project can be logically scheduled, priced, and tracked on a regular basis, an effective, accurate payment schedule can be easily developed for that project. That, of course, depends upon who controls the payments and the nature of the contract agreement regarding progress payments. The simplest payment structure is, of course, full payment upon completion. This system is generally limited to short-term projects, however. Another payment structure, usually seen in commercial construction, is the regular periodic payment of a fixed percentage of the total project cost or lump-sum value. By far the most common payment structure is regular payments based upon the percentage of work completed within the payment period based upon unit price values or a *schedule of values*.

As long as the project stays on schedule and within budget, there should be no substantial difference between costs and revenues. However, in many instances, changes in both time and costs occur with surprising regularity. In such events the project will immediately display a variance between costs and revenues. The knowledgeable contractor will submit requests for payment that are out of conformance with the baseline project schedule and show supporting documentation for the cost difference. In little time, the cost of accounting begins to escalate. If done by hand, over a long construction period, the potential for error becomes staggering. Here the PC and its associated software can more adequately fill the need for progress payment control.

Some progress payment software has been developed in response to the observed need for a quicker and more efficient means of producing accurate progress pay estimates for large jobs. In the past, the usual method of producing pay estimates involved (1) collecting data from field personnel on percentage of work completed, materials used from storage, and change orders for each payment period, and (2) hand calculating and typing of the revised estimate. Most of this work is easily adapted to computers, assuring numerical accuracy and allowing for easy revisions of project data. An interactive program package can reduce the time needed to produce a completed estimate from a week to less than 2 days. Along with reducing turnaround time, there can be substantial reductions in labor and other costs required to produce progress payment estimates.

The basic tool of progress payment control is the accounting process. Simply put, you try to pay only once for something and then pay for it only after you get it. There are as many "fair" ways to accomplish this as there are parties to the contract. The ground rules for progress payments should be written into the contract; in this way, everyone's needs will be served.

## Lump-Sum Projects

On lump-sum contracts, there are two methods available to utilize a PC computer in determining the amount of payment due to the contractor each month:

1. Progress payment program designed for unit price contracts (PROGPAY) but adapted to a lump-sum project by utilizing the values shown on a schedule of values created for payment purposes.

2. Cost loading the network schedule by assigning a cost value to each work activity. Then, if the schedule is being followed faithfully, payment will be computed based upon the number of work items completed each month. (A schedule of values is not used under this plan.)

### Unit-Price Projects

On unit-price projects there is really only one option, namely, the use of a small program expressly created for the purpose of computing progress payments (PROGPAY) based upon the number of units completed of each item on the bid sheet. Cost loading of a CPM for a unit-price job is counterproductive, as it leads to a considerable increase in payment administration costs because of the disparity between the pay-line items as shown in the unit-price bid sheet and the separate work activities shown in the CPM network, neither of which can be effectively correlated. In short, you will be comparing apples with oranges.

## SELECTION OF PC SCHEDULING SOFTWARE

A word of caution if you are planning to buy a CPM program for your personal computer: It seems that a large number of the earlier scheduling programs on the market were created by nonengineer computer programmers to meet design-oriented scheduling needs and who failed to recognize the practical needs of the construction engineers. Some of these programmers appeared to show an elementary knowledge of some facets of the construction industry—a knowledge that was sorely lacking in others.

Several of the programs found by the author are either PERT systems or combinations of PERT/CPM, with far too much of the PERT influence. In the author's opinion, PERT systems have no place as an operational tool for construction scheduling in the field office. PERT was conceived as a project-management scheduling technique for situations in which neither time nor cost could be accurately estimated, and completion times therefore had to be based upon probability. In most construction projects, however, both time and cost can be reliably estimated, and thus the more definitive approach provided by CPM is practical.

It is therefore important to understand that PERT systems involve a "probability approach" to the problems of planning and control of projects and are best suited to reporting on works in which major uncertainties exist. Although there are some uncertainties in any construction project, the cost and time required for each operation involved can be reasonably estimated, and all operations may then be reviewed by CPM in accordance with anticipated conditions and hazards that may be encountered on the site.

PERT, then, is of little value in a construction field office. In fact, if you are obligated to construct an as-built schedule such as that used in claims preparation, such a statistical approach is totally useless. What is actually needed is a program that will allow the user to enter only $i$-$j$ numbers, activity identities, activity durations, and dependencies or job logic and in return receive a report format from the computer that will identify early and late start dates, early and late finish dates, actual start and actual finish dates, total float, and free float. Any of the various CPM formats, whether they be activity-on-arrow, node or precedence diagramming, or activity-on-node, are all quite suitable for field engineering use, as long as they are basically CPM programs, *not* PERT programs.

Before buying software for a PC to use for schedule review, changes, or "what if?" scheduling investigations, it would be wise to check carefully to see that the programs offered are properly suited to construction scheduling. It should be a true CPM system, specifically designed for construction by construction engineers. Far too many of the programs currently offered are designed for project management, design management, or a manufacturing plant, not for actual construction scheduling. There seem to be many people sitting in ivory towers who have never even gotten their boots muddy, trying to second-guess what the field engineer needs. The sooner the programmers get around to actually working with construction engineers to solve construction problems instead of just the design engineers and office-trained project managers, the sooner the problems will disappear. PERT has its place, but not in construction.

### Typical CPM Software Available

Several CPM scheduling programs, which truly reflect the needs of the construction engineer, are available in the software marketplace; most available software, unfortunately, does not. Some even attempt to emphasize PERT in their construction scheduling program. The good ones, however, get right down to the business of scheduling by CPM using either arrow or precedence diagram techniques, or both; these include SureTrak Project Scheduler offered by SureTrak, a Division of Primavera Systems, Inc. (Salt Lake City, UT), Microsoft Project offered by Microsoft Corporation (Redmond, WA), Primavera P3 and P4 (Windows version) offered by Primavera Systems, Inc. (Bala Cynwyd, PA), VUE offered by National Information Systems, Inc. (Cupertino, CA), MSCS Micro and T-Maps offered by McAuto (McDonnel Douglas, St. Louis, MO), and several others. McAuto's MSCS and VUE were programs originally designed for mainframe and minicomputers, which have been scaled down to PC size and offer both precedence diagramming and arrow diagramming capability. The SureTrak and Microsoft Project scheduling programs are based strictly upon precedence diagramming network technique designed especially for PC computers; their prices are considerably less than the MSCS, Primavera P3 or P4, and VUE programs, which offer precedence diagramming in both box node and activity-on-node graphics, in addition to computations for the traditional arrow diagramming ($i$-$j$) format as well. Furthermore, SureTrak is available for less, while Primavera P3 and P4 costs significantly more, and MSCS is even more expensive. One unique feature of SureTrak is that it is advertised by the manufacturer as being compatible with P3.

Although there is a large movement toward the generation of network graphics by computer, principally to keep the cost down, many of the large companies whose business depends entirely on the preparation of construction schedules for contractors still resort to the old tried-and-true hand-drawn networks. There is good reason for the preservation of the hand-drawn networks: They are much easier to follow, as the draftsperson who produced them has the capability of expanding wherever necessary to present the information clearly, while the computer on a complex project creates a document that requires considerable effort and visual skills to follow. The difficulty rests primarily in the area of reading dependency lines that are often too close together and cross other activities, making them very difficult to follow without a magnifying glass and a colored pencil to trace the lines (Figure 12.10). The plotting capabilities of the computers seem to be limited to one or more of three precedence diagramming formats, and none of them seem to have solved those problems.

**FIGURE 12.10** Example of a complex activity-on-node schedule showing the difficulty in reading closely spaced dependency lines on computer-generated graphics.

313

Such programs are available to operate on most of the major microcomputers utilizing MS-DOS, CP/M, and UNIX operating systems, as well as a few others. For microcomputers, the greatest selection available, of course, is written for the various IBM-compatible computers.

Many of the available scheduling programs offered by the software manufacturers refer to all network scheduling diagrams as PERT charts, when in fact they may actually be CPM charts that have been misnamed by the programmer or software supplier because of an unfamiliarity with network scheduling terminology. The only way you can tell if a program is going to provide the desired information is to see it and try it. Some initial confusion seems to result from the similar-sounding terms used by the programmers or software suppliers and the construction engineers. To the programmer and the software supplier, CP/M is a computer operating system having nothing to do with CPM scheduling; to the construction engineer, CPM is a particular type of network scheduling system, whether done manually or by computer.

## PROBLEMS

1. Phased construction is also known by what other name?
2. Name four types of scheduling methods.
3. Line-of-balance scheduling is best adapted to what type of application?
4. What is the principal advantage of the traditional S-curve?
5. What is the primary disadvantage in the use of bar charts for scheduling?
6. Name the types of network scheduling systems in use and state the proper type of work for each system.
7. In computer reports, what is a "sort"?
8. Identify which system of network scheduling is best adapted to each of the following types of work:
   a. Construction scheduling
   b. Research and development
   c. Project management
   d. Fast-track 313construction
9. It is well known that computerized CPM can be used for effective scheduling of time. Name two other applications that are possible using CPM.
10. What is a "critical path"?

# 13

## Fundamentals of CPM Construction Scheduling

Construction projects are complex, and a large job will literally involve thousands of separate operations. If a project is to be completed within the time called for in the contract, the work must be very carefully planned and scheduled in advance. If all the tasks would simply follow each other in consecutive order, the job of scheduling would be much easier. Unfortunately, the problem is not that simple. Each operation within the project has its own time requirement, and often it cannot start until certain other operations have been completed. There are many other tasks, however, that can be carried on simultaneously because they are entirely independent of one another. Thus a typical project involves many tasks that are interdependent as well as many other tasks that are totally independent of one another, and when interrelated in a project, they create a tangled web of individual time and sequence relationships. When all these tasks are superimposed, it becomes obvious that project planning and scheduling is a very complicated and difficult management function.

It is not the intent of this book to go into the subject of CPM scheduling in sufficient depth to enable the resident engineer or inspector to be able to set up a project schedule by CPM, but certainly deep enough so that they should be capable of reading, reviewing, and understanding them. It is often one of the Resident Project Representative's responsibilities to make regular evaluations of the contractor's construction schedules to determine whether they are meeting their schedule requirements and will complete the work within the agreed time. The project representative should know the subject well enough to know what to look for, and be fully capable of recognizing the difference between a logical and an illogical chart.

The traditional basis in past years for scheduling construction work had always been the bar and S-charts. There is no question but that these are still useful tools for showing the established schedule of operations and recording its progress. However, the bar chart falls somewhat short of being an adequate tool for project planning, and the resulting construction schedule is based more upon the contractor's experience and intuition than on any rational analysis of the work to be performed. Its major weakness lies in the fact that it does not show the interrelationships and interdependencies that exist among the various phases of the work. Also, there is no way to determine which operations actually control the overall time progress of the project. The S-curve chart or velocity diagram as a scheduling tool is better suited to linear projects or smaller contracts.

## CPM: WHAT IT IS AND WHAT IT DOES

The CPM is essentially a project management system that covers the construction phase of a project and allows the user to aid the decision-making process by guiding the contractor in selecting the best way to expedite the job and by providing a prediction of future labor requirements as well as equipment needs.

Project planning is the first step in a CPM procedure. This step consists of the following:

1. Identify the elementary work items needed to complete the job.
2. Estimate time durations for each activity.
3. Determine what tasks must be completed before each work item can be started.
4. Establish the logical order in which these work items must be done.
5. Prepare a graphic display in the form of a network diagram.

The next step is the scheduling phase, and it requires an estimate of the time required to accomplish each of the work items previously identified. With the use of the network diagram, computations are made to provide information concerning the time schedule characteristics of each work item and the total time necessary to complete the project.

Although these comments seem to suggest that CPM must follow a definite step-by-step order, this is not the case in actual usage. For example, the five planning steps often proceed concurrently. For the purposes of this discussion, it will be assumed that they are treated separately in the order listed.

The computations previously mentioned are actually only simple additions and subtractions. Although the actual computation is simple and very easy, there are usually so many of them required on an actual project that the process becomes very tedious. For this reason, many contractors use computers to produce their CPM schedules. Furthermore, with the use of the personal computer, the schedule may be updated even on a weekly basis without undue hardship. For more sophisticated schedules, many computer management firms now exist that will provide all levels of service for network scheduling to contractors, architects, and engineers. With the addition of some programmed logic in a computerized network system, complex scheduling problems can be worked out rapidly and optimum solutions can be reached. A task that would be impossible within the allowable time if it had to be done by hand methods can be accomplished in minutes by computer after developing the input data required.

For a full understanding of the method, some understanding of the calculations that are necessary and an understanding of the terminology used are required. In addition, there are many applications of CPM in which manually developed data are adequate and quite usual. Therefore, the following explanations are based upon manual procedures. They are followed by some examples showing how the data developed are printed out when computer methods are used, along with some elementary instructions as to the use of the computer printouts by the Resident Project Representative.

## BASIC PROCEDURE IN SETTING UP A CPM SCHEDULE

Normally, the network scheduling is started right after the award of the project. Because the prime purpose of the system is to produce a coordinated project plan, the principal subcontractors must also be entered into the planning stage. Normally, the general contractor sets the general timing for the project; the individual subcontractors then review their portions of the work, and the needed alterations are made.

The basic procedure used by the planning group is to "talk" the project through first. This way the project is subject to careful, detailed, advance planning. This planning alone justifies the time spent on CPM. Usually, the network diagram is then constructed in a rough form, and the job is broken up into basic elements; then the sequential order of construction operations is discussed. It is often helpful to list the major operations of the project and use them as a means of developing the preliminary diagram.

## PROJECT PLANNING

The first phase of CPM is that of planning. The project must first be broken down into time-consuming activities. An *activity* in CPM is defined as any single identifiable work step in the total project. The extent to which the project is subdivided into activities depends upon the number of practical considerations; however, the following factors must be taken into account:

1. Different areas of responsibility, such as subcontracted work, that are distinctly separate from that being done directly by the prime contractor.
2. Different categories of work as distinguished by craft or crew requirements.
3. Different categories of work as distinguished by equipment requirements.
4. Different categories of work as distinguished by materials such as concrete, timber, or steel.
5. Distinct and identifiable subdivisions of structural work such as walls, slabs, beams, and columns.
6. Location of the work within the project that necessitates different times or different crews to perform.
7. Owner's breakdown for bidding or payment purposes.
8. Contractor's breakdown for estimating or cost accounting purposes.
9. Outage schedules or limiting times that existing utility services may be interrupted to construct the project.

The activities chosen may represent relatively large segments of the project or may be limited to only small steps. For example, a concrete slab may be a single activity or it may be broken into separate steps necessary to construct it, such as erection of forms, placing of steel, placing of concrete, finishing, curing, and stripping of forms or headers.

As the separate activities are identified and defined, the sequence relationships between them must be determined. These relationships are referred to as *job logic* and consist of the necessary time and order of construction operations. When the time sequence of activities is being considered, *restraints* must also be considered; these are the practical limitations that can influence the start of certain activities. For example, an activity that involves the placing of reinforcing steel obviously cannot start until the steel is on the site. Therefore, the start of the activity of placing reinforcing steel is "restrained" by the time required to prepare and approve the necessary shop drawings, fabricate the steel, and deliver it to the job. It is quite common to treat restraints much the same as activities and to represent them as such on the network diagram.

## FUNDAMENTALS OF CPM

The first step in understanding the CPM is to learn the meaning of the terms used, the symbols involved, and the rules of network scheduling. The following paragraphs are presented to define the principal terms and summarize the most important of the rules for network planning and scheduling.

### Activities

After the activities have been identified and their logic established, it is time to construct the job graphically in the form of a network diagram. The basic symbol for an activity is an arrow. It is general practice to think of the arrow as moving from left to right, and that "time" also passes from left to right on the diagram. A basic relationship is that of the event to an arrow or activity. As distinguished from an activity, an event is the instant of time at which an activity is just starting or finishing. An activity is preceded by an event and followed by an event; in other words, it has to have both a starting point and a stopping point. The arrows representing activities are *not* vectors, and their lengths and slopes are *not* significant. Also, the arrows can be straight, bent, curved, or whatever shape the user chooses. The real essence of the diagram is the manner in which the activities are joined together into a total operational pattern or network.

Each activity in a network diagram is shown as an arrow, along with a pair of activity numbers for identification. These are referred to as *i-j* designations. In diagram usage, the letter *i* is used as a general symbol to designate the tail of the arrow or *start* of an activity and the letter *j* is used to designate the head of the arrow or *finish* of the activity.

In the activity arrow in Figure 13.1, the activity is "place concrete" and its *i-j* designation is (9-10). As an illustration of some of the activities that might be involved in a "project" to drill a hole 660mm (24 inches) in diameter by 4.6 m (15 ft) deep and fill it with concrete, the activities involved might be as follows:

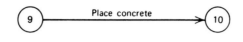

**FIGURE 13.1** Activity arrow.

Approve and sign contract.

Obtain building permit.

Order and deliver drill rig.

Order and deliver concrete.

Locate and lay out the hole.

Drill hole.

Place concrete in hole.

Clean up the site.

## Job Logic

The job logic or time-sequence relationships among the various activities involved in the previously mentioned project are the next steps to determine. The sequence of operations will be the following:

| Activity | Sequence | Symbol | Activity Following |
|---|---|---|---|
| Get signed and approved contract | 1 | SC | BP-OD-OC |
| Get building permit | 2 | BP | LH |
| Subcontract fro drill rig | 2 | OD | DH |
| Subcontract for readily-mixed concrete | 2 | OC | CH |
| Lay out and accurately locate hole | 3 | LH | DH |
| Drill hole | 4 | DH | CH |
| Place concrete in hole | 5 | CH | CU |
| Clean up the construction site | 6 | CU | None |

In elementary form, this is the type of information that is generated while a project is being "talked through." For the purposes of CPM, job logic requires that each of the activities in the network have a definite *event* to mark its starting point. This event may be either the start of the project or the completion of preceding activities. It is not possible in CPM to have the finish of one activity overlap beyond the start of a succeeding activity. When such a condition appears to present itself, it is a sign that the work must be further subdivided. It is a fundamental rule that *a given activity cannot start until all those activities immediately preceding it have been completed.* Normally, the job logic is not written down. It is only for the purposes of presenting a clear example that a separate tabulation is made here. In practice, the arrow diagram is drawn along with the development of the job operational plan (Figure 13.2).

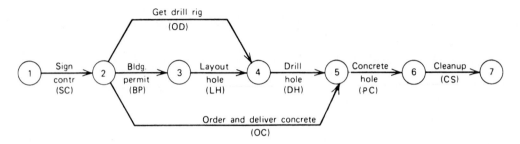

**FIGURE 13.2**　Activity diagram showing job logic of a simple problem.

In the course of explaining the structure of a CPM diagram sufficiently to enable the Resident Project Representative to read and understand the symbolism involved, a few special symbols and conventions will be covered in the following paragraphs.

### Dummy Arrows

Frequently, a dotted- or dashed-line arrow will be found in a CPM arrow diagram. These are the generally accepted symbols for a *dummy arrow*, which is a way of indicating that the completion of one activity restrains the start of two or more other activities. The dummy is nothing more than a slightly awkward way of representing such a dependency.

In Figure 13.3, the dashed arrow (15–16) is an example of a dummy arrow, because the start of (16–20) cannot begin until both (05–15) and (05–16) have been completed, whereas activity (15–20) can begin immediately after (05–15) has been completed, regardless of whether or not (05–16) has been completed. The direction of the arrow indicates the time flow of construction operations, and the sequential order cannot back up against a dummy arrowhead.

Another common usage of dummy arrows is to give each activity its own numerical *i-j* designation for easy identification as a computer "address." In Figure 13.4 three activities are shown that are parallel to one another and share a common start and finish point. As indicated in the figure, however, each of the three activities would have to be identified by the same *i-j* number of (19–25). Although this might be no particular hardship if the network was being prepared manually and the diagram was always in front of the user, if the CPM was being computer generated, there would be no possible way of separating the three

**FIGURE 13.3**　Dummy arrows.

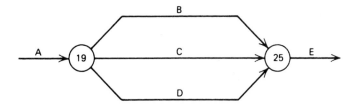

**FIGURE 13.4** Three parallel activities.

activities in the computer, as they would all appear as the same number, thus canceling one another out.

When a situation is encountered such as that illustrated in Figure 13.4, and it occurs fairly frequently, dummy arrows can be utilized as shown in Figure 13.5 to allow separate *i-j* numbers to be assigned to each of the three activities and still show the dependent relationships.

Thus the three parallel activities shown in Figure 13.4 after the introduction of the dummy arrows shown in Figure 13.5 may now be identified as activity (20–25), (19–25), and (21–25), which will satisfy the computer requirement that all activities must have separate *i-j* number identities, while the dashed dummy arrows retain the original relationship of each activity to the others.

## Events

At the ends of each activity arrow are circles (the most common system) or another geometrical figure. These circles are placed at the junction of the arrows and they represent events. As mentioned previously, an "event" is the instant of time at which an activity is just starting or finishing. Although CPM is not basically event oriented, that is, it does not usually emphasize or name the events but merely refers to them by numbers, if some events are particularly important they may be referred to as "milestone events" and may be specially identified and named on the diagram.

The basic rule applying to any event is that all activities leading into an event must be completed before *any* of the activities leading out of the event can be started. This is basic network logic.

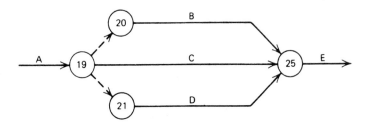

**FIGURE 13.5** Use of dummy arrows to preserve activity identities.

### Event Numbering

In all CPM diagrams, the events are identified by a number. The number assigned to the starting event is referred to as the *i;* the number assigned to the completion of the event is the *j.* The resulting *i-j* number can be used as a name for the activity as well as being used as a storage address in the computer storage register. Most CPM diagrams follow two basic rules in numbering of events.

1. Each activity must have its own *i-j* designation (see Figure 13.5).
2. When event numbers are assigned, the number at the head of the arrow should be greater than the event number at the tail of the arrow.

Although it is possible for a CPM diagram to be prepared using random numbering, especially where an activity was inserted into an arrow network that was already numbered, if rule 2 were strictly applied, all numbers in the entire network would have to be renumbered to allow the new activity to have consecutive *i-j* numbering. In many cases, a CPM network involves thousands of separate activities, and such renumbering would be very impractical. The preferable system of numbering involves the assignment of *i-j* numbers only after the entire network has been completed and is ready for its first computation.

There are two basic practices used in the assignment of *i-j* numbers, the horizontal and the vertical methods (Figure 13.6). In the horizontal method the event numbers are assigned along a line of activities until they meet at a point involving two or more other activities. This is then repeated until all horizontal lines into the junction point have been numbered; then they continue horizontally to the next junction point in the same fashion.

In the vertical numbering method, which is more commonly used, the scheduler numbers all events in vertical fashion, moving from top to bottom and from left to right. However, the basic rule of keeping the *j* value of each activity greater than its *i* value must still be observed. There is actually no significance to the event numbers themselves except as a means of identifying an activity. Often gaps are left in the numbering system so that spare numbers are available for subsequent work refinements or revisions. One advantage to the use of sequential numbering over that of random numbering of activities is that it is easier to locate events and activities on the network diagram, and it also helps to prevent the inclusion of logical loops, which will be discussed next.

### Logic Loops

The logic loop is a paradox in network planning. It indicates the requirement that an activity be followed by another activity *that has already been accomplished.* In Figure 13.7, a simple example of a logic loop is shown. The term *logical loop* is a misnomer, since if anything, a logic loop is extremely *illogical.* Although this is perfectly obvious in the simple example illustrated, logic loops can be inadvertently included in large or complex networks without the scheduler realizing that they are there. Because such loops are representative of impossible conditions, the network planner will take precautions to try to prevent their inclusion. The use of a random *i-j* numbering system allows a greater likelihood of error by allowing logical loops to remain undiscovered, as a computer printout cannot indicate any

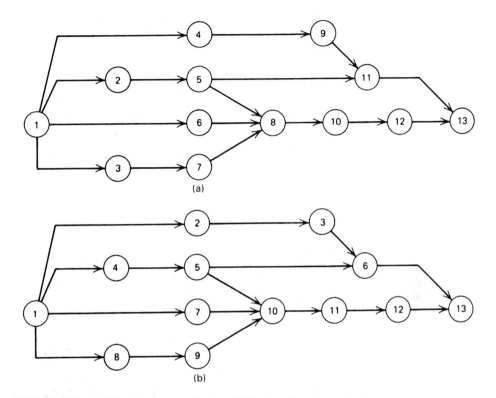

FIGURE 13.6 (a) Vertical event numbering; (b) horizontal event numbering.

clues to its presence under such conditions. It is wise to study the network diagram carefully at the beginning of the job to confirm the logic of its structure.

## Float Time

*Float,* sometimes called *slack,* can best be described as scheduling leeway. When an activity has float time available, this extra time may be used to serve a variety of scheduling purposes. When float is available, the earliest starting time of an activity can be delayed, its duration extended, or a combination of both can occur. To do a proper job of monitoring of the schedules for noncritical items, the Resident Project Representative should understand the working of float times on a project.

FIGURE 13.7 Logic loop.

**FIGURE 13.8**   Graphic illustration of the concept of float.

Arithmetically, float time is easy to compute, as it is simply the difference between the early and late dates for an activity (Figure 13.8). It represents the available time between the earliest time in which an activity can be accomplished (based upon the status of the project to date) and the latest time by which it must be completed for the project to finish by its deadline. There are three important timing facts that can be determined from a CPM network.

1. The earliest time an activity can start and finish.
2. The latest time an activity can start and finish without delaying the project completion.
3. The amount of leeway available in scheduling an item.

There are two types of float time: free float and total float. *Free float* is defined as the amount of time that any activity can be delayed without adversely affecting the *early start of the following activity.* In other words, free float is the least difference between the early finish of an activity and the early start of all following activities. *Total float* is defined as the amount of time that an activity can be delayed without adversely affecting the *overall time for the project completion.* It should be clearly understood that just because an activity has a certain amount of *total float,* it does not necessarily mean that activity can use it all without creating tighter scheduling restraints on all of the other activities. It must be remembered that *total float* is shared with all other activities. Free float, however, is not shared with other activities; thus, it provides a true measure of how much an activity can be delayed or extended without adversely affecting any other activity except to the extent

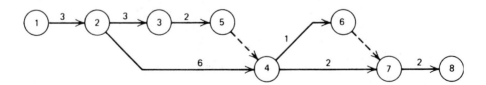

**FIGURE 13.9**   Arrow diagram for CPM network.

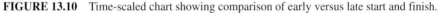

FIGURE 13.10   Time-scaled chart showing comparison of early versus late start and finish.

that it is a part of the total float of preceding activities. In the accompanying illustration in Figure 13.9, an arrow diagram is used to show a CPM network involving seven different activities. The *i-j* numbers are shown in the circles and the numbers on the arrows represent the time required to complete each activity in days.

To illustrate float time, the arrow diagram in Figure 13.9 is time scaled and shown in bar schedule form in Figure 13.10. Each activity is shown on the chart twice: Once plotted for early start and finish (the white bar), and once plotted for late start and finish (the shaded bar).

If a series of activities are on the *critical path* of the project, no float exists; the early and late dates are the same. Sometimes, when a project is behind schedule, the earliest time at which an activity can begin is after the latest time it can be done to remain on schedule. Then, not only does no float exist, but the difference between the early and late dates is less than zero (therefore negative) and is now a measure of how far behind schedule the project is.

## WHO OWNS FLOAT?[1]

Network-based project control systems were developed originally as management tools. They can be abused, however, and some contractors and owners have turned them into

[1]Reprinted with permission from Glen S. K. Williams and Francis L. Smith, "Who Owns Float?" *Power Engineering,* April 1979. Copyright by Technical Publishing, a Division of Dun Donnelley Publishing Corporation, a Company of the Dun & Bradstreet Corporation, 1979; all rights reserved.

weapons, on occasion, for use against one another. The increasing use, or misuse, of network-based management systems often creates as many problems as it solves. We are faced with network schedules prepared more as biased documents to support the originator's right to claims than as management tools to help control the project.

These abuses frequently revolve around float. We define float as scheduling leeway. A more complete definition of float was given earlier in this chapter.

On one hand, a contractor may create an artificial network with multiple critical paths. The intent of the contractor would be to present claims if the owner causes delay on any of the paths. On the other hand, the owner may plan the project duration and then shorten it. The owner's intent would be to obtain a bid on the shortened duration and then to hold the contractor to the time.

Obviously, these practices reduce an otherwise effective management tool to a weapon for justifying or denying claims. The result has been more litigation over more claims than it might even have been possible to resolve by using the management tool correctly.

## Multiple Critical Paths

Most people in the field of planning and scheduling seem to agree that there are large odds against a large CPM network of, say, 10,000 or more activities, having seven different critical paths of exactly the same duration. Yet this situation can sometimes be seen in contractors' networks.

Figure 13.11 is an illustration of what a network with seven critical paths of equal length might look like. In such a network, the originators would develop a true critical path as the first step. Then they would adjust the durations of the other activities to create the seven-critical-path condition.

Very little float is reflected in such a diagram, and the owner is subject to claims at any time that it delays the contractor on any one of the critical paths. This technique invariably gets the contractor off on the wrong foot. The owner's staff members will resent the implication that they are not smart enough to see through the contractor's ploy, and an adversary position is set up that may last for the duration of the contract.

The owner may try to counter the contractor's technique through clauses in the schedule specification that direct the contractor to redraw the network at any time it is behind schedule on the critical path. Obviously, the tactic of eliminating as much float as possible from the network puts the owner at a disadvantage in network analysis.

## Differing Viewpoints

Contractors and owners view the problem differently. A contractor may question if an owner has a right to direct starts or delays for specific purposes. Owners, trying to manage project costs and overall scheduling, may ask if they have the right to force the contractor to start an activity before an established late-start date. Too many of these late starts could cause problems toward the end of the job.

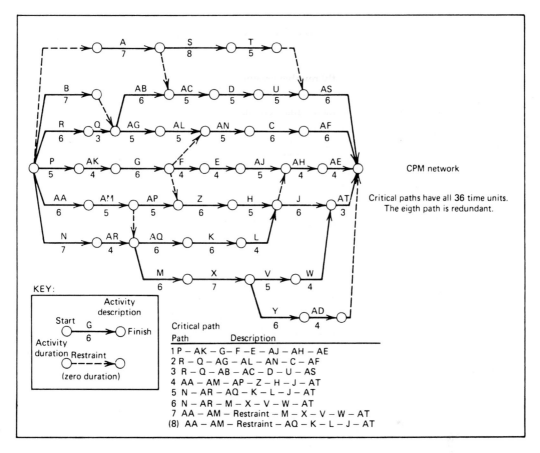

**FIGURE 13.11** Illustration of a CPM network with seven critical paths of exactly the same duration.

For the owner, a week's slippage in a power plant's commercial operation date translates into a loss of several hundred thousand dollars. At the same time, improper or premature activity starts can cause serious hardship for a contractor, who may incur additional expense for equipment, material, labor, and other resources.

The owner's engineers will attempt to resolve these and other scheduling problems and will attempt to gain management control. Usually, the engineer will make the request in the contract for one or more of the several network scheduling techniques currently available. Such specifications would be written with the intent to cover all bases for the owner's protection. With a combination of appropriate general conditions and supplementary general conditions, such specifications can be quite complex.

The contractor, however, using the techniques just described, will manage to circumvent the specifications of the owner, and the whole process can wind up in claims and litigation. Many court decisions have been rendered on such claims, but none seems to have solved the problem.

## Case History

A contractor on a $2 million civil construction project submitted a network that had been prepared with considerable care. The only objective of the plan was to get the job done as efficiently and effectively as possible.

Due to owner-caused delay, the contractor fell behind schedule. Later, the contractor submitted a claim for additional money and a 35-day extension. The owner's engineers analyzed the network and showed that work on the next major milestone on the critical path was delayed only 2 days. The owner contended that was all the contractor was entitled to. The contractor said that it was only through its diligence in accelerating the work that delay was held to only 2 days.

The contractor could not support its 35-day claim because of improper schedule monitoring. The owner's engineers had been able to do a better job of network analysis than had the contractor, and the latter had to settle for the expenses it could prove plus a small sum for supporting its schedule. The contractor felt, correctly so, that it had been penalized for its diligence in maintaining the schedule, despite owner delay.

## Multiple-Critical-Path Case

A contractor on a $12 to $14 million building project submitted a CPM network in compliance with the owner's specifications. There were several zero-float paths—seven critical paths! The contractor was anticipating that the owner would delay one or more of the activities that were a part of these critical paths, thus allowing the contractor to file claims against the owner.

During negotiations, the owner cited the seven critical paths as an unrealistic approach. The contracting firm responded that it was *its* plan of work and the owner had no right to alter it. The negotiation process was soon reduced to a battle of wits.

What had the contractor done to its network, and what might it have achieved? First, it increased the duration of routine concrete pours to three times their normal duration. If requested to shorten this duration, it would request payment for accelerated work. To prevent this, the owner should have the right to refer to standard planning tools such as estimating guidebooks to determine reasonable durations of all activities. Exceptions would be negotiated.

The contractor in the foregoing case used "policy or management constraints" (preferred way of doing work) to consume float. These constraints prevent activities from starting until other preceding activities are sufficiently complete. On detailed analysis, this appeared illogical; however, the contractor was asked to apply work around techniques, and it would counter by saying that the changes to its plan of work would result in extra work and therefore more claims against the owner.

An owner *should* have the right to demand that constraints of this type be removed and the work replanned when the constraint threatened the critical path. Difficulties such as those just described might possibly be overcome with adequate specifications. However, one can hardly hope to anticipate all of the problems that can arise, particularly if the specifications writer has a limited knowledge of all of the tricks that can be used.

The specifications should protect both the owner and the contractor. But it should be remembered that the owner pays for the scheduling system and is entitled to get what it pays for. The specifications should set forth restrictions on falsifying networks to eliminate float. They should spell out what rights the owner has to utilize float to its advantage. They should clarify areas where the owner has the right to apply standard estimating techniques to activities where contractors have obviously set overly long durations to eliminate float.

## Specifications Guidelines

To prevent creation of artificial networks, those schedules traversed by more than one critical path should require a contractual agreement between the owner and the contractor prior to the start of the work or change in work scope.

To prevent manipulation of activity duration, networks with several near-critical paths should be subject to resource (labor-hours, equipment hours, dollars, etc.) and quantity (permanent material) analysis with respect to activity duration. Owners and contractors should be required to review and approve such analyses prior to the start of work or start of change-of-scope work.

Such performance analyses should consider any combination of the following:

- Budgeted rate of quantity installation as a function of time.
- Budgeted rate of resource usage as a function of time. (This can be done by resource scheduling techniques currently available in most CPM processors.)
- Budgeted consumption of resource usage as a function of quantity, type, and time.

The results of these calculations (or other performance calculations) should be agreed upon by all parties to each activity under dispute prior to performing the work.

To predetermine the answer to the question "To whom does float belong?" and prevent improper consumption of float, distributed float calculations can be used. Distributed float allocates float to each and every activity by the following formula.

$$DF = \frac{AD}{PD} \times (TF)$$

where

$$
\begin{aligned}
DF &= \text{distributed float for activity} \\
AD &= \text{activity duration} \\
PD &= \text{path duration} \\
(TF) &= \text{total float}
\end{aligned}
$$

If other than straight-line distribution is required by the owner/contractor agreements, the following formula may be used instead:

$$DF = \frac{AD}{PD} \times (TF) \times f(t) \times f(c)$$

where $f(t)$ and $f(c)$ make the distribution of float sensitive to the activity's location with respect to time (early in the project versus late in the project) and/or the activity's location with respect to its category or phase (engineering, construction, and testing).

Utilization of an approach such as that described can go a long way in predetermining who gets what float, to the mutual satisfaction of all parties.

## PRECEDENCE OR NODE DIAGRAMMING

Another method of network diagraming is called precedence diagraming. Precedence networks are traditionally drawn using squares or rectangular nodes to designate each activity. Arrows are used to show the relationships between the activities. It has thus become known as "activity on node," as opposed to "activity on arrow."

Although it has been said that the job logic is precisely the same, the two methods of drawing networks produce diagrams that are quite different in appearance. In a precedence diagram, the arrow shown in Figure 13.12a would be represented by the rectangular block shown in Figure 13.12b. When two activities are shown in series in the traditional arrow diagram method, they appear as shown in Figure 13.13.

The $j$ node of the first activity becomes the $i$ node of the second activity. The computer relies on this basic principle, to track the relationship between the two activities. Sometimes a dummy must be used, as when the completion of an activity restrains the start of two more activities.

In arrow diagramming, when four activities are combined in a network where one activity shares a dependency on a predecessor activity with another activity, a dummy arrow is introduced into the network, as illustrated in Figure 13.14 to show the relationship, in the illustrated case, of activity 5–10 to the following activities, 10–15 and 25–30. A dummy arrow differs from an activity arrow in that it does not represent time, only dependency, while all other arrows represent both time and dependency. In precedence diagramming, however, the two activities shown in series in Figure 13.13 would be shown as in Figure 13.15.

The line between the two rectangles indicates the relationship between them; in a way, it is a sort of "dummy" arrow. However, explicit dummy activities are not required. In

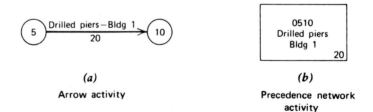

(a)                                                  (b)

Arrow activity                                Precedence network
                                                    activity

**FIGURE 13.12**   Comparison of arrow versus precedence symbols.

**FIGURE 13.13**   Arrow notation of two activities in series.

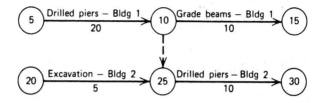

**FIGURE 13.14** Arrow diagram of four activities with dummy arrows to show dependency.

**FIGURE 13.15** Node notation of two activities in series.

**FIGURE 13.16** Node notation of four activities with a restraint.

the example of the four activities shown in Figure 13.14 a precedence diagram version of the same activities and dependencies would appear as shown in Figure 13.16.

The analogy is apparent. If processed on a computer, the output would be identical, except that the *i-j* printout would contain one dummy, the precedence diagram would contain no dummy. However, the printout of the precedence diagram would have to contain a supplementary list of relationships for the user to determine and maintain the logic in the computer memory. With some computer programs, this supplementary list can be quite awkward to use.

## COMPARISON OF NODE AND ARROW DIAGRAMMING

The primary difference between the two methods can be seen in Figure 13.17. Activities can be overlapped using relationships. In the example shown in Figure 13.18 DETAIL ENGRG begins in September and ends in November. DRAFTING begins one month after the start of DETAIL ENGRG and continues on while DETAIL ENGRG is still being done.

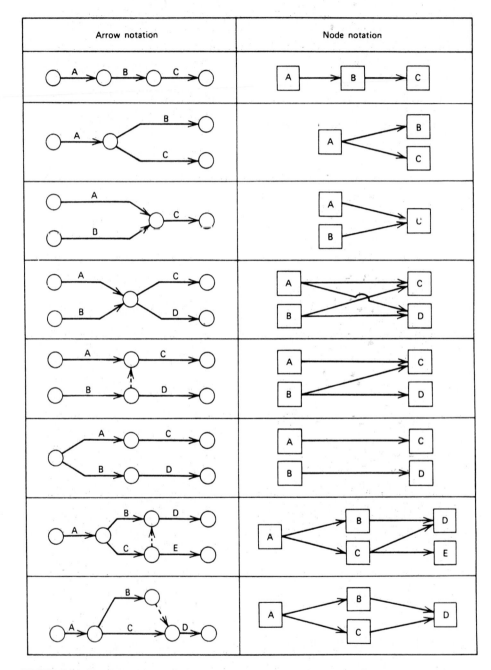

**FIGURE 13.17** Comparison of arrow and node notation. (From Richard H. Clough, *Construction Project Management*. Copyright © 1972 by John Wiley & Sons, Inc. Reprinted by permission of John Wiley & Sons, Inc.)

**FIGURE 13.18** Illustration of activity-on-node format.

This overlapping logic makes it much easier to prepare a precedence diagram. It is not necessary to describe the part of the first activity that must be done before the second activity may start. The arrow diagramming (*i-j*) method requires the planner to carefully describe each logical part of the work. To do so, the planner must learn to think logically. Unless the work is carefully defined into such activities, an *i-j* schedule will not work. The precedence method is much less demanding in that regard. Errors in reasoning and gaps in thinking are less apparent when using the more flexible logic allowed in the precedence method. In short, precedence is easier to learn to use, but harder to use effectively.

The adoption of one diagramming method over another is simply a matter of choice. However, software companies prefer precedence because more people can be trained quickly to begin to use and buy their software. For that reason, the industry is being pushed toward adopting precedence method as the standard. Owners, on the other hand, have been reluctant to depart from the traditional arrow diagramming (*i-j*) method.

## ACTIVITY-ON-NODE FORMAT

Subsequent to the conception of the popular arrow and precedence diagram formats for network graphics, the emergence of practical computer graphics as a meaningful substitute for hand-drafted network diagrams under certain conditions has led to a compromise format containing not only the desirable elements of arrow and precedence diagrams, but some additional attributes as well. In this respect this new hybrid format can be superior to either of its predecessors.

Under this precedence diagram format, which is referred to as *activity-on-node diagramming,* each activity is represented by a long, narrow node resembling a bar on a bar chart. This format, because it is actually a variation of a precedence diagram, does not use dummy arrows, just dependency arrows. Under this format, float time can be represented as a single line following the activity node, which is represented by a bar.

When this is combined with a programmed time line, the resulting time-scaled network becomes understandable by people of any background. If each bar happened to be located on its own separate line and was properly identified in the left margin, the resultant diagram could be viewed as a simple bar chart by non-CPM-trained users by simply ignoring the dependency lines. Some users have actually created what is referred to as "dependency bar charts," which is just another network diagramming format. Those trained on network diagrams of any format can utilize the new scheduling format just as before, whether trained on arrow or node diagramming formats.

While hand-drawn network diagrams are still offered by the major scheduling companies, such as Forward Associates, Ltd. with offices in Florida, Texas, and California, they are falling out of favor with the do-it-yourself scheduler using PC computers because of the labor costs involved. There is no question but that the hand-drawn network is far superior to any computer graphics yet devised, but only experienced scheduling firms who specialize in this area seem to utilize it. In computer graphics available to the PC user, however, in addition to the more traditional formats, virtually all of the available computer network scheduling software now offers activity-on-node format for their computer graphics to complement their network scheduling software package (Figure 13.18). In a delay claim that must be heard by a jury, the activity-on-node format offers something that can be understood by both the layperson who understands a bar chart but knows nothing about network scheduling, and by the more sophisticated juror who understands the significance of a schedule format that has the ability to appeal to nontechnically trained people as well as technically trained people who grasp the significance of the dependency lines that establish job logic.

## READING A MANUAL CPM NETWORK SCHEDULE

As arrow diagramming is frequently utilized, and the logic of an arrow diagram seems more obvious graphically, the emphasis in this book will be placed upon the reading of CPM arrow diagrams and the associated tabular data. The term *critical path,* of course, refers to that portion or those portions of the work that are the bottlenecks in the construction process. Obviously, the total project cannot be completed earlier than those portions of the work that require the most time to complete. On complex schedules it is impossible to determine by examination of the network diagram which paths represent the critical path— thus computers have come into the picture. In this manner, all possible combinations of tasks and activity times, early and late starts and finish dates, and float times can be analyzed by the computer until all of the key times can be determined from the computer printout. In addition, the computer determines the critical path or paths, as the case may be, and any overruns in time along the critical path will result in a schedule overrun.

If performed manually, CPM does not have the benefit of tabular printouts, which give key time data; thus, the user must rely upon observation of the diagram itself. Although on a very simple arrow diagram it may be possible to determine the critical path, it is normally necessary to construct a time-scaled network from the arrow diagram before any true scheduling can be determined. The arrow diagram of Figure 13.19 simply shows the logical relationships between the various project activities.

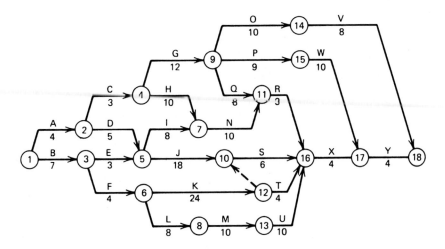

**FIGURE 13.19**   Step 2: Establish job logic and dependencies. (Arrow format)

The basic steps in setting up a manual CPM network can be summarized as follows:

1. Establish activities and activity durations.
2. Determine job logic and construct a dependency network.
3. Prepare a time-scaled diagram of the dependency network, and determine critical path and float times.

Before time scaling the arrow diagram in Figure 13.19, observe the effect of adding activity times from 1-3-6-8-13-16-17-18. Activity B (1–3) has a time of 7 days; activity F (3–6) has an activity time of 4 days; activity L (6–8) has an activity time of 8 days; activity M (8–13) has a time of 10 days; activity U (13–16) has a time of 10 days; activity X (16–17) has a time of 4 days; and activity Y (17–18) has a time of 4 days. Added together they total 47 days. Compare this with the path through 1-3-6-12-16-17-18, which also totals 47 days. From this it might at first appear that both paths are critical and that the minimum time to complete the project was 47 working days.

By plotting each activity on a time-scale chart (Figure 13.20) and adjusting the start and finish times to be compatible with the logic expressed in the arrow diagram, it can be seen that some notable limitations come into view. The chart is based upon early start and

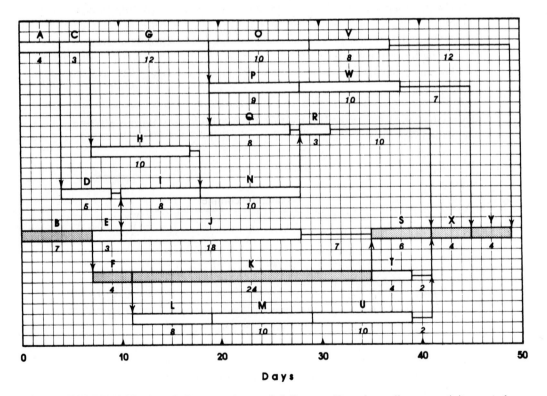

**FIGURE 13.20**   Step 3: Construct time-scaled diagram. (Precedence diagram, activity-on-node format)

finish dates with float time indicated by the single lines. In Figure 13.19 the numbers in the circles represent the *i-j* numbers for the activities, based upon early start and late finish. The numbers under the lines represent the amount of time required in days to complete the activity.

First, the path of 1-2-5 would appear from the arrow diagram to be simply the sum of activity times of A and D, which totals 9 days. Yet it should be noted that path 1-3-5 adds up to 7 days plus 3 days, or a total of 10 days to get from event 1 to event 5. Thus, the controlling time to reach event 5 is of course 10 days, not 9 as it might at first appear, and obviously, path 1-2-5 then includes 1 day of float time.

By careful inspection of the time-scaled network, it can be seen that path B, F, L, M, U, X, Y (1- 3-6-8-13-16-17-18) contains a total of 2 days of total float time. By continuing the inspection of the arrow diagram and the time-scaled chart, it can be further noted that the path through activities B, E, and J (1-3-5-10) cannot proceed past event 10 until the completion of activity K (6-12), as indicated by the dummy arrow. Therefore, event 10 must be delayed until the completion of event 12. (On the time-scaled chart they are equivalent as far as being completed on the same day.)

It should be noted that the path from event 10 to event 16 is a total of 6 days, in contrast to the 4 days required from event 12 to event 16. Also, since both events are held up until the completion of activity K (event 12), the new path becomes (1-3-6-12-10-16-17-18). The new path then follows through activities B-F-K-dummy-S-X-Y, which totals

$$7 + 4 + 24 + 6 + 4 + 4 = 49 \text{ days}$$

*not* the 47 days at first supposed!

It now appears that in comparison with the other paths analyzed, the one discussed is the critical path for this sample project, as all of the other paths contain float time.

Many of the questions that arise in construction involve the establishment of early and late start and finish dates for each activity. These dates represent the earliest or latest that any event can be started or finished without changing the critical path of the project. Any change in the starting time of any event on the critical path must result in a change in the completion date of the project. Thus if activity F (3–6) started 3 days late, the time required to complete the project would be 52 days because activity F is on the critical path. However, if event 11 started 10 days late, the completion date of the project would probably not be affected, as it has 10 days of free float time following it on the time-scaled chart. Note, however, that the early start date for activity R cannot change because it is contingent upon the completion of activities I and N, which allow no time variations.

Other questions may be asked, such as: Before activity R can begin, what other activities must be completed?

Working back from event 11 on the arrow diagram of Figure 13.19, it can be seen that activities N and Q must both be completed first, plus all the activities that must necessarily precede activities N and Q, as outlined in what follows:

1. Working back from event 11, note that N and Q must be done.
2. Then, back from event 9, only activity G must be done.
3. Back from event 7, both activities H and I must be completed.
4. From event 4, only activity C must be done.

**5.** Back from event 5, both activities D and E must be completed.

**6.** Back from event 3, only activity B must be done.

**7.** Finally, back from event 2, only activity A must be done.

Do not overlook the significance of the dummy arrow, however. It should be noted that before any work can proceed beyond event 10, it is required that activity K must be completed. To proceed beyond event 10, not only must activities E and J be completed, but because of the dependency upon completing activity K, all three activities B, F, and K must be completed before activity S can start.

### Float Time in the Sample Problem

As stated earlier, the float of an activity represents the potential scheduling leeway. When an activity has float time available, this extra time may be utilized to serve a variety of scheduling purposes. When total float is available, the earliest start of an activity can be delayed, its duration extended, or a combination of both can occur as long as the late finish time is not exceeded. To do a proper job of scheduling of noncritical activities, it is important that the user understand the workings of float or slack time.

As mentioned previously, the total float of an activity is the maximum time that its actual completion can go beyond its earliest finish time and not delay the entire project. It is the time leeway that is available for that activity if the activities preceding it are started as early as possible and the ones following it are started as late as possible. If all of the available total float is used on one activity, a new critical path is created. The free float of an activity is the maximum time by which its actual completion date can exceed its earliest finish time without affecting either the overall project completion or the times of any subsequent activities. If an operation is delayed to the extent of an activity's free float, the activities following it are not affected, and they can still start at their earliest start times.

Thus, in the illustration in Figures 13.19 and 13.20, the total float of the activity T (12–16) would be as follows:

Critical path from event 12 to event 16 is

$$12(10) \text{ to } 16 = 6 \text{ days time}$$

Completion time for activity T is 4 days

$$\text{Total float time is } (6\text{–}4) \text{ days} = 2 \text{ days}$$

Early start time for activity T (from events 12 to 16):

$$\text{path 1-3-6-12, which totals 35 days}$$

Late start for activity T would be:

$$\text{path 1-3-6-12 plus float time for activity}$$
$$T = (35 + 2) = 37 \text{ days}$$

Thus, as long as the time required to complete activity T does not exceed $(4 + 2) = 6$ days, the critical path time will not change. As soon as activity T goes to 7 or more days, the time to complete the work will change. Similarly, if such would occur on a noncritical path and cause that total path to exceed the original critical path, a new critical path is created. The danger is that if one activity uses all of the total float, it is gone for good. From then on the contractor is on a critical path.

A good example can be seen by considering two sequential activities, such as placing conduit for a concrete pour and actually making the pour. Assume that these activities are not on the critical path and that the difference between the early and the late dates is a total of 10 days. Assuming that no other activities will have any effect on the two mentioned, how much total float does the conduit activity have? The answer, of course, is 10 days—the difference between the early and late start or the early and late finish. Now, how much total float does the pour activity have? The answer to that, too, is 10 days, computed in the same manner. Then, how much total float does the entire sequence of activities have—20 days? *No,* because total float cannot be added; the sequence or chain of activities still has only 10 days.

What if the electrician is 3 days late in starting? As of the time started, there are only 7 days of total float. The general contractor has also been reduced to 7 days of total float. What if the electrician finishes 7 days late? Now the general contractor has *no* float—the contractor is on critical path.

The point is that individual activities do not really have total float individually. Chains of activities have total float, and all of the activities in the chain share the same total float time. If one activity uses it up, it is gone for good and is no longer available for the other activities.

## READING A COMPUTERIZED CPM NETWORK SCHEDULE

By far the majority of cases of CPM scheduling that will be encountered by the Resident Project Representative will involve the use of computer generated scheduling data. Two types of documents will normally be made available to the Resident Project Representative: the arrow diagram and the computer printout of the various types of scheduling data required by the contractor.

Although the majority of the printouts will include contractor cost data as well as time scheduling data, the resident engineer or inspector will probably be interested only in the time scheduling data. Each of the jobs is run through the computer and the data recomputed on a regular basis so that all information is up to date. Of particular concern might be the redistribution of slack times if portions of total slack have been used by certain individual activities. The usual groups of data are sorted and arranged into separate lists, and all such separate lists or "sorts" are printed out separately.

As an example, a CPM schedule prepared for the Aerospace/Mechanical Engineering Building for the University of Arizona provided printouts of the following types of data grouped into separate printouts:

1. Bar chart by early starts (dummies and finished activities omitted)
2. Sort by total slack/late start dates
3. Sort by activity numbers

**4.** Cost by activity numbers

**5.** Schedule of anticipated earnings

In the example of the bar chart in Figure 13.21, it can be seen how the computer can even be used to produce a bar chart from the network analysis data, thus providing the user with several types of statistical data for use in the scheduling operation.

## University of Arizona Project

The CPM network consisted of one 762mm × 1066mm (30 × 42-in) summary network and three 762mm × 1066mm (30 × 42-in) sheets of detailed net for the Aerospace & Mechanical Engineering Building, supplemented by computer printouts covering each reporting period.

On the detailed network plan shown in Figure 13.22, the critical path is indicated by a heavy dashed line. Of particular note on this sheet is the fact that at times there is more than one critical path during this phase of the work. Thus, if any change occurs to delay the work along *any* of the critical paths, that one path will become the only critical path unless similar delays occurred along another path that would exceed those of the one just affected.

By observation, note that the node numbering is based upon the horizontal method (see Figure 13.6b), and that the system of diagramming is an arrow diagram with activity-on-arrow notation. A portion of the same schedule in computer-generated precedence format, is shown in Figure 13.23. The schedule reports (computer printouts) are provided for the following data:

Work item: Sort by *i-j* numbers

Sort by total float

Sort by early finish dates

By observation of each of the computer printouts, it can be seen that the column headings are all identical. The only difference between them is the arrangement of the activities on the sheets. On one, all activities are arranged in numerical order by *i-j* node numbers; in another they are all arranged in the order of dates of early finish of each activity; in another they are all arranged in the order of the amount of float time per activity.

To take just one example, activity 1042–1043 is included in each of the three sample schedule reports shown in Figures 13.24 to 13.26. In each report, the early start date is 23 January 1995 and the early finish date is shown as 3 February 1995. The late start date for the same activity is shown as 26 January and the late finish date as 8 February, and the total float time is 3 days and the free float is shown as zero. Thus, the only difference between the entries on the various report "sorts" is the sequence or arrangement of the data on the sheet.

Note activity 1030–1031 in Figure 13.24. This is a sort by *i-j* numbers. All activities in this report format have been arranged in the numerical order of their activity numbers, as shown in the first two columns headed "I" and "J." Thus, if the user is searching for an activity by its number, it can easily be found by reference to this "sort."

**Forward Associates Ltd.**
CONSULTANTS TO THE CONSTRUCTION INDUSTRY
CALIFORNIA,TEXAS,FLORIDA,WASHINGTON DC,PANAMA
PO BOX 1640,NOVATO,CA,94948 94948 (415) 892-2180

| ACTIVITY ID | EARLY START | EARLY FINISH | 1994 | | | 1995 | | | |
|---|---|---|---|---|---|---|---|---|---|
| | | | NOV | DEC | JAN | FEB | MAR | APR | MAY |
| | | | OWNER | | | | | | |
| 1    2 | 7NOV94 | 7NOV94 | NOTICE TO PROCEED 7NOV94 | | | | | | |
| | | | GENERAL | | | | | | |
| 978  982 | 8NOV94 | 15NOV94 | ☐···DEMOLITION PERMIT | | | | | | |
| 980  982 | 8NOV94 | 22NOV94 | ▮MOBILIZATION | | | | | | |
| 1010 1014 | 9DEC94 | 22DEC94 | ▮ENGINEERING & LAYOUT | | | | | | |
| | | | DEMOLITION | | | | | | |
| 982 1010 | 23NOV94 | 8DEC94 | ▮SITE DEMOLITION | | | | | | |
| | | | CAISSONS | | | | | | |
| 1020 1021 | 23DEC94 | 10JAN95 | ▮DRILL CAISSONS | | | | | | |
| 1022 1026 | 23DEC94 | 10JAN95 | ▮REINFORCE CAISSONS | | | | | | |
| 1024 1026 | 23DEC94 | 10JAN95 | ▮ALL CONCRETE CAISSONS | | | | | | |
| 1060 1066 | 11JAN95 | 25JAN95 | ▨ ·······DRILL CAISSONS | | | | | | |
| 1062 1066 | 11JAN95 | 25JAN95 | ▨ ·······REINFORCE CAISSONS | | | | | | |
| 1064 1066 | 11JAN95 | 25JAN95 | ▨ ·······CONCRETE CAISSONS | | | | | | |
| 1200 1206 | 26JAN95 | 1FEB95 | ▨DRILL CAISSONS 2ND LVL | | | | | | |
| 1202 1206 | 26JAN95 | 1FEB95 | ▨REINFORCE CAISSONS 2ND LVL | | | | | | |
| 1204 1206 | 26JAN95 | 1FEB95 | ▨CONCRETE CAISSONS 2ND LVL | | | | | | |
| | | | EXCAVATION | | | | | | |
| 1012 1016 | 9DEC94 | 15DEC94 | ☐···EXCAVATION | | | | | | BAS |
| 1030 1033 | 4JAN95 | 17JAN95 | ▮ALL EXCAVATE FTGS & PITS | | | | | | |
| 1070 1073 | 26JAN95 | 31JAN95 | ALL EXCAVATE FOOTINGS & ▨ ···!···· | | | | | | |
| 1170 1173 | 20FEB95 | 23FEB95 | ALL PREP SLAB ON GRADE ▮ | | | | | | |
| 1192 1193 | 18APR95 | 8MAY95 | BACKFILL BASEMENT ▨▨ | | | | | | |
| | | | CONCRETE | | | | | | |
| 1036 1040 | 18JAN95 | 24JAN95 | ▮·······ALL CONCRETE FOOTINGS & PITS | | | | | | |
| 1152 1154 | 25JAN95 | 30JAN95 | ▨ ··FORM & PLCE CONCRETE COLUM | | | | | | |
| 1044 1047 | 23JAN95 | 10FEB95 | ▮ALL FORM & PLCE CONC 1ST LVL | | | | | | |
| 1074 1076 | 27JAN95 | 10FEB95 | ALL CONCRETE FOOTINGS & ▨ ··· | | | | | | |
| 1092 1094 | 13FEB95 | 20FEB95 | ALL FORM & PLACE CONC.WALLS 2 ▨ ····· | | | | | | |
| 1082 1094 | 13FEB95 | 21FEB95 | ALL FORM & PLCE CONC COLUMS 2 ▨ ····· | | | | | | |
| 1094 1097 | 22FEB95 | 24FEB95 | FORM & PLACE CONCRETE WALLS 3RD ▨ ··· | | | | | | |
| 1102 1104 | 28FEB95 | 3MAR95 | ALL FORM & PLCE CONC WALLS 4TH LVL ▨ ·!· | | | | | | |
| 1176 1178 | 7MAR95 | 8MAR95 | CONCRETE SLAB ON GRADE ▮ | | | | | | |
| 1180 1184 | 9MAR95 | 29MAR95 | ALL FORM SLAB 2ND LVL (SUSPEND) ▮ | | | | | | |
| 1188 1190 | 21MAR95 | 3APR95 | ALL CONCRETE SLAB 2ND LVL (SUSPENDED) ▮ | | | | | | |
| 1252 1270 | 4APR95 | 10APR95 | ALL FORM & PLACE CONC.WALLS 2ND LVL SO ▮ | | | | | | |
| 1262 1270 | 4APR95 | 10APR95 | ALL CONCRETE COLUMNS 2ND LVL SO ▮ | | | | | | |
| 1254 1255 | 4APR95 | 13APR95 | 2ND LVL SLAB CURE STRIP & BACKSHORE SO ▨ | | | | | | |
| 1270 1277 | 11APR95 | 8MAY95 | ALL FORM 3RD LVL SLABS SOUT ▮ | | | | | | |
| 1276 1280 | 21APR95 | 12MAY95 | ALL CONCRETE SLAB 3RD LVL SOUTH ▮ | | | | | | |

SLETTEN CONSTRUCTION CO.
AEROSPACE/MECH.ENGINEERING BLDG UofA
BC-01 BAR CHART BY RESPONSIBILITY

FORWARD ASSOC LTD- NOVATO, CA (415) 892-2180

(c) Primavera Systems, Inc.

**FIGURE 13.21** Computer printout of bar chart. CPM by Forward Associates, Ltd. Contractor: Sletten Construction Company. Owner: University of Arizona.

341

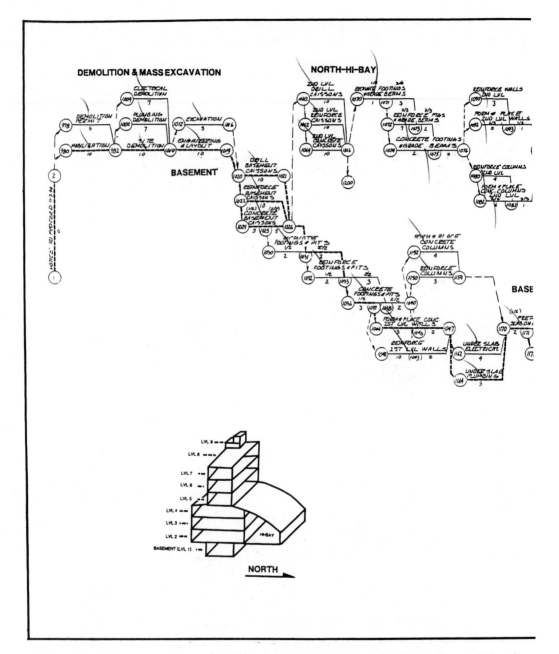

**FIGURE 13.22** Example of hand-drawn network graphics in arrow-diagram format. University of Arizona Aerospace/Mechanical Engineering Building.

FIGURE 13.22 *continued*

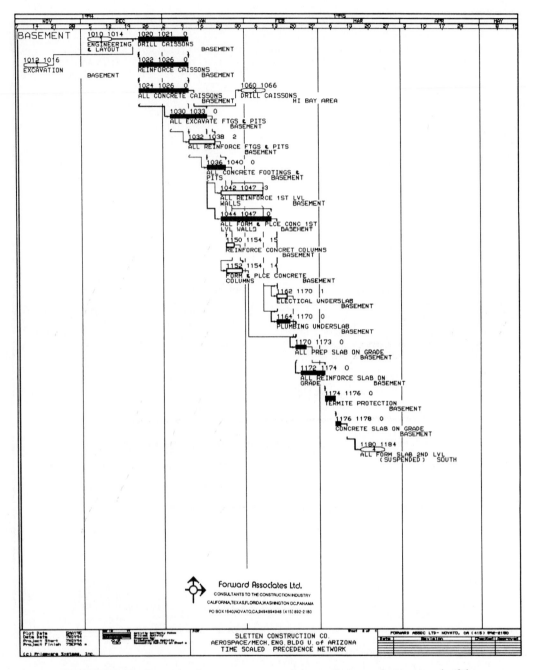

**FIGURE 13.23**  Example of computer-generated time scaled precedence network of the University of Arizona, Aerospace/Mechanical Engineering Building.

SLETTEN CONSTRUCTION CO.

I J SORT

FORWARD ASSOC LTD-CONSTRUCTION CONSULTANTS
CALIFORNIA, FLORIDA, TEXAS, WASHINGTON D.C.
P.O.BOX 1640,NOVATO,CA,94948 (415) 892-2180

U.OF ARIZONA, AEROSPACE & MECH.BLDG

START DATE 07NOV94  FIN DATE 07SEP96*
REPORT DATE 08MAY95  RUN NO.    66
DATA DATE 07NOV94  PAGE NO.    1

| I | J | SCHED DUR | REM DUR | PCT | DESCRIPTION | | EARLY START | LATE START | EARLY FINISH | LATE FINISH | TOTAL FLOAT | FREE FLOAT |
|---|---|---|---|---|---|---|---|---|---|---|---|---|
| 1 | 2 | 1 | 1 | 0 | NOTICE TO PROCEED 7NOV94 | | 07NOV94 | 07NOV94 | 07NOV94 | 07NOV94 | 0 | 0 |
| 2 | 978 | 0 | 0 | 0 | > | | 08NOV94 | 16NOV94 | 07NOV94 | 15NOV94 | 5 | 0 |
| 2 | 980 | 0 | 0 | 0 | > | | 08NOV94 | 08NOV94 | 07NOV94 | 07NOV94 | 0 | 0 |
| 978 | 982 | 5 | 5 | 0 | DEMOLITION PERMIT | | 08NOV94 | 16NOV94 | 15NOV94 | 22NOV94 | 5 | 5 |
| 980 | 982 | 10 | 10 | 0 | MOBILIZATION | | 08NOV94 | 08NOV94 | 22NOV94 | 22NOV94 | 0 | 0 |
| 982 | 1002 | 0 | 0 | 0 | > | | 23NOV94 | 30NOV94 | 22NOV94 | 29NOV94 | 3 | 0 |
| 982 | 1004 | 0 | 0 | 0 | > | | 23NOV94 | 30NOV94 | 22NOV94 | 29NOV94 | 3 | 0 |
| 982 | 1010 | 10 | 10 | 0 | SITE DEMOLITION | | 23NOV94 | 23NOV94 | 08DEC94 | 08DEC94 | 0 | 0 |
| 1002 | 1010 | 7 | 7 | 0 | PLUMBING DEMOLITION | | 23NOV94 | 30NOV94 | 05DEC94 | 08DEC94 | 3 | 3 |
| 1004 | 1010 | 7 | 7 | 0 | ELECTRICAL DEMOLITION | | 23NOV94 | 30NOV94 | 05DEC94 | 08DEC94 | 3 | 3 |
| 1010 | 1012 | 0 | 0 | 0 | > | | 09DEC94 | 16DEC94 | 08DEC94 | 15DEC94 | 5 | 0 |
| 1010 | 1014 | 10 | 10 | 0 | ENGINEERING & LAYOUT | | 09DEC94 | 09DEC94 | 22DEC94 | 22DEC94 | 0 | 0 |
| 1012 | 1016 | 5 | 5 | 0 | EXCAVATION | BASEMENT | 09DEC94 | 16DEC94 | 15DEC94 | 22DEC94 | 5 | 0 |
| 1014 | 1020 | 0 | 0 | 0 | > | | 23DEC94 | 23DEC94 | 22DEC94 | 22DEC94 | 0 | 0 |
| 1016 | 1020 | 0 | 0 | 0 | > | | 16DEC94 | 23DEC94 | 15DEC94 | 22DEC94 | 5 | 5 |
| 1020 | 1021 | 10 | 10 | 0 | DRILL CAISSONS | BASEMENT | 23DEC94 | 23DEC94 | 10JAN95 | 10JAN95 | 0 | 0 |
| 1020 | 1022 | 0 | 0 | 0 | > | | 23DEC94 | 23DEC94 | 22DEC94 | 22DEC94 | 0 | 0 |
| 1021 | 1026 | 0 | 0 | 0 | > | | 11JAN95 | 11JAN95 | 10JAN95 | 10JAN95 | 0 | 0 |
| 1022 | 1024 | 0 | 0 | 0 | > | | 23DEC94 | 23DEC94 | 22DEC94 | 22DEC94 | 0 | 0 |
| 1022 | 1026 | 10 | 10 | 0 | REINFORCE CAISSONS | BASEMENT | 23DEC94 | 23DEC94 | 10JAN95 | 10JAN95 | 0 | 0 |
| 1024 | 1025 | 5 | 5 | 0 | 1/2 CONCRETE CAISSONS | BASEMENT | 23DEC94 | 23DEC94 | 03JAN95 | 03JAN95 | 0 | 0 |
| 1025 | 1026 | 5 | 5 | 0 | 2/2 CONCRETE CAISSONS | BASEMENT | 04JAN95 | 04JAN95 | 10JAN95 | 10JAN95 | 0 | 0 |
| 1025 | 1030 | 0 | 0 | 0 | > | | 04JAN95 | 09JAN95 | 03JAN95 | 06JAN95 | 3 | 0 |
| 1026 | 1031 | 0 | 0 | 0 | > | | 11JAN95 | 11JAN95 | 10JAN95 | 10JAN95 | 0 | 0 |
| 1026 | 1060 | 0 | 0 | 0 | > | | 11JAN95 | 10FEB95 | 10JAN95 | 09FEB95 | 21 | 0 |
| 1030 | 1031 | 2 | 2 | 0 | 1/2 EXCAVATE FTGS & PITS | BASEMENT | 04JAN95 | 09JAN95 | 05JAN95 | 10JAN95 | 3 | 3 |
| 1031 | 1032 | 0 | 0 | 0 | > | | 11JAN95 | 13JAN95 | 10JAN95 | 12JAN95 | 2 | 0 |
| 1031 | 1033 | 4 | 4 | 0 | 2/2 EXCAVATE FTGS & PITS | BASEMENT | 11JAN95 | 11JAN95 | 17JAN95 | 17JAN95 | 0 | 0 |
| 1032 | 1033 | 2 | 2 | 0 | 1/2 REINFORCE FTGS & PITS | BASEMENT | 11JAN95 | 13JAN95 | 12JAN95 | 17JAN95 | 2 | 2 |
| 1033 | 1036 | 0 | 0 | 0 | > | | 18JAN95 | 18JAN95 | 17JAN95 | 17JAN95 | 0 | 0 |
| 1033 | 1038 | 3 | 3 | 0 | 2/2 REINFORCE FTGS & PITS | BASEMENT | 18JAN95 | 18JAN95 | 02FEB95 | 06FEB95 | 11 | 0 |
| 1036 | 1037 | 3 | 3 | 0 | 1/2 CONCRETE FOOTINGS & PITS | BASEMENT | 18JAN95 | 18JAN95 | 20JAN95 | 20JAN95 | 0 | 0 |
| 1037 | 1038 | 0 | 0 | 0 | > | | 23JAN95 | 07FEB95 | 20JAN95 | 06FEB95 | 11 | 0 |
| 1037 | 1042 | 0 | 0 | 0 | > | | 23JAN95 | 26JAN95 | 20JAN95 | 25JAN95 | 3 | 0 |
| 1037 | 1044 | 0 | 0 | 0 | > | | 23JAN95 | 23JAN95 | 20JAN95 | 20JAN95 | 0 | 0 |
| 1038 | 1040 | 2 | 2 | 0 | 2/2 CONCRETE FOOTINGS & PITS | BASEMENT | 23JAN95 | 07FEB95 | 24JAN95 | 08FEB95 | 11 | 0 |
| 1040 | 1043 | 0 | 0 | 0 | > | | 25JAN95 | 09FEB95 | 24JAN95 | 08FEB95 | 11 | 8 |
| 1040 | 1046 | 0 | 0 | 0 | > | | 25JAN95 | 09FEB95 | 24JAN95 | 08FEB95 | 11 | 11 |
| 1040 | 1150 | 0 | 0 | 0 | > | | 25JAN95 | 15FEB95 | 24JAN95 | 14FEB95 | 15 | 0 |
| 1040 | 1152 | 0 | 0 | 0 | > | | 25JAN95 | 14FEB95 | 24JAN95 | 13FEB95 | 14 | 0 |
| 1042 | 1043 | 10 | 10 | 0 | 4/5 REINFORCE 1ST LVL WALLS | BASEMENT | 23JAN95 | 26JAN95 | 03FEB95 | 08FEB95 | 3 | 0 |
| 1043 | 1047 | 2 | 2 | 0 | 5/5 REINFORCE 1ST LVL WALLS | BASEMENT | 06FEB95 | 09FEB95 | 07FEB95 | 10FEB95 | 3 | 3 |
| 1044 | 1046 | 13 | 13 | 0 | 4/5 FORM & PLCE CONC 1ST LVL WALLS | BASEMENT | 23JAN95 | 23JAN95 | 08FEB95 | 08FEB95 | 0 | 0 |
| 1046 | 1047 | 2 | 2 | 0 | 5/5 FORM & PLCE CONC 1ST LVL WALLS | BASEMENT | 09FEB95 | 09FEB95 | 10FEB95 | 10FEB95 | 0 | 0 |
| 1047 | 1162 | 0 | 0 | 0 | > | | 13FEB95 | 14FEB95 | 10FEB95 | 13FEB95 | 1 | 0 |
| 1047 | 1164 | 0 | 0 | 0 | > | | 13FEB95 | 13FEB95 | 10FEB95 | 10FEB95 | 0 | 0 |
| 1060 | 1062 | 0 | 0 | 0 | > | | 11JAN95 | 10FEB95 | 10JAN95 | 09FEB95 | 21 | 0 |
| 1060 | 1066 | 10 | 10 | 0 | DRILL CAISSONS | HI BAY AREA | 11JAN95 | 10FEB95 | 25JAN95 | 23FEB95 | 21 | 0 |

**FIGURE 13.24** CPM sort by *i-j* numbers. CPM by Forward Associates Ltd., Novato, California; Contractor: Sletten Construction Co.; Owner: University of Arizona.

In Figure 13.25, however, the same data used in the sort by *i-j* numbers has now been rearranged by the computer in the order of total float. Thus, if the user reads the two far-right columns headed "TOTAL FLOAT" and "FREE FLOAT," the user can readily locate all activities with the specified amount of float.

Note activity 1042–1043 in Figure 13.24. The total float indicated for this activity is 3 days, yet the amount of free float is zero. This indicates that there is no leeway in the individual schedule for that activity, but any float is the result of slack time somewhere else in the network. By comparison, see activity 1020-1021 in Figure 13.24, which shows that there is no float time of any kind available for this activity. This is an indication that the activity is on the critical path. By locating this activity on the CPM network in Figure 13.22, it can be seen that this is truly the case.

Similarly, in Figure 13.26, the data have again been rearranged, this time in the order of "early finish dates" for each activity. If it is desired to determine all items that will be finished as of any given date, reference to this "sort" will show them.

On the schedule reports shown in Figures 13.24 to 13.26 an example of total and free float for a given activity can be shown. Activities 1004–1010 and 1002–1010 are concurrent, followed by successor activity 1010–1014, which is on critical path, a fact that can be observed on both the printouts and the detailed network plan. Activities 1004–1010 and 1002–1010 each show 3 days of total float and 3 days of free float, followed by activity 1010–1014 which has no float because it is on critical path. In this case, delaying either 1004–1010 or 1002–1010 by 3 days will place that activity on critical path. From the network diagram it is evident that 1010–1014 cannot proceed until all three predecessor activities have been completed. The late finish dates of each of the predecessor activities is shown in the schedule report as 8 December 1994. The early/late start date for 1010–1014, which is on critical path, is shown on the schedule reports as 9 December 1994. The early finish dates of predecessor activities 1002–1010 and 1004–1010 are shown as 5 December 1994, a difference of 3 days between the early finish date of 5 December and the late finish date of 8 December, which accounts for the indicated 3 days float before the early/late start date of critical path activity 1010–1014. Thus any overrun in the completion date of either of the predecessor activities would have an immediate adverse effect on the completion date of the project.

### Kajakai Hydroelectric Project

Another example of a CPM network schedule is that of the Kajakai Hydroelectric Project (Figure 13.27), which, unlike the previous example, only shows major activities such as "structural foundations, Kandahar" in which a single activity includes all of the subsidiary tasks that are sometimes scheduled as separate activities on other projects, such as excavation, build forms, fabricate rebar, erect forms, place rebar, place concrete, and so on.

Of particular note on the Kajakai project is the number of paths shown on the network sheet as being critical; however, many of them involve the ordering and delivery of large fabricated-to-order turbines and generating and transmission equipment as well as heavy earthmoving equipment. Delays in any such items could easily adversely affect the entire project schedule.

```
                              TOTAL FLOAT SORT
              FORWARD ASSOC LTD-CONSTRUCTION CONSULTANTS        START DATE 07NOV94  FIN DATE 07SEP96*
              CALIFORNIA, FLORIDA, TEXAS, WASHINGTON D.C.       REPORT DATE 08MAY95  RUN NO.   64
              P.O.BOX 1640,NOVATO,CA,94948 (415) 892-2180       DATA DATE  07NOV94  PAGE NO.   1
```

| I | J | SCHED DUR | REM DUR | PCT | DESCRIPTION | | EARLY START | LATE START | EARLY FINISH | LATE FINISH | TOTAL FLOAT | FREE FLOAT |
|---|---|---|---|---|---|---|---|---|---|---|---|---|
| 1 | 2 | 1 | 1 | 0 | NOTICE TO PROCEED 7NOV94 | | 07NOV94 | 07NOV94 | 07NOV94 | 07NOV94 | 0 | 0 |
| 2 | 980 | 0 | 0 | 0 | > | | 08NOV94 | 08NOV94 | 07NOV94 | 07NOV94 | 0 | 0 |
| 980 | 982 | 10 | 10 | 0 | MOBILIZATION | | 08NOV94 | 08NOV94 | 22NOV94 | 22NOV94 | 0 | 0 |
| 982 | 1010 | 10 | 10 | 0 | SITE DEMOLITION | | 23NOV94 | 23NOV94 | 08DEC94 | 08DEC94 | 0 | 0 |
| 1010 | 1014 | 10 | 10 | 0 | ENGINEERING & LAYOUT | | 09DEC94 | 09DEC94 | 22DEC94 | 22DEC94 | 0 | 0 |
| 1014 | 1020 | 0 | 0 | 0 | > | | 23DEC94 | 23DEC94 | 22DEC94 | 22DEC94 | 0 | 0 |
| 1020 | 1022 | 0 | 0 | 0 | > | | 23DEC94 | 23DEC94 | 22DEC94 | 22DEC94 | 0 | 0 |
| 1022 | 1024 | 0 | 0 | 0 | > | | 23DEC94 | 23DEC94 | 22DEC94 | 22DEC94 | 0 | 0 |
| 1024 | 1025 | 5 | 5 | 0 | 1/2 CONCRETE CAISSONS | BASEMENT | 23DEC94 | 23DEC94 | 03JAN95 | 03JAN95 | 0 | 0 |
| 1020 | 1021 | 10 | 10 | 0 | DRILL CAISSONS | BASEMENT | 23DEC94 | 23DEC94 | 10JAN95 | 10JAN95 | 0 | 0 |
| 1021 | 1026 | 0 | 0 | 0 | > | | 11JAN95 | 11JAN95 | 10JAN95 | 10JAN95 | 0 | 0 |
| 1022 | 1026 | 10 | 10 | 0 | REINFORCE CAISSONS | BASEMENT | 23DEC94 | 23DEC94 | 10JAN95 | 10JAN95 | 0 | 0 |
| 1025 | 1026 | 5 | 5 | 0 | 2/2 CONCRETE CAISSONS | BASEMENT | 04JAN95 | 04JAN95 | 10JAN95 | 10JAN95 | 0 | 0 |
| 1026 | 1031 | 0 | 0 | 0 | > | | 11JAN95 | 11JAN95 | 10JAN95 | 10JAN95 | 0 | 0 |
| 1031 | 1033 | 4 | 4 | 0 | 2/2 EXCAVATE FTGS & PITS | BASEMENT | 11JAN95 | 11JAN95 | 17JAN95 | 17JAN95 | 0 | 0 |
| 1033 | 1036 | 0 | 0 | 0 | > | | 18JAN95 | 18JAN95 | 17JAN95 | 17JAN95 | 0 | 0 |
| 1036 | 1037 | 3 | 3 | 0 | 1/2 CONCRETE FOOTINGS & PITS | BASEMENT | 18JAN95 | 18JAN95 | 20JAN95 | 20JAN95 | 0 | 0 |
| 1037 | 1044 | 0 | 0 | 0 | > | | 23JAN95 | 23JAN95 | 20JAN95 | 20JAN95 | 0 | 0 |
| 1044 | 1046 | 13 | 13 | 0 | 4/5 FORM & PLCE CONC 1ST LVL WALLS | BASEMENT | 23JAN95 | 23JAN95 | 08FEB95 | 08FEB95 | 0 | 0 |
| 1046 | 1047 | 2 | 2 | 0 | 5/5 FORM & PLCE CONC 1ST LVL WALLS | BASEMENT | 09FEB95 | 09FEB95 | 10FEB95 | 10FEB95 | 0 | 0 |
| 1047 | 1164 | 0 | 0 | 0 | > | | 13FEB95 | 13FEB95 | 10FEB95 | 10FEB95 | 0 | 0 |
| 1164 | 1170 | 5 | 5 | 0 | PLUMBING UNDERSLAB | BASEMENT | 13FEB95 | 13FEB95 | 17FEB95 | 17FEB95 | 0 | 0 |
| 1170 | 1171 | 2 | 2 | 0 | 1/2 PREP SLAB ON GRADE | BASEMENT | 20FEB95 | 20FEB95 | 21FEB95 | 21FEB95 | 0 | 0 |
| 1171 | 1172 | 0 | 0 | 0 | > | | 22FEB95 | 22FEB95 | 21FEB95 | 21FEB95 | 0 | 0 |
| 1172 | 1173 | 3 | 3 | 0 | 1/2 REINFORCE SLAB ON GRADE | BASEMENT | 22FEB95 | 22FEB95 | 24FEB95 | 24FEB95 | 0 | 0 |
| 1173 | 1174 | 4 | 4 | 0 | 2/2 REINFORCE SLAB ON GRADE | BASEMENT | 27FEB95 | 27FEB95 | 02MAR95 | 02MAR95 | 0 | 0 |
| 1174 | 1176 | 2 | 2 | 0 | TERMITE PROTECTION | BASEMENT | 03MAR95 | 03MAR95 | 06MAR95 | 06MAR95 | 0 | 0 |
| 1176 | 1178 | 2 | 2 | 0 | CONCRETE SLAB ON GRADE | BASEMENT | 07MAR95 | 07MAR95 | 08MAR95 | 08MAR95 | 0 | 0 |
| 1178 | 1180 | 0 | 0 | 0 | > | | 09MAR95 | 09MAR95 | 08MAR95 | 08MAR95 | 0 | 0 |
| 1180 | 1181 | 5 | 5 | 0 | 1/3 FORM SLAB 2ND LVL (SUSPENDED) | SOUTH | 09MAR95 | 09MAR95 | 15MAR95 | 15MAR95 | 0 | 0 |
| 1181 | 1184 | 10 | 10 | 0 | 3/3 FORM SLAB 2ND LVL (SUSPENDED) | SOUTH | 16MAR95 | 16MAR95 | 29MAR95 | 29MAR95 | 0 | 0 |
| 1184 | 1189 | 1 | 1 | 0 | 5/5 REINFORCE SLAB 2ND LVL (SUSPENDED) | SOUTH | 30MAR95 | 30MAR95 | 30MAR95 | 30MAR95 | 0 | 0 |
| 1047 | 1162 | 0 | 0 | 0 | > | | 13FEB95 | 14FEB95 | 10FEB95 | 13FEB95 | 1 | 0 |
| 1162 | 1170 | 4 | 4 | 0 | ELECTICAL UNDERSLAB | BASEMENT | 13FEB95 | 14FEB95 | 16FEB95 | 17FEB95 | 1 | 1 |
| 1171 | 1173 | 2 | 2 | 0 | 2/2 PREP SLAB ON GRADE | BASEMENT | 22FEB95 | 23FEB95 | 23FEB95 | 24FEB95 | 1 | 1 |
| 1031 | 1032 | 0 | 0 | 0 | > | | 11JAN95 | 13JAN95 | 10JAN95 | 12JAN95 | 2 | 0 |
| 1032 | 1033 | 2 | 2 | 0 | 1/2 REINFORCE FTGS & PITS | BASEMENT | 11JAN95 | 13JAN95 | 12JAN95 | 17JAN95 | 2 | 2 |
| 982 | 1002 | 0 | 0 | 0 | > | | 23NOV94 | 30NOV94 | 22NOV94 | 29NOV94 | 3 | 0 |
| 982 | 1004 | 0 | 0 | 0 | > | | 23NOV94 | 30NOV94 | 22NOV94 | 29NOV94 | 3 | 0 |
| 1002 | 1010 | 7 | 7 | 0 | PLUMBING DEMOLITION | | 23NOV94 | 30NOV94 | 05DEC94 | 08DEC94 | 3 | 3 |
| 1004 | 1010 | 7 | 7 | 0 | ELECTRICAL DEMOLITION | | 23NOV94 | 30NOV94 | 05DEC94 | 08DEC94 | 3 | 3 |
| 1025 | 1030 | 0 | 0 | 0 | > | | 04JAN95 | 09JAN95 | 03JAN95 | 06JAN95 | 3 | 0 |
| 1030 | 1031 | 2 | 2 | 0 | 1/2 EXCAVATE FTGS & PITS | BASEMENT | 04JAN95 | 09JAN95 | 05JAN95 | 10JAN95 | 3 | 3 |
| 1037 | 1042 | 0 | 0 | 0 | > | | 23JAN95 | 26JAN95 | 20JAN95 | 25JAN95 | 3 | 0 |
| 1042 | 1043 | 10 | 10 | 0 | 4/5 REINFORCE 1ST LVL WALLS | BASEMENT | 23JAN95 | 26JAN95 | 03FEB95 | 08FEB95 | 3 | 0 |
| 1043 | 1047 | 2 | 2 | 0 | 5/5 REINFORCE 1ST LVL WALLS | BASEMENT | 06FEB95 | 09FEB95 | 07FEB95 | 10FEB95 | 3 | 3 |
| 2 | 978 | 0 | 0 | 0 | > | | 08NOV94 | 16NOV94 | 07NOV94 | 15NOV94 | 5 | 0 |
| 978 | 982 | 5 | 5 | 0 | DEMOLITION PERMIT | | 08NOV94 | 16NOV94 | 15NOV94 | 22NOV94 | 5 | 5 |

**FIGURE 13.25** CPM sort by total float. CPM by Forward Associates Ltd., Novato, California; Contractor: Sletten Construction Co.; Owner: University of Arizona.

EARLY FINISH SORT

FORWARD ASSOC LTD-CONSTRUCTION CONSULTANTS          START DATE 07NOV94  FIN DATE 07SEP96*
CALIFORNIA, FLORIDA, TEXAS, WASHINGTON D.C.          REPORT DATE 08MAY95  RUN NO.   65
P.O.BOX 1640,NOVATO,CA,94948 (415) 892-2180          DATA DATE 07NOV94  PAGE NO.   1

| I | J | SCHED DUR | REM DUR | PCT | DESCRIPTION | | EARLY START | LATE START | EARLY FINISH | LATE FINISH | TOTAL FLOAT | FREE FLOAT |
|---|---|---|---|---|---|---|---|---|---|---|---|---|
| 1 | 2 | 1 | 1 | 0 | NOTICE TO PROCEED 7NOV94 | | 07NOV94 | 07NOV94 | 07NOV94 | 07NOV94 | 0 | 0 |
| 978 | 982 | 5 | 5 | 0 | DEMOLITION PERMIT | | 08NOV94 | 16NOV94 | 15NOV94 | 22NOV94 | 5 | 5 |
| 980 | 982 | 10 | 10 | 0 | MOBILIZATION | | 08NOV94 | 08NOV94 | 22NOV94 | 22NOV94 | 0 | 0 |
| 1002 | 1010 | 7 | 7 | 0 | PLUMBING DEMOLITION | | 23NOV94 | 30NOV94 | 05DEC94 | 08DEC94 | 3 | 3 |
| 1004 | 1010 | 7 | 7 | 0 | ELECTRICAL DEMOLITION | | 23NOV94 | 30NOV94 | 05DEC94 | 08DEC94 | 3 | 3 |
| 982 | 1010 | 10 | 10 | 0 | SITE DEMOLITION | | 23NOV94 | 23NOV94 | 08DEC94 | 08DEC94 | 0 | 0 |
| 1012 | 1016 | 5 | 5 | 0 | EXCAVATION | BASEMENT | 09DEC94 | 16DEC94 | 15DEC94 | 22DEC94 | 5 | 0 |
| 1010 | 1014 | 10 | 10 | 0 | ENGINEERING & LAYOUT | | 09DEC94 | 09DEC94 | 22DEC94 | 22DEC94 | 0 | 0 |
| 1024 | 1025 | 5 | 5 | 0 | 1/2 CONCRETE CAISSONS | BASEMENT | 23DEC94 | 23DEC94 | 03JAN95 | 03JAN95 | 0 | 0 |
| 1030 | 1031 | 2 | 2 | 0 | 1/2 EXCAVATE FTGS & PITS | BASEMENT | 04JAN95 | 09JAN95 | 05JAN95 | 10JAN95 | 3 | 3 |
| 1020 | 1021 | 10 | 10 | 0 | DRILL CAISSONS | BASEMENT | 23DEC94 | 23DEC94 | 10JAN95 | 10JAN95 | 0 | 0 |
| 1022 | 1026 | 10 | 10 | 0 | REINFORCE CAISSONS | BASEMENT | 23DEC94 | 23DEC94 | 10JAN95 | 10JAN95 | 0 | 0 |
| 1025 | 1026 | 5 | 5 | 0 | 2/2 CONCRETE CAISSONS | BASEMENT | 04JAN95 | 04JAN95 | 10JAN95 | 10JAN95 | 0 | 0 |
| 1032 | 1033 | 2 | 2 | 0 | 1/2 REINFORCE FTGS & PITS | BASEMENT | 11JAN95 | 13JAN95 | 12JAN95 | 17JAN95 | 2 | 2 |
| 1031 | 1033 | 4 | 4 | 0 | 2/2 EXCAVATE FTGS & PITS | BASEMENT | 11JAN95 | 11JAN95 | 17JAN95 | 17JAN95 | 0 | 0 |
| 1033 | 1038 | 3 | 3 | 0 | 2/2 REINFORCE FTGS & PITS | BASEMENT | 18JAN95 | 02FEB95 | 20JAN95 | 06FEB95 | 11 | 0 |
| 1036 | 1037 | 3 | 3 | 0 | 1/2 CONCRETE FOOTINGS & PITS | BASEMENT | 18JAN95 | 18JAN95 | 20JAN95 | 20JAN95 | 0 | 0 |
| 1038 | 1040 | 2 | 2 | 0 | 2/2 CONCRETE FOOTINGS & PITS | BASEMENT | 23JAN95 | 07FEB95 | 24JAN95 | 08FEB95 | 11 | 0 |
| 1060 | 1066 | 10 | 10 | 0 | DRILL CAISSONS | HI BAY AREA | 11JAN95 | 10FEB95 | 25JAN95 | 23FEB95 | 21 | 0 |
| 1062 | 1066 | 10 | 10 | 0 | REINFORCE CAISSONS | HI BAY AREA | 11JAN95 | 10FEB95 | 25JAN95 | 23FEB95 | 21 | 0 |
| 1064 | 1066 | 10 | 10 | 0 | CONCRETE CAISSONS | HI BAY AREA | 11JAN95 | 10FEB95 | 25JAN95 | 23FEB95 | 21 | 0 |
| 1070 | 1071 | 1 | 1 | 0 | 1/2 EXCAVATE FOOTINGS & GRADE BEAMS | HI BAY AREA | 26JAN95 | 24FEB95 | 26JAN95 | 24FEB95 | 21 | 0 |
| 1150 | 1154 | 3 | 3 | 0 | REINFORCE CONCRET COLUMNS | BASEMENT | 25JAN95 | 15FEB95 | 27JAN95 | 17FEB95 | 15 | 1 |
| 1152 | 1154 | 4 | 4 | 0 | FORM & PLCE CONCRETE COLUMNS | BASEMENT | 25JAN95 | 14FEB95 | 30JAN95 | 17FEB95 | 14 | 0 |
| 1074 | 1075 | 2 | 2 | 0 | 1/2 CONCRETE FOOTINGS & GRADE BEAMS | HI BAY AREA | 27JAN95 | 08MAR95 | 30JAN95 | 09MAR95 | 28 | 7 |
| 1071 | 1073 | 3 | 3 | 0 | 2/2 EXCAVATE FTGS & GRADE BEAMS | HI BAY AREA | 27JAN95 | 03MAR95 | 31JAN95 | 07MAR95 | 25 | 4 |
| 1200 | 1206 | 5 | 5 | 0 | DRILL CAISSONS 2ND LVL | SOUTH | 26JAN95 | 09JUN95 | 01FEB95 | 15JUN95 | 96 | 0 |
| 1202 | 1206 | 5 | 5 | 0 | REINFORCE CAISSONS 2ND LVL | SOUTH | 26JAN95 | 09JUN95 | 01FEB95 | 15JUN95 | 96 | 0 |
| 1204 | 1206 | 5 | 5 | 0 | CONCRETE CAISSONS 2ND LVL | SOUTH | 26JAN95 | 09JUN95 | 01FEB95 | 15JUN95 | 96 | 0 |
| 1042 | 1043 | 10 | 10 | 0 | 4/5 REINFORCE 1ST LVL WALLS | BASEMENT | 23JAN95 | 26JAN95 | 03FEB95 | 08FEB95 | 3 | 0 |
| 1072 | 1073 | 7 | 7 | 0 | 2/3 REINFORCE FTGS & GRADE BEAMS | HI BAY AREA | 27JAN95 | 27FEB95 | 06FEB95 | 07MAR95 | 21 | 0 |
| 1043 | 1047 | 2 | 2 | 0 | 5/5 REINFORCE 1ST LVL WALLS | BASEMENT | 06FEB95 | 09FEB95 | 07FEB95 | 10FEB95 | 3 | 3 |
| 1044 | 1046 | 13 | 13 | 0 | 4/5 FORM & PLCE CONC 1ST LVL WALLS | BASEMENT | 23JAN95 | 23JAN95 | 08FEB95 | 08FEB95 | 0 | 0 |
| 1073 | 1075 | 2 | 2 | 0 | 3/3 REINFORCE FOOTINGS & GRADE BEAMS | HI BAY AREA | 07FEB95 | 08MAR95 | 08FEB95 | 09MAR95 | 21 | 0 |
| 1046 | 1047 | 2 | 2 | 0 | 5/5 FORM & PLCE CONC 1ST LVL WALLS | BASEMENT | 09FEB95 | 09FEB95 | 10FEB95 | 10FEB95 | 0 | 0 |
| 1075 | 1076 | 2 | 2 | 0 | 2/2 CONCRETE FOOTINGS & GRADE BEAMS | HI BAY AREA | 09FEB95 | 10MAR95 | 10FEB95 | 13MAR95 | 21 | 0 |
| 1090 | 1093 | 3 | 3 | 0 | REINFORCE WALLS 2ND LVL | HI BAY AREA | 13FEB95 | 17MAR95 | 15FEB95 | 21MAR95 | 24 | 2 |
| 1080 | 1083 | 4 | 4 | 0 | REINFORCE CONC COLUMNS 2ND LVL | HI BAY AREA | 13FEB95 | 16MAR95 | 16FEB95 | 21MAR95 | 23 | 2 |
| 1162 | 1170 | 4 | 4 | 0 | ELECTICAL UNDERSLAB | BASEMENT | 13FEB95 | 14FEB95 | 16FEB95 | 17FEB95 | 1 | 1 |
| 1092 | 1093 | 5 | 5 | 0 | 2/3 FORM & PLACE CONC.WALLS 2ND LVL | HI BAY AREA | 13FEB95 | 15MAR95 | 17FEB95 | 21MAR95 | 22 | 0 |
| 1164 | 1170 | 5 | 5 | 0 | PLUMBING UNDERSLAB | BASEMENT | 13FEB95 | 13FEB95 | 17FEB95 | 17FEB95 | 0 | 0 |
| 1082 | 1083 | 6 | 6 | 0 | 2/3 FORM & PLCE CONC COLUMS 2ND LVL | HI BAY AREA | 13FEB95 | 14MAR95 | 20FEB95 | 21MAR95 | 21 | 0 |
| 1093 | 1094 | 1 | 1 | 0 | 3/3 FORM & PLACE CONC. WALLS 2ND LVL | HI BAY AREA | 20FEB95 | 22MAR95 | 20FEB95 | 22MAR95 | 22 | 1 |
| 1170 | 1171 | 2 | 2 | 0 | 1/2 PREP SLAB ON GRADE | | 20FEB95 | 20FEB95 | 21FEB95 | 21FEB95 | 0 | 0 |
| 1083 | 1094 | 1 | 1 | 0 | 3/3 FORM & PLCE CONC COLUMS 2ND LVL | HI BAY AREA | 21FEB95 | 22MAR95 | 21FEB95 | 22MAR95 | 21 | 0 |
| 1171 | 1173 | 2 | 2 | 0 | 2/2 PREP SLAB ON GRADE | BASEMENT | 22FEB95 | 23FEB95 | 23FEB95 | 24FEB95 | 1 | 1 |
| 1094 | 1097 | 3 | 3 | 0 | FORM & PLACE CONCRETE WALLS 3RD LVL | HI BAY AREA | 22FEB95 | 23MAR95 | 24FEB95 | 27MAR95 | 21 | 0 |
| 1096 | 1097 | 3 | 3 | 0 | 3/4 REINFORCE WALLS 3RD LVL | HI BAY AREA | 22FEB95 | 23MAR95 | 24FEB95 | 27MAR95 | 21 | 0 |

**FIGURE 13.26** CPM sort by early finish dates. CPM by Forward Associates, Ltd., Novato, California; Contractor: Sletten Construction Co.; Owner: University of Arizona.

**FIGURE 13.27**  Kajakai Hydroelectric Project: 110-kV transmission lines.

**FIGURE 13.27** *continued*

A CPM schedule such as that illustrated for the Kajakai Project is useful only as a conceptual planning tool. It is virtually worthless as an actual scheduling tool, as no actual activities have been shown, only primary project features. Each of the features indicated would require submittal of subroutines that indicate the many activities that make up each of the project features indicated. When requiring a CPM schedule submittal from a contractor, it is wise to follow the Associated General Contractors guide specifications, which recommend that the network be comprised of individual work activities each of which does not exceed 10 days' duration.

## PROBLEMS

**1.** Name the five basic steps in setting up a CPM schedule.

**2.** Define *free float* and *total float.*

**3.** What type of scheduling is defined as an "activity-oriented" system? What type is defined as an "event-oriented" system?

**4.** In what kind of diagramming does an arrow represent both dependency and duration?

**5.** Define a *logic loop.*

**6.** Can a network schedule legitimately contain more than one critical path?

**7.** Under the guide specifications of the Associated General Contractors (AGC) all work activities should be broken down into work activities not exceeding what maximum and minimum number of days?

**8.** In arrow diagraming, the terms $i$ and $j$ are frequently referred to. What do these terms represent?

**9.** Is activity-on-node diagramming more closely related to arrow diagramming or to precedence diagramming?

**10.** What is a dummy arrow?

# 14

## Construction Operations

Although most of the material in this book could be classed as part of the contract administrator's and Resident Project Representative's normal construction operations, separate chapters have been presented to cover material that relates to the more complex functions that are necessary, as well as the more lengthy subjects that require special clarification. Thus, the subject of this chapter is of more general nature. The day-to-day considerations experienced by the Resident Project Representative, along with an understanding of who is responsible for what, are the principal items covered. That is not to imply that the material is unimportant or noncontroversial, as some of the day-to-day activities that must be endured by the Resident Project Representative would challenge the patience of a stone statue.

Following are the paraphrased words of Gene Sheley, editor of *Western Construction* magazine,[1] who admittedly was not thinking about inspectors when he wrote:

> The Resident Project Representative must be an expert in engineering, architecture, construction methods, labor relations, barroom brawls, public relations, and should have an extensive vocabulary in graphic and colorful construction terms. He or she must be able to work closely with contractors, subcontractors, engineers, architects, owners, and agree with frequent directives that make no sense from people who know less than he or she does; he or she must be able to understand then ignore environmental impact reports and regulations without the Sierra Club finding out, and he or she must cooperate with construction superintendents and contractor quality control representatives, and avoid backing his or her automobile into the privy while they are inside.
>
> The resident inspector must have skin like an alligator, the stomach of a billie goat, the temperament of a Presbyterian minister, nerves of chrome-molybdenum steel, the fortitude of Job, and the physical strength to take care of a situation when all else fails. He or she should enjoy

[1]Used with permission of Gene Sheley, Editor, *Western Construction*.

his or her job, and will probably love the working conditions, except for the dust, numbing cold, searing heat, knee-deep mud, mosquitos, rattlesnakes, scorpions, muck-covered office trailers, questionable toilet facilities, and physical assault by frustrated foremen.

If you still want to be a Resident Project Representative or inspector, the job is yours.

## AUTHORITY AND RESPONSIBILITY OF ALL PARTIES

The owner as a contracting party has several especially reserved rights. Depending upon the type of contract and its specific wording, the owner may be authorized to award other contracts in connection with the same work, to require contract bonds from the contractor, to approve the surety proposed, to retain a specific portion of the contractor's monthly progress payments, to make changes in the work, to carry out portions of the work with the owner's own forces in case of contractor default or neglect, to withhold payments from the contractor for adequate cause, and to terminate the contract for cause. The right of the owner to inspect the work as it progresses, to direct the contractor to expedite the work, to use completed portions of the work before contract completion, and to make payment deductions for incomplete or faulty work are also common contractual provisions.

The contract between the owner and the contractor also imposes some responsibilities on the owner. For example, most construction contracts make the owner responsible for furnishing property surveys that describe or locate the project on the site, for making periodic payments to the contractor, and for making land surveys that establish the boundaries of the property upon which the project is to be located. The owner is also obligated to make extra payment in case of eventualities that were not anticipated in the contract, as well as to allow extensions of time to complete the work for such unanticipated conditions.

It is important to note, however, that the owner cannot intrude into the direction and control of the work. By the terms of the usual construction contract, the contractor is classed as an "independent contractor" and even though the owner has certain rights with respect to the conduct of the work, the owner cannot issue direct instructions as to methods or procedures unless specifically provided for under the terms of the contract. The owner does not have the authority to interfere unreasonably with construction operations, or otherwise unduly assume the functions of directing and controlling the work. If the owner were to assume such authority, it would relieve the contractor from the responsibility for the completed work as well as for the negligent acts committed by the contractor in the course of the construction operations—in short, the owner would be acting as a general contractor and would thus have to expect to inherit all of the responsibilities, risks, and liabilities of that position.

### The Architect/Engineer as a Separate Design Organization

Except for cases in which both design and construction are performed by the same contracting party (turnkey construction), or in which the owner has its own in-house design capability, the architect/engineer, as a separate design firm, is not a party to the construction contract, and no contractual relationship exists between the architect/engineer and the contractor. The design firm is a third party that derives its authority and responsibility from its contract with the owner. When private design professionals are utilized by the owner, the construction contract substitutes the architect/engineer for the owner in many important respects under the contract. However, the jurisdiction of the architect/engineer to make determinations and render decisions binding under the construction contract is limited to the specific terms of the construction contract. The architect/engineer often represents the owner in the administration of the contract and acts for the owner in the day-to-day administration of construction operations. In such contracts, the architect/engineer advises and consults with the owner, and communications between the owner and the contractor are usually made through the architect/engineer. Article 9 of the Standard General Conditions of the Construction Contract of the Engineer's Joint Contract Documents Committee (EJCDC) contains typical provisions regarding the architect/engineer's role in construction contract administration.

Construction contracts of this type impose many duties and bestow considerable authority on the architect/engineer. All construction operations are to be constructed under the surveillance of the architect/engineer, who is generally responsible for overseeing the progress of the work. It is normally the architect/engineer's direct responsibility to see that the quality of work and materials are in conformance with the requirements of the drawings and specifications. To assure fulfillment of these conditions, the architect/engineer firm or its Resident Project Representative (resident engineer or inspector) exercises the right of job inspection and approval of materials. In addition, that firm may exercise the privilege of inspecting the contractor's general program of field procedure and even the equipment that is planned for use, as well as the schedule and sequence of operations to complete the work. Should the work be lagging behind schedule, the design firm or its field representative may reasonably instruct the contractor to speed up the work.

The fact that the architect/engineer retains the privilege of approval of the contractor's methods does not mean that they are assuming responsibility for them. The rights of the architect/engineer are essentially those of assuring that the contractor is proceeding in accordance with the provisions of the contract documents, and that the contractor's methods or equipment are capable of accomplishing this objective.

The contract documents often authorize the architect/engineer to interpret the requirements of the contract. The usual wording is that the "decision of the architect/engineer shall be binding and final, and shall bind both parties." Actually, the jurisdiction of the architect/engineer is limited to the settlement of questions of *fact* only, such as what materials, quantities, or quality are required, or whether the work meets the contract requirements. The answers to questions of fact require the professional knowledge and skill of the architect/engineer, and it is proper that they should make such decisions. In the absence of fraud, bad faith, or gross mistake, the decision of the architect/engineer may, in fact, be considered as final unless the terms of the contract contain provisions for appeals or arbitration.

With respect to disputed questions of law, however, the architect/engineer has no jurisdiction. They cannot deny the right of a citizen to due process of law, and the contractor has the right to submit a dispute concerning a legal aspect of the contract to arbitration or to the courts. Whether a particular matter is one of fact or one of legal construction can depend upon the language of the contract. Matters concerning time of completion, liquidated damages, and claims for extra work are usually points of law, not fact.

## The General Contractor

As you might assume from a document prepared by and especially for the owner, the contractor appears to have fewer rights and more obligations under the contract. The contractor's major responsibility, of course, is to construct the project in accordance with the drawings, specifications, and other contract documents. Despite all the troubles, delays, adversities, accidents, and other misoccurrences that may happen, the contractor is generally expected to deliver a completed project in the allotted time—just as if nothing had happened to slow down the work. Although some casualties are considered to be justifiable reasons to receive more construction time, only severe contingencies such as impossibility of performance can serve to relieve the contractor from contractual obligations.

Regardless of how contracts are awarded for a construction project, there should always be one party placed in the position of responsibility for the management and control of construction operations to maintain established work schedules, promote safe working conditions, and avoid unnecessary disputes and conflicts that result in unjustified claims for extra compensation. Such responsibility is normally placed in the hands of a general contractor, except in those states where local laws require separate prime contracts for mechanical and electrical work. The cost of such management and control of construction operations, including the services of a separate person to act as a mechanical work coordinator for major projects, would become a part of the general contractor's bid price. In general, the project should include the services of a separate mechanical work coordinator, but some projects might not require one because the project is too small to justify one, or the mechanical and electrical systems are uncomplicated. The specifying architects/engineers must make their own determination, taking into consideration the percentage of total work contributed by the mechanical and electrical trades as well as the complexity of the design. In all instances, particularly when separate contracts or assigned contracts occur, the mechanical and electrical specifications should contain provisions requiring full and complete cooperation with the general contractor and its mechanical work coordinator.

Under the provisions of Article 6 of the General Conditions of the EJCDC, and similar documents of other agencies, the contractor is expected to give personal attention to the work, and either the contractor or its authorized representative must be on the site at all times during working hours. The contractor is further required to conform to all laws and ordinances concerning job safety, licensing, employment of labor, sanitation, insurance, zoning, building codes, and other aspects of the work. In many cases, failure of the design firm to research restrictions on its project properly results in designs that in themselves are not in conformance with all applicable regulations. Thus, the contractor really inherits a bucket of worms when the contract calls for conformance to some technical requirement, and at the same time requires the firm to conform to all codes and laws that clearly show the original design to be a violation—sometimes, you just cannot win. Many contracts now include tough new rules designed to decrease air pollution, noise pollution, dust, and similar restrictions as well as rules concerning trash disposal, sanitary wastes, pile driving, blasting, riveting, demolition, fencing, open excavations, traffic control, and housekeeping.

The general contractor is further held responsible for and must guarantee all work and materials on the project, whether constructed by the firm's own forces or by subcontractors, because the subcontractors have no contractual relationship with the owner—only with the general contractor. Every restriction in the construction contract that refers to the "contractor" is binding solely upon the general contractor, as far as the owner is concerned. The general contractor may subcontract portions of the work, but the terms of such subcontracts are not subject to review by the owner and are solely an agreement between the general and the subcontractor. Even though a contractor has no direct responsibility for the adequacy of the plans and specifications, it can incur contingent liability for proceeding with faulty work whose defects should be evident to one in that business. Should an instance occur in which the contracting firm is directed to do something that it feels is not proper and is not within the realm of good construction practice, the contracting firm should protect itself by filing a letter of protest to the design firm or the owner through the resident engineer or inspector, stating its position and the facts as it sees them before proceeding with the matter in dispute. If ordered to proceed by the design firm or the owner, the contractor must continue with the work even if it disagrees, or even in case of dispute for other causes. Settlement of disputes then follows concurrently with the prosecution of the work.

Insurance coverage is an important contractual responsibility of the contractor, both as to type of insurance and the policy limits. The contractor is generally required to provide insurance not only for its own direct and contingent liability, but also frequently for the owner's protection. The contractor firm is expected to exercise every reasonable safeguard for the protection of persons and property in, on, and adjacent to the construction site.

Some of the contractor's most important rights concern progress payments, and the contractor's recourse in case the owner should fail to make such payments, as well as the right to terminate the contract for cause, the right to extra payment and extensions of time as provided in the contract, and appeals from decisions of the owner or the design firm. Subject to contractual requirements and limitations in the contract, the contractor is free to subcontract portions of the work, purchase materials where it chooses (but not necessarily the right to select such materials), and to proceed with the work in any way or order that it pleases, if permitted under the terms of the contract documents.

### The Resident Project Representative

The Resident Project Representative normally works as the agent of the owner, the design firm, or a construction management firm, and as such may under the terms of such agency, exercise such authority as is normally reserved to the owner, design firm, or construction firm, as long as they act within the scope of their delegated authority and subject to the restrictions of law that prohibit such persons from performing certain functions reserved by law to the practice of professional engineering or architecture.

The purpose of inspection is to detect, recognize, and report deficiencies in material or workmanship, or noncompliance with applicable plans, specifications, or other contract documents, procedures, standards, codes, or regulations. The resident engineer's or inspector's job is to inspect the workmanship, materials, and manner of construction of all buildings and appurtenant structures, or portions of such structures, to determine whether the requirements described by the plans, specifications, contract documents, codes, ordinances, or other statutory provisions are met by the observed work. This responsibility is basic. Any authority or responsibilities beyond those stated are limited to those delegated by the inspector's employer and should be clearly established before reporting to the job.

### The CQC Representative

A contractor quality control (CQC) representative is a position unique to federal contracts, particularly those with NAVFAC, Corps of Engineers, and NASA. Under a CQC provision, a construction contracting firm has the responsibility to inspect its own work on some federal contracts, and to present for federal acceptance only such work that complies with the contract plans and specifications. Under a contract requiring a contractor quality control program (usually construction projects with a budget estimate of over $1,000,000), the contractor is required to assign a responsible and competent individual to the position of CQC representative, and to delegate to that person certain responsibilities and authority. The primary function of a CQC representative at the site is to assure that all inspections and tests are made and to give all approvals unless specifically reserved to the federal agency. This includes the checking of all material and equipment delivered to the site. One of the objectives is to achieve quality construction acceptable to the agency and to contribute to the contractor's profits by preventing defective work rather than discovering deficiencies that may result in costly removal and replacement. In those cases in which unacceptable work is started or completed, the CQC representative must have the authority to take any action necessary to correct the deficiency event though it means stopping the work of the CQC representative's employer on a particular portion of the job. The CQC representative must also coordinate and assure the performance of all tests required by the specifications. As an agent of the contractor, the CQC representative will be held responsible by the federal agency for any fraudulent acts or certifications. In day-to-day contact with the federal agency involved, the CQC representative works through a federal construction representative assigned to the project.

## TEMPORARY FACILITIES PROVIDED BY THE CONTRACTOR

As a part of each construction contract, the contractor is generally obligated to provide certain facilities and services that are not a permanent part of the facilities to be constructed. In some cases the specifications do not mention the specific items involved, thus needlessly complicating the administration of the contract. (See "Provisions for Temporary Facilities" in Chapter 6 for further details.)

All such items, when properly supported by specifications provisions, become a part of the specific contractual obligations of the contractor. Many of the items so listed are also properly considered as a part of the contractor's mobilization requirements, and as such, it is recommended that the payment provisions of the contract specifically itemize all such facilities and services. Then, in case of failure of the contractor to provide any or all of the items listed, the owner may be justified in withholding all or part of the contractor's initial progress payment. (See "Payment for Mobilization Costs," in Chapter 16 for further details.)

Failure of the owner's architect/engineer to provide such controls over the contractor's mobilization activities frequently results in long delays in providing the Resident Project Representative with a field office and field telephone service. Failure to provide timely communications in itself can be a serious obstacle in the path of the architect/engineer for the development of effective project control.

## TIME OF INSPECTION AND TESTS

The provisions of the various General Conditions of the Construction Contract generally treat the subject of when and under what conditions the inspections and tests will be performed. Although each standard document now in use seems to treat the subject in different words, they all say essentially the same thing. Generally, the provisions cover the following:

1. Contractor must give the architect/engineer timely notice.
2. Tests and inspections required by public agencies must usually be paid for by the contractor.
3. Tests and inspections, other than those mentioned, that are required by the contract documents will be paid for by the owner.
4. Work covered prior to required inspections must be uncovered for inspection and then recovered, all at the contractor's expense.
5. Failure of an inspector to observe a deficiency does not relieve the contractor of obligation for performance.
6. Extra inspections required as the result of a deficiency noted by the inspector must be paid for by the contractor.
7. The contractor firm must provide all materials for testing at its own cost and expense.

The Resident Project Representative is urged to refer to Articles 13.3 through 13.7 of the EJCDC 1910-8 (1996) General Conditions, Article 13.5 of the AIA A201 (1987) General Conditions, and Sub-Clauses 36.3 through 37.5 of the FIDIC (1987) Conditions of Contract for examples of terms covering such inspections. Similarly, the General Conditions of the Contract for Engineering Construction of the Associated General Contractors in collaboration with the American Society of Civil Engineers places similar restrictions upon the contractor in Section 15 of that document.

## CONTRACTOR SUBMITTALS

All submittals from the contractor should be handled in a systematic, consistent, and orderly manner. Changes in systems or procedures during a job lead to confusion, errors, and abuses. There should be no "special cases" or exceptions in the routine established for submittals—these lead to breaks in communication, and occasionally result in gross error. Whenever a Resident Project Representative is provided on a project, the most desirable method is to require that all submittals required under the contract be transmitted directly to that individual, who in turn should forward such items to the project manager of the design firm or owner (see "Handling of Job-Related Information" in Chapter 3 and Figure 3.5). This serves a twofold purpose. First, the Resident Project Representative will be fully aware of the status of all phases of the project; second, it will serve to emphasize to the contractor that the Resident Project Representative speaks for the owner and the design firm and that any efforts to bypass that person will be rejected. Furthermore, it eliminates any arguments that certain submittals were "mailed on time" or that the subcontractors submitted their submittals directly to the design firm or owner.

Often, a contractor making a request that has already been denied by the Resident Project Representative may try to approach the design firm or owner directly *without the knowledge* of the Resident Project Representative. If this procedure is followed, the embarrassing condition of a contractor's proposal being accepted by the project manager after it has already been rejected by the Resident Project Representative will occur. There are subsidiary dangers to that situation, also. Once the contractor is successful, the effectiveness of the Resident Project Representative is diminished measurably, and the project manager will find it necessary to conduct most of the field business personally. It would seem that if a job warrants the presence of a Resident Project Representative, he or she should be provided with the authority necessary to conduct the job efficiently and effectively—otherwise, the design firm or owner should save its money and eliminate the position.

## OPENING A PROJECT

Opening a project requires many details to be completed before the contractor even moves a single piece of equipment onto the project site. Immediately after award of the contract, the contractor is expected to make arrangements for the required policies of insurance, obtain permits, order long-lead purchase items, check the site to determine the availability of storage and work staging areas, make arrangements for off-site disposal of surplus or waste materials, and take care of numerous other tasks.

In addition, the owner and the design firm will usually want to schedule a preconstruction meeting (see Chapter 11). At this time they will be able to meet with the contractor and other key personnel, identify areas of responsibility, establish job philosophy (set the ground rules), set up requirements for on- or off-site job meetings and set the frequency of such meetings, determine who should be in attendance, point out particular problem areas anticipated in construction and discuss any special methods of treatment of such problems, and if necessary, discuss special sequence of operations or scheduling limitations.

Although the practice is not universally followed, it is desirable for the owner, either directly or through the design firm or construction manager, to issue a written Notice to Proceed to the contractor, which will designate the actual beginning of the contract—very important later when attempting to establish the amount of liquidated damages where the contractor has exceeded the contract time. The *Notice of Award* cannot serve as a valid Notice to Proceed, as no contract will have been executed between the owner and the contractor at that time. The Notice to Proceed sets a precise date that the job began and eliminates any later argument over the time of the contract.

The representative of the design firm or owner should visit the site early after the Notice to Proceed has been issued to assure that all the requirements of the contract documents relating to temporary facilities and utilities are being properly implemented. This includes, particularly for the Resident Project Representative, that the proper field office facilities are being provided, that they are on time, that they are separate from those of the contractor (if specified as such), and that telephone service, temporary power, and sanitary facilities have been arranged for so that they will be installed in time. Where initial temporary fencing is required around construction areas, the Resident Project Representative should closely monitor this requirement.

Each of the construction milestones, such as contractor submittals of key items, materials testing, operational tests, reviews and updates required in schedules, delivery dates of major key pieces of equipment, the beginning of new elements of the work, and similar requirements of the contract should be outlined on paper and a calendar established for the systematic control and monitoring of these functions (see Figure 3.3). The procedures for the handling of all communications should be explained at that time, if not previously covered at the preconstruction meeting, and printed directions issued as a guide to the handling of all construction related matters in conformance with the owner agency requirements. A simplified diagram showing the routing of all field communications and submittals is shown in Figure 3.5.

It is quite important that once the communications procedures have been agreed upon, neither the Resident Project Representative nor members of the staff should allow informal changes to occur. Such departures from the formally accepted policy can otherwise be justifiably used by the contractor to allege a lack of communication as a defense in case of a dispute.

## JOB PHILOSOPHY

A *firm but fair* policy should be adopted by the Resident Project Representative to control the work and to require proper workmanship and materials as well as compliance with drawings, specifications, and other contract documents. The Resident Project Representative should provide as much assistance to the contractor as possible to alert the firm to special job requirements or portions of the work requiring more critical control, and to provide any known information that may benefit the contractor in the completion of the work within the terms of the contract. Valid claims for extra work beyond the scope of the contract, as well as unforeseen underground conditions, should be fairly reviewed by the design firm and, if valid, presented to the owner with a recommendation for approval. Invalid claims should be rejected.

The requirement that the resident engineer or inspector be fair in all dealings with the contractor does not mean that he or she should be overly lenient or patronizing, as there is no point in having a Resident Project Representative on the job if he or she is not effective. The basic philosophy is to get a good start on the job. The inspector's attitude at the beginning of each job should be one of *firmness*. This will minimize arguments later during the job. If a job is started in a loose fashion, it is almost impossible to regain proper control later in the work, even by replacing the Resident Project Representative. An incorrect method is easier corrected the first time it is practiced than after it has been in use for a while.

Many organizations formalize the process by the use of a policy manual in which instructions to the inspectors and other field personnel are outlined for constant reference by the field personnel, such as the following:

## *Instructions to Field Personnel*

### Basic Policy

Contractor to be present at meetings and telephone conferences with subcontractors or suppliers.

Job opening philosophy with contractor: Be firm but fair.

### Responsibility and Authority

Be a team member; avoid adversary relationship with the contractor.

Inspections and tests to be made promptly.

Inspect the work as it progresses.

Avoid overly-literal specification interpretation.

No field changes without Project Manager approval.

Followup all required corrective work until completed.

Do NOT supervise any construction nor the contractor's personnel.

No authority to stop the work; notify Project Manager if necessity arises.

No authority to require quality exceeding that covered by the contract.

Instructions to the contractor through Superintendent or Project Manager.

Document all actions taken.

### Documentation

All filed personnel must keep an approved type diary.

Daily and summary reports must be submitted by Resident Project Representative.

Contractor submittals to be documented both coming in and going out.

Substantive content of business telephone calls should be documented in diary.

Keep photographic records of progress and all potential claims issues.

All orders to the contractor must be in writing.

### Communications

Contractor submittals handled only thru Resident Project Representative.

Surveys and special inspections requested thru Resident Project Representative

Orders to contractor from ANY source must be submitted thru the Resident Project Representative.

### Changes

Field orders and change orders must be handled thru Resident Project Representative.

No changes on oral instructions without written confirmation.

No significant deviations from plans and specifications except by change order—even if no cost or time extension is involved.

Emergency changes by Work Directive Change, followed later by a change order.

Feedback report (Report of Field Problem) to be filed on all correctable problems.

Another important philosophy is that the inspector should not become a creature of habit. Do not get into the swing of a regular routine. No one should be capable of anticipating the inspector's moves form one day to the next. All inspection should be at irregular intervals—and, above all, the inspector should be one of the first ones at the job and one of the last to leave. Many substandard details have been accomplished during the brief time between an inspector's early departure and the contractor's release of the crew for the day. Do not get the idea that the Resident Project Representative should become a policeman, nor that everyone in the contractor's camp is out to defraud. The result will be more tension before the job is half over than either the Resident Project Representative or the contractor can handle. By far the majority of contractors and their employees want to do a good job. Remember that they must usually base their judgments upon previous work that they have personally been involved in, and may not recognize the significance of some of the architect or engineer's design requirements. In addition, in most cases the contractor's project manager is an individual with a practical outlook and may not be easily convinced that the architect or engineer's design theory has approached such a degree of exactness as to justify stringent inspection practices and low-tolerance inspection procedures.

## ADMINISTRATIVE ACTIVITIES

The job of the Resident Project Representative involves the handling of numerous administrative responsibilities. All of the items emphasized in the following list are generally necessary to serve the owner's best interests, but care must be exercised to ensure that they are applicable to your situation. Every activity should have a legitimate purpose and objective. There is far too much administrative work needed to be done in the field without being bogged down with "administrivia." Although most of the major tasks have been described in detail, the following list will serve as a summary of the principal administrative activities expected of the Resident Project Representative:

1. Coordinate and provide general direction of work and progress.
2. Review contractor's CPM schedules regularly.
3. Assist in resolution of construction problems.
4. Evaluate contractor claims for the design firm.
5. Maintain log of change orders.
6. Maintain log of contractor submittals.
7. Develop and administer a quality control program.
   (a) Proofs of compliance.
   (b) Qualifications of testing services.
   (c) Define required tests.
   (d) Maintain QC reporting system.
   (e) Maintain QC records of all tests and test results.
   (f) Establish frequency of testing.
8. Physically inspect all construction *every day.*
9. Observe all contractor tests.
10. Maintain daily diary and construction records.
11. Maintain record drawing data.

12. Review contractor progress payment requests.
13. Review contractor's change order requests for design firm.
14. Assure that construction area is safe.
15. Participate in field management meetings.
16. Provide negotiation assistance on contractor claims.
17. Review and recommend contractor value engineering proposals.
18. Supervise inspection forces and field office staff.
19. Report field conditions that prevent original construction.
20. On unit-price projects, obtain accurate field measurements.
21. On all jobs, verify contractor's monthly work quantities.
22. Assist scheduling and ordering required field services.

Although not exhaustive, the foregoing list summarizes the more commonplace activities expected of the Resident Project Representative on a construction project.

## SUSPENSION OR TERMINATION OF THE WORK

Much has been said about not "stopping the work" but little about the related act of "suspending" it. First, the word *suspension* as used in this context should be very carefully qualified. Work may be suspended in whole or in part, and the nature of a suspension is to cease all or part of the work without actual contract termination.

### Suspension of Work by the Owner

The owner may order the contractor in writing to suspend, delay, or interrupt all or part of the work for as long as deemed necessary. However, if the work is delayed or suspended for a longer period than specified, the contractor may claim an adjustment in price for delay damages as well as additional time.

Motives for suspension of the work vary. The owner may have budgetary limits and decide to stop work in certain areas; it may be necessary to update a particular part of some equipment to incorporate state-of-the-art improvements; work may be suspended due to a contractor defaulting or declaring bankruptcy. In the latter case, the bonding company may have to engage another contractor to complete the work—a process that may require additional time and cost.

Under the EPA Clean Water Grant Program, the EPA-required contract provisions or model subagreement clauses contain a clause that the right of the owner (grantee) to suspend or interrupt portions or all of the work temporarily for an appropriate period of time at the convenience of the owner (grantee). In a few cases, the contractor would be entitled to an equitable adjustment for any additional costs caused by such suspension, particularly if the suspended work is on the critical path of the project schedule.

Temporary suspension is subject to the specific terms of the General Conditions of the Contract for each particular project. In general, however, suspensions can be said to fall into two major categories:

1. The first category relates to the failure of the contractor to carry out orders or to perform any provision of the contract. Any letter ordering such suspension must include reference to applicable sections of the specifications and, if possible, state the conditions under which the work may be resumed. Such action must be taken only after careful consideration of all aspects of the problem, and then only under the direct authority of the design firm, construction manager firm, or owner. This is a legally risky area, however, and the EJCDC feels that the right to reject defective work was a sufficient weapon for the architect/engineer, and the severe and more risky right to stop the work should be left to the owner. However, as often stated before, in certain circumstances, moral standards or the law may impose a duty on the architect or engineer for the benefit of employees and third parties to stop work that is being carried on in an unsafe manner, or advise the owner to do so. This is so even when the General Conditions state that safety precautions are the sole responsibility of the contractor (see Article 6.20 of the EFCDC General Conditions of the Construction Contract as an example of typical provisions). The resident engineer or inspector as the authorized on-site representative of the design firm or owner is then the only party who will normally observe such hazards and can serve such notices at the site.

2. The second category under which a suspension may be ordered relates to unsuitable weather or conditions unfavorable for the suitable prosecution of the work. Normally, such suspensions are not necessary for periods of 30 days or less, since these are best handled on a day-to-day basis when determining nonworking days.

   (a) *Suspension of an item or an operation.* A suspension may be ordered that affects an item or several items only if desired. This is usually done when either the work or the public will be adversely affected by continuous operation. Such action is recommended for situations where the probable end result is based upon the architect's or engineer's experience and judgment as opposed to factors that are directly specified. Although this type of suspension is an option generally available only to the design firm or owner, the contractor's opinion on such suspension should also be considered.

   (b) *Suspension of the entire project.* In areas subject to severe weather, it is considered permissible to suspend an entire project if this is considered as being in the best interests of the owner. However, the authority of the architect or engineer to suspend is limited to the specific terms of the contract documents. In some cases it might even be necessary to have the contractor's concurrence to suspend an entire project.

The contractor must be advised of the conditions under which maintenance will be performed during any suspension, and who will be responsible for the condition of the unfinished work during any such suspension. It may be possible under many contracts that the contractor may be entitled to receive extra payments to maintain the project during this time.

When the reason for a suspension no longer exists, or when it can be expected that favorable conditions for resumption of the work will soon prevail, the contractor should be notified in writing. The letter should state the date when the count of working days will be expected to be resumed, and the notice should allow a reasonable amount of time for the contractor to regroup its labor forces and equipment. Generally, 10 working days is considered as a reasonable length of time for this.

## Termination

Some contract documents contain provision allowing the owner to discontinue all or any part of the work being done by a contractor. This greatly reduces owner risk normally associated with such action in the absence of specific terms and conditions in the contract documents. Such termination may be for reasons such as abandoning the work, bankruptcy or insolvency, unnecessary delay of the work, or displaying other conduct detrimental to the execution of the work. The contractor's conduct must be of a very serious nature, however, to warrant such action.

Terminations, suspensions, and extensions of time will necessitate the issuance of a formal change order. Terminations for convenience or default are usually very complex and may require evaluation of the entire project. Other contract provisions can affect the outcome as well. Extensions of time should be fully evaluated and justified. Under federal grant programs, the owner is cautioned against the granting of unwarranted time extensions, as the costs associated with such extensions may not be interpreted as grant-eligible under the applicable grant program.

Whenever time factors are a part of a change order they should be negotiated together with the other factors, not deferred or separately negotiated. In this way, claims for associated costs such as additional overhead during time extensions can be largely avoided. In some cases, however, a contractor may agree on the price for a given change but will be unwilling to be pinned down to a fixed time impact for a given change order, as it may not be possible to anticipate the impact of the proposed change on other elements of the project. In such cases, it may be wise to settle on the price issue and be willing to negotiate the time after all impacts have been determined.

## CONSTRUCTION SERVICES COST MONITORING

One essential task of the project manager during the construction phase is to maintain control of project field service costs as separate and distinct from architect engineer design costs. The amount of the field costs is a function of the size and classifications of the on-site field forces assigned to the project, field office overhead costs, materials and supplies, support services from the home office, auto leases and fuel charges, field office share of corporate general and administrative (G&A) costs, outside consultant or contract services, and job profit.

By not only tabulating the monthly accumulations of budget and actual field service costs, but by graphically plotting each amount on a time versus cost chart, similar in form to the traditional construction S-curve chart, a visual comparison can be made that can clearly indicate not only the status of the contract at any given time, but will also show any change in trend toward either a predicted savings or cost overrun (Figure 14.1). By also

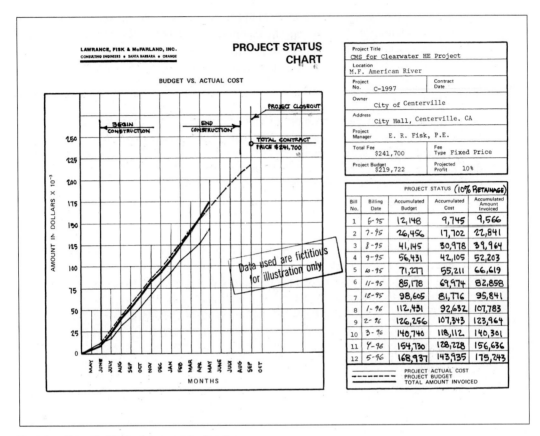

**FIGURE 14.1** Example of a monthly cost report of field services performed by a construction manager.

plotting a curve representing the amounts invoiced to the owner for such field services, an additional dimension is provided.

To prepare and keep up the chart, regular inputs are required by the project manager from the Resident Project Representative on all field costs and hours of work in each classification at the project site. Arrangements should be made by the project manager to assure that all such data are received from the field on a regular, scheduled basis at the end of each month. Generally, the monthly pay estimates of the contractor's work for partial payment are submitted about the 25th of the month, and all submittals are in to the office for payment before the end of the month. Billings from the architect/engineer to the owner, however, usually are based upon the closing date of the end of the month. Therefore, tabulation of these data should not interfere with the Resident Project Representative's review of the contractor's pay requests.

## PROBLEMS

1. True or false? As an accepted standard of quality, a supplier's certificate is an acceptable substitute for a manufacturer's mill test certificate.

2. True or false? As a means of minimizing conflicts between the inspector and the contractor, it is better to set absolute dimensions rather than set tolerance ranges, so that the inspector has a specific value to enforce.

3. Describe the kind of risk involved, if any, where the engineer, the inspector, or the Resident Project Representative is contractually given the right to stop the work.

4. It is a well known principle that the engineer should not tell the contractor how to do the work; but, if the engineer observes that the contractor's construction methods appear to be unable to meet the specifications, what should the engineer do?

5. If the engineer or the owner disputes the work being performed by a subcontractor, with which party should the owner attempt to resolve the issue?

6. Explain the purpose and function of a CQC representative on a NAVFAC or Corps of Engineers contract.

7. Explain the "firm but fair" policy.

8. Describe the responsibilities of the inspector during construction.

9. Is the Resident Project Representative responsible to see that temporary facilities under the control of the contractor are consistent with the provisions of the specifications?

10. Why is it desirable to have all contractor submittals submitted through the Resident Project Representative?

# 15

## Value Engineering

$V$ alue engineering—what is it, and what part does the Resident Project Representative play in its application? The latter question will be answered in this chapter. The first question, however, deserves special consideration. It has been said that value engineering is not the proper role for a project administrator, but rather for the decision maker, such as the project manager. As far as the concept of initiating or granting final approval to a value engineering proposal is concerned, this appears to be true. Nevertheless, it may involve construction methods regarding which the inspector may have valuable knowledge to contribute to the decision maker and, under many federal contracts, it is also a part of the contract requirements of the general contractor to propose value engineering ideas *during the construction phase*. There is no way that a Resident Project Representative can avoid the issue as long as the contractor is involved; thus, it is highly desirable for the inspector to know what value engineering is and how to work with value engineering proposals. In this chapter the resident engineer or inspector will be introduced to the subject in sufficient detail to understand what it is all about and where it fits into his or her responsibility area.

A great deal of lip service has been paid to the concept of value engineering in recent years, and the suggestion is that it is a new, previously undeveloped branch of the construction industry. There are entire engineering organizations devoted solely to the promotion of value engineering and at least one federal agency that lets contracts for large construction projects now requires its use during the design phase of every project. Value engineering concepts are desirable on any project; however, it must be said that all engineering has always involved *value engineering* concepts, although not under that title. In fact, an architect or engineer who did not consider maximum economy and value in the selection and use of construction materials and methods, within the limits dictated by the design, was simply not doing his or her job. Theoretically, during the *design phase* of a project there should be no need for a separate value engineering effort if the architect or engineer is providing competent professional services to the client; however, under the old

**FIGURE 15.1**   Typical EPA Clean Water Grant Project requiring a separate value engineering contract.

EPA Clean Water Grant Program for projects, illustrated in Figure 15.1, a separate contract with an outside consultant was required to provide value engineering.

The concept of providing the value engineering incentives to the construction contractor during the *construction phase* of a project, however, is a more deserving one. Often the selection of materials and methods by the architect/engineer is dictated by an evaluation of the average market conditions or contractor methods. Upon awarding a contract for construction to a specific contractor, the particular skills, equipment, materials sources, and knowledge possessed by that person of the local trade area and labor market can often be used to reduce beneficially the cost of a portion of a proposed project without necessarily compromising the design concepts involved. The final judgment of the acceptability of such suggestions would be up to the architect or engineer and the owner, of course. An example of a value engineering incentive clause in a construction contract is illustrated in Figure 15.2.

## DEFINITION

The first question to arise is usually: What is value engineering, anyway? *Value engineering* is a systematic evaluation of a project design to obtain the most value for every dollar

*ARTICLE 8*

VALUE ENGINEERING INCENTIVE

(a)   Application. This clause applies to a Contractor developed and documented Value Engineering Change Proposal (VECP) which:

(1) requires a change to this contract to implement the VECP; and

(2) reduces the contract price without impairing essential function or characteristics, provided that it is not based solely on a change in deliverable end item quantities.

(b)   Documentation. As a minimum, the following information shall be submitted by the Contractor with each VECP:

(1) a description of the difference between the existing contract requirement and the proposed change, and the comparative advantages and disadvantages of each; justification where function or characteristics of a work item is being altered; and the effect of the change on the performance of the end item;

(2) an analysis and itemization of the requirements of the contract which must be changed if the VECP is accepted and a recommendation as to how to make each such change (e.g., a suggested specification revision);

(3) a separate detailed cost estimate for both the existing contract requirement and the proposed change to provide an estimate of the reduction in costs, if any, that will result from acceptance of the VECP, taking into account the costs of development and implementation by the Contractor (including any amount attributable to subcontracts in accordance with paragraph (f) below);

(4) a prediction of any effects the proposed change would have on related costs to the Government such as Government furnished property costs, and costs of maintenance and operation;

(5) a statement of the time by which a change order adopting the VECP must be issued so as to obtain the maximum cost reduction during the remainder of this contract, noting any effect on the contract completion time or delivery schedule; and

(6) identification of any previous submission of the VECP, including the dates submitted, the agencies involved, the numbers of the Government contracts involved, and the previous actions by the Government if known.

(c)   Submission. 6 copies of each VECP shall be submitted to the Contracting Officer with a copy to the Resident Engineer at the worksite. Proposals shall be processed expeditiously; however, the Government shall not be liable for any delay in acting upon any proposal submitted pursuant to this clause. The Contractor has the right to withdraw, in whole or in part, any VECP at any time prior to acceptance by the Government.

(d)   Acceptance. The Contracting Officer may accept, in whole or in part, by contract modification any VECP submitted pursuant to this clause. The Contracting Officer may accept the VECP even though an agreement on price reduction has not been reached, by issuing the Contractor a notice to proceed with the change. Until a notice to proceed is issued or a contract modification applies a VECP to this contract, the Contractor shall remain obligated to perform in accordance with this contract. Contract modifications made pursuant to this clause will so state. The decision of the Contracting Officer as to the acceptance of any VECP under this contract shall be final and shall not be subject to the "Disputes" clause of this contract.

(1) Definition.

(i)   Instant contract savings to the Contractor (ICS) are the estimated reduction in the Contractor's cost of performance resulting from the acceptance of the VECP. The proposed cost reduction includes estimated allowable Contractor development and implementation costs (CC). The Contractor's development and implementation costs include any subcontractor development and implementation costs (see (f) below). For purposes of this clause, Contractor development costs are those costs incurred after the Contractor has identified a specific VE project and prior to acceptance and implementation by the Government.

**FIGURE 15.2**   Example of value engineering incentive provisions in a federal construction contract.

370

CONTRACT SCHEDULE
SECTION VII - COST & PRICE/PAYMENT
ARTICLE 8 Cont'd

    (ii)   Government Costs (GC) are those NASA costs which directly result from development and implementation of the VECP, such as test and evaluation of the VECP.

  (2) Calculations and Actions.
    Multiply ICS by 45% and GC by 55%. Add these two results, e.g., (.45 ICS + .55 GC) and subtract from the contract price.

(f)   Subcontracts. The Contractor shall include appropriate VE arrangements in any subcontract of $50,000 or greater, and may include such arrangements in contracts of lesser value. To compute any adjustment in the contract price under paragraph (e) above, the Contractor's cost of development and implementation of a VECP which is accepted under this contract shall include any development and implementation costs of a subcontractor, and any VE incentive payments to a subcontractor, which clearly pertain to such VECP. However, no such payment or accrual to a subcontractor will be permitted, either as a part of the Contractor's development or implementation costs or otherwise, to reduce the Government's share.

(g)   Data. The Contractor may restrict the Government's right to use any sheet of a VECP or of the supporting data, submitted pursuant to this clause, in accordance with the terms of the following legend if it is marked on such sheet:

    "This data furnished pursuant to the Value Engineering Incentive clause of contract
    _____ shall not be disclosed outside the Government, or duplicated, used, or disclosed, in whole or in part, for any purpose other than to evaluate a VECP submitted under said clause. This restriction does not limit the Government's right to use information contained in this data if it is or has been obtained, or is otherwise available, from the Contractor or from another source, without limitations. If such a VECP is accepted by the Government under said contract after the use of this data in such an evaluation, disclose any data reasonably necessary to the full utilization of such VECP as accepted, in any manner and for any purpose whatsoever, and have others so do."

In the event of acceptance of a VECP, the Contractor hereby grants to the Government all rights to use, duplicate or disclose, in whole or in part, in any manner and for any purpose whatsoever, and to have or permit others to do so, any data reasonably necessary to fully utilize such VECP.

**FIGURE 15.2** *continued*

of cost. By carefully investigating costs, availability of materials, construction methods, shipping costs or physical limitations, planning and organizing, cost/benefit values, and similar cost influencing items, an improvement in the overall cost of a project can be realized.

    The entire value engineering effort is aimed at a careful analysis of each function and the elimination or modification of anything that adds to the project cost without adding to its functional capabilities. Not only are first costs to be considered, but even the later in-place costs of operation, maintenance, life, replacement, and similar characteristics must be considered. Thus, although the name is new, value engineering is simply a *systematic* application of engineering economy as taught in every engineering course long before anyone ever thought up a catchy name for it.

    The principal difficulty of applying value engineering principles to construction is the problem of having a third party, who may not possess the same degree of expertise in the subject area that the architect or engineer does, cause changes in design that simply substitute the value engineer's judgment for that of the designer—a risky process at best. Theoretically, the value engineer does not actually "cause" a design change, but by placing the architect or engineer in the position of having to defend the original design, the entire production schedule is threatened.

In the construction phase, however, it is a completely new ballgame. Now the value engineer is the contractor, whose experience is in construction methods, techniques, and costs. The contractor's input can often offer the benefit of construction experience and a knowledge of the marketplace and labor force that the designer did not possess. It is here that the greatest cost benefit can result with a minimum of conflict with the designer. Often on federally funded construction contracts, a value engineering incentive clause may be provided, in which the government will allow the contractor to retain a portion of the cost savings realized in any value engineering proposal submitted by the contractor that is accepted and implemented.

Where a voluntary value engineering incentive clause is used in federal contracts, the government is required to share the cost savings with the contractor on a 50/50 percent basis. Where the program is mandatory, the government/contractor share on a 75/25 percent basis [48 CFR 48.104-1].

In public works projects at lower levels of government, application of the principles of sharing value engineering savings varies from state to state. In California, for example, contractor participation in value engineering is optional; however, if it is implemented, the public agency must share the savings with the contractor in the amount of 50 percent of the net savings [CA Public Contracts Code § 7101].

## THE ROLE OF THE RESIDENT PROJECT REPRESENTATIVE

The Resident Project Representative, although generally having no part in the actual submittal of value engineering proposals, may frequently be called upon by the architect or engineer to evaluate a value engineering (VE) proposal that has been submitted by the contractor. It is not being suggested here that the resident engineer or inspector should render judgment in the matter of whether a cost savings proposal is valid, as this would be no better than leaving the matter up to a single individual who did not take part in the actual design, and quite probably did not possess sufficient technical and professional background in the subject area to justify the acceptance of his or her judgment over that of the design engineer. In addition, it should always be remembered that the design engineer is the *engineer of record,* with a license and professional reputation at stake, not that of a value engineer consultant. The inspector's part in this process is to relate to the real world surrounding the assigned project, and evaluate the probable effect of the proposal on the project if it is accepted. All such observations should be written into a memorandum form and submitted to the architect or engineer so that when the final evaluation is made it can be based upon a full knowledge of both the design conditions and the field conditions as communicated by the Resident Project Representative.

## FUNDAMENTALS OF VALUE ENGINEERING

### Function

In value engineering, the *function* is defined as the specific purpose or use intended for something. It describes what must be achieved. For value engineering studies, this function is usually described in the simplest form possible, usually in only two words; a verb and a noun. "Support weight," "prevent corrosion," and "conduct current" are typical expressions of function.

### Worth

*Worth* refers to the least cost required to provide the *functions* that are required by the user of the finished project. Worth is established by comparison, such as comparing it with the cost of its functional equivalent. The worth of an item is not affected by the possibility of failure under the value engineering concept embraced by the federal government. Thus, if a bold supporting a key joint in a large roof truss fails, the entire roof of the structure may be caused to fail. Nevertheless, the worth of the bolt is the lowest cost necessary to provide a reliable fastening.

### Cost

*Cost* is the total amount of money required to obtain and use the functions that have been specified. For the seller, this is the total cost in connection with the product. For the owner, the total cost of ownership includes not only the purchase price of the product, but the cost of the paperwork of including it in the inventory, operating it, and providing support in the form of maintenance and utility services for its total usable life. The cost of ownership may also include a proportional share of expenditures for development, engineering, testing, spare parts, and various items of overhead expense.

### Value

*Value* is the relationship of *worth to cost* as realized by the owner, based upon his or her needs and resources in any given situation. The ratio of *worth to cost* is the principal measure of *value*. Thus, a "value equation" may be used to arrive at a *value index* as follows:

$$\text{value index} = \frac{\text{worth}}{\text{cost}} = \frac{\text{utility}}{\text{cost}}$$

The value may be increased by doing any of the following:

1. Improve the utility of something with no change in cost.
2. Retain the same utility for less cost.
3. Combine improved utility with less cost.

Optimum value is obtained when all utility criteria are met at the lowest overall cost. Although *worth* and *cost* can be expressed in dollars, *value* is a dimensionless expression showing the relationship of the other two.

### The Philosophy of Value

If something does not do what it is intended to do, no amount of cost reduction will improve its value. Any "cost reduction" action that sacrifices the needed utility of something actually reduces its value to the owner. However, costs incurred to increase the functional capacity of something beyond that which is needed amounts to "gilding the lily" and provides little actual value to the owner. Therefore, anything less than the necessary functional capacity is unacceptable; anything more is unnecessary and wasteful.

### Types of Value Engineering Recommendations

Within the Department of Defense and some other federal agencies, there are two types of recommendations that are the result of a value engineering effort:

1. *Value Engineering Proposal (VEP):* a value engineering recommendation that originates from within the government agency itself, or one that was originated by the contractor and may be implemented by unilateral action. A VEP can only relate to changes that are within the terms of the contract and specifications and thus would not require a change order to implement.

2. *Value Engineering Change Proposal (VECP):* a value engineering recommendation by a contractor that requires the owner's approval, and that, if accepted, requires the execution of a change order. This would apply to any proposed change that would require a change in the contract, the specifications, the scope of the work, or similar limits previously established by contract.

## AREAS OF OPPORTUNITY FOR VALUE ENGINEERING

### Value Engineering by the Architect or Engineer

Value engineering is a basic approach that takes nothing for granted and challenges everything on a project, including the necessity for the existence of a product or project, for that matter. The cost of a project is influenced by the requirements of the design and the specifications.[1] Prior to completing the final design the architect or engineer should carefully consider the methods and equipment that may be used to construct the project. Requirements that increase the cost without producing equivalent benefits should be eliminated. The final decisions of the architect or engineer should be based upon a reasonable knowledge of construction methods and costs.

The cost of a project may be divided into five or more items.

1. Materials
2. Labor

---

[1]R. L. Peurifoy, *Construction, Planning, Equipment, and Methods.* Copyright © 1956, McGraw-Hill Book Company, New York. Used with permission of McGraw-Hill Book Company.

**3.** Equipment

**4.** Overhead and supervision

**5.** Profit

Although the last item is beyond the control of the architect or engineer, there is some control possible over the cost of the first four items.

If the architect or engineer specifies materials that must be transported great distances, the costs may be unnecessarily high. Requirements for tests and inspections of materials may be too rigid for the purpose for which the materials will be used. Frequently, substitute materials are available nearby that are essentially as satisfactory as other materials whose costs are considerably higher. The suggestions of the contractor can be of value here.

The specified quality of workmanship and methods of construction have considerable influence on the amount and class of labor required and upon the cost of labor. Complicated concrete structures are relatively easy to design and draw but may be exceedingly difficult to build. A high-grade concrete finish may be justified for exposed surfaces in a fine building, but the same quality of workmanship is not justified for a warehouse. The quality of workmanship should be in keeping with the type of project involved.

Architects and engineers should keep informed on the developments of new construction equipment, as such information will enable them to modify the design or construction methods to permit the use of economical equipment. The resident engineer or inspector is a vital link in the chain of information that supplies the architect and engineer with the latest up-to-date data on construction methods and equipment. The normal *daily construction report* (Figure 4.1) contains sufficient information to keep the architect and engineer adequately informed, and upon noting new methods or equipment in the inspector's report, these leads can be followed to determine the specific capabilities and advantages of each case. For example, the use of a dual-drum concrete paving mixer instead of a single-drum mixer can increase the production of concrete materially, and for most projects will reduce the cost of pavement construction. The use of a high-capacity earth loader and large trucks may necessitate a change in the location, size, and shape of the borrow pit, but the resulting economies may easily justify the change.

The utilization of higher-capacity delivery equipment does not always result in a cost saving, however. On some recent projects in a hot, dry climate as an example, the use of 5.4 $m^3$ (7 cubic yard) transit mixers for delivering concrete to a project proved far more costly than making twice as many trips using 2.3 $m^3$ (3 cubic yard) mixers. The placing requirements involved the construction of thin concrete columns and wall sections with a high concentration of reinforcing steel, with the resultant reduction in the rate of placement. Before a 5.4 $m^3$ (7 cubic yard) truckload of concrete could be completely discharged under the existing conditions, the concrete mix started to set in the delivery vehicles because of the high temperature, low humidity, and 3-hour time span from the addition of water to the mix to the final placement in the forms. Long delivery routes are often the cause of this, combined with slow pour conditions. The resultant frequency of rejection of portions of the 5.4 $m^3$ (7 cubic yard) load (retempering was prohibited by specifications) was more costly than the increase in the number of deliveries and the smaller batch size that allowed the use of a fresh load after every 2.3 $m^3$ (3 cubic yards) placed.

The following are some of the methods that the architect or engineer may use to re-duce the cost of construction:

1. Design concrete structures with as many duplicate members as is practical to al-low the reuse of forms without rebuilding.
2. Confine design elements to modular material sizes where possible.
3. Simplify the design of the structure wherever possible.
4. Design for the use of cost-saving equipment and methods.
5. Eliminate unnecessary special construction requirements.
6. Design to reduce the required labor to a minimum.
7. Specify a quality of workmanship that is consistent with the quality of the project.
8. Furnish adequate foundation information wherever possible.
9. Refrain from requiring the contractor to assume the responsibility for informa-tion that should have been furnished by the architect or engineer, or for the ade-quacy of the design.
10. Use local materials when they are satisfactory.
11. Write simple, straightforward specifications that state clearly what is expected of the contractor. Define the results expected, but within reason permit the contrac-tor to select the methods of accomplishing the results.
12. Use standardized specifications that are familiar to most contractors whenever possible.
13. Hold preconstruction conferences with contractors to eliminate any uncertainties and to reduce change orders resulting from misunderstandings to a minimum.
14. Use inspectors who have sufficient judgment and experience to understand the project and have authority to make decisions.

## Value Engineering by the Contractor

One desirable characteristic of a successful contractor from the standpoint of value engi-neering is a degree of dissatisfaction over the plans and methods under consideration for constructing a project (a characteristic not always appreciated by the architect or engineer). However, complacency by members of the construction industry will not develop new equipment, new methods, or new construction planning, all of which are desirable for pro-viding continuing improvements in the construction industry at lower costs. A contractor who does not keep informed on new equipment and methods will soon discover that his competitors are underbidding him.

Suggestions for possible reductions in construction costs by the contractor include, but are by no means limited to, the following items:

1. Study the project before bidding, and determine the effect of:
   (a) Topography
   (b) Geology
   (c) Climate

    (d) Sources of materials

    (e) Access to the project

    (f) Housing facilities, if required

    (g) Storage facilities for materials and equipment

    (h) Labor supply

    (i) Local services

2. The use of substitute construction equipment that has greater capacities, higher efficiencies, higher speeds, more maneuverability, and lower operating costs.

3. Payment of a bonus to key personnel for production in excess of a specified rate.

4. The use of radios as a means of communications between headquarters office and key personnel on projects covering large areas.

5. The practice of holding periodic conferences with key personnel to discuss plans, procedures, and results. Such conferences should produce better morale among the staff members and should result in better coordination among the various operations.

6. The adoption of realistic safety practices on a project as a means of reducing accidents and lost time.

7. Consideration of the desirability of subcontracting specialized operations to other contractors who can do the work more economically than the general contractor.

8. Consideration of the desirability of improving shop and servicing facilities for better maintenance of construction equipment.

Improvements in the *methods* of construction long the sole domain of the contractor can result in significant savings in the cost of the project. This type of cost saving, if implemented after the award of a contract, is seldom if ever shared with the owner. However, such cost-reducing considerations are an integral part of the competitive bidding system. Thus, the owner benefits in lower bid costs. As an example, an estimator for a contracting firm prepared a bid for a project. When the bids were opened, it was discovered that his firm's bid was so low that the other members of the firm feared that a serious error had been made in preparing the bid. The estimator was called in and asked if he thought that he could actually construct the project for the estimated cost. He replied that he could if he were permitted to adopt the construction methods that he used in estimating the cost. The firm agreed; he was placed in charge of the construction of the project and he completed the work with a satisfactory profit to the contractor. At the same time, the owner benefitted by receiving his project at a low cost.

## METHODOLOGY IN GENERATING VALUE ENGINEERING PROPOSALS

A task that is accomplished in a planned and systematic manner is much more likely to be successful than one that is unplanned and relies upon undisciplined ingenuity. Most successful value engineering (VE) organizations follow a "scientific method" to assure a planned, purposeful approach. This procedure is called a VE *Job Plan.* It is set up as a group action because it is unlikely that a successful value engineering proposal will be the product of a single individual. The group plan produces benefits that the efforts of one or two individuals can seldom match. Among the principal benefits are:

1. More talent is directly applied to the problem.
2. The scope and depth of the effort is increased.
3. More efficient use is made of the available time because problem areas are more readily resolved through direct communications.
4. Team participation provides productive training for those not previously exposed to formal VE training.

Several versions of a VE Job Plan can be found in current publications. Some texts list five phases, some six, and some refer to even more. However, the number of phases is less important than the systematic approach involved. As an example, Figure 15.3 shows a

**FIGURE 15.3**    Value engineering job plan chart (From *Value Engineering,* DOD Handbook 5010.8-H.)

five-phase Job Plan. Although the illustration may suggest otherwise, there are actually no sharp lines of distinction between the phases. They tend to overlap in varying degrees.

An effective value engineering effort must include all phases of the Job Plan. However, the proper share of attention given to each phase may differ from one effort to another. The Job Plan represents a concerted effort to furnish the best answers to the following key questions:

> What is it?
> What *does* it do?
> What *must* it do?
> What does it cost?
> What is it worth?
> What else might do the job?
> What does the alternative cost?
> What will satisfy all of the owner's needs?
> What is needed to put the VE change into effect?

### I. Information Phase

This first phase of the Job Plan has three objectives:

1. Understanding the product being studied
2. Determining the essential functions
3. Estimating the potential value improvement

Both the product itself and the general technical area that it represents must be studied to understand the subject of the VE effort. Data accumulated should include the predicted total cost of ownership; the present configuration; the quality, reliability, and maintainability attributes; the quantity involved; and the background information regarding the reason the product was originally selected (one of the most important considerations of all). It is most important to obtain qualified sources to obtain facts, not opinions. All data must be supported by adequate documentation.

When receiving VE proposals from the contractor, the Resident Project Representative must be assured that the proposal is complete, including all documentation required. The proposal must include a functional analysis, an economic analysis, and a cost analysis to respond to the requirements for submittals of VE proposals.

### II. Speculation Phase

The purpose of the speculation phase is to formulate alternative ways of accomplishing the essential functions (Figure 15.4). The effort begins as soon as enough information has been gathered, reviewed, and understood. The first of four methods used to help answer the basic question "What else might do the job?" raised in this phase is:

**FIGURE 15.4** Proposals to modify details of construction, consistent with design principles, to lessen construction costs are valid considerations for involving the contractor in value engineering.

*Simple comparison:* a thorough search for other things that have at least one significant characteristic similar to the item being studied.

### III. Analysis Phase

The purpose of the analysis phase is to select for further refinement the most promising of the alternatives that were developed during the speculation phase.

During speculation there was a conscious effort to delay judgment so that the creative process would not be inhibited. During the analysis phase those ideas are subjected to a preliminary screening to identify those that satisfy the following criteria:

*Functional comparison:* a creative session in which new and unusual contributions of known things or processes are combined and rearranged to provide different ways of achieving the function.

*Scientific factors:* a search for other scientific disciplines capable of performing the same basic function. This involves contributions from specialists in disciplines not normally considered in the original design.

*Create and refine:* Push to get off the beaten path and create by reaching for an unusual idea or another approach. Refine by strengthening and expanding ideas that suggest a different way to perform the function.

Will the idea work?

Is it less costly than the present design?

Is it feasible to put into effect?

Will it satisfy the owner's needs?

If the answer to any of these is "no," can it be modified or combined with another to give a "yes" answer?

The ideas that survive the initial screening are then rated according to their relative ability to meet the foregoing requirements. The advantages and disadvantages of each are also noted. Preliminary cost estimates are then developed for those ideas that appear technically and economically most promising. Following these preliminary estimates, one or more of the ideas with significant savings potential are selected for further detailed analysis. If relative cost differences among several alternatives are not conclusive at this point, they may all be subject to further analysis.

## IV. Development Phase

In the development phase, the alternatives that have survived the previous selection process are developed into firm recommendations (VE proposals). This portion of the effort includes the development of detailed technical and economic data for the proposal. The proposal should include everything, including total ownership costs. This phase is also devoted to assuring that the proposal satisfies all of the owner's needs. For evaluation of mechanical equipment on a project, a checklist such as the following is often helpful:

Performance requirements

Quality requirements

Reliability requirements

System compatibility

Safety requirements

Maintenance considerations

Logistics support problems

At this stage the value engineering proposal should also include a written discussion designed to satisfy any objections likely to be raised concerning any aspect of the proposal. Conferences with specialists are often helpful in overcoming anticipated objections in advance. If a technical characteristic is either unacceptable or marginal, the alternative should be modified to correct the deficiency wherever possible. If it is not possible to overcome the deficiency, the alternative should be rejected. Of the technically feasible alternatives remaining, only the one that represents the lowest cost is selected for the detailed development of the technical and economic data necessary to support its selection.

If more than one alternative offers the possibility of valid savings, it is common for all of them to be recommended. One becomes the primary recommendation and the others are considered as alternative recommendations and are usually presented in the order of their decreasing savings potential.

## V. Presentation and Follow-up Phase

The final phase of the Job Plan includes the preparation and presentation of the value engineering proposal to those having approval authority. This phase also includes:

Preparing a plan for implementation,
Obtaining a decision regarding disposition of the proposal,
Assisting as needed in the implementation action
Preparing a final report if appropriate

When finally presented for approval, the VE proposal should be self-explanatory and leave no doubt concerning its justification. Only factual and relevant information should be included. All expected technical and cost variations from the existing design must be described. The following checklist represents the minimum information usually included in a value engineering proposal:

Identity of the project
"Before" and "after" descriptions
Cost of the original design
Cost of the proposed design change
Quantity basis for costs
Cost to put VE proposal into effect
Expected savings to the owner
Actions that are necessary to put the change into effect
Suggested schedule for putting the change into effect

The management personnel who are responsible for review and approval must base their judgment entirely upon the documentation submitted with a VE proposal, and this documentation must contain all of the data that the reviewer will need to reach a decision. VE proposals should contain sufficient information to assure the reviewer that:

The performance of the overall project is not adversely affected.
Supporting technical information is complete and accurate.
Potential savings are based upon valid cost analyses.
Feasibility of the proposed change is adequately demonstrated.

Failure to provide adequate VE proposal documentation is a major cause of proposal rejection. An analysis made of 90 rejected contractor-initiated Value Engineering Change

Proposals revealed that approximately 40 percent of the rejections were due to incomplete or inaccurate technical or cost information.

## FIELD RESPONSIBILITY IN VALUE ENGINEERING

As mentioned previously, the resident engineer or inspector's part in the value engineering process is an indirect one. However, participation may be requested in either of two areas: first to assist the architect or engineer in providing valuable, up-to-date construction information on materials, methods, availability, the capabilities of a particular contractor or contractors, and similar field data. In addition, a contractor's judgment may be solicited during both the *information* and *speculation* phases to assist the architect or engineer in his or her own VE proposals. Second, the contractor's comments may be requested to evaluate the contractor's VE proposals and submit commentary to the architect or engineer. In this manner, the Resident Project Representative may perform the function of one of the "specialists" that the architect or engineer may wish to consult during the analysis and evaluation of the contractor's VE proposals.

## PROBLEMS

1. What is value engineering?
2. What is value?
3. How may value be increased?
4. What are the six primary questions to be asked in the preparation of a value engineering Job Plan?
5. What are the primary objectives of the first phase of a Job Plan?
6. Is the practice of value engineering limited to the design professionals, e.g., engineers or architects?
7. Write an example of a "value equation."
8. What are the four fundamental concerns that must be addressed by the value engineer?
9. Name the steps in a five-phase value engineering job plan chart.
10. Explain the philosophy of value.

# 16

## Measurement and Payment

### CONSTRUCTION PROGRESS PAYMENTS

Among the most important items to the contractor are those provisions of the construction contract governing the making of monthly progress payments to the contractor throughout the job (Figure 16.1). The contractor will be expected to submit a request for payment, stating amounts of work completed and the estimated value of such work to the Resident Project Representative approximately 10 days before the payment due date. At this point, the work of the Resident Project Representative is very similar for both a lump-sum and a unit-price contract. Before transmitting the payment request to the owner's or designer's project manager, the Resident Project Representative is generally delegated the task of verifying and evaluating the contractor's payment request. Because of nearness to the work, the Resident Project Representative is often the only representative of the owner or the design firm who can truly verify the actual quantities of the various items of work completed and determine the probable value of such work.

Although a unit-price contract requires extreme care in the verification of the contractor's payment claim, a lump-sum job can usually be handled more informally, as the overage claims will be compensated for ultimately by the fixed-price nature of the contract. Nevertheless, it is undesirable to be so careless as to allow payments in excess of the amounts of work actually done, as first, it cancels the effect of the retention, if any, and second, if the contractor were to default on the contract, the inspector might be in the position of having approved for payment more work than was actually built, thus allowing the defaulting contractor a tidy, unearned profit.

# PROGRESS PAYMENT FLOW DIAGRAM

## For Public Works Contracts

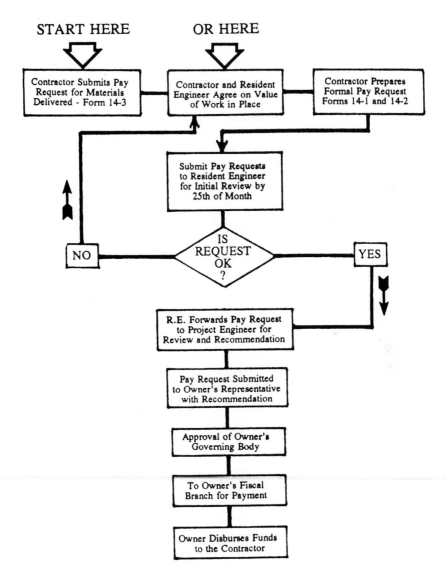

**FIGURE 16.1** Progress payment flow diagram.

## APPROVAL OF PAYMENT REQUESTS

The responsibilities of the Resident Project Representative in the approval stage of contractor partial payment requests are limited to checking quantities and costs prior to submittal to the owner's or designer's project manager with a recommendation for payment if warranted.

The following is a list of possible tasks that might be delegated to the Resident Project Representative during the validation phase of the contractor's payment request:

1. Quantity takeoff of work actually completed as of date of request.
2. Inventory of equipment and materials delivered but not yet used in the work.
3. Field measurements of quantities of work completed or claimed.
4. Construction cost estimate of all completed work, using unit prices in bid or in cost breakdown submitted at beginning of job.
5. Audit of invoices and costs (cost-plus jobs only).
6. Review of claims for extra work and completed change orders.
7. Check of retention amount.
8. On extra work and change orders, check of the method used to determine profit and overhead, material costs, and proper application of each in accordance with the conditions of the contract.
9. Recommendation to the project manager, submitted together with the contractor's payment request (Figures 16.2 and 16.3 or Figure 16.4).

## BASIS FOR PAYMENT AMOUNTS

The basis of all progress payments is a determination, in the field, of the actual quantities of work that have been accomplished as of the date that the payment request is submitted. The accuracy required of these field measurements is determined by the type of contract involved. There are principally three types of construction contracts in current use:

1. Lump-sum contract (fixed price)
2. Unit-price contract
3. Cost plus fixed fee (CPFF)

Although each type of contract may be let on the basis of competitive bids, with the lowest bidder getting the job, several significant differences exist. On a lump-sum contract, the contractor must complete the work for the fixed price shown as long as the scope of the contract has not been altered by change orders. Any cost overruns must come out of the contractor's pocket; similarly, any money that is saved on the job (as long as it conforms to the plans and specifications) belongs to the contractor.

On a unit-price contract, the design firm provides a list of all individual bid items, along with an "engineer's estimate" of the quantities involved. Blanks are provided in the proposal document for the bidder to insert a price per unit for which the contractor agrees

| LAWRANCE, FISK & McFARLAND, INC. | MONTHLY PAYMENT |
| CONSULTING CIVIL & ENVIRONMENTAL ENGINEERS | ESTIMATE SUMMARY |
| Santa Barbara, California | |

| Project Title | | Project No. |
|---|---|---|
| Oakbrook Valve Structure | | 94-132 |

| Contractor | Address |
|---|---|
| ABC Constructors, Inc. | Thousand Oaks, CA |

| Estimate No. | Contract or Spec. No. | Date |
|---|---|---|
| Period 5-26-95 to 6-26-95 | | 26 June 1995 |

| Description | Amounts | | |
|---|---|---|---|
| | Previous | This Month | To Date |
| Total Earnings for Work and Materials Installed........ | 2 328 796.17 | 160 643.90 | 2 489 440.07 |
| Plus _80_% of Invoice Amt for Mat'ls Stored at Site .... | 1 416.07 | 155.79 | 1 571.86 |
| Less Adjustment for Previous Mat'ls invoices ...... | <-0.00> | <-1 416.07> | <-1 416.07> |
| Sub Total ................................ | 2 330 212.24 | 159,383.62 | 2 489 595.59 |
| Less _10_% Retainage ..................... | <-233 021.22> | <15 938.36> | <-248 959.59> |
| Net Earning ................... | 2 097 191.02 | 143 445.26 | 2 240 636.27 |
| Less Previous Payments ........................................................... | | | <-2 097.191.02> |
| Plus: Reduction of Retainage .... | *Data used are fictitious for illustration only* | | 0.00 |
| Net Payment this Estimate ...... | | | 143 445.25 |

| Percent of Time Elapsed | Percent of Work Completed |
|---|---|
| 40% | 47% |

| Contract Completion Data | | Contract Cost Data | |
|---|---|---|---|
| Notice to Proceed Date | 15 Dec 1994 | Amount of Original Contract | 4 671 360.00 |
| Orig. Contract Completion Time | 527 days | Approved Change Orders | 138 785.00 |
| Approved Time Extensions | 42 days | Total Contract Amount | 4 810 145.00 |
| Contract Completion Date | 5 Jul 1996 | | |

| Submitted by (Signature & Title) | Administrative Review - Final Payments |
|---|---|
| M. O. Parker, Resident Engineer | |
| Approved by (Signature & Title) | Approved by - Final Payments |
| R. E. Barnes, Project Manager | |

Fisk Form 14-1

**Purpose:** Summary sheet presented to the City for approval of a Contractor's partial payment during construction.

**Prepared by:** Can be prepared by the Contractor directly, but usually is prepared by the Resident Project Representative from data provided by the Contractor.

**Directed to:** City, Construction Manager, and Project Manager/Engineer.

**Copies to:** Project Manager/Engineer; Contractor; Construction Manager; Resident Project Representative; City; Project Files.

**Comments:** This is a cap sheet, summarizing the itemized pay line items shown on Form 14–2 "Monthly Payment Estimate" breakdown sheets, which must be attached.

**FIGURE 16.2**   Contractor's payment request/approval summary sheet.

LAWRANCE, FISK & McFARLAND, INC.
CONSULTING CIVIL & ENVIRONMENTAL ENGINEERS
Santa Barbara, California

**MONTHLY PAYMENT ESTIMATE**

Project No. 95-130     Contract No. 95-9345     Sheet 1 of 1

Project Title Oakbrook Dam and Appurtenant Works    Contractor ABC Constructors, Inc.    Date 30 June 1995    Estimate No. 15

| PAY ITEM NO. | PAY ITEM | CONTRACT QUANTITY | UNIT | UNIT PRICE | ITEM TOTAL | THIS MONTH QUANTITY | EARNINGS | TO DATE QUANTITY | EARNINGS |
|---|---|---|---|---|---|---|---|---|---|
| 1 | Construction Facilities | --- | LS | --- | 700 000 00 | 0.7% | 4 900 00 | 84.9 % | 594 300 00 |
| 2 | Dewatering | --- | LS | --- | 400 000 00 | 1.25% | 5 000 00 | 77.5 % | 310 000 00 |
| 3 | General excavation | 707 800 | M3 | 2.00 | 1 415 600 00 | 1 191 | 2 382 00 | 498 892 | 497 784 00 |
| 4 | Structure excavation | 76 312 | M3 | 8.00 | 610 496 00 | | | | |
| 5 | Ditch excavation | 8 400 | M3 | 8.00 | 67 200 00 | | | | |
| 6 | Overhaul | 966 690 | M3/KM | 0.15 | 145 003 00 | — | | 510 507 | 76 576 05 |
| 7 | Compacted embankment | 236 400 | M3 | 1.00 | 236 400 00 | — | | 140 808 | 140 808 00 |
| 8 | 450 mm I.D. CMP | 120 | M | 10.00 | 1 200 00 | 26 | 260 00 | 26 | 260 00 |
| 9 | Soil cement | 776 | M3 | 10.00 | 7 760 00 | | | | |
| 10 | Structural concrete | 1 200 | M3 | 90.00 | 108 000 00 | | | | |
| 11 | Backfill concrete | 3 097 | M3 | 65.00 | 201 305 00 | 1 565 | 101 725 00 | 1 565 | 14 725 00 |
| 12 | Access road | --- | LS | --- | 500 000 00 | | | | |
| 13 | Misc. Concrete | 1 543 | M3 | 65.00 | 100 295 00 | — | | 1 013.5 | 65 877 50 |
| 14 | Steel Rebar | 289 475 | KG | 0.38 | 110 000 00 | | | 135 854 | 51 624 52 |
| 15 | Cement | 930 | TONN | 70.00 | 65 100 00 | 184.67 | 12 926 90 | 435 | 30 450 00 |
| 16 | Sump pump | 1 | EA | --- | 3 000 00 | 1 | 3 000 00 | 1 | 3 000 00 |
| | ORIGINAL CONTRACT TOTAL | | | | 4 671 360 00 | | | | |
| | | | | | | | | | |
| | CONTRACT CHANGE ORDERS | | | | | | | | |
| CO1 | Modify field ofc size | --- | LS | --- | <-10 210 00 | | | | <10 210 00> |
| CO2 | Extend 150 mm SN piping | --- | LS | --- | 3 995 00 | | | 3 995 | 3 995 00 |
| CO3 | Drainage modifications | --- | LS | --- | 145 000 00 | 21 % | 30 450 00 | 85 % | 123 250 00 |
| | TOTAL OF APPROVED C.O.'s TO DATE | | | | 138 785 00 | | | | |
| | TOTAL CONTRACT AMOUNT | | | | 4 810 145 00 | | | | |
| | TOTAL FOR WORK & MATLS INSTALLED | | | | | | 160 643 90 | | 2 484 440 07 |
| | | | | | | | | | |
| | MATLS DELIVERED & STORED ON SITE | | | | | | | | |
| 16 | SUMP PUMP | | EA | 1 575.35 | | — | — | 1 | 1 575 35 |
| 8 | 150 mm CMP | | M | 7.44 | | 26 | 194 74 | 52 | 389 48 |
| | TOTAL INVOICE AMT FOR MATLS STORED AT SITE | | | | | | 194 74 | | 1 964 83 |

*Data used are fictitious for illustration only*

**Purpose:** Itemizes work completed to date vs. amount during current pay period.

**Prepared by:** Resident Project Representative from data supplied by the Contractor.

**Directed to:** City, Construction Manager, and Project Manager/Engineer.

**Copies to:** City; Project Manager/Engineer; Construction Manager; Resident Project Representative; Contractor.

**Comments:** Type all pay items from bid sheet or allocation of contract price (Schedule of Values) Form 6–5, including original estimate quantities. Utilize this as a master sheet and reproduce sufficient copies for the entire program term. Each month pay quantities are entered and submitted along with Form 14–1 Monthly Payment Estimate Summary as supporting documentation for the payment requested.

**FIGURE 16.3**   Contractor's pay estimate.

to build the work, which when multiplied by the quantity shown in the engineer's estimate indicates the total amount of its bid for each item. In the example shown in the accompanying illustration (Figure 16.5), the bid sheets that the contractor must fill out to submit the bid already contain a typed-in quantity. The contractor then fills in the price that will be charged for each bid item.

The amount that the contractor shows in the "unit price" column is actually the firm bid. The amount under the "total" column is merely the product of the unit price bid multiplied by the *engineer's quantity estimate*. The actual amount of money that the contractor

## APPLICATION FOR PAYMENT NO. _____

To _____(OWNER)

Contract for _____ .

OWNER's Project No. _____ . ENGINEER's Project No. _____ .

For Work accomplished through the date of _____ .

| ITEM | CONTRACTOR's Schedule of Values | | | Work Completed | |
|------|---------|----------|--------|----------|--------|
|      | Unit Price | Quantity | Amount | Quantity | Amount |
|      | $ |          | $      |          | $      |
| Total (Orig. Contract) |  |  | $ |  | $ |
| C.O. No. 1 |  |  |  |  |  |
| C.O. No. 2 |  |  |  |  |  |

Accompanying Documentation:

_____

_____

_____

_____

GROSS AMOUNT DUE ...................... $_____

LESS _____% RETAINAGE ................... $_____

AMOUNT DUE TO DATE .................... $_____

LESS PREVIOUS PAYMENTS ............... $_____

AMOUNT DUE THIS APPLICATION . ...... $_____

CONTRACTOR'S Certification:

The undersigned CONTRACTOR certifies that (1) all previous progress payments received from OWNER on account of Work done under the Contract referred to above have been applied to discharge in full all obligations of CONTRACTOR incurred in connection with Work covered by prior Applications for Payment numbered 1 through _____inclusive; and (2) title to all materials and equipment incorporated in said Work or otherwise listed in or covered by this Application for Payment will pass to OWNER at time of payment free and clear of all liens, claims, security interests and encumbrances (except such as covered by Bond acceptable to OWNER).

Dated _____ , 19_____   _____
                                                    CONTRACTOR

                               By _____

Payment of the above AMOUNT DUE THIS APPLICATION is recommended.

Dated _____ , 19_____   _____
                                                    ENGINEER

                               By _____

EJCDC No. 1910-8-E (1983 Edition)

Prepared by the Engineers' Joint Contract Documents Committee and endorsed by The Associated General Contractors of America.

**FIGURE 16.4** EJCDC form of Application for Payment, to be used with payment request/approval form shown in Figure 16.1 or equivalent document. (Copyright © 1990 by National Society of Professional Engineers.)

---

**APPLICATION FOR PAYMENT**

**INSTRUCTIONS**

---

**A. GENERAL INFORMATION**

This standard form is intended as a guide only. Many projects require a much more extensive form with space for numerous items, descriptions of Change Orders, identification of variable quantity adjustments, summary of materials and equipment stored at the site and other information. It is expected that a separate form will be developed by Engineer or Contractor at the time Contractor's Schedule of Values is finalized. Note also that the format for retainage must be changed if the Agreement permits (or the Law provides), and Contractor elects, the deposit of securities in lieu of retainage. Refer to Article 14 of the General Conditions for provisions concerning payments to Contractor.

**B. COMPLETING THE FORM**

The Schedule of Values, submitted and approved as provided in paragraphs 2.6.3 and 2.9 of the General Conditions, should be copied in the space indicated on the Application For Payment form. Note that the cost of materials and equipment is often listed separately from the cost of their installation. All Change Orders affecting the Contract Price should be identified and include such supplemental Schedules of Values as required for progress payments.

The form is suitable for use in the Final Application for Payment as well as for Progress Payments; however, the required accompanying documentation is usually more extensive for final payment. All accompanying documentation should be identified in the space provided on the form.

**C. ENGINEER'S REVIEW**

Engineer *must* review all Applications for Payment with care to avoid recommending any payments not yet earned by Contractor. All accompanying documentation of legal nature, such as lien waivers, should be reviewed by an attorney, and Engineer should so advise Owner.

---

**FIGURE 16.4**   *continued*

will finally receive to do the work will be based on the actual *field-measured quantities, not* the quantities shown in the engineer's estimate. However, for the purposes of determining the lowest bid, the quantities shown in the engineer's estimate are used during the bidding so that all bids can be compared on the same basis.

On a cost-plus-fixed-fee project, the contractor agrees to a fixed profit level and is reimbursed for all costs of labor and material at their actual cost, plus the addition of a fixed fee rate for profit. Under this arrangement, the contractor's books must be open to the owner or its representative, and all of the contractor's costs must be regularly audited to establish the amount of progress payments.

### Schedule of Values versus Cost-Loaded CPM Schedule

Often, due to the unfamiliarity of the specification writer with the principles of contract administration, the contract documents ask for information from the contractor that is wholly inconsistent with the type of contract involved. For example, on unit-price contracts, all

# BID SCHEDULE

Schedule of Prices for Construction of

PORTER STREET IMPROVEMENTS

| Item No. | Description | Quantity and Unit | Unit Price | Amount |
|---|---|---|---|---|
| 1. | Excavation and removal of existing asphalt concrete and aggregate base | 1050 m³ | $ 3.92 | $ 4 116.00 |
| 2. | Asphalt concrete paving | 500 t | $ 31.30 | $ 15 650.00 |
| 3. | 6-in Class II Aggregate base | 1500 m² | $ 4.31 | $ 6 465.00 |
| 4. | Junction structure | 1 each | $ 2 000.00 | $ 2 000.00 |
| 5. | Reinforced concrete pipe 600 mm diameter | 120 m | $ 146.25 | $ 17 550.00 |
| 6. | Reinforced concrete headwall | Lump Sum | | $ 2 000.00 |

Data used are fictitious for illustration only

TOTAL $ 47 781.00

NOTE:

All amounts and totals in the Bid Schedule will be subject to verification by the Owner. In case of variation between the unit price and the total shown by the bidder, the unit price will be considered as the bid.

The quantities listed in the Bid Schedule are supplied to give an indication of the general scope of the Work, but the accuracy of these figure is not guaranteed and the bidder shall make his or her own estimates from the drawings.

\* \* \* \* \*

PROPOSAL FORMS
PAGE B-3

FIGURE 16.5    Unit-price bid.

prices are based upon an itemized list of all of the work items or tasks that must be performed under the contract, each with a unit price. In this manner the final price of any line item will simply be the product of the unit price times the actual quantity of that item that was installed or completed. Under this concept, the controlling price is the unit price of each item. Many get mixed up with lump-sum procedures and ask for a schedule of values as well. This is redundant, as the unit-price bid sheet *is* a schedule of values that is tendered with the contractor's original bid.

On a lump-sum project, however, the contractor agrees to do all the work that is defined in the plans and specifications for a fixed price, regardless of quantity variations that are not the result of owner or architect/engineer changes in the work. As a convenience, a schedule of values is invariably requested. In appearance, a schedule of values looks exactly like a unit-price bid, but with several significant differences; prices shown are for convenience in making monthly progress payments only and have no other contractual significance. They cannot legitimately be used to price change orders, for example.

Sometimes confusion results from requests for cost-loaded CPM networks under the assumption that they always result in easier payment administration. This may be true on a lump-sum project, but it has exactly the opposite effect on a unit-price contract, as the cost-loaded network activity items never coincide with the pay line items on unit-price contracts. Some guidelines are offered below:

### Unit-Price Contracts

1. Do *not* call for a cost-loaded CPM schedule; it will conflict with the line items on the unit-price bid sheet.
2. Do *not* call for a Schedule of Values; the original bid sheet serves this purpose.
3. A breakdown of all line items is submitted with the contractor's original bid and is binding for pay purposes throughout the job.

### Lump-Sum Contracts With Cost-Loaded CPM

1. Do *not* ask for a Schedule of Values; the cost-loaded CPM takes its place.
2. Request that a cost-loaded CPM be submitted after execution of the Agreement but before the end of the first pay period.

### Lump Sum Contracts Without Cost-Loaded CPM

1. Do *not* ask for a cost-loaded CPM schedule.
2. Do *not* ask for a bid breakdown with the bid.
3. Request a Schedule of Values after execution of the Agreement but before starting work on the project.

## EVALUATION OF CONTRACTOR'S PAYMENT REQUESTS

### Submittal Requirements

At a prearranged date each month, the contractor is expected to submit a request for payment for all of the work performed during the preceding month (Figure 16.2 or 16.4). Prior to forwarding these payment requests to the owner through the design firm or construction management firm for payment, the Resident Project Representative must check to assure that all items for which the contractor has claimed payment have actually been completed. If a project was contracted for on a lump-sum basis, a reasonable estimate of the fair value of the work that was accomplished might be very difficult, so under the terms of the General Conditions of the Contract for both the EJCDC and the AIA, the contractor is required to submit a schedule of values of the various portions of the work, including quantities where required, so that these values can be used as the basis for determining the amount of progress payments to be made to the contractor each month (see again Figure 11.7). The contractor is normally required to show evidence at the time of submittal of the price break-down that the pricing is correct, and that the total aggregate amount will equal the sum of the total contract amount. Each item should contain its own share of profit at overhead.

## Unit Price Contracts

If a project is based upon a unit-price bid, as many engineering contracts are, the actual unit prices stated in the original bid will be held as the basis for computation of all progress payment amounts. It is essential to note, however, that because a unit-price contract does not have a fixed price ceiling, but the final cost to the owner will be determined by the quantities actually completed, the determination of field quantities must be very precise. This is in direct contrast to the administration of a lump-sum contract, where even if a small error was made one month, it would be compensated for in later payments. The contractor cannot receive more money than the stated fixed price, even if some of the final quantities varied somewhat from the anticipated amounts. Under the concept of a lump-sum contract, the contractor agrees to build a complete project that will perform the intended function indicated in the plans and specifications. Anything that is necessary to accomplish this must be considered as part of the contract, even if not specifically stated. On a unit-price contract, however, the contractor may still be required to construct a complete functional project, but if any variation occurs in the quantities of any of the separate bid items listed, the contractor is entitled to an amount of money equal to the unit price of the bid item multiplied by the actual quantity of that item that was constructed or furnished. In this manner, if the quantity of a bid item exceeds what the original quantity estimate indicated, the contractor will receive more money than that shown in the bid; and if it is less than in the original bid, the amount received will be less than the amount of the bid. All such quantity differences must be based on the unit price stated by the contractor in the bid, as that alone is the controlling amount, not the extension obtained by multiplying the bid price by the anticipated quantity. The one notable exception to this rule is if the quantity overrun or underrun is in excess of 25 percent of the bid item. Then the contractor is entitled to renegotiate its unit price for the item. Although a 15 to 25 percent figure is frequently mentioned in contract documents, in situations where it was omitted, the principle of allowing a price renegotiation in cases in which the actual quantities differed from the anticipated quantities by over 25 percent has been upheld by some state courts. The Associated General Contractors (AGC), on the other hand, recommends a value of 15 percent.

Customary pay line items and units of measure under SI Metric are illustrated on the following pages.

## Equipment and Materials Delivered but Not Yet Used in the Work

The resident engineer or inspector should check the specifications carefully on this point before starting to total the amount of payment due the contractor. Often, certain fabricated items of equipment or certain products are delivered to the site a considerable amount of time before they are actually needed or installed in the work. In some contracts no payment will be made for any such material until it is actually used in the work (such as large pipe mains, which may not be paid for until they have been laid, jointed, backfilled, tested, and paved over; or large pieces of equipment such as motors, generators, valves, or steel plate fabrications that had to be made up especially for the project as opposed to an off-the-shelf item). A second approach to this problem is to allow partial payment for materials or equipment as soon as they have been delivered to the site. In any case, the decision is not for the Resident Project Representative to make, but must be determined by the provisions of the specifications.

Unit prices are often quoted for items as "installed-in-place." Wherever this is the case, it is not reasonable to allow full payment for any material solely on the basis of its having been delivered to the site. If the contract allows any payment at all, and the material is priced as in-place, the contractor should provide a copy of the invoice for the material to support its claim for payment of the delivery and storage of the material at the site. There is considerable justification for allowing some payment for certain types of materials, products, or equipment because the contractor is expected to pay the suppliers within 30 days after delivery in most cases. Thus, if a fabricated item such as mortar-lined-and-coated steel pipe, or precast prestressed roof members, or special pumps or large valves are ordered, there is often a long lead time required in placing the order to be certain of delivery in time. Often, when the item is actually delivered, the work may not yet be far enough along to allow its immediate installation; yet the contractor has already been obligated to make payment. Nevertheless, there is nothing that the inspector can do to alleviate the problem except to read the provisions of the specifications carefully to make certain that such payments can be made under the terms of the contract. It can save a lot of arguments if the inspector can show the contractor the provisions of the specifications that control such payments.

A word of caution at this point. As long as a contract is based upon a lump-sum price, or as long as a unit-price contract shows separate line items for a material and its installation, no particular problem exists other than a need to exercise care in evaluating the amount of work and materials claimed for payment. However, on a unit-price contract where a single line item covers both the cost of the material and its installation, a serious risk of overpayment exists.

Take the example of an underground pipeline under a roadway. Often, a single price may be quoted to cover the cost of the pipe and its installation, including all earthwork and even the pavement over the trench, as would be the case for item 5 in the bid sheet shown in Figure 16.5. In such cases, the price per linear foot of completed pipeline already includes the price of the pipe material. If early payment was allowed for pipe that was delivered to the site but not yet installed, the cost of the pipe would have to be subtracted from the price claimed later for construction of the pipeline in place; otherwise, the contractor would be receiving payment twice for the same pipe.

## Payment for Extra Work and Change Orders

Although in a unit-price contract a prearranged value has been established for each item of work to facilitate the determination of the amount owed to the contractor, and on a lump-sum job, a bid breakdown is often requested to establish a fair price for any work completed, as a means of arriving at the amount to be paid for each monthly progress payment, the cost of extra work that was not included in the original contract must be negotiated separately or a fair method agreed upon for determining its value.

Obviously, if no groundwork were laid to establish a procedure for evaluating and determining the cost of such extra work, the contractor would have the owner "over a barrel," so to speak. Thus, it is common in all standard forms of the General Conditions of a construction contract to specify the means of determining such costs. It should be kept in mind, however, that not all General Conditions treat this subject area in the same way. Many such documents, because they must be universally acceptable, have been so watered down in their provisions that extensive Supplementary General Conditions must be prepared to adapt these provisions to a particular job.

General Conditions documents such as the AIA General Conditions advocate the principle of completing such work on a cost-plus basis with "a reasonable allowance for overhead and profit." Unfortunately, what is reasonable to the contractor may not be considered as reasonable by the owner. Most of the General Conditions used by public agencies for their own use have established fixed policies, and their General Conditions reflect this. An example can be seen in the provisions of the EJCDC *Standard General Conditions of the Construction Contract* for changes in contract price and time shown in Figures 16.6 and 16.7, where a maximum of 15 percent of the actual cost of the work is allowed to cover the cost of general overhead and profit.

Similar, but sometimes considerably more comprehensive, are the provisions for overhead and profit allocation of the various state department of transportation standard specifications for change orders or force account work. The markups involve a percentage added to the cost of labor, which generally varies from agency to agency but is usually 15, 20, 24, or 33 percent, with 20 percent as the most frequently allowed markup. An additional markup of 15 percent is generally applied to the cost of materials and another 15 percent to the equipment rental. Most agencies also allow the general contractor to mark up first-tier subcontractor bids by 5 percent, with no markup allowed for second-tier or lower subcontractors.

As it can be determined from the provisions shown in the accompanying examples, some questions may still be unanswered and are thus subject to negotiation at the time of the owner's incurring the cost of extra work. If all the possible contingencies and conditions could be anticipated, then and only then could a document be produced that would provide a definite answer to any question relating to the cost of such extra work. Obviously, this is an impossible task.

As a part of the contractor's payment request, if extra work authorized by the issuance of a valid change order was completed during the payment period, the resident engineer or inspector must not only evaluate the regular bid items and quantities, but also, under the terms of the specific contract documents controlling the project, must determine the validity of the claims of the contractor for the amount of money claimed for completing such ex-

ARTICLE 10 - CHANGES IN THE WORK; CLAIMS

*10.01 Authorized Changes in the Work*

A. Without invalidating the Agreement and without notice to any surety, OWNER may, at any time or from time to time, order additions, deletions or revisions in the Work by Written Amendment, a Change Order, or a Work Change Directive. Upon receipt of any such document, CONTRAC- TOR shall promptly proceed with the Work involved which will be performed under the applica- ble conditions of the Contract Documents (except as otherwise specifically provided).

B. If OWNER and CONTRACTOR are unable to agree on entitlement to, or on the amount or ex- tent, if any, of an adjustment in the Contract Price or Contract Times, or both, that should be al- lowed as a result of a Work Change Directive, a Claim may be made therefor as provided in paragraph 10.05.

*10.02. Unauthorized Changes in the Work*

A. CONTRACTOR shall not be entitled to an increase in the Contract Price or an extension of the Contract Times with respect to any work performed that is not required by the Contract Documents as amended, modified or supplemented as provided in paragraph 3.04, except in the case of an emergency as provided in paragraph 6.16 or in the case of uncovering Work as provided in paragraph 13.04.B.

*10.03. Execution of Change Orders*

A. OWNER and CONTRACTOR shall execute appropriate Change Orders recommended by EN- GINEER (or Written Amendments) covering:

   1. changes in the Work which are: (i) ordered by OWNER pursuant to paragraph 10.01.A, (ii) required because of acceptance of defective Work under paragraph 13.08.A or OWNER's correction of defective Work under paragraph 13.09, or (iii) agreed to by the parties;

   2. changes in the Contract Price or Contract Times which are agreed to by the parties; and

   3. changes in the Contract Price or Contract Times which embody the substance of any writ- ten decision rendered by ENGINEER pursuant to paragraph 10.05; provided that, in lieu of executing any such Change Order, an appeal may be taken from any such decision in ac- cordance with the provisions of the Contract Documents and applicable Laws and Regulations, but during any such appeal, CONTRACTOR shall carry on the Work and ad- here to the progress schedule as provided in paragraph 6.18.A.

*10.04. Notification to Surety or Insurer*

A. If notice of any change affecting the general scope of the Work or the provisions of the Contract Documents (including, but not limited to, Contract Price or Contract Times) is required by the provisions of any Bond to be given to a surety or by the provisions of any insurance pol- icy to be given to any insurer, the giving of any such notice will be CONTRACTOR's responsi- bility. The amount of each applicable Bond will be adjusted to reflect the effect of any such change.

**FIGURE 16.6**   Example of provisions for Changes in the Work from EJCDC Standard General Conditions of the Construction Contract 1910-8(1995). Copyright © 1995 by the National Society of Professional Engineers.

tra work. In each case, the inspector should consult the project manager of the design firm or the owner to determine the exact terms of the agreement that cover the construction of such extra work, and apply these terms to the evaluation. In any case, the terms of the con- tract General Conditions should be followed carefully, as they form the basis for any spe-

10.05. Claims and Disputes

A. Notice: Written notice stating the general nature of each Claim, dispute or other matter shall be delivered by the claimant to ENGINEER and the other party to the Contract promptly (but in no event later than thirty days) after the start of the event giving rise thereto. Notice of the amount or extent of the Claim, dispute or other matter with supporting data shall be delivered to the EN-GINEER and the other party to the Contract within sixty days after the start of such event (unless allows additional time for claimant to submit additional or more accurate data in support of such Claim, dispute, or other matter). A Claim for an adjustment in Contract Price shall be prepared in accordance with the provisions of paragraph 12.01.B. A Claim for an adjustment in Contract Time shall be prepared in accordance with the provisions of paragraph 12.02.B. Each Claim shall be accompanied by claimant's written statement that the adjustment claimed is the entire adjustment to which the claimant believes it is entitled as a result of said event. The opposing party shall submit any response to ENGINEER and the claimant within thirty days after receipt of the claimant's last submittal (unless ENGINEER allows additional time).

B. *ENGINEER's Decision:* ENGINEER will render a formal decision in writing within thirty days after receipt of the last submittal of the claimant or the last submittal of the opposing party, if any ENGINEER's written decision on such Claim, dispute, or other matter will be final and binding upon OWNER and CONTRACTOR unless:

   1. an appeal from ENGINEER's decision is taken within the time limits and in accordance with the dispute resolution procedures set forth in Article 16, or

   2. if no such dispute resolution procedures have been set forth in Article 16, a written notice of intention to appeal from ENGINEER's written decision is delivered by OWNER or CON-TRACTOR to the other and to ENGINEER within thirty days after the date of such decision and a formal proceeding is instituted by the appealing party in a forum of competent jurisdiction, within sixty days after the date of such decision or within sixty days after Substantial Completion, whichever is later (unless otherwise agreed in writing by OWNER and CON-TRACTOR), to exercise such rights or remedies as the appealing party may have with respect to such Claim, dispute, or other matter in accordance with applicable Laws and Regulations.

C. No claim for an adjustment in Contract Price or Contract Times (or Milestones) will be valid if not submitted in accordance with this paragraph 10.05.

**FIGURE 16.6** *continued*

cific agreement with the owner for establishing the costs of extra work (Figure 16.6 and 16.7.).

Whenever extra work is being performed under the terms of the contract, the Resident Project Representative should keep a daily record of all such work performed and materials furnished for use in checking the contractor's payment requests. Such a record may also be of considerable value in the settlement of claims. A simplified way of documenting such costs is to utilize a daily extra work report designed for this purpose, as illustrated in Figure 16.8.

## PAYMENT FOR MOBILIZATION COSTS

There seems to be an unjustifiable amount of controversy surrounding the concept of allowing a "mobilization" payment to a contractor. By definition, mobilization costs are those

ARTICLE 12 - CHANGE OF CONTRACT PRICE; CHANGE OF CONTRACT TIME

*12.01. Change of Contract Price*

A. The Contract Price may only be changed by a Change Order or by a Written Amendment. Any Claim for an adjustment in the Contract Price shall be based on written notice submitted by the party making the claim to the ENGINEER and the other party to the Contract in accordance with the provisions of paragraph 10.05.

B. The value of any Work covered by a Change Order or of any Claim for an adjustment in the Contract Price will be determined as follows:

1. where the Work involved is covered by unit prices contained in the Contract Documents, by application of such unit prices to the quantities of the items involved (subject to the provisions of paragraph 11.03); or

2. where the Work involved is not covered by unit prices contained in the Contract Documents, by a mutually agreed lump sum (which may include an allowance for overhead and profit not necessarily in accordance with paragraph 12.01.C.2); or

3. where the Work involved is not covered by unit prices contained in the Contract Documents and agreement to a lump sum is not reached under paragraph 12.01.B.2, on the basis of the Cost of the Work (determined as provided in paragraph 11.01) plus a CONTRACTOR's fee for overhead and profit (determined as provided in paragraph 12.01.C).

C. CONTRACTOR's Fee: The CONTRACTOR's fee for overhead and profit shall be determined as follows:

1. a mutually acceptable fixed fee; or

2. if a fixed fee is not agreed upon, then a fee based on the following percentages of the various portions of the Cost of the Work:

   a. for costs incurred under paragraphs 11.01.A.1 and 11.01.A.2, the CONTRACTOR's fee shall be fifteen percent;[1]

   b. for costs incurred under paragraph 11.01.A.3, the CONTRACTOR's fee shall be five percent;

   c. where one or more tiers of subcontracts are on the basis of Cost of the Work plus a fee and no fixed fee is agreed upon, the intent of paragraph 12.01.C.2.a is that the Subcontractor who actually performs the Work, at whatever tier, will be paid a fee of fifteen percent of the costs incurred by such Subcontractor under paragraphs 11.01.A.I and 11.01.A.2 and that any higher tier Subcontractor and CONTRACTOR will each be paid a fee of five percent of the amount paid to the next lower tier Subcontractor;

   d. no fee shall be payable on the basis of costs itemized under paragraphs 11.01.A.4, 11.01.A.5 and 11.01.B;

   e. the amount of credit to be allowed by CONTRACTOR to OWNER for any change which results in a net decrease in cost will be the amount of the actual net decrease in cost plus a deduction in CONTRACTOR's fee by an amount equal to five percent of such net decrease; and

   f. when both additions and credits are involved in any one change, the adjustment in CONTRACTOR's fee shall be computed on the basis of the net change in accordance with paragraphs 12.01.C.2.a through 12.01.C.2.e, inclusive.

[1]Seems low by Western standards, where the labor allowance is seldom less than 20 percent, but ranges as high as 35 percent on some DOT work. In addition, fifteen percent is generally allowed for materials with another 15 percent allowed for equipment. Subcontractor markups under those contracts are usually limited to 5 percent for the first tier and no allowance for second tier subcontractors or below.

**FIGURE 16.7**   Provisions for payments for Extra Work from the EJCDC Standard General Conditions of the Construction Contract 1910-8(1995). Copyright © 1995 by the National Society of Professional Engineers.

E. R. FISK & ASSOCIATES
PO Box 6448 • Orange, CA 92613-6448

**DAILY WORK REPORT**

PROJECT TITLE __PARK ANNEX LIFT STATION__

PROJECT NO. __F 293__ LOCATION __CITY OF MERCED, CA__

WORK PERFORMED BY __ABC CONSTRUCTORS, INC.__

DESCRIPTION OF WORK __HAUL & ERECT CONSTRUCTION SIGNS__

DATE PERFORMED __7 AUG 1989__

DATE OF REPORT __9 AUG 1989__

REPORT NO. __49__

AMOUNT AUTHORIZED $ _____

PREVIOUS EXPENDITURE $ __0__

TODAY $ _____

TO DATE $ _____

CONTRACTOR JOB NO. __87-0157__

CONTRACTOR REPORT NO. _____

| Equip. No. | Equipment | Hours | Hourly Rate | Extended Amounts | P.R. No. | Labor | Hours | | Hourly Rate | Extended Amounts |
|---|---|---|---|---|---|---|---|---|---|---|
| 222 | FLATRACK 19,500 GVW | 8 (10) | 22 80 | 228 00 | | TRUCK DRIVER PAUL MILLIGAN | O.T. Reg. | 8 | 17 25 | 138 00 |
| 111 | PICKUP UNDER 12,000 GVW | 6 (10) | 13 05 | 130 50 | | LABOR FOREMAN JOHN RUSSELL | O.T. Reg. | 6 | 16 44 | 98 64 |
| R-1 | HAND-HELD AUGER UNDER 5-HP | 1-DAY | PER DAY | 6 65 | | LABORER KAHN M TRAN | O.T. Reg. | 8 | 15 94 | 127 52 |
| | | | | | | LABORER GUADALUPE RODRIGUEZ | O.T. Reg. | 6 | 15 94 | 95 64 |
| | Data used are fictitious for illustration only | | | | | LABORER GERALD MADLEY | O.T. Reg. | 6 | 15 94 | 95 64 |
| | | | | 365 15 | | | O.T. Reg. | | | |

MATERIAL and/or WORK done by specialists

| Description | No. Unit | Unit Cost | | |
|---|---|---|---|---|
| LUMBER & HARDWARE SEE ATTACHED INVOICE #27104 | | 225 55 | 225 55 | |

SUB TOTAL __555 44__

Added Percentage – (See Special Conditions) _____ 16% __88 87__

Subsistence _____ No _____ @$ _____

Travel Expense _____ No _____ @$ _____

Other _____

TOTAL COST OF LABOR A __644 31__

B __590 70__

TOTAL COST OF EQUIPMENT, MATERIALS AND WORK

DISTRIBUTION 1. Proj. Mgr. 2. Field Office 3. File

For Office Use Only
Pd. on est. no. _____
Checked by _____

__20__ % ON LABOR COST (A) __128 86__

__15__ % ON EQUIP., MAT'L AND WORK COST (B) __88 61__

TOTAL THIS REPORT __1,452 48__

Submitted – Contractor _____

Recommended – Res. Proj. Representative _____

Wiley-Fisk Form 15-5

**FIGURE 16.8** Record of contractor's costs of extra work, disputed work, delayed work, emergency work, or similar activities for use in computing payments or for defense against claims. (From *Construction Engineer's Complete Handbook of Forms* by Edward Fisk. Copyright © 1992 by Prentice Hall. Reprinted by permission of Prentice Hall.)

initial expenditures that a contractor is obligated to make even before qualifying for a penny of progress payments. It includes the setting up of the field offices; delivering equipment to the job site; obtaining bonds, insurance, and permits; and similar costs. On a heavy construction job the cost can be very large.

Those who naively suggest that it is solely the contractor's problem fail to realize that nothing that the contractor is obligated to do on your project is going to be provided to the owner in the form of a donation. Failure to provide a line item for payment of mobilization simply forces the contractor to prorate its cost over all of the earliest items of construction to get as early a return on its investment as possible. Unfortunately, this also means that the bids will be unbalanced to show a disproportionately high unit cost on many early construction items. Then, in case of a quantity overrun on those items, the owner will be paying a higher cost for the project than is necessary.

It is therefore sensible to provide for payment of mobilization to a contractor as a separate line item. But as we all know, any contracting firm worth its salt will take every opportunity to inflate the unit prices of all first items of construction to obtain front money. Then, if the mobilization item is left open as a competitively bid item, a serious imbalance could result. The solution is simple; include a line item for *mobilization* but type in a fixed *allowance* on the bid sheet for this item. Then every bidder will be able to include the fixed amount of this allowance as a part of its bid, but will be unable to inflate it.

The author once experienced a case involving two earth dams, where the owner's representatives were not very sophisticated in construction contract administration. Initially, they opposed the concept of any mobilization payment but were later convinced that failure to do so on a project involving extensive amounts of heavy earthmoving equipment could have a serious effect on the unit prices of the remaining bid items. The author had careful cost estimates made to show the probable real cost to the contractor of mobilization for each of the dams and included $50 000 for the larger structure and $25 000 for the smaller dam. The amounts involved so shocked the owner's representatives that they insisted upon leaving the mobilization amount blank and calling for competitive bids on the mobilization item. Unfortunately, the local contractors who bid the project took advantage of the situation, as one might expect, and the low bidder on the project had listed $100 000 for mobilization for the larger dam and $75 000 for the smaller one. Thus, the retainage normally collected by the owner became a farce. The contractor was well ahead of the game financially as soon as the first payment was received at the end of the first month of operations.

Some other difficulties have been experienced in the payment of mobilization, too, and perhaps that is one of the reasons for the frequent negative reactions to such payments by architect/engineers. This is the fact that by failure to specify what constitutes "mobilization," the architect/engineer is placed in the position of making a full payment for this line item at the end of the month without even being fully aware of whether or not it had been fully earned.

The solution is simple. Itemize everything in the specification that will be defined as mobilization and then either prorate the mobilization payment at the end of the month for failure to complete all of the listed items, or as the author prefers, provide a lump-sum payment for completion of all of the mobilization items, complete, to qualify for payment of the lump-sum amount for the item.

Although the list of legitimate mobilization items will vary widely from job to job, there are certain basic items of interest to the architect/engineer firm that they may well find it to their advantage to list as required mobilization items. For example, the author has often experienced delays in setting up the engineer's field office and telephone service. If these items were included as mobilization items included in a lump-sum quantity of work that must be completed before the contractor can qualify for any of its mobilization payment amount, there would be more of a tendency on the part of the contractor to meet the required schedule.

Figure 16.9 is a sample specification provision for mobilization that is provided as a guide for the development of similar provisions in the specific job specifications of applicable lump-sum projects. On unit-price projects, a separate specification section entitled "Mobilization" is not used; instead, the provisions of for mobilization are included in the section entitled "Measurement and Payment." The user is cautioned that the example shown in Figure 16.9 may not be suitable for all types of projects in its present form, but

SECTION 01500 - MOBILIZATION

1.01 GENERAL

A. Mobilization shall include the obtaining of all bonds, insurance, and permits; moving onto the site of all plant and equipment; and the furnishing and erecting of plants, temporary buildings, and other construction facilities; all as required for the proper performance and completion of the Work. Mobilization shall include but not be limited to the following principal items:

   1. Moving on to the site of all Contractor's plant and equipment required for first month's operations.

   2. Installing temporary construction power, wiring, and lighting facilities per Section 01510.

   3. Establishing fire protection system per Section 01510.

   4. Developing and installing construction water supply per Section 01510.

   5. Providing field office trailers for the Contractor and the Architect/Engineer, complete with all specified furnishings and utility services including telephones, telephone appurtenances, and copying machines per Section 01550.

   6. Providing all on-site communication facilities as specified per Section 01510.

   7. Providing on-site sanitary facilities and potable water facilities as specified per Section 01510.

   8. Furnishing, installing, and maintaining all storage buildings or sheds required for temporary storage of products, equipment, or materials that have not yet been installed in the Work. All such storage shall meet manufacturer's specified storage requirements, and the specific provisions of the specifications, including temperature and humidity control, if recommended by the manufacturer, and for all security per Section 01600.

   9. Arranging for and erection of Contractor's work and storage yard per Section 01550.

   10. Obtaining and paying for all required permits.

   11. Posting all OSHA required notices and establishment of safety programs.

   12. Have the Contractor's superintendent at the job site full time. (See Article 6 of the General Conditions)

**FIGURE 16.9**  Sample provisions for specifying mobilization in lump sum contracts.

may require editing to fit the requirements of each project. The following list sums up two important differences between lump-sum and unit-price projects.

### Lump-Sum Projects

1. Mobilization terms must be in a separate technical section. Mobilization may be computed as a percentage of project cost.

2. Do *not* include a Section for Measurement and Payment; this is inconsistent with the lump-sum payment principle and does not apply to the Schedule of Values.

13. Submittal of detailed *Preliminary Construction Schedule* for Architect/Engineer's approval within 7 days after execution of the Agreement per Section 01310.

14. Submittal of *Initial Construction Schedule*, embodying all corrections required by the Engineer, within 25 days of date of Notice to Proceed. No payment for Mobilization can be made until this has been approved and submitted per Section 01310.

15. Planning and submittal of proposed design for a Project Sign in accordance with Section 01300, and fabrication and erection of the approved Project Sign in accordance with the requirements of Section 01580.

16. Submittal of a Preliminary Schedule of Values in accordance with the requirements of Article 14.1 of the General Conditions and Section 01300 of the Technical Specifications within 7 days following the date of Notice to Proceed.

B. In addition to the requirements specified above, all submittals shall conform to the applicable requirements of Section 01300 "Contractor Submittals."

1.02 PAYMENT FOR MOBILIZATION

A. The Contractor's attention is directed to the condition that [5][8] per-cent of the total Contract Price will be deducted from any money due the Contractor as initial progress payments until all mobilization items listed above have been completed as specified. The aforementioned amount will be retained by the Owner as the agreed, estimated value of completing all of the mobilization items listed. Any such retention of money for failure to complete all such mobilization items as a lump-sum item shall be in addition to the retention of any payments due to the Contractor as specified in Article 14 of the General Conditions.

B. Payment for mobilization will be made in the form of a single, lump-sum, non-proratable allowance determined by the Architect/Engineer, and no part thereof will be approved for payment under the Contract until all mobilization items listed above have been completed as specified.

**FIGURE 16.9**   *continued*

### Unit-Price Projects

1. Mobilization terms are appropriately covered as a part of Measurement and Payment. Mobilization is included for payment as a separate pay line in the Bid Sheet, with an engineer-determined lump-sum allowance shown in the extension column.

2. Do *not* include a section entitled "Mobilization," as all mobilization terms must be covered in the Measurement and Payment section.

On unit-price contracts where mobilization is included as a bid item, instead of including a section entitled "Mobilization," the measurement and payment section is used to specify the terms and conditions under which the initial payment will be made to the contractor. Figure 16.10 provides an example from a measurement and payment section (the list of 16 required items have been omitted for convenience). In a final specification, the provisions would include the same list as contained in the lump-sum version, except that item 16 is deleted, as there is no requirement for a schedule of values in a unit-price project.

```
SECTION 01028 - MEASUREMENT AND PAYMENT

PART 1 - GENERAL

1.01 SCOPE

A. Payment for the various items of the Bid Sheets, as further specified
   herein, shall include all compensation to be received by the Contractor
   for furnishing all tools, equipment, supplies, and manufactured articles,
   and for all labor, operations, and incidentals appurtenant to the items of
   work being described, as necessary to complete the various items of work
   as specified and shown on the drawings, including all appurtenances
   thereto, and including all costs of compliance with the regulations of
   public agencies having jurisdiction and the Occupational Safety and Health
   Administration of the U.S. Department of Labor (OSHA). No separate payment
   will be made for any item that is not specifically set forth in the Bid
   Sheet(s), and all costs therefor shall be included in the prices named in
   the Bid Sheet(s) for the various appurtenant items of work.

PART 2 - PAYMENT SCHEDULE

2.01 BID SCHEDULE

A. All pay line items will be paid for at the unit prices named in the Bid
   Sheets for the respective items of work. The quantities of work or mater-
   ial stated as unit price items on the Bid Sheets are supplied only to give
   an indication of the general scope of the Work; the owner does not ex-
   pressly nor by implication agree that the actual amount of work or mater-
   ial will correspond therewith, and reserves the right after award to in-
   crease or decrease the quantity of any unit price item of work by an
   amount up to and including 25 percent of any bid item, without a change in
   the unit price, and shall have the right to delete any bid item in its en-
   tirety, or to add additional bid items up to and including an aggregate
   total amount not to exceed 25 percent of the contract price.
B. Quantity variations in excess of the allowable quantity changes specified
   herein shall be subject to the provisions of Article 10 of the General
   Conditions.
```

**FIGURE 16.10**   Sample provisions for specifying mobilization in unit price contracts (*continued on p. 404*).

## PARTIAL PAYMENTS TO THE CONTRACTOR

### *Waiver of Lien Procedure*

Liens exist throughout the United States, but they are not uniform from state to state. As a means of providing some measure of owner protection in the enforcement of contractor and supplier lien rights, many states have enacted preliminary notice requirements (see "Preliminary Notice of Potential Claim" in Chapter 19).

Although it is common to require only a monthly pay estimate from the contractor as a prerequisite to payment, without any specific assurance that the subcontractors and suppliers have been paid for their work, the practice of requiring partial waivers of lien from the prime contractor and all of its subcontractors and suppliers prior to release of partial

2.02 MOBILIZATION (Bid Item No. 1)

A. Measurement for payment for mobilization will be based upon completion of such work as a lump sum, non-proratable pay item, and shall require completion of all of the listed items during the first 25 days following Notice to Proceed.

B. Payment for Mobilization will be made at the lump sum allowance named in the Bid Sheets under Item No. 1, which price shall constitute full compensation for all such work. Payment for mobilization will be made in the form of a single, lump-sum, non-proratable payment, no part of which will be approved for payment under the Contract until all mobilization items listed herein have been completed as specified. The scope of the work included under Pay Item No. 1 shall include the obtaining of all bonds, insurance, and permits; moving onto the site of all plant and equipment; and the furnishing and erecting of plants, temporary buildings, and other construction facilities; all as required for the proper performance and completion of the Work. Mobilization shall include but not be limited to the following principal items:

C. In addition to the requirements specified above, all submittals shall conform to the applicable requirements of Section 01300 Contractor Submittals.

D. No payment for any of the listed mobilization work items will be made until all of the listed items have been completed to the satisfaction of the Engineer.

E. The aforementioned amount will be retained by the Owner as the agreed, estimated value of completing all of the mobilization items listed. Any such retention of money for failure to complete all such mobilization items as a lump-sum item shall be in addition to the retention of any payments due to the Contractor as specified in Article 14 of the General Conditions.

**FIGURE 16.10**   *continued*

payments seems to be gaining ground (Figures 16.11 and 16.12). An attorney should be consulted to ascertain how the procedure may be implemented in each state.

The practice of requiring partial waivers of lien from the prime contractor and each of the subcontractors and suppliers based upon current payment requests, however, imposes harsh penalties upon each of those parties by requiring the prime contractor to pay its subcontractors and suppliers prior to having been paid by the owner, or by requiring the subcontractors and suppliers to waive their lien rights before being paid by the prime contractor, for the prime contractor to receive payment from the owner. The capital required by the prime contractor to pay its subcontractors and suppliers prior to obtaining waivers is quite substantial, and such a practice is unfair to the prime contractor. As a result, the subcontractors and suppliers are frequently pressured into releasing their waivers of lien to the prime contractor without having received payment for the work covered by that specific release and without further assurance that they will be paid when the prime contractor receives payment from the owner.

The Construction Industry Affairs Committee of Chicago studied the problem and offered the following recommendations. The first payment request should be accompanied by the prime contractor's partial waiver of lien only. Each subsequent partial payment should

**CONDITIONAL WAIVER
AND RELEASE UPON PROGRESS PAYMENT**
[California Civil Code §3262(d)1 amended 1993]

Upon receipt by the undersigned of a check from _____

(Maker of Check)

in the sum of $_____ payable to _____

(Amount of Check)                                      (Payee or Payees of Check)

and when the check has been properly endorsed and has been paid by the bank upon which it is drawn , this document shall become effective to release any mechanic's lien, stop notice, or bond right the undersigned has on the job of

_____ located at _____

(Owner)                                                    (Job Description)

to the following extent. This release covers a progress payment for labor, services, equipment, or material furnished to

_____ through _____

(Your Customer)                                        (Date)

only and does not cover any retentions retained before or after the release date; extras furnished before the release date for which payment has not been received; extras or items furnished after the release date. Rights based upon work performed or items furnished under written change order which has been fully executed by the parties prior to the release date are covered by this release unless specifically reserved by the claimant in this release. This release of any mechanic's lien, stop notice, or bond right shall not otherwise affect the contract rights, including rights between parties to the contract based upon a rescission, abandonment, or breach of the contract, or the right of the undersigned to recover compensation for furnished labor, services, equipment, or material covered by this release if that furnished labor, services, equipment, or material was not compensated by the progress payment. Before any recipient of the document relies on it, said party should verify evidence of payment to the undersigned.

Dated_____          _____

(Company Name)

By_____

(Title)

PALM SPRINGS
U-00695

**FIGURE 16.11**   Conditional waiver of lien for progress payment.

## UNCONDITIONAL WAIVER
## AND RELEASE UPON PROGRESS PAYMENT

[California Civil Code §3262(d)2 amended 1993]

The undersigned has been paid and has received a progress payment in the sum of:

$ _1,275.25_    for labor, services, equipment, and material Furnished to:

_XYZ CONSTRUCTORS, INC._
(Your customer)

on the job of _CITY OF PALM SPRINGS_
(Owner)

located at _RAMON ROAD_
(Job Description)

and does hereby waive and release any mechanic's lien, stop notice, or bond right that the undersigned has on the above referenced job to the following extent. This release covers a progress payment for labor, services, equipment, or material furnished to:

_XYZ CONSTRUCTORS, INC._    through _26 JUNE 1995_

only and does not cover any retentions retained before or after the release date; extras furnished before the release date for which payment has not been received; extras or items furnished after the release date. Rights based upon work performed or items furnished under a written change order which has been fully executed by the parties prior to the release date are covered by this release unless specifically reserved by the claimant in this release. This release of any mechanic's lien, stop notice, or bond right shall not otherwise affect the contract rights, including rights between parties to the contract based upon a rescission, abandonment, or breach of the contract, or the right of the undersigned to recover compensation for furnished labor, services, equipment, or material covered by this release if that furnished labor, services, equipment, or material was not compensated by the progress payment.

Dated _3 JULY 1995_        _ABC PAVING CONTRACTORS, INC._
(Company Name)

By _____
(Title)

**NOTICE TO PERSONS SIGNING THIS WAIVER: THIS DOCUMENT WAIVES RIGHTS UNCONDITIONALLY AND STATES THAT YOU HAVE BEEN PAID FOR GIVING UP THOSE RIGHTS. THIS DOCUMENT IN ENFORCEABLE AGAINST YOU IF YOU SIGN IT, EVEN IF YOU HAVE NOT BEEN PAID. IF YOU HAVE NOT BEEN PAID, USE A CONDITIONAL RELEASE FORM.**

Data used are fictitious for illustration only

**FIGURE 16.12**   Unconditional waiver of lien for progress payment.

then be accompanied by the prime contractor's partial waiver and the partial waivers of all subcontractors and suppliers who were included in the *immediately preceding payment request,* to the extent of that payment. Thus, the prime contractor must submit waivers on a current basis, but the subcontractors and suppliers may not be more than one payment late with their partial waivers. Request for final payment would then be accompanied by the final waivers from the prime contractor, the subcontractors, and the suppliers who had not previously furnished such waivers.

Under this procedure, the owner is afforded considerable protection. The owner will not be asked to make final payment until all necessary waivers have been received; the prime contractor will not be asked to make advance payments to secure waivers; and the subcontractors and suppliers will not be placed in a position of surrendering their legal rights without proper consideration.

Copies of sample forms for partial waiver of lien are shown in Figures 16.11 and 16.12. An attorney should be consulted before use, as lien laws vary from state to state.

## Total Cost Pricing of Change Orders

Contractors are sometimes allowed to use the so-called "total cost method" for pricing change orders or delayed work. This approach compares the bid price of the work as bid with the actual cost of doing the work, and charges the increase to the project owner. It is permitted in situations where (1) the nature of the claim makes it very difficult to establish a price within a reasonable degree of accuracy, (2) the contractor's bid price was realistic, (3) the contractor's actual costs were realistic, (4) the contractor's actual costs were reasonable, and (5) the contractor was not responsible for any of the increased costs.

The use of the total cost method reduces the contractor's obligation to link specific costs to specific causes, but it in no way eliminates the need for accurate record keeping. Without good job records, it is impossible to judge how reasonable the contractor's alleged actual costs are or to compare those costs with the original bid. If the cost records are inadequate or nonexistent, a court will not allow the contractor to use the total cost method for pricing its claim [*Appeal of J.D. Abrams, Inc.,* ENG BCA No. 4332 (November 28, 1988)].

## Forward Pricing of Change Orders

Project owners sometimes ask contractors to "forward price" change order work. That is, establish a mutually agreed lump-sum price increase for doing the changed work. The advantage for contractors is that they are relieved of the need to maintain detailed, segregated cost records. The disadvantage is that a misjudgment may prove costly. If unanticipated factors, such as delay and schedule impact drive the costs up, the contractor will still be limited to the agreed-upon fixed-price increase. In such a case, the contractor may wish it had gone to the trouble of tracking and documenting actual costs.

It should be emphasized that a contractor cannot be forced to forward-price change order work. A contractor's refusal to submit to a nonbinding change order estimate or cost proposal may be considered as a breach of contract [*Palmer & Sicard, Inc.,* v. United States, 6Cl.Ct.232(1934)]. A contractor cannot be forced to sign off on a forward-priced change order [*Appeal of Centex Construction Co.,* Inc., ASBCA No. 26830 (April 29, 1983).

## RETAINAGE

The majority of construction projects, particularly public works projects, involve some retention of a portion of earned funds of the contractor. Typically, this has been 10 percent, although 5 percent is not uncommon. In some cases, the retained funds are held throughout the life of the job; in other cases, the amount may be reduced or actually eliminated at some point after the midpoint of the project.

The purpose of the retention of funds is to provide an amount of money that can be available to the owner for the satisfaction of lien claims because of the failure of the prime contractor to pay its subcontractors or suppliers, and as a means of holding the profit that the contractor makes on a given project. In case of default by the contractor, these funds may be utilized by the surety to complete the work.

There is some dispute over the validity of the concept involved, as a project that is protected by payment and performance bonds is already secured against such claims. Because of this, there has been some consideration in recent years to reduce or even eliminate retainage after a project is half over (Figure 16.13). One contractor told me, however, that although a reduction in retainage was welcome, its elimination was not. Otherwise, the argument was that there would be no leverage for withholding a similar amount from the subcontractors.

The amount withheld may, after over a year on a large project, accumulate to a rather large sum. Thus, there may well be some validity in the reduction concept. It should be kept in mind, however, if a project is covered by performance and payment bonds, the permission of the surety company is essential prior to the release or even the reduction of the retention amount. Convenient forms for this purpose are provided in Figure 16.14.

There are two methods of computing retainage. By one method, the amount held at the end of the project is equal to, for example, 10 percent of the entire project cost. On a recent project that the author was involved with, that amounted to over $250,000. Another method allows the retainage to be calculated as a percentage of the current month's billing. In this manner, the owner never holds more than perhaps 10 percent of any month's earnings. In most construction contracts it is the former method that is used.

Both the U.S. government and the American Institute of Architects have approved a procedure recognizing the validity of the concept that the holding of 10 percent during the first half of the work is adequate to assure completion and protection against claims, and that no further retainage is needed. Thus, the owner will be holding a retainage amounting to 5 percent of the entire project cost at the end of the project. Another version of this concept involves the retention of 10 percent retainage until the halfway point, then a refund to the contractor of all but 5 percent. From that point on, the owner continues to withhold 5 percent until the end of the job. This policy applies only if in the judgment of the owner's agent (architect or engineer), performance has been proper and satisfactory progress is being made in the work.

A similar provision should be made for payments to subcontractors by a prime contractor. It is a good idea to furnish to a subcontractor, upon request, information on all payments approved and paid to the prime contractor by the owner as it relates to the work of that subcontractor.

## REQUEST FOR
## ADJUSTMENT OF RETAINAGE

PROJECT TITLE _Emerson Pumping Plant_ _____ PROJECT NO. _89/90-00_ _____

OWNER _____ _City of Thousand Oaks_ _____ CONTRACT NO. _____

PROJECT MANAGER _R. E. Barnes_ _____

CONTRACTOR _____ _XYZ Constructors, Inc., Thousand Oaks, CA_ _____

---

The Contractor, _XYZ Constructors, Inc.,_ _____ hereby requests that the percentage of partial

payment estimates retained by the Owner under the provision of the contract be REDUCED to __50__ % /DISCONTINUED.

by _~signature~_ _____ Date _8-10-90_

Contractor Representative

---

The Surety on the Performance Bond for said project _ABC Indemnity Company, Inc., Los Angeles, CA_
hereby approves the foregoing request.

Power of Attorney
must be attached
to original copy

by _~signature~_ _____ Date _8-14-90_

Attorney-in-Fact

---

Approval **IS** / IS NOT recommended. The percentage of completion as of _18 July_ 19_90_ is _40.4_ % and the

present percentage of elapsed time as of _18 July_ 19_90_ is _56.3_ %

by _~signature~_ _____ Date _8-15-90_

Resident Project Representative

---

Approval **X** / IS NOT recommended;

by _~signature~_ _____ Date _20 Aug 1990_

Project Manager

---

APPROVED / DISAPPROVED

by _~signature~_ _____ Date _8-24-90_

Owner's Representative

---

Distribution: 1. Proj Mgr.
2. Field Ofc
3. File
4. Owner

Wiley-Fisk Form 14-4

**FIGURE 16.13** Example of a Request for Adjustment of Retainage.

# CONSENT OF SURETY
## For Reduction of or
## Partial Release of Retainage

*City of Thousand Oaks*

Project Name___Moorpark Road Improvements_____

Location___Between Thousand Oaks Blvd to Janss Rd_____

Project No.___89/90-00___ Contract No._____

Type of Contract___Lump Sum_____

Amount of Contract___$12,345,570.00_____

In accordance with the provisions of the above-named contract between the Owner and the Contractor, the following named surety:

Guaranteed Indemnity Corp., Los Angeles, CA
_____

on the Bond of the following named Contractor:

XYZ Constructors, Inc., Thousand Oaks, CA
_____

hereby approves a reduction of or partial release of retainage to the Contractor as set forth below:

Continued retention of all monies withheld through 24 Aug 1990. Reduction of future

retention funds to 5 percent monthly for all monies earned subsequent to 24 Aug 1990.
_____

The Surety Company hereby agrees that such reduction of or partial release of retainage to the Contractor shall not relieve said surety company of any of its obligations to the following named Owner as set forth in said Surety Company's bond:

City of Thousand Oaks, a legal entity organized and existing in the County of

Ventura, State of California.
_____

IN WITNESS WHEREOF, the Surety Company has hereunto set its hand and seal this ___12___ day of ___July___ 19_90_

Guaranteed Indemnity Corp.
(Name of Surety Company)

(Signature of Authorized Representative)

(Affix corporate
seal here)

Wiley-Fisk Form 17-4

TITLE___Vice President_____

**FIGURE 16.14** Consent of Surety for reduction or partial release of retainage funds by the owner.

410

Finally, approximately 35 days after the completion of the work, if all lien releases are in and all work completed, and all subcontractors, suppliers, and employees have been paid, obtain the approval of the surety and then release the retention money.

## LIQUIDATED DAMAGES DURING CONSTRUCTION

Traditionally, the assessment of liquidated damages against a contractor for monetary losses suffered by the owner as the result of a contractor's failure to meet the contractual completion date have been computed only for the excess construction time beyond the final specified completion date. Recently, there have been successful actions to collect liquidated damages for failure of a contractor to meet various specified key dates for completion of certain specified portions of the work, affecting the ability of other prime contractors to deliver their portion of the work on time. The effect of delaying other prime contractors can result in added charges for owner-caused delays and in rendering the specified completion dates of the other affected contractors as unenforceable.

Some owners have successfully specified and collected liquidated damages from some of their prime contractors for failure to meet such key dates, and the amount of the liquidated damages was simply deducted from the amount of the progress payment owed the contractor for work done that month. Where the amount of the liquidated damages exceeded the amount of the earned progress payment, it was simply charged as a debit against the contractor's account.

## STANDARD CONTRACT PROVISIONS
## FOR MEASUREMENT AND PAYMENT

Although each set of contract documents treats this subject slightly differently, the provisions of the project documents must be the final determining factor in establishing the method and procedure for handling contractor payment requests. The following references are provided as an aid to comparing the provisions of several General Conditions documents in current use:

1. *EJCDC:* Articles 14.1 through 14.13 of the General Conditions (1996 ed.)
2. *AIA:* Articles 9.1 through 9.10.4 of the General Conditions (1987 ed.)
3. *GSA:* Article 7 of the General Provisions (federal contracts).
4. *FIDIC:* Articles 60.1 through 60.10 of the Conditions of the Contract for Works of Civil Engineering Construction (1987 ed.)

The foregoing are typical of most stock forms of General Conditions, or General Provisions as they are sometimes called.

Similar provisions are made in the various standard specifications, as these documents generally include all general provisions as well as technical ones. The principal difference is that the majority of the standard specifications also contain provisions for measurement methods to be used in determining the payment quantities—an excellent way of minimizing field disputes resulting from disagreements over the method of measurement, which can result in significant differences. The following references are provided as an aid in comparing the measurement and payment provisions of some typical standard specifications:

1. American Public Works Association/Associated General Contractors Standard Specifications for Public Works Construction
   *Measurement of Quantities for Unit-Price Work:* Section 9-1
   *Measurement of Quantities for Lump Contracts:* Section 9-2
   *Payment:* Section 9-3

2. California Department of Transportation Standard Specifications
   *Measurement of Quantities:* Section 9-1.01
   *Payment:* Sections 9-1.02 through 9-1.09

3. Florida Department of Transportation Standard Specifications for Road and Bridge Construction
   *Measurement of Quantities:* Section 9-1
   *Payment:* Sections 9-2 through 9-10

4. Virginia Road and Bridge Specifications
   *Measurement of Quantities:* Sections 109.01 through 109.02
   *Payment:* Sections 109.03 through 109.09

## INTERPRETING THE CONTRACTOR'S BID

### Interpretation of Bidding Errors

If the final-measured amount of earth excavation shown in Figure 16.15 was determined to be 40 000 m³ (52 318 cubic yards) instead of the 39 757 m³ (52 000 cubic yards) estimated by the engineer, the actual payment to the contractor for completing that item would be 40 000 m³ × 3.60 (52 318 cy × 2.75) and he or she would be paid $144 000 instead of the $143 125.20 shown in the totals column of its bid sheet. If the contractor knew in advance that the engineer's estimate was incorrect on this item, it might be worthwhile to place a higher unit price on the item, thus assuring higher profits without placing the firm in a noncompetitive position against the other bidders (see the following section, "Unbalanced Bids").

Often, errors are made in bids submitted and a determination must be made as to the true value of a bid. One common error involves a multiplication of the unit-price and the estimated quantity. In the example in Figure 16.16 it can be seen that the proper product of the unit-price times the quantity should be $575,056 instead of the $175,056 shown.

In some cases, contractors have been allowed to withdraw a bid after opening where a clerical error existed; however, in an apparent equal number of such cases, such withdrawal has been successfully refused. Recent legislative action in some states has made it possible for any contractor to withdraw such an erroneous bid.

| BALANCED BID BASED UPON COMPETITIVE UNIT PRICES | | | | |
|---|---|---|---|---|
| Item No. | Description | Quantity and Unit | Unit Price | Amount |
| 1. | SITE PREPARATION | L.S. | | $   17 500.00 |
| 2. | TEMPORARY SHEETING | 1 133 M2 | $     0.11 | $       124.63 |
| 3. | PERMANENT SHEETING | 6 661 M2 | $    19.50 | $ 129 889.50 |
| 4. | EARTH EXCAVATION | 39 757 M3 | $     3.60 | $ 143 125.20 |
| 5. | ROCK EXCAVATION | 6 881 M3 | $    21.25 | $ 146 221.25 |
| 6. | REINFORCING STEEL | 393 TONN | $   495.80 | $ 194 849.40 |
| 7. | CONDUIT BEDDING | 1 009 M3 | $    17.66 | $   17 818.94 |
| 8. | CONCRETE CONDUIT | 3 884 M3 | $   170.03 | $ 660 396.52 |
| | | TOTAL | $ | 1 309 925.40 |

**FIGURE 16.15**   Balanced bid based upon competitive unit prices

Similarly, where a bid sheet asks for the amount in "words and figures," the *words* will govern over the figures, as there is less chance of error this way. This type of error is likely in either a lump-sum or a unit-price bid amount. If the amount of the bid read

Four thousand two hundred and forty-seven dollars ($40 247.00)

the final amount of the bid would be held as $4247, not $40 247.

### Unbalanced Bids

For unit-price contracts, a balanced bid is one in which each bid item is priced to carry its share of the cost of the work and also its share of the contractor's profit. Occasionally, contractors will raise prices on certain items and make corresponding reductions of the prices on other items, without changing the total amount of the bid for the project. The result is an unbalanced bid. In general, extremely unbalanced bids are considered as undesirable and should not be permitted when detected, although the practice sometimes seems justified from the contractor's viewpoint. Some of the purposes of unbalancing bidding are as follows:

**1.** To discourage certain types of construction and encourage others that may be more favorable to the contractor.

| Item No. | Description | Quantity and Unit | Unit Price | Amount |
|---|---|---|---|---|
| 8. | Concrete Conduit | 5 080 m$^3$ | $ 11320 | $ 115 05600 |

**FIGURE 16.16**   Example of an error in bid computation.

**2.** When the contractor believes that the engineer's estimate for certain items is low, by unbalancing the bid in favor of such items, an increased (unearned) profit in the actual payment of the work can be obtained without increasing the apparent total amount of the bid.

**3.** Unreliable contractors may increase their bid prices for the first items of work to be completed, with corresponding reductions elsewhere in the bid, with the intention of receiving excessive early payments, then defaulting on the contract. This could leave the surety to complete the contract with insufficient funds remaining in the contract.

**4.** By unbalancing the bid in favor of items that will be completed early in the progress of the work, a contractor can build up its working capital (front money) for the remainder of the work. This can also serve to eliminate the financial squeeze caused by the usual 10 percent retention money. This is a fairly common practice.

Of all of the reasons mentioned for unbalancing a bid, only the last item seems to have some justification when dealing with reliable contractors. The expenses of mobilizing the construction plant, bringing the equipment and materials to the site, and the general costs of getting the work started are significant. These items often do not appear on the bid as separate bid items, and therefore are paid for only by adding their cost to the items actually listed. This usually means, however, that they would be paid for only as the work progresses, even though the actual cost to the contractor was all incurred at the beginning of the job. This can cause a hardship on the contractor in that the working capital would be tied up in the work to the sole advantage of the owner.

The prevention of unbalanced bids requires a knowledge of construction costs in the project area so that unreasonable bids on individual items may be detected. An obvious case of unbalanced bidding should be considered as grounds for rejecting the entire bid.[1]

### Example of an Unbalanced Bid

Initially, a contractor must figure its bid normally without unbalancing it to produce a competitive price (Figure 16.15). The price thus determined will become the bottom-line price for the future unbalanced bid. The following example is based upon a partial list of bid items from the low bid for a reinforced box culvert bid in Connecticut in 1976. All original bid items and the quantities are furnished in the bidding documents by the engineer, and the unit-prices and extensions are all filled in by the bidder.

As an example, assume that a bidder, upon carefully studying the plans, discovers that the engineer has made an error in the quantities shown for temporary and permanent trench sheeting. Instead of 1133 m$^2$ (12 200 sq ft) of temporary sheeting and 6661 m$^2$ (71 700 sq ft) of permanent sheeting as the engineer's estimate indicates, totaling 7794 m$^2$ (83 900 sq ft) of trench sheeting all together, let us assume that the bidder has discovered that although the total of 7794 m$^2$ (83 900 sq ft) of sheeting is correct, the engineer has the individual

---

[1]R. W. Abbett, *Engineering Contracts and Specifications* (New York: Wiley, 1963).

| UNBALANCED BID BASED UPON KNOWN QUANTITY ERRORS IN ENGINEER'S ESTIMATE | | | | |
|---|---|---|---|---|
| Item No. | Description | Quantity and Unit | Unit Price | Amount |
| 1. | SITE PREPARATION | L.S. | | $ 23 925.67* |
| 2. | TEMPORARY SHEETING* | 1 133 M2 | $ 45.12 | $ 51 120.96* |
| 3. | PERMANENT SHEETING* | 6 661 M2 | $ 27.23 | $ 181 379.03* |
| 4. | EARTH EXCAVATION | 39 757 M3 | $ 3.60 | $ 143 125.20 |
| 5. | ROCK EXCAVATION | 6 881 M3 | $ 21.25 | $ 146 221.25 |
| 6. | REINFORCING STEEL | 393 TONN | $ 435.80 | $ 171 269.40* |
| 7. | CONDUIT BEDDING | 1 009 M3 | $ 17.66 | $ 17 818.94 |
| 8. | CONCRETE CONDUIT | 3 884 M3 | $ 148.06 | $ 575 065.04* |
| | | | TOTAL  $ | 1 309 925.40 |
| (*Denotes unbalanced bid items) | | | | |

**FIGURE 16.17** Unbalanced bid based upon known quantity errors in the engineer's estimate.

amounts wrong. According to the bidder's estimate, there are actually 6661 m$^2$ (71 700 sq ft) of temporary sheeting and only 1133 m$^2$ (12 196 sq ft) of permanent sheeting. Now, although the price of the temporary sheeting is low because of the contractor's ability to reuse the material, the opportunities presented by the knowledge that the quantities are in error might suggest to the bidder that if its price on this item is high enough, the added quantity over that indicated in the engineer's estimate could be a financial windfall. The bidder, of course, also knows that if that bid item alone is raised, the total bid price will be too high and they may not get the job. Therefore, the prices of certain other items must be reduced to compensate for the raise in the unit-price for temporary sheeting. When completed, the new bid must have the same bottom-line total as the balanced bid.

In the unbalanced bid in Figure 16.17 the bidder has raised the unit-prices of bid items 2 and 3, and compensated by lowering the unit-prices for bid items 6 and 8. At the same time the bidder has increased the amount of money bid for site preparation because it will be the first item completed. In this way it could provide the bidder with additional working capital (front money). Note that the total bid price (bottom line) has remained the same as it was in the original balanced bid in Figure 16.15.

By holding the original competitive bid price, the bidder assures itself of a fair chance of being awarded the job. Then, if this bidder gets the job, the payments to that firm as contractor will be based upon the *actual* quantities of each item of the bid sheet completed (Figure 16.18). Thus, the high bid price on the quantity that the engineer showed as low will yield high unearned profits, which are not reduced significantly by the redistribution of the other bid prices in the unbalanced bid.

A quick comparison of the amount of the contract price that the contractor would have received if the quantities estimated by the engineer were correct with the amount that would actually be claimed by the contractor is shown in the following:

| ACTUAL PAYMENTS TO THE CONTRACTOR | | | | |
|---|---|---|---|---|
| Item No. | Description | Quantity and Unit | Unit Price | Amount |
| 1. | SITE PREPARATION | L.S. | | $    23 925.67 |
| 2. | TEMPORARY SHEETING* | 6 865 M2 | $    45.12 | $ 300 544.32 |
| 3. | PERMANENT SHEETING* | 6 929 M2 | $    27.23 | $   30 851.39 |
| 4. | EARTH EXCAVATION | 39 757 M3 | $     3.60 | $ 143 125.20 |
| 5. | ROCK EXCAVATION | 6 881 M3 | $    21.25 | $ 146 221.25 |
| 6. | REINFORCING STEEL | 393 TONN | $   435.80 | $ 171 269.40 |
| 7. | CONDUIT BEDDING | 1 009 M3 | $    17.66 | $   17 818.94 |
| 8. | CONCRETE CONDUIT | 3 884 M3 | $   148.06 | $ 575 065.04 |
| | | | TOTAL  $    1 408 821.40 | |

**FIGURE 16.18**   Actual payments to the contractor

$1 408 821.40   Amount claimed by the contractor for actual quantities
$1 309 925.40   Original bid price for the project (based upon engineer's quantities)
      98 896.00   Additional unearned profit due to false unit prices

Note that the amount of increase in the price bid for site preparation did not alter the final payment amount; it only provided early money for the contractor to use in its operations.

### Detection of an Unbalanced Bid

There are several ways of detecting an unbalanced bid, depending upon the type of imbalance involved. Using the illustrated example in Figures 16.15, 16.17, and 16.18, however, it is relatively easy to detect a flaw. Generally, an unbalanced bid such as that in the illustration is an indication that the architect/engineer made an error in the preparation of the plans and specifications.

Typically, a bid such as that illustrated stands out when compared with the bids of all other bidders on the same line items. For example, for line items 2 and 3 for Temporary Sheeting and Permanent Sheeting, respectively, the bidder quoted prices of $45.12 and $27.23 per square meter, respectively. While that may not alarm the architect/engineer in that context, if compared with the same items as quoted by all other bidders, the flaw really stands out. For example, on temporary sheeting, if there were five bidders, the bids might be $0.50, $0.10, $1.10, $45.12, and $0.70 per square meter for the same line item. If the architect/engineer tabulates all bids on a Summary of Proposals Received form (Figure 11.7), it will immediately become evident that one contractor's bid appears to be unusually high on this item simply by reading horizontally across the page. Similarly, by comparing the bids for permanent sheeting a similar discrepancy may be noted. Those lines in the form might look like this:

| No. | Item | Bid | | | | |
|-----|------|-----|-----|-----|-----|-----|
| | | **A** | **B** | **C** | **D** | **E** |
| 2 | Temporary sheeting | $0.50 | $0.10 | $1.10 | $45.12 | $6.70 |
| 3 | Permanent sheeting | $13.50 | $18.10 | $14.50 | $27.23 | $19.90 |

By comparing the prices bid for each individual line item on the bid summary (spreadsheet), it quickly becomes evident that one particular bidder appears to have discovered a discrepancy in the documents. This discovery can be put to good use by the architect/engineer, as the bidder has not only made the architect/engineer aware of a probable error in the plans and specifications, but has even told the architect/engineer exactly where the error lies.

The solution depends upon when the discovery was made by the architect/engineer. If discovered prior to award of the contract, the wisest move is to reject all bids, search out and correct the error in the documents, and readvertise the job. If discovered after a contract was let, the only solution is the execution of a change order.

On private work, it is simple merely to reject the bid tendered by the contractor who submitted the unbalanced bid. On public works, however, the task is a little more difficult. As proving the existence of an imbalance is difficult, and because of the necessity of accepting the lowest dollar bidder, the better way is to reject all bids, correct the mistake, and readvertise.

## MEASUREMENT FOR PAYMENT

At first a person may be tempted to think, "What is so difficult about field measurements?" The actual problem is neither with the techniques nor with the accuracy of the measurements as taken, but rather the fact that certain types of measurements may not be representative of the true pay quantities. An example might be the determination of the amount of pipe to be paid for under the construction contract. Often, the contract documents may specify that payment will be made based on the lengths *indicated on the drawings.* It should be noted that the lengths on the drawing are generally shown in *stations,* 100 meter (328.08 ft) increments. Instead of the familiar 100-ft stations widely used in the United States, conversion to SI metric will utilize 100 meter (328.08-ft) stations. Under SI a station value will look something like 2+80.374. Because 100 meters is such a large distance, station tick marks will be at 20 m intervals with annotation at 20 m intervals. The first number in the Station value is the Station number (in 100 m). the next two digits are in meters, and the last 3 digits are in millimeters. The reason that measurements are to the millimeter is to retain the degree of accuracy indicated by measurements to the nearest 100th of a foot.

Now, lengths shown in stations are always *horizontal dimensions.* Thus, they are not representative of the actual lengths of pipe furnished by the contractor! If the pipe is laid in trenches that have a steep profile grade, the contractor must furnish a longer pipe than will show in the plan view, and its bid price must reflect this difference. An inspector who determines the amount of pipe to be paid for on this type of contract by measuring the actual lengths of pipe laid in trenches may be approving an overpayment.

### Determination of Pay Quantities for Pipelines

The example shown in Figure 16.19 is an actual case involving an overflow pipeline from the surge chamber of a hydroelectric powerhouse project. In plan it can be seen that the pipeline is comprised of three reaches of pipe, each at a different slope in a trench on a hillside. The length of the pipe in plan, as determined from the indicated stations, is 175.87 m (577.00 ft) less the length of the upper structure. However, all lengths in stations are horizontal measurements only; thus, the true length is a calculated one. In the example shown, the lower reach of 1200 mm (48-in) diameter pipe has a slope of $S = 0.384$ (same as the tangent of the angle measured off the horizontal). The true length of this pipe *in place* is computed as follows:

**FIGURE 16.19**   Plan and profile of surge chamber overflow pipe.

End station    $= 5 + 77$
Upper station $= 3 + 20$
$\overline{\phantom{xxxxxxxxxx}}$
$2 + 57$ stations $= 257.00$ ft (78.3 m) horizontal length

For $S = 0.384$: vertical slope angle $= 21.00678943°$

$$\text{True length} = \frac{275}{\cos 21.00678943°} = 275.30 \text{ ft (83.91 m)};$$

18.3 ft (5.58 m) longer than indicated in plan view

By computing each reach of the entire length of the pipeline in the same manner, it is found that the actual length of the pipeline *in place* is 602.72 ft (183.71 m) minus the length of the upper structure, or 572.22 ft (174.41 m). This is a total of 25.22 ft (7.69 m) more pipe than indicated from the horizontal dimensions as determined from the plan.

The emphasis on the "in-place" length of a pipe is based upon the fact that the actual delivered lengths of pipe will add up to even more than the indicated 572.22 ft (174.41 m), to allow for fitting the spigot ends into the bell ends of each length of pipe. Thus, the inspector who measures delivered lengths of pipe for payment runs a serious risk of overpayment unless the specifications specifically call for payment to be made on the basis of lengths of pipe as delivered instead of laying length (in-place dimension).

## Determination of Earth and Rock Pay Quantities

It is appropriate to warn of the pitfalls involved in the determination of the quantities of earth or rock excavation or backfill. This is one of the most likely areas for miscalculation. In determining the amounts of excavation and embankment material in construction, an allowance must be made for the difference in space (volume) occupied by the material before excavation and the same material after it has been compacted in embankment. The various earth materials will be more compact in embankment (will occupy less space than they did in their original state) and rock will be less compact (will occupy more space than it did in its original state). This difference in volume between the same material as excavated and as replaced in fill is called *shrinkage* in the case of earth materials, and *increase* or *swell* in the case of rock materials.

The amount of shrinkage depends upon the kind of material and the method of placing it in the fill. Thus, a borrow area needed to provide 19 000 m³ (24 850 cu. yd.) of fill material may have to be capable of yielding 20 600 m³ (26 944 cu. yd.) of borrow material. As it can be seen, the Resident Project Representative who is on a unit-price job must be very careful to measure the material in strict accordance with the measurement for payment instructions of the job specifications. Obviously, a contractor who is excavating borrow material to be used as fill on its project would much rather be paid for the volume of earth embankment material hauled.

The actual percentages can only be determined by a qualified soils engineer; however, the following percentages are from the average of general experience. They express shrinkage in volume of several classes of materials:

| | |
|---|---|
| Fine sand | 6% |
| Sand and gravel | 8% |
| Ordinary clay | 10% |
| Loam | 12% |
| Surface soil | 15% |

If an understanding is reached in the contract to begin with, it does not matter which types of measurements are agreed upon. Thus, the contractor would be able to structure its bid accordingly. But watch for the contractor who wants to change methods of measurement later. Above all, the resident inspector should not yield to any pressure to count scraper or truck loads based upon loose volume!

Another method occasionally suggested by the contractor is that of paying for truck-loads of loose haul material by weight. This sounds acceptable at first, but with earth materials this is an extremely unreliable method. The principal problem lies in the variations of moisture content of the material being weighed. If the contractor uses its water truck extensively during excavation and loading into truck from the borrow area, which might be necessary to loosen some materials, the added weight of the damp or wet materials will be paid for as earth material, when in fact the added weight was actually due to the moisture content of the material. Although the contractor must water the material to achieve proper compaction when he or she is constructing earth embankments, this is usually done at the point of deposit. If, instead, water is added before hauling, on a job where haul materials are paid for by weight, the contractor can realize a tidy profit on the deal. The other way around, money might be lost if unit weight was based upon optimum moisture content and the material was removed and weighed at a lower moisture content.

One common way of combatting the problem is to pay for materials in place *as calculated from the dimensions shown on the plans.* In this manner, the drawings represent "pay lines" and any material in excess of that shown on the plans would not be paid for. This has a disadvantage to the owner; on a heavy earthworks project it would be possible to unbalance the bid to provide a high unit-price on backfill material, then if the contractor overexcavated by a few inches of depth where unit-price payment is also made for excavation, the owner might end up paying twice for the same material.

### Determination of Paving Quantities

On asphalt concrete pavement jobs where the asphalt concrete material was to be paid for by the ton, the inspector should watch closely for overexcavation by as little as 13 mm (1/2 in.) depth. On a large roadway project the cost difference could be great. Similarly, if the price of asphalt concrete is priced by the square yard of material placed to a specific depth, any reduction in pavement thickness would simply assure the contractor the price for a full-depth pavement while allowing the difference between the estimated amount of material specified and the amount actually placed to be pocketed by the contractor.

Many materials are subject to special conditions for the determination of pay quantities. Asphaltic prime coat, for example, is usually measured in gallons. However, the inspector should be certain that the volumes being paid for are based upon the volume that the material occupied at 60 degrees F. If the material is placed hot and the volumetric measurements are made at that time, overpayment could result.

## MEASUREMENT GUIDELINES FOR DETERMINATION OF UNIT-PRICE PAY QUANTITIES

### Bid Items Based Upon Linear Measure

**Pipelines.**   These are often paid for in terms of length in stations (horizontal measure), which is determined from the plans. Could possibly involve field measurements by a survey crew (also horizontal measurements).

Also paid for by measurement along the top of the pipe in place. This method will yield actual laying length. Do not allow measurement along the side of the pipe on the outside of curves. Do not accept lengths of pipe for measurement prior to laying.

Sometimes paid for by measurement in the field, *horizontally* along the center-line alignment of the pipe in place. This should result in the same quantity that would result from the stations indicated on the plans.

**Curbs.**   Curbs are generally measured in the field by measurement along the top edge facing the street. Watch for measurements made at the flow line, as the slope of the curb face may yield a slightly greater quantity this way under certain conditions. Watch for measurements made at the sidewalk side of the top edge of the curbing. In some cases this can cause erroneous lengths also. The important thing is not so much *where* the measurements have been taken, but that all measurements are taken at the *same place* throughout the life of the job.

**Channels.**   Where flood control channels or similar structures are to be lined, be sure to measure at the same location each time. If the point of reference is the toe of a slope, do not permit the measurements to be made on opposite sides, as this will alter the indicated length.

**Sewer lines.**   Measurement of VCP sewer lines is generally made by measurement of the pipe in place. However, do not allow measurements to be made through sewer manholes, as the separate price paid for manhole construction already covers this cost.

**Fencing.**   Measurement of chain link fencing can be accomplished by horizontal measurements or by measuring along the top rail of the fence in place, depending upon the method specified. As in the case of pipelines, the length indicated will be less when measured horizontally.

### Bid Items Based Upon Area Measurements

**Pavements.**   As mentioned before, the measurement of areas for payment usually presents no problem, but particular care must be exercised to assure that the proper pavement thicknesses have been attained. Watch, too, for underruns where the contractor is being paid both for excavation of the roadbed on a volume basis and pavement surfacing on an area basis.

A particular risk is involved where there are separate payments for pavements over small areas, such as trench resurfacing, and for larger paved areas that can be done with a paving machine. On one actual pipeline job in a city street, the unit-price for repavement over trenches was quoted somewhat higher than roadway pavement because it would have to be done using hand methods. The contractor for this project, being an enterprising person, carefully studied the specifications and noted that the earthwork provisions permitted a slope of that portion of the trench walls that were above a plane lying 300 mm (1 ft.) above the pipe, provided that any excess excavation resulting from such methods was to be at the contractor's own expense. The contractor sloped all of the trench walls in the city street area, opening up the entire width of one half of the city street, which he then repaved using a regular paving machine. The specifications for repavement of the area over the pipe trench were based upon the area to be paved, rather than upon the length of pavement to be constructed over trenches. The result was that the contractor not only eliminated the added cost of trench shoring in deep trenches, but also "bought" a street repaving job to repave an entire half of the city street using a paving machine, but performing the work *at unit-prices intended for hand work!* The only excess cost to the contractor was the extra labor of the added excavation involved in the sloping of the sides of the pipe trench and the removal of the additional existing paving. The cost to the city was an additional $15,000, as there was nothing in the contract that would provide legal relief. Thus, the method of measurement for payment purposes can mean significant differences in a project cost. In this case, it was the specifier's fault for not coordinating the paving specification with the earthworks specification. An alert Resident Project Representative noticed this early, but unfortunately, under the terms of the contract specifications, the contractor was fully within legal rights to do this (Figure 16.20).

**FIGURE 16.20**   Effect on contractor's earned payment of sloping trench walls where payment for AC paving was based upon surface area of tonnage instead of linear feet.

***Retaining walls.*** If a retaining wall is to be constructed around the periphery of a property, the inspector should be exceptionally careful of the method of making wall area measurements. If all measurements are around the outside of the wall, the cost to the owner will be excessive. However, if all measurements were on the inside face, the cost to the contractor would be unfair. Each wall surface should be taken as a prism, and any space occupied by the previously measured prism should not be included in any other measurement of adjoining surfaces.

***Volume measurements.*** Be certain of the method of measurement, particularly in the case of earth and rock materials and of materials that must be placed at high temperatures. In many cases, volume measurements will have to be made using a survey crew to take cross sections of the affected area.

If a volume of material is to be placed in accordance with the lines shown on the drawings, be sure to get a survey crew on the site before the work begins, to establish the exact profile of the ground as it existed before the work began; otherwise, disputes may arise concerning the quantities because of a difference of opinion as to the condition that existed prior to the beginning of the work.

***Weight.*** Establish at the beginning of the job what the basis of weight measurement is to be. Under the old English system, which has been converted to metric, a "ton" could have been either the *short ton* of 2000 pounds (907.1847 kg) or the *long ton* of 2240 pounds (1016.0469 kg). Similarly, smaller units of weight needed to be clearly defined under the English system.

The foregoing is not intended to be an exhaustive list of all the special areas of concern, but rather a sampling of some of the more common measurement problems encountered under a unit-price contract project.

## FINAL PAYMENT TO THE CONTRACTOR

After the Certificate of Completion or Substantial Completion has been filed (Chapter 20) the contractor will apply for final payment. Although the form used is the same as that used previously for monthly progress payments, there are several additional requirements that must be complied with before the architect/engineer should issue a final certificate for payment.

1. The contractor must pay all bills or other indebtedness.
2. Under certain contracts he or she must submit receipts, releases, and waivers of liens.
3. Consent of surety must be obtained where a surety is involved.

Under the provisions of the AIA and the EJCDC General Conditions, the final payment is withheld only until the contractor has provided evidence that each of the items in the foregoing list has been complied with. Under the AIA and EJCDC provisions, the making and acceptance of the final payment constitutes a waiver of all claims by the owner against the contractor other than those arising from unsettled liens, from defective work appearing after final payment, or from failure to comply with the requirements of the contract documents or the terms of any special guarantees that are a part of the contract. It is also a waiver of all claims by the contractor against the owner other than those previously made in writing that are still unsettled (Figure 16.21).

Although the holding time for the release of the contractor's final payment under the AIA and the EJCDC contract provisions is not specific but is subject to the time it takes the contractor to submit its documentation, most public agency contracts note a specific period of time before release of the final payment to allow time for any lien holders to file before the owner releases the final payment to the contractor. In this manner, if liens have been filed, or valid claims are presented to the owner for unpaid bills, the owner can pay such indebtedness and deduct all the sums from the money due to the contractor.

Under the provisions for final payment of many other public agency contracts, the owner retains the right to withhold funds to satisfy liens or outstanding bills. In some states, however, this creates a potential problem; the period for the filing of liens against a construction project in many states where a Certificate of Completion or Substantial Completion has been executed and recorded has been established by statute. Because of this fact, many agencies set a holding period for all retention money equal to the statutory period plus 5 or 10 days to allow the lien filing period to close before releasing the contractor's money. In this way, the owner can be assured that all potential lien holders have been satisfied before making final payment to the contractor. Another alternative would be a waiver of claims (see Chapter 20).

As recommended in Chapter 20, it is desirable that a formal Certificate of Completion or Substantial Completion be executed *and recorded* in the county recorder's office. If this is not done, no reasonable retention period of the contractor's final payment may sometimes suffice. It would normally appear to be in the owner's best interest to see that a Certificate of Completion or Substantial Completion is filed and recorded within the statutory time allowed after substantial completion of the work, or to be sure of receiving a release or waiver of claims from the general contractor, all subcontractors, and material suppliers prior to releasing retention money.

### Final Progress Payment

Final payment as referred to in many General Conditions of the Contract is the last progress payment made to the contractor, less retainage, and should not be made until after execution of the Notice of Completion (Substantial Completion). This notice constitutes formal "acceptance" of the Work by the owner.

When computing the contractor's eligibility for the last payment, several items should be considered for deduction *in addition to normal retainage:*

1. Any liquidated damages due to the date of Notice of Completion (Substantial Completion).

*14.07 Final Payment*

A. *Application for Payment*

1. After CONTRACTOR has completed all such corrections identified during the final inspection to the satisfaction of ENGINEER and delivered in accordance with the Contract Documents all maintenance and operating instructions, schedules, guarantees, Bonds, certificates or other evidence of insurance certificates of inspection, marked-up record documents (as provided in paragraph 6.12) and other documents, CONTRACTOR may make application for final payment following the procedure for progress payments. The final Application for Payment shall be accompanied (except as previously delivered) by: (i) all documentation called for in the Contract Documents, including but not limited to the evidence of insurance required by subparagraph 5.04.B.7; (ii) consent of the surety, if any, to final payment; and (iii) complete and legally effective releases or waivers (satisfactory to OWNER) of all Liens arising out of or filed in connection with the Work.

2. In lieu of the releases or waivers of Liens specified in paragraph 14.07.A.I and as approved by OWNER, CONTRACTOR may furnish receipts or releases in full and an affidavit of CONTRACTOR that: (i) the releases and receipts include all labor, services, material and equipment for which a Lien could be filed; and (ii) all payrolls, material and equipment bills and other indebtedness connected with the Work for which OWNER or OWNER's property might in any way be responsible have been paid or otherwise satisfied. If any Subcontractor or Supplier fails to furnish such a release or receipt in full, CONTRACTOR may furnish a Bond or other collateral satisfactory to OWNER to indemnify OWNER against any Lien.

B. *Review of Application and Acceptance*

1. If, on the basis of ENGINEER's observation of the Work during construction and final inspection, and ENGINEER's review of the final Application for Payment and accompanying documentation as required by the Contract Documents, ENGINEER is satisfied that the Work has been completed and CONTRACTOR's other obligations under the Contract Documents have been fulfilled, ENGINEER will, within ten days after receipt of the final Application for Payment, indicate in writing ENGINEER's recommendation *of* payment and present the Application for Payment to OWNER for payment. At the same time ENGINEER will also give written notice to OWNER and CONTRACTOR that the Work is acceptable subject to the provisions of paragraph 14.09. Otherwise, ENGINEER will return the Application for Payment to CONTRACTOR, indicating in writing the reasons for refusing to recommend final payment, in which case CONTRACTOR shall make the necessary corrections and resubmit the Application for Payment.

**FIGURE 16.21**  Provisions for Final payment to the Contractor from the EJCDC Standard General Conditions of the Construction Contract. Copyright © by the National Society of Professional Engineers (*continued on p. 426*).

2. Twice the value of all outstanding punch list items. (In case the punch list items are not completed within the agreed time, the contractor may forfeit this amount.)

3. The value of any lien claims already on file. (In some states, final payment terminates liability of the owner *only* for those contractor claims filed prior to acceptance of final payment by the contractor).

Acceptance of final payment by the contractor may terminate the liability of the owner in some jurisdictions. The final payment should not be approved for payment until

C. *Payment Becomes Due*

1. Thirty days after the presentation to OWNER of the Application for Payment and accompanying documentation, the amount recommended by ENGINEER will become due and, when due, will be paid by OWNER to CONTRACTOR.

14.08. *Final Completion Delayed*

A. If, through no fault of CONTRACTOR completion of the Work is significantly delayed and if ENGINEER so confirms, OWNER shall, upon receipt of CONTRACTOR's final Application for Payment and recommendation of Engineer and without terminating the Agreement, make payment of the balance due for that portion of the Work fully completed and accepted. If the remaining balance to be held by OWNER for Work not fully completed or corrected is less than the retainage stipulated in the Agreement, and if Bonds have been furnished as required in paragraph 5.01, the written consent of the surety to the payment of the balance due for that portion of the Work fully completed and accepted shall be submitted by CONTRACTOR to ENGINEER with the Application for such payment. Such payment shall be made under the terms and conditions governing final payment, except that it shall not constitute a waiver of Claims.

14.09. *Waiver of Claims*

A. The making and acceptance of final payment will constitute:

1. a waiver of all Claims by OWNER against CONTRACTOR, except Claims arising from unsettled Liens, from detective Work appearing after final inspection pursuant to paragraph 14.06, from failure to comply with the Contract Documents or the terms of any special guarantees specified therein, or from CONTRACTOR's continuing obligations under the Contract Documents; and

2. a waiver of all Claims by CONTRACTOR against OWNER other than those previously made in writing which are still unsettled.

**FIGURE 16.21**   *continued*

after formal "acceptance" of the Work by the owner as evidenced by the execution of a formal Notice of Completion (Substantial Completion). From that date forward, the lien law clock starts running, which limits the time for filing of liens or Stop Notices against the project.

## PROBLEMS

1. True or false? Front loading of a bid is always an illegal or unethical form of unbalancing a contractor's bid.

2. Under a unit-price contract with a 25 percent guarantee requirement of all unit prices quoted, the engineer's estimate of earthwork quantities totals 9270 cubic meters. If the actual quantities measured in the field for pay purposes totals 10 650 cubic meters, is a change order justified for the quantity change?

2. Are liquidated damages intended only for missing the completion date of a project, or may they also be established for failure to meet mid-project interface dates?

3. On a unit-price contract, what is the "contract price"?

4. Is measurement for payment of underground pipelines constructed in place in hilly terrain generally based upon true length of the pipe laid or horizontal projected length (station lengths)?

5. On a unit-price contract, if a contractor bids $145.00 per meter for 765 meters of pipe to be constructed in place and incorrectly shows the total amount as $110 952.00, how much money is the contractor entitled to receive?

6. What is a waiver of lien?

7. What means are available to a contractor bidding a unit-price project for recovery of "General Conditions Work" (mobilization, bonds, insurance, cost of permits, and other preconstruction expenses)?

8. Is the final amount paid to a contractor under a unit-price contract limited by the quantities of materials or work shown in the original Bid Schedule?

9. What type of items are recommended for payment to the contractor upon delivery, even before assembly into the constructed work?

10. Is it advisable to use cost-loaded CPM for progress payments to the contractor on unit-price contracts?

# 17

## Construction Materials and Workmanship

Construction materials control is fully one-half of what construction inspection is all about. The other half is control over workmanship. Many inspectors understand quality construction when they see it, or proper materials when they see them, but fail to understand fully what their authority and responsibility requires them to do. The implication often too firmly implanted in some inspectors' minds is that they are on the job to assure that the project will be constructed with only the "best" quality materials and the "highest" quality of workmanship. On numerous occasions, inspectors have been heard to remark, or even interrupt their instructions to say, supposedly reassuringly, "Don't worry about the specs; I'll see that you get a first-class job!"

Reassuring as it may sound at first, it is *not* the proper approach for an inspector to take. The inspector's real authority is *limited* to requiring the contractor to provide all that has been agreed to in writing in the contract documents. If an owner, through lack of funds or otherwise, chooses to purchase less than top-quality goods or to accept adequate but somewhat less than first-class workmanship, it is its prerogative to do so. It would be an overstep of the authority of the inspector to attempt to require the contractor to provide anything in excess of the terms of the approved contract—and certainly would be unfair to the contractor. Remember, one of the basic principles of the law of contracts is that it must involve a meeting of the minds. Thus, anything that is not part of the written terms of the contract is not within the authority of the inspector to attempt to require without a supplemental agreement, such as a change order. If, however, an inspector observed a condition that if performed in strict accordance with the plans and specifications, would result in an unsafe condition or that might be considered as being of questionable judgment, the obligation of the inspector is to bring the matter to the direct attention of the architect or engineer or the owner. Then, if in the judgment of the architect or engineer or the owner a change should be made, it will be executed as a formal change order, with a possible appropriate adjustment in the contract price.

It all comes down to a simple axiom. If a person agrees to buy a Ford, the dealer should not be forced to deliver a Continental for the same price, just because it might represent a higher-quality product in the eyes of the buyer's agent. Similarly, if it is found that the Ford will not do the job but the Continental is required, the buyer must make a new agreement to purchase and pay for the higher-priced product.

In short, the inspector is not on the job to enforce what he or she believes to be proper construction, but rather to obtain the type and quality of construction that has been called for in the plan and specifications. This cannot be emphasized too strongly, as the wise contractor will generally provide exactly what the inspector demands, then file claims for extras for the cost differences between what was provided at the inspector's direction and what was called for in the plans and specifications—and will be entitled to get it.

## MATERIALS AND METHODS OF CONSTRUCTION

Most specifications, in their General Conditions, provide that unless specified otherwise, all workmanship, equipment, materials, and articles incorporated in the work are to be of the best available grade in the local trade area. Materials called for on the drawings that are not called for in the specifications, but that are known to be required for a complete project, are similarly required to be of comparable quality. These phrases are usually found in specifications prepared by someone who does not really know what it takes to make a "complete" project, or how properly to specify quality in a product. The result is one of the all-encompassing generalities such as that noted. It may get the job done, but not without many arguments in the field. It also saves the specifier the embarrassment of having to tell someone how to build something that he or she may not know the first thing about. Apparently, the concept is legally sound, but it puts a considerable added burden upon the Resident Project Representative, who must be the one to interpret the terms "best" and "quality." Generally, an inspector can plan on some arguments over either of these terms, because that which one person considers high quality another may consider substandard and because the construction contract was supposed to represent a "meeting of the minds." Unless both parties agree as to what the terms mean, there may be some doubt concerning that portion of the contract.

Often the specifications provide that all materials furnished must be free of defects or imperfections, and must normally be all new materials. Workmanship, similarly, is often stated in unenforceable terms. Phrases to the effect that "workmanship shall be of highest quality" or that something should be built using the "best workmanship" are almost useless, as the terms cannot be precisely defined, and therefore are largely unenforceable conditions. About all that can be rejected by the inspector under such provisions is craftsmanship that is so obviously defective that even a layman can recognize it.

With the proper specification terms, the inspector has a useful tool that can be used to great advantage. Under the specific terms of a specification that clearly defines the quality of workmanship, an inspector has every right to reject all that does not meet the specified standards—in fact, he or she has an obligation to do so. Specifications such as these are the products of professionals. A good specifications writer is one who has a good understanding of field construction, contract law, and design principles, and a writing ability—a rare breed.

### Interpretation of the Specifications

It should be kept in mind that the designers are the people most familiar with the intent of the contract documents and their provisions. To them, none of the terms seem vague or ambiguous because they understood what it was they were trying to say when they wrote the terms into their specifications. The contractor, however, must attempt to interpret the strict wording of the specifications to prepare the bid, and thus must rely on the ability of the specifications writer to communicate accurately the designer's intent through the wording of the specifications. As a contractor once stated, after being told what was intended by the terms of a specification: "I don't care what was intended—this is *what it says!*" The contractor was right, of course. The contract was to provide what it *said, not* what it should have said. If the designer or owner chooses to interpret the terms differently, they must expect to pay for the privilege.

The courts also respect this concept. They have generally held that, all other things being equal, in case of a dispute over the meaning of the wording of the specifications provisions, the binding interpretation will be in favor of the party who did not write the contract. This means that the judgment stands a good chance of being in the contractor's favor, as the contractor is generally not the party who wrote the contract provisions. In this manner, it is possible that in an imperfectly written set of documents, the contractor may actually be entitled to extra to build the work according to the meaning that the designers intended when they wrote the specifications.

## REQUESTS FOR SUBSTITUTIONS OF MATERIALS

By far one of the most frequent requests received on the job will be requests by the contractor to use substitute materials for those actually specified by the architect or engineer. The conditions controlling the use of such alternative choices of materials differ somewhat between public and private construction contracts, and must be considered separately.

Whenever a substitute is offered, the contractor is obligated to give adequate notice of an intention to offer a substitute—not wait until it is already too late to get delivery in time for the product actually called for. Then, after submittal, sufficient time must be allowed for the architect or engineer to review the technical data submitted by the contractor in support of his or her claim that the product is the equal of the specified one.

On a private project, the design firm may specify a single proprietary item for every item on the project if it chooses to do so, and there is no obligation to anyone except the owner to consider substitutes unless the architect or engineer wishes to do so. Such instructions must be communicated to the inspectors so that they can properly respond to the contractor in case of attempted submittals for consideration as substitutions. Furthermore, if in the judgment of the architect or engineer no substitutes may be considered, then only the specific brand or model of the specified product may be used in the work. All products delivered to the site for use on the work must be rejected if they fail to conform to the specific terms of the plans and specifications.

On public works projects, certain limitations exist all over the United States and in many foreign countries that limit the power of an architect or engineer to specify a single name brand of a product *if equivalent products are on the market.* All specifications for proprietary products in many states, as well as those for use either on federal contracts or contracts by other agencies in which part of the funding is from a federal agency, are required by law to name one or two brand names and the words "or equal" of a product called for by brand name. Also, a prescriptive specification that upon analysis can be seen as applying only to a single brand name is considered the same as calling out only one brand name, and is thus considered illegal. The majority of states have similar laws governing public projects within their jurisdiction, so even without federal funds, these conditions usually prevail on public projects. In certain cases, the law controlling the specifying of brand names allows an exception to the rule (1) if the product specified is required to be compatible with existing facilities, and (2) if the product specified is unique and no other brand is made.

Furthermore, it is the opinion of many competent legal authorities that the specification of several brand names, where one brand is called for by manufacturer and that manufacturer's catalog number, and the remaining brands are called for only by manufacturer's name, is in violation of the intent of the law and will be judged as if no alternatives had been offered. Each product named must include the description in comparable terms. It sounds unreasonable at first, but consider the frequent case of a product called for by catalog number, such as

> Well pump for the emergency water system shall be Jacuzzi 75S6AV15, Byron-Jackson, or approved equal . . .

In the first place, only one *product* has actually been specified. There is no catalog number for the Byron-Jackson unit; thus it is not a product but only the name of a potential *manufacturer* of an "equal" product. Often, a little research turns up the fact that some of the manufacturers named in specifications in this manner do not even manufacture a similar product. The other possibility is that the alternative "product" opens up the specifications so broadly that hardly any offered substitute can be excluded. One of the inherent dangers of the "or equal" concept is that the products named may not be equal at all. Often the designer selected exactly what was wanted in one catalog, then hastily selected what appeared to be an equal from another manufacturer. In doing this, the specifications may have unintentionally broadened to allow any other brand whose characteristics were anywhere within the extremes possessed by either brand. A product that contained all the worst features of both would still have to be considered as acceptable, as the simple naming of a second product that omitted a feature that was in the designer's primary choice of products automatically eliminated that particular feature as a minimum prerequisite for acceptance of a contractor-offered substitute. In some cases, there are also provisions for a public agency to specify a single proprietary product as part of a research or experimentation program in which the single product specified is the article being researched.

Basically, the architect or engineer is considered to be the final judge of the quality of a product, and the courts have often upheld this concept. If in their determination the product offered is not equal, they have the power to reject it summarily. Furthermore, the contractor may be required to carry the burden of the cost that may be necessary to prove equivalency where a laboratory analysis or similar certification is required. A product may be judged as not being equal on the basis of physical or chemical properties, performance, selection of materials, or even due to dimensional incompatibility with the design of the finished structure where the use of the alternative product may require redesign of portions of the structure to accommodate the substitute product. One case in Los Angeles, however, failed to uphold the owner's engineering staff in its refusal of a substitute product when its rejection was on wholly aesthetic grounds, because the specifications in this case had not cited aesthetics as being a proper criterion for the determination of product equivalency [*Argo Construction Co., Inc.,* vs. *County of Los Angeles,* Court of Appeals, 2d Civil No. 32568 (1969)].

In any case, the product offered as a substitute to a specified article must be submitted to the architect or engineer or to the owner, through the Resident Project Representative, for consideration and approval before such a substitute product may be used in the work. The inspector *must* reject any article that fails to satisfy one of the following two requirements:

1. It is the specific product called for in the plans and specifications.
2. It is a substitute product that the architect or engineer or the owner has approved in writing to the contractor.

In the absence of either of these conditions, the substitute product must be rejected by the inspector and required to be removed from the construction site. Failure to observe this requirement may be grounds for withholding partial payment to the contractor, and the inspector should make a careful survey at the time of payment requests to assure that all materials that have been installed or delivered to the site are in fact the same materials that have been specified or allowed by the design firm or the owner in writing as an approved substitute. If the contractor fails to meet these requirements, the inspector should submit a recommendation to the design firm or the owner along with the contractor's payment request that payment be disallowed for the nonconforming portion of the work.

### Time to Consider Substitutions

The construction industry needs generally to be made aware that substitutions proposed by bidders and contractors unduly disrupt the normal bidding and construction processes. Too often, valuable time and efforts of key personnel are wasted in the consideration of such requests that are originated by the proposer solely for his or her own financial benefit. Two factors should be kept in mind before a contractor proposes a substitution. First, there may be several perfectly valid but undisclosed reasons why the selection or specification was established as it was in the first place. Second, and in any case, time and effort will be required for the architect/engineer's and owner's investigation of the proposed substitute product, for which the personnel must be paid, and during which the work and other necessary activities may be delayed.

The claim is often made that all attempts to limit the consideration of substitutions result in a stifling of competition and loss of economy to the owner. This argument might be valid if the efforts of everyone concerned with the problem were without cost and if economics were the only interest of each owner. Everyone knows that the situation is not that simple, yet reasonable competition leading to economy is an important consideration for almost every owner.

There are several distinct periods during the life of a project when unjustified requests for substitutions can be expected to be submitted.

1. Design phase
2. Bidding phase
3. Time between bid opening and award of contract
4. Construction phase

The only time that consideration should be given to evaluation and acceptance of a substitute "or equal" product is either during the design phase or the construction phase just listed. No consideration should be made of any submittal or request for consideration of a substitute product during *any* of the other listed times.

Consideration of an "or equal" product during the bidding phase is not only unfair to the architect/engineer, because it allows too little time for a fair appraisal, but actually places the specifier in a high-risk situation for the benefit of a third party, and it is also quite unfair to the vendors who were willing to spend their own time and money during the design phase to provide data and consultations with the designers for proper application of the products specified (many of which are nonproprietary by nature). Vendors who request consideration of their product as an "equal" during the bidding phase are little more than freeloaders capitalizing on the efforts of the vendors who provided the preliminary design assistance.

Furthermore, these freeloaders are often able to underbid their competitors, as they can deduct an amount from their bid that is equivalent to the money spent by the others in providing design services. The author was personally involved in a case that later ended in litigation, in which consideration of another product was made during the bidding period, and an addendum was issued to the specifications to cover it. The latecomer's product was the lowest priced, of course, but unfortunately, it later failed (even before completion of the project), causing extensive financial loss to both the owner and the architect/engineer, as well as to the contractor and the supplier. Had adequate time been available for study, or had the vendor worked with the architect/engineer firm's specifications engineers during the design phase, the difficulty might never have developed.

The author recalls a recent court case in which the judge ruled against an engineer when a product that had been specified during the bidding phase failed, by stating that it was the engineer's professional obligation to specify only those products that he or she was sure of, and that a specification of one was in a sense a guarantee that the product was suitable for the purpose for which it was specified—despite the fact that the engineer had argued that there was insufficient time to make a proper evaluation of the proposed substitution during the bid period when it had been offered. In case of a vendor's or contractor's inquiry during the bidding phase, the only safe course is to advise all bidders to bid the products specified or proceed at their own risks, and that any requests for substitutions would have to wait until after award before consideration.

On public works projects, there should be no consideration of any substitutions between the bid-opening time and the date of the actual award of the contract. It is, however, both possible and practical in public works construction to limit consideration of proposed substitutes to a 35- to 45-day period just following the signing of the contract, if desired. This would effectively eliminate one of the "squeeze" plays used by some contractors to effect a substitution of a product for their sole personal gain. By this method, the contractor may submit a proposed substitute product at the last minute, claiming that the originally specified product is not available or has a long-lead purchase time that would result in delays to project completion. However, the contractor may offer the substitute product by stating "I can get this right away!" Nevertheless, if it had wanted to do so, the contractor could generally have ordered the specified product months before and met the schedule. As an added squeeze to the owner, this type of contractor might also threaten that if the owner insists on the product originally specified, the long-lead purchase item required will delay the completion of the work, and the owner will be held liable for the contractor's delays.

In such cases, it is the author's viewpoint that if insufficient time is allowed for proper consideration of an "or equal" product, the contractor should be required to submit the originally specified product and be held liable for any delays that might have been caused by its failure to order in time. Furthermore, the contractor should be informed that it will be subject to payment of liquidated damages for any overrun of the project schedule resulting from inability to obtain the product on time due to its failure to place the order early. In practice, it has often been found that this position materially changes the predicted long-lead purchase time, and often the item arrives right on schedule.

## ACCESS TO THE WORK BY QUALITY ASSURANCE PERSONNEL

The contractor is obligated at all times to provide access to the work to the architect/engineer and the owner or their authorized representatives, and the contractor is responsible for their safety while they are at the site. Of course, the contractor may require that all such persons coming onto the site wear appropriate safety devices and conduct their operations in a safe manner. Similarly, the inspector is entitled, normally, to have access to the place of manufacture of materials or equipment that are to be used in the work. Work on offshore facilities may present a problem, however, if the designer or specifications writer neglected to require the contractor to furnish transportation to such facilities (Figure 17.1). In that case, the design firm's or owner's representatives may just have to provide their own boats to get to the project site. The contractor's obligation *to allow* inspector access to the site is not an obligation to provide transportation for the inspector as well, although few contractors will want to risk the adversary relationship that would be the inevitable result in case of refusal. Nevertheless, this is an added risk and cost to the contractor, and where it is a significant amount, the contractor will be justified in claiming extra payment for the service.

## INSPECTION OF MATERIALS DELIVERED TO THE SITE

It is the responsibility of the inspector to inspect promptly all materials delivered to the site *prior* to their being used in the work. The practice of withholding inspection until the job is done, then announcing to the contractor that the work fails to conform to the specifica-

**FIGURE 17.1**  Offshore construction.

tions, is totally unacceptable conduct for a Resident Project Representative. Certain types of intermittent inspection as performed by government agencies, such as building departments, permit this type of inspection, but it is only because the responsibility for on-site quality control is that of the contractor and the owner's representative. A building department's responsibility is limited to assurance that all requirements of the code and the approved plans and specifications have been followed.

In certain cases it may be desirable to perform inspections of materials or fabricated products prior to their delivery at the site. A case in point would be an inspection of the precasting operation at a concrete precasting plant (Figure 17.2). Usually, the product remains in the casting yard for an extended period before delivery to the site, and failure to make early discovery of patent defects may hold up a project for several months while the precasting yard clears the casting beds to work in a new casting schedule and set up the new forms on the beds between other scheduled operations just to recast defective work. In addition, the placement of stirrups and similar conventional reinforcement in pretensioned, precast, prestressed concrete structural members must be carefully checked at the precasting yard before placing concrete, just as it must for cast-in-place conventional concrete. All too often the work of placing such reinforcing steel is not accurately done and can result in major structural failures.

**FIGURE 17.2**   Precast prestressed concrete members at casting yard.

The author was personally involved in one project in which over 80 percent of all roof members on a 61 m × 61 m (200 × 200 ft) roof developed progressive failures that were traced to improper placement of stirrups at the precasting yard. In addition to checking of stirrups, the plant inspection will provide an opportunity to measure the net length of all prestressed beams and girders stored at the plant in time to compare their dimensions with the design spacing of supports to see that adequate bearing will be provided at the ends of all beams and girders. Failure to do this has also resulted in failures at several sites in the past.

## REJECTION OF FAULTY MATERIAL

As described before, the inspector not only has a right to reject faulty materials, but is obligated to do so. Upon the rejection of nonconforming items, they should be clearly and indelibly marked in such manner that the article cannot be used in the work without the mark being clearly visible to the inspector (Figure 17.3). Such marks can be made with an indelible felt-tip pen, paint, or impression-type markers. The inspector should require that all rejected articles be removed from the construction area immediately and placed in a separate pile to be transported off the site the same day. The inspector should assure himself that the rejection marks cannot easily be erased and the nonconforming articles returned to the site as "new material."

```
┌─────────────────────────────────────────────────────────┐
│                                                         │
│          NON-CONFORMING                                 │
│          DO   NOT   USE                                 │
│  The accompanying article fails to conform to the contract requirements │
│  and shall be removed from the site unless approved deviation or │
│  corrective action has been accomplished (KSC Form 8-69)│
│                                                         │
│  ITEM _____      │
│                                                         │
│  DEFECT _____      │
│                                                         │
│  INSP. _____  DATED _____   │
│                                                         │
│  WAIVER REQUEST KSC FORM 869 NO. _____      │
│                                                         │
└─────────────────────────────────────────────────────────┘
```

**FIGURE 17.3**   Example of an inspector's rejection tag.

Acceptability of any material, article, or equipment should be based upon accepted standards of the industry, such as ASTM or trade association standards for the products involved (see "Special Material and Product Standards" in Chapter 6). If additional restrictions are imposed as acceptance criteria, they should clearly be spelled out in the specifications unless the requirements are so common in the industry that they are considered as unquestioned standards of trade.

The contractor should be provided with written notice in each case of noncompliance (Figure 17.4), and each such incident documented and retained in the project files (Figure 17.5a and b) as the data could later be necessary in defense of claims.

## CONSTRUCTION EQUIPMENT AND METHODS

Generally, selection of the type of equipment required to do a job is the responsibility of the contractor. However, if it can be clearly established that the use of a certain piece of equipment to do a specified job will in all probability result in inferior construction quality, it is within the authority of the architect/engineer or owner to require that appropriate changes be made. These instructions would normally be issued through the Resident Project Representative. Also, if the inspector notes that certain equipment, such as a crane, is overloaded and can possibly lead to a serious accident, there is some obligation to interrupt the use of the particular piece of equipment until the hazard has been eliminated.

One example of the right of a design firm or owner to limit the type of equipment to be used on a project concerns a concrete-lined reservoir where a 127 mm (5-inch) thick concrete lining was being placed in 7.3 m (24-ft) square panels joined with PVC waterstops sealed with polysulfide joint sealant. The side walls were sloped to $1\frac{1}{2}$ to 1, and the basin was 4.9 m (16 ft) deep. The concrete lining was to be placed over a layer of polyethylene sheet, and the design requirements prohibited any penetration through the plastic sheet into the earth below. Thus, when the contractor planned to use 3.7 m (12-ft) span mechanical vibratory screeds to span each panel, it was obvious that each panel would have to be screeded

**E. R. FISK & ASSOCIATES**

## NOTICE OF NON-COMPLIANCE

To __L&M Construction Company, Inc.__

___1234 Fontana Street___

___Marysville, CA 90000___

___Attn: Paul Marikian___

| Date |
|---|
| 15 May 1995 |
| Time |
| 09:45 hrs |
| Inspector |
| Jackson |
| ABC Labs, Inc. |

Project Title __Interceptor & Collector Sewers__     Project No. __F-345__

Contractor __Jorgensen & Sons__     Contract No. __95-0005__

You are hereby notified that ☒ tests ☒ inspection that the __trench backfill and compaction__

___between Stations 67+45 and 85+20___

does not conform to the requirements of the Contract Documents. The provision violated is:

Section __02450__     Article/Paragraph __3.4(A)__     under the provisions

of the Contract Documents, the requirements are __sand maust be placed in pipe zone, and after__

__consolidation backfill must be placed in lifts not exceeding 300 mm in depth and__

__compacted to 90 percent per ASTM D 1557-78.__

Noncomplying work may be required to be removed and replaced at no cost to the Owner.

It shall be your responsibility to determine corrective action necessary, and to determine whether you wish to discontinue operations until additional investigations by the Owner or Engineer confirm or refute the initial findings.

*Data used are fictitious for illustration only*

___K. E. Barnes___
Resident Project Representative

Non-compliance notice was received by the Contractor on ___5-15-95___
Date

By ___Harold Martinson___

Title ___PROJ. MANAGER___

Organization ___L&M CONST., INC___

FISK FORM 7-6

**FIGURE 17.4**  Notice to the contractor that work does not comply with specification requirements.

E. R. FISK & ASSOCIATES

**RECORD OF NON-COMPLYING TESTS**

Project Title _Taylor Avenue Reservoir_          Project No. _95-0023_

Contractor _ABC Constructors, Inc._          Type of Work _Concrete and Earthworks_

| GENERAL INFORMATION AS TO TYPE OF TEST RESULTS AND OTHER AVAILABLE PERTINENT DATA (Cite ASTM, ACI, ANSI, AWS, etc, as applicable) | QUANTITY INVOLVED | ACTION TAKEN |
|---|---|---|
| High slump (140 mm) Maximum allowable slump 60 mm ASTM C 143-78 | 5 m³ | Rejected and returned load No adjustment allowed |
| Core taken from panel lining. Permeable concrete in reservoir lining. | 2 panels | Field order issued to remove existing non-complying panels and recast. No adjustment allowed. |
| Backfill in intermediate pipe zone tests at 84% compaction ASTM D 1557-78 mod. to 3 layers | STA 1+63.373 to STA 1+74.955 | Required conditions to be corrected to specified 90 percent. No adjustment allowed. |
| Excavation of reservoir basic shows unforseen large deposit of expansive clay. | 2 800 m³ | Change Order #4 issued to presoak soil, then trim w/Gradall; seal with Visqueen & cast lining concrete while |
|  |  | subgrade is wet. Contract price increased by $23 450 plus additional time of 21 working days. |
|  |  |  |
|  |  |  |
|  |  |  |
|  |  |  |
|  |  |  |
|  |  |  |

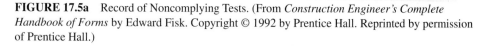
Data used are fictitious for illustration only

FISK FORM 12-8

**FIGURE 17.5a**   Record of Noncomplying Tests. (From *Construction Engineer's Complete Handbook of Forms* by Edward Fisk. Copyright © 1992 by Prentice Hall. Reprinted by permission of Prentice Hall.)

using two passes. This would require the use of steel stakes to support a wood screed upon which one end of the vibratory screed was expected to ride. The result would have required penetration through the polyethylene sheet, as well as some risk of substandard slab thickness in the area of the screed pins due to incomplete filling and consolidation of the screed pin holes. The contractor was informed that the equipment planned on was unsatisfactory and that an alternative method would have to be provided. It should be noted

**RECORD OF DEFECTIVE
MATERIALS AND WORKMANSHIP**

Project Title_Vinson Reservoir_____    Project No._95-0042_____

Location_____Thousand Oaks, CA_____    Project Feature_Basin area walls_____

| DATE | CONTRACTOR | DEFECTIVE CONDITION | RECOMMENDED ACTION TO SECURE CORRECTION |
|---|---|---|---|
| 6-14-95 | ABC Constructor's sub-contractor Specialty Concrete Co. | Waterstop welds are improperly made. Present condition results in unacceptable risk | Complete removal of all defective waterstop joints for a length of not less than 1 meter in each direction from the defective joint. Re-weld per specifications. |
| 8-24-95 | same | Porosity in concrete and excessive bleeding at vertical joints of steel form panels. | Assemble panel sections after thorough cleaning. Use bolts, not standard clamps. No reuse of any warped, bent, or damaged panels. Instruct vibrator operator as to proper method of method of consolidating concrete. |
| | | | |
| | Data used are fictitious for illustration only | | |
| | | | |
| | | | |
| | | | |

FISK FORM 12-7

**Purpose:** Formal notification to the Contractor of defects in his work and the required corrective action.

**Prepared by:** Resident Project Manager and the Project Manager.

**Directed to:** Prime Contractor including defects caused by his subcontractors.

**Copies to:** Prime Contractor, Resident Project Representative; Project Manager.

**Comments:** Documentation of unacceptable work. Any such work is subject to removal and reconstruction, corrective action, or acceptance by the Owner upon consideration of a discount. Must be followed up regularly to assure that corrective action has been taken.

**FIGURE 17.5b**   Record of Defective Materials or Workmanship. (From *Construction Engineer's Complete Handbook of Forms* by Edward Fisk. Copyright © 1992 by Prentice Hall. Reprinted by permission of Prentice Hall.)

here that the Resident Project Representative did not tell the contractor which method to use —only which method was unsatisfactory. It was still up to the contractor to select equipment and methods as long as they were capable of doing a satisfactory job within the terms of the specifications.

Similarly, any Resident Project Representative can influence the methods of construction to be used by the contractor if it can be shown that the proposed method of the contractor will not provide a satisfactory product. As mentioned, however, the resident engineer or inspector must be extremely careful as to how these statements are worded to the contractor. The resident engineer or inspector may indicate that a particular method of construction or piece of equipment is unsatisfactory, but must not go on to the next step and tell the contractor how the work should be done or which particular piece of equipment should be used.

## QUALITY LEVEL AND QUALITY ASSURANCE

### Quality Level

Quality level is the specific degree of excellence, basic nature, character, and kind of performance possessed by a particular item or group of items required by the designer. The minimum quality levels are those called for in the specifications for the project. The items that control quality include the following:

1. Location of the project
2. Magnitude of each phase of construction
3. Availability of local materials
4. Contemplated life of the construction
5. Climatic and operating conditions
6. Cost limitations
7. The desires of the architect or engineer

### Quality Assurance

Each quality level requires sufficient quality control to assure that the established quality levels are met. Quality assurance may be by visual inspection, tests, certifications, reports, shop drawings, and similar procedures. Like the quality level, the quality assurance will vary from project to project. The quality standards that are the means to assure that construction is in conformance with the contract specifications and drawings are the responsibility of the Resident Project Representative. Other quality assurance is provided by the results of tests, samples, shop drawings, and similar procedures.

## QUALITY ASSURANCE PROVISIONS

The following quality control provisions are considered separately from the visual inspection requirements of the Resident Project Representative. They are included in the specifications to assure that the quality of the items specified is actually provided by the contractor. When quality cannot be verified by routine field inspection, the quality assurance for material or equipment must be established by other means to assure satisfactory performance.

## Testing

Testing is limited to those laboratory or field tests actually called for in the specifications, or allowed by them. Such tests may be performed by the contractor, the architect/engineer, the owner, or commercial testing laboratories. The commercial laboratories may be hired by the contractor, the owner, or the design firm, but in each case the project manager and the Resident Project Representative should receive a copy of the test results.

Testing is required for items of work that are critical and are particularly susceptible to unsatisfactory levels of quality, and that cannot generally be detected by observation (Figure 17.6). Examples are concrete, soil compaction, and similar materials. The specifications determine which items are to be tested, which tests and procedures apply, and the required levels of performance. The specification also determines who should perform the test. Testing is necessary for any work that has a history of poor performance and involves an assembly of products furnished by more than one contractor, where the end result is critical.

## Installation in Accordance with the Product Manufacturer's Instructions

In many cases, the specification requires that the product manufacturer provide instructions for the method of installation of products that are installed by subcontractors who are not directly affiliated with the product manufacturer. This provision is supposed to be used only where rigid adherence to the manufacturer's instructions is critical, where product composition and construction create limitations not likely to be understood by the installer, and where installation procedures are complex or subject to significant variations between different manufacturers. Unfortunately, it is also used by lazy specifications writers who either do not know enough about a product to specify it, or who will not take the time to research it.

## Experience Qualification

An experience qualification is a requirement that a firm performing a certain type of work have an established reputation for the successful completion of similar work elsewhere for a specified amount of time. The use of an experience requirement is limited to those fields of work in which the ability to do a certain amount of work in the time normally allowed, as well as competence in performing installations and services, requires a considerable amount of previous experience. Examples of such fields of work include:

1. Metal curtain walls
2. Foundation piles
3. Dewatering

**FIGURE 17.6** Ultrasonic testing of structural field welds.

4. Precast architectural concrete
5. Calking and sealing
6. Spray-on fire protection
7. Laboratory equipment
8. Mechanical and electrical equipment

This type of provision is devised to prevent "fly-by-night" firms from performing work for which they are not qualified or which they may not be able to complete. The disadvantage is that there is still no assurance that the firm selected will remain in business or will stand behind the work it performs. The provision is generally used for work that requires special qualifications for which there are a number of firms of long standing who are generally recognized in the industry as having this special capability, and where there is a history of fly-by-night operators.

### Factory Inspection

Occasionally, a construction contract calls for inspection of production and fabrication facilities at a manufacturer's plant as a part of the quality control requirements of the project. The specification must tell the specific type of inspection to perform. This provision is used for assuring the quality control of custom products of such nature that on-site inspection or testing is either impossible or impractical. This provision is used mostly for large prefabricated products that are fabricated especially for each project, where it is impractical to perform tests and inspection at the job site or at a testing laboratory. Examples of such products are:

1. Precast concrete piles
2. Architectural precast concrete
3. Precast pretensioned concrete members (Figure 17.7)
4. Fabricated steel plate specials
5. Pump station manifolds
6. Concrete or asphalt concrete batch plant facilities
7. Welded steel tanks
8. Hydroelectric project equipment (Figure 17.8)

### Matching Samples on Display during Bidding

Sometimes a contractor is asked to base the quality of a product upon a sample that is placed on display during bidding. This provision is used only where important aesthetic considera-

**FIGURE 17.7**  Precast prestressed concrete members at casting yard.

**FIGURE 17.8**   Factory inspection of a hydroelectric turbine shaft and thrust bearing runner prior to shipment.

tions cannot be adequately specified in words, and for which no known or local appearance standard can be furnished for prospective bidders to examine. To maintain effective quality control during construction, each such sample must later be stored at the construction site for ready reference as a basis of acceptance. Examples of such materials or items are:

1. Natural stone
2. Precast concrete panels with exposed aggregate
3. Concrete finishes
4. Special wood finishes and cabinetry standards

This method allows an effective means to assure that the desired visual characteristics of highly textured or grained materials, which are often difficult to describe verbally, can be provided. Additional advantages when used in public works construction are that trade names can be avoided and that disputes between the Resident Project Representative and the contractor over the appearance of a material surface that may otherwise meet specification requirements can be avoided. The disadvantage is that facilities must be provided in one central location for displays of all samples during bidding, and again at the site during construction. Care must be taken to assure that sample panels represent the full range of colors and textures permitted, and that matching material is obtainable from more than one source in the case of public agency contracts.

## Mock-up

Another method of quality control is the requirement for the contractor to construct a mock-up or a prototype construction assembly that, after approval, will serve as the standard for the same type of construction throughout the project. This method is best used where it is impossible or impractical to specify critical aesthetic characteristics that may be desired, or where an assembly is too large or complex to be fabricated prior to award of the contract. Examples are:

1. Certain masonry or natural stone assemblies
2. Architectural precast concrete

Mock-ups by the contractor prior to construction can be advantageous to control the quality of a complex construction system where the aesthetic and other requirements cannot be described accurately in words or in drawings. The disadvantages are that:

1. The standard of production is established *after award* of the contract.
2. Numerous arguments over fine points of aesthetics may arise.
3. The finally approved mock-up may not conform to other specification requirements.
4. Delays may result while awaiting approvals.
5. Additional costs are normally reflected in the bids.

The use of this system is usually confined to complex exterior wall assemblies on monumental buildings where aesthetics are a major consideration, and where there is no other adequate way to describe the desired appearance.

## Proven Successful Use

Under this provision, the contractor is asked to provide proof that the same type of product or similar products or equipment have been used successfully in similar construction for a specific period of time. The use of this provision is generally limited to mechanical and electrical equipment that requires proof of safe, dependable, continuous operation for a number of years. This provision is not used for those items that would benefit by innovation. The primary advantage of this type of provision is that the risks usually associated with the experimental use of new products are avoided. It has the disadvantage of discouraging innovation, however, and it offers no insurance against faulty installation. It is generally used to specify items such as elevators, electrical equipment, large pumps, water and sewage treatment plant equipment, and similar items that must be in continuous and reliable service for many years. It is not generally used for architectural items or for products for which it is not possible to determine "successful use" clearly.

## Qualified Products List

A *qualified products list* is a provision of the specifications that requires that the procurement of certain contract items be restricted to those items that have previously been tested and approved, and have been included in a list of approved items in the specifications. A qualified products list is not necessarily limited to products that are named in the specifications, but may also be lists of products compiled by independent authorities, such as the Underwriters' Laboratories, which assumes the responsibility for testing and updating their lists. The advantage of using a qualified products list is that the sometimes long, complex, or expensive tests that may otherwise be required have already been performed and do not need to be done for each project. The disadvantages of a qualified products list are:

1. Possibility of less competition
2. Possibility of disclaimer by the contractor for defects in materials furnished under this system
3. Administrative difficulties in maintaining up-to-date lists

## Certified Laboratory Test Reports

This is a requirement by which the contractor is asked to provide a certificate that indicates that a product meets specified quality requirements for performance or physical or chemical standards when the submitted sample is tested in accordance with certain specified laboratory standard tests. Submittal of test reports is required for those standard items for which there is a need for quality control testing but for which the testing of the actual item to be installed cannot be justified. Requirements for this provision normally include a statement calling for exact test methods, minimum level of performance, and identification of the product to be tested to be sure that it is the same as the one to be used in construction. In addition, the tests are required to be performed by a recognized independent testing laboratory acceptable to the design firm or the owner. Examples of materials that may require such certified reports are:

1. Concrete reinforcing steel
2. Structural steel
3. Sound control ratings of materials
4. Fire-spread ratings of materials
5. Polyvinyl chloride materials for waterstops
6. Masonry units

Where the contractor is responsible for obtaining the test reports, the disadvantage is the possible danger of apparent conflict of interest due to the contractor furnishing both the material and the testing. Additionally, the reliability of the testing laboratory could be open to question.

The manner in which this provision appears in specifications varies widely. Some of the more common requirements for certified laboratory test reports that are included in specifications are:

1. Test reports shall be based upon results of tests that have been made within a certain time on materials representative of those proposed for use; or
2. Test reports shall be based upon results of tests made on samples taken from materials proposed for delivery to the job site; or
3. Test reports shall be based upon results of tests made on items installed at the job.

Test reports included in the manufacturer's literature are often worthless, as the tests from which the data were derived are often nonstandard or are designed to dramatize certain properties and to conceal undesirable properties.

## Certificate of Compliance or Conformance

Under these provisions the contractor is required to provide a certificate that says that the product complies with a specified reference standard. It is necessarily limited to products of standard manufacture for which quality can be clearly assured by the manufacturer, installation is not critical, and job testing is neither necessary nor justified. Examples of such products would include:

1. Glass
2. Paint
3. Aluminum windows
4. Wood

The primary advantage is that certificates can usually be obtained with very little if any increase in the price of the product. The disadvantage is that their validity and reliability depend entirely upon the integrity and knowledge of the certifier.

The requirements of the specifications that call for certificates of compliance are normally included only for those times for which the extra costs of certified laboratory costs cannot be justified. Usually, such certificates are reliable when they come from a member of an industry or trade that has a strong association that exerts some policing effort to maintain quality. When they do not come from such a source, their reliability may be subject to question. Generally, a resident engineer or inspector is protected by clauses in the specifications that reserve the right for them to inspect and to test any article over and above the test requirements specified, and that the results of such inspections and tests are also binding upon the contractor. In such cases, the extra testing is usually at the expense of the owner unless it turns up a defect; then, often the contract provisions require payment by the contractor of both the corrective measures and the tests that disclosed the defect.

## Warranties; Guarantees

The terms *warranty* and *guarantee* are often used interchangeably in construction contracts and are used to refer to the maintenance and repair obligations of the contractor for a specific period of time after the completion of construction. The General Conditions of the contract on most projects include specific requirements governing contractor warranties or guarantees. For the purposes of this definition, the term *warranty* will be used to describe this provision.

Two types of warranties are recognized under the law:

1. Implied warranties
2. Express warranties

The term *implied warranties* means that the goods must be capable of passing in trade under the contract description and are fit for the purpose intended. *Express warranties* are those that are specifically set forth in the contract itself; they are in common use for many construction contracts. Warranties are generally for packaged items such as water heaters and compressors. Where the industry practice is to furnish a warranty for an item, the requirement for such a warranty may be included in the specifications. An express warranty is a means of achieving good procurement results by making the contractor responsible for its work and for failures of its work during some part of its useful life. The primary disadvantage of warranties is that they are often unenforceable. Moreover, a warranty clause costs money in the form of higher bid prices, and it cannot be demonstrated that the owner recovers the cost of warranty.

There are several obstacles to the strict enforcement of warranties; some of these obstacles follow:

1. Even in what appears to be a clear-cut contractor responsibility under a warranty, certain action on the part of the owner or design firm may cloud the issue and result in litigation.
2. After acceptance of an item by the owner, the operation and maintenance of the item is performed by other than the contractor's or manufacturer's personnel. Thus, many defects that occur during the warranty period can be argued to result from faulty operation and maintenance by others rather than from a defect in the item itself.
3. Industry is becoming reluctant to accept several of the warranty clauses now in use. In particular, it will not accept the provision relating to third-party damages and the responsibility for an entire building and its contents, including damages to personnel, resulting from the failure of a single item.
4. Warranties of sole-source items are generally unenforceable.
5. In practical application, warranties are generally enforceable only as to defects existing at the time of delivery and acceptance.

Although the warranty clauses usually require the contractor to obtain and enforce warranties normally furnished by manufacturers and suppliers, the exact nature of the warranty is usually not stipulated in the specifications. Therefore, their effectiveness is subject to the wording used by the guarantor and can be expected to be something less than specific. Such a warranty depends almost entirely upon the integrity of the guarantor (the manufacturer or supplier). There are substantial differences in the warranty requirements of public and private agencies in their construction contracts. They range from requiring the contractor to warrant all work as to materials, workmanship, and contractor's design, to requiring the contractor to warrant only mechanical and electrical work. One agency may require the contractor to remedy all damage to equipment, site, buildings, and their contents resulting from a defect, whereas another agency may require the contractor to act as the owner's agent and obtain and enforce the subcontractors' and suppliers' warranties.

## OWNERSHIP OF MATERIALS

Generally, it may be said that the ownership of all materials used in the work or stored at the site is vested in the contractor until final acceptance of the work by the owner at the end of the job. Thus, any risk associated with the protection of the work and the repair of damaged work, or the delivery of damaged materials, is usually the responsibility of the contractor, not the owner. Similarly, the contractor's insurance carrier will normally be called upon to pay the costs of any such claims.

## DELIVERY AND STORAGE OF MATERIALS

There is no firm formula for the determination of which facilities will be accorded the contractor as a working or staging area or for its storage of construction materials. Generally, it is the contractor's responsibility to make its own arrangements for such facilities if provisions have not been made by the owner. Although it is true that most owners do provide space, in some areas no such space is under the owner's direct control; in such cases the contractor must make arrangements for space. Occasionally, this is done by the contractor actually entering into a rental agreement for space, which must accordingly be taken into consideration at the time of figuring the bid.

In no case should any contractor assume that it has the right to block public thoroughfares or to use public property of any kind, including parking lots, for its construction purposes, even when the work is being performed for the owner of the property under consideration, unless specific written authority has been granted. As a means of protecting the owner from such claims, the Resident Project Representative should be assured that the space being used by the contractor for its work area has been properly granted by the owner of the affected property.

## HANDLING OF MATERIALS

The resident engineer or inspector must be concerned not only with the quality of the materials as delivered and their methods of installation, but should require that all such materials be properly handled during delivery, unloading, transporting, storage, and installation so that undue stresses will not result in latent defects that will not be detected until after the project has been signed-off. When in doubt, the resident engineer or inspector should have the design firm or the owner contact the manufacturer of the affected material, who is generally just as interested in its proper handling in the field as is the owner. This is because the manufacturer is often the victim of unjust claims for defective materials when, in fact, the problem may have been due to improper handling during construction.

## PROBLEMS

1. True or false? As an accepted standard of quality, a supplier's certificate is an acceptable substitute for a manufacturer's mill test certificate.

2. List two times during a project (conception to completion) when it is not justified for the engineer or architect to require the contractor to submit its requests for substitutions of products under the provisions for "or equals."

3. Name at least six types of products or fabrications that would be suitable for the engineer or architect to call for inspection at the manufacturing or fabrication plant.

4. True or false? The inspector has no interest in the manner or location of storage of construction materials delivered and stored at the site.

5. Generally, is ownership of materials to be used in the work, and stored at the site, vested in the owner or the contractor?

6. Name the eleven means of establishing quality assurance or compliance described in the text.

7. True or false? An inspector is responsible for securing that the highest possible quality of work be done.

8. Which is more desirable in a specification, to require literal compliance with an absolute dimension or specifying a tolerance range for the inspector to work with?

9. Who is in control of construction means and methods in a construction contract?

10. Name one set of circumstances where it is permissible in a public contract to specify a sole source product without the words *or equal*?

# 18

## Changes and Extra Work

### CONTRACT MODIFICATIONS

A change order is a written agreement to modify, add to, or otherwise alter the work from that set forth in the contract documents at the time of opening bids, provided that such alteration can be considered to be within the scope of the original project; otherwise, a contract modification may be required. It is the only legal means available to change the contract provisions after the award of the contract. Functionally, a change order accomplishes after execution of the Agreement what the specifications *addenda* do prior to bid opening (Figure 18.1), except that an accompanying price change may be involved in a change order. A price change is not necessarily always in the contractor's favor, however, as it could also be in the form of a cash credit to the owner, or it may involve no price change at all.

It is standard practice in construction contracts to allow the owner the right to make changes in the work after the contract has been signed and during the construction period. Depending upon the contract and its specific terms, such changes might involve additions

| ADVERTISING DATE | BID OPENING | AWARD DATE | SIGN AGREEMENT |
|:---:|:---:|:---:|:---:|
| ① | ② | ③ | ④ |
| Changes by Addenda | | No Changes | Changes by Change Order |

**FIGURE 18.1**   Time of changes by addenda versus by change order.

to or deletions from the work, changes in the methods of construction or manner of work performance, changes in owner-furnished materials or facilities, or even changes in the contract time or order of the work. Changes may also be executed to correct errors in the plans or specifications, or they may be the direct result of contractor suggestions that are approved by the owner and the architect/engineer.

## CHANGES IN THE WORK

### Impact Costs

Often, an owner or architect/engineer fails to realize that the cost of changes in the work may well exceed the cost of the immediate change itself. Many change order forms contain an exculpatory clause that precludes a contractor from recovery of impact costs. In some cases, the two parties already agree on the price of a change in both time and dollars, but the contractor wants to reserve the right to file for impact costs. If this is all that the contractor wants, and all of the other terms of the document are acceptable, it may be advisable to accept the change order with that reservation. If the owner does not, the contractor can file a claim anyway (and will, too), but the amount of the new claim will not only be the cost of any potential impact costs, but will include the now-inflated value of the time and dollars that had originally been agreed to. A contractor would be ill-advised to sign off on a change order if it expects to claim any future impact costs.

A California court in *Vanlar Construction, Inc.* v. *County of Los Angeles,* 217 Cal. Rptr.53 (Cal. App. 1985) ruled that a contractor who signed off 81 change orders and seven supplemental agreements had waived its right to any impact costs arising out of the cumulative effect of the numerous changes.

The County of Los Angeles awarded a contract to Vanlar Construction, Inc., to construct a public building. During the course of construction, the county issued 81 change orders and seven supplemental agreements. Each of these documents stated that it covered "all charges direct or indirect arising out of this additional work." Vanlar officials signed off on each document.

After completion of the work, Vanlar brought a claim for the impact costs that were not included in the individual change orders. Vanlar argued that it was impossible to measure the cumulative impact of the changes as each change order was issued, making it necessary to wait until completion of the construction. Vanlar also stated that it was a well-recognized custom of the industry to wait until project completion to submit a claim for impact costs.

The California court ruled that Vanlar's execution of the change orders and supplemental agreements precluded subsequent claims for increased costs arising out of those changes. The documents clearly stated that they covered indirect costs arising out of the extra work. The court also said that because the change orders were clear and unambiguous, Vanlar could not resort to industry custom to explain the intended meaning of those documents.

In the court's words: "If Vanlar contemplated any future claim for impact costs, whether at the time of the first, fiftieth, or the eighty-first change order, it was legally obligated to request that a suitable reservation clause be inserted in each change order and supplemental agreement prior to accepting and signing the change order or supplemental agreement."

If a project owner refuses to agree to appropriate reservation language, the contractor may perform the changed work under protest without signing the change order or agreeing to a price.

### Oral Change Orders

This is risky turf. Despite the fact that the documents require all change orders to be in writing, the actions of both the owner's representative and the contractor can constructively waive that requirement.

In the case of *Udevco, Inc.* v. *Wagner* 678 P.2d 679 (Nev. 1984), the Nevada Supreme Court held that a project owner orally waived a requirement that no extra work be performed without a written change order. In that case, Wosser-Laster Enterprises was awarded a contract by Udevco, Inc. to perform framing work on a condominium project being developed by Udevco. Due to an error in the owner's plans and specifications, the prefabricated roof trusses did not fit. Additionally, the framing had to be modified to accommodate cabinets and doors that did not match the original framing design.

Wosser performed this extra work without first obtaining a written change order as required by the contract. It did so at the oral direction of Udevco's project superintendent, who assured Wosser that it would be paid for the work. When Wosser invoiced the owner for the extra work, however, Udevco denied responsibility for work performed without a change order. Wosser argued that the requirement had been waived, but a trial court disagreed. The trial court ruled that because Udevco never paid for any extra work performed without a written change order, the requirement had not been waived.

Upon appeal, the Supreme Court of Nevada reversed this ruling. One way to waive a change order requirement is to pay for extra work performed without written authorization. The requirement may also be waived by oral agreement, however. The court said: "Whether Udevco made payments or not for extra work is not solely controlling of whether it waived the written change order requirement. . . . After Udevco's express oral waiver and Wosser's reliance thereon, Udevco at that time was bound to pay for extra work, regardless of whether it later failed to pay. . . . We conclude under these facts, as a matter of law, that the parties mutually intended to waive the written change order condition."

### Change Orders

A change order is the formal document that alters some condition of the contract documents. The change order may alter the contract price, schedule of payments, completion date, or the plans and specifications.

**Bilateral change orders.**  The term *change order,* as normally referred to in all except federal contracts, refers to a *bilateral* agreement between the owner and the contractor to effect a change in the terms of the contract. In federal contracts, this document is called a *contract amendment,* as the term *change order* in federal contracts refers to a *unilateral* order to effect a change (Figure 18.2).

| | CHANGE TYPE | PUBLIC (NON-FEDERAL) CONTRACTS AND PRIVATE CONTRACTS | FEDERAL CONTRACTS ONLY (FAR 43.101 and 43.103) |
|---|---|---|---|
| CONTRACT MODIFICATIONS | Bilateral | Change Order | Contract Amendment or Supplemental Agreement |
| | Unilateral | Construction Change Directive | Change Order |

**FIGURE 18.2**    Chart showing the terminology used for the various change documents.

***Unilateral change orders.***    A unilateral change in nonfederal contracts is referred to in the EJCDC contract documents as a *Work Change Directive* (Figure 18.3), and in AIA contract documents as a *Construction Change Directive* (Figure 18.4). In federal contracts, a unilateral change is referred to as a *Change Order* (Figure 18.2). A unilateral contract modification is intended to expedite issuance of a change order to perform emergency work or protested work, and must be replaced by a regular bilateral change order that addresses the effect of the change on contract cost and time before payment can be made to the contractor.

When approved by the owner, the provisions of a change order become a part of the contract. If an approved change order is executed by the contractor, all of its provisions and terms are as binding upon the parties as are those of the original contract.

Each change order must be evaluated individually; however, there are certain basic principles that apply to the handling of all types of change orders.

1. No work should be included beyond the scope of the base contract, particularly on public works contracts.
2. The identity of the individuals authorized to request and approve change orders should be established early. Such information should be provided to the contractor's superintendent or foreman and the owner's Resident Project Representative.
3. During the preconstruction conference, a meeting should be held to establish the change order handling procedures.
4. All changes in the work must be authorized in writing prior to the execution of any change.
5. The scope of a change order must be clear, and a request for a change order proposal should contain enough information to enable the contractor to make a realistic estimate.
6. The contractor should submit its proposal to execute a change order as soon as possible after receiving the request, and the owner's approval or rejection should follow as soon as possible.
7. The proposal should be fair. It should recognize the contractor's right to include overhead and profit percentages in change order estimates and in time and material change order billings. It should also be recognized that the contractor is

**LAWRANCE, FISK & McFARLAND, INC.**
CONSULTING ENGINEERS • SANTA BARBARA • ORANGE

## WORK CHANGE DIRECTIVE

(Instructions on reverse side)                                          No. 7

PROJECT ..ABC Reservoir & Pumping Plant.......................

DATE OF ISSUANCE ...8 June 1990........   EFFECTIVE DATE ...8 June 1990.........................

OWNER ....City of Thousand Oaks, Dept. of Utilities.......................

OWNER's Contract No. ....89/90-00.......................................................

CONTRACTOR ..XYZ Constructors, Inc....  ENGINEER ..Lawrance, Fisk & McFarland, Inc.

You are directed to proceed promptly with the following change(s):
    Install pipe closure on water line shown as abandoned on Dwg. No. C-12
Description: and remove and dispose of damaged materials; Repair damage from water to
    facilities & access road per Attachment A.
Purpose of Work Change Directive:  Unforseen active water line listed as abandoned in
    City records.  Line was actually under pressure & was damanged due to removal attempt.
Attachments: (List documents supporting change)
    Attachment A (Sketch SK-25) showing method & location of closure

If a claim is made that the above change(s) have affected Contract Price or Contract Times any claim for a Change
Order based thereon will involve one or more of the following methods of determining the effect of the change(s).

| Method of determining change in Contract Price: | Method of determining change in Contract Times: |
|---|---|
| ☐ Unit Prices | ☐ Contractor's records |
| ☐ Lump Sum | ☒ Engineer's records |
| ☒ Other ___Time & materials___ | ☐ Other _____ |

Estimated increase (decrease) in Contract Price:
$ 2300.00
If the change involves an increase, the estimated
amount is not to be exceeded without further
authorization.

Estimated increase (decrease) in Contract Times:
Substantial Completion: _unknown_ days;
Ready for final payment: _unknown_ days.
If the change involves an increase, the estimated
times are not to be exceeded without further
authorization.

RECOMMENDED:

  Lawrance, Fisk & McFarland, Inc.
        ENGINEER

By: _____
         (Authorized Signature)
  C. H. Lawrance, Project Manager

AUTHORIZED:

   City of Thousand Oaks
        OWNER

By: _____
         (Authorized Signature)
  Senior Civil Engineer
  Dept. of Utilities

EJCDC No. 1910-8-F (1990 Edition)
Prepared by the Engineers Joint Contract Documents Committee and endorsed by The Associated General Contractors of America.

**FIGURE 18.3**  Example of EJCDC Work Change Directive. (Copyright © 1990 by National
Society of Professional Engineers.)

**WORK CHANGE DIRECTIVE**

**INSTRUCTIONS**

---

**A. GENERAL INFORMATION**

This document was developed for use in situations involving changes in the Work which, if not processed expeditiously, might delay the Project. These changes are often initiated in the field and may affect the Contract Price or the Contract Times. This is not a Change Order, but only a directive to proceed with Work that may be included in a subsequent Change Order.

For supplemental instructions and minor changes not involving a possible change in the Contract Price or the Contract Times a Field Order may be used.

**B. COMPLETING THE WORK CHANGE DIRECTIVE FORM**

Engineer initiates the form, including a description of the items involved and attachments.

Based on conversations between Engineer and Contractor, Engineer completes the following:

METHOD OF DETERMINING CHANGE, IF ANY, IN CONTRACT PRICE: Mark the method to be used in determining the final cost of Work involved and the estimated net effect on the Contract Price. If the change involves an increase in the Contract Price and the estimated amount is approached before the additional or changed Work is completed, another Work Change Directive must be issued to change the estimated price or Contractor may stop the changed Work when the estimated price is reached. If the Work Change Directive is not likely to change the Contract Price, the space for estimated increase (decrease) should be marked "Not Applicable."

METHOD OF DETERMINING CHANGE, IF ANY, IN CONTRACT TIMES: Mark the method to be used in determining the change in Contract Times and the estimated increase or decrease in Contract Times. If the change involves an increase in the Contract Times and the estimated times are approached before the additional or changed Work is completed, another Work Change Directive must be issued to change the times or Contractor may stop the changed Work when the estimated times are reached. If the Work Change Directive is not likely to change the Contract Times, the space for estimated increase (decrease) should be marked "Not Applicable."

Once Engineer has completed and signed the form, all copies should be sent to Owner for authorization because Engineer alone does not have authority to authorize changes in Price or Times. Once authorized by Owner, a copy should be sent by Engineer to Contractor. Price and Times may only be changed by Change Order signed by Owner and Contractor with Engineer's recommendation.

Once the Work covered by this directive is completed or final cost and times are determined, Contractor should submit documentation for inclusion in a Change Order.

THIS IS A DIRECTIVE TO PROCEED WITH A CHANGE THAT MAY AFFECT THE CONTRACT PRICE OR THE CONTRACT TIMES. A CHANGE ORDER, IF ANY, SHOULD BE CONSIDERED PROMPTLY.

**FIGURE 18.3** *continued*

## CHANGE ORDER REQUEST

Project Title ___Tri-City RTD Bus Maintenance Facility___

Project No.___94-2417___ Contract No.___DAA-0-689-94___ Contract Date ___2-18-94___

Contractor ___ABC Constructors and D&F Construction (Jt Venture)___

Proposed By: ___M. O. Parker, Resident Engineer___ Date ___7-28-95___
(Name)

Submitted By: ___E. R. Fisk, Project Manager___ Date ___7-31-95___
(Name)

☐ Owner
☒ Arch. & Engr.
☐ Construction

| Actual job conditions in area of proposed change: Electrical service not yet completed. |
|---|
| All masonry work completed. Rolling steel door installed & operable. |
| Change order justification: |
| Area served by rolling door has no other access or opening. Design of roll-up |
| door installation calls for operating controls to be installed inside the room. |
| Door cannot be operated from outside, as constructed. |

Contractor authorized to proceed with this change ☒ YES ☐ NO on___issuance of change order___

Other contracts involved are as follows (List Contracts by No.):___none___ Is Dwg. Req.? ☐ NO ☒ YES___E-14___
(Sheet No.)

Description of Work to be Performed:

| Drill masonry wall to allow conduit installation from maintenance area into |
|---|
| the secure room and install electrical wiring to allow electrical motor operation |
| or the door to the secure room from the adjacent maintenance room. Install key- |
| operated switch for actuating rolling steel door to the secure area . |
| Power from circuit J-3. |

*Data used are fictitious for illustration only*

Estimated effect on costs of: A&E ___$1,080.00___        Inspection: $ ___$125.00___

Approved ___[signature]___        ___8-11-95___
for Tri-City RTD        (Date)

Fisk Form 15-1

**Purpose:** Describes proposed changes and the justification for them, and authorizes issuance of a change order.

**Prepared by:** Any principal involved in the project: Owner; Engineer; or Contractor.

**Directed to:** Owner.

**Copies to:** Owner; Project Manager; Resident Project Representative; Prime Contractor.

**Comments:** This is merely the first stage in the implementation of a contract change. *This does not constitute a change order.* During final stages, the change order form may be issued by the contractor in the form of a letter proposal, and must address effect on time and cost.

**FIGURE 18.4** Initiator Change Order Request.

entitled to compensation for legitimate time-delay claims, processing of deduct change orders, costs of disposing of removed material, and all other legitimate costs incurred in the execution of the change.

Change orders create additional work for everyone in the industry. One of the most aggravating conditions is the length of time that elapses between the time that a proposed contract modification is announced until the matter is finally rejected or approved as a change order. If the procedures discussed in this chapter are followed, it is possible to minimize the inequities otherwise possible in the administration of a contract change order.

In some cases a situation may arise at the construction site where immediate instruction must be given, and revised drawings and specifications may be unnecessary. In such instances, the Resident Project Representative, upon receiving proper authorization, should prepare an *Initiator Change Order Request* (Figure 18.4) with instructions as to whether the work should proceed immediately or wait until the cost proposals have been approved and a formal contract Change Order (Figures 18.5 and 18.6) issued.

Whereas it is possible, under emergency conditions, to start such extra work under a Work Change Directive (Figure 18.3), it must be emphasized that any work performed beyond the scope of the original contract provisions must be followed up with a confirming change order clearly citing the effect of the change upon both project cost and time of completion. *In no case* should any work beyond the original contract scope or requirements be executed solely upon the authority of a Field Order or Work Change Directive. All such work *must* be supported by a change order. This is for the protection of both the owner and the contractor. The owner has the obligation to review promptly any change order proposals and recommendations and direct the architect/engineer to reject or authorize such change.

Changes frequently have an impact upon the performance of other work that is not in itself changed. The term *impact* refers to the indirect delay or interference that a change on one phase of the work may create on another phase, and the costs of such delay or interference should be recognized as a consequential cost to be considered as a part of direct cost expenses of the contractor, and consideration must be given to allowing for payment of these costs to the contractor.

## TYPES OF CHANGES

### Directed vs. Constructive Change

Before addressing the specific elements of a changes clause in a contract, it is useful to define two basic types of change: directed and constructive.

**Directed changes.**   A directed change is easy to identify. The owner directs the contractor to perform work that differs from that specified in the contract or is an addition to the work specified. A directed change may also be deductive in nature; that is, it may reduce the scope of work called for in the contract.

In the case of a directed change, there is no question that a change occurred. Disagreements tend to center on questions of financial compensation and the effect of the change on the construction schedule.

**FIGURE 18.5** Change Order. (From *Construction Engineer's Complete Handbook of Forms* by Edward Fisk. Copyright © 1992 by Prentice Hall. Reproduced by permission of Prentice Hall.)

# CHANGE ORDER

(Instructions on reverse side)                                                    No. 13

---

PROJECT ... Hydroelectric Project ...

DATE OF ISSUANCE ... 14 May 1990 ...     EFFECTIVE DATE ... 15 May 1990 ...

---

OWNER ... Oakville Power Company ...

OWNER's Contract No. ... 89/90-00 ...

CONTRACTOR ... XYZ Constructors, Inc.     ENGINEER ... Lawrance, Fisk & McFarland, Inc.

---

You are directed to make the following changes in the Contract Documents.

Description:
- Item 1 – Exploratory excavation
- Item 2 – Pipe relocation
- Item 3 – Delete lateral 4A

Reason for Change Order:
Corrective work

Attachments: (List documents supporting change)
Attachment B (Sketch SK-30)

Data used are fictitious
for illustration only

| CHANGE IN CONTRACT PRICE: | CHANGE IN CONTRACT TIMES: |
|---|---|
| Original Contract Price | Original Contract Times |
| $ 65,123,405.00 | Substantial Completion: 1400 <br> Ready for final payment: ___ <br> *days or dates* |
| Net changes from previous Change Orders No. 1 to No. 12 | Net change from previous Change Orders No. 1 to No. 12 |
| $ 62,037.00 | *days* |
| Contract Price prior to this Change Order | Contract Times prior to this Change Order |
| $ 65,185.442.00 | Substantial Completion: 1410 <br> Ready for final payment: 1440 <br> *days or dates* |
| Net Increase (decrease) of this Change Order | Net Increase (decrease) of this Change Order |
| $ 1726.00 | 4 days <br> *days* |
| Contract Price with all approved Change Orders | Contract Times with all approved Change Orders |
| $ 65,187,168.00 | Substantial Completion: 1414 <br> Ready for final payment: 1434 <br> *days or dates* |

RECOMMENDED:                     APPROVED:                      ACCEPTED:

By: _____   By: _____   By: _____
    Engineer (Authorized Signature)   Owner (Authorized Signature)   Contractor (Authorized Signature)

Date: _____       Date: _____         Date: _____

EJCDC No. 1910–8–B (1990 Edition)
Prepared by the Engineers Joint Contract Documents Committee and endorsed by The Associated General Contractors of America.

---

**FIGURE 18.6** Example of the EJCDC Change Order form. (Copyright © 1990 by National Society of Professional Engineers.)

**CHANGE ORDER**

**INSTRUCTIONS**

---

**A. GENERAL INFORMATION**

This document was developed to provide a uniform format for handling contract changes that affect Contract Price or Contract Times. Changes that have been initiated by a Work Change Directive must be incorporated into a subsequent Change Order if they affect Contract Price or Times.

Changes that affect Contract Price or Contract Times should be promptly covered by a Change Order. The practice of accumulating change order items to reduce the administrative burden may lead to unnecessary disputes.

If Milestones have been listed any effect of a Change Order thereon should be addressed.

For supplemental instructions and minor changes not involving a change in the Contract Price or Contract Times, a Field Order may be used.

**B. COMPLETING THE CHANGE ORDER FORM**

Engineer initiates the form, including a description of the changes involved and attachments based upon documents and proposals submitted by Contractor, or requests from Owner, or both.

Once Engineer has completed and signed the form, all copies should be sent to Contractor for approval. After approval by Contractor, all copies should be sent to Owner for approval. Engineer should make distribution of executed copies after approval by Owner.

If a change only applies to Contract Price or to Contract Times, cross out the part of the tabulation that does not apply.

**FIGURE 18.6** *continued*

**Constructive changes.**    A constructive change is an informal act authorizing or directing a modification to the contract caused by an act or failure to act. In contrast to the mutually recognized need for a change, certain acts or failure to act by the owner that increases the contractor's cost and/or time of performance may also be considered grounds for a change order. This is termed a *constructive change* and must be claimed in writing by the contractor within the time specified in the contract documents in order to be considered. The owner should evaluate a change order proposal based on such a claim and can use the same reasoning process as any other proposal. The types of constructive changes may include:

> Defective plans and specifications
> Engineer's interpretation
> Higher standard of performance than specified
> Improper inspection and rejection
> Change in method of performance
> Change in the construction sequence
> Owner nondisclosure
> Impossibility/impracticability of performance

Constructive changes are a major source of construction disputes. A constructive change arises when the contractor alleges that something that the owner has done, or failed to do, has resulted in a de facto change in the contract requirements. The argument, of course, is that the contractor is entitled to extra compensation for performing the work. The owner frequently disagrees that a change in the contract requirements has occurred.

Most constructive changes disputes center around the interpretation of the plans and specifications. It is not surprising that owners and architect/engineers tend to interpret the contract in the manner that will be most beneficial to the project. Contractors, on the other hand, are inclined to read the plans and specifications in a manner that will minimize performance costs. Obviously, the most effective way to prevent constructive change disputes is to have a detailed, carefully prepared scope of work. This does not always happen, of course. Even when it does, disputes may still arise. It is for this reason that a comprehensive changes clause should be included in the General Conditions of any construction contract.

## ELEMENTS OF A CHANGE ORDER

A change order specifies the agreed-upon change to the contract and should include the following information:

> Identification of change order
> Description of change
> Reason for change
> Change in contract price

Change in unit prices (if applicable)

Change to contract time

Statement that secondary impacts are included

Approvals by owner's and contractor's representatives

The owner may require the engineer's signature for internal control, but there is no substitute for the owner's signature.

A change order is a written agreement between the owner and the contractor authorizing an addition, deletion, or revision in the work and/or time of completion within the limits of the terms of the construction contract after it has been executed. It is a specific type of contract modification that does not go beyond the general scope of the existing contract.

The change order generally originates as a claim or recommendation for a change from the contractor or as a request-for-proposal from the owner, seeking a change to the existing contract documents. The change order is necessary to increase or decrease the contract cost or work, interrupt or terminate the project, revise the completion date, alter the design, or in general to implement any deviation from the original contract terms and conditions.

Because change orders are responsible for more disputes than any other single aspect of a construction project, they should be carefully discussed in complete detail so that there is a complete understanding by both the owner and the contractor. Some of the items that are recommended by the Associated General Contractors for discussion include:

1. Percentages for overhead and profit to be applied to change orders; what costs will or will not be included in the change order price.

2. Length of time that a change order proposal price is to be considered as firm.

3. Determination of the individual representative of the owner who is authorized to approve change orders.

4. Procedures to be followed in the submittal of change order proposals.

5. Change order forms to be used (i.e., AIA, NSPE, Federal, Fisk,[1] contractors, or others).

6. Time extensions required, if any—requests made by contractors due to changes in the plans or specifications.

7. The detail required of contractors when submitting change order proposals—will a complete breakdown of all costs be required? Brief description—Descriptive drawings.

8. Overtime necessary due to change orders. Consideration of decreased productivity.

9. When materials or equipment is to be removed due to a change, which party owns the removed items, and who removes them from the site of the job?

10. Responsibility for record drawings brought about due to the change orders.

---

[1]E. R. Fisk, *Construction Engineer's Form Book* (New York: Prentice Hall, 1981, 1992; Englewood Cliffs, NJ: Prentice Hall, 1992).

## *EVALUATING THE NEED*

A contract change order is always used to effect a change within a contract. Such changes should always be in writing. Standard forms such as those shown in Figures 18.5 and 18.6 are readily available for this purpose; however, standard forms are not necessary, as a change order can be in the form of a letter, if desired.

The following are some of the purposes served by change orders:

1. To change contract plans or to specify the method and amount of payment and changes in contract time therefrom.
2. To change contract specifications, including changes in payment and contract time that may result from such changes.
3. To effect agreements concerning the order of the work, including any payment or changes in contract that may result.
4. For administrative purposes, to establish the method of extra work payment and funds for work already stipulated in the contract.
5. For administrative purposes, to authorize an increase in extra work funds necessary to complete a previously authorized change.
6. To cover adjustments to contract unit prices for overruns and underruns, when required by the specifications.
7. To effect cost reduction incentive proposals (value engineering proposals).
8. To effect payment after settlement of claims.

A contract change order is used in most instances when a written agreement by both parties to the contract is either necessary or desirable. Such use further serves the purpose of notifying a contractor of its right to file a protest if it fails to execute a change order.

## *CONSIDERATIONS FOR EVALUATION*

The following are common categories or conditions that generally give rise to the need for a contract change order:

Differing site conditions
Errors and omissions in plans and specs
Changes instituted by regulatory agencies
Design changes
Overruns/underruns in quantities beyond limits
Factors affecting time of completion

It is possible that some change order proposals may fall outside these categories; however, others commonly have characteristics similar to the categories mentioned.

Therefore, they can be related to the reasoning process developed in one or more of the six categories mentioned.

### Evaluation of Delays in the Work

Before it can be determined that a delay in the work was compensable, thereby justifying the issuance of a change order granting both additional time and money to the contractor, the following questions need to be answered:

1. Was the cause of the delay beyond the contractor's control? Did the contractor fail to take normal precautions?
2. Was the contractor ready and able to work?
3. Did the contractor submit a detailed schedule projecting project completion within the allotted time? Was the schedule updated regularly? Did the updated schedule justify a time extension?
4. Did this schedule contain a critical path analysis or equivalent?
5. Has the contractor maintained sufficient forces in those operations along the critical path where needed to meet target dates?
6. How have causes, other than normal weather, beyond the control and without the fault or negligence of the contractor affected target dates along the critical path?
7. Has the contractor proven "unusually severe weather" with such information as climatological data, return probability of severe storms, or flood depth data?
8. Did the weather phenomenon actually delay operations along the critical path or in secondary operations?
9. Was the contractor shut down for other reasons?

## CHANGE ORDERS FOR DIFFERING SITE CONDITIONS

Justification for the issuance of a change order to compensate the contractor for a differing site condition will be influenced by the specific terms of the Contract Documents. Some guidelines follow that suggest special areas of concern to be evaluated prior to issuance of a change order to cover extra work resulting from a differing site condition:

1. What is the differing site condition?
2. What is the site condition shown on the plans?
3. What sections of the specifications are applicable?
4. Do the parties have the latest revised issues of the plans and specifications?
5. Have the parties checked all of the plan references? Plans are usually grouped by specialty: architectural, site, plumbing, mechanical, structural, electrical, special and standard details. A critical note or dimension on one of the specialty drawings may solve the whole puzzle of need and responsibility.

6. Has the inspection staff provided adequate data? If not, correct that situation immediately. The next claim could be much larger.

7. Why was the condition shown differently by the design?

8. Was provision made for this situation in the contract documents?

9. Did the construction contractor encounter unstable soils, rock excavation, or subsurface structures where no careful prebid site inspection and contract documents could have predicted their existence?

10. Was the construction contractor forced to employ unusual construction techniques and equipment to overcome the obstacles encountered?

11. Can the construction contractor's performance, selection of construction procedures, and responses to site conditions be evaluated by the architect/engineer (or possibly a third party) experienced in modern construction techniques?

## Subsurface Investigations

Prior to the determination of the validity of a contractor's request for a change order to compensate the contractor for a differing site condition, the architect/engineer and the owner should consider the following questions before assuming that the responsibility is all on the shoulders of the contractor:

1. Were borings made or test holes dug, displayed correctly, available to all bidders, or proper kind and depth, spaced at reasonable intervals? Contract documents often have disclaimers regarding differing subsurface conditions, but these are not always as enforceable as they may appear.

2. Was the overall subsurface investigation in proportion to the type and magnitude of the project?

3. Was the geologic history of the site incorporated into the subsurface investigation data displayed in the contract documents?

4. Although not part of the evaluation, the owner should consider whether additional subsurface investigation should be initiated immediately to minimize future claims and delays.

## Inclusion of Soils Reports in Contract Documents

Whenever the owner or the architect/engineer knows of or is in the possession of soils reports, logs of borings, asbestos reports, hazardous waste reports, or similar knowledge about a construction site, it is under obligation to make full disclosure of all such documents to the bidders on a project. This is normally done through the medium of identifying them by title, origin, and date in the Notice Inviting Bids, and at the same time cautioning the bidder that they are *not a part of the contract documents,* and are identified for the convenience of the bidders. Usually, exculpatory language is included to the effect that the owner or its architect/engineer makes no representations regarding such data, and that the bidder must interpret and draw his or her own conclusions therefrom. Recent issues of EJCDC

General Conditions, however, do allow the contractor's reliance on certain limited technical information, but not upon any interpretations contained in the report. It is again emphasized in the contract documents that the soils reports, for example, should *not* be a part of the contract documents. Inclusion of such documents as a part of the contract documents invariably lead to claims for extra work and change orders.

### Evaluation of a Claim of Differing Site Conditions

Once the information on differing site conditions has been assembled, the owner should be in a position to determine if the site conditions differed materially from those indicated in the contract or those ordinarily encountered and whether this will justify an increase in the construction contractor's cost or the time to complete the work.

The owner or its architect/engineer should be able to determine whether a change order is justified by a careful review of the contractor's supporting documentation, including reports, pictures, plans, and whatever is appropriate to demonstrate where and how actual conditions deviated from the plan or from conditions that should have been anticipated.

### Other Influences on Change Order Justification

Prior to filing a request for a change order due to alleged differing site conditions, the architect/engineer should determine whether or not the contractor complied with the following:

1. Did the construction contractor promptly and before such conditions were disturbed comply with the owner's modification requirements?
2. Did the construction contractor make a site inspection and evaluation of conditions prior to bidding?
3. Is the construction layout correct? Who performed the construction staking; who checked the staking?
4. Did utility companies respond and locate their respective facilities? Did the construction contractor protect or obliterate utility reference stakes and use suitable construction techniques to protect structures and utilities?

## STARTING THE CHANGE ORDER PROCESS

### Initiation of Change Orders

Change orders are usually initiated by construction personnel at the project site (Figure 18.7). However, changes are also requested from various other sources, such as the contractor, the design firm, outside public agencies, or private individuals. In any case, they must be authorized by the owner before any change order authorizing extra work is valid. A proposed contract change order is written only after the designers have given consideration as to the necessity, propriety, other methods of accomplishing the work, method of compensation, effect on contract time, estimate of cost, the contractor's reaction to the proposed change, and the probability of final approval.

# FLOW DIAGRAM - CHANGE ORDER PROCEDURE

## *For Non-Emergency Changes Involving Time and Cost*
(For emergency changes use a Work Directive Change Form)

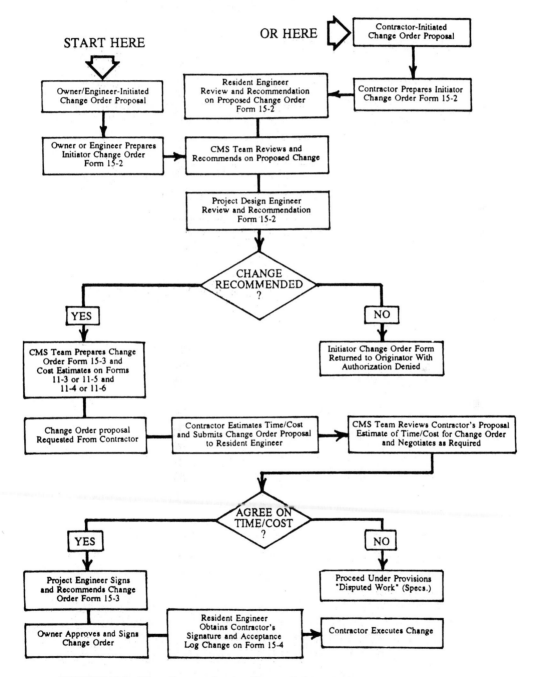

**FIGURE 18.7** Flow diagram showing Change Order procedure.

Any change in the work that involves a change in the original contract price must be approved in writing by the owner before a change order can be executed. If it is not the owner who signs, then the party who does sign for him or her must have written authorization from the owner to sign on his or her behalf. The architect or engineer of record, by virtue of their positions alone, have no authority to order changes to the contract. If they do act in this manner, they must be authorized in some way to act in the owner's behalf.

### Change Order Preparation

A change order must be clear, concise, and explicit. It must tell the contractor what is to be done, where or within what limits, when the work is to be performed, if the order of the work is affected, how the contractor will be paid, and what consideration will be given to contract time (extensions, etc.).

For users of the current EJCDC documents, the Work Change Directive (Figure 18.3) was developed for use in situations involving changes in the Work which, if not processed expeditiously, might delay the project. The AIA counterpart is called a Construction Change Directive. Such changes are often initiated in the field and may affect contract price or time. This form is not a Change Order, however, but only a directive to proceed with the Work that may be included in a subsequent Change Order. Unfortunately, the AIA form confuses the issue somewhat by having a block where the contractor can sign the document. If both parties are to sign the change document, you may as well issue a regular change order; after all, the purpose of that document is to allow the issuance of a unilateral order to perform the Work. The EJCDC, AIA, and Federal forms for implementing changes in the contract are:

**Bilateral Contract Modification**
Change Order EJCDC Document 1910-8-B
Change Order AIA Document G701
Federal Contract Modification
Change Order-Fisk Form 15-2

**Unilateral Contract Modification**
Work Change Directive EJCDC Document 1910-8-F
Construction Change Directive AIA Document G714
Federal Change Order
Work Directive Change-Fisk Form 15-3

Although the use of the Change Order and the Work Change Directive is quite clear and it satisfies all the requirements for documenting and executing an amendment to the contract provisions, the same cannot necessarily be said of a Field Order. The Field Order is supposed to be an order from the architect/engineer to the contractor that either interprets the contract documents or orders minor changes in the work without changing either the contract sum or the contract time. As a document to interpret the contract provisions, it serves its purpose admirably well. However, any document that changes any of the provisions of the plans, specifications, or other contract documents *is* a change order no matter what you may choose to call it. As such, in the absence of a written authorization from the owner that allows the architect/engineer unilaterally to make such changes, only the owner can execute this document.

On a recent project where a Field Order was used, it was desired to make a minor change in the work, for which there would be no additional charge by the contractor. When confronted with this document, the contractor asked that a formal change order be issued instead, even though the terms had been agreed to previously and no charge was being made for the changes.

The contractor was not only legally right in requesting a formal change order, but wise to do so. A formal Change Order provides the written authorization of the owner to make a change in the contract provisions; it states the effect on the contract sum, if any; it specifies the effect on contract time, if any; and could serve to release the contractor from liability that might result from making the change.

Any document that alters the terms of the original contract *in any way* must be considered as a Change Order. As such, the document must either be signed by the owner or by someone with the power of attorney to act for him. The architect/engineer's Field Order only provides for the signature of the architect/engineer and thus does not satisfy this requirement unless the architect/engineer also possesses written authority of the owner to execute such changes on his or her behalf. Even then, if a change in the work is intended, as opposed to an interpretation of the contract documents, it is still far more desirable to utilize the Change Order form for this purpose as a protection to all parties to the contract, even though there will be no change in contract price or time.

The AIA Construction Change Directive differs, principally, from the form of the EJCDC Work Change Directive (Figure 18.3) in that it provides for the written acceptance by the contractor.

There are only four basic steps involved in the execution of a nonemergency change order, although the in-house procedures of an organization may expand on this to satisfy their own procedural requirements. The four basic steps are:

1. Change order request by initiator (may be initiated by contractor or architect/engineer) for architect/engineer and owner's approval.
2. Upon approval of initiator request, discuss with contractor and draft a change order proposal document citing the effect of the change on contract time and cost.
3. Contractor submits a signed change order proposal to the owner, showing all costs and additional time required.
4. Owner accepts proposal by signing the proposal and orders execution of the work described.

## COST OF DELAYS CAUSED BY CHANGE ORDERS

Often, the execution of a change order involves slowdowns or delays of the contractor's operations. It should be kept in mind that all such delays involve extra cost to the contractor and, as such, the costs are recoverable by the contractor. In a case involving construction delays resulting from defective specifications for an FAA Air Force Traffic Control Center, the U.S. Court of Claims rules ruled that a contractor working on a government contract is entitled to the extra costs incurred as a result of the government's defective specifications, even if only part of the job is delayed [*Chaney and James Construction Co., Inc., v. United States,* U.S. Court of Claims No. 150–67 (Feb. 20, 1970)].

This lends even more importance to the inspector's obligation to record all equipment and workers at the site, and to note whether such equipment is being used on that day or not (Chapter 4). Such information can be the basis for defending claims of excessive charges for delays caused by extra work.

---

## PROBLEMS

1. A Work Change Directive under the EJCDC documents must be signed by which party or parties?

2. Who can initiate a change order, the owner, engineer, Resident Project Representative, or the contractor?

3. What is a change order?

4. True or false? A change order can be issued at any time after award of the contract.

5. What is a Work Change Directive?

6. Under what conditions may an oral change order be valid and binding, even if the contract states that all changes must be in writing?

7. What is a constructive change?

8. Name at least three conditions that may justify the issuance of a change order.

9. May change orders be issued between the time of opening bids and the execution of the Agreement?

10. What are the principal issues that must be addressed in a change order?

# 19

## Claims and Disputes

## FIVE PRINCIPLES OF CONTRACT ADMINISTRATION

Construction contracts are subject to broader principles of interpretation than most other contracts. There are five basic rules of contract interpretation that are quite important in construction contracts. The courts are frequently unfamiliar with the specialized rules that have evolved in the construction industry and often rely upon the testimony of experts in the subject area to guide them in forming a decision.

A written contract is merely a form of documentation of the conditions agreed upon by the parties. However, it reflects the understanding that each party had with regard to the wording of the documents. If every written contract was clear, unambiguous, and complete, the rules of contract interpretation would be unnecessary, as the intent and understanding of the parties would be self-evident. Unfortunately, this is not the case.

In any construction contract, it is almost inevitable that the written documents will not adequately address every single matter. There may be gaps, conflicts, or subtle ambiguities. The five principles mentioned here are used to help resolve such problems. They are little more than applications of common sense in an effort to determine the intentions of the parties from a written document that does not adequately express those intentions.

### 1. The Document Must Be Read as a Whole

Often in a construction dispute, each party concentrates on some narrow provision of the specifications, general conditions, or drawings that seems to support his or her position. The attitude is: "There it is in writing."

The law recognizes that the intentions of the parties cannot be determined by examining one small part of a document by itself. Every provision of the document is presumed

**473**

to have meaning; therefore, no provision should be presumed to be meaningless or super-
fluous. The document must be considered in its entirety.

## 2. The Document Will Be Construed against the Drafter

This is a well-known principle but must be recognized in any dispute as to the meaning of
the wording used in the document. There may be latent ambiguity; the contract may be subject to more than one reasonable interpretation, and a court is often faced with the burden
of choosing between the two.

In such a situation, the document is interpreted in favor of the party that did not draft
the document. The reasoning behind this principle is that the party that drafted the document had ample opportunity to avoid ambiguity and clearly express the intended meaning,
but failed to do so. The nondrafting party did not have such an opportunity; they reasonably
assumed that the contract language meant a certain thing, and in court that interpretation
must prevail.

This means that in construction contracts the contractor's reasonable interpretation
will usually prevail over that of the owner or the architect/engineer, and in the case of prime
contractor/subcontractor relations, the subcontractor's reasonable interpretation will usually prevail over that of the prime contractor. Although not necessarily so in all cases, contracts are usually prepared by owners or architect/engineers, and subcontracts are usually
prepared by prime contractors.

## 3. The Document Supersedes All Previous Discussions

The bottom line here is that any oral commitments made prior to the execution of an agreement are nonbinding, as the written document is presumed to constitute the entire agreement.

Basically, the rule is that the document speaks for itself. However, when it does not
speak for itself, or when it is so inarticulate that no one knows what it means, oral testimony
is permitted to determine the intended meaning of the parties. This is a well-known exception to the *parol evidence* rule. After hearing the expert testimony, the final interpretation
of the contract will probably be decided based upon the respective credibility of each
party's expert testimony. Unfortunately, this does not assure that justice will be served, as
in the author's experience a case was reviewed in preparation for an appeal of an earlier decision in which the court heard conflicting opinions of two experts. The courts said that it
had heard two experts testify as to the opposite opinion on a crucial issue, and the court was
being called upon to determine which expert was correct. Unfortunately, said the court,
lacking specific technical knowledge of the subject matter, the court's only recourse was to
accept the opinion of the expert "who sounded most credible." Unfortunately, in our review
of the case, it was found that the most credible, or most articulate, was the one whose testimony was in error. Unfortunately, it was too late to change that, as the decision had already been rendered, so the case was decided on the strength of erroneous testimony.

## 4. Specific Terms Govern over General Terms

Sometimes there will be a conflict between two different provisions of a written agreement.
The courts rule that the more specific term should govern over the general term. The rea-

soning behind this is that a narrowly drafted provision was customized to fit a specific situation and thus reflects more accurately the parties intentions that a "general" or "boilerplate" provision of the contract.

On construction contracts, this is often applied by making handwritten or typewritten provisions prevail over conflicting provisions found in the preprinted sections of the contract. Similarly, job-specific Supplementary General Conditions will prevail over the General Conditions.

### 5. Document Must Be Read in the Context of the Trade

This is another commonsense rule. If a word or phrase has a commonly accepted meaning in the construction industry, that meaning must be applied when reading and interpreting construction contracts.

---

## CONSTRUCTION PROBLEMS

Every construction project seems to include its share of problems. To one way of thinking, perhaps if it were not for these problems, the job of Resident Project Representative might never have been conceived. A good Resident Project Representative is not simply a person who has the unique ability to solve problems, for generally the contractor can do this. It is the inspector's ability to apply personal experience and knowledge to the project, to look ahead, anticipate the occurrence of various events resulting from the various approaches that the contractor might take, evaluate these conditions, and offer constructive assistance in seeing that the potential problems either never occur or are minimized. An inspector who lacks this quality contributes nothing to the project—but is simply an added cost.

To help you understand fully their application to the terms of the construction contract, several terms frequently used in this book will be defined. This chapter is divided into two major classifications. The first deals with the definition and the administrative procedures involved in the handling of protests, claims, and disputes under the terms of the construction contract; the second addresses itself to the methods available for the settlement of such differences, as well as an explanation of the principle of arbitration under the rules of the American Arbitration Association, which is receiving growing respect as a fast, economical, and fair method for the resolution of construction contract disputes.

---

## PROTESTS

The term *protests* as used here refers to disputes arising out of the issuance of a contract change order by the architect or engineer against the objections of the contractor. The terms of the contract documents for the orderly filing of written protests by the contractor as a means of establishing its claims for additional compensation or time to complete the work or claims of unfair treatment under the terms of the contract, short of turning the problem over to arbitration, is normally covered in the General Conditions (boilerplate). In Articles 9.11 through 9.12 and Article 16 (including Exhibit GC-A) of the EJCDC Standard General Conditions of the Construction Contract (1990 Edition), and in Sub-Clauses 67.1 through

67.4 of the FIDIC Conditions of Contract (1987 Edition) the procedures for the handling of protests and disagreements are specified in detail, up to and including referring the matter to binding arbitration. An example of the current provisions of the 1990 edition of the EJCDC General Conditions for dispute resolution is illustrated in Figure 19.1.

The normal procedure is for the Resident Project Representative to discuss with the contractor any objections to a particular change order or other directions of the architect/engineer. If the contractor's objections can be satisfied by minor changes in the provisions of a proposed change order or direction and such changes do not violate the contract provisions (this includes plans, specifications, addenda, previous change orders, codes, permit provisions, or similar constraints), the change should normally be discussed with the architect/engineer's or owner's project manager and with their concurrence the change should normally be made. This will often avoid a formal protest, which is often costly even to the winner.

In the event that the Resident Project Representative cannot satisfy the contractor's objections, the project manager should be consulted to explore other possible means of settlement. When neither the Resident Project Representative nor the project manager can resolve the problem through normal procedures, the pending change order or other direction of the architect/engineer or the owner should be issued in its original form and the contractor reminded of the provisions of the contract documents that require the contractor's conformance with any such order of the architect/engineer or owner even if the contractor disagrees with it, under penalty of being considered in default on the contract. It should also be carefully noted in the Resident Project Representative's or inspector's diary that such a reminder was given to the contractor. This does not take away the contractor's right to file a letter of protest that could be used as a later basis of claims against the owner, provided that such letter is submitted within the time schedules that are specified in the General Conditions of the construction contract.

When a protest letter is received from the contractor, it should be examined carefully prior to acknowledgment of its receipt to assure that the basic requirements of the specifications are included in the contractor's letter. The architect/engineer or owner should then review the merits of the contractor's protest. If the architect/engineer or owner decides that the protest is without merit, they should issue a letter to the contractor advising of its rights under the contract to file legal claims. Normally, if the contractor fails to file claims in accordance with the provisions of the contract, especially as to the time of filing, it may waive its rights under the contract.

## CLAIMS

### Potential Claims

The term *potential claim* applies to any differences arising out of the performance of the work that *might* reasonably lead to the later filing of a formal claim by the contractor if the difference cannot be resolved in the field.

It should be the policy of the architect/engineer or owner to consider the merits of a potential claim at the earliest possible time. As soon as the Resident Project Representative has knowledge of the existence of a dispute that may lead to the filing of a potential claim,

## EXHIBIT GC-A to General Conditions of the Agreement Between OWNER and CONTRACTOR Dated_____
### For use with EJCDC No. 1910-8 (1990 ed.)

DISPUTE RESOLUTION AGREEMENT

OWNER and CONTRACTOR hereby agree that Article 16 of the General Conditions to the Agreement between OWNER and CONTRACTOR is amended to include the following agreement of the parties:

16.1. All claims, disputes and other matters in question between OWNER and CONTRACTOR arising out of or relating to the Contract Documents or the breach thereof (except for claims which have been waived by the making or acceptance of final payment as provided by paragraph 14.15) will be decided by arbitration in accordance with the Construction Industry Arbitration Rules of the American Arbitration Association then obtaining, subject to the limitations of this Article 16. This agreement so to arbitrate and any other agreement or consent to arbitrate entered into in accordance herewith as provided in this Article 16 will be specifically enforceable under the prevailing law of any court having jurisdiction.

16.2. No demand for arbitration of any claim, dispute or other matter that is required to be referred to ENGINEER initially for decision in accordance with paragraph 9.11 will be made until the earlier of (a) the date on which ENGINEER has rendered a written decision or (b) the thirty-first day after the parties have presented their evidence to ENGINEER if a written decision has not been rendered by ENGINEER before that date. No demand for arbitration of any such claim, dispute or other matter will be made later than thirty days after the date on which ENGINEER has rendered a written decision in respect thereof in accordance with paragraph 9.11; and the failure to demand arbitration within said thirty days' period will result in ENGINEER's decision being final and binding upon OWNER and CONTRACTOR. If ENGINEER renders a decision after arbitration proceedings have been initiated, such decision may be entered as evidence but will not supersede the arbitration proceedings, except where the decision is acceptable to the parties concerned. No demand for arbitration of any written decision of ENGINEER rendered in accordance with paragraph 9.10 will be made later than ten days after the party making such demand has delivered written notice of intention to appeal as provided in paragraph 9.10.

16.3. Notice of the demand for arbitration will be filed in writing with the other party to the Agreement and with the American Arbitration Association, and a copy will be sent to ENGINEER for information. The demand for arbitration will be made within the thirty-day or ten- day period specified in paragraph 16.2 as applicable, and in all other cases within a reasonable time after the claim, dispute or other matter in question has arisen, and in no event shall any such demand be made after the date when institution of legal or equitable proceedings based on such claim, dispute or other matter in question would be barred by the applicable statute of limitations.

16.4. Except as provided in paragraph 16.5 below, no arbitration arising out of or relating to the Contract Documents shall include by consolidation, joinder or in any other manner any other person or entity (including ENGINEER, ENGINEER's Consultant and the officers, directors, agents, employees or consultants of any of them) who is not a party to this contract unless:

16.4.1. the inclusion of such other person or entity is necessary if complete relief is to be afforded among those who are already parties to the arbitration, and

16.4.2. such other person or entity is substantially involved in a question of law or fact which is common to those who are already parties to the arbitration and which will arise in such proceedings, and

16.4.3. the written consent of the other person or entity sought to be included and of OWNER and CONTRACTOR has been obtained for such inclusion, which consent shall make specific reference to this paragraph; but no such consent shall constitute consent to arbitration of any dispute not specifically described in such consent or to arbitration with any party not specifically identified in such consent.

16.5. Notwithstanding paragraph 16.4 if a claim, dispute or other matter in question between OWNER and CONTRACTOR involves the Work of a Subcontractor, either OWNER or CONTRACTOR may join such Subcontractor as a party to the arbitration between OWNER and CONTRACTOR hereunder. CONTRACTOR shall include in all subcontracts required by paragraph 6.11 a specific provision whereby the Subcontractor consents to being joined in an arbitration between OWNER and CONTRACTOR involving the Work of such Subcontractor. Nothing in this paragraph 16.5 nor in the provision of such subcontract consenting to joinder shall create any claim, right or cause of action in favor of Subcontractor and against OWNER, ENGINEER or ENGINEER's Consultants that does not otherwise exist.

16.6. The award rendered by the arbitrators will be final, judgment may be entered upon it in any court having jurisdiction thereof, and it will not be subject to modification or appeal.

**FIGURE 19.1** Provisions for dispute resolution in the 1990 edition of the EJCDC General Conditions of the Construction Contract.

16.7.   OWNER and CONTRACTOR agree that they shall first submit any and all unsettled claims, counterclaims, disputes and other matters in question between them arising out of or relating to the Contract Documents or the breach thereof ("disputes"), to mediation by The American Arbitration Association under the Construction Industry Mediation Rules of the American Arbitration Association prior to either of them initiating against the other a demand for arbitration pursuant to paragraphs 16.1 through 16.6, unless delay in initiating arbitration would irrevocably prejudice one of the parties. The respective thirty and ten day time limits within which to file a demand for arbitration as provided in paragraphs 16.2 and 16.3 above shall be suspended with respect to a dispute submitted to mediation within those same applicable time limits and shall remain suspended until ten days after the termination of the mediation. The mediator of any dispute submitted to mediation under this Agreement shall not serve as arbitrator of such dispute unless otherwise agreed.

ARTICLE 16—DISPUTE RESOLUTION

---

If and to the extent that OWNER and CONTRACTOR have agreed on the method and procedure for resolving disputes between them that may arise under this Agreement, such dispute resolution method and procedure, if any, shall be as set forth in Exhibit GC-A, "Dispute Resolution Agreement," to be attached hereto and made a part hereof. If no such agreement on the method and procedure for resolving such disputes has been reached, and subject to the provisions of paragraphs 9.10, 9.11, and 9.12, OWNER and CONTRACTOR may exercise such rights or remedies as either may otherwise have under the Contract Documents or by Laws or Regulations in respect of any dispute.

*Decisions on Disputes:*

9.11.   ENGINEER will be the initial interpreter of the requirements of the Contract Documents and judge of the acceptability of the Work thereunder. Claims, disputes and other matters relating to the acceptability of the Work or the interpretation of the requirements of the Contract Documents pertaining to the performance and furnishing of the Work and Claims under Articles 11 and 12 in respect of changes in the Contract Price or Contract Times will be referred initially to ENGINEER in writing with a request for a formal decision in accordance with this paragraph. Written notice of each such claim, dispute or other matter will be delivered by the claimant

to ENGINEER and the other party to the Agreement promptly (but in no event later than thirty days) after the start of the occurrence or event giving rise thereto, and written supporting data will be submitted to ENGINEER and the other party within sixty days after the start of such occurrence or event unless ENGINEER allows an additional period of time for the submission of additional or more accurate data in support of such claim, dispute or other matter. The opposing party shall submit any response to ENGINEER and the claimant within thirty days after receipt of the claimant's last submittal (unless ENGINEER allows additional time). ENGINEER will render a formal decision in writing within thirty days after receipt of the opposing party's submittal, if any, in accordance with this paragraph. ENGINEER's written decision on such claim, dispute or other matter will be final and binding upon OWNER and CONTRACTOR unless: (i) an appeal from ENGINEER's decision is taken within the time limits and in accordance with the procedures set forth in EXHIBIT GC-A, "Dispute Resolution Agreement," entered into between OWNER and CONTRACTOR pursuant to Article 16, or (ii) if no such Dispute Resolution Agreement has been entered into, a written notice of intention to appeal from ENGINEER's written decision is delivered by OWNER or CONTRACTOR to the other and to ENGINEER within thirty days after the date of such decision and a formal proceeding is instituted by the appealing party in a forum of competent jurisdiction to exercise such rights or remedies as the appealing party may have with respect to such claim, dispute or other matter in accordance with applicable Laws and Regulations within sixty days of the date of such decision, unless otherwise agreed in writing by OWNER and CONTRACTOR.

9.12.   When functioning as interpreter and judge under paragraphs 9.10 and 9.11, ENGINEER will not show partiality to OWNER or CONTRACTOR and will not be liable in connection with any interpretation or decision rendered in good faith in such capacity. The rendering of a decision by ENGINEER pursuant to paragraphs 9.10 or 9.11 with respect to any such claim, dispute or other matter (except any which have been waived by the making or acceptance of final payment as provided in paragraph 14.16) will be a condition precedent to any exercise by OWNER or CONTRACTOR of such rights or remedies as either may otherwise have under the Contract Documents or by Laws or Regulations in respect of any such claim, dispute or other matter pursuant to Article 16.

**FIGURE 19.1**   *continued*

**478**

the situation should be discussed with the contractor. If the Resident Project Representative determines that the contractor's preliminary arguments are valid, such corrective measures should be taken as are within the scope of the inspector's authority under the contract, including the possibility of making recommendation to the architect/engineer or owner to submit change orders to alleviate the problem.

In the event that the Resident Project Representative cannot resolve the differences in the field, the problem should be discussed with the architect/engineer or the owner. If the differences still cannot be resolved within the terms of the contract, the contractor should be reminded of the provisions of the contract documents relating to the time and methods for it to file claims, and such reminder should be recorded in the Resident Project Representative's diary.

Upon receipt of a potential claim in writing from the contractor, and prior to submitting it to the architect/engineer or owner for review, it should be reviewed by the Resident Project Representative to see that it contains the basic information necessary, such as the reasons that the contractor believes additional consideration is due. It should also be reviewed to determine that the timeliness of the submittal is in accordance with the terms of the contract documents. If the contractor's letter is not sufficiently complete with respect to the nature of the claim, the architect/engineer or owner should request in writing that the contractor submit additional data before further processing of the contractor's claim.

Each potential claim should be reviewed by the architect/engineer or owner. If after this review the potential claim is considered as being without merit, an answering letter should be sent to the contractor. The letter should include the statements referred to under "protests" in previous paragraphs. If the contractor's notice of potential claim does not meet the requirements for timeliness as set forth in the specifications, the architect/engineer or owner should advise the contractor in writing of this deficiency.

### Early Claims Reporting

The professional liability underwriters would prefer to have claims overreported rather than underreported, as it is better to report a dispute situation before it becomes an actual claim than to wait until it is a very hot issue and the battle lines have been drawn. The claims department of a professional liability insurance company can usually give counsel on methods of reducing exposure, or at least on keeping things fair. In addition, their claims department can advise on methods for mitigating damages (if any) so that whoever is finally held responsible, the financial burden will be less. By spotting a dispute before it becomes a claim and reporting it to the architect/engineer or owner, a monumental amount of later grief may be avoided.

### Insurance Claims

Sometimes, through oversight or lack of understanding of contract practice, issues can arise that may spell latent financial disaster for the owner. On one occasion, the author was engaged by an insurance company in southern California to investigate a project that had just suffered major fire damage resulting from an arsonist who set the blaze about 4:00 p.m. on a Thanksgiving day when no one was at the site, resulting in a near total loss of a project that was at that time about 70 percent completed (Figure 19.2). The initial thrust of the investigation was to determine whether the project was a total loss, hence a higher payoff by the insurance carrier, or whether any remaining portions of the structure were salvageable. Copies of the policies and project drawings were made available and a detailed field investigation was started. Assisted by CTL laboratories (a subsidiary of the Portland Cement Association) the author made a thorough examination of the structural properties of the remaining portions of the concrete and concrete block portions of the structures, with a determination that there was a salvage value of over $300,000. All wood and steel members were a total loss, and the only surviving remnants of the structure were the reinforced concrete parking garage structure and some peripheral concrete block buildings.

The surprise came, however, when the insurance policy and the construction contract documents were examined. The policy involved appeared to be a standard builder's-risk fire policy. Although it was purchased by the owner, not the contractor, this is not unusual. The insurance industry informed me that often, the owner buys the policy; otherwise, the contractor buys the policy. The problem occurred because the policy terms and conditions were not included in the construction contract documents by the architect, and the en-

**FIGURE 19.2**   Fire damage to a project under construction. Owner suffered total loss due to failure to include policy provisions in the construction contract.

dorsements called for a 1.8 m (6-ft) chain link fence to be erected around the project and *24-hour security guard service.* Investigation showed that the project was fenced but no security guard service was provided. However, because the terms of the policy were not specified as a part of the contractor's construction documents, it was not the contractor's responsibility to provide either guard service or fencing. The contractor provided fencing on its own to protect its equipment, but was possibly completely unaware of the insurance endorsement requirements. Thus, the obligation to assure that the job was properly policed rested completely upon the shoulders of the owner, who unknowingly thought the contractor was obligated to provide security guards. The author's recommendation here was that the insurance company deny the entire claim because of the breach. A court of law later reached the same conclusion.

The lesson here is that whenever the owner elects to purchase its own policy of insurance on a construction project, it should make certain that its architect/engineer includes the terms and conditions imposed in the policy as a part of the contractor's obligation under the construction contract.

## CLAIMS AND DISPUTES

The term *claim* applies to differences that *are* developed during the life of the contract under protests and potential claims, and that are not yet resolved at the time the contractor returns the proposed final estimate of the amount of additional money or time asked for. In other words, a protest or potential claim does not become a claim until the contractor repeats its objections by notifying the architect/engineer or owner at the time the proposed final estimate for such claim is returned to the architect/engineer.

Whether it is the competitive bidding process, increased competition, or just part of the growing trend toward more litigation, more and more projects are being affected by claims and disputes. Very often, a majority of contractor claims and disputes arise out of poorly drafted or ambiguous contract documents. Disagreements between the contractor and the owner, and increasingly including the architect/engineer, regarding interpretation of the plans and specifications, what should be considered as extra work to the contract, payment for contract work and change orders, extensions of time, damages for delay caused by either the owner or the contractor, changed or unforeseen conditions, performance of subcontractors, compliance with contractual requirements, partial acceptance of a project by the owner, and similar problems seem to be increasing. When such claims or disputes arise, the owner and architect/engineer must pay careful attention to the procedures set forth in the contract documents for the handling of claims and disputes.

### Contractor Must Alert Owner

Typically, contract documents require a contractor to alert the owner and/or the architect/engineer immediately, or within a certain number of days, of any potential claim or dispute when it arises. Contracts normally require that any claim or dispute must be submitted to the architect/engineer or owner's representative as the first step in the claims resolution process. Contracts often set forth an appeals procedure so that the contractor can proceed with its claim or dispute if the architect/engineer's decision is unfavorable. When all administrative steps set forth in the contract documents have been exhausted, the contractor may then, and only then, resort to the courts or arbitration, if provided for under the contract. The procedural steps set forth in the contract must be followed by the contractor. Failure to follow these steps could in itself be considered as a breach of the contract by the contractor.

### Administrative Procedures

A contractor must exhaust all of its administrative remedies before resorting to the courts and must strictly adhere to any claim procedures mandated by law. For example, in addition to the claims and disputes provisions outlined in the typical owner contract, some states require that a claim first be filed by the contractor against the appropriate owner, with that owner subsequently rejecting the claim within a prescribed time, before the contractor has the right to take the matter to court. A contractor's failure to follow mandated government claims procedures can result in the contractor being barred from recovery on its claim.

### Work Performed under Protest

Except for total nonpayment by the owner, or due to particular circumstances under a specific contract, the contractor cannot refuse to proceed with the work on the project when a claim or dispute arises. Normally, the contractor must continue its operations despite any claims or disputes. Generally, the contractor must perform any disputed work under protest and must still complete the project on schedule, leaving any unresolved claims or disputes until after the project has been completed.

When a claim or dispute arises, or when the contractor foresees that it will arise, the contractor must take two immediate steps. First, the contractor must give the owner notice of any claim or dispute, or any potential claim or dispute, as soon as possible. Most contracts contain very specific requirements for "Notice of Claims" or "Notice of Potential Claims" that set forth specific time frames within which a contractor must notify the owner. Although the courts have varied in their interpretation and enforcement of such time requirements, a contractor runs a risk when its claims are not filed in accordance with contractual requirements.

### Owner Must Have Opportunity to Correct

Regardless of any contractual language regarding the time for making claims, common sense and equitable principles dictate that once a contractor becomes aware of a claim or a potential claim, it must be communicated to the owner. For example, if the owner's actions in some way delay the contractor and the project, the owner must be advised of the situation in order for the owner to have an opportunity to correct or alleviate the problem. If a contractor does not give notice to the owner that it is being delayed at the time that the delay is occurring, the contractor will have very little chance of recovering damages incurred as a result of such delay after the project is complete. Without proper notice, the owner will argue, and rightfully so, that it cannot be held liable to the contractor for a delay that it was never made aware of and never had an opportunity to do anything about.

### Contractor's Right to File Claims

Contractors are entitled to file any real and provable claim that arises during the course of a project. Claims should not be made or taken "personally," as they are simply the means available to the parties to the contract to be able to adjust the contractual and economic relationship between them to meet changing conditions. However, the filing of claims is not a proper way for the contractor to make up for a bad bid, or to recoup losses incurred on the project. Ultimately, it is the integrity of the contractor that dictates what claims are and are not made against an owner. In general, if a contractor only presents claims to an owner that are legitimate and verifiable, it will stand a better chance of having those claims, and all other claims it files, settled in an equitable manner. If, on the other hand, the contractor makes it a practice to file claims for any and all reasons, some less legitimate than others, the contractor runs the risk of prejudicing its legitimate claims and reducing the possibility of resolving them without litigation—a very costly and delayed process for both parties.

A contractor is entitled to pursue every legitimate claim that it has, but must recognize that the owner is entitled to proper notice and adequate proof of the claim before the owner has any obligation to pay on the claim. Contrary to a bidding situation where the contractor assumes only the best-case circumstances, a contractor's claim is generally estimated by assuming only the worst-case circumstances in the determination of estimated impact costs yet to be incurred.

Particular attention should be paid to situations where claims are directly related to the actions or inactions of the owner's representatives or agents. Claims that sometimes arise as a result of the obligations of the owner's architect/engineer to design a portion of a project properly are assertable against the owner, and under some circumstances, directly against the architect/engineer.

Although claims often provide the contractor with an opportunity to attempt to make up for mistakes made in its bid or in the construction of the project, it is not a good practice for a contractor to make more claims simply to make up for mistakes and errors. No purpose will be served by a contractor who turns a project into a battleground to cover losses incurred as a result of its own mistakes and errors.

## DIFFERENCES BETWEEN THE PARTIES

In general, most claims issues will fall into approximately ten classifications, with numerous variations possible within each category.

1. Owner-caused delays in the work.
2. Owner-ordered scheduling changes.
3. Constructive changes.
4. Differing site conditions.

5. Unusually severe weather conditions.
6. Acceleration of the work; loss of productivity.
7. Suspension of the work; termination.
8. Failure to agree on change order pricing.
9. Conflicts in plans and specifications.
10. Miscellaneous problems.

## Owner-Caused Delays

The majority of all claims involve at least some elements of delay, even if the primary issue is one of the other categories. Most contractors fail to realize the potential for recovery of losses in this sensitive claims area, until they have consulted a claims specialist.

Delay claims fall into three categories, nonexcusable, excusable, or compensable. Nonexcusable delay is one that is caused by factors within the contractor's reasonable control. Essentially, this means that the delay is the contractor's fault, so the contractor will be unable to recover additional time or additional compensation.

A delay that is caused by factors beyond the contractor's reasonable control, but is not the result of the owner's actions or failure to act, is considered excusable. An excusable delay entitles the contractor to an extension of time but to no additional compensation for the cost of the delay (Figure 19.3).

## Contractor Entitled to Complete Early

An unusual twist on the delay issue is that where a contractor plans to finish a project ahead of schedule. In some cases, an owner has been known to object to early completion of a pro-

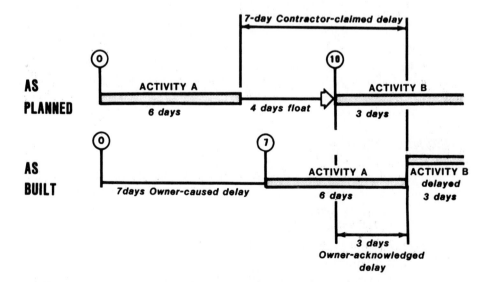

**FIGURE 19.3** Example of disputed time in an owner-caused delay.

ject for varied reasons. However, it should be kept in mind that an owner may be held liable for hindering early completion of a project [*Appeal of CWC, Inc.,* ASBCA No. 264342 (June 29, 1982)]. CWC, Inc., was prime contractor for renovation of certain military buildings. The contract required the government to arrange access to the individual buildings within two weeks after receiving a request from the contractor. In several instances, however, the government failed to provide access in a timely manner.

The contractor finished the entire project in less than the allowed time and prior to the completion date indicated in the contractor's own schedule. Nevertheless, the contractor submitted a claim for the increased costs caused by the government's delay. The Armed Services Board of Contract Appeals recognized the claim and issued the following statement: "Barring express restrictions in the contract to the contrary, a construction contractor has the right to proceed according to his [or her] own job capabilities at a better rate of progress than represented by his [or her] own schedule. The government may not hinder or prevent earlier completion without incurring liability." The bottom line here is that if the owner has reason to require the contractor to conform to a scheduled completion date, allowing neither delays or early completion, this requirement must be clearly spelled out in the contract documents.

### Sources and Causes of Time-Related Disputes

All too often, owners and architect/engineers automatically blame the contractor for virtually all construction delays. Although that is often a well-founded accusation, there are many sources and causes of time-related disputes, as indicated in the following list:

| Source | Cause |
|---|---|
| Owner | 1. Lack of expertise |
| | 2. Long line of authority in project organization |
| | 3. Delayed approvals of schedules and change orders |
| | 4. Slow change order processing |
| | 5. Failure to obtain permits |
| | 6. Irrelevant milestone dates in documents |
| Contract Documents | 1. Inadequate scheduling clauses |
| | 2. Directing work sequence by owner or architect/engineer |
| | 3. Drawings not indicating interfaces |
| | 4. Permitting responsibilities vague |
| | 5. Milestone dates and interface clauses |
| | 6. Leverage for enforcement of schedule specification |
| | 7. Coordination inadequately specified |
| Construction Manager | 1. Lack of expertise in schedule management by designer |
| | 2. Implementation of specifications |
| | 3. Inadequate record keeping |
| | 4. Inadequate schedule updates and progress monitoring |
| | 5. On-site coordination |
| | 6. Job meetings |

Contractor
1. Noncompliance with specifications
2. Schedule updates not done
3. Reluctance to cooperate and coordinate
4. Failure to meet milestone dates
5. Not following permit requirements

## Compensable versus Noncompensable Delays

A delay that is considered compensable is one where the owner has failed to meet an obligation stated or implied in the construction contract. If a delay is considered compensable, the owner must grant a time extension and reimburse the contractor for the increased cost caused by the delay. If a contractor experiences concurrent delays where one is compensable and the other is merely excusable, no compensation is allowed. Similarly, on concurrent delays where one is caused by the contractor and the other by the owner, the delay is considered neither excusable nor compensable to the extent of the overlap or concurrency. [*Appeal of Rivera General Contracting,* ASBCA No. 25888 (April 30, 1985)]. It should be stressed that these definitions are general in nature. The parties have great latitude to contractually determine whether or not the contractor will be entitled to additional compensation, an extension of time, or nothing at all.

If an event delays an activity on the critical path, the entire project completion date will be delayed. To avoid delay, it is necessary to accelerate the performance of a subsequent critical activity or adjust the sequence of work activities to compensate for the delay. If a delay occurs to an activity not on the critical path, however, the impact is cushioned by the available free-float time. Delays to a noncritical activity, which do not exceed the amount of free-float for that activity, will not result in a delay to the completion date of a project. If, however, a delay to a noncritical activity directly caused an increase in the contractor's costs, such costs may be recovered by the contractor if the delay was the owner's responsibility. This, of course, is a matter requiring very clear proof to overcome the presumption that delays to noncritical activities do not result in delay-related costs. Although an owner-caused delay to a noncritical activity that used only free-float time may not be justification for an extension of time, such delays may still be compensable when they cause the contractor to accelerate the work, cause inefficiency or disruption, or delay some specific activity and thus cause extended costs, such as cost of equipment rental. In addition, such delay is not necessarily measured from the time that the contract documents required the project to be completed, but rather from the time that the contractor could have completed the project, from a completion date earlier than the one indicated in the contract documents [*Metropolitan Paving Co.* v. *United States,* 325 F.2d 241 (1963)]. The most valuable tools for the defense of a claim are properly prepared CPM schedules.

Delays are the most prevalent problem on construction projects. A variety of factors in an ongoing project can lead to a delay. Typical of the types of delays that might be caused by an owner include the following:

1. Late approval of shop drawings and samples
2. Late approval of laboratory tests
3. Delays in answers to field inquiries by the contractor

**4.** Changes in the contractor's method of doing the work
**5.** Variation in estimated quantities
**6.** Interference with the contractor during construction
**7.** Owner-caused schedule changes
**8.** Design changes
**9.** Changes in inspection level
**10.** Failure to provide for site access
**11.** Lack of required rights-of-way
**12.** Interference by other contractor's or owner's forces

A contractor may jeopardize its claim, however, by being the cause of nonexcusable delays of its own. Such delays are frequently the result of any of the following causes:

**1.** Late submittal of shop drawings
**2.** Late procurement of materials or equipment
**3.** Insufficient personnel
**4.** Unqualified personnel
**5.** Inadequate coordination of subs or other contractors
**6.** Subcontractor delays
**7.** Late response to owner and architect/engineer inquiries
**8.** Construction not conforming to contract requirements, making repeated reworking necessary

### *Attendance at Site Visit*

From time to time, owners and architect/engineers feel that they will better protect the owners' interests by requiring all bidders to attend a prebid site visit. This is obviously based upon the presumption that the contractor might have a stronger claim for differing site conditions if he or she failed to attend a scheduled prebid site tour. However, it appears that the owner may not be as vulnerable as at first thought. In a 1986 case, the Comptroller General ruled that a contractor's failure to attend a prebid site visit is not a valid reason to reject an otherwise acceptable low bid [*Matter of Arrowhead Construction, Inc.*, Comp. Gen. No. B-220386 (January 8, 1986)].

In the subject case, the government requested bids for construction of a paint booth. The Notice Inviting Bids required all bidders to attend a site visit on a designated date. When the government announced its intention to award the contractor to a bidder that did not attend the site visit, the second-lowest bidder protested. The Comptroller General denied the protest.

The decision was that a bidder that fails to attend a prebid site visit does so at its own risk and will be held responsible for any information that it could reasonably determine from that inspection. According to the Comptroller General, the site inspection does not relate to the responsiveness of the bid. Even when the Notice Inviting Bids expressly requires attendance at a prebid inspection, failure to attend is not a valid basis for rejection of an otherwise responsive bid.

## HOME OFFICE OVERHEAD

The costs of delays involve many elements. Naturally, the direct costs are affected, but a contractor's work efficiency, construction schedule, available favorable weather, impact costs, and even home office overhead may be affected. Normally, most contract documents specify the limits of overhead charges that may be levied for force account work, but it should be kept in mind that such limitations apply only to a contract that is completed within the specified time. If the owner causes a compensable delay that forces the contract into a longer time frame, the contractor may be entitled to unabsorbed or extended home office overhead.

### The Eichleay Formula for Home Office Overhead

The most common way of computing the value of extended home office overhead is based upon the use of the *Eichleay Formula*. The validity of this formula was challenged successfully in February 1983 but was reborn a year later when the U.S. Court of Appeals for the Federal Circuit reinstated it [*Capital Electric Co.* v. *United States,* Appeal No. 83-965 (February 7, 1984)]. The Eichleay formula is a method of calculating home office overhead damages in delays, suspensions, or extensions of work. Such damages have usually been called "extended" home office overhead.

The Eichleay formula is commonly expressed as follows:

(a) $\dfrac{\text{Contract billings}}{\text{total billings for the contract period}} \times \dfrac{\text{total overhead for}}{\text{the contract period}} = \dfrac{\text{overhead allocable}}{\text{to the contract}}$

(b) $\dfrac{\text{Allocable overhead}}{\text{Days of performance}} = \text{daily contract overhead}$

(c) Daily contract overhead $\times$ number of days of delay = amount claimed (total added overhead)

The Eichleay formula requires proof of actual damage, however. The Armed Services Board of Contract Appeals ruled that although the use of the Eichleay formula is well recognized in a suspension-of-work situation, the contractor must still show that it was unable to fill in with other work during the suspension period.

In one instance, a contract awarded to Ricway, Inc. at an army ordnance facility, the government issued a stop work order during construction, which remained in effect for 95 days. Ricway later submitted a claim for its unabsorbed home office overhead, computed according to the Eichleay formula.

The board acknowledged that Eichleay is an appropriate measure of unabsorbed home office overhead but said that it cannot be applied automatically. First, the contractor must show that it incurred actual damage, that is, that the contractor was unable to obtain other contracts that could have absorbed the contractor's overhead during the suspension period. [*Appeal of Ricway, Inc.,* ASBCA No. 29983 (February 1986)].

## Unabsorbed Home Office Overhead

*Unabsorbed* home office overhead is computed in a similar manner but relates only when the direct cost base is not large enough to absorb the fixed overhead (an indirect cost) at the contractor's "normal" absorption rate. Fixed overhead is an indirect cost in that it is a cost incurred for the benefit of more than one cost objective or project. Direct costs, of course, are always identified with separate projects. However, indirect costs cannot be identified in this manner, and as a result must be allocated or distributed in a logical manner among all of the contractor's projects.

The allocation of indirect costs is usually done by using a certain "base," for example, labor cost, contract billings, machine hours, or a similar base. The Eichleay formula uses *contract billings* as a base. A ratio of the base for a specific project to the total base for all projects is used to allocate the indirect cost. This is called *absorption costing;* the distributed cost is absorbed by the projects.

## Underabsorption of Overhead

One of the problems with the Eichleay formula as a means of calculating underabsorbed home office overhead is that it does not truly reflect underabsorption of overhead. Assuming that a contractor can offer proof of entitlement, the Eichleay formula results in recovery regardless of whether there was an actual underabsorption of home office overhead. For example, if the delay is caused by the influx of a large amount of extra direct costs as a result of numerous change orders, the contractor's base for absorbing home office overhead may actually increase to the extent that overhead is overabsorbed despite the extended duration of the project. In other words, the contractor was not prevented from obtaining additional work and forced to allocate an unfair amount of overhead to the project. Instead, the contractor may have obtained plenty of additional work through additional change orders to which the contractor may have been able to allocate home office overhead.

As an example, consider a fictitious project that we shall call Project A. If work on Project A is suspended, the contractor cannot earn any revenue, and its billings decrease. However, during the suspension period, the contractor continues to incur the fixed overhead that was originally allocated to Project A prior to its suspension. This fixed overhead for the now suspended Project A is *unabsorbed* during the suspension period; there is no Project A revenue to absorb these overhead costs. In other words, the unabsorbed overhead of Project A must now be absorbed by the remaining projects. However, as the actual allocation base during suspension is less than that of the as-planned base, the remaining projects must support more overhead than was originally planned, or is "normal." For example, let us say that the normal overhead rate is 10 percent for all projects. Without Project A, it increases to 15 percent for the remaining projects. The suspension causes the overhead rate to increase. In this example, the overhead rate "differential" is a 5 percent increase.

It should be pointed out that overabsorption can also occur, such as when the base increases. For example, let us say that the suspended work of Project A is performed during a later period. Fixed overhead remains as planned, but the billings *increase*. Thus, the allocation base is higher than the as-planned base. Then, while the overhead rate may have been 10 percent, with a larger base it may actually drop to 5 percent. The overhead rate differential is then a 5 percent *decrease*. This is called *overabsorption* of fixed overhead.

Because the damages computed through the Eichleay method bear no relationship to actual absorption rates, contractors with home office overhead claims may be forced to rely upon other methods, such as two examples of construction delayed projects can illustrate. The first method is known as the *Comparative Absorption Rate* method (Figure 19.4). Under this method the underabsorbed overhead is determined by finding the difference between overhead actually incurred and overhead that would have been incurred if the contractor had been able to maintain a reasonable absorption rate. The second method is known as the *Burden Fluctuation* method (Figure 19.5). It has been used by Boards of Contract Appeals in calculating manufacturers' underabsorbed overhead claims. This method determines the underabsorbed overhead by finding the increase in absorption rate and allocating that increase to work on other projects that were forced to bear more than their fair share of overhead expenses. An Eichleay calculation for each of the two examples is provided for further comparison.

Example 1 in Figure 19.4 illustrates a project that could have been performed by the contractor for $400 000 over a four-month duration, assuming no change orders were issued and no suspensions of work or other delays were encountered. The contractor in this example has a fixed home office overhead rate of $40 000 and regularly does $500 000 worth of total business per month, including the subject project. These data appear under the heading "Potential Performance" and reflect what would have happened if there had been no changes or delays caused by the owner on this project.

In the actual performance of the work, the contractor experienced no changes; however, there was a one-month suspension of work during the third month of the project. This resulted in a one-month delay to the contractor in question and the inability to take on $100 000 in new work after the planned completion date had passed. Under the Eichleay theory, the contractor would have a claim for only $6667 of extended overhead, based upon the one-month delay.

A comparison of absorption rates reveals that the contractor, in fact, suffered $8000 in underabsorbed overhead during the delay. This figure was arrived at by calculating a reasonable overhead rate, based upon what the contractor's overhead absorption rate would have been, had it not been for the delay. In this case, the rate equals 8 percent. By applying that rate to the actual billings for the actual period, the contractor can arrive at a reasonable total overhead of $192 000, which is $8000 less than the amount of overhead that the contractor had to absorb. In other words, the contractor was unable to maintain the 8 percent absorption rate during the delay. Had the contractor been able to maintain that rate, only $32 000 would have been expended on home office overhead during the delay.

Under the Burden Fluctuation method shown in Example 1 in Figure 19.4, the contractor would claim a 0.33 percent increase in its overhead rate. By applying that percentage increase to the work that had to bear the extra overhead cost, the contractor could claim $6600. Regardless of the method used, this example presents a classic case of underab-

---

*Example No 1:* A $400 000, 4-month contract with a one-month suspension and no change orders.

|  | MO. 1 | MO. 2 | MO. 3 | MO. 4 | MO. 5 |
|---|---|---|---|---|---|
| **POTENTIAL PERFORMANCE** | | | | | |
| Home Office Overhead | $ 40 000 | $ 40 000 | $ 40 000 | $ 40 000 | $ 40 000 |
| Contract Billings | $100 000 | $100 000 | $100 000 | $100 000 | — |
| Other Contract Billings | $400 000 | $400 000 | $400 000 | $400 000 | $500 000 |
| Total Billings | $500 000 | $500 000 | $500 000 | $500 000 | $500 000 |
| **ACTUAL PERFORMANCE** | | | | | |
| Home Office Overhead | $ 40 000 | $ 40 000 | $ 40 000 | $ 40 000 | $ 40 000 |
| Contract Billings | $100 000 | $100 000 | — | $100 000 | $100 000 |
| Other Contract Billings | $400 000 | $400 000 | $400 000 | $400 000 | $400 000 |
| Total Billings | $500 000 | $500 000 | $400 000 | $500 000 | $500 000 |

### METHOD #1—EICHLEAY FORMULA

$$\frac{\$400\ 000\ (\text{Contract Billings})}{\$2\ 400\ 000\ (\text{Total Billings})} \times \$200\ 000\ (\text{Total Overhead}) = \$33\ 333\ (\text{Allocable Overhead})$$

$$\frac{\$33\ 333\ (\text{Allocable Overhead})}{5\ (\text{Months of Performance})} \times \$6667\ (\text{Monthly Contract Overhead})$$

$$\times\ 1\ \text{Month Delay} = \$6667\ \text{Claim}$$

### METHOD #2—COMPARATIVE ABSORPTION RATES

$$\frac{\$200\ 000\ (\text{Potential Total Overhead})}{\$2\ 500\ 000\ (\text{Potential Total Billings})} = 8\%\ \text{Reasonable Overhead Ratio}$$

8% (Reasonable Overhead Ratio) × $2 400 000 (Actual Total Billings)

$$= \$192\ 000\ (\text{Reasonable Total Overhead})$$

$200 000 (Actual Total Overhead) − $192 000 (Reasonable Total Overhead)

$$= \$8000\ \text{Underabsorbed Overhead Claim}$$

### METHOD #3—BURDEN FLUCTUATION

$2 400 000 (Total Billings) − $400 000 (Contract Billings)

$$= \$2\ 000\ 000\ (\text{Other Billings})$$

$$\frac{\$200\ 000}{\$2\ 400\ 000}\ (\text{Actual Overhead Rate}) - \frac{\$200\ 000}{\$2\ 500\ 000}\ (\text{Potential Overhead Rate}) =$$

8.33% − 8.00% = 0.33% (Burden Fluctuation)

.33% × $2 000 000 = $6600 Underabsorbed Overhead Claim

---

**FIGURE 19.4**  Comparative Absorption Rate method of computation. (Reprinted with permission from Phillip R. McDonald, Esq., for *Construction Claims Monthly,* 951 Pershing Drive, Silver Spring, MD 20910.)

sorption of home office overhead. Recovery, however, would be clearly dependent upon proof that additional work could have been obtained in other contracts had it not been for the delay on this project.

Example 2 in Figure 19.5 is based upon the same contract and contractor described in Example 1, but on a different type of delay. The actual performance included no

*Example No 2:* A $400 000, 4-month contract with no suspension of work and change orders worth $110 000 including $10 000 overhead mark-up. Potential performance is the same as Example No. 1.

|                          | MO. 1      | MO. 2      | MO. 3      | MO. 4      | MO. 5      |
| ------------------------ | ---------- | ---------- | ---------- | ---------- | ---------- |
| **ACTUAL PERFORMANCE**   |            |            |            |            |            |
| Home Office Overhead     | $ 40 000   | $ 40 000   | $ 40 000   | $ 40 000   | $ 40 000   |
|                          |            |            |            |            |            |
| Contract Billings        | $ 75 000   | $ 75 000   | $125 000   | $135 000   | $100 000   |
| Other Contract Billings  | $400 000   | $400 000   | $400 000   | $400 000   | $400 000   |
| Total Billings           | $475 000   | $475 000   | $525 000   | $535 000   | $500 000   |

### METHOD #1—EICHLEAY FORMULA

$$\frac{\$510\ 000\ \text{(Contract Billings)}}{\$2\ 510\ 000\ \text{(Total Billings)}} \times \$200\ 000\ \text{(Total Overhead)} = \$40\ 637\ \text{(Allocable Overhead)}$$

$$\frac{\$40\ 637\ \text{(Allocable Overhead)}}{5\ \text{(Months of Performance)}} \times \$8127\ \text{(Monthly Contract Overhead)}$$

$$\times\ 1\ \text{Month Delay} = \$8127\ \text{Claim}$$

### METHOD #2—COMPARATIVE ABSORPTION RATES

$$\frac{\$200\ 000\ \text{(Potential Total Overhead)}}{\$2\ 500\ 000\ \text{(Potential Total Billings)}} = 8\%\ \text{(Reasonable Overhead Ratio)}$$

$$8\%\ \text{(Reasonable Overhead Ratio)} \times \$2\ 510\ 000\ \text{(Actual Total Billings)}$$

$$= \$200\ 800\ \text{(Reasonable Total Overhead)}$$

$$\$200\ 000\ \text{(Actual Total Overhead)} - \$200\ 800\ \text{(Reasonable Total Overhead)}$$

$$= (\$800)\ \text{Underabsorbed or } \$800\ \text{Overabsorbed Overhead}$$

### METHOD #3—BURDEN FLUCTUATION

$$\$2\ 510\ 000\ \text{(Total Billings)} - \$510\ 000\ \text{(Contract Billings)} = \$2\ 000\ 000\ \text{(Other Billings)}$$

$$\frac{\$200\ 000}{\$2\ 510\ 000}\ \text{(Actual Overhead Rate)} - \frac{\$200\ 000}{\$2\ 500\ 000}\ \text{(Potential Overhead Rate)} =$$

$$7.97\% - 8.00\% = (0.03\%)\text{(Burden Fluctuation)}$$

$$(.03\%) \times \$2\ 000\ 000 = (\$600)\ \text{Underabsorbed or } \$600\ \text{Overabsorbed Overhead}$$

**FIGURE 19.5** Burden fluctuation method of computation. (Reprinted with permission from Phillip R. McDonald, Esq., for *Construction Claims Monthly,* 951 Pershing Drive, Silver Spring, MD 20910.)

suspension of work and resulted in the increase of the contract price by $110 000 for change orders, including $10 000 of overhead markup. Under the Eichleay formula, the contractor would have an extended home office overhead claim of $8127 despite the fact that change orders resulted in additional direct charges that could absorb the contractor's overhead.

Calculating the contractor's damages by comparing absorption rates shows that the contractor actually did not suffer from underabsorption of home office overhead. Instead of absorbing the overhead at the normal rate of 8 percent, the contract, with the help of changes, was able to absorb overhead at the rate of 7.97 percent. This resulted in $800 of overabsorbed overhead. Moreover, if the $10 000 markup on the changes was required to be set off against the contractor's claim, the contractor would actually have absorbed its overhead at the rate of 6.8 percent. The Burden Fluctuation method would similarly reveal an overabsorption of overhead in the amount of $600, based upon the 0.03 percent decrease in the contractor's overhead rate.

The results obtained for the two examples through the Absorption Rate or Burden Fluctuation methods vary greatly, but the results obtained by using the Eichleay formula do not. This illustrates some of the objections to using Eichleay. The contractor in Example 1 who experiences a one-month suspension without receiving any extra work clearly suffers more damages than the contractor in Example 2, who receives extra work extending its contract through changes; yet the Eichleay formula would give the second contractor a larger recovery.

### Flaws in Use of the Various Computation Methods

Several criticisms can be raised about the Burden Fluctuation method. Some of these criticisms also apply to the basic Eichleay approach. First, the use of a differential is not a cost accounting method but an approximation method that is based upon certain assumptions.

Burden Fluctuation assumes that all of the overhead rate differential is due to the one impacted project. It does not consider other factors that may impact a contractor's overhead costs, such as other sour jobs that a contractor may have. It may, therefore, overcompensate the contractor.

The normal rate is an *averaged* rate for all jobs. Different projects may, in fact, have overhead rates lower or higher than the average rate. How, then, is the normal rate for a particular job calculated? Even knowing the contractor's cost records and the nature of the indirect costs, it is difficult to find a way to know *directly* which part of fixed overhead differential is due to impacts, delays, suspensions, extensions, and so on, of one particular project.

Second, the unabsorbed overhead determined by the Burden Fluctuation method would be expected to be reduced by the amount of money received by the contractor on Change Orders.

Third, the Burden Fluctuation method does not account for the growth-decay bell curve of costs. This also applies to Eichleay.

Fourth, the method does not account for variable overhead costs. Burden Fluctuation treats all overhead costs as fixed, introducing some distortion.

Fifth, some home office overhead costs may be attributed directly to specific jobs or distributed on some percentage-of-effort basis instead of by allocation formula.

Sixth, a more appropriate base than total costs may be found to allocate overhead. One suggestion might be to use labor costs as a base. This would have the effect of overcompensation of a contractor on a labor-intensive job, or undercompensation of a contractor on a material-intensive job.

Thus, there are problems with the Burden Fluctuation method. The Eichleay method has some of the same problems. However, Burden Fluctuation does answer in part those complaints that the daily rate method of Eichleay is not related to actual costs. Through the use of actual overhead rates, the Burden Fluctuation method is more closely tied into actual costs.

While under certain circumstances, either the Burden Fluctuation method or the Comparative Absorption Rate formulas might be preferred to the Eichleay approach, in the sense of producing a more convincing claim, each of the alternative approaches is capable of producing claims that are inconsistent with the facts regarding a particular contractor's business, and thus may be unreasonable. The distortion is most likely when dealing with a large-volume contractor.

As an example, consider a large contractor (300 million per year) whose $11 million, 20-month contract (which represents only a small fraction of the company's business) is affected by differing site conditions and takes 30 months for completion while generating $2 million through change orders. Plotted against these data, the expected performance on such a contract might be compared to actual performance as shown in Figure 19.6.

| EXPECTED PERFORMANCE: 20 MONTHS, $11 MILLION | | |
|---|---|---|
| | **First Year** | **Second Year** |
| **Potential Performance** | **Mo. 1–12** | **Mo. 13–20** |
| Home Office Overhead | $1 M/month | $1.3M/month |
| Contract Billings | $550 000/month | $550 000/month |
| Other Billings | $25M/month | $27M/month |
| Total Billings | $25.55M/month | $27.43/month |

| ACTUAL PERFORMANCE: 30 MONTHS, CHANGE ORDERS OF $2 MILLION | | | |
|---|---|---|---|
| | **First Year** | **Second Year** | **Third Year** |
| **Actual Performance** | **Mo. 1–12** | **Mo. 13–24** | **Mo. 25–30** |
| Home Office Overhead | $1M/month | $1.3M/month | $1.35M/month |
| Contract Billings | $433 333/month | $433 333/month | $435 333/month |
| Other Billings | $25M/month | $27M/month | $22M/month |
| Total Billings | $25.43M/month | $27.43M/month | $22.43M/month |

**FIGURE 19.6**  Comparison of home office overhead expected and actual performance. (Reprinted with permission from Lawrence C. Melton, Esq., "Common Sense about Home Office Overhead." Volume 7, Number 6, June 1985, *Construction Claims Monthly,* 951 Pershing Drive, Silver Spring, MD 20910.)

By comparing the expected and actual performance charts, it can be seen that (1) the contractor earned $116 667 per month less than projected from the extended (delayed) contract; (2) home office overhead increased each year (no direct correlation with the extended contract earnings; and (3) other billings were higher than projected for one year, and lower than projected for the last 10 months (no direct correlation with extended contract earnings).

Thus, at some time during the delay, additional work was available to absorb overhead costs (overabsorption), but at other times the delayed contract had to support more than its projected portion of the overhead pool (underabsorption). Based upon these facts, the owner might argue that home office costs were covered despite the extended performance.

If the delay occurred during the first year of performance, when other contract earnings were higher than projected, the owner's argument might be meaningful, but still might not constitute an equitable basis for denying the payment of home office overhead to the contractor. Any overabsorption in the first year is caused not by the delayed contract, which is still earning less per month than reasonably projected, but by other factors, such as the contractor's managerial expertise or good fortune. For the owner to deny an equitable adjustment on that basis would be to let the owner take advantage of the contractor's good fortune or good business judgment to avoid paying for the logical consequences of the delay.

In the second year, the owner forced the contractor into a time of high overhead and low earnings that could not have been anticipated. Overabsorption in the first year, which was not caused by the owner, is balanced by underabsorption in the second year, which was a direct consequence of the owner-caused delay. The Eichleay formula ignores these considerations and bases its computation of the contractor's award on the actual allocated overhead expense and the number of compensable delays during the delay period. In comparison with the Burden Fluctuation method and the Comparative Absorption Rate, the Eichleay formula not only gives a smaller recovery, but is more realistic.

| | | |
|---|---|---|
| *Eichleay* | $201 196 | ($671/day × 300 calendar days) |
| *Comparative Absorption Rate* | $3.4M | ($11 333/day) |
| *Burden Fluctuation* | $2.94M | ($ 9 827/day) |

While admittedly crude in terms of the number of variables it considers, the Eichleay formula per diem approach gives a daily value for home office support, such as management and clerical salaries, rent, computers, and so on, that bear a reasonable relationship to the value of the affected work (3.65 percent).

## SCHEDULING CHANGES

Any scheduling change can have an important effect on project operations. When scheduling changes are implemented as a result of constraints created by the owner or architect/engineer, the basis for a contractor claim may exist. Whenever the owner or the architect/engineer issues any change order, field order, or work directive, or whenever a constructive change condition exists in any of the following areas, the contractor will begin to consider the impact of such action by the owner or architect/engineer upon its project costs and profitability.

The areas of primary sensitivity include owner- or architect/engineer-caused delays, requirements to deviate from the schedule, orders to expedite the work, job interference by the owner or architect/engineer, owner constraints on scheduling interfaces, late availability of owner-furnished material, owner-imposed acceleration or deceleration, impractical or impossible milestones, extra work, schedule impacts, sequence of construction by owner or architect/engineer, changes in completion dates, time extensions, utilization of scheduling float time, and schedule approvals. If a CPM schedule is not available during the job, any consistent scheduling method that illustrates the delay will help support the claim.

Any change in the schedule imposed by either the owner or the architect/engineer can become a basis for potential claim by the contractor. The best way to assure a sound, defensible claim is to utilize CPM scheduling techniques. This form of scheduling documentation offers the greatest protection.

The routine approval of contractor-prepared schedules can be the most costly mistake an owner can make. In the absence of a thorough review by an experienced, competent individual, contractually required schedules can become the primary source of documentation for successful contractor claims. The contractor can simply unveil its prebid, preconstruction, and progress schedules and compare them with the as-built or adjusted schedules. The comparison can be very graphic and may have a significant impact on a panel of arbitrators or a jury. As the owner had approved the contractor's schedules, the owner is left in a rather weak position.

As a job progresses, time extensions may be granted by the owner or architect/engineer. These would result in changes in the schedule and could result in revised interface dates or changed completion dates. The contractor will probably keep a close watch on the status of the schedules that it submits to the owner or architect/engineer for approval. Departures in the contractor's schedule from the schedule originally intended by the owner may be considered as a contract amendments after approval by the owner. If a contractor submits a shorter schedule than that originally called for under the contract, and it is approved by the owner or its architect/engineer, any liquidated damages provided under the contract may now be applied to the early finish date shown in your own shortened schedule.

There is no question that the only way for a contractor to make a profit on a project is to get in and get out in the shortest possible time, thus reducing the home office overhead allocated to that project.

## CONSTRUCTIVE CHANGES

A *constructive* change is an informal act authorizing or directing a modification to the contract caused by the owner or architect/engineer through an act or failure to act. In contrast to the mutually recognized need for a change, certain acts or a failure to act by the owner that increases the contractor's cost and/or time of performance may be considered as grounds for a change order. This is termed as a constructive change; however, it must be claimed in writing by the contractor within the time specified in the contract documents;

otherwise, the contractor may waive its rights to collect. Types of typical constructive changes may include:

Defective plans and specifications

Architect/engineer's interpretations of documents

Higher standard of performance than specified

Improper inspection and rejection

Change in the method of performance by owner

Change in construction sequence by owner

Owner nondisclosure of pertinent facts

Impossibility or impracticability of performance

An example of a constructive change resulting more *from failure to act* is the *Appeal of Continental Heller Corp.* [GSBCA 7140 (March 23, 1984)], where the government's failure to grant a legitimate request for a time extension has been held to be a constructive acceleration of the work schedule.

Continental Heller Corp. was awarded a contract for construction of a federal building in San Jose, California. Heavy rains at the start of the project made it impossible for the excavation subcontractor to proceed.

Nevertheless, the contracting officer insisted that the contractor stay on schedule and refused to grant a time extension until the contractor documented both the site conditions and the status of the activity on the critical path. An extension was finally granted 16 months after completion of the excavation. In the meantime, however, the subcontractor had switched to a more expensive method of excavation in order to remove the saturated soil in accordance with the original schedule.

The Board of Contract Appeals of the General Services Administration found classic elements of a construction acceleration case. The delay was excusable, yet the government forced the contractor to adhere to the original performance period, thereby causing the contractor to incur additional costs. Continental Heller was awarded $113 165 plus interest.

The Board of Contract Appeals, referring to the belated time extension granted to the contractor 16 months later, said: "As a defense to a claim of constructive acceleration, a belated time extension is worthless. . . . It had to have been clear to anyone who did not sleep through the entire two days that the soil at the site was saturated with moisture and could not be compacted as required. The government could not, by continually insisting on documentation of what was already known, justify its refusal to grant a time extension."

## Differing Site Conditions

Sometimes referred to as "changed conditions" or "unforeseen conditions," the term *differing site conditions* is typically used in all federal contracts, and there is a growing trend by many public agencies and a few private owners to adopt similar wording. Failure of an owner to provide payment for differing site conditions places the contractor in a difficult position. If the owner takes a hard-line position on this issue, the contractor may find it necessary to seek relief from the court, a process that is both lengthy and costly to both parties.

The federal policy is to make adjustments in time and/or price where unknown subsurface or latent conditions at the site are encountered by the contractor. The purpose is to have the owner accept certain risks and thus reduce the large contingency amounts in bids to cover such unknown conditions. The federal government and many local agencies include provisions in their construction contracts that will grant a price increase and/or time extension to a contractor who has encountered subsurface or latent conditions.

Under the definitions for differing site conditions in Chapter 6, an existing underground pipeline that either was not shown on the drawings at all or that was incorrectly located on the contract drawings would be a Type 1 differing site condition. Unusually severe weather conditions for the time of year and location of a given project may well fall into a Type 2 differing site condition. The discovery of expansive clays in the excavation area, if not normally encountered in the location where the project was planned, and if not detected during soil investigations may be either a Type 1 or 2 condition, depending upon circumstances. However, the discovery by the contractor of a permafrost condition in the tropics, for example, would most certainly be a Type 2 differing site condition.

### Unusually Severe Weather Conditions

Severe rains or similar weather that prevents work from being done, or which in any way delays the project, may not always be excusable delays, and in some cases may be ruled excusable only and not compensable.

In the *Appeal of Inland Construction, Inc.* [ENG BCA 5033 (October 11, 1984)], a contractor was denied a differing site condition claim because the board found that the increased costs were caused by unusually severe rainfall, an event "which only entitles the contractor to an extension of time." In another case, although the contractor was delayed by rain, its claim of excusable delay was denied because the severity of the storm could have been foreseen by the contractor [*Appeal of B. D. Click Co., Inc.,* ASBCA 24586 (July 27, 1984)]. In that case, the Board of Contract Appeals ruled that weather delays are excusable only when the weather is abnormal. In the words of the board, "No matter how severe or destructive, if the weather is not unusual for the particular time and place, or if the contractor should have reasonably anticipated it, the contractor is not entitled to relief." Nevertheless, the owner or architect/engineer should document all weather delays as they occur. Determination of compensability can be made at a later date.

### Acceleration of the Work

Acceleration of the work is usually the result of an attempt by the contractor to take whatever means and measures are necessary to complete the work sooner than would normally be expected for a given project under stated conditions, or an attempt by the contractor to take extra measures to make up for delays, whatever the cause, by utilizing whatever means are at its disposal to accomplish the objective.

There are two types of acceleration:

1. Directed acceleration
2. Constructive acceleration

They are largely self-defining, but briefly, a "directed acceleration" occurs when the owner or architect/engineer specifically orders a contractor to speed up the work. The U.S. District Court outlined the necessary elements of a claim for constructive acceleration. "Constructive acceleration is present when (1) the contractor encountered an excusable delay entitling it to a time extension; (2) the contractor requested an extension; (3) the request was refused; (4) the contractor was ordered to accelerate its work, that is, to finish the project as scheduled despite the excused delays; and (5) the contractor actually accelerated the work."

In considering acceleration, the first consideration must be whether the so-called "acceleration" is the result of an order from the owner to a contractor who is behind schedule to get back onto schedule, or an order from the owner or architect/engineer to the contractor requiring a contractor either directly or constructively to complete the work prior to the scheduled completion date.

If a contractor is behind schedule and it is the desire of the owner or architect/engineer to require the contractor to get back on schedule, it is sometimes necessary to direct the contractor to take whatever means are necessary to assure completion by the originally scheduled completion date. Herein lies an administrative risk for the Resident Project Representative or contract administrator. If an order is issued to the contractor directing it to accelerate the work so as to catch up or make up for delays or lost time, the risk is that the contractor will perform as directed, then submit a claim for directed acceleration, arguing that although it appeared from the original schedule that it would not complete on time, actually the contractor may claim that there was no risk of failing to complete on time at all. The contractor might state that in the absence of the acceleration order it would have finished on time anyway. The proper handling of a situation such as this is not to issue an acceleration order (even though acceleration is justified or needed), but to send a letter to the contractor calling attention to the fact that completion by the scheduled date will be required, and that "according to the schedule it appears that the contractor will be unable to complete the project by the completion date indicated in the contract. Please resubmit a revised schedule showing how the contractor plans to complete the project by the scheduled date." This leaves the means and methods to the contractor, as it should be.

Often the problem starts in the design office. Project completion dates or time available to complete is frequently established by a designer who has little field experience, and thus is hardly qualified to properly establish the time needed to build a project. Typically, the time allotted to complete a project, as established by a designer, is either too short or too long.

If insufficient time is allotted to the completion of a project, all of the bidders will be forced to bid the job as accelerated work, thus increasing the costs materially. One indication that this may be happening is evident when all of the bids are in and although they are grouped close together (a good sign of competent documents), they are considerably in excess of the amount of the engineer's estimate of anticipated project cost. This can be evidence that all of the bidders are bidding the job as accelerated work, thus increasing the cost of construction above that for a job completed within a normal schedule.

Another risk surfaces here as well. After figuring a bid for a job as being all accelerated work, a bidder may look in the contract documents to determine how much liquidated damages are being assessed in case of a completion delay. Upon finding daily liquidated damages to be assessed as somewhat less than $500 or $600 per day, the bidder now refigures the bid.

In the foregoing example, let us assume that we plan to build a project that on a normal schedule should take 16 months to complete, but the contract documents actually indicate that completion must be within 14 months. The bidder will first figure the bid for completion in 14 months, including the two months' acceleration of work that is necessary to complete by the required 14 months. Then the bidder may check the amount of liquidated damages called for in the documents. Let us say that the amount of liquidated damages was only $300 per day. An enterprising bidder will now go back to its 14-month bid and refigure the costs for completion in 16 months instead of the required 14 months. Then the bidder will determine that the difference in time between the time that was allowed by the owner for completion versus the time that a job such as that should normally take was two months, or 66 working days. The bidder may now multiply 66 times $300 per day and add the amount of liquidated damages to its total bid price for doing the work in 16 months, and submit it as its bid price.

The problem is, of course, that the cost of acceleration at $300 per day is considerably less than the daily cost to the contractor of acceleration; thus, the bidder submits a bid claiming that it will complete on time, when in fact it planned from the very beginning to complete the work two months late and pay liquidated damages costs. The owner and the designer, unfortunately, are the only persons who were unaware that the project was destined to be late before it was even started. Generally speaking, any job that has a Resident Project Representative operating out of an on-site field office can justify in excess of $1000 per day of liquidated damages without difficulty. Only then will liquidated damages serve as a deterrent to the contractor for finishing late.

A related condition called "deceleration" can also be experienced on a project. This occurs when a contractor is directed in writing or constructively to slow down its job progress. Many of the same considerations that apply to acceleration also apply to deceleration.

In preparing a claim for acceleration or deceleration, it should be borne in mind that the costs to the contractor for going into premium time, such as working an extended workweek, cannot be computed simply as including the added hourly costs multiplied by the additional hours. Studies have shown that as the workweek is extended, there is an accompanying loss in worker productivity. Furthermore, as the extended overtime is continued, the productivity rate continues to drop.

### Productivity Losses

Scheduled overtime is not often seen on competitively bid lump-sum contracts, as most contractors are well aware of the negative effects of overtime on cost and productivity. Simple arithmetic shows that premium pay for double time or time and one-half makes overtime work much more expensive. However, people who insist on overtime seldom realize that other costs associated with overtime may be even more significant than premium pay. Premium pay affects only overtime hours, but continuing of scheduled overtime drastically affects costs of all hours. All available research findings indicate a serious inverse ratio between the amount and duration of scheduled construction overtime and the labor productivity achieved during both regular and overtime hours.

In the first few weeks of scheduled overtime, total productivity per person is normally greater than in a standard 40-hour week, but not as much more than the number of additional work hours. After seven to nine consecutive 50-or 60-hour weeks, the total weekly productivity is likely to be no more than that attainable by the same work force in a 40-hour week.

Productivity will continue to diminish as the overtime schedule continues. After another 8 weeks or so of scheduled overtime, the substandard productivity of later weeks can be expected to cancel out the costly gains in early weeks of the overtime schedule, so that the total work accomplished during the entire period over which weekly overtime was worked will be no greater, or possibly even less, than if no overtime had been worked at all.

When the loss of productivity is added to the higher wage cost (including premium pay), productive value per wage dollar paid after several weeks of scheduled overtime drops to less than 75 percent for five 10-hour days, less than 62 percent for six 10-hour days, and less than 40 percent for seven 12-hour days. When an overtime schedule is discontinued, it has been found that there was a dramatic jump in productivity per hour after return to a 40-hour week.

Construction delay claims involving acceleration of the work usually include claims for loss of productivity, which often exceed all other claimed amounts. The following breakdown of a claim on a treatment plant project serves to point out the relative magnitude of the claim for loss of productivity as compared with the other issues shown:

| | |
|---|---:|
| 1. Extended project overhead | $1 019 099 |
| 2. Unabsorbed home office overhead | 227 620 |
| 3. Labor escalation | 142 430 |
| 4. Material escalation | 148 329 |
| 5. Labor loss of productivity | 2 442 409 |
| 6. Subcontractor claims | 920 407 |
| SUBTOTAL | 4 900 284 |
| 7. Profit and overhead on items 1 to 5 | 1 298 575 |
| 8. Unresolved changes | 157 993 |
| 9. Interest on money | 1 073 897 |
| 10. Additional bond premium | 11 844 |
| TOTAL CLAIM | $7 442 593 |

### Suspension of the Work; Termination

The work on the project can usually be suspended by the owner for any one or more of several reasons. In each case, the owner or architect/engineer should keep detailed cost isolation records of all activities affected by the suspension. It should be kept in mind that suspension of the work for any amount of time such that the completion date is extended may impact the contractor's costs through unabsorbed home office overhead and the real possibility of missing other projects due to the delay.

The contractor may also claim the effect upon its organization of the costs related to dismantling operations, mobilization or demobilization, direct costs, settlement expenses, escalation costs, prior commitments, post-termination continuing costs, unabsorbed overhead, unexpired leases, severance pay, implied agreements, restoration work, utility cutoff, inventory, replacement costs, and all other allocable costs. On suspensions of the work, be certain that all such orders are in writing and that a careful record is kept of its total effect on the contractor's time and costs.

### Failure to Agree on Change Order Pricing

One of the most common causes of contractor claims occurs during attempts to price change orders. All too often, owner change orders contain a waiver clause that requires the contractor to guarantee that the price and time named in each individual change order represents the total cost to the owner for that change, and the contractor waives any rights to impact costs.

This, unfortunately, leaves the contractor with only one recourse—the claims process. The owner and architect/engineer should take note of the settlement ordered in at least one contract dispute. In the *Appeal of Centex Construction Co., Inc.* [ASBCA 26830 (April 29, 1983)] the Armed Services Board of Contract Appeals ruled that the government may not force a contractor to "forward price" its impact costs when pricing a government-directed change.

In that case, Centex Construction Co., Inc., was a prime contractor on a military construction project. The government ordered a number of changes and asked Centex to submit cost proposals under the terms of its contract. Centex listed the *direct* costs of performing the changed work but did not list delay damages and other impact costs. When a change order was issued, Centex refused to release its right to submit a claim for impact costs.

Centex stated that it was impossible to forecast such costs accurately, particularly when an ongoing series of changes is involved. The Appeals Board agreed with Centex, stating:

> While it might be good contract administration on the part of the government to attempt to resolve all matters relating to a contract modification [change order] during the negotiation of the modification, use of a clause which imposes an obligation on the contractor to submit a price breakdown required to "cover all work involved in the modification" cannot be used to deprive the contractor from its right to file claims.

### Conflicts in Plans and Specifications

This is an often misunderstood area in contractor claims. However, the probability of recovery by the contractor as the direct result of such conflicts is good insofar as the settlement is limited to the cost difference between the project cost as the plans and specifications are interpreted by the owner or architect/engineer and the contractor.

Public works contracts are called *contracts of adhesion,* which is a term applied to contract documents that are drawn by one party and offered to the other party on a take-it-or-leave-it basis, where there can be no discussion of terms nor contract modifications by the other party. The contractor, however, does have one advantage. In case of ambiguity, the court will interpret the contract in the contractor's favor. This does not relieve the contractor from the obligation of building the work in accordance with the interpretation of the architect or engineer, but only assures that the contractor will get paid for its trouble.

Frequently, the contractor will find in the specifications that outdated standards are specified, or that products are named that no longer exist. Often, the specifications will contain references stating that wherever codes or commercial standards are specified, the contractor is obligated to use the latest issue of that standard existing at the time that the project went to bid. Unfortunately, in many cases the designers failed to consider the fact that the design was based upon an old standard that exists in their files, or a standard that was current during the design phase, but which later may have been updated by the sponsoring agency without the designer's knowledge. Occasionally, serious difficulties arise from such practices, and the contractor certainly should have the right to the project cost difference resulting from the error.

Perfect specifications are hard to find. In fact, there has never been one known to the author, so the contractor must make a reasonable interpretation at the time of bidding the job and will then be in a good position for recovery if a variance exists. The contractor's interpretation must be based upon what a reasonable person would interpret the documents to mean; then the contractor will have the court on its side.

A contractor should never attempt to construct any questionable area without first submitting to the owner or architect/engineer for clarification or notifying them of an error. In many contract forms, failure to do this may serve as a bar to full recovery of contractor costs.

## Miscellaneous Problems

Problems may arise that are directly related to the conduct of the owner's representative on the job, such as issuing changes in the work that are of such magnitude as to constitute a cardinal change (creating a breach of contract) or indirectly related, where one contractor may negligently delay another, which may result in the owner seeking recovery from the negligent contractor in order to pay the contractor that was harmed.

Some of the types of problems that may fall into this category include the following:

Damage to work by other prime contractors
Breach of contract
Cardinal changes
Work beyond contract scope
Beneficial use of the entire project before completion
Partial utilization of the project before completion
Owner nondisclosure of site-related information
Owner's failure to make payment when due

## RESOLVING DIFFERENCES

Even if a perfect set of contract documents were to be devised, there would still be disagreements between parties. Disagreements may arise between the contractor and the architect/engineer or owner concerning the interpretation of the contract; what constitutes extra work on the contract; payment for changes; extensions of time; damages for owner-directed acceleration or slowdown; costs occasioned by owner-caused delay; defective drawings or specifications; and changed conditions (sometimes referred to as unforeseen conditions, based upon the logic that the conditions have not actually "changed" but were that way all the time; discovery of the difference between the actual conditions and the way they were represented in the specifications or drawings is referred to under this concept as "unforeseen" differences). Similar matters may affect contract cost or time required to complete the work. Contract documents routinely include procedures to be followed in the settlement of such claims and disputes. The greatest difficulty arises from the fact that there is no uniform method of handling such unforeseen conditions, and numerous books and technical articles have been written about it; many cases are brought to suit over such differences; and the matter is not much closer to the development of a fair and equitable contract provision that will apply to all such cases than it was at the beginning.

Although their provisions may vary, construction contracts typically require the contractor to notify the architect/engineer immediately upon recognizing a situation that can lead to a claim or dispute. In cases of conflicts between the drawings and the specifications (a frequent cause of difficulty), it is the obligation of the contractor to notify the architect/engineer immediately without going further with what it knows to be improper work.

A word of caution at this point. The Resident Project Representative should always be aware of the possibility that a contractor who is alert for extras may recognize a defect in the plans or specifications, yet hastily construct the work exactly as shown on the defective documents, knowing all the time that it will be directed to remove such work and reconstruct it later as soon as the architect/engineer or owner discovers the same defect. A situation such as this could be a race between the contractor and the inspector to see if the contractor can get the incorrectly specified or detailed work constructed before the inspector notices it and reports it to the architect/engineer or owner. The logic of the plan is simple. If a contractor can feign ignorance of the problem and simply claim that it was just following the plans and specifications (which, undoubtedly, it would be) then, when the architect/engineer or owner discovers the defect in the plans and specifications and orders the newly constructed work to be removed and reconstructed, the contractor will willingly rebuild the work in any manner subsequently ordered by the architect/engineer or owner—followed later by bills for extra work, which, of course, the owner then becomes obligated to pay.

If a dispute cannot be settled with the architect/engineer or owner, and they order the contractor to continue with the work as directed by the architect/engineer or owner, the contractor cannot usually refuse without becoming potentially liable for breach of contract. Although the contractor may perform such work under written protest, it must continue to do the work and keep the operation on schedule, relying on the contractual remedies in the contract documents to settle the question of compensation or additional time.

## *Resolution by Negotiation*

Although the individual provisions may vary, most construction contracts for public works contain language regarding the method of resolution of claims, either by litigation or arbitration. In the construction industry, there appears to be far more emphasis on the resolution of disputes by arbitration. Unfortunately, in a contract of adhesion (which includes any public works contract) the contractor is not offered a choice, except in those states where arbitration statutes prohibit contract provisions that agree at the time of signing the contract to submit to binding arbitration on future disputes.

Yet, in many cases, neither arbitration nor litigation is the sensible answer. Keep in mind that if the owner or architect/engineer goes to court or to arbitration, the costs on smaller claims may exceed the settlement, even if they win: Whenever the value of a claim is under $50 000 or even $100 000, it is doubtful whether either party can ever win financially. The only true winners will be the lawyers and claims consultants (Figure 19.7). Fighting for principles may be a fine hobby for another Howard Hughes, but to most people and organizations it is financially unsound. The only economically sound solution is to negotiate.

Negotiation involves compromise, so it should be entered into with that in mind. Remember that claims in the dollar range mentioned previously cannot ever be won by anyone except the lawyers, so even if a party collected only 10 cents on the dollar, they would actually be ahead financially. Put up a good fight; do some hard bargaining, but be prepared to compromise. It should also not be forgotten that unless a little is left on the table for the

IF YOUR CLAIM GETS TO COURT

THERE WILL BE ONLY ONE WINNER...

...THE LAWYERS

**FIGURE 19.7**   If your claim gets to court, there will be only one winner—the lawyers.

other party to save face, they may be forced into arbitration or litigation—a position that neither party can afford.

## *PREPARATIONS FOR CLAIMS DEFENSE*[1]

### *Documentation*

One of the most important things to be considered in presenting any claim is documentation. In cases other than construction, very often the facts can be reconstructed from public records, police documents, or witnesses. The data required to support construction claims cannot generally be reconstructed after the fact without careful documentation. One of the most important functions of the Resident Project Representative is the establishment and implementation of procedures for documenting what may eventually become a claim. Figure 19.8 is a checklist that can be used to check present documentation policies for their potential usefulness in the defense of claims.

An owner would be wise to have its legal counsel investigate any engineering problem that might be likely to lead to a claim. Although there are instances where the architect/engineer can function effectively without the aid of legal counsel by making engineering determinations and documenting them for future use by legal counsel, there are very few instances where the attorneys should be involved in a potential construction claim without the advantage of the objective input of the architect/engineer. If negotiation fails, the documented data may be of considerable later value in litigation or in arbitration. The author recalls a few instances where failure of the firm's inspector to keep a diary or other daily record placed the employer in an indefensible position, and the firm was persuaded by its legal counsel to accept whatever out-of-court settlement could be reached, as they had no case at all if they went to court.

Organized documentation of the facts surrounding the alleged wrongdoing is the single most important weapon in a case. There is nothing that can replace regular, detailed record keeping during construction. The tremendous volume of documentation is common to all projects, good and bad; therefore, the key is in the organization of the various documents. It is an important duty of the Resident Project Representative and the project manager to provide or assist the attorney in producing a chronologically organized summary of facts of the dispute. At an early stage, the attorney should obtain copies of documents and other information held by the contractor through a pretrial process of discovery before they can be disturbed.

Another important source of evidence is the live witness, including the expert witness. The owner and architect/engineer should provide their attorneys with a list of all potential witnesses, including those who may testify against the claim, since it is equally important that the opposition's strengths are known early in the case. A live witness is especially important where the dispute concerns an oral agreement, such as an oral change order, for which there is no subsequent written memorandum. The exact spoken words can

[1]Adapted from I. M. Fogel, "The Claims Engineer," *The Military Engineer,* 457, September-October 1978, pp. 341–342. Copyright © 1978, The Society of American Military Engineers, Alexandria, VA. Reproduced by permission.

CHECKLIST

I. *Prebid*
  A. Invitation, notice, Dodge or other reports
  B. Meetings—minutes
  C. Site visits—notes/minutes/photographs
  D. Proposed schedules and sequences
  E. Estimates and back-up work sheets

II. *Bid*
  A. Copy of *all* papers submitted or issued (bid or proposal)

III. *Post-bid/Precontract*
  A. Negotiation meetings—notes and minutes
  B. Scheduling sessions—notes and minutes
  C. Cost-reduction calculations
  D. Bonds—payment and performance

IV. *Contract Signing*
  A. Check all contract documents

V. *Construction*
  A. Owner/consultants/construction manager/general contractor/subcontractor/controlling agency correspondence files
  B. Schedules
  C. Job meetings and conferences—notes and minutes
  D. Oral instructions
  E. Field orders
  F. Drawing logs
  G. Submittal logs (samples—shop drawings)
  H. Change estimates—including *all* calculations
  I. Extra work—costs
  J. Field survey book and computations
  K. Cost records
  L. Job diaries/logs
  M. Photographs

VI. *General*

WRITE

A. If no minutes are prepared, prepare memos for your own files. Confirm decisions, instructions, or orders.

B. Read the minutes. If you do not agree, write.
C. Answer all correspondence.
D. Maintain chrono and subject files.

**FIGURE 19.8**   Checklist of documentation for claims protection.

also provide valuable evidence where the dispute involves some subject matter that was left out of the written memorandum, either by error or because it was not directly relevant to the agreement. Given a solid reputation, the most important qualification of a person who will serve as an expert witness is integrity. The soundness of the integrity of the expert witness will be tested by the opposition in many ways, but most importantly by questioning the witness as to whether or not he or she is too closely connected with the case to give an impartial opinion.

In addition to proving the defendant's liability, the plaintiff is faced with the task of establishing the validity of the damages claimed. The general rule is that the prevailing party may recover whatever damages that may reasonably be supposed within the contemplation of the parties at the time that the contract was made. This is the most complex and time-consuming phase of construction litigation. Often, the case is split into two separate trials, one for determining liability and the other for determining the damages. The advantages of separating the trial into two separate actions are that the determination of liability issues may narrow and simplify preparation for the damages phase; that it may enable the parties to get an earlier determination of the entire dispute by settlement after the liability issue has been decided; and that it may reduce the number of parties involved in the damages phase. The greatest disadvantage is that separation into two separate actions may delay final resolution.

### Burden of Proof

Generally, it is the plaintiff who has the burden to prove its claim. Where the contractor succeeds in proving substantial compliance against the owner's claim of nonperformance, the burden of proof reverts to the owner to prove its claim for residual defects.

### Method of Presentation

The ordinary fact finder, whether it be a jury panel or a judge, is not likely to be familiar with the technical and administrative details of construction. Therefore, the factual issues must be presented in a simple, concise manner. Photographic evidence and charts are very effective in conveying the facts. Actual site visits may save time and energy consumed in otherwise describing the general physical conditions. An expert witness who can translate technical concepts into simple language is an invaluable evidentiary aid.

### Evidence

In all disputes, regardless of the method of resolution, the prevailing party will be the one that can better support its burden of proof of its allegation. In preparing to bring a dispute to some kind of resolution, the contractor must assure that it is equipped with all of the necessary evidence in support of its claim or defense, and anticipate what the opponent will produce as evidence of their position on the claim. The following is a checklist of the possible sources of evidence that should be used in the course of dispute settlement:

> **Documentation**
> 1. Bid documents
> 2. Boring logs and soils reports
> 3. Drawings: as-planned
> 4. Drawings: as-built
> 5. Specifications
> 6. General and supplemental general conditions
> 7. Schedule: as-planned (CPM, etc.)
> 8. Schedule: as-built (progress charts)
> 9. Addenda
> 10. Change orders
> 11. Instructions and directives
> 12. Inspection records
> 13. Contractor's logs
> 14. Architect/engineer's or owner's diaries (through deposition)

15. Correspondence files
16. Check registers
17. Purchase orders
18. Shipping and delivery tickets
19. Time cards
20. Person-loading charts
21. Memoranda (including memos to file)
22. Site photographs
23. Testing results
24. Public records

**Witnesses**
1. Contractor's project personnel
2. Owner's project personnel
3. Architect/engineer personnel
4. Construction manager personnel
5. Subcontractors
6. Inspectors
7. Suppliers
8. Testing lab personnel
9. Consultants (expert witnesses)
10. Adverse witnesses

There is no claims protection or support without adequate documentation. It is the single most important thing that an owner and architect/engineer can do prior to the existence of a claim to provide the attorney with the tools needed for an owner or architect/engineer to defend or prosecute its case, whether it be in arbitration or litigation.

## Estimates

Invariably, every claim seems to include some form of estimate. An objective review of the source material and methods upon which the estimate was based will often show up weaknesses or deviations from accepted industry practice. In any case, it is extremely difficult to determine the amount of a claim or counterclaim without preparing careful estimates of the work involved.

## Schedules

Another of the items of construction that seems to contribute to the most controversy is scheduling. Scheduling controversies arise not only from poor planning, on occasion, but also from disagreement over construction methods or sequences of operations. Often, these disputes occur where a project is constructed under multiple prime contracts, such as those commonly experienced in a professional construction management (PCM) contract. The absence of any contractual relationship between the individual prime contractors or the architect/engineer has been the root cause of numerous disputes.

Scheduling techniques such as CPM or other network scheduling systems and their associated computer-generated printouts have only served to compound the problem. Often the owner has stacks of computer printouts that it either does not want or does not know how to read. Yet somewhere in that stack of paper may well be the key to success in the defense of claims being made against it. The question of scheduling methods of operation and the impact of deviating from the anticipated schedule requires a careful analysis to determine the reasonableness of the originally anticipated schedule in conjunction with the planned methods of operation. The analysis of every schedule-related problem is unique, and every such analysis should include a review of the anticipated sequence and schedule together with a review of the actual progress of the work. The review must include an analysis of any delay and impact caused by all parties to the progress of the project.

## Costs

It is in the presentation of cost data and their supporting documentation that most construction claims are the weakest. A carefully detailed reconstruction of all construction activities and their related costs must be made and presented so that they can be clearly identified for use in negotiating affirmatively or defensively. Construction-related organizations are reported to be poor in their cost record-keeping systems (or lack of systems) and a lack of ability to relate costs to possible claims areas. An accounting firm is not the answer either, as often those cost items relating to potential claims are not identified by an accounting firm because most accounting firms are not familiar with the cost control procedures for construction contracts.

### Claims Administration

There are several common forms of settlement of contractor claims costs. Principally, these include lump-sum settlements with or without qualification, and time and materials settlements. The type of settlement generally favored under Clean Water Grant Projects is the lump-sum approach. With that type of settlement the owner and the contractor reach an agreement on the total amount of money and time required to complete the work. This agreement may be reached either prior to or after the work has been completed, with the advantage that it places a price ceiling on the entire dispute, and on Clean Water Grant Projects facilitates the grantees application for funding from the administrators of the funding.

The most desirable form of a lump-sum settlement is the so-called "no fault" settlement, which allows resolution of the dispute without determination of fault. With this type of settlement, in exchange for the issuance of a change order, the contractor gives a full accord and satisfaction and a waiver of all claims arising out of the incident.

A variation of the no fault settlement is one wherein the owner may obtain a unilateral reservation of legal rights that will enable the owner to sue for a portion of the claim settlement after full payment has been made to the contractor upon completion of the project. This type of solution is of special value on Clean Water Grant Projects by helping to solve the contractor's cash flow problems related to the claim and gives the owner a chance to recover funds that may later be determined to be ineligible for payment by the administrators of the grant funds.

With the time and material settlements, the contractor performs the work and submits documented charges for all materials, labor, and equipment used on the affected work. This type of settlement has one advantage, namely, the opportunity for the contractor to begin work without prior negotiation of costs involved. It has a disadvantage as well. By this method a contractor can artificially increase the cost and time required to complete the work and inflate the costs submitted to the owner for payment.

A similar approach is sometimes referred to as *force account.* This is based upon a contractual agreement whose terms are generally spelled out in the General Conditions of the Contract for payment of extra work. It is generally applied in conditions involving an unexpected condition that leads to extra work and involves a prearranged formula for reimbursing the contractor for the costs of labor, materials, and equipment plus a fixed percentage for overhead expenses and profit, and the allowable surcharge that will be permitted to be applied to the billings of its subcontractors and suppliers. A contractor does not waive its rights to claim extra costs over and above the amount allowed by force account, if it can be justified and verified; however, it is contractually bound to proceed with the extra work as long as the owner continues payments to the contractor under the formula. The advantages and disadvantages are similar to those for time and materials settlements as described above. It should be kept in mind that a force account settlement is open-ended as opposed to a lump-sum settlement which may cover all costs of an item of extra work.

## THE USE OF PROJECT RECORDS IN LITIGATION

### Planning Strategy

Before a dispute even reaches the courtroom, the value of project records becomes quite evident. During the early stages of case preparation they can be used in helping define the issues of a complaint. They are essential to the establishment of the facts in a case and to the planning of litigation strategy. In addition, project records are valuable as an aid to weighing the credibility of an additional source.

### Prelitigation Use of Records

During the prelitigation phase of case preparation, the project records are invaluable in the preparation of interrogatories and depositions, for without competent and thorough documentation, key issues could easily be overlooked. They are also of considerable value during the preparation of the trial outline itself.

### The Litigation Process

Initially, the project records may be used to define contractual parameters within which the parties should function. Then, during litigation, these records may be used to define relevance and establish probative value of facts under dispute.

The value of the records does not end here. They are also used to establish credibility or, conversely, for impeachment. Project records are also of considerable value in ascertaining the true impact (damages) from the harm that was alleged or suffered.

### Records Are Your First Line of Defense

The construction environment of today is far too complex and vulnerable to claims to leave matters to be settled orally in the field. All matters of substance should always be in writing, and it is better to document too much than too little.

If sufficient documentation is maintained, many potential claims problems can be resolved equitably without resorting to the courts. The same records that can assist in the resolution of difficulties in the field can be used to support your position if a claim later goes to litigation or arbitration. Many of the records that are kept in the normal course of business are admissible as evidence in litigation or arbitration, so it is important that sufficient data be recorded and that the documents meet certain standards to be meaningful. Diaries can normally be used by a witness during testimony as an aid to his or her memory if such diaries meet the prescribed requirements for credibility. In some cases, such diaries are admissible as evidence in their own right as a record kept in the normal course of business.

Properly kept records are the first line of defense. Don't lose a case before it even starts by failure to develop and implement an effective record-keeping system. It is equally important that all parties working on a project be thoroughly indoctrinated in the proper use of the record-keeping system. The best system in the world is of no value if not faithfully used.

## ORDER OF PRECEDENCE OF CONTRACT DOCUMENTS

To assist in the resolution of field disputes in cases where a discrepancy exists between the various parts of the contract documents, it is desirable to establish some system of order to indicate the relative order of importance of each. Although through legal precedent some degree of order has already been established, many General Conditions cite the specific order so that a dispute may be settled without the need for interpretation or arbitration.

Although a specific listing of order, if specified in the contract documents, will govern over any policy listed here, the following guide is based upon the NSPE General Conditions, with some modifications.

> The contract documents are complementary; what is called for in one is as binding as if called for in all. If the contractor finds a conflict, error, or discrepancy in the contract documents, it should be called to the attention of the engineer in writing before proceeding with the work affected thereby. In resolving such conflicts, errors, and discrepancies, the documents should be given preference in the following order:
>
> 1. Agreement
> 2. Specifications
> 3. Drawings

Within the preceding elements, further preference can be established as outlined in the following breakdown of a typical set of public works contract documents (on private contracts it is uncommon to have the Notice Inviting Bids, the Instructions to Bidders, and the Bid or Proposal as a part of the contract documents):

Within the specifications, the order of precedence is as follows:

1. Change Orders or Work Change Directives
2. Agreement
3. Addenda
4. Contractor's Bid or Proposal
5. Supplementary General Conditions (Special Conditions)
6. Notice Inviting Bids
7. Instructions to Bidders
8. General Conditions of the Contract
9. Technical Specifications
10. Standard Specifications
11. Contract Drawings

With reference to the drawings, the order of precedence is as follows:

1. Figures govern over scaled dimensions.
2. Detail drawings govern over general drawings.
3. Change order drawings govern over contract drawings.
4. Contract drawings govern over standard drawings.
5. Contract drawings govern over shop drawings.

The acceptance of shop drawings that deviate substantially from the requirements of the contract documents must be accompanied by a written change order.

## OBLIGATIONS OF THE CONTRACTOR

As might be expected from a document prepared by the owner, the contractor's rights under the terms of the construction contract documents are often few and its obligations many. However, certain standard forms of General Conditions of the Construction Contract, such as those of the AIA, the EJCDC, and many public agencies, provide fairly equitable conditions for all parties to the contract, which is one reason that builders generally favor such standard forms over those typewritten, do-it-yourself varieties produced by the usually well meaning but often poorly informed specifier or even attorney who is unfamiliar with construction contract requirements.

The contractor is expected to give its personal attention to the work, and either the contractor or its authorized representative must be on the construction site at all times that work is being performed there. Some contractors will leave the job site without adequate supervision in an attempt to entice the resident engineer or inspector into directing some of the construction work (actual direct supervision). Such action by the resident engineer or inspector would then shift a portion of the job responsibility to the owner or the architect/engineer. In cases of defects in construction in which the inspector has exercised such supervision, the contractor has grounds for being legally relieved of the financial responsibility of correcting such defects.

In addition to the requirements for providing continuous, adequate supervision, the contractor is also required to conform to all laws and ordinances concerning job safety, licensing, employment of labor, sanitation, insurance, zoning, building codes, environmental conditions, and similar constraints.

The general contractor, as the only party with a direct contractual relationship with the owner for construction, is responsible for and must guarantee all materials and workmanship, whether constructed by its own forces or by its subcontractors. The resident engineer or inspector should check the specifications thoroughly, as they may contain a provision that the contractor must arrange for an extension of the performance bond through the entire guarantee period, usually one year from the date of completion of the work and its acceptance by the owner. The requirement may call for the bond in the full amount of the original contract price or may allow a reduced amount such as 5 or 10 percent for the term of the guarantee period.

Even though the contractor normally has no direct responsibility for the plans and specifications, it can incur a contingent liability for proceeding with faulty work whose defects should be obvious to one in its business. Thus, if the contractor is asked to do something that it feels is improper or not in accordance with good construction practice, the contractor is entirely within its rights to submit a letter of protest to the architect/engineer or owner stating its position before proceeding with the matter in dispute. If after the contractor has submitted its written protest, the architect/engineer or owner prefers to require that the contractor proceed anyway, the contractor has protected itself in case of later flaws that may develop. It may even be possible that the insuring firm could get out of paying a claim if a flaw developed later as a direct result of not heeding the contractor's advice—a matter for the courts to decide.

Insurance coverage is an important contractual responsibility of the contractor, both as to type of insurance and policy limits. The contractor is required to provide insurance not only for its own direct and contingent liability, but also frequently for the owner's protection. The contractor is expected to exercise every reasonable safeguard for the protection of persons and property in, on, and adjacent to the construction site.

Some of the most important of the contractor's rights include progress payments, recourse by the contractor if the owner fails to make payments, termination of the contract for cause, rights to extensions of time and extra payment as provided, and appeals from the decisions of the owner and the architect/engineer. Subject to contractual requirements and contractual limitations and, in the case of public works contracts, subject to the local laws concerning the use of subcontractors, the general contractor is normally free to purchase materials from any source it wishes, and to schedule work in any manner that it sees fit in the absence of any contractual provisions to the contrary.

## *ALTERNATIVE METHODS FOR DISPUTE RESOLUTION*

Figure 19.9 shows a simplified summary of the principal methods available to the contractor for resolution of construction disputes.

## *ARBITRATION OR LITIGATION?*[2]

Many standard forms of construction contracts include provisions for binding arbitration of any future disputes. It is also the declared public policy of the federal government and many states to require arbitration in public contracts. Yet we find that most insurance carriers try to avoid arbitration wherever possible.

Parties to the construction process often gain a false sense of security from having an arbitration clause in their contracts. There is no perfect method for dispute resolution. Whether it is arbitration or litigation, the choice between the two is much like the choice of whether to be put to death in a gas chamber or in an electric chair. Under both arbitration and litigation the parties are asking an outside party to resolve their disputes. Common sense dictates that the quickest and most economical way of resolving a dispute is for the parties to resolve the dispute themselves, without the intervention of others.

Is arbitration the best method for resolving construction disputes? The answer is a definite "maybe." The proponents of arbitration hail it as being speedy and economical. Experience has shown, however, that this is not always true, especially in the larger cases. Arbitration can be extremely lengthy, expensive, and by its very nature can lead to inconsistent results. One arbitration case in which the author was involved lasted over five years, mostly because of hearing delays and the difficulty of scheduling hearing dates that were mutually acceptable to the arbitrators, the parties to the arbitration, and their attorneys who also had to weave their arbitration schedule in and out of equally demanding court appearance dates—many of which occurred on short notice, thus forcing the arbitration to be rescheduled.

### *Inconsistent Results*

One difficulty is that the arbitrators are not bound by rules of evidence, or for that matter any previously rendered decisions, whereas under English common law principles, a court is obligated to be bound by previous decisions rendered in its state for similar circumstances.[3]

Consider also the case where an owner demands a general contractor to arbitrate a claim that the work performed by one of its subcontractors is defective. If the subcontract does not provide for arbitration, or if both arbitration agreements do not provide that third

---

[2]Postner and Rubin, Attorneys at Law, New York, NY. Reproduced by permission.

[3]Excluding the state of Louisiana, which does not operate under English common law, due to its French origins.

| Time | Settlement Cost | Binding Nature | Appeal |
|---|---|---|---|
| **Negotiation** | | | |
| 1. Dependent on the parties' negotiators' objectives, attitude, and other factors.<br>2. Can be very fast. | 1. Minimal.<br>2. Cost of compromised settlement. | 1. Take it or leave it.<br>2. May lead to an agreement. | 1. Waived if agreement is reached.<br>2. Arbitration or litigation if no agreement. |
| **Mediation** | | | |
| 1. Same as negotiation.<br>2. There may be some limitations imposed by the mediator's schedule.<br>3. Usually fast. | 1. Mediator's compensation, if any. | 1. Take it or leave it.<br>2. May lead to an agreement.<br>3. Moral pressure to reach an agreement. | 1. (same as above) |
| **Mediation-Arbitration** | | | |
| 1. Speed depends on the procedure used.<br>2. If formalities can be waived, resolution is fast. | 1. Mediator's compensation, if any. | 1. May be agreed in advance in most states, that parties will be bound to the decision. | 1. (same as above) |
| **Arbitration** | | | |
| 1. Faster than litigation.<br>2. Rules may impose some limitations.<br>3. Availability and schedule of arbitrators is a problem.<br>4. Preparation may take several months. | 1. Filing fee.<br>2. Arbitrator's compensation after 2nd day.<br>3. Attorney fees if any. | 1. May be nonbinding or binding according to contract. | 1. No review of merits in court.<br>2. Arbitrator not required to explain award. |
| **Litigation** | | | |
| 1. May take up to 5 years or more to reach a trial.<br>2. Preparation itself may take years. | 1. Prohibitively expensive, both in terms of attorney's fee and time costs. | 1. Binding | 1. Full appeal. |
| **Drop Claim/Concede** | | | |
| 1. None | 1. Value of claim. | 1. Contractual agreement by mutual accord.<br>2. Waivers. | 1. None, right waived in most cases. |

**FIGURE 19.9**   Construction claims resolution alternatives.

parties which have an interest in the issue to be arbitrated can be joined as parties to the arbitration, the general contractor may be unable to join the subcontractor in the arbitration with the owner over the subcontractor's work.

If this occurs, the arbitrators in the proceeding between the owner and the general contractor could find that the subcontractor's work was defective. This decision would not be binding on the subcontractor, however, who might convince a different panel of arbitrators that he or she was not responsible for the defects claimed. The general contractor would then be liable to the owner for the cost of correcting the defective work, although it will be unable to recover these costs from the subcontractor.

A parallel situation is one where an owner finds a defect in the work. The contractor claims that the defect was due to faulty design; the architect/engineer claims that it was due to defective work. In this connection it should be noted that standard AIA documents have been worded specifically to prevent consolidation or joinder of the architect/engineer along with the contractor in a single arbitration proceeding.

## Cost of Arbitration

Arbitration is not always economical. The filing fees for initiating arbitration with the American Arbitration Association (AAA) greatly exceed the fees to file a complaint in most state courts. Under the rules of the AAA, the filing fee for a $100 000 claim is $1500. By contrast the fee for filing a complaint in most state courts is under $100. An additional expense of arbitration is the fee paid to the arbitrators, which can range from $300 to $1500 or more per day, depending upon the number and experience of the arbitrators. Other costs may include charges for a hearing room and a written transcript.

## Speedy Results?

Another problem with arbitration is that the hearings are not normally held on a day-to-day basis. This is because arbitrators have their own business affairs to conduct, and it is rare to be able to schedule more than two hearings on consecutive days. This means that an arbitration that involves four days of hearings may actually take two or three months before the hearings are completed. Similarly, a large complex arbitration requiring 30 days of hearings (not unusual) can take upward of three years to resolve. It should be noted, too, that with hearings so far apart, the attorneys for the parties have the opportunity to prepare more, thus further increasing the cost of arbitration.

## Discovery

Proponents of arbitration cite the fact that there is no discovery in arbitration, an expensive and time-consuming process involved in almost every lawsuit which is frequently the subject of abuse or overkill by one or both sets of lawyers. As a practical matter, however, discovery actually occurs in an arbitration during the hearings. Thus the time which is saved in arbitration by having no discovery beforehand is more often than not lost in the extension of the arbitration hearings themselves. It should also be noted that discovery in a lawsuit often discloses valid claims or defenses which can lead to settlement discussions. This opportunity is often lost in arbitration.

### Arbitrary Arbitrators

Arbitrators are normally not bound by rules of law. For example, as an owner you may have insisted that your construction contracts include a clause providing that the contractor shall not be entitled to any damages for delay. While the courts have held such clauses as enforceable in the face of contemplated delays, there is nothing to prevent an arbitrator from ignoring the clause and awarding the contractor damages for such delays.

## THE MEDIATION PROCESS

Mediation is a process in which a trained third-party neutral attempts to assist the parties to a dispute in reaching an agreement that resolves the dispute. Another way of saying it is that mediation is a particular form of settlement negotiation in which a trained third-party neutral intervenes by agreement of the parties in order to guide and facilitate the parties' negotiations toward an agreement that resolves the dispute.

### Why Is a Mediator Needed?

A mediator is needed when one or more of the following circumstances or desires exist:

1. Parties are unable to narrow the gap between the expectations of one group and the inflexibility of the other.
2. Too many issues are open and the parties are unable to get movement going.
3. The parties wish the mediator to explore and narrow the differences between them.
4. There is a desire to resolve a problem mutually and end a dispute amicably.
5. It is desired to furnish the parties with a realistic look at the demands and possibility of obtaining them.
6. There is a wish to give the parties some idea of how their positions look to an impartial person.
7. The parties wish a mediator to be used as a conduit through which private, confidential disclosures can be made without jeopardizing their original positions.
8. There is a wish to avoid negative consequences, such as a lawsuit.

### Mediation as Distinguished from Arbitration

Like arbitration, mediation is a private, unofficial, confidential means of dispute resolution. Like arbitration, mediation is generally favored by modern law. And like arbitration, it generally promises savings in time and cost as compared with civil litigation. Yet mediation differs from arbitration in a number of important ways, including:

1. An arbitrator has final power of decision, subject only to very limited judicial review; a mediator has absolutely *no* power beyond the power of illumination and persuasion.

2. An arbitrator normally takes a rather passive role, leaving it largely to the parties to present and press their cases; a mediator is normally an active intervenor in, and principal shaper of, the process.

3. Although arbitration is more informal than civil litigation, and the usual order of proceedings is generally predictable and tracks the usual order of proceeding in litigation, the order of proceeding in a mediation is much less structured than either arbitration of litigation.

4. The arbitrator avoids all ex-parte communication with the parties on the merits of the dispute or the parties' positions; the mediator will virtually always caucus privately with each party for the express purpose of learning as much as they are willing to disclose about their private views and interests with respect to the dispute.

5. Although an arbitration is normally a private proceeding, information about it may become public knowledge in some circumstances: for example, if the losing party seeks to have a court vacate the award. Mediations are settlement discussions and, as such, some information about them are inadmissible.

6. Perhaps most important, the arbitrator imposes upon the parties a decision that he or she has made and that may please neither party; the mediator, if successful, guides the parties to a decision that they can have a major role in shaping and which, by definition, they both agree.

### Use of Mediation as a Dispute Resolution Tool

Mediation is generally used first. Its use may precede either arbitration of litigation. It may be used, however, even after an arbitration or litigation has been initiated but prior to an award. Since a mediation is treated as a settlement negotiation, evidence concerning it is not admissible in any subsequent arbitration of litigation.

---

## SETTLEMENT OF DISPUTES BY ARBITRATION

In overturning a decision rendered by the California Supreme Court [*Southland Corporation* v. *Keating*, 52 U.S.L.W. 4131 (January 23, 1984)] the U.S. Supreme Court ruled that the Federal Arbitration Act [9 USC Sec 1–4] takes precedence over state statutes prohibiting arbitration of certain disputes. Although the case did not involve a construction dispute, it has significant implications for the construction industry.

### Business Disputes

In the world of business, disputes are inevitable. One person may understand rights and obligations differently from another no matter how carefully a contract is written. This could lead to delayed shipments, complaints about the quality of the work, claims of non-performance of the terms of the contract, and similar misunderstandings. Even with the best of intentions, parties often perform less than they promise.

Such controversies seldom involve great legal issues. On the contrary, they generally deal with the same facts and interpretation of contract terms that owners and contractors are used to dealing with every day. Therefore, when disputes arise out of day-to-day activities, the parties frequently like to settle them privately and informally. This is what commercial arbitration is for.

## What Is Arbitration?

Arbitration is the voluntary submission of a dispute to one or more impartial persons for final and binding determination. It is private and informal and is designed for quick, practical, inexpensive settlements. But at the same time, arbitration is an *orderly* proceeding, governed by the rules of procedure and standards of conduct that are prescribed by law. The most commonly used arbitration procedures are those administered by the American Arbitration Association. Both the AIA and the EJCDC General Conditions call for arbitration under the Construction Industry Arbitration Rules of the American Arbitration Association. The association does not act as arbitrator. Its function is to *administer* arbitrations in accordance with the agreement of the parties and to maintain panels from which arbitrators may be chosen.

The arbitrators are quasi-judicial officers. Their decisions represent their judgments of the rights of the parties to a dispute. One significant difference between the rules that govern civil action in court and an arbitration proceeding is that, in arbitration, the strict rules of evidence do not apply. The arbitrator's guiding principle is to hear all the evidence that may be material and to hear no arguments or evidence from one side that the other has no opportunity to comment upon or to rebut.

The arbitrator is the final judge of matters considered. His or her decision will not be reviewed on its merits where procedures were fair and impartial. More than a hundred years ago, in 1854, the U.S. Supreme Court said:

> If an award is within the submission, and contains the honest decision of the arbitrators, after a full and fair hearing of the parties, a court of equity will not set it aside for error, either in law or in fact. A contrary course would be a substitute of the judgment of the chancellor in place of the judges chosen by the parties, and would make an award the commencement, not the end, of litigation.

Most arbitration cases are heard by a panel of three arbitrators, each usually representing a different field of specialization. Unless the agreement of the parties requires a unanimous decision, the arbitrators are governed by majority rule, both in procedural decisions and in rendering the award. In some cases, usually those in which the amount in question is relatively small, a single arbitrator may serve if desired by the parties. When three-person boards are used, it is customary for one of the arbitrators to serve as a chairperson, whose powers, however, are exactly the same as those of the other two.

## Authority of the Arbitrator

The arbitrator has broad powers to determine matters of fact, law, and procedure. This decision-making authority must be exercised by the arbitrator alone to the best of its ability, and it may not be delegated to others. It would render his or her award subject to attack in court if, for example, the arbitrator sought clarification of a point of law by outside consultation. Under the rules of arbitration, the award must be in writing, and it must represent the judgment of at least the majority of the board unless the contract of the parties requires a unanimous decision. The arbitrator must word the award clearly and definitely and must answer all the questions but may not deal with any matter not submitted to arbitration. The relief granted in the judgment must be consistent with the contract and may include specific performance as well as monetary damages. Arbitrators are not required to write opinions explaining the reasons for their decisions. As a general rule, their awards consist of a brief direction to the parties on a single sheet of paper. There are a number of reasons for this. One is that written opinions might open avenues for attack on the award by the losing party.

As stated earlier, arbitrators are the final judges of all matters of both fact and law before them. Courts will not review their decisions on the merits of the case even when the arbitrators have come to a conclusion that is different from that which the court might have reached. In particular, courts are concerned only with the face of the award itself, not any additional explanatory matter.

The members of the National Panel of Arbitrators of the American Arbitration Association volunteer their time and talent without any fee, although on hearings that last for more than one day, some payment is made. There is an administrative fee that must be paid to the American Arbitration Association for handling claims; however, the amount is relatively small. The American Arbitration Association was founded in 1926 as a private, nonprofit organization "to foster the study of arbitration, to perfect its techniques and procedures under arbitration law, and to advance generally the science of arbitration."

## Arbitration Agreements Regulated by Law

Commercial arbitration agreements today are recognized by statute by the U.S. Arbitration Act and in all but one state. However, the extent to which these agreements are enforceable differs widely. In overruling common law, many states distinguish between agreements to submit present disputes to arbitration and agreements to arbitrate unknown disputes that might arise in the future. The most modern arbitration laws provide that all agreements to arbitrate, whether of present or future controversies, are valid, irrevocable, and enforceable. In some other states, the laws merely provide that present and known disputes are arbitrable when the parties agreed by contract to arbitrate them. In cases of present disputes, however, many statutes require that the arbitration agreement be made a rule of court before it becomes irrevocable and enforceable.

Some confusion has been caused by some writers who state that in some of these older laws, agreements to arbitrate future disputes are void. In most states such agreements are valid in the sense that it is permissible to enter into such agreements. The only problem that remains is the one of enforcing it.

For the basis of comparison, the various arbitration laws of the different states will be divided into two groups. The breakdown will be based upon those states that have, by statute or judicial law, changed the common law rule of revocability that permitted either party to an arbitration agreement to terminate it at his or her will at any time prior to the rendition of an award.

### Group I: Statutes Allowing Arbitration of Present and Future Disputes

The first group of states will be those in which there is specific authority by statute or judicial ruling that holds that an arbitration clause in a commercial contract for *construction* is valid, irrevocable, and enforceable. The 44 states listed, as well as Puerto Rico, the District of Columbia, and the federal government, have statutes that conform to or embody features that are essentially similar to "modern arbitration law" in which all written agreements to arbitrate, whether present controversies or future controversies between the contracting parties, are valid, irrevocable, and enforceable.

The 44 states, Puerto Rico, the District of Columbia, and federal law in Group I are as follows:[4]

1. *Alaska* Alaska Stats. Ann. §09.43.010 et seq. (1968)* (4).
2. *Arizona* Ariz. Rev. Stats. §12–1501 et seq. (1962)* (4).
3. *Arkansas* Ark. Stats. Ann. §34–511 et seq. (1971)* (2, 4, 7).
4. *California* Cal. Code of Civil Procedure §1280 et seq. (1961).
5. *Colorado* Colo. Rev. Stats. §13–22–201 (1975). *
6. *Connecticut* Conn. Gen. Stats. Ann. §52–408 et seq. (1958).
7. *Delaware* Del. Code Ann., Title 10, §5701 et seq. (1973)* (4).
8. *Florida* Fla. Stats. Ann. §682.01 et seq. (1969).
9. *Hawaii* Hawaii Rev. Stats. §658–1 et seq. (1955).
10. *Idaho* Idaho Code, Chap. 9, §7–901 et seq. (1975)* (4).
11. *Illinois* Ill. Rev. Stats. Chap. 10, §101 et seq. (1961).*
12. *Indiana* Ind. Stats. Ann. §344–2–1 et seq. (1968)* (3, 5, 6).
13. *Iowa* Iowa Code §679A.1 et seq.
14. *Kansas* Kansas Stats. Ann., Chap. 5, §401 et seq. (1973)* (2, 4, 7).
15. *Kentucky* Ky. Rev. Stat. Ann.; [1984 Ky. Acts ch. 278].
16. *Louisiana* La. Rev. Stats. §9:4201 et seq. (1948)* (4).
17. *Maine* Me. Rev. Stats. Ann., Title 14, §5927 et seq. (1967)* (8).
18. *Maryland* Md. Courts and Judicial Proceedings §3–201 et seq. (1965)* (4).
19. *Massachusetts* Mass. Ann. Laws, Chap. 251 §1 et seq. (1960)* (4).
20. *Michigan* Mich. Compiled Laws Ann. §600.5001 et seq. (1963).
21. *Minnesota* Minn. Stats. Ann. §572.08 et seq. (1957).*
22. *Missouri* Mo. Ann. Stats. §§435.350 to 435.470 (1980).
23. *Montana* Mont. Code Ann. Chap. 27 [S.B. 110(1985)].
24. *Nevada* Nev. Rev. Stats., Chap. 38, §38.015 et seq. (1967).*

---

[4]Asterisks indicate laws that are referred to as the Uniform Arbitration Act. Numbers following * indicate statute exclusions as to (1) Insurance, (2) Leases, (3) Labor Contracts, (4) Loans, (5) Sales, (6) Torts, (7) Uninsured Motorists, and (8) Doctors and Lawyers.

25. *New Hampshire* N.H. Rev. Stats. Ann. §542:1 et seq. (1955).
26. *New Jersey* N.J. Stats. Ann. §2A:24–1 et seq. (1952).
27. *New Mexico* N.M. Stats. Ann. 44–7–1 et seq.
28. *New York* N.Y. C.P.L.R. §7501 et seq. (1920).
29. *North Carolina* No. Carolina Gen. Stats., §1–567.1 et seq. (1973)* (4).
30. *Ohio* Ohio Rev. Code Ann. §271 1.01 et seq. (1955).
31. *Oklahoma* Okla. Supp. 1978, §801 et seq., Title 15 (1978)* (2, 4).
32. *Oregon* Ore. Rev. Stats. §33.210 et seq. (1955).
33. *Pennsylvania* Pa. Stats. Ann., Title 22, §7301 et seq.
34. *Rhode Island* R.I. Gen. Laws §10–3–1 et seq. (1956).
35. *South Carolina* S.C. Code of Laws §15–48–10 et seq. (1978)* (2, 4, 7, 9).
36. *South Dakota* S.D. Comp. Laws §21–25A–1 et seq. (1971)* (2).
37. *Tennessee* Tenn. Code. Ann. §29–5–301 et seq.
38. *Texas* Tex. Rev. Civ. Stat. Ann. art. 224 et seq.
39. *Utah* Utah Code Ann. [tit. 78, ch. 31(a) (1985)].
40. *Vermont* Vt. Stat. Ann. tit. 12, §5651 et seq.
41. *Virginia* Va. Code, Vol. 2 §8–503 et seq. (1986).
42. *Washington* Wash. Rev. Code §7.04.010 et seq. (1943).
43. *Wisconsin* Wisc. Stats. Ann. §788.01 et seq.
44. *Wyoming* Wyo. Stats. §1–36–101 et seq.
    *District of Columbia* D.C. Code Ann. §16–4301 et seq.
    *Puerto Rico* Puerto Rico, Title 32, §3201 et seq. (1951).
    *United States Code* United States Arbitration Act, 43 Stat. 883, 9 U.S.C.A. §1 et seq. (1925).

## Group II: Statutes Allowing Arbitration of Present Disputes Only

The six states listed below have statutes that provide essentially that agreements to arbitrate *present* controversies are valid. The following list indicates the states in Group II in which arbitration statutes exist, but they contain varying restrictions that could affect the application of a future arbitration clause in the General Conditions of a *construction contract:*

1. *Alabama* Code of Alabama, §6–6–1 et seq.
2. *Georgia* Ga. Code §9–9–1 et seq.
3. *Mississippi* Miss. Code Ann., Chap. 15, ¶ 11–15–1.
4. *Nebraska* Nebr. Rev. Stats. ¶ 25–2103.
5. *North Dakota* N. Dak. Rev. Code, Chap. 32–29, ¶ 32–29–01.
6. *West Virginia* W.V. Code, Chap. 55, Art. 10, ¶ 55–10–1.

## PRELIMINARY NOTICE OF POTENTIAL CLAIM

Most states require subcontractors and material suppliers to notify the prime contractor, owner, or surety of a potential lien or bond claim. There are, however, a limited number of states that have preliminary notice requirements. In these states, notice of any potential claim must be given before or within 60 days of first beginning the performance of the subcontractor's work. The following is a summary of the states and their requirements for the preliminary notice.

**Private Construction Projects: Mechanic's Liens**

| State | When | To Whom |
|---|---|---|
| Arizona | Within 20 days of first performance | Owner, prime contractor, and construction lender |
| Arkansas | Before performance | Owner of reservation of right to file lien |
| California | Within 20 days of first performance | Owner, prime contractor, and construction lender |
| Florida | Within 45 days of first performance | Owner, prime contractor, and all non-privity entities |
| Michigan | Within 20 days of first performance | Prime contractor and designee named in owner's notice of commencement |
| Minnesota | Within 45 days of first performance on small projects only | Owner |
| Montana | Within 20 days of first performance | Serve owner and file with county clerk |
| Nevada | Within 31 days after first performance | Owner |
| New Hampshire | Before performance | Owner |
| New Jersey | Before performance | File |
| North Dakota | Prior to furnishing labor or materials | Owner |
| Texas | No later than the 15th day of the 2nd month following each month in which labor/materials have been furnished | Original contractor |
| Utah | Within 45 days of first performance | File at county recorder |
| Washington | Within 60 days of first performance | Owner |
| Wyoming | Within 60 days of first performance (only for contracts of more than $5000) | Prime contractor or its agent |

**Public Construction Projects: Public Bond Claim**

| State | When | To Whom |
|---|---|---|
| Arizona | Within 20 days of first performance | Owner, prime contractor, and construction lender |
| Florida | Within 45 days of first performance | Owner, prime contractor |
| Michigan | Within 30 days of first performance | Prime contractor |
| Montana | Within 30 days of first performance | Prime contractor |
| Nevada | Within 30 days of first performance | Prime contractor |
| Texas | On or before the 15th day of the 2nd month following each month in which labor and/or materials were furnished | Prime contractor and surety (in 3rd month) |
| Utah | Within 45 days of first performance | Prime contractor |
| Washington | Within 10 days of first performance | Prime contractor |

**Public Construction Projects: Lien Against Public Funds**

| State | When | To Whom |
|---|---|---|
| California | Within 20 days of first performance | Prime contractor or public agency |
| Washington | Within 60 days of first performance | Prime contractor |

## PROBLEMS

1. What are the four principal methods available for the resolution of construction claims?
2. Under the principle of full disclosure of all site information to the bidder/contractor, should a copy of the soils reports be included in the Contract Documents to assure that the contractor will be aware of it?
3. Of the four claims resolution alternatives discussed in the book, which two are considered as binding?
4. What are the chances of a successful appeal of an award under American Arbitration Association rules?
5. Where a contract document lists an order of precedence, what effect does that provision have on disputes related to conflicts between the different documents?
6. In a construction claim, is the burden of proof on the plaintiff or the defendant?

7. Can recovery of contractor costs be made under a "Type 2 Differing Site Conditions" clause for weather related delays?

8. Show how extended home office overhead is computed under the Eichleay formula.

9. What is the difference between compensable and noncompensable delays?

10. Name the five principles of contract administration.

11. A contractor is working on a $500 000 construction contract which was scheduled to be completed within 12 months; however, the owner delayed the contractor one month. Using the Eichleay formula, compute the amount of reimbursement that the contractor can claim for home office overhead if the contractor's total billing for the contract period was $10 000 000 and the total overhead for the contract period was $300 000.

# 20

## Project Closeout

### ACCEPTANCE OF THE WORK

At first it would seem that all that would be necessary to close out a project would be to inspect it, accept it for the owner, and see that the contractor receives the final payment. But what about all the guarantees, operating instructions for equipment, keying schedule, record drawings, bonds, and similar items that must be accounted for first? What about liens that may have been filed against the property by subcontractors? Each of these items will require careful handling to assure the owner of a quality product that is free of encumbrances and that will be backed up by the guarantees that were called for in the original documents.

Acceptance of the work and final payment to the contractor must proceed in accordance with the terms of the construction contract documents. Although the methods may vary somewhat from job to job, basically they all begin with a request from the contractor to make a final inspection of the work. Generally, there may be at least two inspections required to close out the project. The first will establish those areas still requiring correction or other remedial work, and the final inspection will be a checkoff to assure that all work is substantially complete and that all corrections have been made.

The checkoff list, or "punch list" as it is normally called, is a detailed list made near the end of the project, showing all items still requiring completion or correction before the work can be accepted and a *Certificate of Completion* issued. Before acceptance, all workmanship must meet specified standards, all work must be installed and complete, and all equipment must be tested and operational.

In some cases it is possible to accept a project as being "substantially complete" if only minor items remain to be finished. This simply means that the project is close enough to being completed that it can be put to use for the purpose it was intended, and that all remaining incomplete work is comprised of relatively minor items that the contractor agrees

**527**

to correct while the structure is occupied: for example, maybe the wrong wall switch plates were installed. In this case, the owner could use the building while waiting for the contractor to receive the proper wall plates and replace them.

If a *Certificate of Completion or Substantial Completion* is filed, and written on the certificate is a complete list of all work remaining to be done to complete the project, anything that is not indicated on the list of deficiencies requiring correction on the Certificate of Substantial Completion is considered as being satisfactory as is. Often, retention funds are held for 35 to 45 days after completion and are not released until correction of all remaining deficiencies and waiver of liens. Final payment, as it is often defined, does not include the release of retainage held during the project, which generally amounts to about 5 to 10 percent of the total cost of the project. The retainage is usually held for an additional 30 to 40 days to cover the lien filing period and to assure the completion of remaining punch list work.

## GUARANTEE PERIOD

Generally, the work covered in a construction contract includes a stated guarantee period, which is frequently one or two years. In some cases, the overall project may be guaranteed for only one year, although certain portions of the work may be covered by supplementary guarantees for longer periods. Normally, there is no need to withhold payment from the contractor for the purpose of assuring performance during the stated guarantee period, as the performance bond may be written to cover this period. Although some contracts call for 100 percent of the performance bond to be continued in force during the entire guarantee period (a costly arrangement for the contractor), many contracts allow for a reduced portion of the performance bond to cover any defects noted during the guarantee period. After all, if the project is 100 percent complete, there is little reason to believe that it will *all* fail. Thus, many such bonds are reduced to 10 percent or some other reduced percentage of the performance bond during the guarantee period. This seems quite reasonable, because frankly, if a significant percentage of failures were noted in the first year following completion, it would certainly appear to cast doubt over the quality of the inspection that was provided. As an alternative to the surety bond, some owners require the contractor to post a cash bond to cover the guarantee period.

The contractor's warranty does not imply liability, however, for the adequacy of the plans and specifications unless they were prepared by the contractor personally, or unless the contractor agreed to guarantee their adequacy. A contractor is only required to construct in accordance with the terms of the contract documents, and when this is done, the contractor cannot ordinarily be held to guarantee that the architect's or engineer's design will be free from defects or that the completed job will accomplish the purpose intended. The contractor is responsible only for the quality of the workmanship, the quality of the materials used, and for performance of the contract. It should be kept in mind that in the evaluation of the adequacy of the contractor's work, the standard of comparison should not be based on the previous experience of the inspector as to what is considered to be inferior work, but rather upon specific or substantial conformance with the terms set forth in the contract documents. The contractor can only be obligated to perform that which it specifically agreed to do in the written contract; anything required of the contractor that is beyond this would be valid grounds for a claim for additional compensation.

In Wisconsin, a court ruled that a contractor does not absolutely guarantee its work against defects or losses prior to the owner's final acceptance [*E. D. Wesley Co.* v. *City of New Berlin,* 215 N.W.2d 657 (1974)]. The case involved a problem with a booster pump and the owner withheld the contractor's final payment. The city maintained that because *it had not yet accepted the work,* the contractor was absolutely liable for all repair costs. The court found that the damage was not caused either by a defect in the pump or by the contractor in its installation. Therefore, the court ruled that the damage was not within the scope of the contractor's liability either before or after acceptance of the work.

## CONTRACT TIME

Most contracts are quite specific regarding the amount of construction time allowed to complete the work, and many provide for the payment of "liquidated damages" by the contractor to the owner for failure to complete on time or, in some cases, to complete portions of the work that interface with other contract schedules where multiple prime contracts have been executed. It should be noted, however, that in the absence of a provision establishing "time as the essence of the contract," neither the beginning date nor the date of completion can be considered to create an absolute schedule for the purpose of imposing the provisions of a liquidated damages clause for exceeding the specified completion dates. According to a ruling by the Supreme Court of Nebraska, time is not of the essence in a construction contract unless specifically stated in the contract documents [*Kingery Construction Co.* v. *Scherbarth Welding, Inc.,* 185 N.W.2d 857 (1971)]. If a contractor's failure to complete a project on schedule was the result of delays that occurred because of the owner's action, however, a North Carolina Court of Appeals has ruled that the contractor would not be liable for liquidated damages [*Dickerson, Inc.* v. *Bd. of Transportation,* Court of Appeals of North Carolina (June 18, 1975)].

When computing contract time, particular attention should be paid to the contract wording—is it "calendar days" or "working days"? If it is working days, particular care will have to be taken to determine the definition of a working day. Generally, this will have to be resolved by checking the master labor agreement for the area involved to see what is considered a holiday and what is not. The easiest time to compute is *calendar* days, as this method includes all days, including Saturdays, Sundays, and holidays.

Normally, construction time is computed from the date on the written Notice to Proceed given to the contractor at the beginning of the job (Figure 11.16). If no such notice was issued, the determination of the actual contract period may be indefinite. Preferably, a Notice to Proceed should be issued at the beginning of each project to assure a complete understanding as to the actual date construction work was authorized to begin (see "The 5-Step Process of Initiating a Project" in Chapter 1). The Notice to Proceed should not be confused with the Notice of Award (Figure 11.14)—the latter document simply establishes the identity of the contractor who will be given the contract to do the work and obligates the owner to sign the contract. It does not establish the date of starting construction, as no contract exists at that time. Once a contract has been signed, however, most specifications require that the contractor begin work within 10 or 15 days after the signing of the agreement. If this takes the place of a formal Notice to Proceed, then to compute the completion date, you will have automatically to allow the contractor an additional 10 or 15 days added to the contract term to allow for the latest date they could begin the work. As stated before, unless time is stated as the "essence of the contract" in the contract documents, there is always the possibility that a contractor may be reasonably secure from charges of liquidated damages for relatively minor time overruns.

In the absence of a formal document that specifically identifies the date upon which all work was completed, the establishment of the date of completion of a project may be more difficult. It is in the owner's best interests to file a formal certificate of completion upon completing the project. This should be filed as early as possible before the release of the contractor's final payment and retention money. The filing and recording of such a notice generally sets the lien law "time" running in the owner's favor. Sufficient holding time should be provided in the specifications to enable the owner to retain the contractor's final payment until a waiver of claims or final payment of all subcontractors and material suppliers has been made; otherwise, the contractor will have received the final payment and all of the retainage money, and the owner will be encumbered with stop notices or liens on its property. Of course, the owner has legal recourse to recover from the general contractor, but that could be a long and costly process. Meanwhile, the owner would be obligated to pay the liens filed by the subcontractors and suppliers to clear title to its own property (see "Final Payment to the Contractor" in Chapter 16).

## LIQUIDATED DAMAGES FOR DELAY

On many projects, where time is the essence of construction, the owner and the contractor agree under the contract terms that if the contractor fails to complete the project by the stipulated date, it is financially liable to the owner for a preagreed sum for each day beyond the specified completion date that it takes the contractor to finish the work. This amount of money represents the financial losses to the owner for such delays, and because it is difficult to determine the real values of the owner's losses, the preagreed sum is used in lieu of a determination of the actual damages suffered. This assessment is referred to as *liquidated damages,* and it is common practice throughout the construction industry to require that the contractor pay the owner this fixed sum of money for each calendar day that it exceeds the specified date of completion.

When provided for by contract, liquidated damages are enforceable at law provided that they represent a reasonable measure of the anticipated damages that the parties agree to at the time of executing the agreement. To collect, the owner simply deducts the amount of accumulated liquidated damages from the sum due to the contractor at the time of final payment. In recent years, some organizations also have successfully assessed liquidated damages for failure of the contractor to meet specified key dates for completion of certain specified portions of the work that affect the ability of other prime contractors to deliver their portions of the work on time (see "Liquidated Damages During Construction" in Chapter 16). Once established under the contract, it is enforceable as long as the date was missed, even if the owner suffered no loss at all.

It should be emphasized that the courts enforce liquidated damages only when they appear to represent reasonably the actual damages expected to be suffered by the owner based on the information available at the time of bidding. When it has been established that the amount was excessive and unreasonable, the courts have ruled that such payment by the contractor to the owner constituted a *penalty* and was not enforceable. Another thing that is considered by the court is whether *time* was the essence of the contract. In the absence of anything in the terms of the contract to specify this, the owner is placed in a weak position to sustain its rights to liquidated damages for time overruns [cf. *Kingery Construction Co. v. Scherbarth Welding, Inc.,* 185 N.W.2d 857 (1971)].

The estimated amount of the liquidated damages per day may be a function of many things. It can represent the loss of rental fees in an apartment, utility fees for a public utility company, or any other losses to the owner in connection with a revenue-producing project. Similarly, it can be keyed to daily costs to the owner of interest on loans or investment as a direct result of the failure of the contractor to finish the project on time.

## CLEANUP

In addition to the requirement that the job site be kept clean during the progress of the work, the contractor is similarly obligated to clean up the construction site thoroughly at the end of the job before the work can be accepted. The final cleanup is of significantly greater proportions than previous cleanup work, as all of the various items of demobilization rightfully are included under the cleanup category. This includes removal of temporary utilities, haul roads, temporary fences, field offices, detours, stockpiles, surplus materials, scrap, replacement of landscaping where it had been temporarily removed, street cleaning, and the obtaining of releases from the various city, county, or other governmental authorities having jurisdiction.

The contractor is obligated to clean up the site of its own operations as well as all areas under the control of the owner that may have been used by the contractor in connection with the work on the project, and should be required to remove all temporary construction, equipment, waste, and surplus material of every nature unless the owner has approved otherwise in writing. Final acceptance of the work should be withheld until the contractor has satisfactorily complied with all of the requirements for final cleanup of the project site (Figure 20.1). This includes cleanup of city streets as well, where dirt or other deposits have accumulated as a result of the contractor's operations.

Disposal of all waste and refuse should be at the contractor's expense. No waste or rubbish of any nature should be allowed to be buried or otherwise disposed of at the site except upon receipt of written approval of the owner.

## THE PUNCH LIST

There is probably no period during construction that is troubled with more time-consuming delays and the resulting exasperation than the period involving the corrective work prior to final acceptance. Theoretically, if every trade performed its work in strict compliance

**FIGURE 20.1**   Example of a project site properly cleaned up before acceptance by the owner (Quincy Reservoir, City of Aurora, Colorado). Engineer: J. M. Montgomery Consulting Engineers, Inc.

with the contract requirements and the best of craftsmanship, what is known as a *punch list* might never have come to exist. Thus, it should be the objective of everyone connected with a project to minimize the number of punch lists required.

### Punch List Obligations of the Contractor and Subcontractors

It is the contractor and its subcontractors who must assume the greatest responsibility for the existence of work that must be corrected. More critical, exacting, and progressive supervision is required of the contractor so that all the trades will perform their work in accordance with the highest standards of quality workmanship. To that end, the following procedures are recommended:

1. The contractor should carefully check its own work and that of the subcontractors while the work is being performed.
2. From the very beginning of a project, it is suggested that the contractor's superintendent prepare and maintain a written record of deficiencies observed as the job progresses to preclude their being overlooked or forgotten.

3. Unsatisfactory work should be corrected immediately and not permitted to remain and become a part of the punch list.

4. Corrections should be made before any particular subtrade leaves the project. Unless this is done, the door is left open for later evasion and disclaiming of responsibility for extended delays.

5. During the finishing stages of the project, the contractor should make frequent and periodic inspections with the subcontractors and the Resident Project Representative to check progressively for and correct any faulty work.

6. When the contractor has decided that the project has been completed satisfactorily in accordance with the terms of the contract, the architect/engineer should be notified, through the Resident Project Representative, for the purpose of obtaining acceptance of the work.

## Punch List Obligations of the Architect/Engineer

The architect/engineer can also make a positive contribution toward the efficient handling of the final inspection process by following a few simple procedures of its own.

1. During the progress of the work, the Resident Project Representative or the inspectors should make frequent and careful inspections of all work and should point out any deficiencies as they are discovered instead of waiting to place the items on the punch list.

2. During the finishing stages of the work, the contractor and the Resident Project Representative, accompanied by any affected subcontractors, should make frequent and careful inspections of the work to check progressively for and assure the correction of any faulty or deficient work.

3. When the contractor has determined that the work has been completed satisfactorily in accordance with the terms of the contract, he or she should promptly notify the Resident Project Representative (Figure 20.2).

4. Upon receiving such notification from the contractor, the Resident Project Representative should notify the project manager and promptly make arrangements for the *prefinal inspection* of the work. The representatives of the contractor and the subcontractors should participate in the inspection tour to respond to any questions that may be raised by the representatives of the architect/engineer.

5. Preferably prior to, but in no case later than during, the *prefinal inspection* period, dates should be established for equipment testing, systems validation, acceptance periods, warranty dates, and instructional requirements that may not have been agreed upon previously.

6. Following the prefinal inspection of the work, the Resident Project Representative should prepare a punch list setting forth in accurate detail any items of work that have been found not to be in accordance with the requirements of the contract documents (Figure 20.3). Following preparation of the punch list, the

## CONTRACTOR'S CERTIFICATION
## OF COMPLETION

TO: Mr. L.B. Farrington
General Manager
ABC Mutual Water District
123 Central Avenue
Winchester, Indiana 00000

DATE 9 August 1990

PROJECT Pyramid Pumping Plant

JOB NO. C1234-87

CONTRACT NO. W1234-5678

ATTN: Resident Project Rep.

OWNER ABC Mutual Water District

FROM: L&M Construction Company, Inc.

(Firm or Corporation)

This is to certify that I, Delbert C. Martin    am an authorized

official of L&M Construction Company, Inc.

working in the capacity of Vice President of Operations

and have been properly authorized by said firm or corporation to sign the following statements pertaining to the subject contract:

I know of my own personal knowledge, and do hereby certify, that the work of the contract described above has been performed, and materials used and installed in every particular, in accordance with, and in conformity to, the contract drawings and specifications.

The contract work is now complete in all parts and requirements, and ready for your final inspection.

I understand that neither the determination by the Engineer-Architect that the work is complete, nor the acceptance thereof by the Owner, shall operate as a bar to claim against the Contractor under the terms of the guarantee provisions of the contract documents.

BY Delbert C. Martin

Delbert C. Martin

TITLE Vice President, Operations

FOR L&M Construction Company, Inc.

DISTRIBUTION: 1. Proj. Mgr.
2. Field Ofc.
3. File

Wiley-Fisk Form 17-2

**FIGURE 20.2** Contractor's notification to the owner and architect/engineer that the work is certified to be complete.

**PUNCH LIST**

E. R. FISK & ASSOCIATES
P.O. Box 6448 • Orange, CA 92613-6448

Project __Zone 3 Booster Pumping Station__ No. __532-52__

Location __Mission Viejo, Orange County, CA__

Date __11 Dec 1989__

Inspection was conducted at above project by __R. M. Bendix__ at __10:00am__ o'clock this date.

REPRESENTATION

| CONTRACTOR-OWNER | ENGINEER-ARCHITECT |
|---|---|
| Contractor: Farris & Booth, Inc | Design: E. R. Fisk & Associates |
| Owner: Santa Ana Water District | Staff Spec.: J. F. Beardsley |
| Improvement District No. 1 | Job Supervisor: R. M. Bendix |

The following items are to be corrected or completed to comply with the contract documents:

| Type of Inspection | Check | Final X | 1 Yr. Guar. | Guar. |
|---|---|---|---|---|

| NO. | ITEM |
|---|---|
| 9 | Cracked globe on vapor-proof fixture in lower gallery |
| 13 | Field coating req'd for damaged shop coat on LPG tank |
| 17 | Replace defective stair tread |
| 18 | Replace door No. 2 stop w/331ES or 431ES |
| 19 | Finish paint access panels after factory prime |
| 20 | Readjust swing of Door No. 5 |
| 21 | Master keying not in accordance w/Spec |
| 28 | Readjust air systems to within 5% of design requirements |
| 31 | Provide handwheel for emergency manual operation of plug valve motor operator as per spec. |
| 37 | Adjust access MH cover to finish grade |
| 39 | Replace existing welded gate post with spec. one-piece hot-dip galv.-after-fab post |
| 40 | Cleanup premises. Remove & dispose of all debris |
| 41 | Remove temp. power facilities |
| 43 | Retest standby engine-generator set on auto mode |
| 44 | Pump station system control check & validation test |

Data used are fictitious for illustration only

DISTRIBUTION:
1. Project Manager
2. Contractor's Representative
3. Resident Project Representative
4. File

Wiley-Fisk Form 17-1

**FIGURE 20.3** Example of a final punch list showing use of the same item numbers that appeared on the first list. (From *Construction Engineer's Complete Handbook of Forms* by Edward Fisk. Copyright © 1992 by Prentice Hall. Reprinted by permission of Prentice Hall.)

contractor, the subcontractors, the Resident Project Representative, and the architect/engineer's project manager shall meet to make a tour of the entire project and identify and explain all of the items on the punch list. At that time the architect/engineer representatives should be ready to answer any questions that might arise so that there will be no misunderstanding of what is required before the project can be accepted as complete.

7. If the contractor gives notice that a major subcontractor has completed its punch list items, the Resident Project Representative should inspect that portion of the work, and if those items are found to be satisfactory, the contractor and subcontractor should be advised accordingly. If some items of work still remain to be picked up, the cycle should be repeated with a new punch list until all of the items on the list have been satisfactorily corrected.

8. Each punch list should be dated and signed by the person who prepared it, and all items on the original list should be numbered consecutively. Upon issuance of any subsequent punch lists containing only the remaining uncorrected items, the original item numbers should be retained to assure proper identification. If additional items are later discovered, they should be added to the end of the list and assigned item numbers in sequence following the last number used on the *original list*. All punch lists should be dated and signed. Failure to do so has sometimes resulted in unfavorable actions when a case went to arbitration to resolve a dispute.

9. When advised by the contractor that all punch list items have been completed, the architect/engineer representatives, accompanied by the contractor and subcontractors, should conduct the *final inspection* of the work. Then, if all punch list items have been completed satisfactorily, the Certificate of Completion should be issued.

10. If, following the *final inspection* of any portion of the work, there remains a question as to whether one or more punch list items have not been properly completed, but otherwise the overall project is substantially complete, the owner, through its architect/engineer, may issue a *Certificate of Substantial Completion* noting the uncompleted punch list items. Final payment of any retainage for that portion of the work should be paid after deducting an amount that the architect/engineer reasonably estimates will more than cover the cost of the completion of the remaining punch list items. Any such amounts withheld should be retained only until completion of such items to the satisfaction of the architect/engineer.

11. If the owner or installer of the owner's equipment and furnishings should damage any work that was completed and accepted previously, the owner should be advised accordingly and made aware of its obligation to bear the responsibility of repair costs for any such damaged work.

12. When preparing the punch list or any subsequent updates of the punch list, items of maintenance or any work damaged by the owner after he or she has taken occupancy or beneficial use should not be included. Should the owner want the contractor to repair or replace any such damaged work, he or she should be separately reimbursed for such costs through the issuance of a formal change order.

If these procedures are followed, it is reasonable to assume that the initial punch list will be minimal and that there should be no more than one additional punch list between the period of initial occupancy or use and final acceptance. The issuance of multiple punch lists in series is considered by many to be a sign of improper project control, and it is considered as unnecessary under good field management by both the contractor and the staff of the architect/engineer. However, there is no fixed limit to the number of punch lists that can be—and often are—used.

## PREPARATIONS FOR CLOSEOUT

Contrary to the layman's belief, the resident engineer's or inspector's job is not finished when the contractor completes the work at the site and a Certificate of Completion is executed. It is only then that the work of closing out the project *really* begins. The field staff must be reduced to the minimum number of persons necessary to complete the closeout activities; all office equipment must be returned to the office that supplied it; telephone and utility services must be terminated; radio paging devices or similar communications equipment must be returned and their contracts terminated; project records must be transferred into the office of the resident engineer's or inspector's employer; and a copy of a complete field office inventory should precede the return of all supplies and equipment and records of the field office.

Notices of address change should be sent to all parties who were previously addressing correspondence to the field office, and a closing schedule should be sent to the design firm and the owner so that appropriate plans can be made for the smooth transition of field personnel being released from the closing project into another assignment. Generally, the closeout will be accomplished by one or two persons: the Resident Project Representative and, if the work load warrants, a field clerk-typist.

The closeout period may actually begin several weeks to a month before the contractor completes the work on the project and can often extend for a month after completion of the work. In many cases the Resident Project Representative will be required to assure that all construction data have been posted on a copy of the plans showing the actual manner and location of all work as actually completed. These are referred to as "record drawings" and they are normally in the form of red pencil marks on a set of prints of the contractor's. These are often required to be turned over to the architect or engineer or owner when completed, and from these the architect or engineer or the owner may be required to have their draftsmen revise the original tracings to reflect recorded field information.

A summary of the principal closeout activities for a medium-sized to large project is shown in the flow diagram illustrated in Figure 20.4 and in the following list. Although some of the items may vary from job to job and the order may vary somewhat, the tasks do not vary significantly.

1. Perform closeout inspections as outlined under "The Punch List" in the preceding section of this chapter.
2. During the closeout inspection phase of a project, careful notes should be kept by each inspector in the field diary of all corrective, remedial, or extra work

# CLOSEOUT PROCEDURE

## For Public Capital Construction Contracts

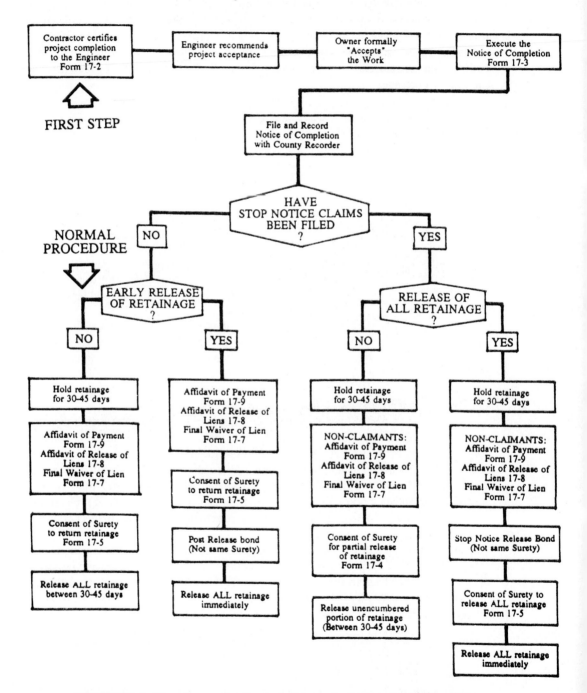

**FIGURE 20.4**  Flow diagram showing typical closeout procedure for public projects.

required to meet acceptance standards, and these data should be used to develop a preliminary list of all items still requiring completion or correction before acceptance of the work. The contractor must make corrections before the final inspection date.

3. Begin a partial reduction of field office inspection staff if the project is large enough to require several full-time inspectors in addition to the Resident Project Representative.

4. Begin an inventory of all architect/engineer or owner property in the field office. List separately all office equipment, records and reports, supplies, field inspection and testing equipment, vehicles, cameras and photographic supplies, office furniture, and other property.

5. Complete final reduction of the field office inspection staff to the minimum number of persons necessary to complete the closeout administrative activities.

6. Prepare for final inspection. The final inspection team should include the same persons who participated in the prefinal inspection. All items indicated as requiring correction on the preliminary punch list should be reinspected, and all tests that were originally unsatisfactory should be conducted again. Tests should not only include run-up of motors, pumps, air-conditioning systems, fire protection systems, communications systems, and similar installed work, but should include the testing of fail-safe devices, switches, controls, and other emergency devices. In addition, all doors should be operated, all locksets operated, and any other moving parts operated to assure that they will function properly before acceptance of the work. A final punch list should be developed for any outstanding deficiencies still requiring correction.

7. The contractor's record drawing set should be checked to see that all changes and variations from the original contract drawings have been marked on the set of prints or tracings that it may be required to submit under the terms of the contract. If properly completed, these should be turned over to the Resident Project Representative for transmittal to the architect/engineer or owner.

8. Prior to acceptance of the work, the Resident Project Representative should obtain the following items from the contractor if required under the contract:

Guarantees

Certificates of inspection

Operating manuals and instructions for equipment items

Keying schedule

Maintenance stock items; spare parts; special tools

Record drawings

Bonds (roof bonds, maintenance bonds, guarantee bonds, etc.)

Certificates of inspection and compliance by local agencies

Waivers of liens (varies from state to state)

Consent of Surety for Final Payments

9. If all work has been substantially completed and all punch list items accomplished to the satisfaction of the inspecting team, a *Certificate of Completion* or

*Substantial Completion* (Figures 20.5 and 20.6) should be prepared. If some items remain to be corrected and the owner elects to move into the facilities prior to their completion an attachment may be made to the *Certificate* listing all remaining remedial work required to be done, as noted on the final punch list. Either a *Certificate of Completion* or a *Certificate of Substantial Completion* may serve to certify fulfillment of the contract by the contractor. (See "Completion versus Substantial Completion" later in this chapter.) Execution of a *completion* or *substantial completion* notice constitutes acceptance by the owner of the work *as is*—the presumption being made that it is contractually complete. (See definition of the terms *Completion* and *Substantial Performance* as quoted from Black's Law Dictionary later in this chapter.) Under such conditions, in many cases the contractor may have no further obligations under the contract except possibly to satisfy any claims made under the provisions of the guarantee or any exceptions taken by supplemental agreement.

An owner who unqualifiedly accepts the work and makes final payment on a construction contract without taking exception to any part of the work has been held by the Montana Supreme Court to waive the owner's right to demand correction or get damages for defects in the work that are known at the time. Furthermore, such flaws do not fall under the coverage of the guarantee clause [*Grass Range High School District No. 27* v. *Wallace Diteman, Inc.,* Supreme Court of Montana, 465 P. 2d 814 (1970)].

10. Receive the contractor's request for its final progress payment. This does *not* include a release of its retainage money at this time, however. Figure 20.4 is a flow diagram illustrating the typical closeout steps involved in public agency contracts.

11. Check all work quantities and the value of the work completed from the punch list, retaining funds for those portions of the work named as still required to be done on the Certificate of Substantial Completion.

12. Submit contractor's payment request to the owner through the design or construction management firm with recommendation to pay, if warranted, less the retainage specified in the contract plus an amount sufficient to cover double the cost of remaining punch list items.

13. Obtain signatures of the architect/engineer, the contractor, and the owner or their authorized representatives on the Certificate of Completion or Certificate of Substantial Completion, then file the certificate for recording in the office of the county recorder, where it serves as a public record and puts all potential lien holders on notice that their lien filing period has begun.

14. Notify owner, through the architect/engineer, that the building or other project is ready for occupancy or beneficial use, subject to completion of pickup work during occupancy.

15. If using a contractor-furnished field office, terminate any architect/engineer or owner obligations for telephone or other utility services to the field office. Transfer all records, supplies, equipment, and all other items on the inventory to the architect/engineer's or owner's office. Move into other quarters during the fi-

# CERTIFICATE OF SUBSTANTIAL COMPLETION

PROJECT ...................................

DATE OF ISSUANCE ........................................................................................

OWNER ..........................................................................................................

OWNER's Contract No. ...........................

CONTRACTOR ................................. ENGINEER ...........................................

This Certificate of Substantial Completion applies to all Work under the Contract Documents or to the following specified parts thereof:

TO ...............................................................................................................

OWNER

And To ..........................................................................................................

CONTRACTOR

The Work to which this Certificate applies has been inspected by authorized representatives of OWNER, CONTRACTOR and ENGINEER, and that Work is hereby declared to be substantially complete in accordance with the Contract Documents on

...........................................<br>DATE OF SUBSTANTIAL COMPLETION

A tentative list of items to be completed or corrected is attached hereto. This list may not be all-inclusive, and the failure to include an item in it does not alter the responsibility of CONTRACTOR to complete all the Work in accordance with the Contract Documents. The items in the tentative list shall be completed or corrected by CONTRACTOR within _____ days of the above date of Substantial Completion.

EJCDC No. 1910–8-D (1990 Edition)
Prepared by the Engineers Joint Contract Documents Committee and endorsed by The Associated General Contractors of America.

**FIGURE 20.5** EJDC Certificate of Substantial Completion. (Copyright © 1990 by National Society of Professional Engineers.)

From the date of Substantial Completion the responsibilities between OWNER and CONTRACTOR for security, operation, safety, maintenance, heat, utilities, insurance and warranties and guarantees shall be as follows:

RESPONSIBILITIES:

OWNER: _____

_____

_____

CONTRACTOR: _____

_____

_____

The following documents are attached to and made a part of this Certificate:

*[For items to be attached see definition of Substantial Completion as supplemented and other specifically noted conditions precedent to achieving Substantial Completion as required by Contract Documents.]*

This certificate does not constitute an acceptance of Work not in accordance with the Contract Documents nor is it a release of CONTRACTOR's obligation to complete the Work in accordance with the Contract Documents.

Executed by ENGINEER on        . . . . . . . . . . . . . . . . . . . . . . . . , 19 . . . . .

. . . . . . . . . . . . . . . . . . . . . . . . . . . . . . . . . . . . . . . . . . . . . . . . . . . . .
ENGINEER

By: . . . . . . . . . . . . . . . . . . . . . . . . . . . . . . . . . . . . . . . . . . . . . . . .
(Authorized Signature)

CONTRACTOR accepts this Certificate of Substantial Completion on . . . . . . . . . . . . . . . . . . . . . . , 19 . . . . .

. . . . . . . . . . . . . . . . . . . . . . . . . . . . . . . . . . . . . . . . . . . . . . . . . . . . .
CONTRACTOR

By: . . . . . . . . . . . . . . . . . . . . . . . . . . . . . . . . . . . . . . . . . . . . . . . .

OWNER accepts this Certificate of Substantial Completion on . . . . . . . . . . . . . . . . . . . . . . . . , 19 . . . . .

. . . . . . . . . . . . . . . . . . . . . . . . . . . . . . . . . . . . . . . . . . . . . . . . . . . . .
OWNER

By: . . . . . . . . . . . . . . . . . . . . . . . . . . . . . . . . . . . . . . . . . . . . . . . .
(Authorized Signature)

**FIGURE 20.5**   *continued*

542

**FIGURE 20.6** Notice of Completion (substantial completion) suitable for either buildings or engineering works.

nal administrative functions involved in the termination of all owner/contractor obligations.

**16.** If final completion of all pickup work noted on the Certificate of Substantial Completion has been accomplished, and if no liens have been filed during the holding period specified in the contract for making final payment, the architect/engineer may recommend to the owner that all remaining retainage funds be released. Prior to releasing retainage, however, the following certificates should be executed by the contractor and its surety, by all subcontractors and all suppliers: final waiver of lien and a properly signed Consent of Surety for Final Payment.

**17.** The making of the final payment and release of retainage by the owner will normally constitute a waiver of further claims by the owner, except those arising from:

(a) Unsettled liens or stop notice claims.

(b) Faulty or defective work appearing after substantial completion.

(c) Failure of the work to comply with the requirements of the contract documents.

(d) Terms of special guarantees required by the contract documents.

The making of final payment will also constitute a waiver of all claims by the contractor *except* those previously made and still unsettled.

## COMPLETION VERSUS SUBSTANTIAL COMPLETION

Substantial completion is based on the owner being able to use the project for the purposes intended and that the remaining activity of the contractor will not interfere with such use. The definitions of AIA and EJCDC vary slightly in their definition as to what "substantial completion" actually is; the AIA definition in Document A201 (1987) states that substantial completion is the stage in the progress of the Work when the Work or designated portion thereof is sufficiently complete in accordance with the Contract Documents so that the owner can occupy or utilize the work for its intended use.

Then AIA has another "stage" of completion, called "Final Completion," which they define as that stage of the Work where the Architect finds the Work acceptable under the Contract Documents and the Contract fully performed. At that point the architect issues a final Certificate for payment and a statement that the Work has been completed in accordance with the terms and conditions of the Contract Documents.

Particular note should be made of the AIA references to both "Substantial Completion" and "Final Completion" as though they represented two separate stages of completion of a project, notwithstanding the legal definitions to the contrary of "completion" and "substantial performance" in *Black's Law Dictionary*. In this area, the AIA documents create some confusion with the wording used in contract law, in particular the definitions established under the lien laws of the various states.

It is possible, of course to have a different definition for substantial completion and substantial performance if they are carefully defined in the contract; however, this leads to confusion and ultimately into litigation. It is much more economical to avoid such confusion of terms in the contract documents.

The EJCDC definition of substantial completion is more consistent with the legal definition of substantial performance of a contract. In EJCDC Document 1910-8(1996) the language has been improved since the 1983 edition. Article 14.04 is reproduced in Figure 20.7.

There is no attempt by EJCDC to suggest two stages of completion. Substantial Completion is recognized as contractual fulfillment of the obligation of the contractor to the owner, and that the existence of small defects or omissions will not jeopardize that. It has been held in law that once substantial completion has been achieved and acknowledged, a contractor cannot be defaulted for failure to pick up the remaining punch list items, quite inconsistent with the AIA definition. The EJCDC addresses the subject of "Final Payment

---

*14.04. Substantial Completion*

A. When CONTRACTOR considers the entire Work ready for its intended use CONTRACTOR shall notify OWNER and ENGINEER in writing that the entire Work is substantially complete (except for items specifically listed by CONTRACTOR as incomplete) and request that ENGINEER issue a certificate of Substantial Completion. Within a reasonable time thereafter, OWNER, CONTRACTOR and ENGINEER shall make an inspection of the Work to determine the status of completion. If ENGINEER does not consider the Work substantially complete, ENGINEER will notify CONTRACTOR in writing giving the reasons therefor. If ENGINEER considers the Work substantially complete, ENGINEER will prepare and deliver to OWNER a tentative certificate of Substantial Completion which shall fix the date of Substantial Completion. There shall be attached to the certificate a tentative list of items to be completed or corrected before final payment. OWNER shall have seven days after receipt of the tentative certificate during which to make written objection to ENGINEER as to any provisions of the certificate or attached list. If, after considering such objections, ENGINEER concludes that the Work is not substantially complete, ENGINEER will within fourteen days after submission of the tentative certificate to OWNER notify CONTRACTOR in writing, stating the reasons therefor. If, after consideration of OWNER's objections, ENGINEER considers the Work substantially complete, ENGINEER will within said fourteen days execute and deliver to OWNER and CONTRACTOR a definitive certificate of Substantial Completion (with a revised tentative list of items to be completed or corrected) reflecting such changes from the tentative certificate as ENGINEER believes justified after consideration of any objections from OWNER. At the time of delivery of the tentative certificate of Substantial Completion ENGINEER will deliver to OWNER and CONTRACTOR a written recommendation as to division of responsibilities pending final payment between OWNER and CONTRACTOR with respect to security, operation, safety and protection of the Work, maintenance, heat, utilities, insurance and warranties and guarantees. Unless OWNER and CONTRACTOR agree otherwise in writing and so inform ENGINEER in writing prior to ENGINEER's issuing the definitive certificate of Substantial Completion, ENGINEER's aforesaid recommendation will be binding on OWNER and CONTRACTOR until final payment.

B. OWNER shall have the right to exclude CONTRACTOR from the Site after the date of Substantial Completion, but OWNER shall allow CONTRACTOR reasonable access to complete or correct items on the tentative list.

---

**FIGURE 20.7** Provisions for Substantial Completion from the EJCDC Standard General Conditions of the Construction Contract 1910-8(1996). Copyright © 1996 by the National Society of Professional Engineers.

and Acceptance" as opposed to AIA's "Final Completion and Final Payment," thus not necessarily agreeing that the Work is acceptable merely because "substantial completion" has been achieved. This difference is normally resolved either by the contractor's completion of the outstanding punch list items, or by a *quanti minoris* settlement wherein the owner withholds an amount of money from the retainage equal to substantially more than the value of the remaining punch list items as a cash settlement for failing to complete these items.

Both the AIA and EJCDC publish a document entitled *Certificate of Substantial Completion* but no document called *Notice of Completion* or *Notice of Final Completion.* Under the EJCDC terms stated earlier, this document is adequate, as EJCDC recognizes substantial completion as "completion." However, the AIA documents leave some doubt. In fact, in California, where such documents are required by law to be recorded with the office of the county recorder within 10 days of actual completion, the recorders have generally refused to recognize and record a "substantial" completion document, stating simply, "come back when it is finished." The layperson does not generally recognize the significance of the legal terminology involved in certifying project completion and does not realize that substantial performance of a contract is defined in law as completion of a contract. (See *Black's Law Dictionary* definitions of "completion" and "substantial performance" quoted below.)

The provisions of the EJCDC Standard General Conditions of the Construction Contract for "substantial completion" are reasonable and accurate, but the AIA provisions leave the actual interpretation of the term *substantial completion* to the architect/engineer using the documents.

As if to further complicate matters, the courts have their own definition of substantial completion, which appears to differ materially from the interpretations of the term by the architect/engineers using the AIA and the EJCDC. Some documents tend to confuse the unwary by treating the term *substantial completion* as if it meant "nearly finished" as opposed to *final completion,* a term that seems predicated on the concept of absolute performance of the contract in every detail. Unfortunately, this leads many owners and architect/engineers astray, as the courts take a different and considerably more liberal view as to when a construction contract is done. The term *substantial completion* as applied to a construction contract means "substantial performance" of the terms of the contract. *Black's Law Dictionary* defines "completion" and "substantial performance" as follows:

COMPLETION. The finishing or accomplishing in full of something theretofore begun; *substantial performance of what one has agreed to do;* state in which no essential element is lacking. Flad v. Murphysboro & S.I.R. Co., C.C.A.Ill., 283 F. 386, 390.

SUBSTANTIAL PERFORMANCE. Exists where there has been no willful departure from the terms of the contract, and no omission in essential points, and the contract has been honestly and faithfully performed in its material and substantial particulars, and the only variance from the strict and literal performance consists of technical or unimportant omissions or defects. Cotherman v. Oriental Oil Co., Tex.Civ.App., 272 S.W. 616, 619; Brown v. Aguilar, 202 Cal. 143, 259 P. 735, 737; Cramer v. Esswein, 220 App.Div. 10, 220 N.Y.S. 634; Connell v. Higgins, 170 Cal.541, 150 P. 769, 774. Performance except as to unsubstantial omissions with compensation therefor, Cassino v. Yacevish, 261 App.Div. 685, 27 N.Y.S. 2d 95, 97, 99. (Equitable doctrine of "substantial performance," protects against forfeiture, for technical inadvertence or trivial variations or omissions in performance. Sgarlat v. Griffith, 349 Pa. 42, 36 A.2d 330, 332.)

The word *completion,* then, properly means that a project is finished when all of the work of any substantial nature has been done, regardless of whether a few minor pickup or call-back items remain to be done. It is the interpretation of the term *minor* that seems to be causing problems for many architects or engineers. The work done in the following cases offers an example of the courts' interpretation of the term *minor.* In each of these cases, the court held that the remaining punch list item was sufficient to *prevent* "completion" of the work, because it was a specified item and the contractor failed to make an honest attempt to meet the terms of the contract.

> Application of a second coat of paint on the porch floors and steps, where the second coat was required by the specifications. [*Rockwell* v. *Light* (1907) 6 Cal.App.563, 92 Pac 649] Installation of soap dispensers which were specified in the contract. [*Lewis* v. *Hopper* (1956) 140 Cal.App.2d 365, 295 Pac. 2d 93.]

Some architect/engineers attempt to issue a Notice of Substantial Completion prematurely, such as in the case of a wastewater treatment plant where the owner wanted to issue the Notice of Substantial Completion as soon as the plant was operable but before completion of fencing, paving, and landscaping. This, however, did not meet the legal criteria for substantial completion, and the owner incurred the risk of being vulnerable to liens filed later than the normal filing time if a claimant could succeed in having a court invalidate a prematurely issued Notice of Substantial Completion.

It should also be kept in mind that the contractor's failure to complete remaining punch list items after the issuance of a Notice of Substantial Completion may not be used as grounds for declaring the contractor in default. Substantial completion in the eyes of the court may be viewed as "completion" of the contract, and as such the contractor can no longer be declared in default for failure to perform subsequent to the date of substantial completion [*Appeal of Wolfe Construction Co.,* ENG BCA No. 3610 (June 29, 1984)] (Figure 20.8). In a conflicting opinion, the Veterans Administration Board of Contract Appeals ruled that a contractor *may* be terminated for default by failing to meet a deadline for completion of punch list items. [*Appeal of Dimarco Corp.* VABCA No. 1953 (June 22, 1984)]

Certain other facts are worthy of consideration before executing a Notice of Substantial Completion. If the contractor is to be excluded from the area involved except for access necessary to correct or complete the pickup work items on the punch list, it will be necessary for the architect/engineer or owner to indicate who will have the responsibility for maintenance, heat, and utilities for the area involved. The extent to which the issuance of a Certificate of Substantial Completion will affect the insurable interest of the owner and the contractor in the project should be discussed with an insurance counselor.

The execution of a Certificate of Substantial Completion releases the contractor of all responsibility and obligation for further maintenance of the work, and ownership of the project passes to the owner. It is important to see that the owner is fully aware of the significance of this document in terms of its added responsibility. Normally, a Certificate of Substantial Completion will relieve the contractor of the hazards of liquidated damages for any work

**FIGURE 20.8**   75MGD (ult.) water treatment plant for the City of Escondido, Vista Irrigation District, California, "substantially completed." (From J. M. Montgomery Consulting Engineers, Inc., Pasadena, California.)

performed subsequent to its execution. Thus it certainly seems to be in the contractor's best interest to obtain such a certificate as early as possible. As for a deficiency noted on the punch list that required the replacement of a piece of defective equipment, it would seem within reason that the guarantee period for the affected equipment should begin after the receipt of the replacement equipment and conclusion of a satisfactory operational test.

## SUBSTANTIAL COMPLETION VERSUS BENEFICIAL OCCUPANCY OR USE

The meaning of *substantial completion* as it applies to a construction project has been found to be somewhat ambiguous. Although the AIA and EJCDC General Conditions both provide a good definition and are quite acceptable as far as they go, they do not determine the responsibilities of the owner, architect/engineer, and contractor, nor do they recommend how certain matters should be resolved.

By a general definition, the owner's occupancy of a project prior to its being 100 percent complete may be defined as "beneficial occupancy." Thus the terms *substantial completion* and *beneficial occupancy* (or "use") are complementary.

The date of *substantial completion* or *beneficial occupancy* will normally establish the beginning of the specified period on the guarantees, unless a prior commitment has been made for acceptance of a portion of the total project (or *partial occupancy* or use). This concept is not uncommon in large residential tract housing and apartment complexes, where completed units are generally accepted and placed for sale while other portions of the project are in various stages of completion. It is *important* on tract work to identify the specific units that are accepted and cover in the specifications who is responsible for security, maintenance, heat, and general care during the period between the substantial completion of the early units and the date of sale and eventual move-in by the new owners. It should clearly be established that after acceptance of a single structure as being substantially complete, the owner will accept total responsibility for the building. Otherwise, the difficulty may arise, as it did on a case where the author was the arbitrator, where certain apartment units were substantially completed but no separate certificates had been issued, yet a final punch list had been satisfactorily completed. Both the contractor and the sales agency denied responsibility for weather damage occurring to some of the units because of lack of heat and for doors left open during the rainy season. The units were completed by the contractor, so no further maintenance was being provided. Furthermore, the sales agency had been leaving the doors open, causing some of the units to suffer severe weather damage. This condition existed for over six months with some of the completed units. The judgment was in favor of the contractor in this case, as there is no reason, contractually or morally, why the contractor had to play nursemaid to the owner's buildings while the owner was not only trying to sell them, but was not even showing normal consideration and care when an apartment was shown to a prospective buyer.

One solution, or an approach to one at least, is to execute a separate Certificate of Substantial Completion for each apartment unit as it is completed. Then the responsibility clearly passes to the owner, where it belongs.

The laws appear to provide generally that when a work of improvement consists of separate residential units, the owner may record a Notice of Completion as each unit is finished. Similarly, a subdivider may record separate Notices of Completion covering each house in the subdivision as it is finished rather than waiting until the entire subdivision is completed.

In one sense, a condominium project also consists of separate residential units. Each condominium is a residential unit that may be owned separately from the other condominiums in the project. However, in a California decision, it has been held that an apartment-type condominium, at least, is a single project requiring one Notice of Completion at the end of the entire job [*McGillicuddy Construction Co.* v. *Noll Recreation Association, Inc.,* 31 Cal. App. 3d 891, 107 Cal. Rptr. 899 (1973)].

Immediately following *substantial completion* or *beneficial occupancy,* the owner must assume the complete responsibility for the maintenance and operation of all fuel and service utilities. The owner will normally also become responsible for all maintenance and damage and/or wear and tear and, with the exception of items that are specifically under guarantee or warranty, the cost of repairs or restoration during the period between *substantial completion* and *final completion.* The owner should also have the responsibility to have in effect all necessary insurance for protection against any losses not directly attributable to the contractor's negligence.

The contractor must be required to arrange a schedule so that punch list items will be completed within the designated time by working during regular working hours. If the architect/engineer determines that the work interferes with the beneficial use of the project, and the owner is unable to adjust the operations to permit the contractor to perform punch list work during regular working hours, the architect/engineer must certify to the owner that this work must be performed on an overtime basis, and the owner should compensate the contractor for the additional expense.

The purpose of retention is both as a hedge against lien claims and a guarantee to the owner that sufficient funds will remain to pay another party to complete the work or correct unsatisfactory items if the contractor refuses to make or delays making the corrections for an unreasonable length of time. If all lien waivers have been received, the amount of the retention should be adjusted so that the sum has a direct relation to the value of the work included on the punch list. It is recommended that the proper amount of retention to cover punch list items be equal to approximately twice the value of the punch list items, as determined by the architect/engineer.

## BENEFICIAL USE/PARTIAL UTILIZATION

Generally, during the administration of a construction contract for a project such as a water or wastewater treatment plant addition, it will be necessary for the owner to begin to use completed portions of the new facilities well before total project completion.

This creates a very sensitive, high-risk relationship between the parties to the contract, as several serious problems can and often do occur as a result of such utilization.

1. Identification of latent defects in equipment are almost impossible, and malfunctions are generally claimed to be the result of improper maintenance of equipment being utilized by the owner.
2. Equipment warranty dates are in question.
3. Maintenance responsibility frequently becomes a controversial issue between the contractor and the owner.
4. Security of the site and the on-site safety responsibility is no longer a clear-cut issue during beneficial use. Generally, the owner will inherit these risks.
5. One of the principal risks involved in items 3 and 4 is that each party will assume that the other is responsible for maintenance, security, and safety, and then neither party will perform. This can result in increasing the severity of the problem and increasing the volume and magnitude of disputes and claims.

It is recommended that wherever practical the owner first be advised against assuming the risk of taking beneficial use or partial utilization unless the owner is fully prepared to accept all attendant risks from the contractor.

If the owner does elect to utilize any portion or portions of a project prior to total project completion, the following guidelines are suggested:

1. Issue a letter to the contractor advising that the owner will take beneficial use of a particular described portion of the Work as of a specified date. This will serve to begin the product warranty date if it has not already begun upon purchase by the contractor. This should not affect the contractor's normal one-year guarantee period, dated from the *completion* date of the total project. This letter will place all parties on notice that the owner is taking partial utilization and has agreed to accept certain responsibilities (Figure 20.9).

2. A copy of this letter should be sent to the owner's operations and maintenance department.

3. The letter to the contractor should indicate that a particular portion of the Work is designated as being "sufficiently complete so as to allow beneficial use by the owner."

4. Be careful of the word *complete* in any notice to the contractor. The term *operationally complete* should be avoided in favor of terms utilizing the words *beneficial use* or one of their variants.

5. Do not refer to the act of taking "beneficial use" as constituting "preliminary acceptance." The term *acceptance* should not be used in any context at this stage of the project, as it has a strict legal meaning on public works projects.

6. Advise the owner to take positive steps to take over maintenance of any affected equipment.

7. Advise the owner to take positive steps to institute security measures, as necessary, to protect the equipment in use.

8. The owner should be advised not to occupy or use any portion of the Work until after official notification of beneficial use has been made to the contractor.

Such notification serves a dual purpose. It not only alerts the owner's operational and maintenance staff that they are under obligation to maintain the equipment now being utilized by the owner, but it also affords the owner the opportunity to establish in writing the limits of responsibility that the owner will accept, without making a big issue of it.

In the current edition of the Standard General Conditions of the Construction Contract published by the EJCDC, the subject is recognized and an orderly procedure for administering a contract involving partial utilization is specified (Figure 20.10).

## LIENS AND STOP ORDERS

Mechanic's lien laws applicable to construction are designed to protect subcontractors, material suppliers, laborers, and in some cases architects, engineers, and other design professionals who contribute to a work of improvement. These individuals and entities are all potential lien claimants on the projects they worked on. Due to the wide variation in state laws, it is impossible to do more than discuss lien rights generally.

Although public property is not subject to liens, some states have lien laws that entitle an unpaid claimant to place a lien on public funds that may be due a contractor. Under

```
                                    UTILITIES DEPARTMENT
    10 August 1990                   DONALD H. NELSON, DIRECTOR

    XYZ Constructors, Inc.
    1000 Magnolia Street
    Camarillo, CA 90000

    Attention: Mr. Conrad W. Belker
               Project manager

    Dear Mr. Belker:

    The City plans to take beneficial use of a portion of the Lakeside
    Treatment Plant Addition prior to completion of the remaining
    portion of the project by utilizing or placing into service the
    following items during the period when your firm will be working
    elsewhere on the site.

         Pump Nos. 203 and 205 and appurtenance piping from valve
         17 to valve 27 and from the pumps to, but not including,
         the circuit breaker controlling said pumps.

    In consideration of such beneficial use, the City hereby accepts
    responsibility for the maintenance and protection of the specific
    portion of the project so used. It is further understood that the
    manufacturer's warranties on any piece of equipment placed into
    beneficial use by the City will commence as of the date of this
    Notice of Beneficial Use.

    The Contractor shall retain full responsibility for satisfactory
    operation of the total project, however, and the Contractor's one-
    year maintenance and repair period and/or guarantee provided under
    the Contract Documents shall commence only after acceptance by the
    City and issuance of a final Notice of Completion for the entire
    project. Such guarantee of total systems operation shall include
    that portion or portions of the Work previously placed into
    beneficial use by the City.

    Very truly yours,


    WENDELL T. RIGBY
    SENIOR CIVIL ENGINEER

    WTR:db

    CC: O&M Department
```

**City of Thousand Oaks**

**Purpose:** Notice to Contractor that the City will take Beneficial Use/Partial Utilization of a portion of the project prior to completion of the remaining portion of the project.

**Prepared by:** Project Manager/Engineer, Construction Manager, or Resident Project Representative.

**Directed to:** Primarily to the Contractor, but in reality also intended to place the City's Operations and Maintenance personnel on ''Notice'' as well.

**Copies to:** Contractor, City, Project Manager/Engineer, Resident Project Representative.

**Comments:** Notice to Contractor that the City will accept certain responsibilities for items placed into beneficial use; that it is understood that warranties will commence on those items; and, that the City will accept responsibility for providing all maintenance, security, and safety related to the affected portions of the Work after the date of this letter. Contractor is reminded that his or her project guaranteed or maintenance and repair agreement still covers the affected items during the normal one year post construction period.

**FIGURE 20.9** Notice of taking beneficial use of a part of a project (partial utilization).

---

*14.05. Partial Utilization*

A.  Use by OWNER at OWNER's option of any substantially completed part of the Work which has specifically been identified in the Contract Documents, or which OWNER, ENGINEER and CONTRACTOR agree constitutes a separately functioning and usable part of the Work that can be used by OWNER for its intended purpose without significant interference with CONTRACTOR's performance of the remainder of the Work, may be accomplished prior to Substantial Completion of all the Work subject to the following conditions.

1.  OWNER at any time may request CONTRACTOR in writing to permit OWNER to use any such part of the Work which OWNER believes to be ready for its intended use and substantially complete. If CONTRACTOR agrees that such part of the Work is substantially complete, CONTRACTOR will certify to OWNER and ENGINEER that such part of the Work is substantially complete and request ENGINEER to issue a certificate of Substantial Completion for that part of the Work. CONTRACTOR at any time may notify OWNER and ENGINEER in writing that CONTRACTOR considers  any such part of the Work ready for its intended use and substantially complete and request ENGINEER to issue a certificate of Substantial Completion for that part of the Work. Within a reasonable time after either such request, OWNER, CONTRACTOR and ENGINEER shall make an inspection of that part of the Work to determine its status of completion. If ENGINEER does not consider that part of the Work to be substantially complete, ENGINEER will notify OWNER and CONTRACTOR in writing giving the reasons therefor. If ENGINEER considers that part of the Work to be substantially complete, the provisions of paragraph 14.04 will apply with respect to certification of Substantial Completion of that part of the Work and the division of responsibility in respect thereof and access thereto.

2.  No occupancy or separate operation of part of the Work may occur prior to compliance with the requirements of paragraph 5.10 regarding property insurance.

---

**FIGURE 20.10**   Provisions for Partial Utilization from the EJCDC Standard General Conditions of the Construction Contract 1910–8 (1996). Copyright © 1996 by the National Society of Professional Engineers.

such schemes, the unpaid claimant advises the agency of its claim in accordance with the statutory notice requirements, and then the agency must stop further disbursements to the contractor of the affected funds until payment has been received by the claimants. Generally, once a claim has been made, the lien claimant must foreclose on its lien within a set time period in order to collect; otherwise, the rights will be lost. The agency must hold the liened funds until the lien has been satisfied through foreclosure, at which time the funds are paid over to the claimant. California, Louisiana, New York, and Texas are examples of four states that have provisions allowing liens to be filed against construction funds. In California, a lien against construction funds is accomplished by the use of a *Stop Notice,* which, when served, gives the agency notice to stop payment to the contractor.

### Lien Waivers

A contractor may be asked to submit lien waivers as a condition of receiving payment. Although this is not at all uncommon at the end of the job, it is becoming increasingly popular as partial waivers of lien on a monthly basis, each covering only the value of the currently completed month's work.

There are basically two types of waivers of lien and two versions of each.

1. Conditional waiver and release upon receipt of progress payment upon final payment (Figure 20.11).
2. Unconditional waiver and release upon receipt of progress payment upon final payment (Figure 20.12).

A contractor will generally be asked to submit lien waivers for itself and each of its subcontractors before the owner will issue a check. Some owners don't seem to have the least bit of sympathy for the fact that it demands an unconditional release—they could refuse to pay at all, and the contractor would have no recourse for collection. The answer, of course, is either use the unconditional lien waivers when receiving payment in person, trading the contractor's lien release for the owner's check, or if being paid by mail, submit only a conditional waiver and release. A contractor is not at risk as long as conditional waivers are used, but should not consent to submitting unconditional releases unless the transaction is being handled in person and the check is tendered at the same time that the release is submitted.

## FINAL PAYMENT AND WAIVER OF LIENS

On public projects the closeout procedure is often more complex. A typical closeout procedure on a public works project is illustrated in Figure 20.4. Although mechanics liens cannot be applied to public agencies, the lien laws of a number of states do provide the means to allow access to, or freezing of, public funds (Chapter 19). The lien laws throughout the country are by no means uniform. Lien rights, however, are based on the contract and provide for a lien on the property improved. Stop notices or "freeze orders" may also provide for a lien on funds payable by virtue of the improvement. A lien is only an additional remedy for securing payment of labor and materials furnished on a project. A final of lien (Figures 20.11 and 20.12) is a receipt for an exact sum of money paid as of a certain date for certain services, labor, and material that were supplied under the contract for a specific improvement and property (see "Measurement for Payment" in Chapter 14).

If such a receipt is made for funds received by the contractor in payment for its work, any claim of lien to the extent of such payment against the money owed is waived. To implement this effectively in each state, a local attorney should be consulted, as the laws vary from state to state.

Every time a payment is made to a contractor, you should insist on a corresponding waiver of lien rights. Progress payments should result in partial lien waivers, and final payment should result in a full waiver and release.

Along with each lien waiver, you should insist on an affidavit from the contractor swearing that all subcontractors and suppliers who furnished labor or materials for the work covered by the owner's payment have been paid in full. This should include an indemnification provision whereby the contractor agrees to reimburse the owner if any of the subs or suppliers later assert a lien. It is important for each administrator of a construction contract to become familiar with the lien laws of your own state. It should be kept in mind that even

**Purpose:** Protect the City from lien (stop notice) claims.

**Prepared by:** Prime and Subcontractors; Suppliers.

**Directed to:** City's Representative.

**Copies to:** City; Project Manager or Construction Manager; Surety Company; Contractor.

**Comments:** Application for final payment should be accompanied by final waivers of lien from the Prime Contractor, all Subcontractors, and Suppliers who have not previously furnished such final waivers. If partial lien waivers have been used, the amount of such final lien waiver would not be required to exceed the last month's payment. *NOTE: That a conditional waiver does not become effective unless or until AFTER the funds have been credited to the lienholder's account.*

**FIGURE 20.11**   Conditional waiver of lien for final payment.

## UNCONDITIONAL WAIVER
## AND RELEASE UPON FINAL PAYMENT

[California Civil Code §3262(d)(4)]

The undersigned has been paid in full for all labor, services, equipment or material

furnished to ___XYZ Constructors, Inc.___

on the job of ___City of Thousand Oaks Street Widening___
<br>(Your Customer)

located at ___Janss Road at Drake___
<br>(Owner)

<br>(Job Description)

and does hereby waive and release any right to a mechanic's lien, stop notice, or any right against a labor and material bond on the job, except for disputed claims for extra work in the amount of

$ __5,278.43__ .

Dated: __7 Aug 1990__          ABC Paving Contractors, Inc.
<br>(Company Name)

By ___O. C. Johnson___

(Title) Vice Pres.

**NOTICE TO PERSONS SIGNING THIS WAIVER: THIS DOCUMENT WAIVES RIGHTS UNCONDITIONALLY AND STATES THAT YOU HAVE BEEN PAID FOR GIVING UP THOSE RIGHTS. THIS DOCUMENT IS ENFORCEABLE AGAINST YOU IF YOU SIGN IT, EVEN IF YOU HAVE NOT BEEN PAID. IF YOU HAVE NOT BEEN PAID, USE A CONDITIONAL RELEASE FORM.**

Thousand Oaks
Form 17-7b

**Purpose:** Protect the City from lien (stop notice) claims.

**Prepared by:** Prime and Subcontractors; Suppliers.

**Directed to:** City's Representative.

**Copies to:** City; Project Manager or Construction Manager; Surety Company; Contractor.

**Comments:** Application for final payment should be accompanied by final waivers of lien from the Prime Contractor, all Subcontractors, and Suppliers who have not previously furnished such final waivers. If partial lien waivers have been used, the amount of such final lien waiver would not be required to exceed the last month's payment. *NOTE: That an unconditional waiver waives rights unconditionally and the person signing it gives up all rights whether they have been paid or not.*

**FIGURE 20.12**   Unconditional waiver of lien for final payment.

individuals may be able to assert lien rights over the owner's property due to failure of their contractor employer to pay them wages due them.

It is important to note, however, that on projects for which the contractor has provided surety bonds, it is essential to obtain a written release or *consent of surety* prior to release of the final payment to the contractor (Figure 20.13).

## STOP NOTICE RELEASE BOND

Most states that have statutory provisions enabling lien claimants to lien construction funds usually have provisions to help the contractor protect itself against fraudulent, improper, or disputed claims. In some states, if the contractor posts a bond in a specified amount to cover the amount of the lien, the agency is then free to release the construction funds that have been held up in accordance with the original lien. However, it should be noted that agencies will often demand that all liens and lien-related issues be resolved by the contractor before the project is accepted and final payment is made.

One method open to a public agency to allow the release to the contractor of retainage funds being held to cover stop notice claims is through the acceptance of a *Stop Notice Release Bond* from a reputable surety company in favor of the general contractor. A public agency that honors a Stop Notice Release Bond by releasing retainage funds to the contractor may be relieved of any liability resulting from the stop notice. The public agency is no longer a stakeholder when it accepts a release bond. Its duty has been discharged by release of the withheld funds, and the claimant must then look to the surety company for payment. Under such conditions, the claimant has no right of action against the public agency [*Cal-Pacific Materials Co.* v. *Redondo Beach City School Dist.,* 94 Cal. App. 3d 652, 156 Cal. Rptr. 590 (1979)].

## POST COMPLETION

As soon as the contractor's final payment and release of retainage have been made, another, and final, phase of the project begins. At this point, assuming that all contractual obligations of both parties have been met, the project manager takes over all of the activities on the project, and the Resident Project Representative is completely phased out in most organizations.

The visual satisfactions of watching the project develop into reality are now gone, and in its place is the rather mundane task of bookkeeping and report writing. Of the several tasks that must be accomplished during this period, the most prominent ones are:

1. Financial accounting of the entire project, summarizing all costs, expenditures, overhead, profit, and other cost-related items for the entire life of the project.
2. Preparation of the final project report to the management team of the architect/engineer's or owner's organization.
3. Assembly, organization, analysis, and filing of complete project records for the master file. These are quite important, as they may yet be needed by the legal department in case of later claims.

**CONSENT OF SURETY**
**For Final Payment**

City of Palm Springs

Project Name ___1991 Expansion of Palm Springs Convention Center___

Location ___277 North Avenida Caballeros___

Project No. ___CP90-38___ Contract No. _____

Type of Contract ___Construction___

Amount of Contract ___$5,678,000.00___

In accordance with the provisions of the above-named contract between the Owner and the Contractor, the following named surety:

___Guaranteed Indemnity Corporation, a legal entity organized and existing in the___

___City of Los Angeles, State of California.___

on the Payment Bond of the following named Contractor:

___XYZ Constructors, Inc., a California Corporation, organized and existing in___

___The City of Santa Ana, California___

hereby approves of final payment to the Contractor, and further agrees that said final payment to the Contractor shall not relieve the Surety Company named herein of any of its obligations to the following named Owner: as set forth in said Surety company's bond:

___City of Palm Springs, a legal entity, organized and existing in the County___

___of Riverside, State of California.___

IN WITNESS WHEREOF, the Surety Company has hereunto set its hand and seal this ___20th___ day of ___August 1990___ 19___

Guaranteed Indemnity Corporation
(Name of Surety Company)

(Signature of Authorized Representative)

(Affix corporate seal here)

TITLE ___Vice President___

Wiley-Fisk Form 17-5

**Purpose:** The surety's financial interest could be jeopardized by premature final payment by the owner.

**Prepared by:** Surety company upon specific request of the contractor.

**Directed to:** Owner's Project Manager.

**Copies to:** Surety company; owner; Project Manager; Resident Project Representative.

**Comments:** Final payment by owner, prior to a consent of the surety, could place owner in a vulnerable position in case contractor fails to pay his subcontractors or suppliers.

**FIGURE 20.13** Consent of Surety for final payment to the contractor.

## PROBLEMS

1. What types of coverage are provided under a guarantee? What types under a warranty?

2. Under a liquidated damages clause, is it necessary to prove that the owner suffered a loss to be entitled to withhold liquidated damages?

3. Is it necessary to include a provision for a bonus clause in order to have a valid liquidated damages clause?

4. Define "substantial completion."

5. In a construction contract, list the effects of achieving substantial completion upon the contract requirements for project insurance, liquidated damages, time for filing lien claims, processing of payments, and retainage.

6. What is the effect of "beneficial use" on the foregoing list of contract requirements?

7. Define the difference between a conditional and an unconditional waiver of lien.

8. Define "punch list" and indicate the principal elements that a punch list must contain.

9. What phrase regarding time must be included in the contract to support a liquidated damages claim?

10. Liquidated damages are intended to represent anticipated losses to the owner based upon circumstances existing at the time the contract was made. List at least five types of potential losses to the owner that would qualify for determination of such potential losses.

# Bibliography

ACRET, J. *California Construction Law Manual,* 3rd ed. Colorado Springs, CO: Shepard's/ McGraw-Hill, 1982.

ANTILL, J. M. AND WOODHEAD, R. W. *Critical Path Methods in Construction Practice,* 3rd ed., New York, NY: Wiley, 1982.

ASCE Committee on Specifications, "Summary Report of Questionnaire on Specifications (Contractor Returns)," ASCE Vol. 104, No. C03, Proceedings Paper No. 14001, September 1978, pp. 353–359.

ASCE Committee on Specifications, "Summary Report of Questionnaire on Specifications (Owner and Owner Representative Returns)," *Journal of the Construction Division,* ASCE Vol. 105, No. C03, Proceedings Paper No. 14799, September 1979, pp. 163–186.

ASKEN, G. "Resolving Construction Contract Disputes Through Arbitration." *Delays and Disputes in Building Construction,* New York, The American Arbitration Association, 1981.

Associated General Contractors of America. "Standard Form of Agreement Between Owner and Construction Manager (Guaranteed Maximum Price Option)," AGC Document No. 8. Washington, D.C.

BARRIE, D. S. AND PAULSON, B. C. JR., "Professional Construction Management," *Journal of the Construction Division,* Vol. 102 No. C03, Proceedings of the American Society of Civil Engineers, September 1976, pp. 427, 428.

BECKMAN, N. W. *Negotiations, Principles, and Techniques.* Lexington, MA: Heath.

*A Businessman's Guide to Commercial Arbitration and A Manual for Commercial Arbitrators and Construction Industry Arbitration Rules,* New York, The American Arbitration Association, 1981.

*California Public Contract Law Conference,* published papers, Sacramento, CA, April 1970, pp. 3, 4.

CASEY, J. J. (President, Gordon H. Ball, Inc., New York, NY). "Identification and Nature of Risks in Construction Projects: A Contractor's Perspective." *Construction Risks and Liability Sharing* (ASCE Conference, (January 1979) published papers, Vol. 1, pp. 17–23.

*CIAC Construction Industry Affairs Committee of Chicago,* Recommendations No. 3, *Management Control of Construction Operations.*

*CIAC Construction Industry Affairs Committee of Chicago,* Recommendations No. 7, *Construction Contract Change Orders.*

*CIAC Construction Industry Affairs Committee of Chicago,* Recommendations No. 8, *Punch List.*

*CIAC Construction Industry Affairs Committee of Chicago,* Recommendations No. 9, *Substitutions.*

*CIAC Construction Industry Affairs Committee of Chicago,* Recommendations No. 12, *Construction Completion Schedules Related to Building Costs.*

*CIAC Construction Industry Affairs Committee of Chicago,* Recommendations No. 13, *Waiver of Lien Procedure.*

*CIAC Construction Industry Affairs Committee of Chicago,* Recommendations No. 16, *Bonds.*

CLARKE, J. R., ESQ. *Commentary on Contract Documents.* 1990 ed. Washington, D.C., Professional Engineers in Private Practice, a practice division of the National Society of Professional Engineers, Washington, D.C.

CLARKE, J. R., ESQ. *Focus on Shop Drawings,* 1990 ed., prepared for Engineer's joint Contract Documents Committee, published by the National Society of Professional Engineers, Washington, D.C.

CLOUGH, R. H. *Construction Contracting,* 5th ed., New York, Wiley, 1986.

CLOUGH, R. H. *Construction Project Management,* New York, Wiley, 1972.

COFFIN, R. A. *The Negotiator: A Manual for Winners.* New York, AMACM, a Division of American Management Associations, 1973.

COLLINS, F. T. *Network Planning and Critical Path Scheduling,* Berkeley, CA: Know-How Publications, 1964.

Contractor's State Licensing Board, Sacramento, CA. *California Contractor's License Law and Reference Book.*

Construction Claims Monthly, April 1983, *Differing Site Conditions.*

Construction Claims Monthly, August 1983, *Recent Decisions Affecting Recovery of Home Office Overhead,* by Robert G. Watt, Esq., and David C. Romm, Esq.

Construction Claims Monthly, December 1983, *Recovery of Home Office Overhead—A Different Point of View,* by Phillip R. McDonald, Esq.

Construction Claims Monthly, July 1984, *The Return of Eichleay: Is it Here to Stay,* Part II, by W. John Irwin II, P. E. and *Denial of Time Extension is a Constructive Acceleration.*

*Construction Claims Monthly,* 951 Pershing Drive, Silver Spring, MD 20910, Phone (301) 587–6300.

Constructability Task Force "Guidelines for Implementing a Constructability Program," Publication 3–2, July 1987, Construction Industry Institute, The University of Texas at Austin, Austin, Texas 78705.

*CSI Manual of Practice,* Vol. 2, "Formats: Specifications and Manuals," Washington, D.C., The Construction Specifications Institute, Inc.

Department of the Navy. "Quality Level and Quality Control" NAVFAC P–455, *Construction Engineering Handbook,* July 1974 ed., Book 1—General Requirements, Naval Facilities Engineering Command, Alexandria, VA.

DIXON, S. A. AND CROWELL, R. D. *The Contract Guide,* 1993, Design Professionals Insurance Company (DPIC), Monterey, CA.

*EJCDC Standard General Conditions of the Construction Contract,* prepared by the Engineer's Joint Contract Documents Committee, as issued and published by Professional Engineers in Private

Practice, a practice division of the National Society of Professional Engineers; American Consulting Engineer's Council; American Society of Civil Engineers; and the Construction Specifications Institute, approved and endorsed by the Associated General Contractors of America (1996 Edition).

Engineers Joint Contract Documents Committee (EJCDC), *Standard Forms of Agreement,* Document No. 1910–1–A (1996 Edition).

*FIDIC Conditions of Contract for Works of Civil Engineering Construction,* Parts I and II, Federation Internationale des Ingenieurs-Conseil Fourth Edition 1987, Lausanne, Switzerland.

FISK, E. R. *The Use of Project Records for Litigation,* a technical paper presented at the ASCE Construction Division Committee on Professional Construction Management Symposium on *Liability and the Construction Manager,* held at the October 17–21, 1983 ASCE Convention and Exposition held in Houston, TX.

FISK, E. R. *Construction Engineer's Complete Handbook of Forms,* New York: Prentice Hall, 1981, 1992.

FISK, E. R. "Designer Evaluation of Contractor Comments on Specifications," *Journal of the Construction Division,* ASCE Vol. 104, No. C01, Proceedings Paper No. 13585, March 1978, pp. 77–83; presented at the October 17–21, 1977, ASCE National Convention and Exposition, held at San Francisco, CA (Preprint No. 2930).

FISK, E. R. "Evaluation of Owner Comments on Specifications," *Journal of the Construction Division,* ASCE Vol. 106, No. C04, Proceedings Paper 15875, December 1980, pp. 469–476; presented at the April 2–6, 1979, ASCE Spring Convention, held at Boston, MA.

FISK, E. R. "Inspector Training and Knowledge of Specifications," a technical paper presented at the Feb. 16–18, 1981, ASCE Construction Division Committees on Inspection and Specifications Specialty Conference on *Reducing Risk and Liability Through Better Specifications and Inspection,* held in San Diego, CA.

FISK, E. R. *Management Systems for Claims Protection,* a technical paper presented at the March 17–19, 1982, ASCE Construction Division Committee on Professional Construction Management Specialty Conference on *Engineering and Construction Projects—The Emerging Management Roles,* New Orleans, LA.

FISK, E. R. *Project Administration,* a technical paper presented at the April 15–17, 1985 ASCE Construction Division Committee on Contract Administration Specialty Conference on *The Resident Engineer,* Tampa, FL.

FISK, E. R. *Risk Management and Liability Sharing,* a technical paper presented at the May 1–3, 1985, Annual State Conference of the Arizona Water & Pollution Control Association (AWPCA) held at Lake Havasu, AZ.

FISK, E. R. "Specifications-Design professionals Forgotten Challenge," *Journal of the Construction Division,* ASCE Vol. 102, No. C02, Proceedings Paper 12171, June 1976, pp. 303–306; presented at the November 3–7, 1976, ASCE National Convention and Expo, held at Denver, CO (Preprint No. 2522).

FISK, E. R., "Construction Contracts and Specifications for California Public Works Projects," a technical book, Brea, CA 1990.

FISK, E. R. AND CALHOUN, J. C. *Contracts and Specifications for Public Works Projects,* New York, Wiley, 1991.

FISK, E. R. AND NEGELE, J. R. *Contractor's Project guide to Public Works Contracts,* New York: Prentice Hall, 1987.

General Services Administration, Public Buildings Service, Project Management Division, Washington, D.C. *Guide Specifications,* U.S. Army, Corps of Engineers.

GORDON, C., P. E. "Accident Prevention," Unpublished paper.

HAMMOND, D. G. (Vice President, Daniel, Mann, Johnson, & Mendenhall, Baltimore, MD) "Minimizing Risks and Mitigating Losses," *Construction Risks and Liability Sharing* (ASCE Conference, January 1979) published papers Vol. 1, pp. 133–143.

HOWELL, E. B. AND HOWELL, R. P. *Untangling the Web of Professional Liability,* San Francisco, CA, Risk Analysis and Research Corporation Publication, Design Professionals Insurance Company.

HUIE, W. S. (Partner, Kutak, Rock, & Huie, Atlanta, GA) "Identification and Nature of Risks," *Construction Risks and Liability Sharing* (ASCE Conference, January 1979) published papers Vol. 1, pp. 15–27.

JACOBY, H. J. (Chairman, Grow Tunneling Corporation, New York, NY) "Summary Session Commentary," Vol. 2, pp. 178–183.

KARP, HILARY. "The Hot States: States Requiring Preliminary Notices," *Network 50 News,* Network 50, Inc., Highland Park, IL 60035.

KUESEL, T. R. (Senior Vice President, Parsons, Brinckerhoff, Quade, & Douglas, Inc., New York, NY) "Allocation of Risks," *Construction Risks and Liability Sharing* (ASCE Conference, January 1979) published papers Vol. 1, pp. 51–60.

*Managing Construction of Clean Water Grant Projects,* a clean water grant program guideline by Division of Water Quality, California State Water Resources Control Board, March 1979.

McLEAN, R. C. "Construction Planning and Scheduling" from Havers and Stubbs (eds.), *Handbook of Heavy Construction,* 2nd ed., NY: McGraw-Hill, 1971.

NADEL, N. A. (President, MacLean Grove & Company, Inc., New York, NY) "Allocation of Risks— A Contractor's View," *Construction Risks and Liability Sharing* (ASCE Conference, January 1979) published papers Vol. 1, pp. 61–67.

National Joint Guideline. "Overtime, Construction Costs and Productivity," American Subcontractor's Association, Associated General Contractors of America, and Associated Specialty Contractors, Inc., 1979.

The National Society of Professional Engineers, *Professional Index of Private Practice,* Washington, D.C.

NAVFAC Construction Quality Control Manual, NAVFAC P–445, Department of the Navy, Naval Facilities Engineering Command, Alexandria, VA.

NEAL, RICHARD H. AND DAVID E., "Construction Planning," London: Thomas Telford.

*Network Float—What Is It and Who Owns It?* and *Some Comments on the Precedence Diagraming Technique of Network Analysis Systems,* Dallas, TX: Winn & Associates, 1976. (Now Forward Associates, Ltd., Novato, CA, 1991.)

NSPE/PEPP *Guidelines for Development of Architect/Engineer Quality Control Manual.* Washington, D.C., Professional Engineers in Private Practice, a Division of National Society of Professional Engineers, NSPE Pub. No. 1957, January 1977.

O'BRIEN, J. J. *CPM in Construction Management,* 2nd ed., New York: McGraw-Hill, 1971.

PEURIFOY, R. L. *Construction Planning, Equipment, and Methods,* New York: McGraw-Hill, 1956.

*Prevention, Management and Resolution of Construction Contractor Claims On Clean Water Grant Projects,* Vol. I— Discussion (California State Water Resources Control Board, Division of Water Quality, June 1980).

SEARLES, W. H., IVES, H. C. AND KISSAM, P. *Field Engineering,* 22nd ed., New York: Wiley.

SNELL, F. *How to Win the Meeting.* New York: Hawthorne.

State of California, Department of Transportation, *Construction Manual,* Section 1–60 Safety; issued by the Division of Construction and Research, Office of Construction, Sacramento, CA, 1990.

State of California, Department of Transportation, *Construction Manual,* Section 2–08 Prosecution and Progress; issued by the Division of Construction and Research, Office of Construction, Sacramento, CA, 1990.

State of California, Department of Transportation, *Construction Manual,* Section 2–70 Protests, Potential Claims, and Claims; issued by the Division of Construction and Research, Office of Construction, Sacramento, CA, 1990.

Sweet, Justin, "Sweet on Construction Industry Contracts: Major AIA Documents," Wiley Law Publications, John Wiley & Sons, New York 1987.

*The Uniform Arbitration Act.* New York: The American Arbitration Association, 1990.

U.S. Army Corps of Engineers, *Resident Engineer's Management Guide,* pamphlet EP 415–1–260, dated 6 December 1990.

U.S. Army Management Engineering Training Agency, *Principles and Applications of Value Engineering,* Department of Defense Joint Course Book, Vol. I, Rock Island, IL.

U.S. Government Printing Office, *Value Engineering,* Department of Defense Handbook 5010.8–H, 12 September 1968, Superintendent of Documents, Washington, D.C.

U.S. Department of the Interior, Bureau of Reclamation, *Metric Manual,* by L. D. Pedde, W. E. Foote, L. F. Scott, D. L. King, and D. L. McGalliard, Bureau of Reclamation, Engineering and Research Center, Denver Federal Center, P.O. Box 25007, Denver, CO 80225, Attn: 922, dated 1978.

# Index

**565**

# Forms Index